IFIP Series on Computer Graphics

Editors
J. L. Encarnação
G. G. Grinstein

B. Falcidieno T.L. Kunii (Eds.)

Modeling in Computer Graphics

Methods and Applications

With 54 Figures

Springer-Verlag
Berlin Heidelberg New Yor
London Paris Tokyo
Hong Kong Barcelona
Budapest

Dr. Bianca Falcidieno
Istituto per la Matematica Applicata
C.N.R.
Via De Marini, 6
Torre di Francia
16149 Genova, Italy

Prof. Dr. Tosiyasu L. Kunii
University of Tokyo
Dept. of Information Science
Faculty of Science
7-3-1 Hongo, Bunkyo-ku
Tokyo 113, Japan

ISBN-13: 978-3-642-78116-2 e-ISBN: 978-3-642-78114-8
DOI: 10.1007/ 978-3-642-78114-8

Softcover reprint of the hardcover 1st edition 1993

Typesetting: Camera-ready by authors; Cover design: H. Lopka, Ilvesheim
Printing: Mercedes-Druck, Berlin; Binding: Lüderitz & Bauer, Berlin
33/3020 5 4 3 2 1 0 Printed on acid-free paper

Preface

In the history of technology, many fields have passed from an initial stage of empirical recipes to a mature stage where work is based on formal theories and procedures. This transition is made possible through a process called "modeling". Also Computer Graphics as a separate field of Computer Science makes extensive use of formal theories and procedures of modeling, often derived from related disciplines such as mathematics and physics. Modeling makes different application results consistent, unifying varieties of techniques and formal approaches into a smaller number of models by generalizing and abstracting the knowledge in Computer Graphics.

This volume presents a selection of research papers submitted to the conference "Modeling in Computer Graphics : Methods and Applications" held at the Research Area of the National Research Council in Genoa, Italy, on June 28 - July 1, 1993. This meeting was the ideal continuation of a previous conference organized in Tokyo, Japan, in April 1991. The success and the variety of research themes discussed at that meeting suggested to promote a new working conference on methods and applications of modeling to be held in Italy two years later.

In response to the call for papers, 45 high-quality original research papers were submitted from 16 different countries, 1 from Australia, 1 from Canada, 3 from China, 5 from France, 3 from Germany, 3 from Israel, 5 from Italy, 6 from Japan, 1 from Macedonia, 1 from the Netherlands, 2 from Portugal, 1 from Romania, 2 from Spain, 1 from Switzerland, 2 from the UK and 8 from the USA. The amount and distribution of the proposals shows the wide international coverage of research in this area.

After extensive and thorough review, 27 papers were selected for presentation at the conference and also for printing in this book. To highlight areas of particular importance, 3 additional papers were invited.

This volume is divided in two parts: Methods of Modeling and Modeling for Applications. The first part includes new advances in modeling tools derived from closely related disciplines. It contains the first 6 chapters: Mathematical Modeling for Vision and Graphics (Chapter 1), Modeling with Constraints (Chapter 2), Modeling of Dynamic Objects (Chapter 3), Geometric Modeling (Chapter 4), Surface Modeling as a Creative Tool (Chapter 5), Curve and Surface Modeling (Chapter 6).

Part 2 on Modeling for Applications presents modeling techniques devised for specific applications. It includes three chapters: Modeling for Animation (Chapter 7), Modeling for CIM Applications (Chapter 8) and Modeling for Rendering Complex Objects (Chapter 9).

The conference was promoted by IFIP WG 5.10, under the auspices of TC5 and organized by the Institute for Applied Mathematics of the C.N.R. with the cooperation of the Research Area of Genova.

Many people have contributed to the preparation of the conference. First of all we would like to thank the authors who submitted papers and the invited speakers, secondly we want to thank the members of the conference committees and the external reviewers for their efforts in setting the standard for the quality of papers in this volume. Our special thanks are due to Marinella Pescaglia and Sandra Burlando for running the conference secretariat so effectively and to all assistants and students of the I.M.A. Computer Graphics group for their collaboration to the conference organization.

Bianca Falcidieno Tosiyasu L. Kunii

Programme Committee

Programme Chairpersons

Bianca Falcidieno (Italy) Tosiyasu L. Kunii (Japan)

Members

Sabine Coquillart (France)
Umberto Cugini (Italy)
Rae Earnshaw (UK)
José Encarnação (Germany)
Olivier Faugeras (France)
Michael Groß (Germany)
Leonidas Guibas (USA)
Christoph Hoffmann (USA)
Masa Inakage (Japan)
Nadia Magnenat-Thalmann (Switzerland)
Jarek Rossignac (USA)
Hans-Peter Seidel (Germany)
Wolfgang Straßer (Germany)
Tapio Takala (Finland)
Zesheng Tang (China)
Daniel Thalmann (Switzerland)
Marco Tomljanovich (Italy)
Vincent Torre (Italy)

List of External Reviewers

C. Bajaj
J. D. Boissonnat
P. Brianzi
W. Broonsvort
R. Caracciolo
L. Casu
W. Dai
L. De Floriani
T. De Martino
G. Dodero
W. H. Du
G. Fasciolo
S. Filippi
R. Fischer
F. Folini
A. Fortunato
R. Franklin
F. Giannini
C. Gold
P. Gugliermero
S. Haas
S. Haßinger
A. Kaufman
M. Ippolito
A. Luciani
K. Minamida
T. Mora
M. Mukherjee
P. Mussio
G. Nagy
C. Pienovi
H. Prautzsch
M. Protti
E. Puppo
T. Recio
A. Requicha
A. Rossi
C. Sacchi
H. Saji
H. Sato
M. Spagnuolo
S. Takahashi
P. Vallebona
R. Veltkamp
F. Winkler

Local Arrangement Committee

Chairperson : Michela Spagnuolo
Members: Caterina Pienovi, Teresa De Martino, Franca Giannini

Secretariat

Marinella Pescaglia, Sandra Burlando

Conference Organization

IFIP TC 5/WG 5.10

Institute for Applied Mathematics
National Research Council, Genoa

Genoa Research Area - C.N.R.

Table of Contents

Part 1: Methods of Modeling

Chapter 1: Mathematical Modeling for Vision and Graphics

Chapter 2: Modeling with Constraints

Chapter 3: Modeling of Dynamic Objects

PART 1

Methods of Modeling

Chapter 1

Mathematical Modeling for Vision and Graphics

Area Guide Map Modeling by Manifolds and CW-Complexes

TOSIYASU L. KUNII and SHIGEO TAKAHASHI
Department of Information Science, Faculty of Science
The University of Tokyo, Tokyo, 113 Japan

ABSTRACT

From ancient times, area guide maps have been drawn intuitively without appropriate modeling. Understanding such maps and developing guide map CAD require clear modeling. This paper presents the model of area guide maps using manifolds and CW-complexes. The process of drawing an area guide map is modeled as that of creating a manifold. First, we represent the surface shape of an area as a CW-complex. Then, we glue the CW-complexes representing the areas into a manifold. Surface shapes in the overlaps are blended by a partition of unity. The mechanism to project a surface shape from multiple views is installed. Finally, the area guide map is generated automatically.

Keywords: area guide map modeling, CW-complexes, manifolds, partition of unity

1. INTRODUCTION

In drawing the area guide maps, what features are extracted to characterize the land undulations? We will first extract the characteristic points such as mountain tops, mountain passes, and lakes. These characteristic points can be regarded as peaks, passes, and pits, which are called singular points. With singular points, the land surface can be described as a CW-complex (Shinagawa, Kergosien and Kunii 1991) . The guide maps feature these characteristic points.

Further, the area guide maps are not described by the projection from only one view point, but by the projections from multiple view points. For example, a mountain is usually described as seen from the foot to show the mountain skyline clearly. Lakes are described as seen from heights not to get the scene barred by the surrounding mountains. In this way, the areas are described separately with the different views, and then put together into a guide map in a way similar to gluing charts together to obtain a manifold. Each area can be considered as an open neighborhood, and the gluing process can be considered as a coordinate map. In the following, this paper assumes that area guide maps are constructed by these processes.

When we model area guide maps by CW-complexes and manifolds, first, we code the surface shapes of the individual areas separately. In this part, we use the Morse theory (Milnor 1963) and the Reeb graph (Reeb 1946) to code each surface shape as a CW-complex. Then, we glue these surface shapes together to construct the whole map. In the overlapping areas, the surface shapes are blended in an appropriate way with a partition of unity. The projection from multiple views are also realized for both the perspective projection and the parallel projection. Finally, the area guide maps are automatically generated.

2. IMPLEMENTION OF MANIFOLDS IN COMPUTERS

In this section, we explain how to implement the concept of manifolds in computers.

2.1 Concept of Manifolds

Let's have a review on the definition of manifolds(See Fig. 1). Readers can also refer to some books (Wasserman 1992) . A manifold consists of an atlas that is a set of charts. A chart is a pair of an open neighborhood and a coordinate map. These notations are indicated in Fig. 1. We denote the open neighborhood and the coordinate map as U_i and φ_i respectively, where i is the index number. The charts are represented as (U_i, φ_i), and the atlas is the set $\{(U_i, \varphi_i) | i \in I\}$ where I is a set of integer numbers. Each open neighborhood U_i is mapped from the global coordinate system to the local by the coordinate map φ_i.

2.2 Implementation of Manifolds

We explain how to implement the manifolds in computers. Since manifolds are constructed from open neighborhoods and coordinate maps, we first consider how to implement these two elements.

The open neighborhood U_i is represented as an inverse image of a 3-D local coordinate system. The surface shape in the local coordinate system $\varphi_i(U_i)$ is expressed by the surface equation $z_i = f_i(x_i, y_i)$. The surface equation is assumed to be continuous and differentiable. There exists a mapping from a point p_i on the local (x_i, y_i)-plane to a height value f_i.

The coordinate map φ_i is represented as a 4×4 matrix M_i in the homogeneous coordinate system. A 4×4 matrix includes a translation with a scale transformation and a rotation. We also assume that we can change the charts smoothly over the global coordinate system. Later, this is defined as C^r-compatibility formally. This assumption enables us to define an atlas as a collection of charts.

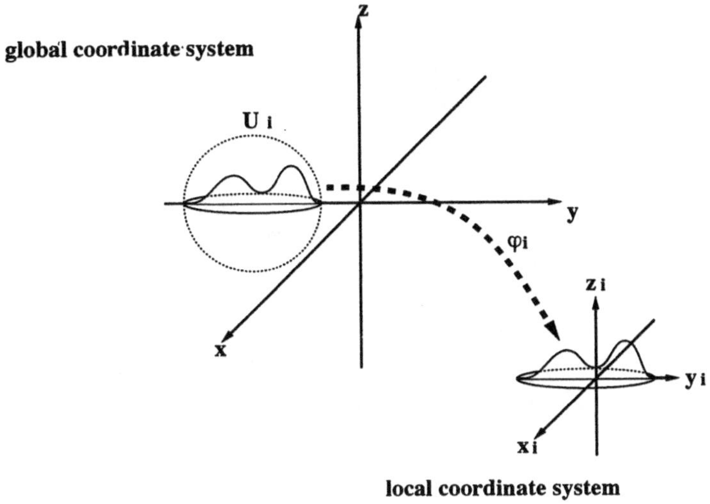

Fig. 1. The concept of a manifold

Atlas

index	surfaces in neighborhood	coordinate maps
0	$z_0 = f_0(x_0, y_0)$	$\varphi_0 \quad (M_0)$
1	$z_1 = f_1(x_1, y_1)$	$\varphi_1 \quad (M_1)$
2	$z_2 = f_2(x_2, y_2)$	$\varphi_2 \quad (M_2)$
⋮	⋮	⋮

Table 1. An atlas represented as the array of charts in computers

Now we are ready to define the data structure of a chart and an atlas. An atlas, a set of charts, is stored as an array in computers. Table 1 illustrates an atlas in array structure. The elements of the atlas as the array correspond to the charts. Each array has the surface equations of individual local coordinate systems, and the coordinate maps represented as 4×4 matrices.

2.3 Coordinate Transformations

First, we define the C^r-compatibility as follows (Wasserman 1992) .

Definition 1 (C^r-Compatibility) *A pair of charts (U_i, φ_i) and (U_j, φ_j) are said to be C^r-compatible if the following conditions are satisfied.*

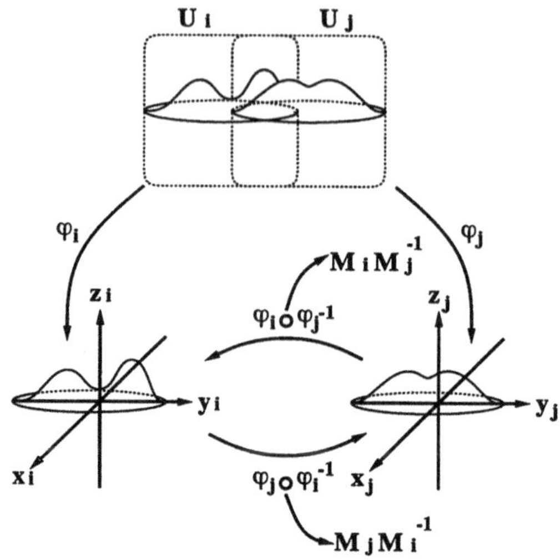

Fig. 2. The coordinate transformation in $U_i \cap U_j$

1. $U_i \cap U_j \neq \emptyset$.

2. The coordinate transformations $\varphi_j \circ \varphi_i^{-1}$ *and* $\varphi_i \circ \varphi_j^{-1}$ *is* C^r *on* $U_i \cap U_j$.

Thus, to realize the compatibility among charts is equivalent to implementing the coordinate transformations. In our system, the product of two corresponding matrices represents the coordinate transformation. Fig. 2 illustrates the coordinate transformation in $U_i \cap U_j$. The coordinate transformation $\varphi_j \circ \varphi_i^{-1}$ is represented as $M_i M_j^{-1}$. The same is true for the reverse transformation. In this way, the coordinate transformation in the overlapping area of two open neighborhoods is implemented.

3. SHAPE DESCRIPTION IN THE CHARTS

In describing the land undulations in each area, we pay attention to the characteristic points such as peaks, passes, and pits. These points are called the singular points. This section describes the surface codings by singular points. From the Morse theory, we can regard the surface of the area under consideration as a CW-complex.

3.1 Morse Theory

First, we introduce the Morse theory as a tool of surface coding with singular points. Readers can refer to the book (Milnor 1963) for more details.

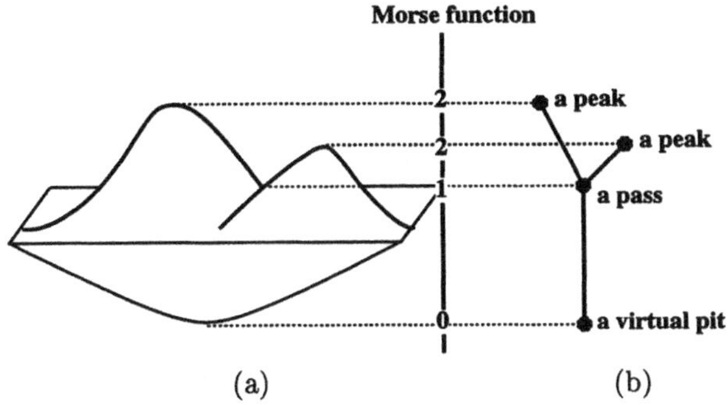

Fig. 3. (a) The example of a mountain shape and (b) its Reeb graph

Theorem 2 (Morse Theory) *Let M be a compact, smooth, and closed manifold, and f be a Morse function of M. If the indices of singular points are r_1, r_2, $\cdots$, and r_k respectively, M is homotopy equivalent to the finite CW-complex that is decomposed into a r_1-cell, a r_2-cell, $\cdots$, and a r_k-cell. In other words, the following is satisfied;*

$$M \simeq e^{r_1} \cup e^{r_2} \cup \cdots \cup e^{r_k}.$$

Consider a mountain shape with a virtual pit and put the Morse function as illustrated in Fig. 3(a). Along the direction of the Morse function, we can scan the singular points whose indices are 2, 2, 1, and 0. Hence, the surface can be decomposed into two 2-cells, one 1-cell, and one 0-cell according to the Morse theory. Based on the Morse theory, the compact smooth surface can be regarded as a CW-complex.

3.2 Reeb Graph

The Morse theory tells us the number of decomposed cells and their dimensions, but cannot tell us how to glue the cells. To fill the lack of this information, we use the Reeb graph. The definition of the Reeb graph is as follows (Reeb 1946) .

Definition 3 (Reeb Graph) *Let $f : M \to \boldsymbol{R}$ be a function on a compact manifold M. The Reeb graph is the quotient space of the graph of f in $M \times R$ by the equivalence relation given below :*

$$(X_1, f(X_1)) \simeq (X_2, f(X_2)),$$

which holds if and only if $f(X_1) = f(X_2)$ and X_1, X_2 are in the same connected component of $f^{-1}(f(X_1))$.

Fig. 3(b) presents the Reeb graph of the mountain shape. With the Reeb graph, the structure of the cells is determined.

3.3 Morse Theoretical Coding

The Morse theoretical coding is presented by (Shinagawa, Kergosien and Kunii 1991) . In this coding, a simple height function is used as a Morse function. Along the height function from the top to the bottom, we can describe the dimensions of cells and a way to glue them to the existing surface. Since the cross sectional structure of the surface changes at the singular points, the Morse theoretical coding is sufficient to describe the changes of cross sectional contours. The Morse theoretical coding represents also the inclusion relations of the contours by tree structures. To visualize the topological structure of surfaces, the Morse theoretical coding uses the icon representation of the Reeb graph. In this way, cells are glued along the height function to construct the whole surface. This paper uses this surface coding to describe the surface shapes of the charts.

4. HOW TO OVERLAP THE CHARTS

As mentioned earlier, the process of drawing area guide maps amounts to creating an atlas from the charts. Since the surface shapes are described individually in the charts, different surface shapes can exist in the overlapping areas. Hence, our next problem is how to overlap the surface shapes in the charts.

4.1 The Partition of Unity

To solve this problem, we blend the surface shapes in the overlapping areas. Here, surface shapes must change smoothly over the whole global area. For this blending, we use the partition of unity.

The definition of the partition of unity is as follows (Hirsch 1976) .

Definition 4 (Partition of Unity) *We define the support* $\mathrm{Supp}\, f$ *of a continuous real valued function* f *to be the closure of* $f^{-1}(\boldsymbol{R} - 0)$. *Let* M *be a* C^r *manifold,* $0 \leq r \leq \infty$, *and* $\mathcal{U} = \{U_i\}_{i \in \Lambda}$ *be an open cover. A* C^r *partition of unity subordinate to* $\mathcal{U}$ *is a family of* C^r *maps* $\lambda_i : M \rightarrow [0,\ 1]$, $i \in \Lambda$ *such that the following conditions hold:*

$$\mathrm{Supp}\, \lambda_i \subset U_i \qquad (i \in \Lambda),$$

$$\{\mathrm{Supp}\, \lambda_i\}_{i \in \Lambda} \quad \textit{is locally finite},$$

and

$$\sum_{i \in \Lambda} \lambda_i(x) = 1 \qquad (x \in M).$$

The following functions are examples of the partition of unity.

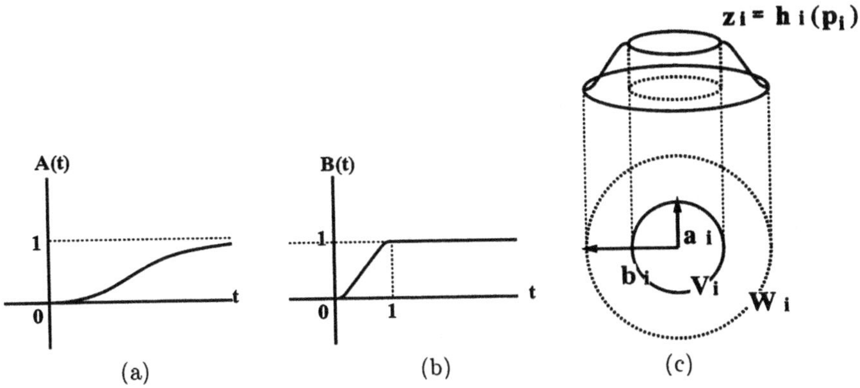

Fig. 4: The blending functions for the partition of unity: (a) the shape of the blending function $A(t)$, (b) the shape of the blending function $B(t)$, and (c) the shape of the blending function $h_i(p_i)$

- Bernstein basis function
- B-spline basis function
- Gaussian basis function

The next step is to construct the partition of unity in our case.

4.2 Blending of Surface Shapes

The approximations for blending of surface shapes are explained in (Hirsch 1976) . First, we define the exponential function $A(t)$ indicated below.

$$A(t) = \begin{cases} 0 & t \leq 0 \\ e^{-\frac{1}{t}} & 0 < t \end{cases}$$

The shape of this function is shown in Fig. 4(a). You can see that this function is C^∞.

We define the second function $B(t)$ from the first as follows.

$$B(t) = \begin{cases} 0 & t \leq 0 \\ \frac{A(t)}{A(t)+A(1-t)} & 0 < t < 1 \\ 1 & 1 \leq t \end{cases}$$

The shape of this function is shown in Fig. 4(b). After simple calculations, we can see that this function is C^∞.

Then, we define the function $C_i(t)$ in each local coordinate system $\varphi_i(U_i)$,

$$C_i(t) \quad = \quad B(\frac{b_i - t}{b_i - a_i})$$

where the real numbers a_i and b_i are defined in each local coordinate system and satisfy the condition $0 < a_i < b_i < 1$. We also define the areas V_i and W_i as

$$\begin{aligned} V_i &= \{(x_i,\ y_i,\ z_i) \in U_i | \sqrt{x_i^2 + y_i^2} \leq a_i\} \\ W_i &= \{(x_i,\ y_i,\ z_i) \in U_i | \sqrt{x_i^2 + y_i^2} < b_i\} \end{aligned}$$

Let p_i be a point on the (x_i, y_i)-plane in the local coordinate system. The function h_i is defined as

$$h_i(p_i) = \begin{cases} 1 & p_i \in V_i \\ C_i(\sqrt{x_i^2 + y_i^2}) & p_i \in W_i - V_i \\ 0 & \text{otherwise} \end{cases}$$

in each local coordinate system. The shape of h_i is shown in Fig. 4(c). With this definition, each point p_i on the local coordinate system has the weight $h_i(p_i)$ for surface blending.

We are now ready to consider how to blend the surface shapes in the charts. Let p be a point on the (x, y)-plane in the global coordinate system, and let I_p be a set of indices $\{i \,|\, p \in U_i\}$. If the open neighborhood U_i includes the point p, the set I_p includes the index i. The equation of the surface in the global coordinate system can be defined as,

$$f(x, y) = \frac{\sum_{i \in I_p} h_i(x_i, y_i) \cdot f_i(x_i, y_i)}{\sum_{i \in I_p} h_i(x_i, y_i)},$$

where $x_i = \varphi_i(x),\ y_i = \varphi_i(y)$. Fig. 5(a) helps us to comprehend this overlapping. As you see, the equation of this surface is C^∞. In this way, the surface shapes can be blended with the partition of unity.

Actually, the blending defined above is homotopic. The homotopy of the blending is defined in Fig. 5(b). Thus, the partition of unity among the charts is defined as the homotopy among the charts.

4.3 Weight Assignment

Our method still gives the same weights to all of the charts. We can assign different weights to the charts for the control of the height values. Let w_i be the weight parameter of the chart (U_i, φ_i). The equation of the surface in the global coordinate system can be modified as follows.

$$f(x, y) = \frac{\sum_{i \in I_p} w_i \cdot h_i(x_i, y_i) \cdot f_i(x_i, y_i)}{\sum_{i \in I_p} w_i \cdot h_i(x_i, y_i)},$$

where $\quad x_i = \varphi_i(x),\ y_i = \varphi_i(y)$.

The weight parameters give us flexibility to blend surface shapes. For example, we suppose that each chart has the different reliability in the exactness of the parts of the chart. We can assign the larger weights to the more reliable parts of the chart for more accurate blending.

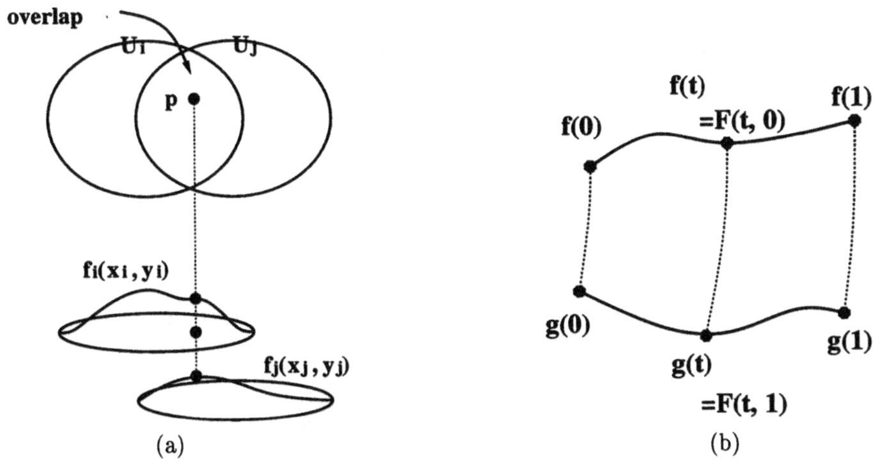

Fig. 5. (a)The blending of the surface shapes, and (b) the homotopy of blending

4.4 Restrictions in the Overlapping Areas

In blending the surface shape in the overlapping areas, it is possible that new singular points appear or existing singular points disappear. Since we code the topological structure with singular points, we need to maintain the singular points in any glued surface. For this purpose, we show that it is sufficient to keep the sign of the gradient in the fixed direction in the overlapping areas. If this condition is satisfied, no singular points appear in the overlapping areas because the sign of the partial derivative in this direction does not become 0.

To satisfy this restriction, we define rules as followings.

1. Any point on the (x, y)-plane in the global coordinate system is covered with three or less open neighborhoods(See Fig. 6(a)).

2. There exists a partial order between the two charts that have the overlapping area with each other. This paper denotes the partial order between the two charts as $(U_i, \varphi_i) \succ (U_j, \varphi_j)$. Fig. 6(b) represents the example. In this case, the partial order relations are $(U_1,\ \varphi_1) \succ (U_2,\ \varphi_2)$, $(U_1,\ \varphi_1) \succ (U_3,\ \varphi_3)$, $(U_1,\ \varphi_1) \succ (U_4,\ \varphi_4)$, $(U_2,\ \varphi_2) \succ (U_4,\ \varphi_4)$, and $(U_3,\ \varphi_3) \succ (U_4,\ \varphi_4)$.

3. Let U_i and U_j have the partial order $(U_i, \varphi_i) \succ (U_j, \varphi_j)$. We define one direction in the overlapping area $U_i \cap U_j$. The following rules are satisfied in this overlapping areas.

   - (U_i, φ_i) and (U_j, φ_j) have the same sign "$-$" of the gradient.

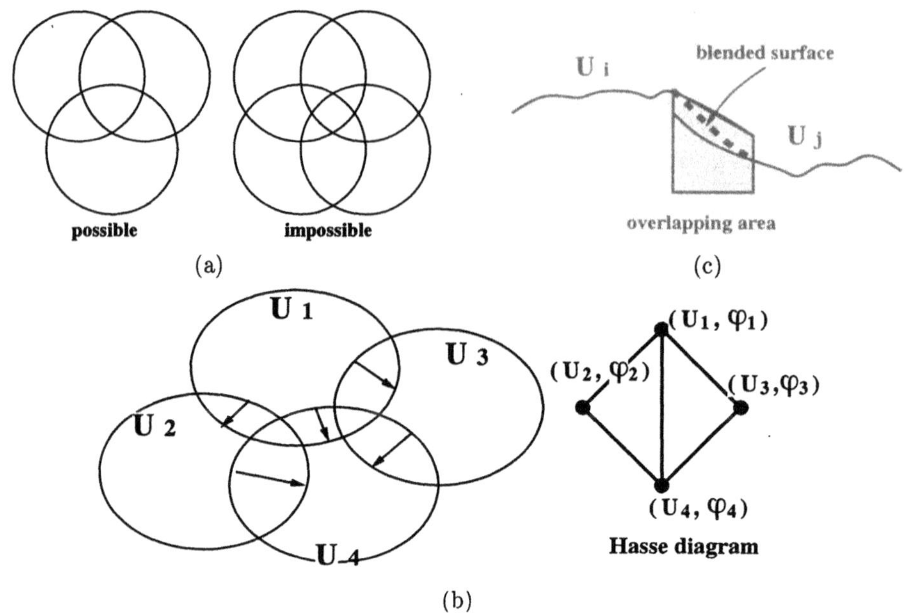

Fig. 6. The rules for restrictions in the overlapping areas.

- Let $p = (x, y)$ be a point of the (x, y)-plane in the global coordinate system. Here, $f_i(p) > f_j(p)$ is satisfied where $f_i(p)$ and $f_j(p)$ is the height values in the open neighborhoods U_i and U_j respectively. Fig. 6(c) indicates this rule.

These rules satisfy the initial restriction in the overlapping areas. Our system supports the interface to satisfy these rules for gluing the charts with fixed gradient in the overlapping areas.

5. PROJECTIONS FROM MULTIPLE VIEWS

Area guide maps are generally drawn based on the projections from multiple views. Mountains are seen from the oblique views. Lakes are seen from the top. From such considerations, each chart has its own view point or direction. Hence, our next problem is how to define the continuous and differentiable views between the charts. In the following, we will discuss this problem in the following two cases. One is the perspective projection and the other is the parallel projection.

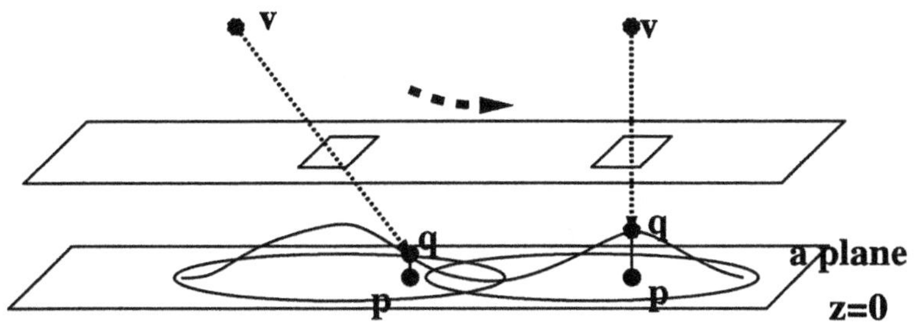

Fig. 7. View blending in perspective projection

5.1 Perspective Projection

In the case of perspective projection, the view point and the reference point are crucial because these two points determine the view line. First, we make some assumptions.

- The reference point is on the blended surface in the global coordinate system.
- Each chart (U_i, φ_i) has its own view point v_i.
- The view plane is parallel to a plane $z = 0$ and has an intersection point with the view line.

Then, we can find the desired view point in the same way as blending the surface shapes of the charts. In Fig. 7, given a reference point q, let p be the vertically projected point on a plane $z = 0$ from the reference point q. By the partition of unity, the view point v of the reference point q is defined as

$$v(x, y) = \frac{\sum_{i \in I_p} h_i(x_i, y_i) \cdot v_i}{\sum_{i \in I_p} h_i(x_i, y_i)},$$

where $I_p = \{i \mid p \in U_i\}$, $x_i = \varphi_i(x)$, and $y_i = \varphi_i(y)$.

Fig. 7 represents this blending of view points in perspective projection. Since edge points are continuous and differentiable, we can find the desired view point through this equation.

We can also assign the weight parameters to the view points. Let the chart (U_i, φ_i) have the weight parameter w_i' of perspective projection. The view point is modified as

$$v(x, y) = \frac{\sum_{i \in I_p} w_i' \cdot h_i(x_i, y_i) \cdot v_i}{\sum_{i \in I_p} w_i' \cdot h_i(x_i, y_i)},$$

where $I_p = \{i \mid p \in U_i\}$, $x_i = \varphi_i(x)$, and $y_i = \varphi_i(y)$.

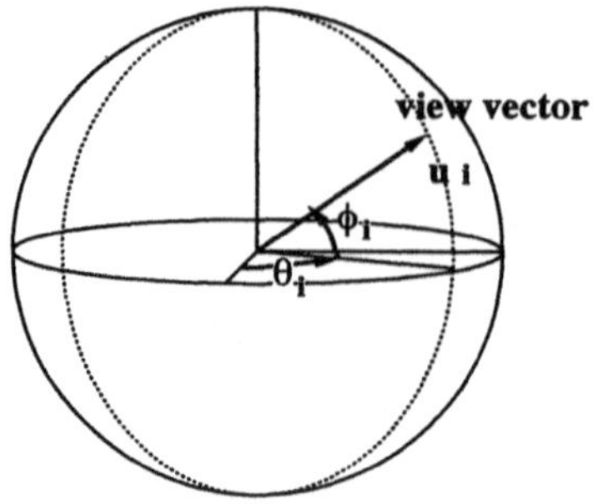

Fig. 8. The angle with two parameters in parallel projection

5.2 The Parallel Projection

Once the view direction is fixed, the way of parallel projection is determined. Hence, our concern is only the direction of the view line. In order to determine the direction of parallel projection, the unit vector from the origin to the unit sphere is considered. We make some assumptions as followings.

- Each chart (U_i, φ_i) has its own direction u_i, which is the above unit vector.
- The unit vector u_i has the form

  $$u_i = (\cos\Theta_i \cos\Phi_i,\ \sin\Theta_i \cos\Phi_i,\ \sin\Phi_i),$$

  with two parameters Θ_i and Φ_i(See Fig 8).

The problem left is how to find the continuous and differentiable functions of these two parameters Θ_i and Φ_i. We can also use the partition of unity to find the desired angles. The view direction u is defined as

$$u = (\cos\Theta \cos\Phi,\ \sin\Theta \cos\Phi,\ \sin\Phi),$$

where

$$\begin{aligned} \Theta &= \frac{\sum_{i\in I_p} h_i(x_i, y_i) \cdot \Theta_i}{\sum_{i\in I_p} h_i(x_i, y_i)} \\ \Phi &= \frac{\sum_{i\in I_p} h_i(x_i, y_i) \cdot \Phi_i}{\sum_{i\in I_p} h_i(x_i, y_i)}. \end{aligned}$$

Let w'' be the weight parameter of the chart (U_i, φ_i) of parallel projection. With this parameter, the angles Θ and Φ are represented as

$$\begin{aligned} \Theta &= \frac{\sum_{i\in I_p} w_i'' \cdot h_i(x_i, y_i) \cdot \Theta_i}{\sum_{i\in I_p} w_i'' \cdot h_i(x_i, y_i)} \\ \Phi &= \frac{\sum_{i\in I_p} w_i'' \cdot h_i(x_i, y_i) \cdot \Phi_i}{\sum_{i\in I_p} w_i'' \cdot h_i(x_i, y_i)} \end{aligned}$$

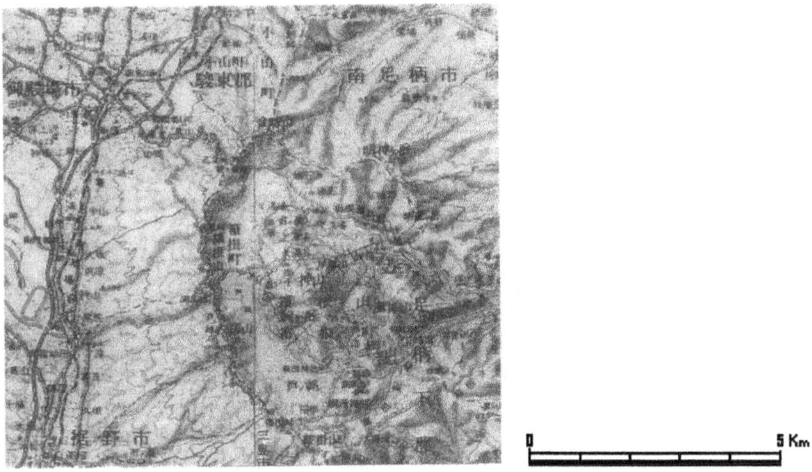

Fig. 9. The map around the Lake Ashinoko

As we have seen, we can find the desired view, and surface shapes are projected from multiple views.

6. EXAMPLES

We apply our model to the automatic generation of area guide maps. Fig. 9 shows the map around the Lake Ashinoko, which is a famous tourist area having a scenic crater lake. Fig. 10 and Fig. 11 are the results of the generation as the candidates of the basic image to draw the area guide maps around the lake. Fig. 10 shows the images of perspective projection with one view point and with multiple view points. Fig. 11 shows the images of parallel projection with one direction and with multiple directions. In Fig. 10(a) and Fig. 11(a), the mountain obstructs the lake because the land shape is projected from one view point or direction. In Fig. 10(b) and Fig. 11(b), on the contrary, the whole lake can be seen because the area including the lake has a different view point or direction.

7. CONCLUSIONS

This paper presents the model of area guide maps based on the concept of manifolds. The shape description of the charts with CW-complexes and manifold is explained. The blending method of surface shapes and views is represented. Automatic generation of area guide maps is also implemented.

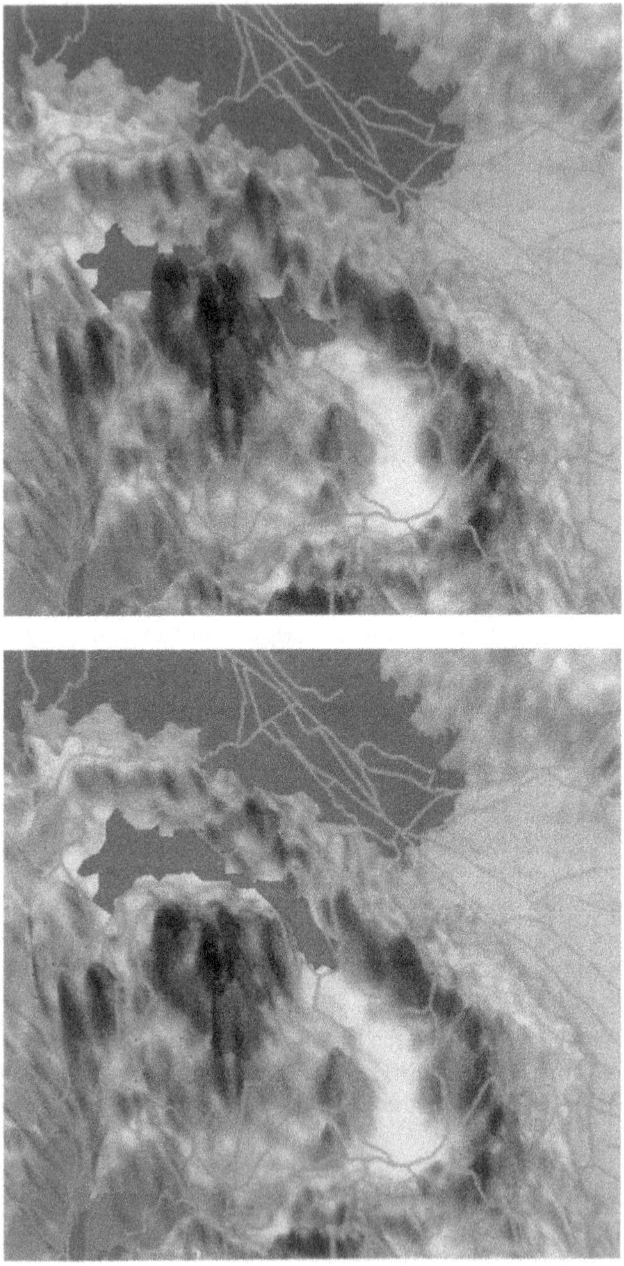

(a)

(b)

Fig. 10: The image of the perspective projection with (a) one view point and (b) multiple view points

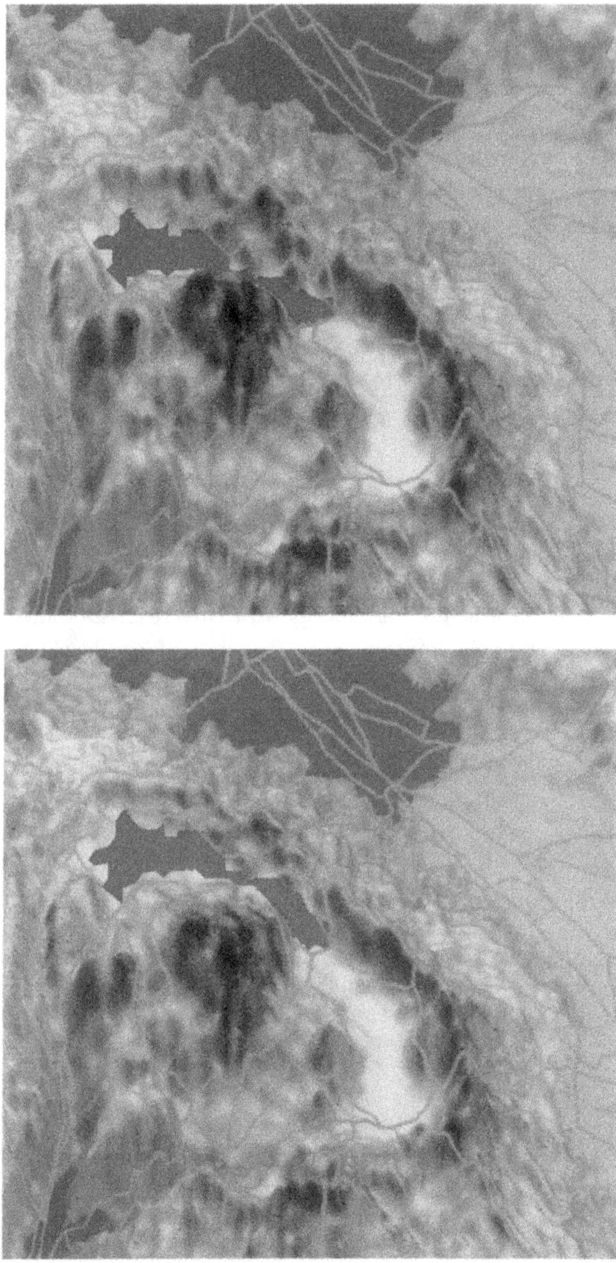

(a)

(b)

Fig. 11: The image of the parallel projection with (a) one view direction and (b) multiple view directions

Our research directions are as follows:

- Reconstruction of the global Reeb graph from the local
  In gluing the charts, we set the restrictions of fixed gradients. Under this condition, it is possible to reconstruct the global Reeb graph from the local.

- Application of this model to the non-Cartesian coordinate system
  In area guide map modeling, the global coordinate system is a simple Cartesian coordinate system. For example, the modeling of facial expressions needs the curved coordinate system to represent a human face properly.

- Animation with blended views
  The view blending enables us to animate the change of the vision. Projections of teeth from multiple views are good examples, because front teeth and back teeth have the different views.

ACKNOWLEDGEMENTS

We gratefully acknowledge helpful discussions with Dr. Yoshihisa Shinagawa and Miss Saeko Miyoshi on several points of this paper. The data of land height around the Lake Ashinoko is provided by Japan Map Center. We also like to thank Mr. Akihiro Miyazawa of RICOH Co., Ltd. for the data conversion from magnetic tapes. Finally, we wish to express our gratitude to Silicon Graphics for the IRIS workstations.

REFERENCES

Hirsch MW (1976) *Differential Topology.* Springer, New York Berlin Heidelberg London Paris Tokyo.

Milnor J (1963) *Morse Theory.* Princeton University Press, New Jersey.

Reeb G (1946) Sur les points singuliers d'une forme de Pfaff completement integrable ou d'une fonction numerique [On the Singular Points of a Completely Integrable Pfaff Form or of a Numerical Function]. *Comptes Rendus Acad. Sciences Paris*, 222:847–849.

Shinagawa Y, Kergosien YL, Kunii TL (1991) Surface Coding Based on Morse Theory. *IEEE Computer Graphics and Applications*, 11(5):66–78.

Wasserman RH (1992) *Tensors and Manifolds.* Oxford University Press, New York Oxford.

The Elementary Equation of the Conjugate Transformation for the Hexagonal Grid

Z.J. Zheng and A.J. Maeder

Victorian Centre for Image Processing and Graphics, Department of Computer Science, Monash University, Clayton Vic. 3168, Australia

ABSTRACT: In this paper the conjugate transformation of the hexagonal grid is described and its elementary equation is defined. Two strategies are used to extend a matrix morphology into the conjugate transformation. First, the conjugate classification represents 128 structuring elements of the kernel form of the hexagonal grid to a tree of six levels. Each node of a given level is a class of structuring elements with a calculable index. Two conjugate nodes of the same level with the same index can be distinguished by two conjugate sets of $2*n$ classes respectively. Second, by considering each element which has six neighbours as a state for any Boolean matrix of the hexagonal grid, it can be transformed into an index matrix relevant to a specific level of the classification. From the index matrix, two sets of Boolean matrices (feature matrices) can be constructed with the same number of classes on the level. Depending on simpler algebraic properties of feature matrices, dilation and erosion can be unified to one operation, reversion, in the elementary equation. The reversion has a self-duality property with a space of 2^{2*n} functions in which only a total of 2^{n+1} functions are dilation and erosion. In addition, several images generated by applying morphological operations using an implemented prototype of the conjugate transformation and their running complexities compared with a matrix morphology, are illustrated. Owing to the class representation, the new scheme has more than a 4-8 speed-up ratio for the general applications.

Key words: *cellular automata, matrix mathematical morphology, matrix Boolean algebra, image analysis, structuring elements, elementary equation, conjugate classification, conjugate transformation*

Introduction

In the past three decades, mathematical morphology has been developed and a number of basic theorems have been proved by Hadwiger (1957), Matheron (1975) and Serra (1982). A concise treatment of the algebraic properties of erosion, dilation, opening and closing for binary and gray-scale N-dimensional sets, has been taken placement by Haralick *et al.*(1988) and more recently, a matrix morphology has been defined and developed by Wilson (1992). From the algebraic point of view, a matrix morphology is an extensive Boolean matrix algebra relative to a state set of structuring elements.

It is well-known that dilation and erosion are two elementary equations of the mathematical morphology. Depending on the two elementary equations and structuring elements, other functions of mathematical morphology can be constructed, for example opening and closing. There is a duality relationship between dilation and erosion in the form of the complementary and transpose operations. Under traditional schemes of mathematical morphology, if we decompose a complex operation, then it can be reduced to a sequence of dilations and erosions and a state set of structuring elements. In such schemes, dilation or erosion will increase or decrease the number of 1-elements in the matrix monotonicly for any Boolean matrix and a given structuring element. If we let $\mathbf{X}$ be a matrix of a binary image, $\mathbf{0}$ be a 0 matrix and $\mathbf{1}$ be a 1 matrix, then the convergent ranges of dilations and erosions can be shown in Figure 1.

$$\mathbf{0} \overset{Erosions}{\longleftrightarrow} \mathbf{X} \overset{Dilations}{\longleftrightarrow} \mathbf{1}$$

Figure 1: Convergent Ranges of Dilations and Erosions

From the linguistic point of view, dilation and erosion are preferable for describing the operations related to 1-elements rather than 0-elements which are usually regarded as background.

In this paper, a new scheme for describing matrix morphology, the *conjugate transformation*, and its *elementary equation* are defined and investigated on the hexagonal grid. The conjugate transformation is an extended structure of a matrix morphology. It manages a state set of structuring elements as two conjugate class sets, each set containing the same number of classes. If a state of structuring elements is in the k-th class, then its conjugate state (reversing all elements of the state from 1 to 0 or 0 to 1) must be in the k-th conjugate class of structuring elements. Using Boolean matrix operations, for any matrix, each class of structuring elements can decompose the matrix to be a feature matrix. Two class sets of structuring elements are represented to two sets of feature matrices. Depending on the feature matrices and the original image, Boolean matrix operations can be carried out.

For the conjugate transformation, we would like to restrict our representation to the hexagonal grid since we have already established the conjugate classification of the kernel form of the hexagonal grid (Zheng and Maeder 1992). Comparable representations for other regular plane lattices also exist (Zheng 1993 thesis).

We use two strategies to extend the Boolean matrix scheme of mathematical morphology to the conjugate transformation. Firstly, for any Boolean matrix **X** of the hexagonal grid, an element of **X** has the kernel form composed of the given element and six neighbouring elements around it. The kernel form is a *structuring form*, the given seven elements are a *state* of the kernel form, and the state is a *structuring element* (a total of 128 states in the kernel form). Because each element and six neighbouring elements of **X** can correspond to the centre element and six neighbourings of the kernel form, each element of the matrix has a state and the matrix is extended to a state matrix. The state matrix can be organised by a classification. Then, each class of the state matrix can be transformed to a Boolean matrix (or a *feature matrix*) with the same domain as **X**. Since centre elements of the kernel form of **X** can be assigned to 0 or 1, there are two fundamental groups of feature matrices: a matrix (or a conjugate matrix) corresponds to a feature matrix of a class of the state matrix in which their centre elements are equal to 1 (or 0). Using matrix representation, one class of structuring elements on **X** maps correspond to one feature matrix. Therefore, whole classes of the conjugate classification on **X** correspond to two feature matrix sets. Secondly, we combine dilation and erosion to be a unique operation: reversion. In order to reverse a class (or classes) of structuring elements from **X**, it is convenient to use the elementary equation to reverse each element of **X** corresponding to a matrix (or matrices) of two feature matrix sets on **X**.

The elementary equation has self-duality and balanced representation for both 1 and 0 structuring elements. Since the elementary equation can increase and decrease both 0 and 1 elements of **X**, besides typical monotonic functions of dilation and erosion, other functions of the elementary equation have recursive or cyclic properties.

This paper is composed of five sections. In section one, the essential relations between the conjugate classification and respected matrix representation for each class are explained and defined. In section two, the basic algebraic properties of feature matrices are investigated. In section three, the elementary equation of the conjugate transformation is defined and analyzed. In section four, several sample cases of applications, their timing measurements and speed-up ratios (such as the edge detections, noise filters and dynamic patterns generated by an implemented prototype of the conjugate transformation based on the elementary equation and a matrix morphology), are illustrated; and in section five the main contributions of the paper are summarised.

1 Matrix Representations of the Conjugate Transformation

The hexagonal grid plays a significant role in two dimensional image domains. How to represent the fundamental grouping of seven adjacent grid points (the *kernel form*) for the hexagonal grid is a key issue of any descriptive and analytic task on such images. In order to satisfy different circumstances (such as cellular automata, mathematical morphology and parallel Boolean logic computation), several representations for the kernel form of the hexagonal grid applicable to the binary images, have been developed. Examples are Boolean logic (look-up table), symmetric function (Gardner 1971), crossing number (Preston and Duff 1984, pp43-44), Golay transformation [Golay 1969] and conjugate classification (Zheng and Maeder 1992).

1.1 The Conjugate Classification of the Kernel Form

The *kernel form* of the hexagonal grid is a point with six neighbouring points around it. When each point is allowed to assume values of only 0 or 1, there is a total of 128 states corresponding to unique instances of the kernel form. From the state set of 128 states and the inclusion relation of set theory, we can use a tree of six levels to represent the conjugate classification. Each level contains the same of the 128 states and each node is a subset of states. Any two nodes in the same level do not contain the same state. If we let the 128 state set be the root, then the first level can be divided into one state set G and one conjugate state set $\widetilde{G}$ dependent on the value of the centre point (1 or 0). The second level of 14 nodes $\{_pG,_p\widetilde{G}\}$ can be distinguished by p, the number of connections, $0 \leq p \leq 6$, that is, the number of six neighbouring points with the same value of the centre point. The third level of 22 nodes $\{^q_pG\}$ and $\{^q_p\widetilde{G}\}$ is related to q which is the number of branches, $0 \leq q \leq 3$ (the number of runs of the six neighbouring points with the same value of the centre point in each state). The fourth level of 28 nodes $\{^q_pG^s\}$ and $\{^q_p\widetilde{G}^s\}$ has the property of rotational invariant in which any two states in a node can be congruent by rotation, s denotes the number of spins, $s \in \{0,1\}$. The fifth level of 128 leaves $\{^q_pG^s_r\}$ and $\{^q_p\widetilde{G}^s_r\}$ has the simple relation to the respected state, and r denotes the number of rotations $0 \leq r \leq 6$. In short, the conjugate classification is a tree of six levels: one root, 2 nodes, 14 nodes, 22 nodes, 28 nodes and 128 leaves. Each node of the tree is a class of states with 1-5 calculable parameters.

We would like to restrict our investigation to what we term the fundamental structure of the conjugate classification: that is, the substructure of the tree from root to the third level of 22 nodes $\{^q_pG\}$ and $\{^q_p\widetilde{G}\}$. We would expect the entire tree structure would have similar algebraic properties to the fundamental structure. The fundamental structure of the conjugate classification is shown in Figures 2 and 3, where each node contains one state from a rotation invariant class as a representative.

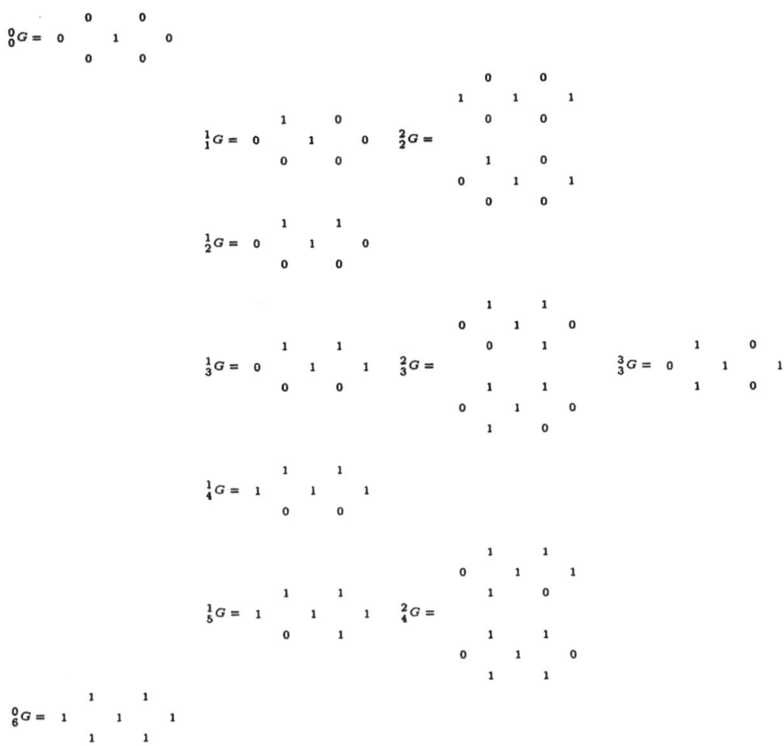

Figure 2: The 11 classes of the Fundamental Structure of the Kernel Form

1.2 The Feature Matrix of the Conjugate Classification

Since the conjugate classification is only a representation for the kernel form of seven points, it is necessary to extend the relations from the kernel form to provide two sets of feature matrices. This is done by following the two steps discussed below.

First, let $\mathbf{X}$ be a Boolean matrix on the hexagonal grid, $\mathbf{X}[i,j] \in \{0,1\}$ be an element at position $[i,j]$ of $\mathbf{X}$, and $\mathbf{X}_{i,j}$ be a *state* in which $\mathbf{X}[i,j]$ is the centre element of the kernel form. If all seven elements of $\mathbf{X}_{i,j}$ have defined positions in $\mathbf{X}$ and fixed values (they are *well-defined* in $\mathbf{X}$) then $\mathbf{X}_{i,j}$ is a *regular* kernel form. However, if $\mathbf{X}[i,j]$ is well-defined and one of its neighbouring elements is not well-defined (i.e. does not have a defined position in $\mathbf{X}$ and a fixed value), then it is a *border* element of $\mathbf{X}$ and $\mathbf{X}_{i,j}$ is an *irregular* kernel form.

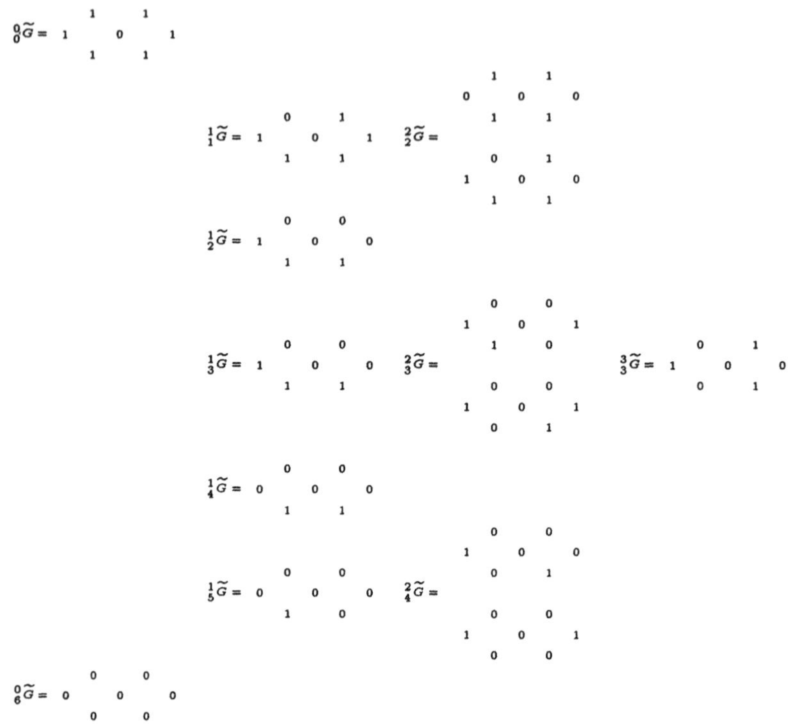

Figure 3: The 11 conjugate classes of the Fundamental Structure of the Kernel Form

Definition 1.2.1 *For any irregular* $\mathbf{X}_{i,j}$, *if* $\mathbf{X}[k,l] \in \mathbf{X}_{i,j}$ *and* $\mathbf{X}[k,l]$ *is not a well-defined element of* $\mathbf{X}$ *then for* $\forall \mathbf{X}[k,l]$, *let*

$$\mathbf{X}[k,l] = \begin{cases} 0 & \textit{if } \mathbf{X}[i,j] = 1; \\ 1 & \textit{if } \mathbf{X}[i,j] = 0. \end{cases}$$

From the above extension, each $\mathbf{X}_{i,j} \in \mathbf{X}$ becomes the regular kernel form.

Second, let $\{G_i\}_{i=0}^{n(v)}$ and $\{\widetilde{G}_j\}_{j=0}^{n(v)}$ be two node sets in a v-th level of the conjugate classification and let a node G_i have a conjugate node $\widetilde{G}_i$ and vice versa. Having selected an element (a node) from $\{G_i\}$ or $\{\widetilde{G}_j\}$ as a class of structuring elements, it is natural to establish a Boolean feature matrix to represent a class of structuring elements as follows.

For any $\mathbf{X}$, let $G_k(\mathbf{X})$ (or $\widetilde{G}_k(\mathbf{X})$) be a feature matrix of G_k (or $\widetilde{G}_k$) and $G_k(\mathbf{X})[i,j]$ (or $\widetilde{G}_k(\mathbf{X})[i,j]$) be the $[i,j]$-th *entry* (element) of the feature matrix. (Definition 1.2.2)

Definition 1.2.2 *For any $[i,j]$ entry of $G_k(\mathbf{X})$ or $\widetilde{G}_k(\mathbf{X})$, let*

$$G_k(\mathbf{X})[i,j] = \begin{cases} 1 & \textit{if } \mathbf{X}_{i,j} \in G_k; \\ 0 & \textit{otherwise;} \end{cases}$$

or

$$\widetilde{G}_k(\mathbf{X})[i,j] = \begin{cases} 0 & \textit{if } \mathbf{X}_{i,j} \in \widetilde{G}_k; \\ 1 & \textit{otherwise.} \end{cases}$$

Given the definition of a feature matrix, all elements of the hexagonal grid are assumed to have proper values even for any entry of an uncertain element beyond the border of $\mathbf{X}$. It is convenient to describe two constant matrices to be $G_0(\mathbf{X}) = \mathbf{0}$ and $\widetilde{G}_0(\mathbf{X}) = \mathbf{1}$ respectively.

Proposition 1.2.3 *For any $\mathbf{X}$ on the hexagonal grid, there are two feature matrix sets for each level in which one matrix set is composed of $2, 8, 12, 15$ or 65 feature matrices corresponding to 1 through 5 levels of the conjugate classification respectively.*

Proof: By the classification, there are two $n(v)$ classes on the v-th level, $n(v) = \{1, 7, 11, 14, 64\}$, $1 \leq v \leq 5$ corresponding to the same number of non-constant matrices that is, $\{G_i(\mathbf{X})\}_{i=1}^{n(v)}$ or $\{\widetilde{G}_i(\mathbf{X})\}_{i=1}^{n(v)}, n(v) \in \{1, 7, 11, 14, 64\}$ respectively and only one constant matrix can be put in a feature matrix set. □

2 Algebraic Properties of the Feature Matrices

2.1 Operations of the Feature Matrices

In order to carry out Boolean matrix operations, it is necessary to extend three elementary Boolean operations ($\neg, \cap, \cup$ or NOT, AND, OR) to matrix descriptions.

Definition 2.1.1 *For three Boolean matrices $\mathbf{X}, \mathbf{Y}$ and $\mathbf{Z}$,*

$$\begin{aligned} \mathbf{X} &= \neg\mathbf{Y}, \ \textit{if } \forall[i,j], \mathbf{X}[i,j] = \neg\mathbf{Y}[i,j]; \\ \mathbf{X} &= \mathbf{Y} \cap \mathbf{Z}, \ \textit{if } \forall[i,j], \mathbf{X}[i,j] = \mathbf{Y}[i,j] \cap \mathbf{Z}[i,j]; \\ \mathbf{X} &= \mathbf{Y} \cup \mathbf{Z}, \ \textit{if } \forall[i,j], \mathbf{X}[i,j] = \mathbf{Y}[i,j] \cup \mathbf{Z}[i,j]. \end{aligned}$$

For a given level, the number of the feature matrices, $n(v)$, is constant so this is simply denoted by n.

Proposition 2.1.2 *For any matrix $\mathbf{X}$, suppose $G(\mathbf{X}) = \cup_{i=0}^{n} G_i(\mathbf{X})$ and $\widetilde{G}(\mathbf{X}) = \cap_{i=0}^{n} \widetilde{G}_i(\mathbf{X})$, then*

$$G(\mathbf{X})[i,j] = \begin{cases} \mathbf{X}[i,j] & \textit{if } \mathbf{X}[i,j] \textit{ can be well-defined;} \\ 0 & \textit{otherwise;} \end{cases}$$

$$\widetilde{G}(\mathbf{X})[i,j] = \begin{cases} \mathbf{X}[i,j] & \textit{if } \mathbf{X}[i,j] \textit{ can be well-defined;} \\ 1 & \textit{otherwise.} \end{cases}$$

Proof: $\{G_k(\mathbf{X})\}_{k=1}^n$ (or $\{\widetilde{G}_k(\mathbf{X})\}_{k=1}^n$) is made of a complete set of feature matrices for all 1-elements (or 0-elements) of $\mathbf{X}$. For any element $\mathbf{X}[i,j]$, if the state of $\mathbf{X}_{i,j} \in G_k$ (or $\widetilde{G}_k$), then there is one 1-element (or 0-element) on $G_k(\mathbf{X})[i,j]$ (or $\widetilde{G}_k(\mathbf{X})[i,j]$), since all 1 elements (or 0 elements) of $\mathbf{X}$ have this property and so they can be regenerated by applying the OR operation (or AND operation) on feature matrices of $G_k(\mathbf{X})$ (or $\widetilde{G}_k(\mathbf{X})$), $1 \leq k \leq n$. For any entry of a non-well-defined element, it has been assumed to be 0 in each entry of $G_k(\mathbf{X})$ or to be 1 in each entry of $\widetilde{G}_k(\mathbf{X})$. □

Corollary 2.1.3 *For any* $\mathbf{X}$, $G(\mathbf{X})$ *and* $\widetilde{G}(\mathbf{X})$, $\mathbf{0} \subset G(\mathbf{X}) \subset \mathbf{X} \subset \widetilde{G}(\mathbf{X}) \subset \mathbf{1}$. *i.e.*

$$\begin{aligned} G(\mathbf{X}) &= \widetilde{G}(\mathbf{X}) \cap G(\mathbf{X}); \\ \mathbf{X} &= \mathbf{X} \cup G(\mathbf{X}) \\ &= \mathbf{X} \cap \widetilde{G}(\mathbf{X}); \\ \widetilde{G}(\mathbf{X}) &= G(\mathbf{X}) \cup \widetilde{G}(\mathbf{X}). \end{aligned}$$

Corollary 2.1.4 *For any* $\mathbf{X}$, *if we ignore all elements beyond the border of* $\mathbf{X}$, *or all elements of* $\mathbf{X}$ *each element can have the regular kernel form, and so*

$$\mathbf{X} = G(\mathbf{X}) = \widetilde{G}(\mathbf{X}).$$

Corollary 2.1.5 *For a general condition, if we have to determine an element beyond* $\mathbf{X}$ *on the grid or* $\mathbf{X}$, *there is an irregular kernel form then*

$$\mathbf{X} \neq G(\mathbf{X}) \neq \widetilde{G}(\mathbf{X}).$$

To generate any Boolean matrix from its feature matrices is a useful property. It makes it possible to use two conjugate sets of feature matrices to represent a Boolean matrix equation in a more convenient form to satisfy multi-requirements of applications.

Using three operations of Boolean matrix, the conjugate operation $\tilde{}$ can be investigated in detail.

Proposition 2.1.6 *For two forms of feature matrices* $G_i(\mathbf{X})$ *and* $\widetilde{G}_i(\mathbf{X})$, *the conjugate symbol* $\tilde{}$ *reverses both a feature matrix and the original matrix,*

$$\widetilde{G}_i(\mathbf{X}) = \neg G_i(\neg \mathbf{X}); \tag{1}$$

$$G_i(\mathbf{X}) = \neg \widetilde{G}_i(\neg \mathbf{X}). \tag{2}$$

Proof: Because each 0 element of $\tilde{G}_i(\mathbf{X})$ describes the i-th class of a 0 element in $\mathbf{X}$, the operation of $\neg\mathbf{X}$ changes all 0 elements of $\mathbf{X}$ to be 1 elements on which the feature matrix of the i-th class of 1 elements, can be calculated. Since each 1 element of $G_i(\neg\mathbf{X})$ describes a corresponding 0 element of $\tilde{G}_i(\mathbf{X})$, another $\neg$ operation has to be performed. The conjugate operation reverses both a feature matrix and the original matrix and so it is a double reversing operation. □

2.2 The Properties of the Feature Matrices

Using the elementary operations on Boolean matrices, more detailed operations of feature matrices can be investigated. To illustrate the operations on two feature matrices, we have four groups of equations.

Proposition 2.2.1 *For any $G_i(\mathbf{X})$ and $G_j(\mathbf{X})$,*

$$G_i(\mathbf{X}) \cap G_j(\mathbf{X}) = \begin{cases} \mathbf{0}, & i \neq j; \\ G_i(\mathbf{X}), & i = j; \end{cases} \tag{3}$$

$$G_i(\mathbf{X}) \cap \neg G_j(\mathbf{X}) = \begin{cases} G_i(\mathbf{X}), & i \neq j; \\ \mathbf{0}, & i = j; \end{cases} \tag{4}$$

$$\neg G_i(\mathbf{X}) \cap G_j(\mathbf{X}) = \begin{cases} G_j(\mathbf{X}), & i \neq j; \\ \mathbf{0}, & i = j; \end{cases} \tag{5}$$

$$\neg G_i(\mathbf{X}) \cap \neg G_j(\mathbf{X}) = \begin{cases} ?, & i \neq j; \\ \neg G_i(\mathbf{X}), & i = j; \end{cases} \tag{6}$$

$$G_i(\mathbf{X}) \cup G_j(\mathbf{X}) = \begin{cases} ?, & i \neq j; \\ G_i(\mathbf{X}), & i = j; \end{cases} \tag{7}$$

$$G_i(\mathbf{X}) \cup \neg G_j(\mathbf{X}) = \begin{cases} \neg G_j(\mathbf{X}), & i \neq j; \\ \mathbf{1}, & i = j; \end{cases} \tag{8}$$

$$\neg G_i(\mathbf{X}) \cup G_j(\mathbf{X}) = \begin{cases} \neg G_i(\mathbf{X}), & i \neq j; \\ \mathbf{1}, & i = j; \end{cases} \tag{9}$$

$$\neg G_i(\mathbf{X}) \cup \neg G_j(\mathbf{X}) = \begin{cases} \mathbf{1}, & i \neq j; \\ \neg G_i(\mathbf{X}), & i = j. \end{cases} \tag{10}$$

Proposition 2.2.2 *For any $\tilde{G}_i(\mathbf{X})$ and $\tilde{G}_j(\mathbf{X})$,*

$$\tilde{G}_i(\mathbf{X}) \cup \tilde{G}_j(\mathbf{X}) = \begin{cases} \mathbf{1}, & i \neq j; \\ \tilde{G}_i(\mathbf{X}), & i = j; \end{cases} \tag{11}$$

$$\widetilde{G}_i(\mathbf{X}) \cup \neg\widetilde{G}_j(\mathbf{X}) = \begin{cases} \widetilde{G}_i(\mathbf{X}), & i \neq j; \\ \mathbf{1}, & i = j; \end{cases} \tag{12}$$

$$\neg\widetilde{G}_i(\mathbf{X}) \cup \widetilde{G}_j(\mathbf{X}) = \begin{cases} \widetilde{G}_j(\mathbf{X}), & i \neq j; \\ \mathbf{1}, & i = j; \end{cases} \tag{13}$$

$$\neg\widetilde{G}_i(\mathbf{X}) \cup \neg\widetilde{G}_j(\mathbf{X}) = \begin{cases} ?, & i \neq j; \\ \neg\widetilde{G}_i(\mathbf{X}), & i = j. \end{cases} \tag{14}$$

$$\widetilde{G}_i(\mathbf{X}) \cap \widetilde{G}_j(\mathbf{X}) = \begin{cases} ?, & i \neq j; \\ \widetilde{G}_i(\mathbf{X}), & i = j; \end{cases} \tag{15}$$

$$\widetilde{G}_i(\mathbf{X}) \cap \neg\widetilde{G}_j(\mathbf{X}) = \begin{cases} \neg\widetilde{G}_j(\mathbf{X}), & i \neq j; \\ \mathbf{0}, & i = j; \end{cases} \tag{16}$$

$$\neg\widetilde{G}_i(\mathbf{X}) \cap \widetilde{G}_j(\mathbf{X}) = \begin{cases} \neg\widetilde{G}_i(\mathbf{X}), & i \neq j; \\ \mathbf{0}, & i = j; \end{cases} \tag{17}$$

$$\neg\widetilde{G}_i(\mathbf{X}) \cap \neg\widetilde{G}_j(\mathbf{X}) = \begin{cases} \mathbf{0}, & i \neq j; \\ \neg\widetilde{G}_i(\mathbf{X}), & i = j. \end{cases} \tag{18}$$

Proposition 2.2.3 *For any $G_i(\mathbf{X})$ and $\widetilde{G}_j(\mathbf{X})$,*

$$G_i(\mathbf{X}) \cap \widetilde{G}_j(\mathbf{X}) = G_i(\mathbf{X}); \tag{19}$$

$$G_i(\mathbf{X}) \cap \neg\widetilde{G}_j(\mathbf{X}) = \mathbf{0}; \tag{20}$$

$$\neg G_i(\mathbf{X}) \cap \widetilde{G}_j(\mathbf{X}) = ?; \tag{21}$$

$$\neg G_i(\mathbf{X}) \cap \neg\widetilde{G}_j(\mathbf{X}) = \neg\widetilde{G}_j(\mathbf{X}); \tag{22}$$

$$G_i(\mathbf{X}) \cup \widetilde{G}_j(\mathbf{X}) = \widetilde{G}_j(\mathbf{X}); \tag{23}$$

$$G_i(\mathbf{X}) \cup \neg\widetilde{G}_j(\mathbf{X}) = ?; \tag{24}$$

$$\neg G_i(\mathbf{X}) \cup \widetilde{G}_j(\mathbf{X}) = \mathbf{1}; \tag{25}$$

$$\neg G_i(\mathbf{X}) \cup \neg\widetilde{G}_j(\mathbf{X}) = \neg G_i(\mathbf{X}). \tag{26}$$

Proposition 2.2.4 *For any $\widetilde{G}_i(\mathbf{X})$ and $G_j(\mathbf{X})$,*

$$\widetilde{G}_i(\mathbf{X}) \cap G_j(\mathbf{X}) = G_j(\mathbf{X}); \tag{27}$$

$$\neg\widetilde{G}_i(\mathbf{X}) \cap G_j(\mathbf{X}) = \mathbf{0}; \tag{28}$$

$$\widetilde{G}_i(\mathbf{X}) \cap \neg G_j(\mathbf{X}) = ?; \tag{29}$$

$$\neg\widetilde{G}_i(\mathbf{X}) \cap \neg G_j(\mathbf{X}) = \neg\widetilde{G}_i(\mathbf{X}); \tag{30}$$

$$\widetilde{G}_i(\mathbf{X}) \cup G_j(\mathbf{X}) = \widetilde{G}_j(\mathbf{X}); \tag{31}$$

$$\neg\widetilde{G}_i(\mathbf{X}) \cup G_j(\mathbf{X}) = ?; \tag{32}$$

$$\widetilde{G}_i(\mathbf{X}) \cup \neg G_j(\mathbf{X}) = \mathbf{1}; \quad (33)$$

$$\neg\widetilde{G}_i(\mathbf{X}) \cup \neg G_j(\mathbf{X}) = \neg G_j(\mathbf{X}). \quad (34)$$

There is a total of 32 equations(3-34) and two groups of equations-(3-10 and 11-18) and (19-26 and 27-34)-have the duality property. If we simply exchange each item of $< G_k(\mathbf{X}), \cap, \cup, 0 >$ to $< \widetilde{G}_k(\mathbf{X}), \cup, \cap, 1 >$ respectively, then one group of equations can be directly changed to another group of equations.

We call an equation of two matrices an *independent* equation, if it cannot be reduced to one of two constant matrices or one of two selected matrices. Otherwise, it is a *dependent* equation.

Corollary 2.2.5 *For any two feature matrices, only eight independent equations under* $\{\neg, \cap, \cup\}$ *operations can be established. They are*

$$\begin{aligned}
\neg G_i(\mathbf{X}) \cap \neg G_j(\mathbf{X}) &= \widetilde{G}_i(\neg\mathbf{X}) \cap \widetilde{G}_j(\neg\mathbf{X}); \\
G_i(\mathbf{X}) \cup G_j(\mathbf{X}) &= \neg\widetilde{G}_i(\neg\mathbf{X}) \cup \neg\widetilde{G}_j(\neg\mathbf{X}); \\
\neg\widetilde{G}_i(\mathbf{X}) \cup \neg\widetilde{G}_j(\mathbf{X}) &= G_i(\neg\mathbf{X}) \cup G_j(\neg\mathbf{X}); \\
\widetilde{G}_i(\mathbf{X}) \cap \widetilde{G}_j(\mathbf{X}) &= \neg G_i(\neg\mathbf{X}) \cap \neg G_j(\neg\mathbf{X}); \\
\neg G_i(\mathbf{X}) \cap \widetilde{G}_j(\mathbf{X}) &= \neg G_i(\mathbf{X}) \cap \neg G_j(\neg\mathbf{X}); \\
G_i(\mathbf{X}) \cup \neg\widetilde{G}_j(\mathbf{X}) &= G_i(\mathbf{X}) \cup G_j(\neg\mathbf{X}); \\
\widetilde{G}_i(\mathbf{X}) \cap \neg G_j(\mathbf{X}) &= \neg G_i(\neg\mathbf{X}) \cap \neg G_j(\mathbf{X}); \\
\neg\widetilde{G}_i(\mathbf{X}) \cup G_j(\mathbf{X}) &= G_i(\neg\mathbf{X}) \cup G_j(\mathbf{X}).
\end{aligned}$$

It is interesting that only 8 equations are independent, while other equations are dependent. Considering the number of equations in a general condition for four groups of two Boolean matrices under $\{\neg, \cap, \cup\}$ operations, there must be 32 independent equations. It is obvious that the conjugate structure has a simpler organization than a general structure of Boolean matrices.

3 The Elementary Equation of the Conjugate Transformation

Since two feature matrix sets are generated from the original matrix, each feature matrix keeps the site information for a class of structuring elements being a Boolean matrix and three Boolean matrix operations can be performed.

Let the *conjugate transformation* be an extensive Boolean matrix structure in which, for any $\mathbf{X}$ on a given domain, it uses $\mathbf{X}$ as an original matrix, $\{G_i\}_{i=0}^n, \{\widetilde{G}_i\}_{i=0}^n$ as two class sets of structuring elements to represent two sets of feature matrices. Using algebraic language, a conjugate transformation CT can be defined as:

$$CT = (\mathcal{X}, \mathcal{C}, \neg, \cap, \cup).$$

Where $\mathcal{X}$ is a fixed domain of Boolean matrices on a specific grid, $\mathcal{C}$ is a conjugate classification of structuring elements and $\{\neg, \cap, \cup\}$ are the elementary operations of Boolean matrices.

The simpler algebraic properties of feature matrices make it possible to establish a more efficient scheme for changing the relevant parts of the original image. For convenience of descriptions to the conjugate transformation, we use the following notations:

Let $I = \{0, 1, \cdots, n\}$ be the index set of the feature matrices, $A, B \subseteq I$ be two index sets. For any given $< A, B >$,

$$< A, B > = \{G_i\}_{i \in A} \cup \{\widetilde{G}_j\}_{j \in B}.$$

The first parameter of $< A, B >$ is an index set of feature classes for 1 elements and the second one is an index set of feature classes for 0 elements.

For example, if $A = \{0, 2, 4\}$ and $B = \{1, 6\}$, then

$$< A, B > = \{G_0, G_2, G_4, \widetilde{G}_1, \widetilde{G}_6\}.$$

For any matrix $\mathbf{X}$, $< A, B > (\mathbf{X})$ is a feature matrix set

$$< A, B > (\mathbf{X}) = \{G_i(\mathbf{X})\}_{i \in A} \cup \{\widetilde{G}_j(\mathbf{X})\}_{j \in B}.$$

From the notations above, it is possible to define a new operation called *reversion* (denoted by $\natural$) to reverse selected parts from the original image on a Boolean matrix structure.

Definition 3.0.6 *For a Boolean matrix* $\mathbf{X}$ *and a feature matrix set of* $< A, B > (\mathbf{X})$, $F(< A, B > |\mathbf{X})$, *the* elementary equation *of the conjugate transformation is defined as:*

$$\begin{aligned} F(< A, B > |\mathbf{X}) &= \mathbf{X} \natural < A, B > (\mathbf{X}) & (35) \\ &= \mathbf{X} \cap (\cap_{i \in A} \neg G_i(\mathbf{X})) \cup (\cup_{j \in B} \neg \widetilde{G}_j(\mathbf{X})). & (36) \end{aligned}$$

Proposition 3.0.7 *The elementary equation is a Boolean matrix equation. It reverses the selected parts of* $< A, B > (\mathbf{X})$ *and keeps other elements of* $\mathbf{X}$ *invariant.*

Proof: The equation (36) is a Boolean matrix equation. It is composed of Boolean matrices and connected by three Boolean operations. Let $\mathbf{Y} = F(< A, B > |\mathbf{X})$ be an output matrix, if $\mathbf{X}[k, l]$ is an element of the i-th class and $i \in A$, then only the operation of $\cap \neg G_i(\mathbf{X})$ makes the

$[k,l]$ element of $\mathbf{Y}$ from 1 to 0. However, if $\mathbf{X}[k,l]$ is an element of the j-th class and $j \in B$, then the operation of $\cup\neg\widetilde{G}_j(\mathbf{X})$ changes the $[k,l]$ element of $\mathbf{Y}$ from 0 to 1. For an element $\mathbf{X}[k,l]$ not in selected classes, $\neg G_i(\mathbf{X})[k,l] = 1$ and $\neg\widetilde{G}_j(\mathbf{X})[k,l] = 0$ the value of $\mathbf{Y}[k,l]$ is equal to $\mathbf{X}[k,l]$. □

Proposition 3.0.8 *The elementary equation is a self-duality equation. It can keep the invariant form under* $\neg$ *operation. For any* $\mathbf{X}$ *and* $< A, B >$*, the duality variables are* $\neg\mathbf{X}$ *and* $< B, A >$*.*

$$\neg F(< A, B > |\mathbf{X}) \quad = \quad F(< B, A > |\neg\mathbf{X}). \tag{37}$$

Proof: From the definition of the elementary equation and basic operations of Boolean matrices, we have the following: (the rule of the deduction is indicated by ** $\cdots$ **)

$$\begin{aligned}
\neg F(< A, B > |\mathbf{X}) &= \neg(\mathbf{X}\natural < A, B > (\mathbf{X})) \\
&= \neg(\mathbf{X} \cap (\cap_{i\in A}\neg G_i(\mathbf{X})) \cup (\cup_{j\in B}\neg\widetilde{G}_j(\mathbf{X}))) \\
&\quad \text{** de Morgan's law **} \\
&= (\neg\mathbf{X} \cup (\cup_{i\in A} G_i(\mathbf{X}))) \cap (\cap_{j\in B}\widetilde{G}_j(\mathbf{X})) \\
&\quad \text{** Distributive law **} \\
&= \neg\mathbf{X} \cap (\cap_{j\in B}\widetilde{G}_j(\mathbf{X})) \cup (\cup_{i\in A} G_i(\mathbf{X})) \cap (\cap_{j\in B}\widetilde{G}_j(\mathbf{X}))) \\
&\quad \text{** Equation (19) **} \\
&= \neg\mathbf{X} \cap (\cap_{j\in B}\widetilde{G}_j(\mathbf{X})) \cup (\cup_{i\in A} G_i(\mathbf{X})) \\
&\quad \text{** Equations (1) and (2) **} \\
&= \neg\mathbf{X} \cap (\cap_{j\in B}\neg G_j(\neg\mathbf{X})) \cup (\cup_{i\in A}\neg\widetilde{G}_i(\neg\mathbf{X})) \\
&= \neg\mathbf{X}\natural < B, A > (\neg\mathbf{X}) \\
&= F(< B, A > |\neg\mathbf{X}). \square
\end{aligned}$$

Proposition 3.0.9 *For a given* $< A, B >$*, if* $A = \{0\}$ *(or* $B = \{0\}$*) then* $F(< A, B > |\mathbf{X})$ *is a dilation equation (or an erosion equation) for* $< A, B > (\mathbf{X})$*.*

Proof:

$$\begin{aligned}
F(< \{0\}, B > |\mathbf{X}) &= \mathbf{X} \cap \neg G_0(\mathbf{X}) \cup (\cup_{j\in B}\neg\widetilde{G}_j(\mathbf{X})) \\
&= \mathbf{X} \cup (\cup_{j\in B}\neg\widetilde{G}_j(\mathbf{X})); \\
F(< A, \{0\} > |\mathbf{X}) &= \mathbf{X} \cap (\cap_{i\in A}\neg G_i(\mathbf{X})) \cup \neg\widetilde{G}_0(\mathbf{X}) \\
&= \mathbf{X} \cap (\cap_{i\in A}\neg G_i(\mathbf{X})). \square
\end{aligned}$$

Proposition 3.0.10 *For any* $\mathbf{X}$ *in the same conditions of Corollary 2.1.4, then four extreme matrices,* $\{\mathbf{X}, \mathbf{1}, \mathbf{0}, \neg\mathbf{X}\}$*, can be generated from the elementary equation. These correspond to* $< A, B > = < \{0\}, \{0\} >, < \{0\}, I >, < I, \{0\} >$ *or* $< I, I >$ *conditions respectively.*

Proof: Under the condition of the corollary, we have the following:

$$\begin{aligned}
F(<\{0\},\{0\}>|\mathbf{X}) &= \mathbf{X}\cap\neg G_0(\mathbf{X})\cup\neg\tilde{G}_0(\mathbf{X}) \\
&= \mathbf{X}\cap\mathbf{1}\cup\mathbf{0} \\
&= \mathbf{X}; \\
F(<\{0\},I>|\mathbf{X}) &= \mathbf{X}\cap\neg G_0(\mathbf{X})\cup\neg\tilde{G}(\mathbf{X}) \\
&= \mathbf{X}\cap\mathbf{1}\cup G(\neg\mathbf{X}) \\
&= \mathbf{X}\cup\neg\mathbf{X} \\
&= \mathbf{1}; \\
F(<I,\{0\}>|\mathbf{X}) &= \mathbf{X}\cap\neg G(\mathbf{X})\cup\neg\tilde{G}_0(\mathbf{X}) \\
&= \mathbf{X}\cap\neg\mathbf{X}\cup\mathbf{0} \\
&= \mathbf{0}; \\
F(<I,I>|\mathbf{X}) &= \mathbf{X}\cap\neg G(\mathbf{X})\cup\neg\tilde{G}(\mathbf{X}) \\
&= \mathbf{X}\cap\neg\mathbf{X}\cup G(\neg\mathbf{X}) \\
&= \mathbf{0}\cup\neg\mathbf{X} \\
&= \neg\mathbf{X}.\square
\end{aligned}$$

Proposition 3.0.11 *For any* $\mathbf{X}$ *and a given* n*, we can generate a set of* 2^{2*n} *functions from the elementary equation of the conjugate transformation.*

Proof: For a total of $2*(n+1)$ feature matrices, two constant matrices with dependent properties cannot be selected independently. For the other $2*n$ matrices, there are two possibilities, they can either be selected or not selected. Each selected condition corresponds to a function. □

4 Sample Pictures and Measurements

Using the feature matrices and the elementary equation, different operations can be constructed. We have implemented a prototype of the conjugate transformation and a matrix morphology for binary images on the hexagonal grid in an X-windows environment. In order to illustrate some operations based on using the conjugate transformation, we use four sets of sample pictures of binary images (Appendix A). It is more convenient to see the effects of the operations directly from these pictures than from an abstract algebraic equation. Three kinds of applications of the four sets of sample pictures are:

1. Two sets of pictures for edge detections (Figure 4 and Figure 5);
2. One set of pictures for smoothings (Figure 6);

3. One set of pictures for dynamic patterns (Figure 7).

Let ${}^{q}_{p} = <{}^{0}_{0}, {}^{0}_{6}, {}^{1}_{1}, {}^{1}_{2}, {}^{1}_{3}, {}^{1}_{4}, {}^{1}_{5}, {}^{2}_{2}, {}^{2}_{3}, {}^{2}_{4}, {}^{3}_{3}> = <1,2,3,4,5,6,7,8,9,10,11>$, then three groups of processed functions can be described by the form of the elementary equation as:

$$\text{Figure 4} = \begin{cases} A = \{1,2,3,5,6,7,8,9,10,11\}, B = \{0\}; & \text{Picture (b)} \\ A = \{1,2,3,4,6,7,8,9,10,11\}, B = \{0\}; & \text{Picture (c)} \\ A = \{1,2,3,4,5,8,9,10,11\}, B = \{0\}; & \text{Picture (d)} \\ A = \{1,2,3,8,9,10,11\}, B = \{0\}; & \text{Picture (e)} \\ A = \{2\}, B = \{0\}; & \text{Picture (f)} \\ A = \{4,5,6,7\}, B = \{0\}; & \text{Picture (g)} \end{cases}$$

$$\text{Figure 5} = \begin{cases} A = \{0\}, B = \{1,2,3,5,6,7,8,9,10,11\}; & \text{Picture (b)} \\ A = \{0\}, B = \{1,2,3,4,6,7,8,9,10,11\}; & \text{Picture (c)} \\ A = \{0\}, B = \{1,2,3,4,5,8,9,10,11\}; & \text{Picture (d)} \\ A = \{0\}, B = \{1,2,3,8,9,10,11\}; & \text{Picture (e)} \\ A = \{0\}, B = \{2\}; & \text{Picture (f)} \\ A = \{0\}, B = \{4,5,6,7\}; & \text{Picture (g)} \end{cases}$$

Figure 6 (b)-(e) $A = \{1,3,4\}, B = \{1,3\}$;

Figure 7 (b)-(g) $A = \{1,2,3,7\}, B = \{5,8,9,10,11\}$.

As a basis for comparison, it is helpful to use the language of 'the game of life' to describe the function of Figure 7(b)-(g) as follows:

Death conditions: For 1-elements,

1. Less than two 1-neighbour; ($A = \{1,3\}$)
2. More than four 1-neighbours. ($A = \{2,7\}$)

Birth conditions: For 0-elements,

1. Three 0-elements; ($B = \{5,9,11\}$)
2. Two branch states. ($B = \{8,9,10\}$)

A comparison of Figure 7 (f) and (g) reveals that a colony of pictures does not grow infinitely to the outside, their borders of the colony are restricted by envelopes and its inner structure keeps changing dynamicly. The function has more invariant properties than the original game of life [Kunii and Takai (1989)]. Depending on the elementary equations, more detailed dynamic patterns of the cellular automata, can be constructed.

Table 1: Time Measurements of Two Schemes

Function	Class	State	CT(unit)	Morph(unit)	Speed-up	Figure
Full Edges	1	1	86	38	0.44	Fig.4 & 5(f)
One Feature	1	6	86	230	2.6	Fig.4 & 5(b)(c)
Two Features	2	12	105	470	4.4	Fig.4 & 5(d)
Block Edges	4	24	142	968	6.8	Fig.4 & 5(e)(g)
Smoothing	5	20	167	805	4.8	Fig.6(b)
Dynamic Pattern	9	52	256	2269	8.8	Fig.7(b)

Note: Where *Class* is the minimized number of relevant classes for the function; *State* is the minimized number of involved states; *CT* is the average number of time units by the Conjugate Transformation; *Morph* is the average number of the time units by the Mathematical Morphology and *Speed-up* is equal to Morph/CT. The *unit* of the measurement time is 1/60 second and the number is the sum of CPU and system CPU units measured by the standard function 'times'. *Figure* declares the processed pictures.

In the mentioned functions, each function can be described as a unique $< A, B >$ scheme or a form of feature matrices corresponding to a specific operation. From the computational viewpoint, it is more economical for some applications to use feature matrices themselves representing the functions directly. Figures 4 and 5 are good examples. Figure 4(b), $F(<\{1,2,3,5,6,7,8,9,10,11\},\{0\}>|\mathbf{X}) = \frac{1}{2}G(\mathbf{X})$, is equivalent to a single feature matrix.

Because of the capability of the class representation to states, the conjugate transformation of the hexagonal grid has significant speed-up ratios compared with the same function performed by the standard implementation of mathematical morphology. The measuring results are listed in Table 1 which illustrates the numerical measurements of the speed-up ratio of running times of two compared schemes on IRIX 4.0.5 System V, Silicon Graphics.

5 Conclusion

In order to overcome two weaknesses of mathematical morphology, a new scheme of matrix mathematical morphology, the *conjugate transformation* and its *elementary equation*, are defined and investigated on the hexagonal grid. The conjugate transformation manages a state set of structuring elements as two conjugate class sets (each set contains the same number of classes). Since the conjugate classification is a hierarchical structure, it is possible to establish a connection from a class of structuring elements on a certain level of the classification to a calculable index of the class. Related to the index set, for any matrix, each class of structuring elements can decompose the matrix into a feature matrix. Two conjugate class sets of structuring elements are transformed to two sets of feature matrices. Depending on the feature matrices and the original matrix, Boolean matrix operations can be constructed. The greatest advantage of the conjugate transformation is that it can process all 1-elements and 0-elements equivalently and the elementary equation has the self-duality properties. Another advantage is that the transformation can be divided into different levels from one class contained in half of the structuring elements to a class contained in only one of the structuring elements. Since the index function is not a Boolean function, our structure has a more extensive framework than previous structures. The universal form of the elementary equation provides a space of 2^{2*n} functions to support different applications. As shown in various examples, each function for an application can be expressed in a simple and concise form with clearly geometric and topological meanings. The class representation guarantees a higher efficiency for common conditions involving multi-structuring elements. Furthermore, it is a general structure for image analysis operations on binary images.

Acknowledgements: The first author would like to express gratitude to the financial support of ADCSS Awards and Monash University Department of Computer Science Scholarship for him towards the undertaking of this work, Prof. Terry Caelli, Dr. Les Kitchen for suggestions to the edge detections and Mrs. Patrizia Rossi for proofreading and editing this paper.

REFERENCES

M. Gardner(1971). "On Cellular Automata, Self-reproduction, the Garden of Eden and the Game 'life'," *Scientific American* 224(2), pp112-117.

M.J.E. Golay(1969). "Hexagonal Parallel Pattern Transformations" *IEEE Trans. Comput.* Vol.18, pp733-740.

H. Hadwiger(1957). *Vorlesungen über Inhalt, Oberfläche, und Isoperimetrie* Berlin: Springer-Verlag, pp. 142-150.

R.M. Haralick, S.R. Sternberg and X. Zhuang(1988). "Image analysis using mathematical morphology," *IEEE Trans. Patt. Anal. Machine. Intell.*, Vol. 9, no. 4, pp. 632-550.

T.Y. Kunii and Y. Takai (1989). "Cellular Self-Reproducing Automata As a Parallel Processing Model for Botanical Colony Growth Pattern Simulation" *New Advances in Computer Graphics: Proceedings of CG International'89*, R.A. Earnshaw and B. Wyvill(Eds.), pp7-22, Springer-Verlag Tokyo.

G. Matheron(1975). *Random Sets and Integral Geometry*, New York: Wiley.

K. Preston, Jr and M.J.B. Duff(1984). *Modern Cellular Automata: Theory and Application* Plenum Press, New York.

S.S. Wilson(1992). "Theory of Matrix Morphology" *IEEE Trans. Patt. Anal. Machine. Intell.*, Vol. 14 no. 6, pp 636-652.

Z.J. Zheng and A.J. Maeder(1992). "The Conjugate Classification of the Kernel Form of the Hexagonal Grid" *Modern Geometric Computing for Visualization*, T.L. Kunii and Y. Shinagawa (Eds), Springer-Verlag, Tokyo, pp73-89.

Z.J. Zheng (1993). "The Conjugate Transformation of the Regular Plane Lattices for Binary Images" Ph.D Thesis (not submitted), Department of Computer Science, Monash University.

Appendix A.

SET ONE: Figures 4.

(a) The Original Image $\mathbf{X}$

(b) $\frac{1}{2}G(\mathbf{X})$

(c) $\frac{1}{3}G(\mathbf{X})$

Figure 4: Edge Detections for Black Elements(1-elements) (a)-(g). (a) original images (256×256); (b)-(g) sample images and (e) = (b) $\cup$ (c) $\cup$ (d); (g) = (a) $\cap\neg$ (e).

(d) $\frac{1}{4}G(\mathbf{X}) \cup \frac{1}{5}G(\mathbf{X})$

(e) Block Edges of (a)

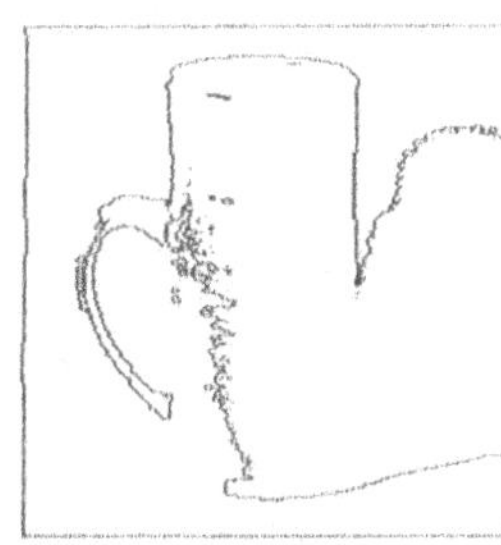

(f) Full Edges of (a)

(g) Erosion of Block Edges to (a)

SET TWO: Figure 5.

(a) The Original Image X

(b) $\frac{1}{2}\widetilde{G}(\mathbf{X})$

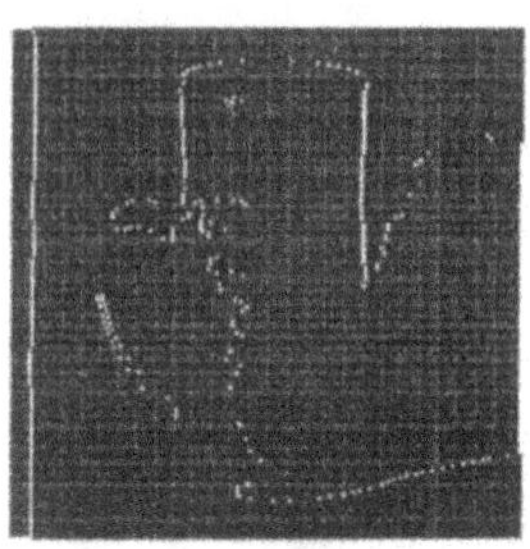

(c) $\frac{1}{3}\widetilde{G}(\mathbf{X})$

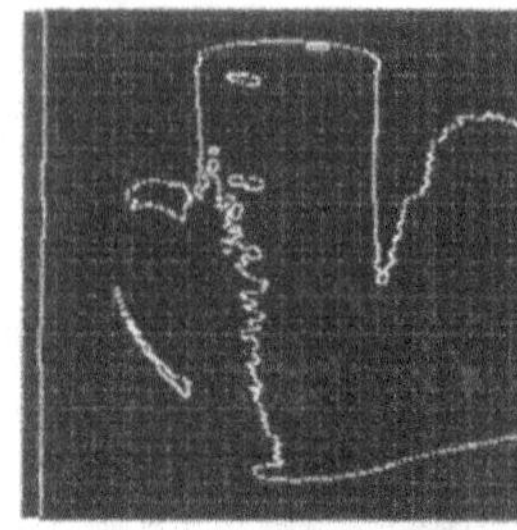

(d) $\frac{1}{4}\widetilde{G}(\mathbf{X}) \cap \frac{1}{5}\widetilde{G}(\mathbf{X})$

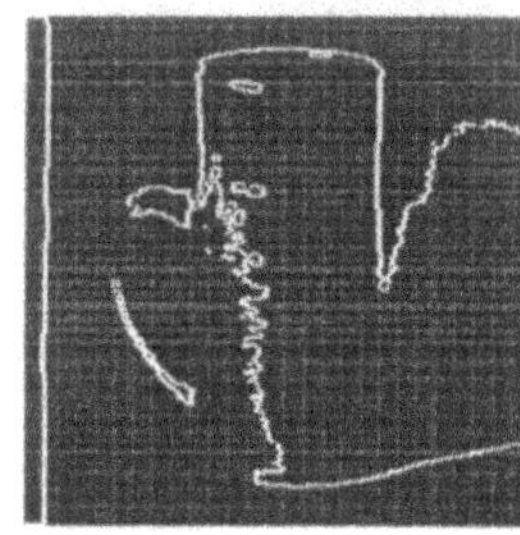

(e) Block Edges of (a)

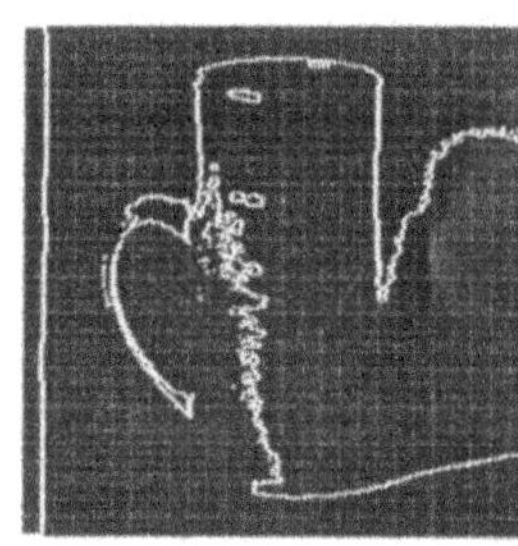

(f) Full Edges of (a)

(g) Dilation of Block Edges of (a)

Figure 5: Edge Detections of White Elements(0-elements) (a)-(g). (a) original images (256×256); (b)-(g) sample images and (e) = (b) $\cap$ (c) $\cap$ (d); (g) = (a) $\cup\neg$ (e).

SET THREE: Figure 6.

(a) The Original Image X

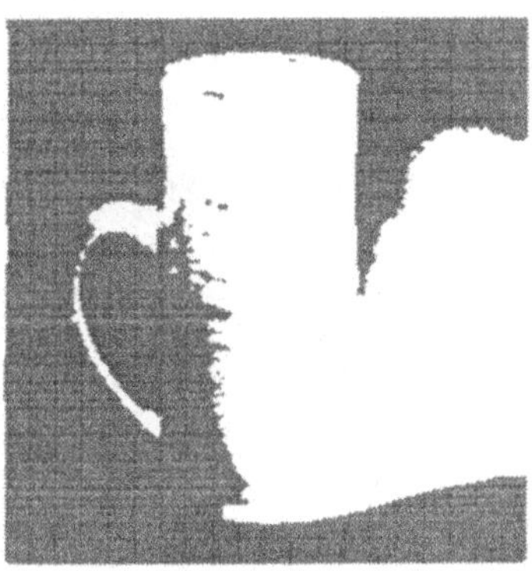

(b) The first smoothing to (a)

Figure 6: Smoothing Operations (a)-(e). (a) original image 256 × 256; (b) once, (c) twice, (d) five and (e) ten recursions.

(c) The second smoothing to (a)

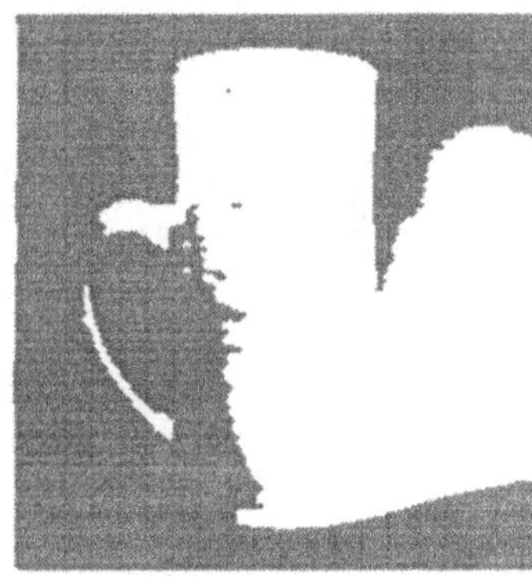

(d) The fifth smoothing to (a)

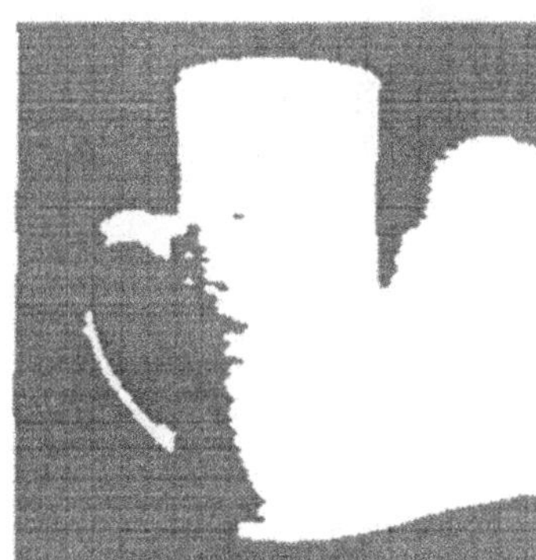

(e) The tenth smoothing to (a)

SET FOUR: Figure 7.

(a) The Original Image X

(b) The Dynamic Pattern of (a)

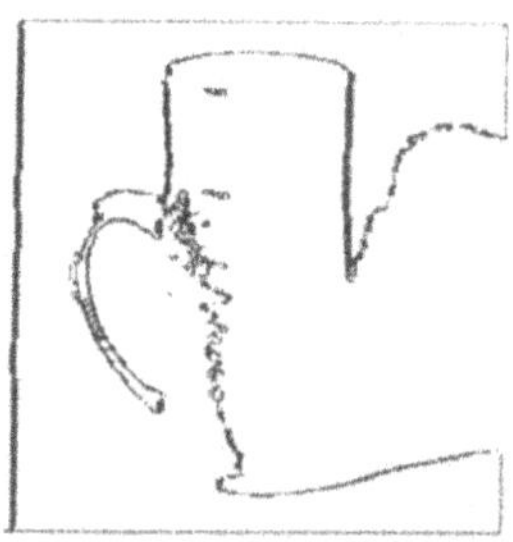

(c) The second recursion of (a)

Figure 7: Dynamic Patterns (a)-(g). (a) original image 256 × 256; (b) 1, (c) 2, (d) 5, (e) 20, (f) 100 and (g) 180 recursions to (a).

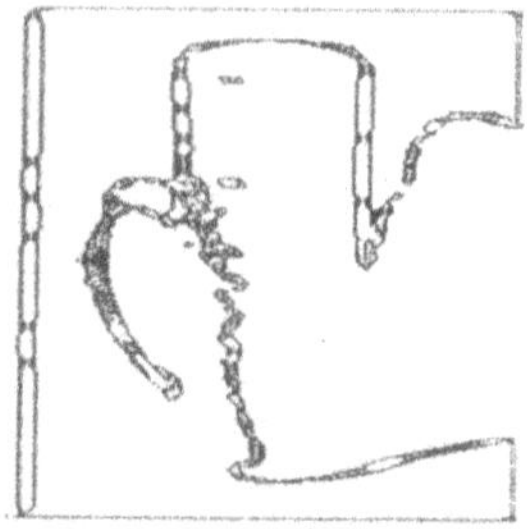

(d) The fifth recursion of (a)

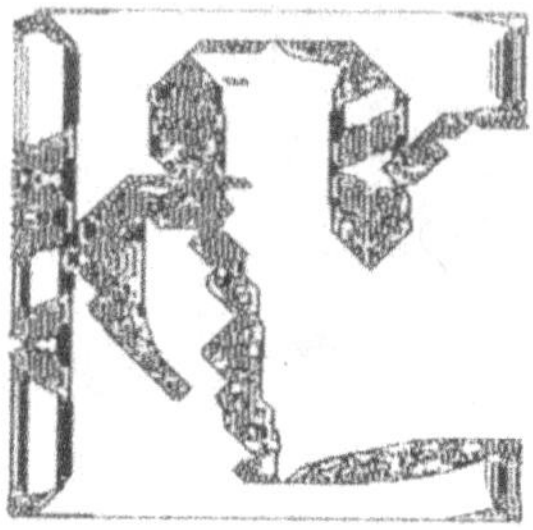

(e) The 20-th recursion of (a)

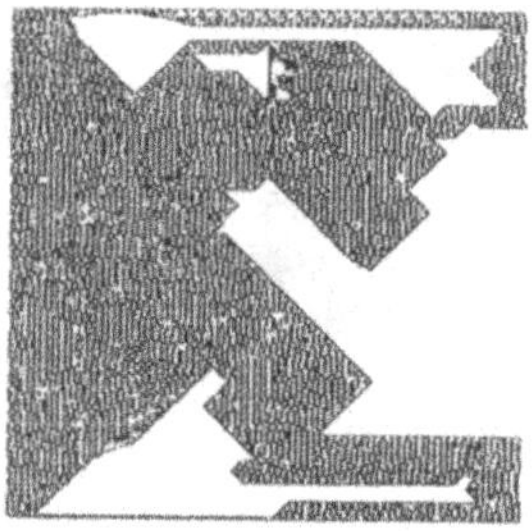

(f) The 100-th recursion of (a)

(g) The 180-th recursion of (a)

Generating Views of $3D$ Objects from Viewer-Centered Representations

Ronen Basri

Dept. of Applied Math.

The Weizmann Institute of Science

Rehovot 76100, Israel

Abstract

Computer vision and graphics applications involve generating views of $3D$ objects. We present a scheme for generating views of objects from viewer-centered representations. In this scheme an object is modeled by a small number of views with the correspondence between the views. Novel views of the object are generated by linearly combining the model views. The scheme handles rigid objects accurately and was extended to handle objects with smooth bounding surfaces and articulated objects. To construct models for this scheme, the correspondence between the model views should be recovered. The paper concludes with an algorithm to achieve such correspondence.

1 Introduction

Computer vision and graphics applications involve generating views of $3D$ objects. Computer vision applications often are required to recognize objects seen at some previously unseen view. A common approach to recognition identifies an object if a view of the

[0]This report describes research done in part at the Massachusetts Institute of Technology within the Artificial Intelligence Laboratory and the McDonnell-Pew Center for Cognitive Neuroscience. Support for the laboratory's artificial intelligence research is provided in part by the Advanced Research Projects Agency of the Department of Defense under Office of Naval Research contract N00014-91-J-4038.

object that matches the observed image can be generated (e.g., Basri and Ullman, 1988; Chien and Aggarwal, 1987; Faugeras and Hebert, 1986; Fischler and Bolles, 1981; Huttenlocher and Ullman, 1990; Lamdan *et al.*, 1987; Lowe, 1985; Thompson and Mundy, 1987; Ullman, 1989). In graphics applications, views of objects are generated to illustrate the appearance of the objects from different perspectives or to create a sense of continuous motion between isolated frames (e.g., Poggio and Brunelli, 1992). This paper presents an efficient and simple scheme for generating views of $3D$ objects from small sets of their images.

Existing approaches for generating views of $3D$ objects handle the problem by storing and manipulating detailed $3D$ descriptions of the objects. A common approach represents an object by a set of volumetric (Bajcsy and Solina, 1987; Binford, 1971; Brown, 1981; Nevatia and Binford, 1977; Requicha and Voelcker, 1977; Marr and Nishihara, 1978), surface (Brady *et al.*, 1985; Sederberg *et al.*, 1984), or wire (Baker, 1977) primitives. To generate a view, the primitives are translated and rotated in $3D$ and then projected to the image plane. Recognition systems often store only the identifiable features (such as corners and line segments) of the object (e.g., Fischler and Bolles, 1981; Huttenlocher and Ullman, 1990; Lamdan *et al.*, 1987; Lowe, 1985). The assumption in these systems is that objects in the world are sufficiently different, and therefore such compact representations would suffice to identify the objects uniquely. These representations are all called *object-centered* since they model an object independent of view.

Viewer-centered representations propose an alternative approach for generating views of $3D$ objects. In this approach an object is represented by a set of its views. Additional information (such as depth) may or may not be stored with the views. Other views of the object are obtained by manipulating the model views. Viewer-centered representations are generally less concise than object-centered descriptions, but they generally are easier to construct and manipulate. An example for a viewer-centered representation is found in (Thompson and Mundy, 1987). In this system an object is modeled by 5184 (72×72) views obtained by rotating the object about the vertical and the horizontal axes by $5°$ intervals. Other views of the object are obtained by selecting one of the images, and then rotating, translating, and scaling the image in $2D$.

The scheme presented in this paper also uses viewer-centered representations, but it requires only a small number of views. In this scheme an object is modeled by a small set of views with the correspondence between the views. Novel views are generated by applying linear combinations to the stored views. The method has several advantages over existing methods. First, it requires only a small number of views to represent an object. Second, the process of generating views is computationally simple. Third, explicit $3D$ representations are not used. Fourth, as is shown below, the method handles rigid (polygonal) objects accurately under weak-perspective projection (orthographic projection followed by a uniform scaling). Finally, the system can also handle rigid objects with smooth bounding surfaces and articulated objects.

The rest of the paper proceeds as follows. In Section 2 the method for generating views by combining model views is presented, and in Section 3 the problem of model construction is discussed.

2 Generating Views by Combining Model Views

The scheme for generating views of $3D$ objects is based on the following observation. If a view is represented by vectors that contain the position of feature points in the image, then the novel views of objects can be generated by linearly combining small numbers of the objects' views. In Section 2.1 we show that using this scheme correct views of rigid (polygonal) $3D$ objects can be generated. Extensions to rigid objects with smooth bounding surfaces and to articulated objects are briefly mentioned in Section 3.2. A detailed description of the scheme can be found in (Basri, 1993; Ullman and Basri, 1991).

2.1 Rigid Objects

We begin with the following definitions. Given an image I containing n feature points, $p_1 = (x_1, y_1)$, ..., $p_n = (x_n, y_n)$, a *view* V_I is a pair of vectors $\vec{x}, \vec{y} \in \mathcal{R}^n$, where $\vec{x} = (x_1, ..., x_n)^T$ and $\vec{y} = (y_1, ..., y_n)^T$ contain the location of the feature points, p_1, ..., p_n, in the image. A *model* is a set of views $\{V_1, ..., V_k\}$. The location vectors in these views are ordered in correspondence, namely, the first point in V_1 is the projection of the same physical point on the object as the first point in V_2, and so forth. The objects we consider undergo rigid transformations, namely, rotations and translations in space. We assume that the images are obtained by weak-perspective projection, that is, orthographic projection following by a uniform scaling.

Below we show that the novel views of a rigid object can be expressed as linear combinations of a small number of its views. The proof proceeds in the following way. First, we show (Theorem 1) that the set of views of a rigid object is contained in a four-dimensional linear space. Any four linearly independent vectors from this space therefore can be used to span the space. Consequently, we show (Theorem 2) that two views suffice to represent the space. Any other view of the object can be expressed as (two) linear combinations of the two basis views. Finally, we show (Theorem 3) that not every point in this $4D$ space necessarily corresponds to a legal view of the object. The coefficients satisfy two quadratic constraints. These constraints depend on the transformation between the model views. A third view can be used to derive the constraints.

Theorem 1: The views of a rigid object are contained in a four-dimensional linear space.

Proof: Consider an object O that contains n feature points $P_1 = (X_1, Y_1, Z_1)$, ..., $P_n = (X_n, Y_n, Z_n)$. Let I be an image of O obtained by a rotation R, translation $\vec{t}$, and scaling s, followed by an orthographic projection, Π. Let $p_1 = (x_1, y_1)$, ..., $p_n = (x_n, y_n)$ be the projected location in I of the points P_1, ..., P_n respectively. For every $1 \leq i \leq n$

$$p_i = s\Pi(RP_i + \vec{t}) \tag{1}$$

more explicitly, these equations can be written as

$$\begin{aligned} x_i &= s(r_{11}X_i + r_{12}Y_i + r_{13}Z_i + t_x) \\ y_i &= s(r_{21}X_i + r_{22}Y_i + r_{23}Z_i + t_y) \end{aligned} \tag{2}$$

where $\{r_{ij}\}$ are the components of the rotation matrix, and t_x, t_y are the horizontal and the vertical components of the translation vector. (Under weak-perspective projection the depth component of the translation vector, t_z, affects only the value of s.) Since these equations hold for every $1 \leq i \leq n$, we can rewrite them in a vector notation. Denote $\vec{X} = (X_1, ..., X_n)^T$, $\vec{Y} = (Y_1, ..., Y_n)^T$, $\vec{Z} = (Z_1, ..., Z_n)^T$, $\vec{1} = (1, ..., 1)^T$, $\vec{x} = (x_1, ..., x_n)^T$, and $\vec{y} = (y_1, ..., y_n)^T$, we obtain that

$$\begin{aligned} \vec{x} &= a_1\vec{X} + a_2\vec{Y} + a_3\vec{Z} + a_4\vec{1} \\ \vec{y} &= b_1\vec{X} + b_2\vec{Y} + b_3\vec{Z} + b_4\vec{1} \end{aligned} \tag{3}$$

where

$$
\begin{aligned}
a_1 &= sr_{11} & b_1 &= sr_{21} \\
a_2 &= sr_{12} & b_2 &= sr_{22} \\
a_3 &= sr_{13} & b_3 &= sr_{23} \\
a_4 &= st_x & b_4 &= st_y
\end{aligned} \tag{4}
$$

The vectors $\vec{x}$ and $\vec{y}$ can therefore be expressed as linear combinations of four vectors, $\vec{X}$, $\vec{Y}$, $\vec{Z}$, and $\vec{1}$. Notice that changing the view would result merely in a change in the coefficients. We can therefore conclude that

$$\vec{x}, \vec{y} \in span\{\vec{X}, \vec{Y}, \vec{Z}, \vec{1}\} \tag{5}$$

for any view of O. Note that if translation is omitted the views space is reduced to a three-dimensional one. □

Theorem 2: The views space of a rigid object O can be constructed from two views of O[1].

Proof: Theorem 1 above establishes that the views space of a rigid object is four-dimensional. Any four linearly independent vectors in this space can be used to span the space. The constant vector, $\vec{1}$, belongs to this space. Therefore, only three more vectors are remained to be found. An image supplies two vectors. Two images supply four, which is already more than enough to span the space (assuming the two images are related by some rotation in depth, otherwise they are linearly dependent). Let $V_1 = (\vec{x}_1, \vec{y}_1)$ and $V_2 = (\vec{x}_2, \vec{y}_2)$ be two views of O, a novel view $V' = (\vec{x}', \vec{y}')$ of O can be expressed as two linear combinations of the four vectors $\vec{x}_1$, $\vec{y}_1$, $\vec{x}_2$, and $\vec{1}$. The remaining vector, $\vec{y}_2$, already depends on the other four vectors. □

Up to this point we have shown that the views space of a rigid object is contained in a four-dimensional linear space. Theorem 3 below establishes that not every point in this space corresponds to a legal view of the object. The coefficients of the linear combination satisfy two quadratic constraints.

Theorem 3: The coefficients satisfy two quadratic constraints, which can be derived from three images.

[1]This lower bound was independently noticed by Poggio (1990)

Proof: Consider the coefficients a_1, ..., a_4, b_1, ..., b_4 from Theorem 1. Since R is a rotation matrix, its row vectors are orthonormal, and therefore the coefficients satisfy the following quadratic constraints

$$\begin{aligned} a_1^2 + a_2^2 + a_3^2 &= b_1^2 + b_2^2 + b_3^2 \\ a_1 b_1 + a_2 b_2 + a_3 b_3 &= 0 \end{aligned} \tag{6}$$

Choosing a different basis to represent the object (as we did in Theorem 2) will change the constraints. The constraints depend on the transformation that separates the model views. Given an object $O = (\vec{X}, \vec{Y}, \vec{Z})$, let $V_1 = (\vec{x}_1, \vec{y}_1)$ and $V_2 = (\vec{x}_2, \vec{y}_2)$ be two model views of O such that $\vec{x}_1 = \vec{X}$, $\vec{y}_1 = \vec{Y}$, and V_2 is obtained by a rotation U, translation $\vec{t}'$, and scaling s'. According to Theorem 2, a novel view $V' = (x', y')$ of O can be expressed as

$$\begin{aligned} \vec{x}' &= \alpha_1 \vec{x}_1 + \alpha_2 \vec{y}_1 + \alpha_3 \vec{x}_2 + \alpha_4 \vec{1} \\ \vec{y}' &= \beta_1 \vec{x}_1 + \beta_2 \vec{y}_1 + \beta_3 \vec{x}_2 + \beta_4 \vec{1} \end{aligned} \tag{7}$$

for some $\alpha_1, ..., \alpha_4$, $\beta_1, ..., \beta_4$. Plugging the value of $\vec{x}_2$

$$\begin{aligned} \vec{x}_2 &= s'(u_{11}\vec{X} + u_{12}\vec{Y} + u_{13}\vec{Z} + t'_x) \\ \vec{y}_2 &= s'(u_{21}\vec{X} + u_{22}\vec{Y} + u_{23}\vec{Z} + t'_y) \end{aligned} \tag{8}$$

into Eq. 7, we obtain

$$\begin{aligned} \vec{x}' &= (\alpha_1 + \alpha_3 s' u_{11})\vec{X} + (\alpha_2 + \alpha_3 s' u_{12})\vec{Y} + (\alpha_3 s' u_{13})\vec{Z} + (\alpha_4 + \alpha_3 s' t'_x)\vec{1} \\ \vec{y}' &= (\beta_1 + \beta_3 s' u_{11})\vec{X} + (\beta_2 + \beta_3 s' u_{12})\vec{Y} + (\beta_3 s' u_{13})\vec{Z} + (\beta_4 + \beta_3 s' t'_x)\vec{1} \end{aligned} \tag{9}$$

which contains the explicit values of the coefficients $a_1, ..., a_4$, $b_1, ..., b_4$ from Eq. 6. Substituting these values into Eq. 6, we obtain the following constraints on $\alpha_1, ..., \alpha_4$, $\beta_1, ..., \beta_4$:

$$\begin{aligned} \alpha_1^2 + \alpha_2^2 + \alpha_3^2 - \beta_1^2 - \beta_2^2 - \beta_3^2 = 2(\beta_1\beta_3 - \alpha_1\alpha_3)u_{11} + 2(\beta_2\beta_3 - \alpha_2\alpha_3)u_{12} \\ \alpha_1\beta_1 + \alpha_2\beta_2 + \alpha_3\beta_3 + (\alpha_1\beta_3 + \alpha_3\beta_1)u_{11} + (\alpha_2\beta_3 + \alpha_3\beta_2)u_{12} = 0 \end{aligned} \tag{10}$$

where u_{11} and u_{12} are the two upper left components of U. To derive the constraints, the values of u_{11} and u_{12} should be recovered. A third view can be used for this purpose. When a third view of the object is given, the constraints supply two linear equations in u_{11} and u_{12}, and, therefore, in general, the values of u_{11} and u_{12} can be recovered from the two constraints. This proof suggests a simple, essentially linear structure from motion algorithm that resembles the method used in (Huang and Lee, 1989; Ullman, 1979), but the details will not be discussed further here. □

The scheme therefore is the following. An object is modeled by a set of views, with the correspondence between the views, together with the two constraints. Novel views of

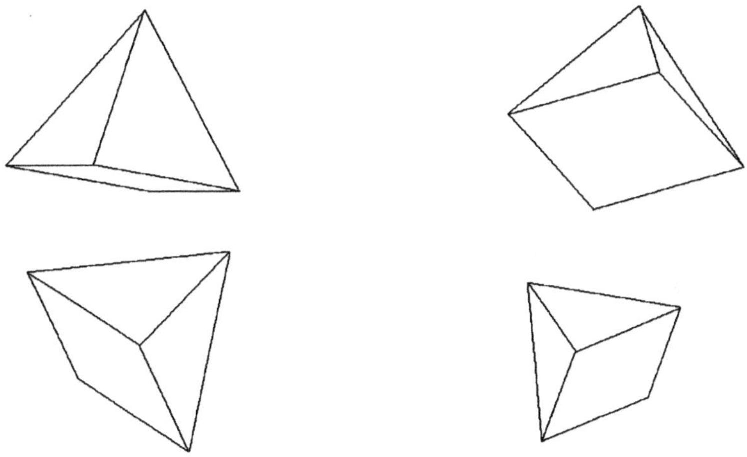

Figure 1: Generating views of a pyramid. Top: two model pictures of a pyramid. Bottom: two of their linear combinations.

the object are generated by linearly combining the model views. Applying the quadratic constraints to the coefficients guarantees that the novel views in fact represent a rigid transformation of the object. In recognition applications, the obtained views are compared with the actual image, and if a satisfactory match is achieved the object's identity is determined. Figure 1 shows the application of the linear combination scheme to an artificially made object.

Although two views are sufficient to represent an object, in order to reduce noise and occlusion one may seek to use additional views to improve the accuracy of the model. The problem is then the following. Given l view vectors $\vec{v}_1, ..., \vec{v}_l$, recover the nearest four-dimensional hyperplane to these vectors. The obtained hyperplane is the linear sub-space that best explains the view vectors. The nearest hyperplane can be found by applying principal components techniques. A detailed algorithm can be found in (Ullman and Basri, 1991) (see also Tomasi and Kanade, 1991).

For transparent objects, a single model is sufficient to predict their appearance from all possible viewpoints. For opaque objects, due to self occlusion, a number of models is required to represent the objects from all aspects. These models are not necessarily independent. For example, in the case of a convex object as few as four images are sufficient to represent the object from all possible viewpoints. A pair of images, one from the "front" and another one from the "back" contains each object point once. Two such pairs contain two appearances of all object points, which is what is required to obtain a complete representation of all object points. For concave objects additional views may be required.

Note that positive values of the coefficients ("convex combinations") correspond to interpolation between the model views, while extrapolation is obtained by assigning one or more of the coefficients with negative values. This distinction between intermediate views and other views is important, since if two views of the object come from the same aspect (namely, include the same parts of the object), then intermediate views are likely to also come from that aspect, while in other views other aspects of the objects may be observed.

A method that approximates the space of views of an object from a number of its views using Radial Basis Functions (Poggio and Girosi, 1990) was recently suggested (Poggio and Edelman, 1990). Similar to our method, the system represents an object by a set of its familiar views with the correspondence between the views. The number of views used for this approximation, between 10 to 100, is much larger than the number required under the linear combinations scheme. The system, however, can also handle perspective views of the objects.

2.2 Extensions

We have shown in the previous section that the linear combinations scheme accurately handles rigid (polygonal) objects under weak-perspective projection. The scheme can also handle objects that undergo general affine transformation in $3D$, rigid objects with smooth bounding surfaces, and articulated objects. This is achieved by changing the number of model views, or by changing the functional constraints. A brief description is given below.

The scheme can be extended to handle objects that undergo general affine transformation in $3D$ (including stretch and shear) simply by ignoring the quadratic constraints. In this case two views are required to span the space, and every point in this space represents a legal view of the object.

The scheme can also be extended to handle rigid objects with smooth bounding surfaces. The problem with such an object is that its contours appear in different locations on the object at different views. Using three rather than two views (the space of views for such objects is six- rather than four-dimensional), the curvature of the points along the contour is (implicitly) taken into account, providing a better prediction of the contour position following rotation. For details see (Basri and Ullman, 1988; Basri, 1992; Ullman and Basri, 1991).

Finally, articulated objects can also be modeled by our scheme. An articulated object is a collection of links connected by joints. Each link is a rigid component. It can move independently of the other links when only its joints constrain its motion. The space of views of an articulated object with l links is at most $(4 \times l)$-dimensional. The joints contribute additional constraints, some of which may be linear, and they reduce the rank of the space, others are non-linear, in which case they are treated in the same way the quadratic constraints are treated in the rigid case. For example, an object with two rigid links connected by a rotational joint can be modeled by a six-dimensional linear space (Basri 1993). Three views can be used in these cases to span the space. Articulated objects with different numbers of links or with different types of joints require different number of views. Advance knowledge of the number of links and the type of joints, however, is not required. When sufficiently many views are presented, the correct rank of the views space can be recovered using principal components analysis.

Figure 2 shows the application of the scheme to several objects with smooth bounding surfaces and to articulated objects. The figure shows views of the objects generated by combining several model views and the matching of these views to actual contour images of the objects.

In our implementation we considered only the contour points of the object. The method, however, can be used in conjunction with other methods to obtain richer appearances of the objects. For instance, texture mapping can be applied to the surfaces between the contours or illumination patterns can be constructed on these surfaces. A scheme that recovers the illumination in lambertian surfaces by linearly combining three gray-level images was recently proposed (Moses, 1992; Shashua, 1991).

3 Model Construction

To use the scheme for generating views of $3D$ objects, models for the objects first must be constructed. As is mentioned above, objects are modeled in our scheme by sets of

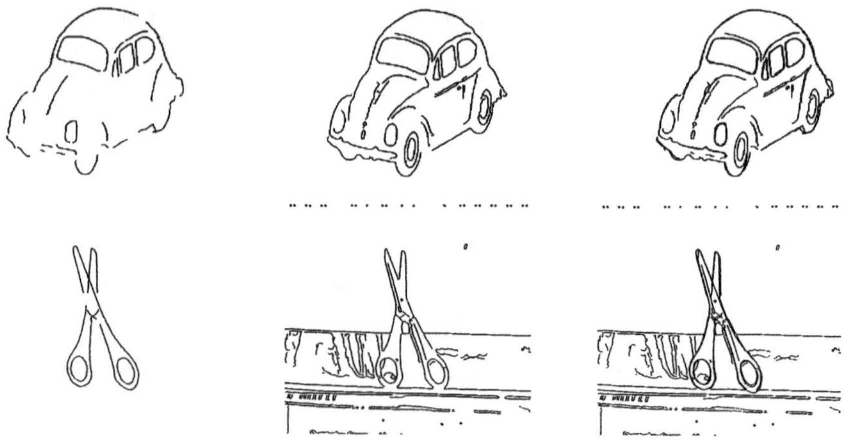

Figure 2: Generating views of a VW car and a pair of scissors. Top: matching the model to a picture of the VW car. A linear combination of model images (left), an actual edge image (middle), and the two images overlayed (right). Bottom: matching a model to a picture a scissors. A linear combinations of model images (left), an actual edge image (middle), and the two images overlayed (right). The prediction images and the actual ones align almost perfectly.

their views with the correspondence between the views. The difficult part of constructing object models, therefore, is resolving the correspondence between views. This difficulty exists also in schemes that use object-centered models, since correspondence is required for recovering the $3D$ shape of the objects from sets of $2D$ images.

In this section we outline an algorithm for recovering full point-to-point correspondence between images. Given two images of an object, the algorithm proceeds in three steps. First, the epipolar lines in the two images are computed. This can be done either by calibrating the camera externally or by tracking the position of four identifiable points in the images. (Under weak-perspective projection four non coplanar points are sufficient to recover the epipolar lines (Huang and Lee, 1989; Lee and Huang, 1990).) Next, the correspondence between contours is resolved. At this stage topological criteria, such as whether the contour is long or short, closed or straight, can be used. Also, if the object is opaque the order of the contours along the epipolar lines is preserved. Finally, point-to-point correspondence is resolved by intersecting the contours with the epipolar lines. This procedure would work unless the contours coincide with the epipoles.

The epipolar constraint is the following. Given two images I_1 and I_2 of an object obtained by applying a rigid (or even affine) transformation to the object, it is possible to slice the images into straight lines $\{l_i^1\}$ and $\{l_i^2\}$ respectively, such that every point on l_i^1 corresponds to a point on l_i^2 and vice versa. Consequently, once the epipolar lines are recovered, the process of resolving the correspondence between the images is reduced to resolving the correspondence within pairs of epipolar lines.

Under weak-perspective projection, epipolar lines are parallel to each other, and four pairs of corresponding points can be used to recover the epipoles (Huang and Lee, 1989; Lee and Huang, 1990). This can be derived directly from Theorem 1. Since the views of a rigid object are embedded in a four dimensional space, two images I_1 and I_2 provide four vectors $\vec{x}_1$, $\vec{y}_1$, $\vec{x}_2$, and $\vec{y}_2$, which, together with the constant vector $\vec{1}$, must be linearly dependent. In other words, there exist nonzero scalars a_1, a_2, b_1, b_2, and c such that

$$a_1\vec{x}_1 + a_2\vec{y}_1 + b_1\vec{x}_2 + b_2\vec{y}_2 + c\vec{1} = 0 \tag{11}$$

The coefficients are determined (up to a scale factor) by four non coplanar points. The epipolar line are immediately derived from this equation. If we fix some point in the first image we obtain a line equation for the corresponding point in the second image.

The epipolar lines break the transformation that relates the images into its planar components and its non planar ones. The planar components can be recovered from the epipolar lines, while the non planar ones cannot be determined from two images. Suppose the two images are related by a rotation R, translation $\vec{t}$, and scaling s. The translation component perpendicular to the epipolar line is given by c. (The translation components can be discarded altogether if we consider differences between points rather than their actual location.) The values of the other coefficients are given below.

$$\begin{aligned} a_1 &= sr_{32} \\ a_2 &= -sr_{31} \\ b_1 &= r_{23} \\ b_2 &= -r_{13} \end{aligned} \tag{12}$$

The scale factor is therefore given by the ratio

$$s = \sqrt{\frac{a_1^2 + a_2^2}{b_1^2 + b_2^2}} \tag{13}$$

The relative angle between the epipolar lines determines the planar parts of the rotation, as explained below. Rotation in $3D$ can be decomposed into a sequence of three successive rotations: a rotation about the Z-axis by an angle α, a second rotation about the Y-axis by

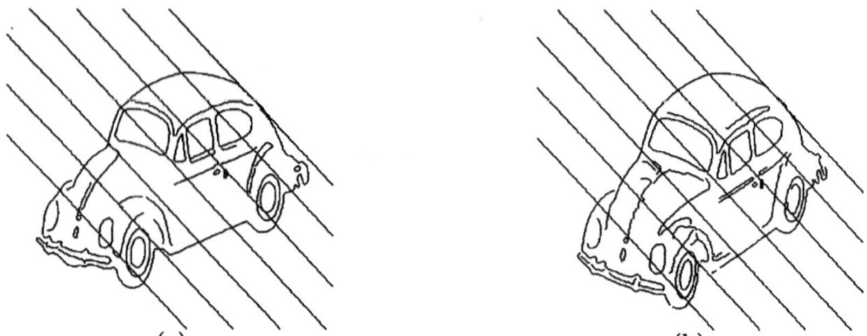
(a) (b)

Figure 3: Epipolar lines in two orthographic projections of a VW car. Note the fact that corresponding points lie along the epipolar lines.

an angle β, and a third rotation about the Z-axis by an angle γ. Under this decomposition the following identities hold

$$\begin{aligned} r_{32} &= \sin\alpha\sin\beta \\ r_{31} &= -\cos\alpha\sin\beta \\ r_{23} &= \sin\beta\sin\gamma \\ r_{13} &= \sin\beta\cos\gamma \quad . \end{aligned} \tag{14}$$

We therefore obtain that

$$\begin{aligned} \alpha &= \tan^{-1}\tfrac{a_1}{a_2} \\ \gamma &= -\tan^{-1}(-\tfrac{b_1}{b_2}) \end{aligned} \tag{15}$$

while β cannot be determined.

We can visualize this decomposition in the following way. After compensating for the translation and scale changes, we first rotate the image P_1 by α. Consequently, the epipolar lines in P_1 point to the horizontal direction. Next, we rotate the second image, P_2, by $-\gamma$. As a result, the epipolar lines in P_2 also point horizontally. The images obtained in this process are related by a rotation about the vertical axis, which is a rotation in depth. Following such a rotation the points move horizontally, namely, along the (rotated) epipolar lines. This motion cannot be recovered since it depends both on the angle of rotation, β, and on the depth of the points.

Figure 3 shows the epipolar lines in a pair of VW images. It can be seen that, in general, using the epipolar lines, when the correspondence between contours is given, point-to-point correspondence is uniquely determined.

4 Summary

We have presented a scheme for generating views of $3D$ objects. An object is modeled in this scheme by a small set of its views with the correspondence between the views. Novel views of the object are generated by linearly combining the model views. The scheme handles rigid objects accurately and was extended to handle rigid objects with smooth bounding surfaces and articulated objects.

To build models for the scheme, full point-to-point correspondence between the model views should be recovered. This can be done by matching the contours in these views using topological criteria and then intersecting the contours with the epipolar lines.

The scheme can be used for object recognition and graphics applications. In recognition, given an image, a system would attempt to generate a view of the object that matches the image. In graphics applications, the scheme can be used for presenting an object from several perspectives and for generating interframe views for creating a continuous sense of motion. Unlike in existing schemes, explicit $3D$ representations of the objects are not used. Additional research is required here for effectively handling the different aspects of the objects.

Acknowledgments

I wish to thank Shimon Ullman for his advice and Yael Moses for her comments on earlier drafts of this paper. A partial version of this paper were reported in C. H. Chen, L. F. Pau and P. S. P. Wang (Eds.), *Handbook of Pattern Recognition and Computer Vision*, World Scientific Publishing Company, Singapore.

References

Bajcsy, R. and Solina, F. (1987) Three dimensional object representation revisited. *Proc. of 1st Int. Conf. on Computer Vision, London* 231–240.

Baker, H. (1977) Three-dimensional modeling. *Proc. 5th Int. Joint Conf. on Artificial Intelligence (Cambridge, Mass., Aug 22-25)* 649–655.

Basri, R. and Ullman, S. (1988) The alignment of objects with smooth surfaces. *Proc. of 2nd Int. Conf. of Computer Vision, Florida* 482–488.

Basri, R. (1992) The alignment of objects with smooth surfaces: error analysis of the curvature method. *Proc. Computer Vision and Pattern Recognition, Urbana.*

Basri, R. (1993) Viewer-centered representations in object recognition: a computational approach. To appear in C. H. Chen, L. F. Pau and P. S. P. Wang (Eds.), *Handbook of Pattern Recognition and Computer Vision*, World Scientific Publishing Company, Singapore.

Binford, T. O. (1971) Visual perception by computer. *IEEE Conf. on Systems and Control*

Brady, M., Ponce, J., Yuille, A., and Asada, H. (1985) Describing surfaces. *Computer Vision, Graphics, and Image Processing* 32:285–349.

Brown, C. M. (1981) Some mathematical and representational aspects of solid modeling. *IEEE Trans. on Pattern Analysis and Machine Intelligence* 3(4).

Chien, C. H. and Aggarwal, J. K. (1987) Shape recognition from single silhouette. *Proc. of 1st Int. Conf. on Computer Vision, London* 481–490.

Faugeras, O. D. and Hebert, M. (1986) The representation, recognition and location of 3D objects. *Int. J. Robotics Research* 5(3):27–52.

Fischler, M. A. and Bolles, R. C. (1981) Random sample consensus: a paradigm for model fitting with application to image analysis and automated cartography. *Com. of the A.C.M.* 24(6):381–395.

Huang, T. S. and Lee, C. H. (1989) Motion and Structure from Orthographic Projections. *IEEE Trans. on Pattern Analysis and Machine Intelligence* 11(5):536–540.

Huttenlocher, D. P., and Ullman, S. (1990) Recognizing Solid Objects by Alignment with an Image, *Int. J. Computer Vision* 5(2):195–212.

Lamdan, Y., Schwartz, J. T., and Wolfson, H. (1987) On recognition of 3-D objects from 2-D images. *Courant Inst. of Math. Sci., Rob. TR 122.*

Lee, C. H. and Huang, T. S. (1990) Finding point correspondences and determining motion of a rigid object from two weak perspective views. *Computer Vision, Graphics, and Image Processing* 52:309–327.

Lowe, D. G. (1985) Three-dimensional object recognition from single two-dimensional images. *Courant Inst. of Math. Sci., Rob. TR 202*

Marr, D. and Nishihara, H. K. (1978) Representation and recognition of the spatial organization of three-dimensional shapes. *Proc. of the Royal Society, London* B200:269–294.

Moses, Y. (1992) *Doctorate Dissertation, The Weizmann Institute of Science*, Rehovot, Israel.

Nevatia, R. and Binford, T. O. (1977) Description and recognition of curved objects. *Artificial Intelligence* 8:77–98.

Poggio, T. (1990) 3D object recognition: on a result by Basri and Ullman, *TR 9005-03, IRST, Povo, Italy.*

Poggio, T. and Edelman, S. (1990) A network that learns to recognize three-dimensional objects, *Nature* 343:263–266.

Poggio, T. and Girosi, F. (1990) Regularization algorithms for learning that are equivalent to multilayer networks, *Science* 247:978–982.

Poggio, T. and Brunelli, R. (1992) A Novel Approach to Graphics. *M.I.T., A.I. Lab, Memo 1354, CBIP paper 71.*

Requicha, A. and Voelcker, H. (1977) Constructive solid geometry. *Tm-26, Production Automation Project, University of Rochester, NY.*

Sederberg, T. W., Anderson, D. C., and Goldman, R. N. (1984) Implicit representation of parametric curves and surfaces. *Computer Vision, Graphics, and Image Processing* 28:72–84.

Shashua, A. (1991) Illumination and view position in 3D visual recognition. In Moody, J.E., Hanson, S.J., and Lippmann, R.P., (eds.), *Advances in Neural Information Processing systems 4 (NIPS-4)*, San Mateo, CA: Morgan Kaufmann publishers 404–411.

Thompson, D. W. and Mundy, J. L. (1987) Three dimensional model matching from an unconstrained viewpoint. *Proc. of IEEE Int. Conf. on robotics and Automation*, 208–220.

Tomasi, C. and Kanade, T. (1991) Factoring image sequences into shape and motion, *IEEE Workshop on Visual motion*, Princeton, NJ, 21–29.

Ullman, S. (1979) The Interpretation of visual motion. *M.I.T. Press.*

Ullman, S. (1989) Aligning pictorial descriptions: an approach to object recognition. *Cognition* 32(3):193–254.

Ullman, S. and Basri, R. (1991) Recognition by linear combinations of models. *IEEE Trans. on Pattern Analysis and Machine Intelligence* 13(10):992–1006.

Chapter 2

Modeling with Constraints

A System for Constructive Constraint-Based Modelling

Lluis Solano Pere Brunet
Software Department. Polytechnical University of Catalunya.
Diagonal 647, 08028 Barcelona. Spain.
E-mail: solano@lsi.upc.es
brunet@lsi.upc.es

ABSTRACT

The paper discusses proposed solutions for constraint-based modelling, with special emphasis on constructive approaches. A new constructive scheme that overcomes a number of the present limitations is proposed. It is based on a non-evaluated, constructive solid model. The proposed approach supports instantiation of pre-defined models, parametric geometric operations in 1D, 2D and 3D, variable topologies, and operations with structural constraints. The EBNF specification of the model definition language is presented and discussed through several examples.

Keywords: Geometric modelling, solid modelling, CAD, constraint-based modelling, parametric design.

1. INTRODUCTION

Present CAD systems can be very useful for the design and representation of specific, final products. However, they still have a number of drawbacks that must be solved in order to use them in practical design applications. There is a need for facilities for conceptual design, and better tools for the generation of the design are required. On the other hand, the use of previous designs in a new one is not always supported. Finally, in most CAD systems it is necessary to define the exact size and location of every geometric element and/or part. This is of course too rigid in many applications, where the interest of the user is to generate a prototype model from a number of shape specifications, and then adjust it through shape modification tools in order to optimize the performances of the product.

Parametric CAD systems can design general objects that represent a family of different objects, sharing the same topological constraints but having different geometry [CFV88]. Given a set of specific parameters, particular components of the family are obtained. Parametric models store the geometry of the object together with variable dimension parameters [RSV89], [Rol91a]. Parametric design increases the flexibility in the design process, by defining the geometry and geometric constraints without specifying the set of concrete dimensions of the object.

Parametric design [Rol91a] is becoming a useful methodology for conceptual design, tolerance analysis, efficient design of families of parts, representation of standard parts and features in libraries, kinematics simulations, and assemblies design. Several parametric design approaches have been proposed that will be reviewed in section 2.

The present paper proposes a constructive definition of the object model that overcomes a number of the present limitations of parametric systems. It supports instantiating of pre-defined models, parametric geometric operations in 1D, 2D and 3D, variable topologies and operations with structural constraints. Next section discusses some of the well-known approaches for parametric design, focusing on constructive schemes and comparing their performances and limitations. The proposed constructive scheme is then presented in section 3. Section 4 presents and discusses several connected examples, introducing the definition language of the object models.

2. PROPOSED SCHEMES AND CONSTRUCTIVE APPROACHES IN PARAMETRIC DESIGN

Roller [Rol91a] proposes a classification of parametric design approaches into variants programming, numerical constraint solvers, expert systems and constructive schemes. In variants programming, the user must write a procedure in a certain programming language whenever he wants to define a parametric object. Variants programming is widely used in CAD systems through macro definition languages, mainly for the definition of parts libraries. The main drawback of this approach however is, that it is not practical for non-expert users.

The numeric constraint solver approach or algebraic method, translates all the dimensional constraints into a set of equations. The shape of a part can be defined and modified based on a set of characteristic points of the geometric model. An algebraic system of equations relates the characteristic points to the constraints. The geometry of a specific part is computed by solving the system of equations with an iterative numerical method.

Several versions of this approach have been proposed [HiB78] [LiG81] [LiG82] [LeA85] [Nel85] [Owe91] [Ser91].In this method the number of equations and variables grows fast with the number of geometric elements and constraints involved. The numerical resolution needs good starting points in order to converge and the computational cost is expensive.

From the user's point of view, it is difficult to express a design in terms of a system of equations that reflects the relationship between the geometric entities of the design. Furthermore, the user doesn't have any feedback about inconsistent shapes or unexpected solutions.

Another approach in parametric design, is the use of an expert system in order to create a geometric model based on a set of constraints. The constraints are thus expressed as rules or predicates [Ald88] [Sun88] [SAK90] [Yak90]. Given the constraints and the starting points, an inference engine is used to determine sequentially the unknown positions of the geometric elements.

This method allows to use more complex constraints. However it needs a large number of predicates for simple shapes [Yak90]. The expert system approach doesn't seem to support incremental design. Moreover, it doesn't support cyclic constraints and it is expensive in memory and computations.

In the constructive approach the sequence of interaction performed by the user in order to define an object is recorded by the system. The design sequence is described interactively and graphically by the user. The previous works using this method can be classified into two main groups according to the way the user's actions are recorded. In the first group the interactive design generates a procedural description of the modelling operations of an object [RBN89] [Emm89] [Emm90] [Kon90] [Rol90] [Rol91b]. In the second group the design sequence is used for the management of a data structure that reflects the relationships between the geometric elements [Ros86] [CFV88] [GZH88].

There are many aspects that characterize a constructive method, however the most significant ones are:

- Whether the method generates a procedure or manages directly a data structure.
- The dimensionality of the method (2D/3D).
- The existence of mechanisms to detect inconsistencies.
- The need to specify all constraints.
- The possibility of instantiating other objects during the building of a new object (instantiating previous models).
- The existence of a mechanism to validate the parameters of an object or to fix their range of validity.
- The ability to detect and support topological changes.
- Whether it is possible to parametrize modelling operations.

Table 1 discusses these aspects in relation to the most representative methods in the constructive approach.

The result of the interaction with the user, together with an accurate set of parameters can be used in order to generate any object of a specific family. In general, this approach is based on the idea of programming with example [GPG90]. The user defines an example which is recorded by the system. It is thus necessary to keep the history of the design [YKH87] and this can be performed by recording the modelling operations and constraints.

The design of an object is incremental. The design is a sequence of states that converges towards the final object. Every state is characterized by a set of geometric elements and constraints. The evolution between states is done through modelling operations and by adding new constraints.

Table 1.

	CFV88	Emm90	GZH88	Kon90	RBN89	Rol91a
Kind of method	estruct.	proc.	estruct.	proc.	proc.	proc.
Dimensionality	2D	3D	3D	2D/3D	2D	2D
Inconsis.detection	?	yes	?	yes	yes	yes
All constraints	yes	no	no	yes	?	yes
Inst. previous model	no	yes	no	no	yes	no
Validate parameters	no	yes	no	no	yes	no
Parametrize mod. op.	no	yes	?	?	yes	yes
Detect topol. changes	?	?	yes	?	yes	yes

The designer uses modelling operations and constraints while he is building the object in a natural way. The constructive approach preserves the user's traditional working enviroment and encourages his hability to decompose a problem into subproblems. In this sense it can be said that the system assists the user in the design of a solution. The geometric elements on which the system is based are simple user sketches whose exact sizes and positions are not needed. It is only necessary to define constraints. Under this perspective, the system doesn't need expert users and the user interface plays an important role. When the interactive design is finished, it can be immediately evaluated in order to modify the design sequence or to perform a new design of a part. Unfortunately, the classical constructive approach doesn't support circular constraints, that must be solved simultaneously.

3. THE CONSTRUCTIVE PARAMETRIC SOLID MODEL

A constructive parametric solid model (CPSM) can be defined as the procedural description of the sequence of modelling operations and constraints performed by the user during the interactive design of a parametric object. It must be observed that the constructive parametric solid model is transparent to the user; the user simply interacts with the system through the graphical user interface in order to generate a particular object that will become the representative of the parametric family. The CPSM can be considered as a generic model of the whole family of objects. The CPSM is a procedural description with a set of formal parameters. Instances - specific object models - of the CPSM are obtained by fixing the values of its formal parameters. The design process when using a constructive parametric solid model involves the following steps:

- A particular object of the parametric family of objects is designed through a graphical user interface and using available modelling operations and constraints. Dimensions and operation parameters can be either constant, related to other dimensions through constraints, or defined as a function of the formal parameters of the model. Constraints can be introduced at any moment during the design process. The corresponding constructive parametric solid model which tracks the design process is automatically generated. The contructive parametric solid model is represented by a sequence of statements from a definition language [SoB92]. Modelling operations and contraints are expressed through procedure calls in the language. This kind of ERep (Editable Representation) has the advantage of being editable, suitable for archival and transmission, it supports both generic and specific designs, and records the conceptual construction steps [RBN89] [HoJ92]. The formal description of the constructive solid model in a simple case with a limited set of basic geometric elements is presented in the appendix.

- The constructive parametric solid model can be evaluated in order to generate specific objects. Different sets of parameter values generate different specific objects, all of them from the same parametric family.

Therefore, the proposed parametric system consists of two modules:

- The module that generates the constructive parametric solid model depicted by a sequence of avalaible modelling operations and constraints. Figure 1 shows the generic structure of this module. The user chooses the modelling operations and constraints through a grafical user interface. A model generator translates it and generates the CPSM that represent the generic object.

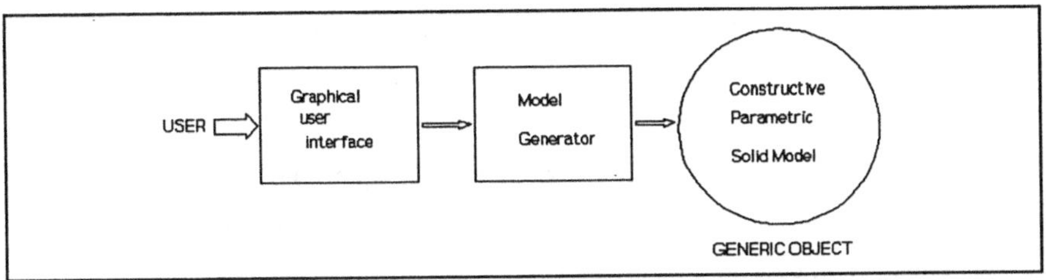

Figure 1. Generation of the Constructive Parametric Solid Model.

The evaluation module which generates specific object models with a particular geometry and topology given a set of parameter values. This module (figure 2) includes a translator that generates an internal model representation. The validation and evaluation of the CPSM is done on this internal model representation model. With specific parameter values, the evaluation module produces a particular object model.

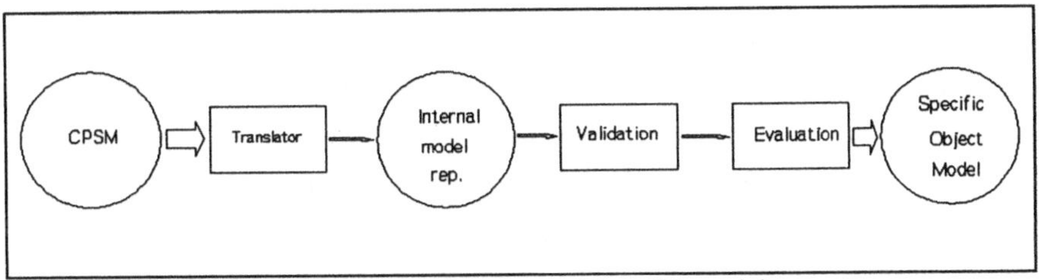

Figure 2. Evaluation of the constructive parametric solid model.

It is possible to define assemblies using instances of previously defined parametric models, which are available through a models library. In addition to the representation of a generic object through modelling operations and constraints, the constructive parametric solid model includes information on the explicit geometry of the element which was generated during its design phase. As a consequence, the system can automatically deal with underconstraint situations.

The domain of the proposed constructive parametric solid model is obviously limited by the power of the underlying language. On the other hand, it presents the following advantages:

- It represents the conceptual construction steps, in an incremental way.
- Intermediate models can be stored in generic object libraries, and they can be instantiated in later designs.
- It uses a scheme based on the design with example. Having always the default geometry of the specific object designed by the user, it automatically supports underconstraint cases.
- The system is structured three independent modules: the interaction module, the internal model representation, and the validation and evaluation module.
- The generic model CPSM is an editable representation, able for archive and transmission.
- The CPSM has a uniform representation for geometries of different dimensions. It is therefore a global approach involving 2D and 3D parametric design.
- It supports structural parameters, that is, parameters in geometric operations (2D to 2D, 2D to 3D or 3D to 3D operations).

The present approach is in some sense parallel to that of [HoJ92], [RBN89], [Emm90]. Hoffman-Juan presents a general framework for ERep languages in solid modelling, Rossignac et al. and Van Emmerick propose an specific language for the representation of the model. Rossignac et al. proposes to record the parameterized sequence of design operations. However, his approach is oriented to intensional model and feature-based design. Van Emmerick's approach works directly in 3D, but the user can only interact with a set of characteristic points of the model (geometric tree). Our approach is adressed to the design of generic objects in terms not only of modelling operations but also constraints. The user can interact with the whole geometry of the specific object being designed. The presented model covers both 2D and 3D parametric design.

3.1. USER INTERACTION AND MODEL GENERATION

The user interacts with the system through a graphical user interface. The user interface is an independent proces that manages and parses the operations provided by the user. Furthermore, the user interface manages the visualization of the model in progress. From the user operations the system generates the statements of the representation model through the following steps:

- The user interacts with the already designed geometry, and defines new operations and constraints.
- The system automatically generates the language description of the new designed features, and assigns symbolic names to any new geometric element.
- In parallel, an specific object model is stored with the explicit geometry given by the user interaction, in order to visualize it during the next interactive design steps.

The set of basic geometric elements that can be used in modelling operations and constraints include 0D elements (points), 1D elements (lines and edges), 2D elements (planes, polygons and circles) and 3D elements (polyhedra, etc). All of them must be instantiated and are parametrically defined. They act as primitives within the final constructive parametric solid model. Modelling operations can either keep the dimension of the operands (for instance, in the case of boolean set operations between 3D elements) or increase it (like in sweep operations that transform a 2D element onto a solid). Modelling operations can be parametric operations, that is, the result depends not only on the operands but also on the value of a number of formal parameters.

Both the interaction process and the structure of the constructive parametric solid model can be clarified through the design of a simple object. A family of 'L-shaped' solids is to be generated. Being L the edge size of the square faces, figure 3, the heigh of the part must be 2*L and its length must be 2*L*F, F>0.5 (figure 3-a). Different specific objects from the same parametric family can be obtained by giving particular values to the parameters L and F. The design process starts by instantiating a square (one of the supported 2D parametric objects) and performing a sweep operation in order to generate a parametric prism with a general heigh H. The system automatically generates the corresponding constructive parametric solid model of the prism (see appendix) according to the following sequence of user's actions:

- select 'define new model' and enter its name.
- select 'define a regular polygon'.
- enter the parameters involved.
- select 'generate solid by parallel sweep' and define the parameters as:
    - select the polygon just generated
    - define the value of the sweep as a parameter of the model.

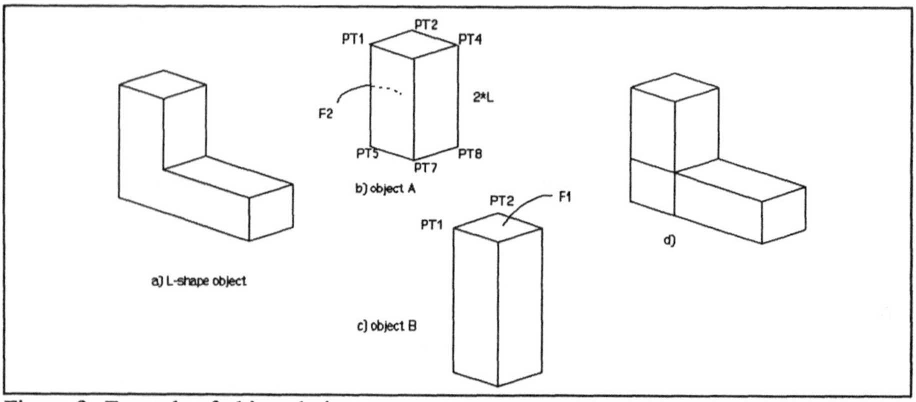

Figure 3. Example of object design.

The result generated by the system is:

```
model square_prism (L,H) {
   A:= Reg_pol (4, L, point(0., 0., 0.) )
   B:= Paral_sweep ( A, H)
}
```

When the user chooses an avalaible modelling operation or constraint, he has to define the involved parameters. Thus can be done by,

- an specific value. It is the case of the number '4' in the previous sequence.
- a symbol that identifies a formal parameter of the model wich will appear on the heading of the CPSM. In the previous example the parameter 'L'.
- a function or expression that computes and returns the parameter value. It is the case of the function 'point' that creates a point located by the user on the graphic screen.

The following options are therefore possible in the previous example:

- A:= Reg_pol (4, 16, point(0.0, 0.0, 0.0))

  where the length of the polygon edge has been fixed to 16.
- A:= Reg_pol (4, 2*L-H, point(0.0, 0.0, 0.0))

  in this case the number of sides is 4 and the polygon edge size is the evaluation of 2*L-H.

The parameter A in the Paral_sweep operation indicates that the polygon to be operated is the result of the Reg_pol invocation. Now, the user can simply ask for two instances of square_prism and define in a graphic way a number of constraints in order to fix the relative location of both prisms. The final object is generated by means of a boolean union operation. The constructive parametric solid model that will be obtained for the final L-shaped object will be,

```
model L_object (L,F) {
        A:= square_prism (L, 2*L)
        B:= square_prism (L, 2*L*F)
        Equal_normal (A.F2, B.F1)
        Coincident_2P (A.P5, B.P1)
        Coincident_2P (A.P6, B.P2)
        C:= Union (A, B)
    }
```

In this second step, three constraints have been introduced. First, the user selects the top faces of both prisms, figures 3-b and 3-c, and asks for coincidence of the normal vectors. Then, coincidence of the point 5 of prism A with point 1 of prism B is required, and the same with point 6 of prism A and point 2 of prism B, figures 3-b and 3-c. The user works by graphically selecting the points to be coincident, and the system generates the corresponding constraint sentences in the model description by using the point ordering in the data structure associated to the square_prism model, figure 3. The set of imposed constraints produces the relative location of the prisms indicated in figure 3-d, while the final union operation generates the model of the parametric object in figure 3-a. It must be observed that the spatial location of the generated object is irrelevant in most cases. Both prisms have been designed in a general location, but the right assembly has been obtained by means of the imposed constraints.

3.2. INTERNAL MODEL DATA REPRESENTATION AND EVALUATION

Given a set of defined parameter values, the CPSM can be evaluated to an specific object (fig.2). The evaluation process includes the following steps:

- An internal model representation is generated automatically from the CPSM. This representation keeps both the default geometry of the object and the constraints between geometric elements.
- The internal model representation is validated in order to detect inconsistencies and overconstraints.
- Finally, a numerical evaluator generates the specific object model from the internal representation and the parameter values. The evaluator first deals with non cyclic constraints, and solves the remaining nonlinear equations from cycles in a second step.

The internal model representation consists of a graph containing all points that have appeared in the CPMS design process. Nodes of the graph contain:

- The point coordinates (Initially they contain the default geometry of the points).
- A list of constraints concerned with the point. Every constraint includes pointers to other graph nodes involved in it.

More specific aspects of the internal model representation are presented in a forecoming paper.

4. EXAMPLES AND DISCUSSION

In this section we present both the design process and the generation of the constructive parametric solid model of the family of objects shown in figures 5 and 6. The first step consists on the generation of the parametric polygon indicated in figure 4-a. The model depends only on a single parameter, the heigh H. The user directly draws the closed polygon using a graphical user interface, and afterwards indicates several constraints on the vertical dimensions. The resulting constructive model of the parametric polygon includes both the input polygon with the specific coordinates input by the user, and the distance constraints,

```
Model bell_poly (H) {
 A:= Closed_pol (Hor_edge (Point(0.,0.,0.), Point(3.,0.,0.) ),
            Ver_edge (Point(3.,0.,0.), Point(3.,2.,0.) ),
            Hor_edge (Point(3.,2.,0.), Point(2.,2.,0.) ),
```

```
        2P_edge (Point(2.,2.,0.), Point(0.,16.,0.) ),
        2P_edge (Point(0.,16.,0.), Point(-2.,17.,0.)),
        Ver_edge(Point(-2.,17.,0.),Point(-2.,18.,0.)),
        Hor_edge (Point(-2.,18.,0.), Point(-4.,18.,0.)),
        Ver_edge (Point(-4.,18.,0.), Point(-4.,15.,0.)),
        Hor_edge (Point(-4.,15.,0.), Point(-2.,15.,0.)),
        2P_edge  (Point(-2.,15.,0.), Point(0.,0.,0.)) )
    Y_dist (A.PT2, A.PT7, H)
    Y_dist (A.PT2, A.PT3, .1*H)
    Y_dist (A.PT3, A.PT5, .8*H)
    Y_dist (A.PT7, A.PT10, .15*H)
    Y_dist (A.PT6, A.PT7, .05*H)
    X_dist (A.PT6, A.PT10, 0.)
    X_dist (A.PT1, A.PT5, 0.)
}
```

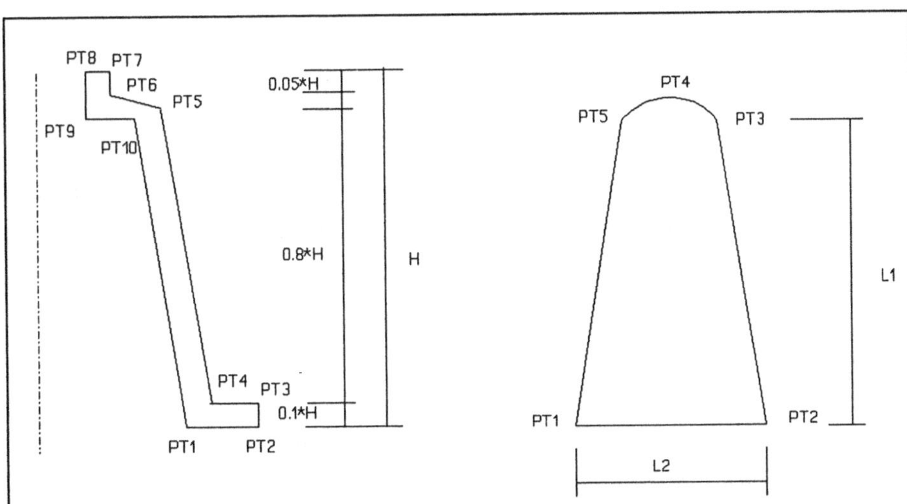

Figure 4. Parametric polygons.

It must be observed that the use of primitives like Hor_edge and Ver_edge in the input process of the polygon adds a number of implicit constraints between consecutive points of the polygon. Every geometric element has a default explicit geometry. In this way, edge sizes not forced by constraints will keep their input values.

Now, the 3D solid 'bell' can be generated by means of a rotational sweep. A rotation axis must be supplied, and the distances from certain polygon points to the axis must be incorporated to the model in the form of constraints. However, when more than two distances from points to the axis are indicated, they act as additional constraints that force the shape of the swept polygon. In the present example, the user instanciates a bell_polygon with 2*D heigh and gives two extra constraints in order to shape the width of the bell. The generated model will be,

```
Model bell (D) {
    e:= 2P_axis ( Point(0.,0.,0.), Point(0.,30.,0.) )
    A:= bell_poly (2*D)
    Point_axis_dist (A.PT1, e, D)
    Point_axis_dist (A.PT9, e, D/3.)
    Point_axis_dist (A.PT6, e, .66*D)
    Point_axis_dist (A.PT2, e, 1.25*D)
    B:= Rotation_sweep (A, e, 360.)
}
```

A second solid will be generated through a parallel sweep operation from the parametric polygon in figure 4-b. The initial parametric 2D polygon is designed in the same way as bell_poly, being the only difference that, now, the polygon includes three straight edges plus an arc. Corresponding constraints include dimension constraints, simmetry of the central point A.PT4, specification of the slant angles at both sides, and tangency of the arc. This last constraint is finally represented in the model in terms of trigonometric functions,

```
Model 2D_window (L1, L2) {
  A:= Closed_pol(Hor_edge(Point(0.,0.,0.), Point(6.,0.,0.)),
          2P_edge(Point(6.,0.,0.), Point(4.5,12.,0.)),
          3P_arc (Point(4.5,12.,0.), Point(3,13.5,0.), Point(1.5,12.,0.)),
          2P_edge  (Point(1.5,12.,0.), Point(0.,0.,0.)))
  X_dist (A.PT1, A.PT2, L2)
  Y_dist (A.PT2, A.PT4, L1)
  Y_dist (A.PT4, 2P_point(A.PT1, A.PT2, .5), 0.)
  Edge_angle (A.ED1, A.ED2, 80.)
```

```
   Edge_angle (A.ED1, A.ED4, 80.)
   Y_dist (A.PT3, A.PT5, 0.)
   Y_dist (A.PT4, A.PT5, (A.PT3.X, A.PT5.X)*.5*(1/cos(80.)-1/tan(80.)))
 }
```

Now, the swept object 3D_window is generated by a simple instatiating operation of the previous model plus a parallel sweep,

```
 Model 3D_window (L1,L2) {
   B:= 2D_window (L1,L2)
   C:= Paral_sweep (B, 10.*L1)
 }
```

Finally, the generation of the final object is performed through the difference between instances of the bell and 3D_window. Specific values of the parameters are supplied to the operating objects, as functions of the formal parameters of final_object. Locating both objects in the right place for the boolean difference involves a graphical selection of the bottom faces of each objects - the corresponding faces in the associated data structure are A.F2 and B.F3 -, and a selection of the top face of the bell. The constructive parametric solid model which results for the final object is,

```
 Model final_object (D,L) {
   A:= bell (D)
   B:= 3D_window (L,.25*L)
   Equal_normal (A.F2, B.F3)  /* bottom faces */
   P1:= Centroid (A.F2)
   P2:= Centroid (B.F3)
   P3:= Centroid (A.F4)        /* top face of A */
   Coincident_2P (P2, 2P_point (P1, P3, .12) )
   C:= Difference (A, B)
 }
```

All intermediate models are stored on a model library, and can be instantiated in different applications. Several models, like bell_poly and 2D_window, are 2D models, while bell or 3D_window represent parametric solids. Any model is a non-evaluated representation of the parametric family, and can be evaluated by means of a geometric interpreter, figure 2.

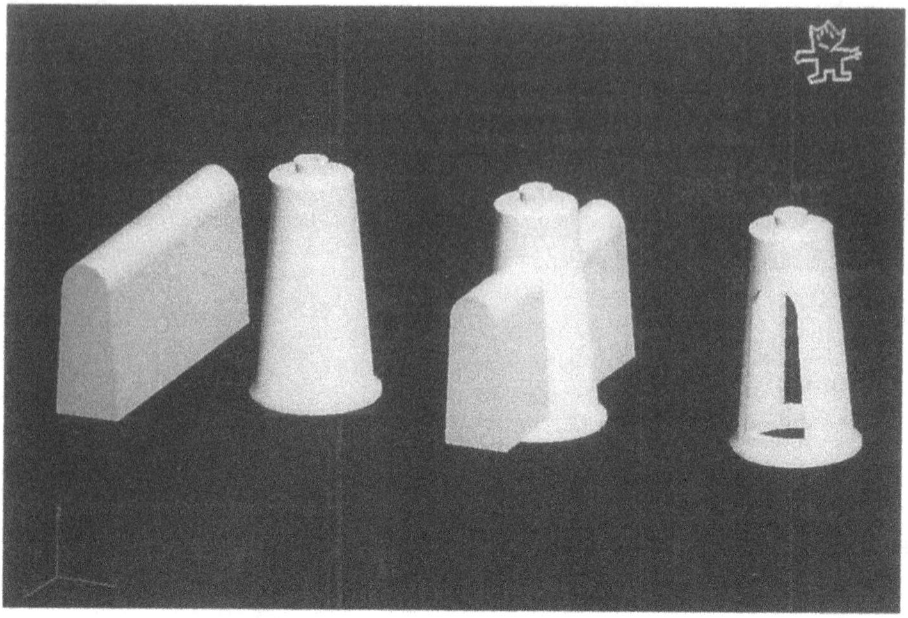

Figure 5. The boolean difference between the objects generated in figure 4 defines a family of parametric objects.

5. CONCLUSIONS

A new constraint-based modelling scheme has been proposed, based on the definition of constructive parametric solid models. A non-evaluated procedural model of the parametric family is automatically generated during the design process of a single object of the family. General modelling operations together with geometric constraints can be mixed with no restriction during the design step.

Constructive parametric solid models support instantiating of predefined models, variable topologies, parametric geometric operations in 1D, 2D and 3D, and operations with structural constraints. A specification of the model definition language has been presented and discussed through several examples.

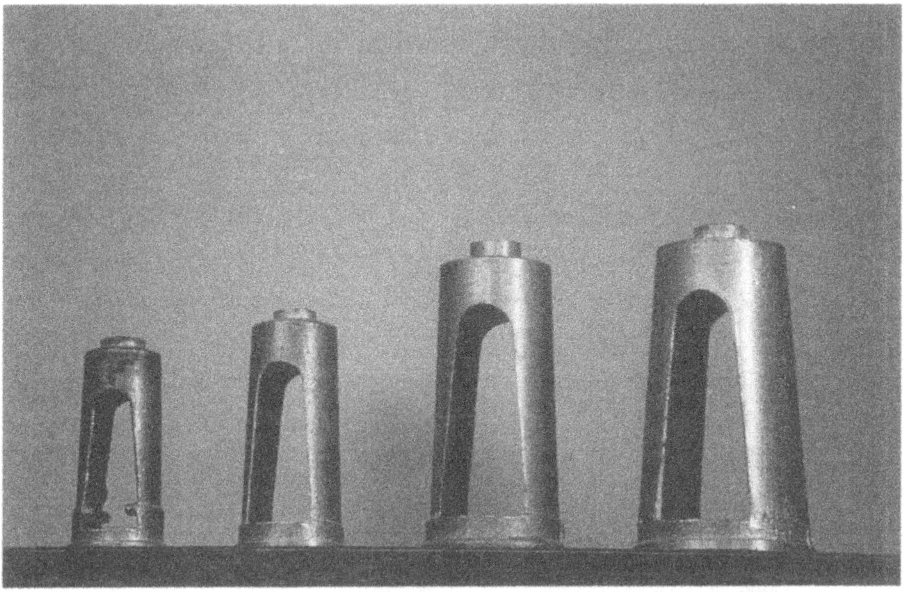

Figure 6. Several real objects from the parametric family defined in figure 5.

Future work will involve the analysis of constraints consistency, the generation of specific tools for the detection of overconstraints, efficient mechanisms for deletion and editing of geometric parts, and aspects related to the validity and range of the parameters. On the other hand the set of supported modelling operations and geometric constraints will be extended beyond the kernel that has been presented in the appendix.

6. REFERENCES

[Ald88] B.Aldfeld
Variation of geometries based on a geometric-reasoning method. CAD, vol.20, no.3, April 1988.

[CFV88] U.Cugini, F.Folini, I.Vicini
A Procedural System for the Definition and Storage of Technical Drawings in Parametric Form. Proceedings of Eurographics'88, pp.183-196, North-Holland, 1988.

[Emm89] M.J.G.M.van Emmerick
Graphical Interaction on Procedural Object Descriptions. Theory and Practice of

Geometric Modelling, W.Strasser, H.P.Seidel (eds), pp.469-482, Springer-Verlag,1989.

[Emm90] M.J.G.M.van Emmerick
Interactive Design of Parameterized 3D models by direct manipulation. PhD thesis, Delft University Press, 1990.

[GPG90] P.Girard, G.Pierra, L.Guittet
End User Programming Enviroments: Interactive Programming-on-example in CAD Parametric Design. Proceedings of Eurographics'90, pp.261-274, North-Holland, 1990.

[GZH88] D.C.Gossard, R.P.Zuffante, H.Sakurai
Representing Dimensions, Tolerances, and Features in MCAE Systems. IEEE CG&A, March 1988.

[HiB78] R.C.Hillyard,I.C.Braid
Characterizing non-Ideal Shapes in Terms of Dimensions and Tollerances. ACM Computers Graphics, vol.12, no.3, August 1978.

[HoJ92] C.M.Hoffmann, R.Juan
ERep. An editable high-level representation for geometric design and analysis. Technical Report CSD-TR-92-055. CAPO Report CER-92-24. Purdue Unversity, August 1992.

[Kon90] K.Kondo
PIGMOD: Parametric and Interactive Geometric Modeller for mechanical Design. CAD, vol.22, no.10, December 1990.

[LeA85] K.Lee, G.Andrews
Inference of the Positions of Components in an assembly: part 2. CAD, vol.17, no.1 January/February 1985.

[LGL81] V.C.Lin, D.C.Gossard, R.A.Light
Variational Geometry in Computer Aided Design. ACM Computer Graphics, vol.15, no.3, August 1981.

[LiG82] R.A.Light,D.C.Gossard
Modification of geometric models through variational geometry. CAD, vol.14, no.4, July 1982.

[Nel85] G.Nelson
Juno, a constraint-based graphics system. SIGGRAPH'85, vol.19, no.3, pp.235-243, San Francisco. July 22-26, 1985.

[Owe91] J.C.Owen
Algebraic Solution for Geometry from Dimensional Constraints. Proceedings of Symposium on Solid Modelling Foundations and CAD/CAM Applications. J.Rossignac, J.Turner (eds). Austin, June 5-7, pp.397-407, ACM Press 1991.

[RBN89] J.R.Rossignac, P.Borrel, L.R.Nackman
Interactive Design with Sequences of Parameterized Transformations. Intelligent CAD Systems II. V.Akman, P.J.W.ten Hagen, P.J. Veerkamp (eds), pp.93-125, Springer-Verlag, 1989.

[Rol90] D.Roller
A System for Interactive Variation Design. Geometric Modelling for Product Engineering. M.J.Wozny,J.U.Turner, K.Preiss (eds), pp.207-219, North-Holland, 1990.

[Rol91a] D.Roller
Advanced Methods for Parametric Design. Geometric Modelling. Methods and Applications. H.Hagen, D.Roller (eds), pp. 251-266, Springer-Verlag, 1991.

[Rol91b] D.Roller
An approach to computer-aided parametric design. CAD, vol.23, no.5, June 1991.

[Ros86] J.R.Rossignac
Constraints in Constructive Solid Geometry. Proc. of the 1986 Workshop on Interactive 3D Graphics. F.Crow and S.M.Pizer (eds), pp.93-110, ACM Press.1986.

[RSV89] D.Roller, F.Schonek, A.Verroust
Dimension-driven Geometry in CAD: A Survey. Theory and Practice of Geometric Modelling. W.Strasser, H.P.Seidel (eds), pp.509-523, Springer-Verlag 1989.

[SAK90] H.Suzuki, H.Ando, F.Kimura
Geometric Constraints and Reasoning for Geometrical CAD Systems. Comput.&Graphics, vol.14, no.2, 1990.

[Ser91] D.Serrano
Automatic Dimensioning in Design for Manufacturing. Proc. of Symposium on Solid Modelling Foundations and CAD/CAM Applications. J.Rossignac, J.Turner (eds) Austin, June 5-7, pp.379-386, ACM Press 1991.

[SoB92] L.Solano, P.Brunet
A Language for Constructive Parametric Solid Modelling. Research Report LSI-92-24. Polytechnical University of Catalunya. Dec, 1992.

[Sun88] G.Sunde
Specification of Shape by Dimensions and Other Geometric Constraints. Geometric Modelling for CAD Applications. M.J.Wozny, H.W.McLaughlin, J.L.Ecarnacao (eds), pp.199-213, North-holland 1988.

[YaK90] Y.Yamaguchi, F.Kimura.
A Constraint Modelling System for Variational Geometry. Geometric Modelling for Product Engineering. M.J.Wozny,J.U.Turner, K.Preiss (eds), pp.221-233, North-Holland 1990.

[YKH87] Y.Yamaguchi, F.Kimura, P.J.W. ten Hagen
Interaction Management in CAD Systems with History Mechanism. Proc. of Eurographics'87, pp.543-554, North-Holland 1987.

APPENDIX
CONSTRUCTIVE SOLID MODELLING LANGUAGE.

In this section we present part of the formal specification of the constructive solid modelling language. For a full definition see [SoB92].

A model is defined as a sequence of statements. The model has a name given by an identifier and a list of formal parameters that are used in order to evaluate the model. Every statement can be a modelling operation or a constraint.

```
model ::= Model model_id "(" formal_parameter_list ")" "{" statement_list "}".
formal_parameter_list ::= parameter_id { , parameter_id }.
statement_list ::= statement { "<CR>" statement }.
model_id ::= identifier.
parameter_id ::= identifier.
```

Every statement in the model is a modelling operation or a constraint:

```
statement ::= operation
        | constraint.
identifier ::= letter { letter | digit }.
```

The modelling operations supported can be unary or binary:

```
operation ::=  unary_op
        | binary_op.
```

Unary operations involve one geometric element:

```
unary_op ::=  creation
            | geometric_transf
            | section
            | copy.
```

Binary operations involve two geometric element:

```
binary_op ::=  boolean_op.
```

Some possible operations in order to create geometric elements are:

```
creation ::=  identifier ":=" cr_geometric_element
        | model_instantiating.
cr_geometric_element ::=  cr_0D_element
                | cr_1D_element
                | cr_2D_element
                | cr_3D_element.
cr_0D_element ::=  cr_point.
cr_1D_element ::=  cr_edge
            | cr_line
            | cr_axis.
cr_2D_element ::=  cr_polygon
            | cr_cercle
            | cr_arc
            | cr_plane.
cr_point ::=  Point "(" real_exp, real_exp, real_exp ")"
        | 2P_point "(" point_exp, point_exp, real_exp ")"
        | Centroid "(" polygon_exp ")"
        | Point_edge "(" edge_exp, real_exp ")"
        | 4P_point"("point_exp, point_exp, point_exp,
                point_exp,real_exp,real_exp,real_exp,real_exp")".
cr_edge ::=  2P_edge "(" point_exp, point_exp ")"
        | Hor_edge "(" point_exp, point_exp ")"
        | Ver_edge "(" point_exp, point_exp ")".
cr_line ::=  2P_line "(" point_exp, point_exp ")"
        | Hor_line "(" point_exp ")"
        | Ver_line "(" point_exp ")".
```

```
        | Para_line "(" line_exp, point_exp ")"
        | Perp_line "(" line_exp, point_exp ")".
cr_polygon ::= cr_regular_polygon
          | cr_close_polygon.
cr_regular_polygon ::= Reg_pol "(" sides_num, long, point_exp ")".
cr_closed_polygon ::= Closed_pol "(" edge_list | point_list ")".
cr_arc ::= 3P_arc "(" point_exp, point_exp, point_exp ")".
cr_axis ::= 2P_axis "(" point_exp, point_exp ")"
        | Edge_axis "(" edge_exp ")".
cr_polyhedron ::= regular_polyh
            | paral_sweep
            | rotat_sweep.
```

The geometric elements are expressed as (a non exhaustive list follows):

```
point_exp ::= identifier
          | cr_point
          | point_id.
edge_exp ::= identifier
        | cr_edge
        | edge_id.
polygon_exp ::= identifier
          | cr_polygon
          | polygon_id.
axis_exp ::= identifier
        | cr_axis
        | axis_id.
point_id ::= identifier "."PT point_model.
edge_id ::= identifier "."ED edge_model.
polygon_id ::= identifier "."F polygon_model.
```

The solid object creation could be:

```
paral_sweep ::= Paral_sweep "(" polygon_exp, real_exp ")".
rotat_sweep ::= Rotation_sweep "(" polygon_exp, real_exp ")".
model_instantiating ::= model_id "(" parameter_list ")".
parameter_list ::= expression {, expression}
expression ::= real_exp
          | integer_exp.
```

Binary operations are defined as:

```
bool_op ::= identifier ":=" union
                | intersection
                | difference.
union ::= Union "(" element_exp, element_exp ")".
intersection ::= Intersection "(" element_exp, element_exp ")".
difference ::= Difference "(" element_exp, element_exp ")".
```

And the presently supported constraints are:

```
constraint ::= distance
        | angle
        | coincidence.
distance ::= 2_points_d
        | point_axis_d.
2_points_d ::= 2P_dist "(" point_exp, point_exp, real_exp ")"
        | X_dist "(" point_exp, point_exp, real_exp ")"
        | Y_dist "(" point_exp, point_exp, real_exp ")"
        | Z_dist "(" point_exp, point_exp, real_exp ")".
point_axis_d ::= Point_axis_dist "("point_exp,axis_exp,real_exp")".
angle ::= 3P_angle "(" point_exp, point_exp, point_exp,real_exp")"
        | Edge_angle "(" edge_exp, edge_exp, real_exp ")".
coincidence ::= points_coincidence
        | normals_coincidence.
points_coincidence ::= Coincident_2P "(" point_exp, point_exp ")"
        | Coincident_X "("point_exp, point_exp")"
        | Coincident_Y "(" point_exp, point_exp ")"
        | Coincident_Z "(" point_exp, point_exp ")".
normals_coincidence ::= Equal_normal"(" normal_exp, normal_exp")"
        | Angle_normal"("normal_exp, normal_exp,real_exp")"
        | Perpe_normal"("normal_exp,normal_exp")"
        | Opposite_normal"("normal_exp,normal_exp")".
normal_exp ::= edge_exp
        | polygon_exp.
```

CONSTRAINED OPTIMIZATION IN SURFACE DESIGN

Michael Kallay,
EDS, C4 Technology West
13555 SE 36th ST. Suite 300
Bellevue, WA 98006
e-mail kallay@c4west.eds.com
phone US 206-562-4541

Abstract: Constrained optimization is used for interactive surface design in our new surface editor. It allows designers to modify B-spline surfaces to satisfy their design intents, expressed as geometric constraints. The restrictions on the set of constraints are few. In the special case of no constraints a surface can be faired to remove design flaws.

Introduction

In their introduction to my favorite geometric modeling textbook [Faux & Pratt, 1987], the authors make the distinction between a "**surface fitting** system", which "performs what a numerical analyst would refer to as two dimensional interpolation", and a "**surface design** system", which allows the designer to modify it through "an interactive process, amounting to a dialogue between the designer and the computer." A surface fitting system typically has a very rigid template for its input, because it uses a closed formula to compute the surface. Coon's formula, for example, requires a closed chain of 4 curves. Other fitting systems solve linear equations, but that requires an exact match between the number of interpolation conditions (equations) and the number of unknowns.

The flexibility offered on the other hand by "surface design" systems is achieved by allowing the designer to directly manipulate (B-spline or Bézier) control points. Unfortunately, the effect on the surface of moving a single control point is highly unpredictable. To make things worse, a surface computed by a surface fitting scheme often has hundreds of control points. Modifying such a surface in any useful way must involve the coordinated manipulation of scores of control points, a hopeless task if done manually. By exposing the control points to the designer we have forgotten that they are nothing but the surface's mathematical coefficients; they should not be confused with design tools.

This work presents a new B-spline surface design scheme that combines the flexibility of control point manipulation with the precision of surface fitting. This scheme accepts the design intent in the form of exact geometric constraints. There is no restriction on the number of constraints, and only one restriction on their types: they must be expressed as linear equations in the surface's control points. This covers point and curve interpolation, surface normal direction at a point, etc. If there is no conflict among the constraints, they will be satisfied exactly, otherwise they will be satisfied in a least squares sense. By designating the boundaries of the affected region on the surface, the designer is free to make the changes as local or global as he pleases. Control points are kept where they belong: in the engine room.

The key to this flexibility is in treating the equations as the constraints in a constrained optimization problem, with a fairing goal function. This eliminates the need for a fully determined linear system, and allows the scheme to live with as few constraints as the designer wishes to supply. In fact, the set of constraints may be empty, and then the surface will be faired, to remove design flaws.

Previous Work

Using optimization in surface design is not a new idea. Unconstrained optimization has been proposed for curve and surface fairing in [Farin & Sapidis,1989], [Hagen & Schulze, 1987], [Kallay & Ravani, 1990] and [Lott & Pullin, 1988]. Since there is no exact definition for fairness, it is difficult to decide which goal function should be used to achieve a fair surface. For comparison, let us recall how curves are faired.

Thin elastic strips of wood were historically used for designing ship hull and airplanes. Elastic strips tend to minimize their bending energy, and curves of least energy are considered fair. When computers started to replace wooden splines in curve design, it was computationally too expensive to minimize the elastic energy, which is proportional to the length integral of the squared curvature. As it turned out, the elastic energy's cheaper "cousin", the integral of the squared second derivative of the curve mapping, provides an acceptable fairness criterion ([Faux & Pratt, 1987]). This integral is not a geometric property of the curve, it depends on its parameterization, but the true curve of least energy is usually outside the space of curves used in CAD, i.e. piecewise rational curves, while the curve that minimizes the cheaper functional is a cubic spline.

Choosing a goal function for surface fairing, we must again choose between a true geometric goal function and a cheap parameterization-dependent one. Lott and Pullin in [1988] chose the purist path, minimizing the elastic energy of the surface, which is proportional to the area integral of the sum of the squares its principal curvatures. Their results were good, but the method is computationally too costly for interactive design. In analogy to using the integral of the squared curvature for fairing curves, integrals of quadratic functions of the surface's partial derivatives were explored in [Hagen &Schulze, 1987] and [Kallay & Ravani, 1990], but these methods were implemented only for some restricted classes of surfaces. Here it is done for the workhorse of CAGD: tensor product B-spline surfaces with any degrees and knot sequences.

The idea of using constrained optimization for general interpolation schemes has been suggested in [Ferguson & Grandine, 1990]. The goal function was not specified in the paper, but it was, as in [Lott & Pullin, 1988], purely geometric. As a result, the computations were too expensive for interactive design. Using a quadratic functional, the surface design scheme presented in [Celinker & Gossard, 1991] is sufficiently fast for interactive design. Its practicality is limited, though, by two factors. First, it restricts the types of input constraints: Only such constraints are accepted that directly eliminate some variables. Second, the surface in [Celinker & Gossard, 1991] is represented as a finite-element mesh, commonly used for structural analysis, but rarely for design and manufacture. Our scheme accepts any number of linear equality constraints of any type, and works on B-spline surfaces.

The Variables

Suppose we are given a tensor-product B-spline surface

$$\mathbf{S}_0(u,v) = \sum_{ij} \mathbf{C}_{ij} N_{ij}(u,v), \tag{1}$$

where N_{ij} are the B-spline basis functions, and $\mathbf{C}_{ij}$ their control points. We need to compute the control points of a new modified surface $\mathbf{S}(u,v)$ that satisfies a given set linear equality constraints in the control points $\mathbf{C}_{ij}$. The designer wishes to restrict all changes to a specified region on the surface. Let K be the set of indices ij of those basis functions that vanish outside the specified region. For ij in K, write the coefficients of the target surface $\mathbf{S}$ as $\mathbf{C}_{ij}+\mathbf{D}_{ij}$. The modified surface will then be

$$\mathbf{S}(u,v) = \mathbf{S}_0(u,v) + \sum_{k \in K} \mathbf{D}_k N_k(u,v). \tag{2}$$

The perturbation vectors $\mathbf{D}_k$ will be the variables of the constrained optimization problem. Note that the index k ranges in the set K of pairs of integers. The conversion from the double index (i,j) of a control point to a single index k (as required by the solver) is done by a C macro.

The Goal Function

When a flat thin elastic plate at $z = 0$ is deformed to the shape of the surface $z(x,y)$, its bending energy (under some simplifying assumptions) is proportional to the area integral of $(\frac{\partial^2 z}{\partial x^2})^2 + 2(\frac{\partial^2 z}{\partial x \partial y})^2 + (\frac{\partial^2 z}{\partial y^2})^2$. The first term in our goal function is the sum of these "thin-plate" energies of the coordinates of surface mapping (also used in [Celinker & Gossard 1991]). The second term is the squared deviation from the original surface (used in [Lott & Pullin, 1988]). Our goal function is therefore:

$$F = \int\int w(\frac{\partial^2 \mathbf{S}}{\partial u^2}\cdot\frac{\partial^2 \mathbf{S}}{\partial u^2} + 2\frac{\partial^2 \mathbf{S}}{\partial u \partial v}\cdot\frac{\partial^2 \mathbf{S}}{\partial u \partial v} + \frac{\partial^2 \mathbf{S}}{\partial v^2}\cdot\frac{\partial^2 \mathbf{S}}{\partial v^2}) + (\mathbf{S} - \mathbf{S}_0)\cdot(\mathbf{S} - \mathbf{S}_0)\,du\,dv. \tag{3}$$

The weight w is at the user's diposal, expressing the relative importance assigned to fairing versus adherance to the original design; a large w represents greater emphasis on fairing.

We did experiment with some other, somewhat more geometric quadratic goal functions. For example, the true elastic energy of the surface (under some simplifying assumptions) is proportional to the area integral of $(\frac{\partial^2 \mathbf{S}}{\partial u^2}\cdot\mathbf{N})^2 + 2(\frac{\partial^2 \mathbf{S}}{\partial u \partial v}\cdot\mathbf{N})^2 + (\frac{\partial^2 \mathbf{S}}{\partial v^2}\cdot\mathbf{N})^2$, where $\mathbf{N}$ is the surface normal. We tried to minimize the quadratic function obtained by fixing $\mathbf{N}$ in several ways: The normal of the original surface, or its local or global average. However, the simple-minded (and cheapest) approach, of fairing the sum of the energies of the surface's coordinate functions, seems to produce better looking surfaces, perhaps because it "fairs" the parameterization as well as the geometry.

Unconstrained fairing: The Equations

Write the first integrand as

$$\sum_{i=0}^{2} E_i \frac{\partial^2 \mathbf{S}}{\partial u^{2-i} \partial v^i} \cdot \frac{\partial^2 \mathbf{S}}{\partial u^{2-i} \partial v^i}, \tag{4}$$

where $E_0 = E_2 = 1$ and $E_1 = 2$.

In terms of our optimization variables $\mathbf{D}_k$, the, goal function expands to:

$$F = \int\int w \sum_i E_i\left(\frac{\partial^2 \mathbf{S}_0}{\partial u^{2-i} \partial v^i} + \sum_{k \in K} \mathbf{D}_k \frac{\partial N_k}{\partial u^{2-i} \partial v^i}\right) \cdot \left(\frac{\partial^2 \mathbf{S}_0}{\partial u^{2-i} \partial v^i} + \sum_{l \in K} \mathbf{D}_l \frac{\partial^2 N_l}{\partial u^{2-i} \partial v^i}\right) +$$

$$\left(\sum_{k \in K} \mathbf{D}_k N_k\right) \cdot \left(\sum_{l \in K} \mathbf{D}_l N_l\right) = \int\int w\left(\sum_i E_i \frac{\partial^2 \mathbf{S}_0}{\partial u^{2-i} \partial v^i} \cdot \frac{\partial^2 \mathbf{S}_0}{\partial u^{2-i} \partial v^i} + \right.$$

$$2\sum_{i,k} E_i \mathbf{D}_k \cdot \frac{\partial^2 \mathbf{S}_0}{\partial u^{2-i} \partial v^i} \frac{\partial^2 N_k}{\partial u^{2-i} \partial v^i} + \left.\sum_{i,k,l} E_i \mathbf{D}_k \cdot \mathbf{D}_l \frac{\partial^2 N_k}{\partial u^{2-i} \partial v^i} \frac{\partial^2 N_l}{\partial u^{2-i} \partial v^i}\right)$$

$$+ \sum_{k,l} \mathbf{D}_k \cdot \mathbf{D}_l N_k N_l du dv = \sum_{k,l} A_{kl} \mathbf{D}_k \cdot \mathbf{D}_l + 2\sum_k \mathbf{b}_k \cdot \mathbf{D}_k + c, \tag{5}$$

where:

$$A_{kl} = \sum_i E_i \int\int w \frac{\partial^2 N_k}{\partial u^{2-i} \partial v^i} \frac{\partial^2 N_l}{\partial u^{2-i} \partial v^i} + N_k N_l du dv, \tag{6}$$

and

$$\mathbf{b}_k = \sum_i E_i \int\int w \frac{\partial^2 \mathbf{S}_0}{\partial u^{2-i} \partial v^i} \frac{\partial^2 N_k}{\partial u^{2-i} \partial v^i} du dv, \tag{7}$$

and c doesn't depend on the variables $\mathbf{D}_k$.

The necessary optimization conditions are the linear equations, one for every $l \in K$:

$$\sum_k A_{kl} \mathbf{D}_k + \mathbf{b}_l = \mathbf{0}. \tag{8}$$

Since the goal function is quadratic, this condition is also sufficient, and the minimum is global.

Note that A is a symmetric matrix of scalars, while the unknowns $\mathbf{D}_k$ and the right hand side $\mathbf{b}_k$ are columns of 3-dimensional vectors. The matrix A is sparse, due to the compact support of the B-spline basis functions.

Constraints

The surface $\mathbf{S}$ interpolates a given point $\mathbf{Q}$ if there exists a parameter pair (u,v) such that $\mathbf{S}(u,v) = \mathbf{Q}$. This equation is linear in the surface's control points, but not in u and v. It is therefore common practice in interpolation schemes to apply some heuristic procedure for assigning a parameter pair (u,v) to $\mathbf{Q}$. In our surface editor (u,v) is the parameter pair of the point on $\mathbf{S}$ nearest to $\mathbf{Q}$. The equations are then

$$\sum_{k\in K} \mathbf{D}_k N_k(u,v) = \mathbf{Q} - \mathbf{S}_0(u,v). \tag{9}$$

If we require $\mathbf{S}$ to interpolate a curve $\mathbf{R}(t)$, again we need a procedure for defining a curve $(u(t),v(t))$ in the surface's domain, to make the condition $\mathbf{S}(u(t),v(t)) = \mathbf{R}(t)$ linear. Given such a procedure, the problem can be reduced to a multiple point interpolation constraint if both curves are B-splines. To see that, raise degrees if necessary, so that $\mathbf{R}(t)$ and $\mathbf{S}(u(t),v(t))$ have the same degree d, and refine them to make their knots compatible. If the curves $\mathbf{S}(u(t),v(t))$ and $\mathbf{R}(t)$ agree on $d+1$ points in each span then the curves must coincide. The curve interpolation condition is therefore equivalent to $d+1$ point interpolation conditions per span.

In our implementation the curve $(u(t),v(t))$ in the surfaces domain is defined by an approximate projection of $\mathbf{R}$ on $\mathbf{S}$. In other words, $(u(t),v(t))$ is computed so that $\mathbf{S}(u(t),v(t))$ is an approximation of $\mathbf{R}(t)$.

Meeting a prescribed surface normal direction at a given point is equivalent to the surface partial derivatives being perpendicular to the given normal. This can be expressed as linear equations in the control points. This type of constraint has not been implemented in our editor yet.

Once the constraints have been gathered as a list of linear equations

$$\sum_k \mathbf{P}_{ik}\cdot\mathbf{D}_k = q_i, \tag{10}$$

their origin no longer matters. This allows mixing different types of geometric constraints. The resulting equality constraints are handled with Lagrange multipliers λ_i, one for every constraint. The constrained problem reduces to the unconstrained problem

$$\min(F + \sum_i \lambda_i(\sum_k \mathbf{P}_{ik}\cdot\mathbf{D}_k - q_i)) \tag{11}$$

in the variables $\mathbf{D}_k, \lambda_i$ (see [Gill, Murray & Wright, 1981]). The minimality conditions are obtained by equating to zero the partial derivatives of (11) with respect to the coordinates of $\mathbf{D}_k$ and λ_i. The equations are all linear.

In the presence of conflicting constraints, we must replace these constraints with the minimality conditions for the sum of the residues

$$min \sum_i(\sum_k \mathbf{P}_{ik}\cdot\mathbf{D}_k - q_i)^2. \tag{12}$$

These conditions are again linear. The resulting linear system may still be singular, but the equations are no longer conflicting. Our solver returns the least norm solution.

Implementation and Results

Our surface editor was implemented as a prototype within GM's Corporate Graphics System (CGS). It seems to produce good looking surfaces, as the following examples illustrate, and our own color curvature-plots verify. In its unconstrained mode, it very effectively removes undesired wiggles from a surface. The typical response time is not longer than a few seconds, even on a Sun SPARC station 1.

First we see the lines of maximum curvature on a bicubic surface of 7 by 8 spans, modeling a car body surface. The lines are disrupted by a flaw in the surface:

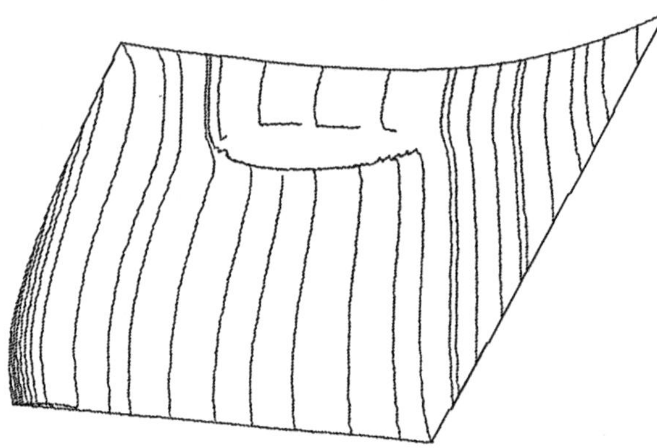

After unconstrained fairing, the lines of curvature flow smoothly. Position and the first two derivatives were preserved along three boundaries, by clamping the three raws or columns of control points adjacent to those boundaries. The boundary near the flaw was free to move.

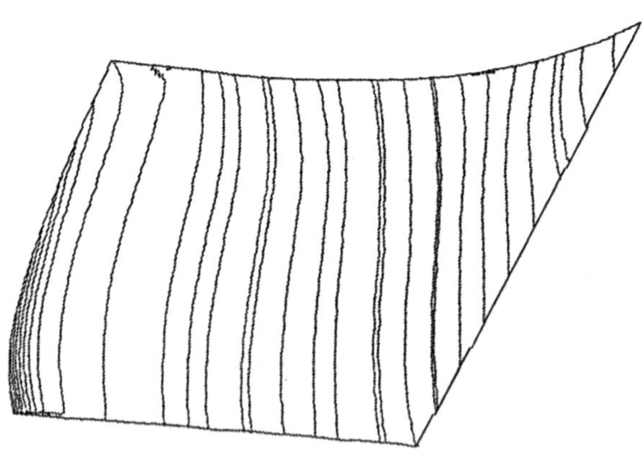

Next we see the same surface with a single point interpolation constraint.

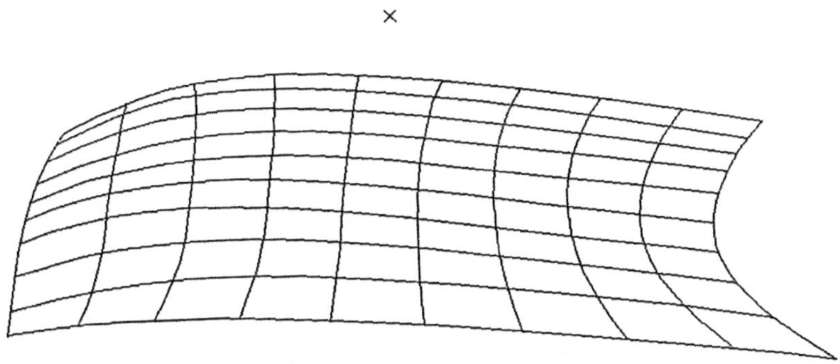

The modified surface interpolates the point. The entire surface was changed, preserving position and the first two derivatives along all boundaries. The three rows (or columns) of control points adjacent to the boundaries were not included in the optimization process.

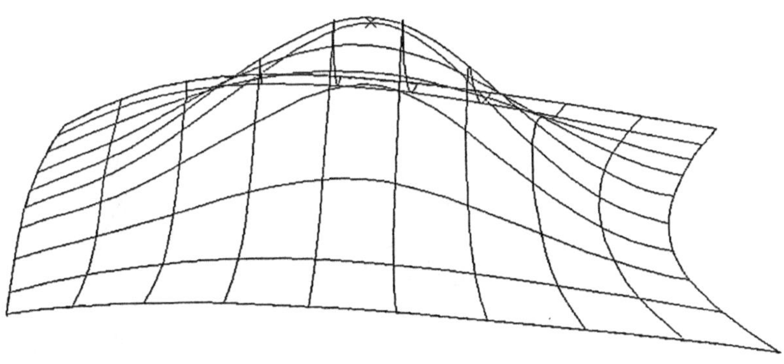

Finally, here is the same base surface with 7 target curves to interpolate. All the control points are subject to optimization here, imposing no boundary conditions. Note that the intersection pattern of the curves is a far cry from the regular mesh required by most surface fitting schemes: There is a curved quadrangle with its two diagonals, and an additional arc hovering.

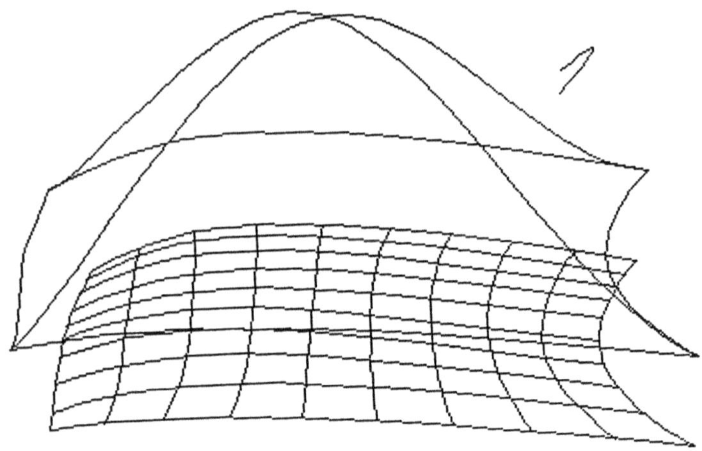

Here is the modified surface. The problem was overconstrained — 462 constraints were imposed on 330 variables. As a result, the surface looks like a short blanket pulled over big feet: It visibly misses the boundary in the area marked by the arrow.

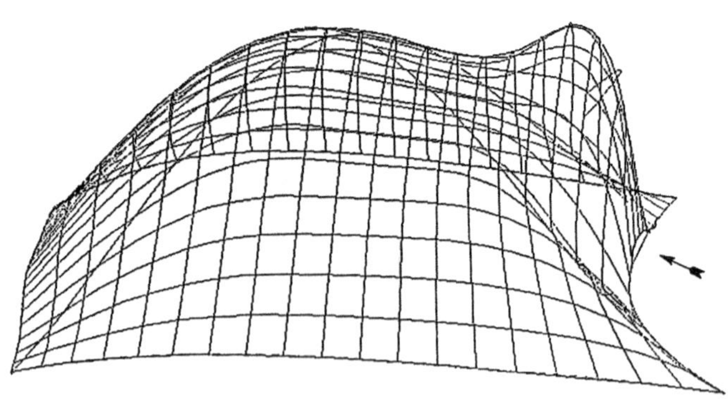

Acknowledgement

This project was funded by General Motors; Jeff Stevens kept us on practical tracks, with his deep understanding of geometric algorithms and designing cars. The equations are solved by the Harwell Library's MA27 subroutines; Nick Gould and John Reid (Rutherford Appleton Lab) were very helpful in showing us how to use them for our problem. Mark Hickman, who did much of the programming, was infinitely patient and resourceful on the rocky road from theory to usable software.

In a recent paper, published after this paper was submitted, Welch & Vitkin present a similar method [1992] in a more general context, with the additional capability of local refinement.

References

Celinker, G. and Gossard, D. (1991) Deformable curve and surface finite-elements for free-form shape design, ACM Computer Graphics, 25 pp. 157-266.

Farin, G, and Sapidis, N. (1989) Curvature and fairness of curves and surfaces, IEEE Computer Graphics and Applications 20 pp 52-57.

Faux, I.D., and Pratt, M.J. (1987) Computational Geometry for Design and manufacture, Ellis Horwood.

Ferguson, D. R. and Grandine, T. A. (1990) On the construction of surfaces interpolating curves: I. A method for handling nonconstant parameter curves, ACM Transactions on Graphics 9 pp 212-225.

Gill, P.E, Murray, W. and Wright, M.H (1981) Practical Optimization, Academic Press.

Hagen, H. and Schulze, G. (1987) Automatic smoothing with geometric surface patches, CAGD 4 231-236.

Kallay, M. and Ravani, B. (1990) Optimal twist vectors as a tool for interpolating a network of curves with a minimum energy surface, CAGD 7, pp 465-473.

Lott, N. J, and Pullin, D. I. (1988) Method for fairing B-spline surfaces, CAD 20 pp 597-604.

Welch, W., and Witkin, A. (1992) Variational surface design, SIGGRAPH, pp 157-166.

Adaptive Range Data Approximation by Constrained Surface Triangulation

Xin CHEN and Francis SCHMITT

École Nationale Supérieure des Télécommunications
46 Rue Barrault 75013 PARIS - FRANCE

1. Introduction

Polyhedral approximation of range data has the advantage of being simple to obtain from raw data and of being capable of approximating any sampled surface to the desired precision. Among different possible polyhedral approximation schemes, surface triangulation is a popular one due to its efficiency in computing and storage. Surface triangulation has been used to solve many problems, such as definition of the object shape [BOIS-84], digital terrain modeling [FOWL-79], control of the automatic machining of surfaces [JERA-89], smooth interpolation between 3-D points [LAWS-77], approximation of the digitized object surfaces [FAUG-84,DELI-91], and computer graphics.

Different methods have been proposed to construct a surface triangulation-based approximation to a set of range data. Faugeras *et al* [FAUG-84] presented a technique to approximate 3-D objects without holes. De Floriani *et al* [DEFL-85] designed an algorithm to approximate surfaces defined over an arbitrarily shaped domain. Lee *et al* [LEE-89] introduced an approximation scheme for visual communication purposes. Recently, Delingette *et al* [DELI-91] proposed a deformable model based on surface triangulation to approximate a set of sampled surface points.

However, all these schemes suffer from a common problem: they cannot reflect surface characteristics of the objects, i.e., points and edges where the triangular patches join generally have no physical significance. In this paper, we propose a method for constructing a polyhedral surface model from a range image constrained to its surface characteristics. These characteristics are firstly extracted from the range image. A triangulation-based surface approximation of range data is then constructed to embed this edge-junction graph, i.e., the polygonal approximation of the extracted surface characteristics are embedded as edges of the surface triangulation. The construction of this approximation is adaptive in the sense that an initially rough approximation is progressively refined at the locations where the approximation accuracy does not meet the requirements.

We organize the paper as follows: Section 2 presents the general idea of our surface approximation scheme. Section 3 discusses how to extract surface characteristics from a range image. Section 4 presents an adaptive surface approximation scheme based on the idea of a constrained surface triangulation. Section 5 gives the experimental results followed by Section 6 which concludes the paper.

2. General Idea

Our aim is to construct a triangulation-based surface approximation of a set of dense sampled surface data arranged in the form of an image. The main issue involved in this problem is how to choose from a range image a subset of data points which allows the construction of a triangulation-based surface approximation to within a predefined error tolerance. We use an adaptive refinement technique to solve this point selection problem.

Because surface triangulation is a piecewise representation, the refinement of a triangulation-based surface approximation can be performed locally. We examine the approximation error of each triangular patch; if the error for a patch is greater than a predefined tolerance, we locally refine the surface approximation around this patch. The refinement can be achieved by adding new points to the triangulation. Thus, the point selection strategy is as follows: *each time the approximation accuracy for a triangular patch is greater than a given tolerance, the data point which is worst approximated by this patch will be added to refine the approximation.* This point selection strategy is adaptive in the sense that it is only performed at the locations where the approximation is not satisfactory.

Such an approximation scheme has already been used by several authors to obtain a triangulation-based surface approximation [FAUG-84,DEFL-85,SCHM-91a]. However, it has been criticized for its inability to reflect characteristic features of object surfaces [FAN-90]. Specifically, the points and edges where the approximating triangular patches are joined generally have no *physical* significance. To remedy this defect, we propose to first extract from range images the surface characteristics which reflect significant object shape features. These characteristics are then embedded into a triangulation-based surface approximation in such a way that the subsequent adaptive refinement will not destroy them.

We have considered two kinds of surface characteristics: surface discontinuities and curves of surface curvature extrema. Surface discontinuities of type C^0 and C^1 often indicate physical events on object surfaces. For example, C^0 discontinuities often indicate the occlusion of two surfaces or the self-occlusion of a surface; while C^1 discontinuities often correspond to a vivid edge on the object surface. The curves of surface curvature extrema correspond to surface ridge or valley lines and have been considered as important shape descriptors. Examples of these three types of surface characteristics are shown in **Fig. 1**.

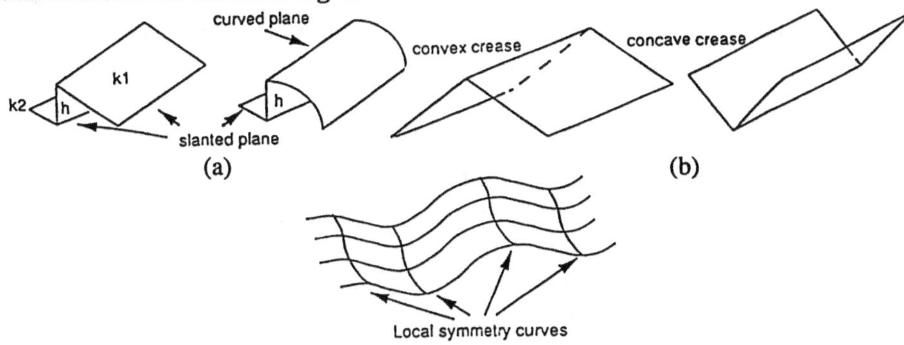

(a) (b) (c)

Fig. 1 *(a) C^0 and (b) C^1 surface discontinuities. (c) Surface curvature extrema.*

In the next section, we describe how to extract such surface characteristics from a range image.

3. Extraction and Organization of Surface Characteristics

Because surface characteristics play a crucial role in the final surface description, their extraction constitutes a key step in our surface approximation scheme. We expect that an extraction process will satisfy the following requirements:

1) The localization of edges, especially those corresponding to surface discontinuities, must be as precise as possible.
2) The labeling of edge types must be correct.

In general, there are two kinds of methods for extracting surface characteristics: region-based or edge-based. Edges detected by region-based methods often do not correspond to the real surface characteristics, especially when there is an over-segmentation. In contrast, edge-based methods provide edges which correspond more closely to the reality. We therefore chose to use edge-based methods.

Although edge-based methods using curvature computation [FAN-87,PONC-87] satisfy requirement 2, they suffer from an edge displacement problem: the computation of the surface curvatures is highly noise sensitive, an image smoothing is thus needed to decrease the effects of noise; however, such smoothing often works blindly to cross the potential surface discontinuities and thus causes edge displacement.

The quality of today's range images allows us to use relatively simple techniques to extract the edges of surface discontinuities without smoothing data [GODI-89]. We thus adapt a two-step strategy to extract surface characteristics: we first detect the surface discontinuity edges and organize them in such a way that missing edges are recovered and spurious edges eliminated. We then smooth range data without crossing these extracted edges. The surface curvatures are finally computed and edges corresponding to curves of maximum curvature extrema detected. In the following subsections, we present these steps in more detail.

3.1 Extraction of C^0 and C^1 Discontinuity Edges

Geometric model fitting methods have been proposed to detect edges in intensity images. The basic idea of such methods is to fit predefined edge models to data, and then make a decision to accept or reject the presence of such models. Geometric model fitting provides an explicit mechanism for **classifying** the detected edges. We have chosen a method proposed by Leclerc [LECL-87] to detect discontinuity edges.

A naive method of using the geometric model fitting to detect a C^0 discontinuity of a 1-D function at a point p would be as follows: we fit a curve to the points in a neighborhood left of p, and fit a separate curve to a neighborhood right of p. Then we compare statistically the limits of these two curves when they approach p. If they are significantly different, we declare that at p there is a C^0 discontinuity. The same process can be used to detect a C^1 discontinuity. An apparent drawback of this method is that for a point near a discontinuity, its left- or right-hand neighborhood will overlay this discontinuity. Therefore, the approximated curve for the points falling in this neighborhood is not a correct estimate of the underlying function, and the statistical tests of significance are inapplicable. If we could eliminate those points whose neighborhoods overlay a C^0 or C^1 discontinuity, we would be left only with the points whose two-side estimated curves are correct. The statistical test could then be applied on them to decide whether they are discontinuity points or not. We have therefore the following discontinuity detection procedure for 1-D sampled points.

1). Fit a curve to each of the left- and right-hand neighborhoods for every point;

2). Eliminate those points whose neighborhoods overlay a discontinuity;

3). Apply a statistical test on remaining points to see if there is a discontinuity.

To perform step 1, polynomial of degree 1 is fitted to the left- and right-hand neighborhoods of a given size for every point. The sum of the fitting errors of these two fits are calculated and stored. The elimination of false points in step 2 is done by taking into account the fact that when a fitting crosses a discontinuity, the sum of the fitting errors is generally very high. Thus by performing a non-minimum suppression on the values of the sum of the fitting errors through the sequence of points, we can eliminate those false points. For step 3, an $F-test$ is performed on the two fitted curves at each point to decide whether there is a discontinuity or not.

This 1-D procedure is applied in two passes to detect surface discontinuities in a range image: the first pass for each row, and the second pass for each column. Note that with this method, detected edge points can be labeled as C^0 or C^1 type. For C^1 edge points, we can further decide whether they are convex or concave by comparing their fitted curves at their left- and right-hand neighborhoods. Results of applying this detection method to an example object is shown in **Fig. 2**.

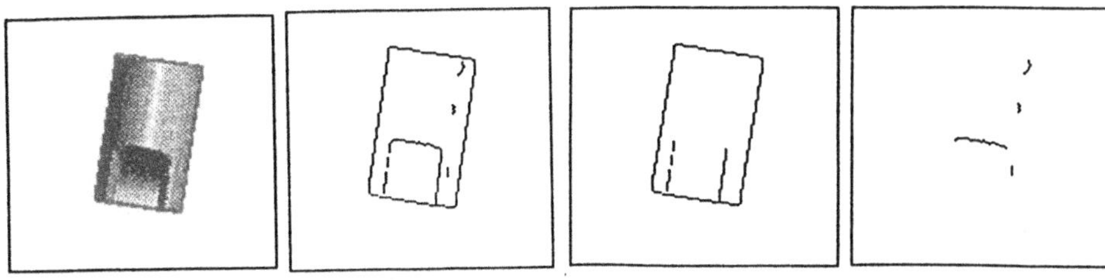

(a) (b) (c) (d)

Fig. 2 *Edge extraction for an example object. (a) Shaded display of range image. (b) Joint view of C^0 and C^1 edge points. (c) C^0 edge points. (d) C^1 edge points.*

3.2 Organization of C^0 and C^1 Discontinuity Edges

After the extraction of discontinuity edge points, we can link them into edges of the same label on the basis of 8-connectivity. This linking is performed in such a way that the range values of the resulting edges are continuous in depth. Edges are oriented so that the surface closest to the sensor is to the right of the oriented edges. If two edges of different types or more than two edges meet together, a junction is created. An initial edge-junction graph is then obtained. Some faults are often present in such an initial graph (see **Fig. 3**(a)). For example, junctions may be lost due to a complex surface geometry around surface vertices; edges may be fragmented due to the presence of noise; or spurious edges may appear due the presence of noise or to an invalid edge model.

The aim of the organization process is to construct from these detected edges a final edge-junction graph in which missing edges are recovered and spurious edges are eliminated. Our edge organization process [CHEN-92] builds an edge-junction graph by using both the knowledge of a junction dictionary [MALI-87] and the principles of generic geometrical regularity obtained in perceptual organization studies [LOWE-85,MOHA-92].

The edge-junction graph is a planar undirected graph similar to the one proposed in [GODI-89]. Its nodes represent junctions while its arcs represent edges. Each edge is labeled as *convex*(+), *concave*(−), *occluding*(→), or *limb*(→→), the range value and the image coordinates of its ordered associated points are also stored. Each junction is labeled according to the junction dictionary, its position and its connection with edges are stored. We see that such an edge-junction graph encodes the quantitative position information as well as the qualitative type descriptors of edges and junctions. The final edge-graph results for the previous object are shown in **Fig. 3**(b).

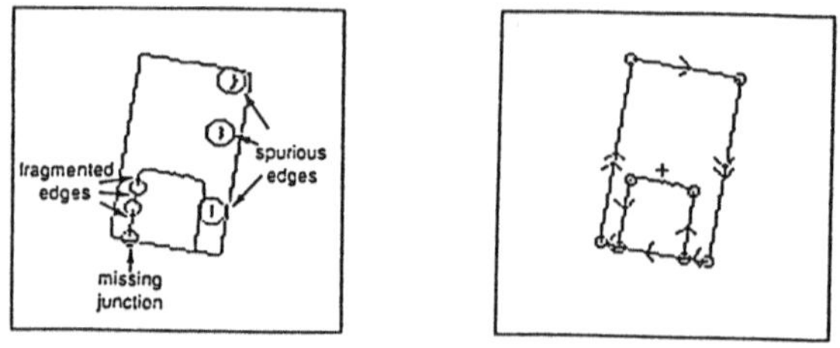

(a) (b)

Fig. 3 *(a) Faults in edge extraction. (b) Final edge-junction graph with labeled edges.*

3.3 Extraction of Curves of Surface Curvature Extrema

Because extrema of the minimum curvature are very sensitive to noise, only the extrema of the maximum curvature are extracted.

To smooth a range image, we use a binomial mask [BESL-88]. This smoothing is designed not to cross the discontinuity edges previously detected.

The calculation of the principal curvatures and directions on this smoothed image is then performed by first fitting an orthogonal polynomial surface of degree 2 to a local neighborhood of each point, and then differentiating the resulting surface to obtain the partial derivatives necessary for the curvature computation.

To detect edge points corresponding to the curves of curvature extrema, we use an efficient structural technique [HORA-89] which provides connected edges. A detection result is shown in **Fig. 4**(a). The detected edge points are linked and added into the edge-junction graph (**Fig. 4**(b)).

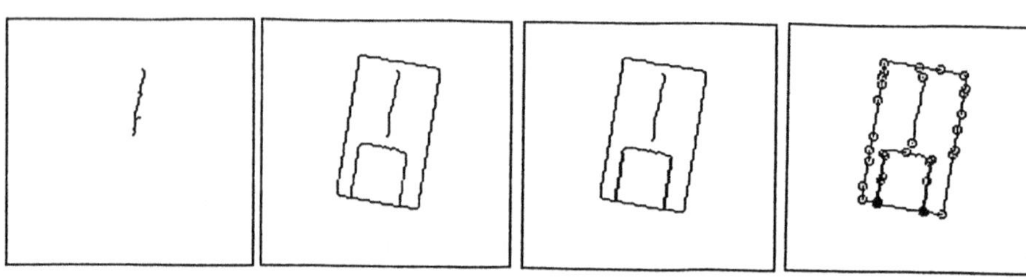

(a) (b) (c) (d)

Fig. 4 *(a) Edges of maximum curvature extrema. (b) All detected edges. (c) Doubling of C^0 edges. (d) Junctions after polygonalization*

3.4 Final Organization

So far, for objects in a range image, we have extracted the edges of their surface characteristics and structured them into an edge-junction graph. However, such an edge-junction graph cannot be directly used for constructing a surface approximation.

We still need two special processing steps: the doubling of the C^0 edge points and the polygonization of the extracted surface characteristics.

C^0 edges are caused by the occlusion of object surfaces. Thus, along a C^0 edge there are two surfaces meeting it. In the edge-junction graph constructed above, a detected C^0 edge belongs to the limit of the surface which is closer to the sensor. We thus need to double this C^0 edge in the farther surface in order to provide boundary limits for both adjacent surfaces. These boundary limits will be used in the surface construction process presented in the next section. As the detected edges have been oriented in such a way that the surface closest to the sensor is on their right, we can easily double a C^0 edge at its left side when we follow it along the defined orientation and orient the doubled edge in the reverse direction. If an object is totally contained inside a range image, we discard the background surface. In **Fig. 4**(c), two interior C^0 edges have been doubled.

For our surface reconstruction process, we also need to polygonize the extracted surface characteristics. This polygonization is performed on the 3-D coordinates of the extracted edges. An algorithm for 2-D curve approximation [DUDA-73] has been generalized for 3-D curve approximation. The algorithm provides a continuous polygonal approximation in which the extremities of each 3-D line segments lie on the 3-D digital curves. For extremity, a corresponding junction is created in the edge-junction graph. An example is shown in **Fig. 4**(d).

4. Adaptive Approximation by Constrained Surface Triangulation

In order to embed the pre-extracted surface characteristics, a triangulation-based surface approximation requires the notion of a constrained triangulation. In this section, we first define this notion and then present procedures for iteratively constructing such a triangulation. Based on these procedures, we describe an adaptive method for approximating digital surfaces.

4.1 Constrained 2-D Triangulation and Surface Triangulation

Since our input is a range image, we can use a 2-D triangulation method to construct a surface triangulation. To construct a surface triangulation constrained to the pre-extracted surface characteristics then becomes to construct a 2-D triangulation constrained to the projection in the image domain of these characteristics. Such a set of projected surface characteristics is represented by $\boldsymbol{D} = (\boldsymbol{S}, \boldsymbol{V})$ where $\boldsymbol{S}$ is a set of the 2-D projections of 3-D segments and $\boldsymbol{V}$ is the union of the set of the extremities of $\boldsymbol{S}$ and the set of projections of the isolated characteristic points.

A 2-D triangulation $\boldsymbol{T}$ constrained to a given $\boldsymbol{D} = (\boldsymbol{S}, \boldsymbol{V})$ is a triangulation in which segments in $\boldsymbol{S}$ are embedded as its edges and points in $\boldsymbol{V}$ are embedded as its vertices.

It is easy to see that a given input data $\boldsymbol{D}$ can be triangulated in different ways. However, it can be shown that for any triangulation of $\boldsymbol{D}$, the number of triangles $N_t = 2n - n_b - 2$, and the number of edges $N_e = 3n - n_b - 3$ is fixed, where $n = |\boldsymbol{V}|$ and n_b is the number of points situated on the convex hull of $\boldsymbol{V}$.

Now suppose that a constrained triangulation $\boldsymbol{T}$ has been constructed for an input data $\boldsymbol{D}$. A surface triangulation is obtained by backprojecting $\boldsymbol{T}$ to the 3-D space using the range value associated with each data point in $\boldsymbol{V}$ (**Fig. 5**). In the following, we will note $\boldsymbol{T}$ a 2-D triangulation, $\boldsymbol{ST}$ the surface triangulation obtained by backprojecting $\boldsymbol{T}$, t_i a triangle of $\boldsymbol{T}$, and st_i a triangle of $\boldsymbol{ST}$.

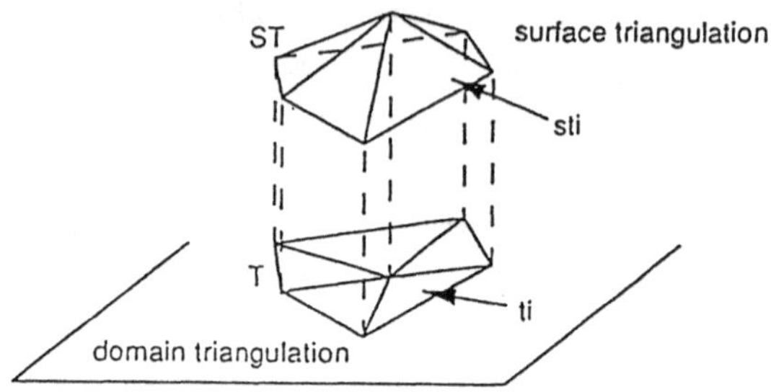

Fig. 5 *Surface triangulation* $\boldsymbol{ST}$ *obtained by backprojecting 2-D triangulation T.*

4.2 Incremental Construction of a 2-D Locally Optimal Triangulation

Because there are many ways to triangulate a given input data $\boldsymbol{D}$, we would like to find a way to decide which one is the best. This needs a global criterion which can measure the "goodness" of a triangulation. The following idea was originally proposed by Lawson for 2-D triangulations [LAWS-77] and then adapted by Lee for 2-D constrained triangulations [LEE-86].

Suppose $\alpha(t)$ is a numerical measure of the goodness of a triangle t. Then associated with a triangulation $\boldsymbol{T}$, we can define an *index vector* $\boldsymbol{\alpha}(\boldsymbol{T}) = (\alpha_1, \ldots, \alpha_{N_t})$, where $\{ \alpha_i \}$ are obtained from $\{ \alpha(t_i) \}$ by putting them in increasing order. Note that the dimension of this vector is fixed because N_t remains the same for any triangulation of $\boldsymbol{D}$. We can now compare the goodness of two different triangulations by using the standard **lexicographical order** of their associated index vectors: $\boldsymbol{a} < \boldsymbol{b}$ means that for some integer m, we have $a_i = b_i$ for $i = 1,\ldots,m-1$ and $a_m < b_m$. So a triangulation $\boldsymbol{T}$ is said to be an **optimal triangulation** of an input data $\boldsymbol{D}$ with respect to a given $\alpha(t)$ iff $\boldsymbol{\alpha}(\boldsymbol{T}) \geq \boldsymbol{\alpha}(\boldsymbol{T}')$ for any other triangulation $\boldsymbol{T}'$ of $\boldsymbol{D}$.

However, it might be difficult to obtain such an optimal triangulation in practice. In most cases, we will be satisfied with a *locally optimal* triangulation. We first define the notion of a *locally optimal edge*. An edge e is said to be locally optimal with respect to a measure $\alpha(t)$ if one of the following conditions holds: i) e is a constrained edge; ii) The quadrilateral Q formed by two triangles sharing e is not strictly convex.

iii) Q is strictly convex, e is not a constrained edge, and $\alpha(\boldsymbol{T}) > \alpha(\boldsymbol{T}')$ where $\boldsymbol{T}'$ is obtained from $\boldsymbol{T}$ by **swapping** e with the other diagonal of Q (**Fig. 6**). Based on this notion, a triangulation $\boldsymbol{T}$ of an input data $\boldsymbol{D}$ is said to be locally optimal with respect to a measure $\alpha(t)$ if all edges of $\boldsymbol{T}$ are locally optimal with respect to $\alpha(t)$.

Fig. 6 *Two ways to triangulate a strictly convex quadrilateral.*

This swapping technique can be used to iteratively construct a locally optimal triangulation: *We first construct an initial but incomplete triangulation which includes all rest points or segments in its interior. We then update this triangulation by adding remaining points or segments, and at each iteration apply the swap operation to make the current triangulation locally optimal.* The worst-case complexity of the algorithm is $O(n^2)$ [LAWS-77].

The realization of this algorithm needs two procedures: one for inserting a new point into an existing constrained triangulation (ADD_POINT), another for inserting a segment (ADD_SEGMENT). The point insertion procedure can be implemented by means of a stack in which edges to be tested for the local optimization are placed.

The segment insertion procedure we use is a modified version of the one proposed by De Floriani and Puppo [DEFL-88]. Its basic idea is to first insert two endpoints v_1 and v_2 of a segment s by ADD_POINT procedure. Then the segment s itself is inserted. To insert s, those triangles of $\boldsymbol{T}$ intersected by s are collected which form an influenced polygon R with s as one of its diagonals. Thus s splits R into two polygons R_1 and R_2 which are then triangulated separately. After this, the swap operation is applied to the newly generated edges until they are locally optimal. In [DEFL-88], an algorithm of time complexity $O(n^2)$ was used to triangulate R_1 and R_2. We use instead an algorithm of $O(n)$ [TOUS-82] for the same purpose. The local optimization step is implemented by means of a stack as in the point insertion procedure.

To construct an initial triangulation, we can simply use four corners of the image domain to form two triangles. We now turn to define $\alpha(t)$.

4.3 Triangulation with Different Criteria

Different definitions of $\alpha(t)$ give different criteria for obtaining a locally optimal triangulation. Many measures have been proposed in the literature [CHEN-92]. We introduce two of them below. One is in 2-D, the other is in 3-D.

It has long been recognized that 2-D **thin** triangles should be avoided because they can cause a problem for spline approximation or for graphic rendering algorithms. The minimum interior angle of a triangle can be used to measure its thinness. This leads to the max-min angle criterion of Lawson [LAWS-77] where $\alpha(t)$ is defined to be the minimum interior angle of t. Using this criterion leads to the so-called 2-D Delaunay triangulation which has also been proved to be a global optimal one with respect to $\alpha(t)$ so defined.

The above criterion is a 2-D one which uses a numerical quantity defined on the t_i of $\boldsymbol{T}$. Similarly, we can define a 3-D criterion using a quantity defined on the st_i of $\boldsymbol{ST}$. Dyn, Levin, and Rippa [DYN-90] introduced a criterion called the quasi-G^1 continuity criterion. It is based on a numerical measure defined on the common edge of two adjacent surface triangles. The index vector for a triangulation is then defined on all internal edges of $\boldsymbol{T}$

$$\boldsymbol{\alpha}(\boldsymbol{T}) = (\alpha(e_1),\ldots,\alpha(e_{N'_e})),$$

where N'_e is the number of internal edges equal to $N_e - n_b$. Now let e be an internal edge of $\boldsymbol{T}$ and let t_1 and t_2 be the two triangles sharing the edge e. Then $\alpha(e) = 180 - \theta$, where θ is the angle between the normals of st_1 and st_2 (**Fig.** 7). $\alpha(e)$ is in fact the angle between the planes supporting these two triangles. Maximizing $\alpha(e)$ will result in a triangulation in which the normal to the surface triangulation minimizes its direction changes when crossing the edges of the triangulation.

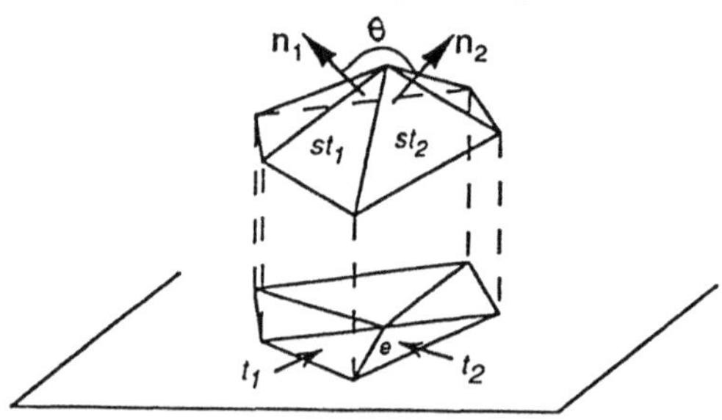

Fig. 7 *Angle between two neighboring surface triangles.*

4.4 Adaptive Surface Approximation by Surface Triangulation

We now describe an adaptive surface approximation scheme which makes use of the procedures ADD_POINT and ADD_SEGMENT and the two triangulation criteria presented above. In this description, the function ERROR(st) returns the approximation error for a surface triangle st; FIND_POINT(st) finds the coordinates v of the point worst-approximated by st; ε is a given error tolerance. Two lists, namely ACTIVE_LIST and DEFINITIVE_LIST, are used to store the surface triangles which need or needn't be refined.

Adaptive Refinement of a Surface Triangulation

```
1. Initialization
    1.1 construct an initial triangulation T constrained to the
        approximated surface characteristics;
    1.2 for each triangle t_i ∈ T do
            if ERROR(st_i) > ε do Add t_i to ACTIVE_LIST;
            else do              Add t_i to DEFINITIVE_LIST;
        end for

2. Patch Refinement
    while (NOT_EMPTY(ACTIVE_LIST)) do
        2.1 t ← remove a triangle from ACTIVE_LIST;
        2.2 v ← FIND_POINT(st);
        2.3 ADD_POINT(T,v);
        2.4 for each new triangle t_i do
                if ERROR(st_i) > ε do Add t_i to ACTIVE_LIST;
                else do              Add t_i to DEFINITIVE_LIST;
            end for
    end while

3. Characteristics Refinement
    if REQUEST do
        3.1 refine the approximation of surface characteristics with new error tolerance;
        3.2 remove old constraints of surface characteristics from T;
        3.3 for each new refined segment s_i do
            3.3.1 ADD_SEGMENT(T,s_i);
            3.3.2 for each new triangle t_i do
                      if ERROR(st_i) > ε do Add t_i to ACTIVE_LIST;
                      else do              Add t_i to DEFINITIVE_LIST;
                  end for
        3.4 goto 2.
    else finish.
```

To estimate the approximation error ERROR(st_i) for a surface triangle st_i, we must define a partition of the image domain with respect to a triangulation $\boldsymbol{T}$. This partition is obtained by associating with each triangle t_i, the coordinates of the sampled points which are enclosed by t_i (see **Fig. 8**). Let C_i be the set of coordinates associated with t_i. C_i may be empty. In this case, the approximation error of st_i will be considered as zero. Otherwise, we define the approximation error of st_i as

$$ERROR\,(st_i) = \max_{v \in C_i} \varepsilon(v).$$

$\varepsilon(v)$ is the error associated with the coordinates v of a point and is defined as

$$\varepsilon(v) = \mid z_v - f_v \mid,$$

where z_v is the range value at v, and f_v the value of st_i at v (see **Fig. 8**).

When calculating ERROR(st_i), we register the coordinates of the point which is worst approximated by st_i. The function FIND_POINT(st) is then trivial.

Step 3 is an optional process for refining the approximation of the surface characteristics (specified by the logical variable *REQUEST*). If at a certain refinement stage, the user requires that the original polygonization of the surface characteristics be refined, this process can be turned on. The refinement of this polygonization is realized by just adding new knots. The removal of a previously constrained segment from the triangulation ***T*** is very simple. We just consider this segment as an ordinary edge of ***T*** and apply the local optimization procedure to locally optimize ***T***.

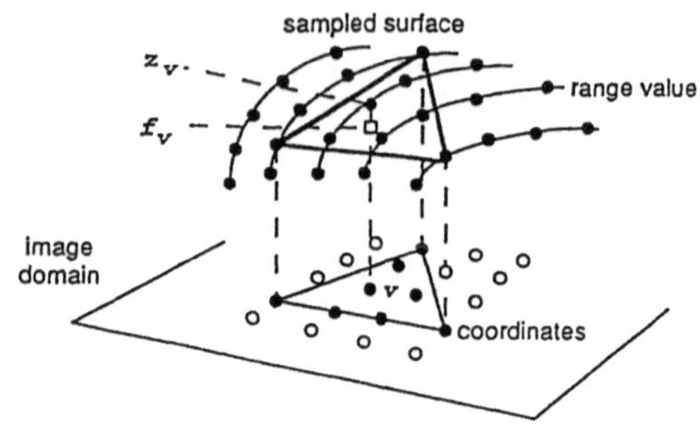

Fig. 8 *Partition of image domain with a triangulation and definition of* $\varepsilon(v)$.

Different strategies are possible for choosing the next triangle to refine. For example, we can sort the triangles in ACTIVE_LIST based on their approximation error in a descending order. In this way, the worst approximated triangle will be first refined each time. However, the additional computation cost is needed. In the results presented below, we used a simple strategy in which the first triangle in list is taken.

5. Experimental Results

The proposed scheme has been applied to several range images from the *NRCC* range image database [RIOU-88]. We present some of them as examples to illustrate various aspects of this scheme. These range images are originally coded in 16 bits and have been requantized into 8 bits. In the following, we first present the various results of the adaptive approximation phase for the example image discussed above. We then present the results on both the characteristic extraction phase and the adaptive approximation phase for other objects.

Block Image 1

The object of the previous example is a subpart of the *NRCC* range image "BLOC 27" (**Fig. 9**(a)). Its extracted surface characteristics have been shown in **Fig. 4**(b).

Beginning from a polygonization of the surface characteristics with an error tolerance of 4 sampling units (61 segments in **Fig. 9**(b)), the adaptive surface approximation scheme with the max-min angle criterion was first applied by setting the logical variable *REQUEST* to *false*. This resulted in 160 triangles when $\varepsilon = 4$ (**Fig. 9**(e)) or 349 triangles when $\varepsilon = 2$ (**Fig. 9**(h)). *REQUEST* was then set to *true* with a new polygonization error tolerance equal to 2, the approximation scheme was applied and resulted in 84 segments (**Fig. 9**(c)) and 205 triangles when $\varepsilon = 4$ (**Fig. 9**(f)) or 373 triangles when $\varepsilon = 2$ (**Fig. 9**(i)).

The adaptive approximation with the quasi-G^1 continuity criterion was then applied with $REQUEST = false$ on the polygonization results shown in **Fig. 9**(b), which resulted in 134 triangles when $\varepsilon = 4$ (**Fig. 9**(d)) or 273 triangles when $\varepsilon = 2$ (**Fig. 9**(g)). We see that the number of triangles was reduced compared to the results obtained above. We have found that for surfaces having a preferred direction (the example object has a cylindrical surface), using the quasi-G^1 continuity criterion results in less number of triangles. By examining the domain triangulations in **Fig. 9**, we see that the shape of the triangulations shown in **Fig. 9**(d) and (g) follow better the preferred direction of the example object.

Due to the limited space, we will present only two surface approximation results for other objects which are obtained by using the max-min angle criterion.

Block Image 2

This block object is also a subpart of the *NRCC* range image "BLOC 27". From **Fig. 10**(b) and (c), we see that the C^0 and C^1 discontinuity edges have been very well detected. Because the object is composed of only planar surfaces, no curvature extremum edge is detected. The polygonal approximation of the left- and right-side edges of the object has resulted in many edge segments (**Fig. 10**(g)). This is because the quantization of a strongly slanted surface can result in an aliasing phenomenon.

Telephone Image

This is the *NRCC* range image "TELE 1". The telephone wire has been masked out and the background set to zero. Four false C^1 discontinuity edges have been detected on the telephone (**Fig. 11**(c)) The reason is that for a surface curved like a smooth roof, our detector will detect a false C^1 discontinuity edge along the roof when the image resolution is not high enough. Solving such ambiguities necessitates *a priori* knowledge of the object surfaces and the image acquisition setup.

Face Image

This is the *NRCC* range image "FACE 30" (**Fig. 12**). Because the image consists of many curved surfaces, we did not use the detected C^1 discontinuity edges which were mostly false. The most interesting results about this image are the edges of maximum curvature extrema at the "eye", "nose", and "mouth" parts of the face, which are meaningful enough for recognizing the face.

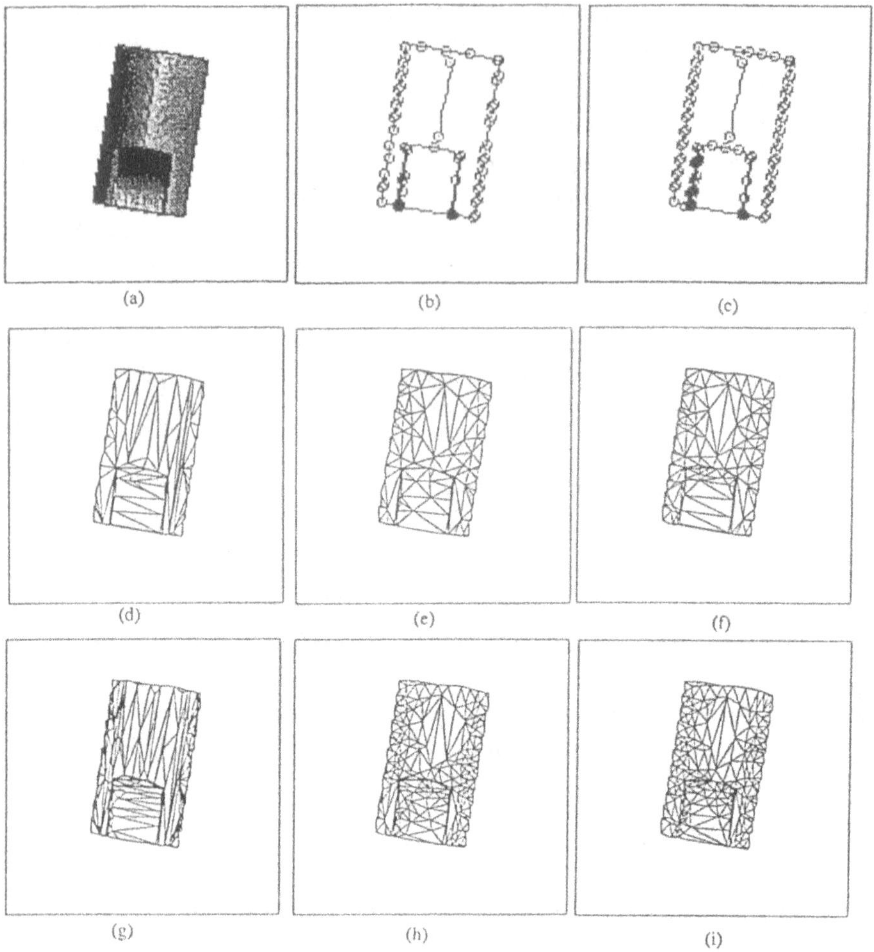

Fig. 9 *"BLOCK 1": (a) shaded display of the range image; (b) (c) Polygonization results with ε set to 4 and 2, respectively; (d) (g) triangulation with the quasi-G^1 continuity criterion performed on (b) with ε set to 4 and 2, respectively; (e) (h) triangulation with the max-min angle criterion performed on (b) with ε set to 4 and 2, respectively; (f) (i) triangulation by max-min angle criterion performed on (c) with ε set to 4 and 2, respectively;*

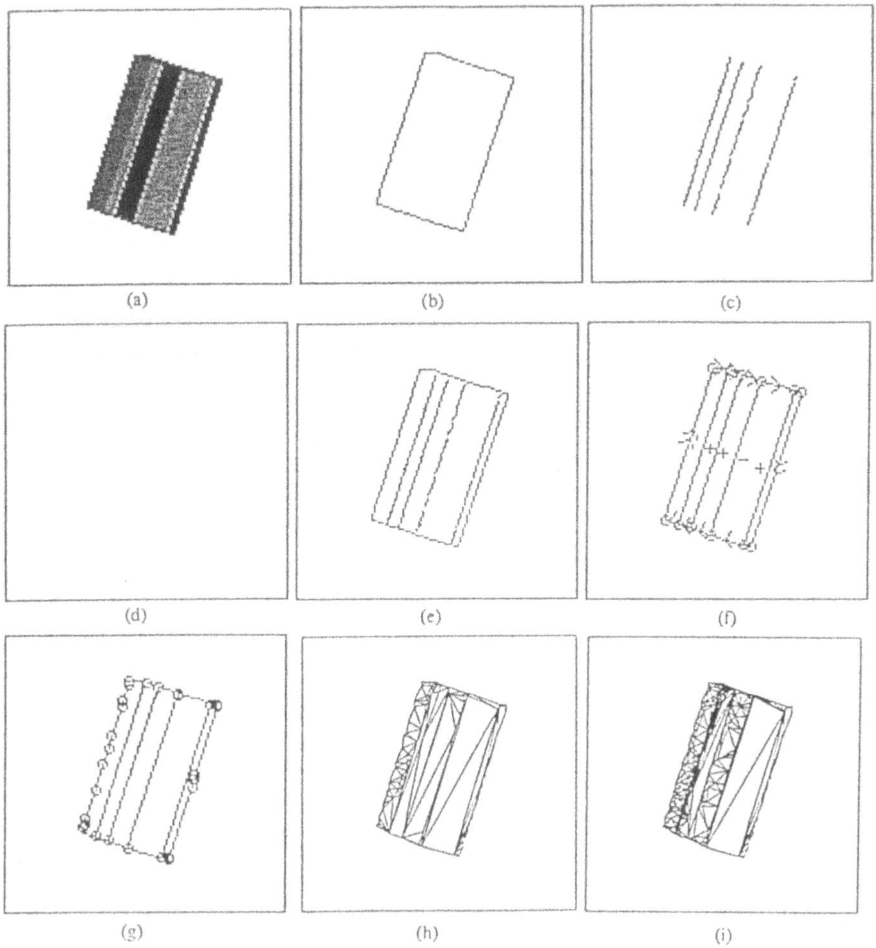

Fig. 10 *"BLOCK 2": (a) shaded display of the range image; (b) (c) C^0 and C^1 discontinuity edges, respectively; (d) maximum curvature extrema; (e) complete set of extracted edges; (f) edge-junction graph with labeled edges; (g) polygonization; (h) (i) domain triangulation with error tolerance set to 4 and 2 units, respectively.*

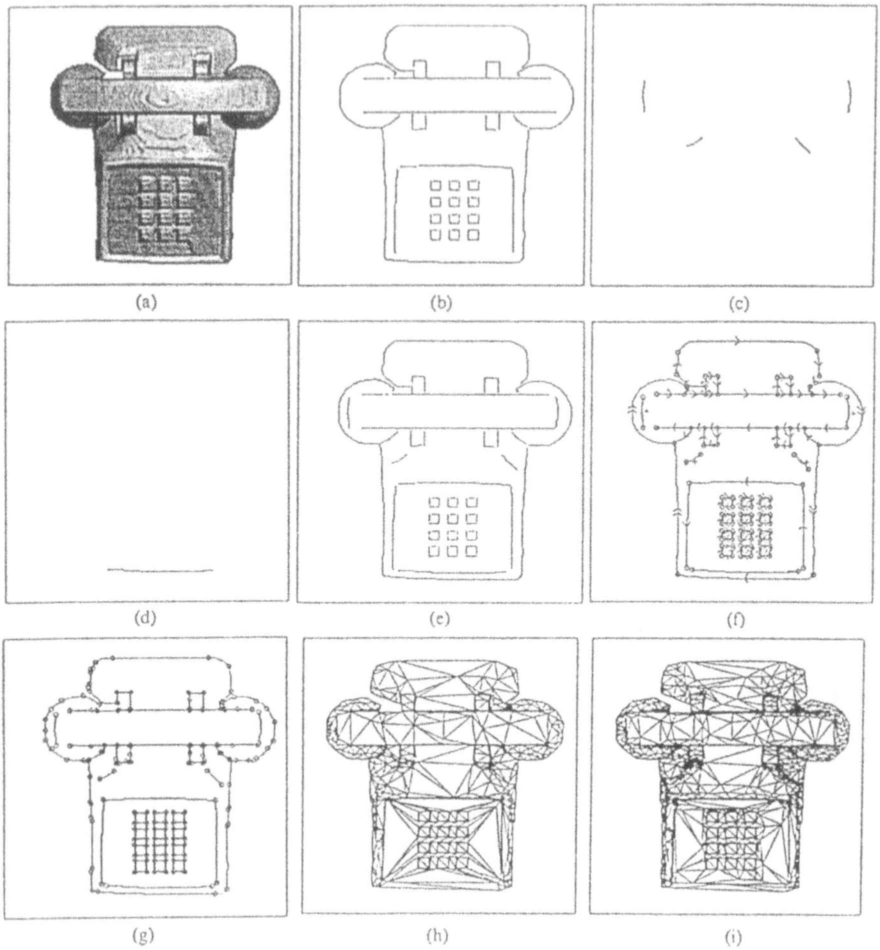

Fig. 11 *"TELEPHONE": (a) shaded display of the range image; (b) (c) C^0 and C^1 discontinuity edges, respectively; (d) maximum curvature extrema; (e) complete set of extracted edges; (f) edge-junction graph with labeled edges; (g) polygonization; (h) (i) domain triangulation with error tolerance set to 4 and 2 units, respectively.*

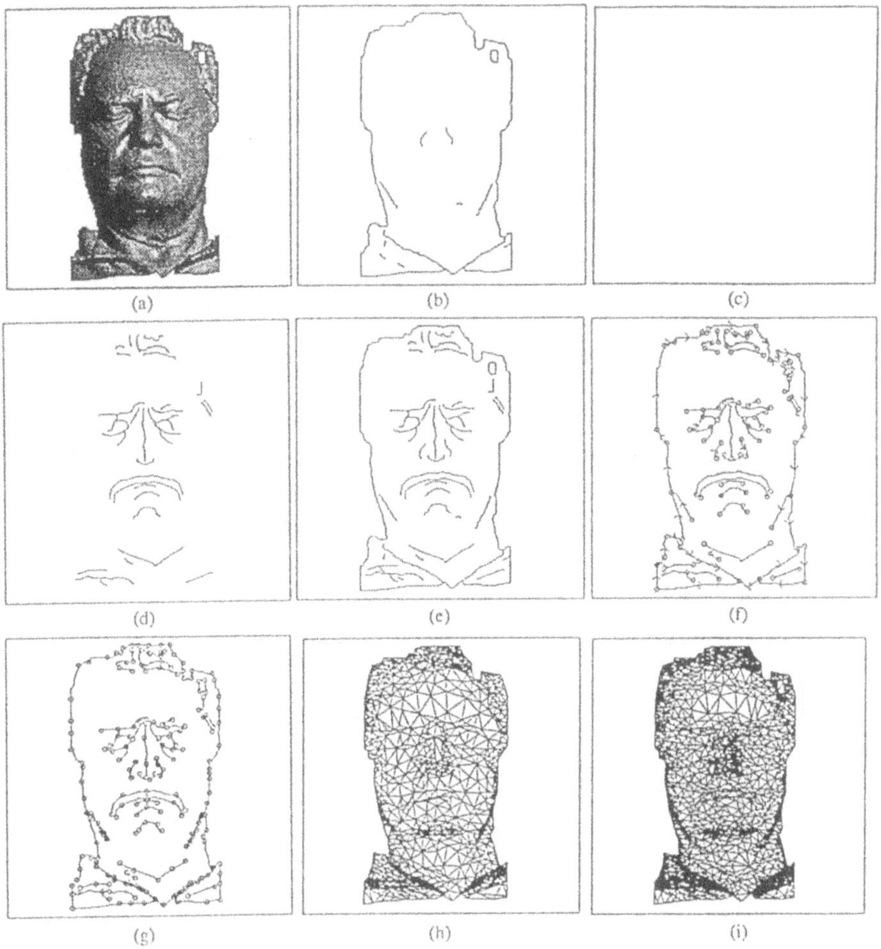

Fig. 12 *"FACE": (a) shaded display of the range image; (b) (c) C^0 and C^1 discontinuity edges, respectively; (d) maximum curvature extrema; (e) complete set of extracted edges; (f) edge-junction graph with labeled edges; (g) polygonization; (h) (i) domain triangulation with error tolerance set to 4 and 2 units, respectively.*

6. Conclusion

In this paper, we have proposed an adaptive surface approximation scheme based on a constrained surface triangulation. A significant feature distinguishing this scheme from the other ones [FAUG-84,DEFL-85,LEE-89,DELI-91] is that the constructed surface model embeds pre-extracted surface characteristics. Such surface models can be used for many applications. For example, for a face image segmented into its composite subparts like "nose", "eye", and "mouth", the extracted subpart boundaries can be embedded into the constructed face model. This model would be very useful for face animation where the face models have frequently been constructed manually [THAL-88].

One possible extension of this work is to use smooth rather than flat surface primitives in the approximation scheme. We have already used a triangular Gregory-Bézier patch model in a non-constrained surface approximation scheme [SCHM-91b]. A constrained piecewise surface constructed with such a patch model can have various degrees of continuity depending on the locations and the types of the detected surface characteristics. Preliminary results have been obtained and will be reported elsewhere [CHEN-92].

REFERENCES

[BESL-88] **P.J.Besl and R.C.Jain,** *"Segmentation through variable-order surface fitting",* IEEE Trans. on Pattern Anal. Machine Intell., vol. 10, no. 2, pp. 167-192, 1988.

[BOIS-84] **J.D.Boissonnat,** *"Geometric structures for three-dimensional shape representation",* ACM Trans. on Graphics, vol. 3, no. 4, pp. 266-286, 1984.

[CHEN-92] **X.Chen,** *"Vision-based geometric modeling",* Ph.D dissertation, École Nationale Supérieure des Télécommunications, PARIS-FRANCE, 1992.

[DEFL-85] **L.De Floriani, B.Falcidieno, and C.Pienovi,** *"Delaunay-based representation of surfaces defined over arbitrarily shaped domains",* Comput. Vision, Graphics, and Image Processing, vol. 32, 127-140, 1985.

[DEFL-88] **L.De Floriani and E.Puppo,** *"Constrained Delaunay triangulation for multiresolution surface description",* in Proc. of 9th Int. Conf. on Pattern Recognition, 1988, pp. 566-569.

[DELI-91] **H.Delingette, M.Hebert, and K.Ikeuchi,** *"Shape representation and image segmentation using deformable surfaces",* in Proc. of IEEE Conf. on Computer Vision and Pattern Recognition, Hawaii, June 1991, pp. 467-472.

[DUDA-73] **R.Duda and P.Hart,** *"Pattern classification and scene analysis",* Wiley-Interscience, New York, 1973.

[DYN-90] **N.Dyn, D.Levin, and S.Rippa,** *"Data dependent triangulations for piecewise linear interpolation",* IMA Journal of Numerical Analysis, vol. 10, pp. 137-154, 1990.

[FAN-87] **T.J.Fan, G.Medioni, and R.Nevatia,** *"Segmented descriptions of 3-D surfaces"*, IEEE J. Robotics and Automation, pp. 527-538, Dec., 1987.

[FAN-90] **T.J.Fan,** *"Describing and recognizing 3-D objects using surface properties"*, Springer-Verlag, 1990.

[FAUG-84] **O.D.Faugeras, M.Hebert, P.Mussi, J.D.Boissonnat,** *"Polyhedral approximation of 3-D objects without holes"*, Comput. Vision, Graphics, and Image Processing, vol. 25, 169-183, 1984.

[FOWL-79] **R.F.Fowler and J.J.Little,** *"Automatic extraction of irregular digital terrain models"*, Computer Graphics, vol. 13, pp. 199-207, 1979.

[GODI-89] **G.D.Godin and M.D.Levine,** *"Structured edge map of curved objects in a range image"*, in Proc. Conf. Computer Vision and Pattern Recognition, 1989, pp. 276-281.

[HORA-89] **P.Horain,** *"Extraction des arêtes dans des images de distance"*, in Proc. 7e congrès de Reconnaissance des Formes et Intelligence Artificielle, Paris, 1989, pp. 63-72.

[JERA-89] **R.B.Jerard, R.L.Drysdale, K.Hauch, B.Schaudt, and J.Magewick,** *"Methods for detecting errors in numerically controlled machining of sculptured surfaces"*, IEEE Trans. on Computer Graphics & Applications, vol. 9, pp. 26-39, January 1989.

[LAWS-77] **C.L.Lawson,** *"Software for C1 surface interpolation"*, In Mathematical Software III (J.R.Rice, eds.) Academic Press, pp. 161-164, 1977.

[LECL-87] **Y.G.Leclerc and S.W.Zucker,** *"The local structure of image discontinuities in one dimension"*, IEEE Trans. on Pattern Anal. Machine Intell., vol. 9, no. 3, pp. 341-355, 1987.

[LEE-86] **D.T.Lee and A.K.Lin,** *"Generalized Delaunay Triangulation for Planar Graphs"*, Discrete Comput. Geom., vol. 1, pp. 201-217, 1986.

[LEE-89] **D.Lee, T.Nishida, and Y.Kobayashi,** *"Object representation for 3-D visual communications"*, in Proc. of 1989 ITEJ National Convention, pp. 437-438, 1989.

[LOWE-85] **D.G.Lowe,** *"Perceptual organization and visual recognition"*, Hingham, MA: Kulwer Academic, 1985.

[MALI-87] **J. Malik,** *"Interpreting line drawings of curved objects"*, International Journal of Computer Vision, vol. 1, pp. 73-103, 1987.

[MOHA-92] **R.Mohan and R.Nevatia,** *"Perceptual organization for scene segmentation and description"*, IEEE Trans. on Pattern Anal. Machine Intell., vol. 14, no. 6, pp. 616-634, 1992.

[PONC-87] **J.Ponce and M.Brady,** *"Toward a surface primal sketch"*, in Three-Dimensional Machine Vision (T.Kanade, eds.), New York: Kluwer Academic, 1987, pp. 195-240.

[RIOU-88] **M.Rioux and L.Cournoyer,** *"The NRCC three-dimensional image data files"*, Technique report CNRC 29077, 1988.

[SCHM-91a] **F.Schmitt and X.Chen,** *"Fast segmentation of range images into planar regions"*, in Proc. of IEEE Conf. on Computer Vision and Pattern Recognition, Hawaii, USA, June 1991, pp.710-711.

[SCHM-91b] **F.Schmitt, X.Chen, and W.H.Du,** *"Geometric Modelling from range image data"*, in Proc. of Eurographics'91, Vienna, Austria, Sept. 1991, pp. 317-328.

[THAL-88] **N.M.Thalmann, H.T.Minh, M. de Angelis, and D.Thalmann,** *"Human prototyping"*, **in Proc. of CG International'88, pp. 74-82, 1988.**

[TOUS-82] **G.T.Toussaint and D.Avis,** *"On a convex hull algorithm for polygons and its application to triangulation problems,* Pattern Recognition, vol. 15, no. 1, pp. 23-29, 1982.

Collinearity Constraints on Geometric Figures

Maharaj Mukherjee
Indian Institute of Technology
Kharagpur, India

George Nagy
Rensselaer Polytechnic Institute
Troy, NY, USA

1 Introduction

The preservation of collinearity relationships under geometric operations is important in computer-graphics applications that manipulate line arrangements in engineering drawings and geographic information systems. Finite-precision computer implementations of these operations do not generally preserve these relationships. We show that for a wide class of line arrangements, any specified collinearity relationships can be preserved, without extending the precision, at the expense of a bounded displacement of the vertices of the arrangement.

Consider a set of points on the integer grid subjected to a projective transformation. The transformed points will have rational-valued coordinates. If we wish to store these coordinates with the same number of digits as the original data, as is customary in most graphics environments, we must approximate the rational-valued coordinates by integers. This is the case whether we use "integer" or "floating-point" computer arithmetic. The most common methods of approximation are *truncation* and *round-off* (Figure 1a). These methods do not necessarily preserve the collinearity relationships that may have existed among certain subsets of the original point set. Thus, the primary reason for using projective transformations is lost.

Our objective is to preserve at least some of the collinearity relationships by resorting to a more refined approximation. The collinearity relationships that we attempt to preserve are those that are the immediate consequence of the input specifications that postulate that certain subsets of points lie on a straight line. For instance, the point of intersection of two line segments will lie on both approximated lines, provided that the intersection point is explicitly represented as collinear in the original data structure (Figure 1b). *Derived* relations, such as those postulated by Pascal's and Desargues' theorems [Coxeter 61], may be lost, unless the vertices resulting from the construction are explicitly specified to be collinear.

Collinearity constraints that intrinsically cannot be represented by discrete points with rational coordinates do exist. Consider, for example, the sets {AOF, COH, EOJ, GOB, IOD, ABDE, CDFG, EFHI, GHJA, IJBC}, where the points A....J form the vertices of a five-pointed star and O is the "center". We do not attempt to approximate *overconstrained* line arrangements.

Even rotations can be approximated by rational transformations [Franklin 84]. Collinearity also plays an important role in Boolean operations that require intersecting pairs of line segments. The failure of preserving collinearity can often be observed in the output of drawing software, where the underlying integer grid (the display screen or 300 dpi printer) is far coarser than the internal 16-bit or 32-bit representation. We are concerned with both *visible distortions* and with inaccuracies in the data structure, which may give rise to *inconsistent topology* or incorrect answers to *geometric queries*.

Our approximation strategy is based on the continued-fraction expansion of the slope of a line. We have previously applied continued-fraction expansions to vertex approximations governed by location constraints [Mehta 91, Mukherjee 92b] rather than incidence constraints. The derivation of the approximation of a single set of collinear points is given in [Mehta 92], and the graph representation for line arrangements is introduced in [Mukherjee 92a]. Here we demonstrate a new back-tracking algorithm for approximating a certain class of line arrangments, which yields much lower error than our earlier single-pass method and seems to us eminently practical.

The computational complexity of the algorithm and the bound on the maximum error (i.e., the error of approximation of the point with the maximum error) are both linear in terms of the number of vertices in the figure. The bound on the maximum error is also proportional to the square-root of the largest integer used in the computation. We argue that the class of geometric figures that the algorithm can approximate corresponds to those that usually occur in engineering applications.

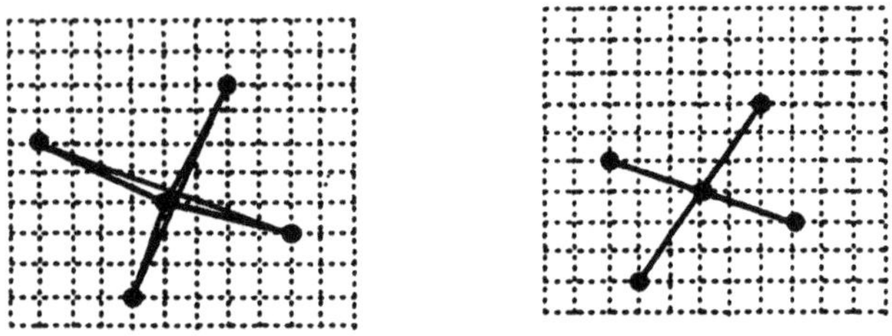

(a) (b)

Figure 1. Round-off destroys the collinearity between the end-points of two lines and their point of intersection (a). The collinearity may be preserved by small displacements of the end-points (b).

2 Approximation of a set of collinear points

Consider a set of n collinear points p_i with rational coordinates. Without loss of generality, we let the points p_i lie on a ray L in the first quadrant. (We can translate any point set or rotate it by multiples of $\pi/2$ without error.) Let the slope of this ray be c/d. Thus,

$$p_i = (a_i/b_i\, c,\ a_i/b_i\, d), \qquad i = 1,2,\ldots,n$$

where a_i, b_i, c and d are all integers smaller than N, the largest representable integer (in contemporary digital computers, N is typically 2^{16} or 2^{32}).

We will approximate ray L by another ray L' with slope c'/d'. Each point p_i will be approximated by point q_i, where

$$q_i = (e_i', f_i'),\ \text{where } e_i', f_i', \text{ are integers smaller than N, and } e_i'/f_i' = c'/d'.$$

Therefore the points q_i have integer coefficients, and the error of approximation is:

$$E = \max_i \left[\, (e_i' - a_i/b_i\, c)^2 + (f_i' - a_i/b_i\, d)^2 \,\right]^{1/2}$$

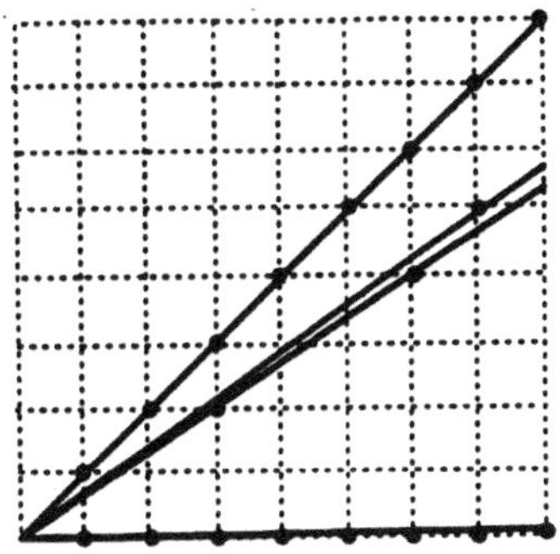

Figure 2. Successive approximations to a ray with slope c/d = 5/7 = 0 + 1/(1 + 1/(2 + 1/2)). The approximating rays straddle the original ray with increasing offset and decreasing integer spacing.

3 Continued fraction approximation

Our objective is to choose c' and d' so as to minimize the *least upper bound* on E. Consider the continued fraction expansion of c/d:

$$c/d = u_m + 1/(u_{m-1} + 1/(u_{m-2} + 1/\ldots.1/u_0))$$

We obtain the slopes for successive approximating lines by omitting terms from the end. For the example of Figure 2, the slopes of the successive approximating lines are:

$$c/d = c_0/d_0 = 5/7;\quad c_1/d_1 = 2/3;\quad c_2/d_2 = 1/1;\quad c_3/d_3 = 0/1.$$

As we omit terms by setting successive u_j's equal to infinity, each slope will differ more and more from the original slope c/d. The final approximation is either the horizontal or the vertical axis, depending on whether u_m is 0 or not. (Note that we have assumed that approximating line passes through the origin.) At the same time, the magnitudes of the numerators and denominators of the successive approximations of the slope decrease, increasing the density of integers on the approximating ray. On an approximating ray with slope c_j/d_j, the distance between integers is $(c_j^2 + d_j^2)^{1/2}$.

For any point p_i, the error E has two components (Figure 3):

1. The distance from p_i to the closest point q'_i on the approximating ray; and

2. The distance from q_i' to the nearest integer q_i on the approximating ray.

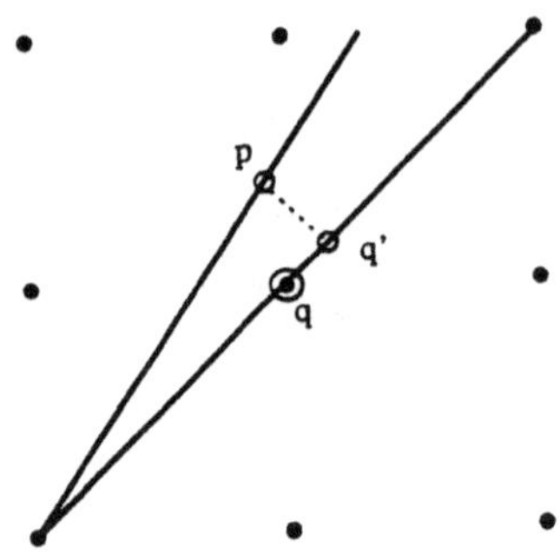

Figure 3. The error of approximation of an arbitrary point on the ray has two components: the offset |p - q'|, and the distance |q' - q| to the nearest integer on the approximating ray.

The first of these components, called *offset*, increases approximately linearly on successive approximations (as terms are omitted from the expansion) because of the increase in the (small) angle between L and L'. The offset is also proportional to the distance of p_i from the origin (which is bounded by the length D of the line). The second component is, in the worst case, inversely proportional to the density $(c_j^2 + d_j^2)^{-1/2}$ of integer points on the approximating ray, which increases as the square root of the sine of the angle between the rays [Metha 92]. The key equality, $[(c_j^2 + d_j^2)(c_{j+1}^2 + d_{j+1}^2)]^{-1/2} = \sin|\theta_{j+1} - \theta_j|$, is an immediate consequence of the unit-area property of lattice cells on the integer grid.

Instead of finding the minimum value of the sum of the two orthogonal components, we minimize the maximum of the two. The minimum of the maxima occurs when the two components are equal and can be shown to be $O(D^{1/3})$, where D is the length of the line in units of integers. Figure 4 shows the offset o_j and the half-spacing s_j plotted against the difference t_j between the slopes of the original and the approximating ray, where

$$o_j = (c_0^2 + d_0^2)^{1/2} \sin(|\tan^{-1} c_0/d_0 - \tan^{-1} c_j/d_j|),$$

$$s_j = 1/2\,(c_j^2 + d_j^2)^{1/2},$$

$$t_j = |c_0/d_0 - c_j/d_j|\,.$$

This simple calculation does not take into consideration that the approximation is not continuous, and that it is therefore possible that the theoretical minimum occurs *between* successive approximations. The absolute worst-case error is $O(D^{1/2})$ [Metha 92]. However, the worst case applies only to some very special lines.

An algorithm based on the above bound allows us to approximate any line segment L with only one point fixed (above, it is the origin). We call lines of this type *one-constrained.* Regardless of where the collinear points are located on L, the error is bounded by $N^{1/2}$. The time complexity of the computation for n collinear points is $O(n + \log N)$, because $\log N$ is the maximum number of terms in the continued fraction expansion of a fraction with numerator and denominator bounded by N [Knuth 81].

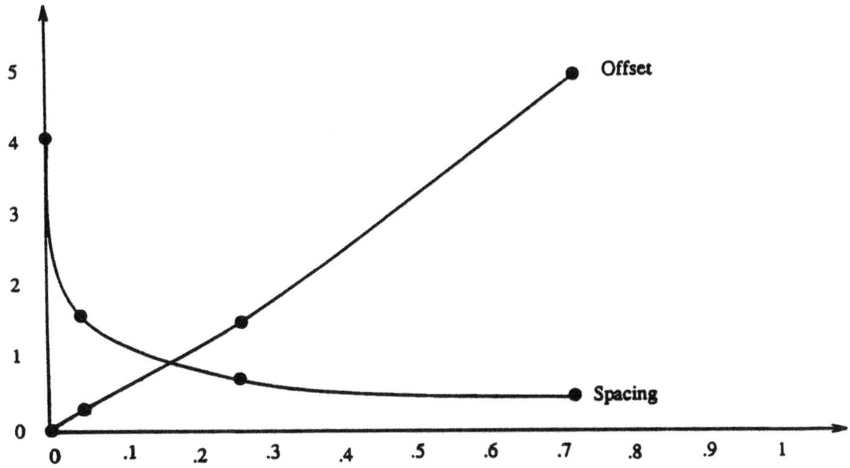

Figure 4. The offset increases and the spacing decreases as a function of the absolute value of the difference between the slopes of the original and the approximating ray.

4 Approximation of two-constrained line segments

Consider now a line segment L_1 whose end-points are constrained to lie on two other line-segments, L_2 and L_3 (Figure 5). We call such line segments *two-constrained.* The nominal position of L1 is defined by the best approximations of its end-points, as given by the approximations of L_2 and L_3, respectively. To approximate L_1, we shift its end-points along the constraining lines L_2 and L_3 in either direction from their nominal positions. For each integer position of either end-point, the deviation of every point on L_1 is determined. If the maximum error is within a preset bound, the algorithm proceeds to the next line to be approximated.

The maximum deviation of the end points is also governed by the preset bound: once it is reached without obtaining an acceptable approximation for all the points on L_1, nothing further can be done without backtracking to alter L_2 and L_3.

As in the case of a one-constrained line, the maximum error has two components. The *offset* in the location of the endpoints is introduced by the approximation of L_2 and L_3 in the previous stages, and is bounded by $O(N^{1/2})$. The other component of the error depends on the sparsity of integers on L_1, which in turn depends on its slope. The slope of L1 depends on the constraining integer points on L_2 and L_3.

5 Graph representation of a line arrangment

We approximate the lines that form geometric figures in such an order that we never have to approximate any but one-constrained and two-constrained lines. Line-arragements where such an order exists are called ***under-constrained*** line arrangments. Most engineering drawings, circuit diagrams, flow charts, etc., are of this type. Meccano constructions also generally correspond to underconstrained arrangments, since building an over-constrained arrangment would generally require solving a difficult integer-programming problem! However, see Figure 6 for the simplest example of an arrangement that is over-constrained, and perhaps try to construct it with a Meccano set. This arrangement occurs repeatedly in the one mentioned in the Introduction.

We represent a line-segment arrangement by a graph G(V, E), with V the set of nodes, and E the set of arcs. Each collinear set is a node in V, and a point shared by two collinear sets is an arc. If a point is common to more than two collinear sets, we represent it by a hyper-arc. The graph representation does not have any dangling edges or vertices, neither does it have any self loops. Line arrangements that can be approximated by successive approximations of one-constrained and two-constrained lines can be characterized recursively in terms of this graph representation.

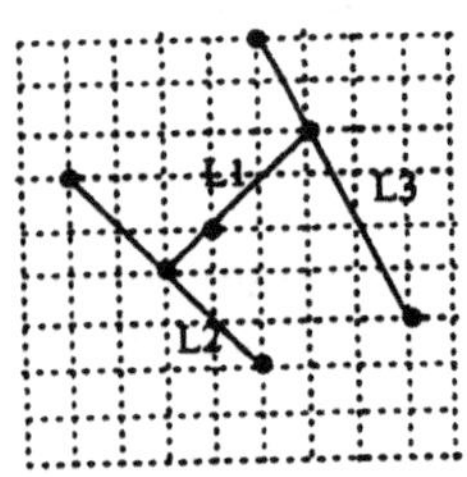

Figure 5. An approximating point with integer coordinates on line L1, whose end-points are constrained to be incident on previously approximated lines L2 and L3.

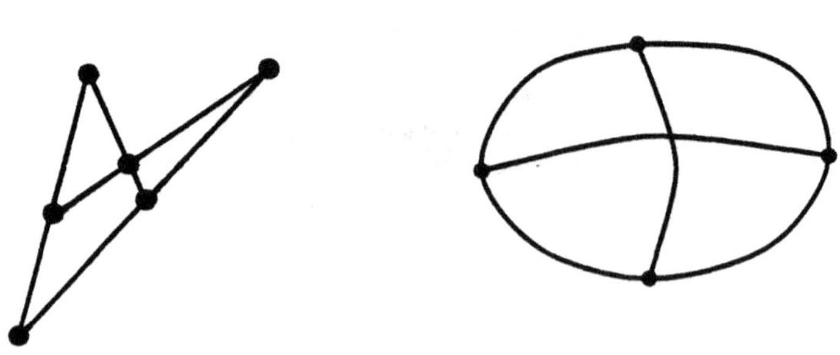

Figure 6. The simplest example of an over-constrained line arrangment, and its graph representation.

Under-Constrained Graph:
A graph G(V,E) is under-constrained if there exists some node v in V, such that degree(v) <= 2, and G-v is an under-constrained graph.

We now present an algorithm for the approximation of a line arrangement characterized by an under-constrained graph. This algorithm approximates the two-constrained lines in arbitrary order. The slope of each line is expanded in a continued fraction, and the integer point on the resulting line nearest to each vertex on the original line is determined.

1. Obtain the Graph-Representation and sort the nodes according to their degrees.

2. While the Graph contains a node

   Find a node of degree < = 2
   if there exists such a node
   push the node on to a stack
   else declare: OVERCONSTRAINED and exit.

3. While the stack is not empty

   Pop a node from the stack
   Approximate all points on the line.

6 A back-tracking algorithm for approximation

The above algorithm does a good job approximating line segments in a local sense. It fails, however, when points on these line segments define further lines, which may also contain points that lie on still other lines as well. In the simplest instance, the density of integer points on a line L1 is not taken into account in the approximation of two one-constrained lines L2 and L3, which contain the end-points of L1. Therefore the error of points on L1 may be unacceptably large.

In the drawings that we have studied to date, the portions that were difficult to approximate were not uniformly distributed throughout the drawing, but confined to isolated patches. It makes therefore sense to devote more computing resources to these areas.

Our back-tracking algorithm is similar in spirit to Dobkin's and Silver's approximation of iterated pentagons [Dobkin 88]. We check on approximating each point on a line whether the error is acceptable. If it is not, we perturb the location of the parent lines, and try again. This is done recursively, so that all possible configurations - subject to the chosen order of approximating the lines - are tried. This algorithm tends to distribute the errors uniformly along all the lines. We have found that a few iterations normally suffice to reduce the error considerably. The algorithm is given overleaf.

1. Obtain the Graph-Representation and sort the nodes by their degrees.

2. If it is underconstrained, then obtain the list of lines.

3. Recursively approximate the lines.

```
recursively_approximate(line)
        if(test.condition(line))
                if(line->next_line <> NULL)
                        recursively_approximate(line->next_line)
                else "DONE"
        else
                if(line->previous_line <> NULL)
                        recursively approximate(line->previous_line)
                else "TRY ANOTHER ERROR BOUND"


test_condition(line)
        update_slope_list(line);
                while (slope_list(line) <> NULL and check_error(line) > Bound
                get_next_slope(line)
                approximate_all_points(line);
        if(done)
                return(1)
        else
                return(0).
```

7 Experimental results

We show results on two geometric figures, a Howe truss and an airport layout (Figure 7). Both figures are represented on a 1000 x 1000 grid: any finer grid would preclude visual observation of the deviations. The maximum diameters of both drawings are between 500 and 600 grid units.

In each case, the figures are represented by a set of infinite lines with rational-valued slopes. The vertices are then obtained by intersection. The results obtained by round-off are shown in Figure 8, by the one-pass algorithm in Figure 9, and by the backtracking algorithm in Figure 10. The corresponding maximum deviations are shown in Table I. When the bound is decreased further than the minimum values shown, the backtracking algorithm does not find a solution.

Table I - Maximum Error in Vertex Placement

Truss (N = 1000)

	MAX-ERROR
One-pass	41
Bound = 45	38
Bound = 30	14
Bound = 15	14

Airport (N = 1000)

	MAX-ERROR
One-pass	65
Bound = 30	24
Bound = 20	18
Bound = 10	8

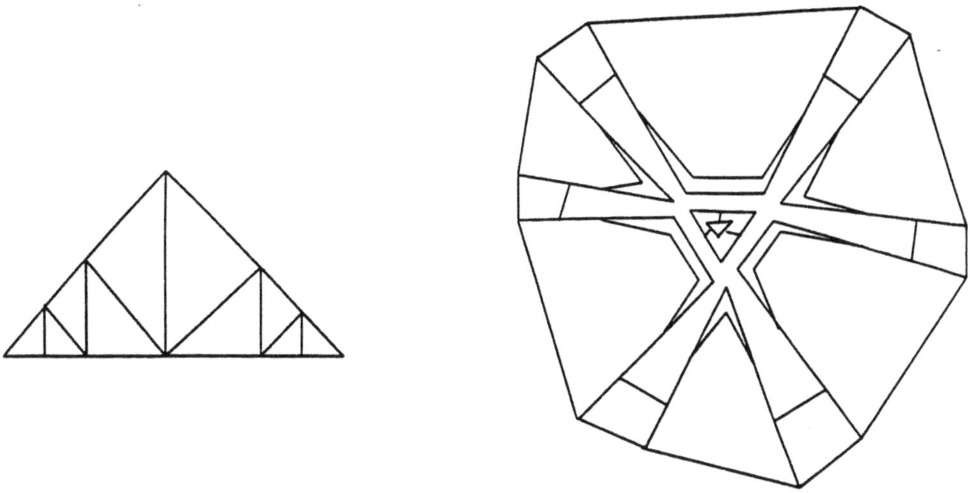

Figure 7. Two line drawings: a Howe truss and an airport layout.

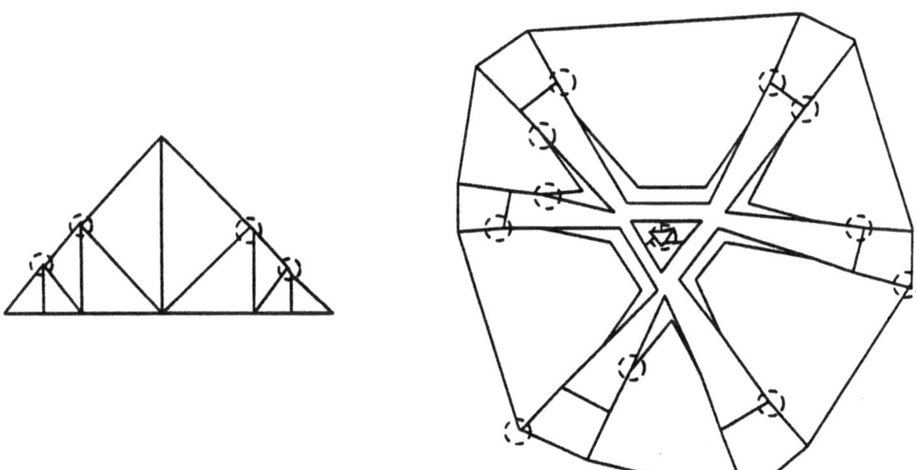

Figure 8. The results of scaling up and down the figures by a factor of 5, using round-off. The geometric errors introduced by round-off are circled.

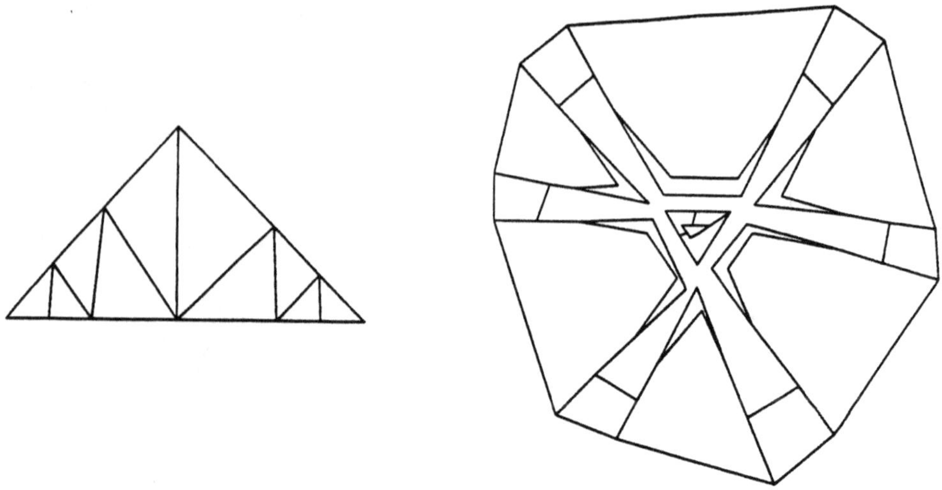

Figure 9. Approximating the figures after scaling, using the single-pass algorithm that preserves the specified collinear relations.

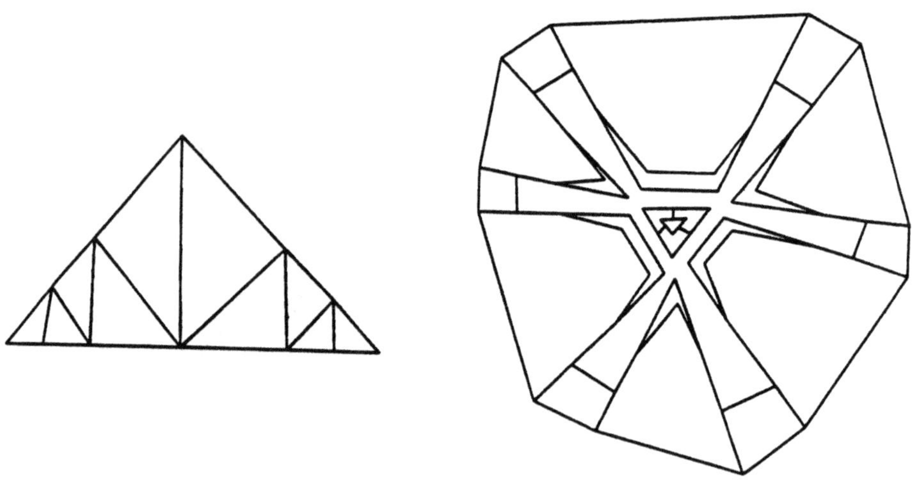

Figure 10. Approximating the figures after scaling with back-tracking. The displacements of the vertices are less than in Figure 9.

8 Conclusion

We have shown that the continued-fraction expansion is a useful tool for preserving collinearity constraints. Eventually we hope to extend our results to incidence constraints for parallel and perpendicular lines, and to coplanarity constraints in three dimensions.

Even the absolute worst case bound of $O(D^{1/2})$ yields a useful engineering approximation. Few engineering designs require dimensioning tolerances smaller than 1 part in 10,000, i.e., 1 micron in a part with a 1 cm diameter (comparable to the coefficient of thermal expansion). Suppose that the error of approximation is of the same order as the tolerance:

$$D^{1/2} / D = 1/10^4 > 1/2^{16}.$$

Then $D < 2^{32}$, which is a reasonable degree of precision for integer representation in any contemporary computer.

9 Acknowledgments

This work was partially supported by the National Science Foundation Information, Robotics, and Systems grant IRI-8704718; and by a New York State Science and Technology Foundation grant to the Rensselaer Center for Advanced Technology. Some of the material presented in this paper is a result of work jointly done with Prof. S. Mehta, University of Poona.

10 References

Coxeter, H.S.M. (1961) *Introduction to Geometry*, John Wiley & Sons.

Dobkin, D., Silver, D. (1988) Recipes for geometry and numerical analysis - part I: An empirical study, *Proceedings of the ACM Symposium on Computational Geometry*, Champaign-Urbana, Illinois, pp. 93 - 105.

Franklin, W.R. (1984) Cartographic errors symptomatic of underlying algebra problems, *Proceedings of the International Symposium on Spatial Data Handling*, pp. 190 - 208, Zurich, Switzerland.

Knuth, D.E. (1981) *The Art of Computer Programming - Seminumerical Algorithms* (Vol. II), Addison Wesley, Reading, Massachusetts.

Mehta, S., Mukherjee, M., Nagy, G. (1991) Constrained integer approximation to planar line intersections, *Information Processing Letters*, V.40, N. 3, pp. 137-139.

Mehta, S., Mukherjee, M., Nagy, G. (1992) Integer approximation of collinear rational points, Rensselaer Polytechnic Institute *Computational Geometry Laboratory Technical Report #92-1122*.

Mukherjee, M., Nagy, G. (1992*a*) Collinearity constraints on spatial subdivision algorithms with finite precision, *Proc. Int. Symp. on Spatial Data Handling*, Charleston, pp. 424-433.

Mukherjee, M., Mehta, S., Nagy, G. (1992*b*) Integer approximation to the intersection of three planes with planar constraints, in *Computer Graphics and Mathematics*, Ed: B. Falcidieno, I. Herman, C. Pienovi, Springer-Verlag, pp 3-22.

Chapter 3

Modeling of Dynamic Objects

Animation of Interacting Objects with Collisions and Prolonged Contacts

STÉPHANE JIMENEZ AND ANNIE LUCIANI
ACROE (Ministère de la Culture) - LIFIA (IMAG)
46 av. Félix Viallet - 38031 Grenoble-Cedex, France
Email : acroe@lifia.imag.fr - Fax : (33) 76 57 46 02 - Tel : (33) 76 57 46 69

Abstract
In this paper, we present the development of an interaction simulation model between deformable objects which deal with both collisions and prolonged contacts. The model involves reaction forces (in the normal direction) and friction forces (in the tangential direction). Friction forces are classified as either kinetic friction when the objects are slipping on each other, and static friction when the objects are stuck. This model is developed in the framework of a modular system for dynamic simulations: The Cordis-Anima system.
In a first part, we will consider the existing physically based methods for movement generation in computer animation and their capacity to tackle the problem of interacting objects. These methods are essentially based on a continuous representation of matter. Then we will present the general context in which our interaction model was developed: a formalism for discrete structural modelling specially directed towards the representation of interactions. The third part is devoted to the description of our interaction model. And finally, we will describe several simulations achieved thanks to the modelor-simulator Cordis-Anima and using our surface interaction model: several kind of wheel drive vehicles crossing over various terrains.

Key-Words : Physical modeling - Animation - Robotics

I. The problem of interaction in computer animation

At present the use of movement generation models based on Newtonian mechanics for the creation of computer animated images is widespread. Models of this type, all designated by the generic term of physical models have been developed basically for the purpose of creating sequences of realistic movements automatically.

I.1 Continuous models

For about a century now, engineer mechanics has offered numerical models based on a continuous representation of matter enabling the explicit calculation of the movements of certain objects when they are submitted to a set of forces [Bam81, Cia85]. Over the last few years, a great deal of the work carried out by computer animation researchers has consisted in adapting and applying these mechanical theories to the computer context. One of the major problems that arises here is hidden behind the term 'interaction'. Indeed, the theories of mechanics specify how to calculate a movement from a given set of forces, but they generally omit to be more specific about the way these forces appear in the mechanical system in question.

Today, there are several methods based either on forces or on impulses for the calculation of the dynamic behavior of interacting rigid objects [Hah88, Dum90, MW88, BB88, Bar89-90]. However, most of them propose distinct models for collisions, i.e. instantaneous (high speed) collisions and for prolonged contacts, while others merely omit this last case. More recently, Baraff [Bar91] proposed an analytical method for the calculation of static and dynamic friction forces during prolonged contacts between non-penetrating rigid objects. But, as a consequence of choosing the context of purely undeformable objects, Baraff has to deal with indeterminate and inconsistant contact situations and cannot define a unified model.

These different methods have enabled the production of very satisfactory sequences of rigid object animation. However they are totally inadequate when the interacting objects are deformable. In fact, classical mechanics offer no general method for the description of collisions between two deformable objects. In computer animation, only the case of instant collisions has been treated in a relatively general manner [MW88, Gas89] (we must point out that M.P.Gascuel proposed a hybrid model made of a discrete deformable skin surrounding an articulated rigid body. see §I.2). But, most of the time, the foregoing techniques are limited to interactions between a deformable object and a rigid polygonal object and are well adapted only to the specific application they were designed for [GTT89, TPBF87, PB88].

Thus, it appears that, although continuous models can directly access a representation of the dynamic characteristics of certain classes of objects, they are not well adapted to interacting objects, and all the less to complex interactions involving subtle phenomena, for example those relating to the microscopic roughness of the surfaces in contact.

I.2 Discrete models

Discrete models represent a totally opposite approach. In fact, at a first stage, the discrete model does not deal with the object's shape. The shape is a result of an interpretation of the physical model's behavior. The aim is no longer to superpose an analytic mechanical model on a given geometrical model but rather to represent interacting physical systems directly from a spatially dicretized model, i.e. by organizing elementary physical primitives. There are only a few applications of this type of model for computer animation. In fact, they are used principally when it is not possible to represent the desired phenomenon with a continuous model, and they are implemented specifically for a given context [TPF89, Mil88, CHP89, VG91]. An interesting approach based on a layered model using structured discrete model can be found in [Gas89]. The proposed method deal with the interactions between articulated bodies having a more or less thick elastic skin, while taking into account the relative stiffness of the objects and various propagation modes for the deformation.

Finally, it appears that if certain methods are interested in dealing with non penetrating objects, none of them has tackled the problem of interaction in general .

II. Cordis-Anima: modular system for animation by discrete physical models

For about ten years, the researchers of the ACROE have been working on the elaboration of a general formalism and computation methods for a physical object modeler-simulator [CFL81,

CLF84, Luc85, LJC91]. The purpose of this work is the development of a complete system for animation and music synthesis. (This aspect will not be discussed in this paper but both applications share a large common basis). The major characterisitics of this system can be summed up by the two following paradigms:

- *Modularity* : the system must enable the operator to construct all types of objects from a given set of components (physical primitives). It follows that any sub-object of this system must have the same communicational properties as the object itself.
- *Experimentability* : the transition between the specification of the model and the simulation algorithms that implement it must be as quick and as flexible as possible. In this way, at any stage of the modelling, the operator can carry out a great number of simulations in order to refine the model.

The above prerequisites directed the choice of representation towards discrete models, i.e. towards a discretization of matter as set of material points and an explicit expression of the interactions between these points.

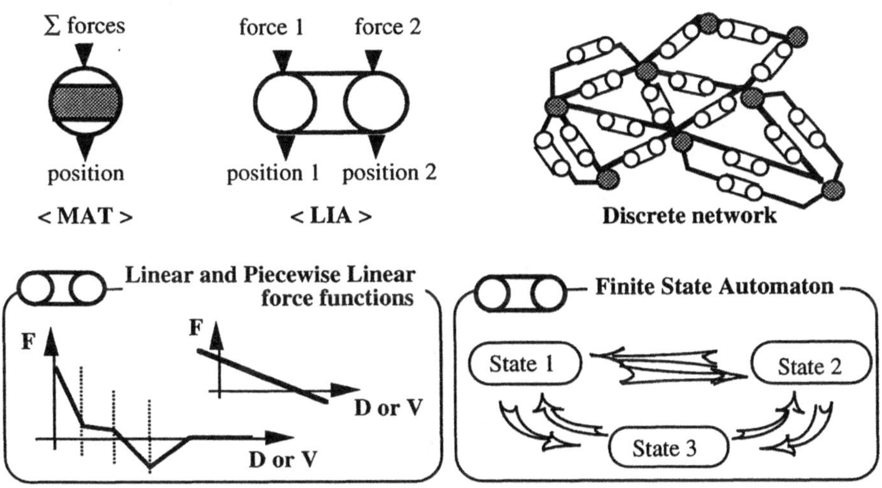

figure 1 : Cordis-Anima general formalism

With the Cordis-Anima formalism, all objects are represented by a discrete network consisting of only two types of components which are idealized representations of basic physical objects: the matter component (<MAT>), which represents a punctual mass (no spatial dimension) and the link component (<LIA>) which represents the interactions between punctual masses (figure 1). In the simplest case, the link component represents a spring or a damper (which have no inertia).

The combination of primary viscous-elastic behavior is done in a natural way with the Cordis_Anima formalism. Two punctual masses can be connected by several link component, the resulting force being the sum of the forces produced by each link. Moreover, link components must enable the representation of any type of discontinuity, such as those involved in collisions. Therefore, besides linking mass components, they must fulfil another logical function. This function consists in making these links according to a state automata logic with or without memory, in order to modify the behavior of the material according to the values of certain of the system's variables as distances, relative speeds or forces (figure 1). The model presented in the following paragraph is based on the foregoing mechanism.

III. Interaction model taking into account surface friction

III.1 The standpoint of classical physics

This model involves particularly the microscopic roughness of the surfaces in contact. When two pieces of matter are in contact, several phenomena may occur, but all raise a common problem: how to know what is happening on the borderline between the two objects (figure 2).

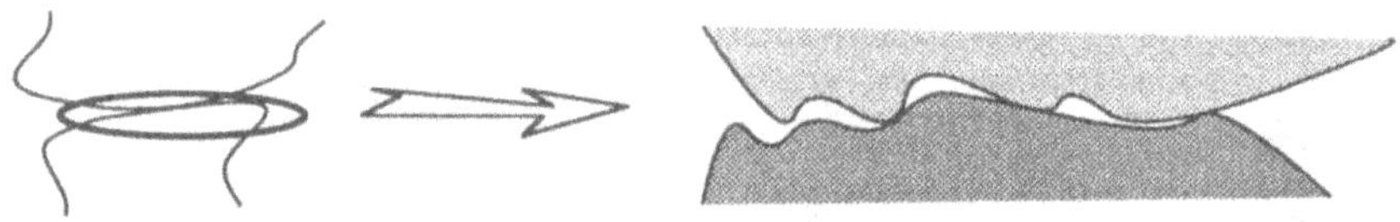

figure 2: the microscopic roughness of the surfaces

The phenomena that can be observed when the objects are brought into contact result from a great number of interactions between the different rough patch of the surfaces in contact, and this all the way to the molecular level. At present it does not exit any characterization of these miscroscopic interactions called cohesion or 'adhering'. That is the reason why all these contact situations have been characterized at a macroscopic level, i.e. by a set of experimental laws. The most widespread among these laws is known as the **Coulomb model.**

According to this model, there are two states in contact situations: a **'kinetic state'**, in which both surfaces in contact are slipping on each other, and a **'static state'** in which they are not (They stick together). These two states are associated respectively with two friction coefficients μ_k and μ_s (for most of the known materials μ_k is smaller than μ_s).

III.2 The algorithmic model

The algorithmic model that we have developed from the Coulomb model and that we habve called "the dry friction model", follows a previous work on surface interactions involving viscous friction (damping forces) [JLR91].

The objects in contact are modelled with agglomerates [LJR91]. They are presented as a set of punctual masses associated with visco-elastic interaction modules (link components) that define a spatial bulk. In the case of more or less cohesive objects, these masses would be linked together by cohesive interactions (calculated according to piecewise linear force functions). The agglomerate is a physical model of matter which enables the generation of fixed obstacle borderlines as well as mobile and deformable objects of various shapes [JLL 91-92] (figure3). Indeed the *agglomerate* is a model that allows the construction of pieces of heterogeneous matter presenting non-linear visco-elastic properties, pasty plasticities and fractures. This is why it is specially suitable for representing various kind of natural terrain.

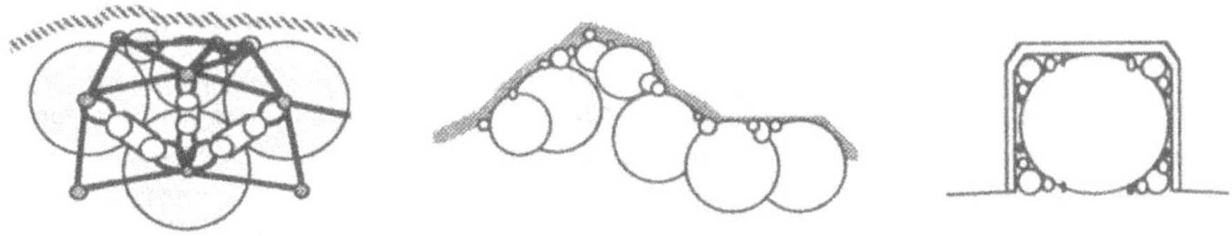

figure 3 : a model of agglomerate : mobile body and rigid (ground type) fixed obstacles.

The algorithm that we have developed controls the relative position of the bodies and the interaction forces (should they be free or in contact and should the contact be a collision or a prolonged contact.) Therefore it is composed of a three state automata defined within the Cordis-Anima formalism (see preceding paragraph and figure 1). The first state correspond to the case in which the bodies dont touch each other (according to their specific spatial bulk), the two others deal with colliding bodies and with bodies in resting contact. In this last case, the static contact state is involved when the relative splip is small whereas the slipping contact state correspond to large slip. To each state is associated a specific force calculation (figure 4).

The free state: the bodies are not in contact, the interaction force equals zero.	**F = 0**
The state of slipping contact: the bodies are in contact with a non-zero slipping speed (i.e. Speed > threshold), the force is composed of a non-penetration-force and of a force which opposes to the relative motion of the surfaces.	**F = Non-penetration + resistance to the surfaces' motion**
The state of static contact: the bodies are in contact but with a slipping speed near zero (the speed will be compared with a threshold), the force is composed of a non-penetration-force and of a gripping-force.	**F = Non-penetration + adhesion**

figure 4: the three state automaton - free, static contact and slipping contact.

The automaton controls the transitions between these different states according to the results of tests carried out on the system's variables: the distance between the two interacting masses, the relative tangential speed at the contact point and the value of the non-penetration-force. It should be pointed out that the apparent volume of our objects is only a result of the visco-elastic component set between each couple of interacting mass, and which define a spatial bulk. Indeed the surface of our objects is no more than an interaction border on which there is no mass. Therefore, in order to localize the interaction on the surface of contact, it is necessary to use a material point at the place where this interaction occurs. In order to achieve this, the algorithm that we have developed generates a virtual point which is used for the calculation of the adhesion force in the case the automaton is set to the static contact state.

III.2.1 Calculation of the non-penetration-force: F_{np}

As stated above, a visco-elastic interaction component is set between each couple of masses which are supposed to interact. In the case of structured (strongly cohesive) agglomerate, this component is only set between the masses of the skin-deep layer. This interaction component provides each interacting masses with a non-penetration area. In the simplest case, the forces which result from this spatial bulk is computed according to an 'elastic-buffer' model (figure 5), but we could use piecewise linear approximation of any function (e.g. an exponential-buffer instead of an elastic one). When prolonged contact occurs between the interacting objects, the force produced by the 'elastic-buffer' corresponds to the normal surface reaction.

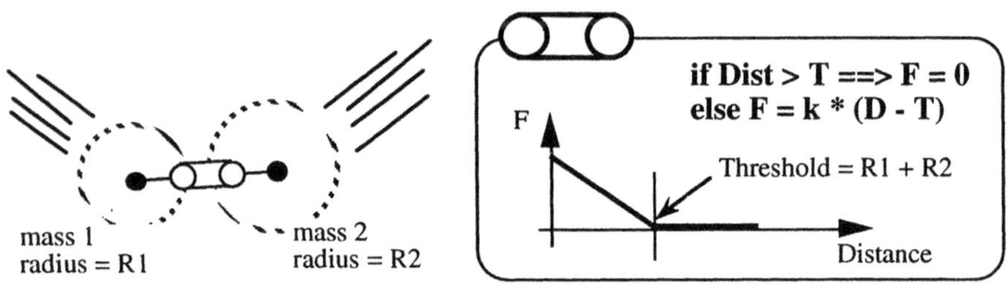

figure 5: the elastic buffer.

III.2.2 Calculation of the slipping-force: F_{slip}

As the slipping-force opposes the relative slipping of the surfaces in contact, its direction is the opposite of the tangential speed. According to the Coulomb Model, this force is proportional to the normal reaction. This slipping-force calculation is illustrated in figure 6.

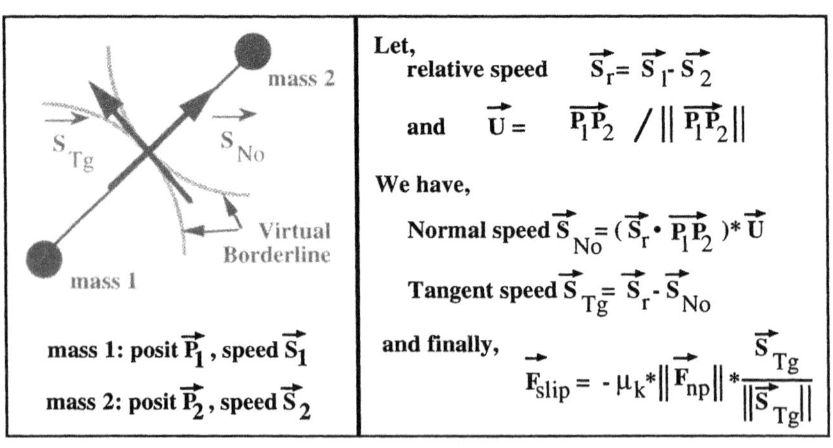

figure 6: slipping-force calculation

III.2.3 Calculation of the gripping-force (static contact): F_{grip}

The algorithm described in this paper only concerns point-surface interactions. With the Cordis-Anima formalism, this comes down to decide that one of the two interacting masses is bearing a given (non-empty) non-penetration area while the other is not. With the elastic-buffer model described above for example (figure 5), it comes down to choose $T = R_1$ and $R_2 = 0$. Let us explain now how to compute the gripping-force in this case.

As stated above, the automaton needs to generate a virtual point when the static contact state is reached, i.e. when the relative tangent speed of the bodies in contact becomes lower than a given velocity threshold. In the point-surface case the virtual point's position is equal to the position of the point at the time it begins to interact with the surface (figure 7).

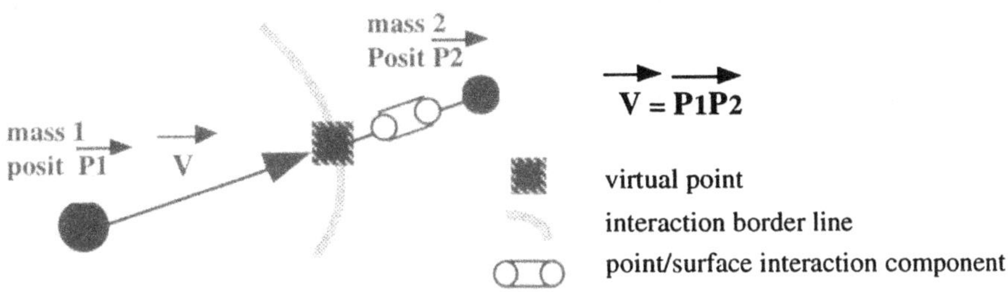

figure 7: Introduction of a virtual (contact) point

Once the virtual point position is defined, the gripping-force is calculated according to a gripping (visco-élastic) component, e.g. a spring-damper unit, fixed between the interacting point and its associated virtual point. The automaton leaves the static contact state, and thus disables the gripping component, as soon as the gripping-force becomes larger than a force threshold (the de-grip threshold) whose value is given by the coulomb model:

$$\textbf{Force Threshold} = \mu s * F_{np}$$

This force threshold and the formula used to calculate the slipping-force F_{slip} (figure 6) characterize the Coulomb model.

III.3 Application : simulation of wheeled vehicles crossing over various terrains

The surface interaction algorithm was used to achieve the simulation of the interactions between vehicle wheels and various terrains composed of fixed and mobile elements.

Several models for the physical simulation of vehicles have already been proposed by several researchers for the purpose of computer animation [AD92], scientific simulation for automobile industry [ADH91] and driving simulator systems [DBD88]. In each case the vehicle was modeled as a set of linked rigid bodies according to modern car manufacturers' specifications (the model developed for the purpose of animation is a simplified version of the one used for scientific simulation). To simulate the interactions with the terrain (typically road-tire interactions) the authors use behavorial laws (i.e. experimental data giving the forces as functions of normal reaction, slip angles, etc..) while the vehicle model itself only presents punctual wheels.

The purpose of the simulation tests that we have realized was rather to assess vehicle concepts defined in the framework of the development of autonomous planetary mobile robots intended to progress over little known natural terrain. This work was done within the 'VAP' project of the French Spatial Agency (CNES).

In the particular case of a vehicle in a natural environment the interactions with the terrain, which depend on the latter's physical characteristics, are of prime importance and moreover there exists no experimental data about the interactions with natural terrain such as muddy, sandy or rocky grounds. For that, we need explicit physical models for the wheels, for various kinds of rocks and deformable grounds, and for multi-punctual interactions between all these elements. Beside this we used relatively simple models, from a mechanical and functional point of vue, which correspond to the proposed vehicle concepts.

The model of vehicle presented here has four independant wheels each equipped with a motor, and an articulated chassis. The wheels are more or less deformable according to the kind of tires and present a set of masses on their edge (figure 8).

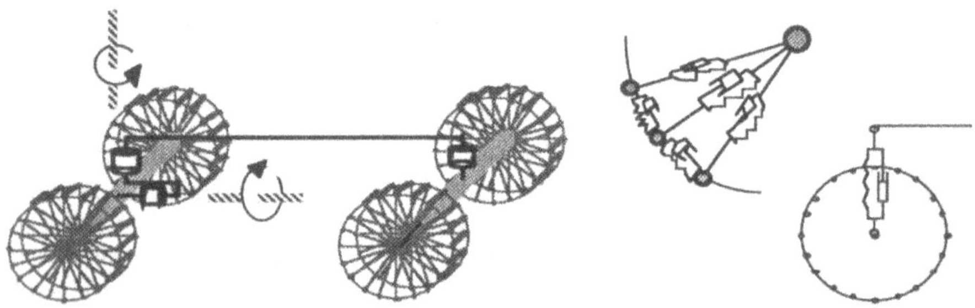

figure 8 : the general structure of the vehicle

The surface interaction module presented above was set between each wheel mass and the elements making the ground. Figure 9 illustrates the principle of introducing a virtual physical point in this case. It must be pointed out that this approach correspond to an adaptative discretization of the surface of the terrain.

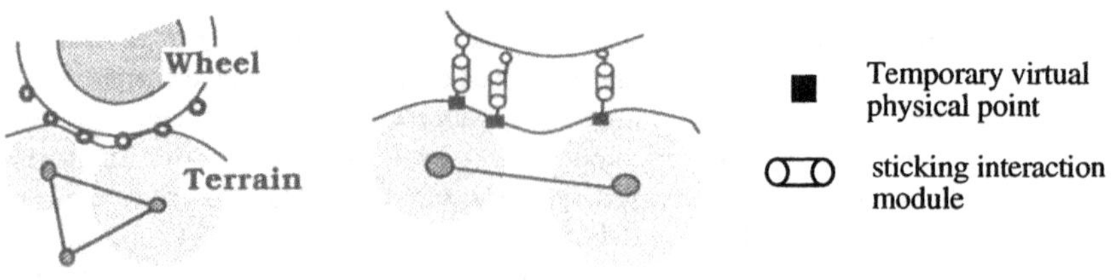

figure 9 : Interaction modules set between the wheel mass and the terrain.

The resulting simulations have been particularly realistic. Notabbly they show that the wheels spin or skid in extreme situations, i.e. when the slope is too abrupt or when the accelerations are too sudden. It aslo can be observed how hightly deformable terrains, e.g. non cohesive grounds or rigid grounds covered with mobile pebbles can severely entail the performance of the locomotion system.This type of behavior can not be represented if the static part of adhesion friction is not taken into account and of course, even less with behavorial laws.

IV. Implementation and Experiments

The general approach for animation using dicrete physical model described in this paper is implemented and tested through the Cordis-Anima modeler/simulator [Luc 91.2]. The working environment of this system includes a VAX 730, an Evans & Sutherland PS350 graphic workstation, an array processor AP120, and gestural retroactive devices which have been fully described in previous papers [Cad 81, Cad 84] . The fast communications between the simulation processor (AP120), the graphic workstation and the retroactive device are performed thanks to several dedicated processors. The whole system provides the user with real-time simulation capabilities and with multi-modal communication tools.

IV.1 2D simulations of various deformable terrains

In these experiments we have used a 2D version of the vehicle presented above which is composed of two driving wheels and a rigid chassis (figure 10). The model of the wheels consist of set of punctual masses distributed on the outline of the wheel and connected by elatic-viscous connectors as shown in the diagram on figure 8. As the wheels and the terrain are deformables, multi-punctual wheel-ground contacts can occur. The movements are generated using two independant torque generator with speed command (see the 3D vehicle command law described in the following paragraph).

We have made experiments involving terrains with complex outline, some of them made of plane ground littered with various size fixed blocks and others with mobile blocks (figure 11). Between these two extreme cases, we have experimented several kinds of deformable terrain. Non cohesive terrain can be characterized by parameters like compacity, internal friction, resistance to shearing of or pressure-sinking law. According to the Cordis-Anima formalism, these models are all made of several layers, each ones being made of a network of connected punctual masses. These layers are characterized by the involved connectors representing the non-linearities associated to the object boundaries -like internal friction-, or connectors defining some structural modifications (elastic and plastic deformation properties), see [Luc 91.1]. The different layers are combined to make up a terrain model capable of deep or superficial deformations and presenting a given 'state of surface'.

IV.2 Motion control for the 4-Wheel drive vehicle

As we have said above, the vehicle has four independant driving wheels and is provided with an anti-rolling articulation on the front axle-tree. This articulated structure allow to continuously maintain a sufficient number of contact points between the wheels and the ground when getting over some natural obstacles (rocks, small hills and hollows ...). This is achieved by automatically modifying the configuration of the articulated mechanical structure under the effect of gravity and of reaction forces produced by the wheels/ground interactions (figure 12). The two axle tree are swivelling in the chassis plane, which allow, as well as the possibility to apply different speed commands on each wheel, to follow the desired trajectory. But the counterpart of this great manoeuvrability is the deep complexity of the command to apply to the locomotion system. As mentionned before, we have apply only constant speed command law and we have coupled together the pair of torque generator of each axle-tree while the swivel-articulations was locked. And in fact this is the minimum to do to make the vehicle go straight ahead (figure 13).

Acknowledgement

The research carried out by the ACROE/LIFIA team is mainly supported by the French 'Ministère de la Culture'. The work presented in this paper has been partly supported by the CNES (French spatial agency) through the RISP national project. It also has been partly supported by the Rhône-Alpes Region through the IMAG/INRIA Robotics project SHARP.

We wish to thank the referees for their helpful comments and A. Habibi for helping us to produce the english version of this paper.

References

[AD92] B. ARNALDI and G. DUMONT - "Vehicle simulation versus vehicle animation" - EuroGraphics'92 Workshop on Animation and Simulation, Cambridge, England, 5-6 Sept. 1992.

[ADH91] B. ARNALDI, G. DUMONT and G. HEGRON - "Animation of Physical Systems from Geometric, Kinematic and Dynamic Models" - *Modeling in Computer Graphics*, pp.37-53 - Springer Verlag 1991 (Proceedings of the IFIP WG 5.10 Working Conference, Tokyo, Japan, April 1991).

[Bam81] Y. BAMBERGER - "Mécaniques de l'ingénieur" , T1 & 2 - ed. Hermann 1981.

[Bar89] D. BARAFF - "Analytical methods for Dynamic Simulation of Non-Penetrating Rigid Bodies" - *Computer Graphics*, 23 (3) july 89, pp.223-232 (Proceedings of SIGGRAPH'89).

[Bar90] D. BARAFF - "Curved surfaces and Coherence for Non-penetrating rigid body simulation" - *Computer Graphics*, 24 (4) august 90, pp.19-28 (Proceedings of SIGGRAPH'90).

[Bar91] D. BARAFF - "Coping With Friction for Non-penetrating Rigid Bodies Simulation" - *Computer Graphics*, 25 (4) july 91, pp.31-40 (Proceedings of SIGGRAPH'91).

[BB88] R. BARZEL and A.H. BARR - "A modeling system based on dynamics constraints" - *Computer Graphics*, 22 (4) august 88, pp.179-188 (Proceedings of SIGGRAPH'88).

[CHP89] J.E. CHADWICK, D.R. HAUMANN and E. PARENT - "Layered construction for deformable animated characters" - *Computer Graphics*, 23 (3) july 89, pp.243-252 (Proceedings of SIGGRAPH'89).

[CFL81] C. CADOZ, J.L. FLORENS and A. LUCIANI - "Synthèse Musicale par Simulation des mécanismes instrumentaux: Tranducteurs Gestuels Rétroactifs pour l'étude du Jeu Instrumental" - Revue d'Acoustique n° 59 - 1981.

[Cia85] P.G. CIARLET - "Elasticité Tridimensionnelle" - Eds Masson 1985.

[CLF84] C. CADOZ, A. LUCIANI and J.L. FLORENS - "Responsive input devices and sound synthesis by simulation of instrumental mechanisms : the Cordis system" - Computer Music Journal - N°3 - 1984- reprint in "Music Machine" - MIT Press

[DBD88] R. DEYO, J.A. BRIGGS and P. DOENGES - "Getting Graphics in Gear: Graphics and Dynamics in Driving Simulation" - *Computer Graphics*, 22 (4) august 88, pp.317-326 (Proceedings of SIGGRAPH'88).

[FC90] J.L. FLORENS and C. CADOZ - "Modèles et simulation en temps réel de corde frottées" - Proceedings 1er Congrés Français d'acoustique, Editions de physique - SFA -Lyon, avril 1990.

[Gas89] M.P. GASCUEL - "OSEA - Un nouveau modèle de matière pour traiter les collisions entre objets déformables" - in PIXIM 89, pp.309-324, Paris, France, October 89.

[GTT89] J.P. GOURRET, N. MAGNENAT-THALMAN and D. THALMAN - "Simulation of Object and Human Skin Deformations in a Grasping Task" - *Computer Graphics*, 23 (3) july 89, pp.21-30 (Proceedings of SIGGRAPH'89).

[Hah88] J. K. HAHN - "Realistic animation of rigid bodies" - *Computer Graphics*, 22 (4) august 88, pp.299-308 (Proceedings of SIGGRAPH'88).

[JLL91] S. JIMENEZ, A. LUCIANI and Ch. LAUGIER - "Physical modeling as an help for planning the motions of a land vehicle" - Proceedings of the IEEE/RSJ Internationnal Workshop of Intelligent Robots and Systems - IROS'91, Osaka, Japan, November 1991, pp.1461-1466.

[JLL92] S. JIMENEZ, A. LUCIANI and Ch. LAUGIER - "Teleprogramming the motions of a planetary robot using physical models and dynamic simulation tools" - Proceedings of the IEEE/RSJ Internationnal Conference of Intelligent Robots and Systems - IROS'92, Raleigh, NC, july 1992, pp.1383-1390.

[JLR91] S. JIMENEZ, A. LUCIANI and O. RAOULT - "Physical simulation of land vehicles with obstacle avoidance and various terrain interactions" - EuroGraphics'91 Workshop on Animation and Simulation - Vienna, Austria, 1, 2 sept. 1991.

[Luc85] A. LUCIANI - "Un outil informatique d'images animées - modèle d'objets, langage, contrôle gestuel en temps réel" - Thèse Doctorat Informatique - INP-Grenoble - 1985.

[LJR91] A. LUCIANI, S. JIMENEZ, O. RAOULT, C. CADOZ and JL. FLORENS - "An unified view of multitude behaviour, flexibility, plasticity and fractures: balls, bubbles and agglomerates" - *Modeling in Computer Graphics*, pp.54-74 - Springer Verlag 1991 (Proceedings of the IFIP WG 5.10 Working Conference, Tokyo, Japan, April 1991).

[LJC91] A. LUCIANI, S. JIMENEZ, C. CADOZ, JL. FLORENS and O. RAOULT - "Computational Physics: A Modeler-Simulator for Animated Physical Objects." - EuroGraphics'91 - European Computer Graphics Conference, Vienna, Austria, Sept. 1991.

[Mil88] G. MILLER - "The motion dynamics of snakes and worms" - *Computer Graphics*, 22 (4) august 88, pp.169-178 (Proceedings of SIGGRAPH'88).

[MW88] M. MOORE and J. WILHELMS - "Collision detection and response for computer animation" - *Computer Graphics*, 22 (4) august 88, pp.289-298 (Proceedings of SIGGRAPH'88).

[PB88] J.C. PLATT and A.H. BARR - "Constraint methods for flexible models" - *Computer Graphics*, 22 (4) august 88, pp.279-288 (Proceedings of SIGGRAPH'88).

[TPBF87] D. TERZOPOULOS, J. PLATT, A. BARR and K. FLEISCHER - "Elastically Deformable Models" - *Computer Graphics*, 21 (4) july 87, pp.204-214 (Proceedings of SIGGRAPH'87).

[TPF89] D. TERZOPOULOS, J. PLATT and K. FLEISCHER - "Heating and melting deformable models (from goop to glop)" - Proceedings of Graphics Interface'89, june 89, pp. 219-226.

[VG91] L. VELHO and J.M. GOMES - "A Dynamics Simulation Environment for Implicit Objects using Discrete Models" - EuroGraphics'91 Workshop on Animation and Simulation - Vienna, Austria, 1, 2 sept. 1991.

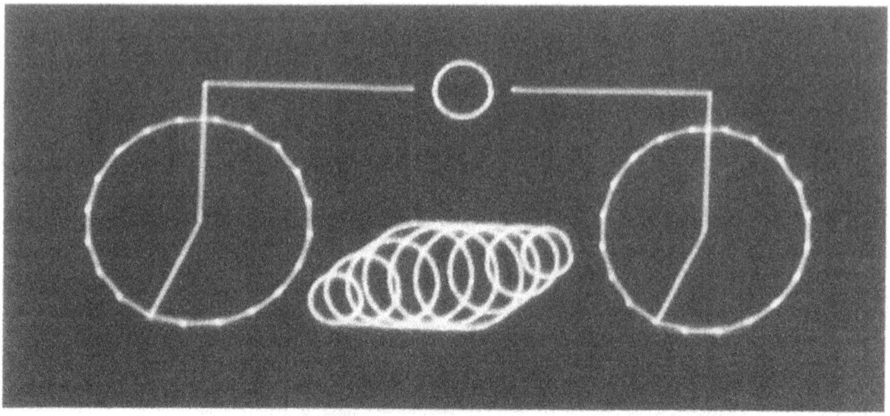

figure 10: the 2D-version of the wheel-drive vehicle and a mobile block resting on the ground.

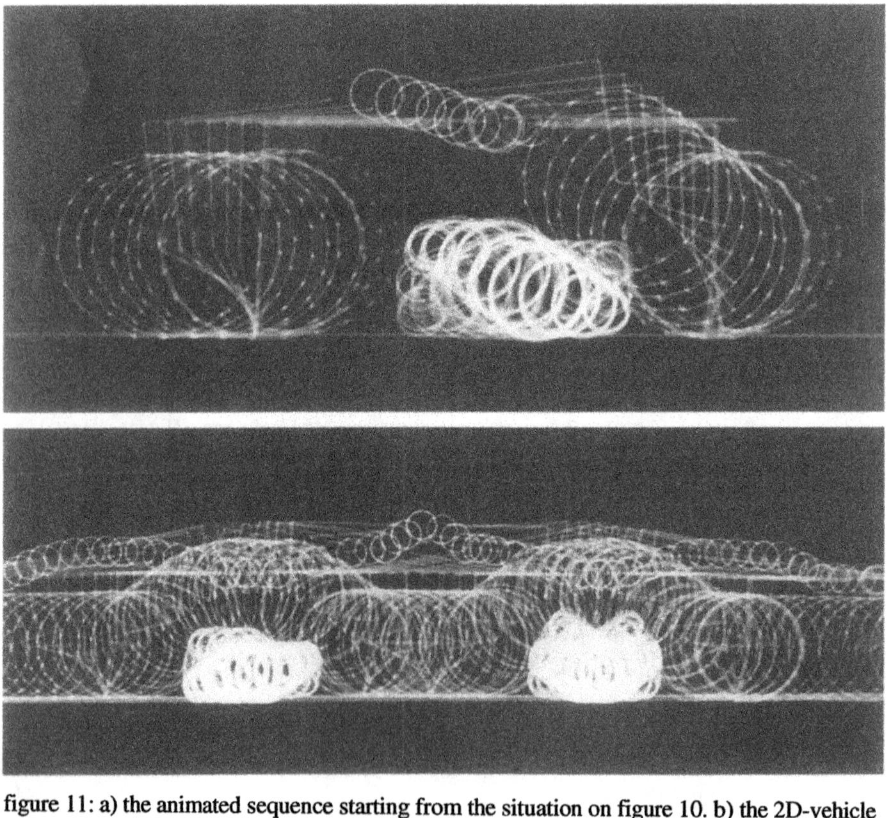

a)

b)

figure 11: a) the animated sequence starting from the situation on figure 10. b) the 2D-vehicle crossing over two successive mobile blocks. (movement from right to left).

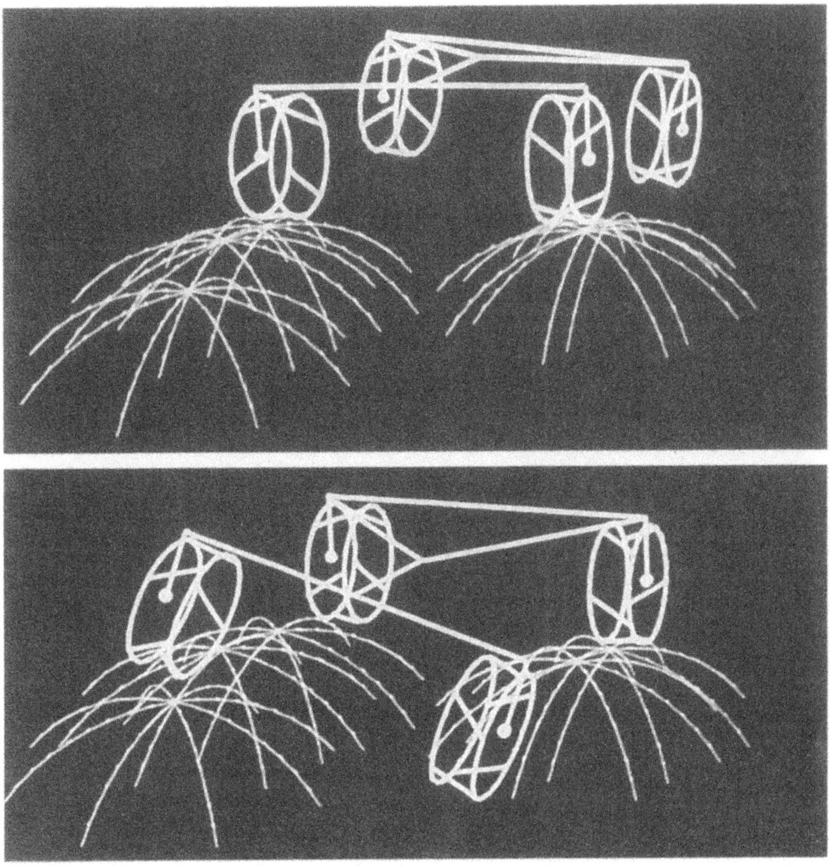

figure 12.a and 12.b: the 4-wheel-drive vehicle and spherical rigid small hills (the chassis adapts its configuration to the shape of the ground).

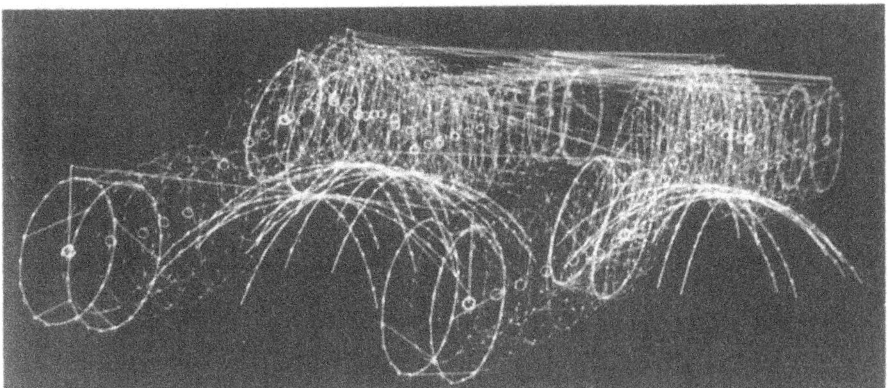

figure 13: the movements of the 4-wheel-drive vehicle when getting over the small hills.

Hexadecimal-Tree: A Time-Continuous 4D Interference Check Method

Naota Inamoto
NEC Corporation
2-11-5 Shibaura, Minato-ku
Tokyo 108 Japan
inamoto@ccs.mt.nec.co.jp

Abstract
I propose a new 4D interference check method among multiple 3D moving objects. One characteristics of this method is using hexadecimal-tree as a 4D spatial index. Another characteristics is using 4D polyhedron to avoid direct treatment of curved surfaces which are boundaries of 4D motion trajectories. Based on an appropriate 3D geometric modeling system, I experimented on this method in a very simple case. I report its results.

1. Introduction

4D interference check is required in many research areas. For example, the robotics area requires it because robots must not injure human beings, objects and themselves. Collision-free path planning also requires it because planning itself is including 4D interference check. Grasping planning also requires it to obtain the contact positions. Movability check of mechanical parts and possibility check of mechanical assembly also requires it. In the computer animation area, 4D interference check is necessary to avoid physically impossible scenes in which an object crosses another object [Moor88].

But there are many difficulties in the 4D interference check. At first, it is very difficult for human to understanding 4 dimensional space. Second, it is difficult to treat curved trajectories of 3D moving object. Third, there are few geometric modeling systems which are fit good for the achievement of 4D interference check. At last, amount of computation is very large.

I use the 3D geometric modeling system based on the graph-based tool [Inam89] to experiment on the 4D interference check method.

2. Related Work

Most current methods for interference check are 3D interference check [Boys79, Nobo87]. If such 3D interference check methods are extended to 4D, time will be sampled appropriately and 3D interference check will be performed at the each sampling point. However, they can not be said to be a reliable check because such methods may fail to find the interference between two sampling points. Figure 1 (a) shows this situation. To perform the reliable check, continuous-time must be considered as shown in Figure 1 (b).

(a) Discrete-time (b) Continuous-time

Figure 1 Discrete-time and continuous-time

There are related works in the area of collision-free path planning [Taka89, Fuji89, Sing87, Kamb86, Loza79]. However, they are theoretical rather than experimental. Most of them are 2D. Moving objects in them are usually simple shapes or points. They can not treat complex shapes which appear in a practical world.

The octree was proposed for a 3D solid approximation [Jack80, Meag82, Yama84] or a 3D spatial indexing method [Fuji85]. However, octree is not suitable for rotations which usually often appear in representative 6-degree-of-freedom robot manipulators. It is because the octree is a set of cubes.

The concept of S-boundary and active zone [Came89] based on CSG representation was also proposed for set operations and interference check. However, they can treat only 3D solids and can not treat moving objects.

There had been no reliable (time-continuous) 4D interference check methods which treat moving 3D complex-shape objects.

3. A New 4D Interference Check Method

In this section, I explain overview of a new 4D interference check method. This method is a time-continuous method and treats moving polyhedral complex-shape objects.

The feature of this method is the use of *hexadecimal-tree* for a hierarchical 4D spatial index. The hexadecimal-tree is the extension of an 3D octree [Jack80, Meag82, Yama84] to 4D. Hexadecimal-tree is defined as follows:

hex = <Homo, x, y, z, t, width, interval>
where x,y,z and t mean the hypercube position,
width and interval mean the hypercube size
hex = <Hetero, hex_0, ... , hex_{15}>
for each $i \in [0, 15]$; hex_i is hexadecimal-tree.

The most significant advantage of hexadecimal-tree is that it makes interference check time-continuous. Another advantage of hexadecimal-tree is that hypercube division occurs only if there is collision possibility in the hypercube. Another advantage of hexadecimal-tree is that it makes space and time complexity linear about number of elements of objects.

For determining exactly whether interference occurs or not, it is necessary to solve complex mathematical equations which represents the boundary surfaces of motion trajectories. Solving such equations is not practical. To avoid complex equations, the new method uses a set of hypercubes which may intersect trajectory boundary. For judging the intersection, the new method uses maximum velocity of moving objects. At first, I explain mechanism of intersection judgement in 2D and show how the new method is time-continuous. Figure 2 shows a 2D point trajectory.

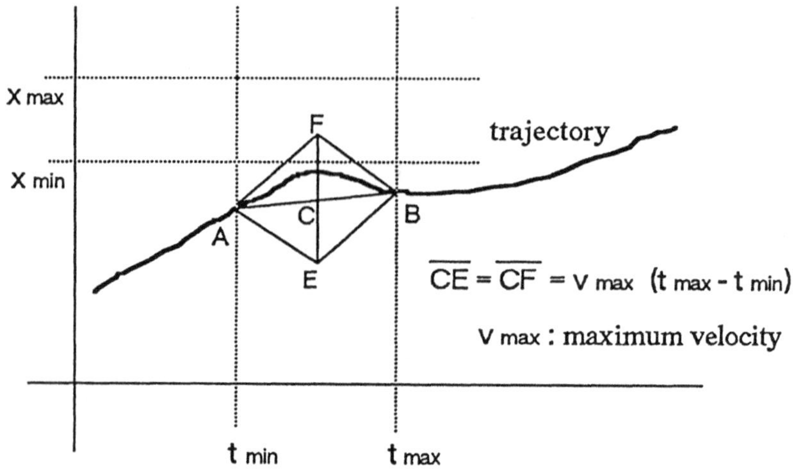

Figure 2 A curved trajectory

The moving point is at A when time is t_{min}. The moving point is at B when time is t_{max}. If you create polygon AEBF by using the maximum velocity, the moving point must be in the polygon AEBF during time is in the section [t_{min}, t_{max}]. If an object does not intersect the polygon AEBF, the object must not intersect the moving point in the time section [t_{min}, t_{max}]. This is time-continuous check. The length of an error bar EF is adaptively decreased by division of the time section. In the case of 4D, the problem is more difficult, but the basic concept is the same.

I explain the algorithm of a new method with a hexadecimal-tree spatial index. The new method checks interference among multiple moving polyhedral objects. In the algorithm, faces whose trajectories may intersect a hypercube corresponding to a hexadecimal-tree node are linked to the hexadecimal-tree node. There is no interference in the hypercube if no face is linked to the hexadecimal-tree node, or if all faces linked to the hexadecimal-tree node belongs to the same object. In other cases, some objects may intersect each other. Initial step of the algorithm obtains the size of the 4D trajectory box covering all trajectories of all faces of all moving polyhedral objects, and creates the root node of the hexadecimal-tree spatial index, and links all moving faces to it. Algorithm 1 shows this step.

```
create_hexad(world)
{
        S_index = create_node()->self;
        for all object in world {
        for all 4D_face in motion of object {
                create_arc(S_index, 4D_face);
        }}}
        set size to S_index;
}
```

Algorithm 1

The function create_node() creates a root of hexadecimal-tree. In the experiments, motions of objects are described by point-to-point motion. The point-to-point motions are specified by a sequence of pairs of time and C-space variables. A variable *4D_face* indicates a pair of an object face and one time section of the object point-to-point motion. The function create_arc() links all face trajectories to the root node of the hexadecimal-tree.

When some objects may intersect each other in the hypercube corresponding to a hexadecimal-tree node, the hypercube is divided into 16 child hypercubes. Interference possibilities between each child hypercube and trajectories of faces linked to the hexadecimal-tree node are investigated. When there is interference possibility, the face is linked to the child hexadecimal-tree node. Algorithm 2 shows this step.

```
divide_hexad(hypercube) {
        create 16 child hypercubes;
        for all child_hypercube in hypercube {
          for all 4D_face intersected by hypercube {
                if inter_face4D_hypercube( 4D_face, hypercube) then
                        create_arc(child_hypercube, 4D_face);
          }
        }
        for all 4D_face intersected by hypercube {
                        delete_arc(hypercube, 4D_face);
        }
}
```

Algorithm 2

In the case that the size of a hypercube is lower than the division limit, the algorithm judges that there will be interference in the minimum hypercube. In the case that there is no interference in all leaf hexadecimal-tree nodes, the algorithm judges that there is no interference. This judgement is reliable. Algorithm 3 shows this step.

```
inter_check(hypercube) {
        if not exist two objects
                such that both objects intersect hypercube then
                                        return NOT_INTERSECT;
        if size of hypercube < minimum acceptable distance then
                                        return WILL_INTERSECT;
        divide_hexad(hypercube);
        for all child_hypercube in hypercube {
                result = inter_check(child_hypercube);
                if result is WILL_INTERSECT then break;
        }
        return result;
}
```

Algorithm 3

I explain the method which investigates interference possibility between a hypercube and a face trajectory. To check interference between a hypercube and a face trajectory, the method checks interference between the hypercube and each edge trajectory of the face, and checks interference between the face and each cube edge at the first and the end time of the hypercube. This method will miss the cases such that whole of the hypercube is in the face trajectory. However, these cases can be ignored by the following reason: If there is interference, an edge of a polyhedral object and a face of another polyhedral object must exist such that they intersect each other at a certain time. The algorithm never miss the hypercube in which this intersection occurs even if division of the hypercube is repeated recursively. Therefore, the algorithm is reliable.

I explain the method which checks interference between a hypercube and each edge trajectory of a face. Generally, an edge trajectory consists of a complex curved surface. To avoid the direct treatment of the complex curved surface, the method approximates the edge trajectory by 6 triangles using the maximum velocity of moving objects. Figure 3 shows a moving polyhedral object. An edge which is E at the time t_{min} is E' at the time t_{max}. $[t_{min}, t_{max}]$ is the time section of the hypercube. At the time $(t_{min}+t_{max})/2$, the start and the end points of the edge are in the cubes whose size is $2V_{max}(t_{max}-t_{min})$.

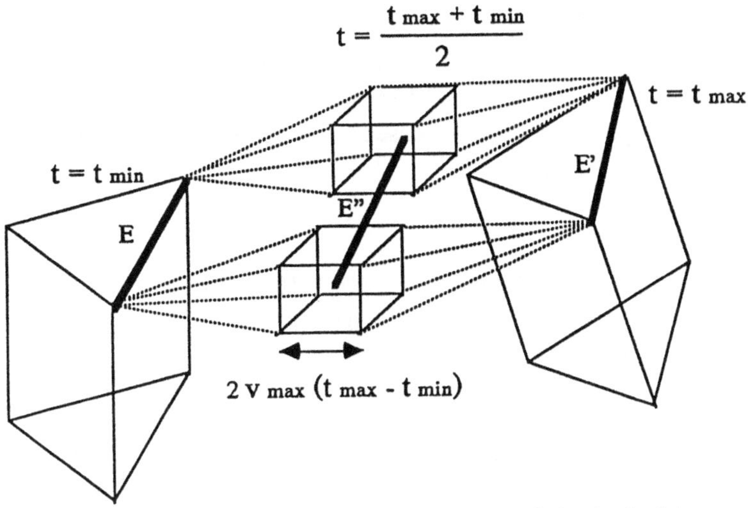

Figure 3 An edge trajectory of moving polyhedral object

The approximation by triangles is performed as the face trajectory enlarges. Figure 4 shows how to perform triangulation.

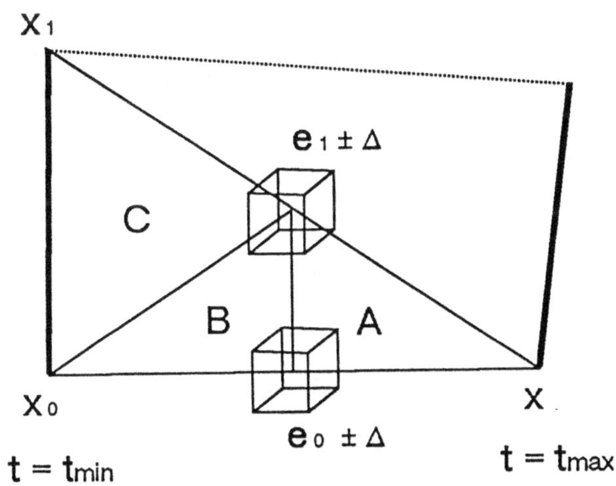

Figure 4 Triangulation of an edge trajectory

At first, the diagonal X_1X is selected as the middle point of the diagonal is outside the face trajectory. Secondary, the triangle X_0X_1X is divided into 3 areas A, B and C. The other triangle is also divided into 3 areas. The edge trajectory may intersect the hypercube if the following equations are satisfied:

$$[X_{min}]_i \le [(1-r)\{(1-p)x + p(e_0 + \Delta)\} + r\{(1-p)x + p(e_1 + \Delta)\}]_i$$
$$[(1-r)\{(1-p)x + p(e_0 - \Delta)\} + r\{(1-p)x + p(e_1 - \Delta)\}]_i \le [X_{max}]_i$$

(These equations correspond to the triangle A in Figure 4)

$$[X_{min}]_i \le [(1-r)\{(1-p)x_0 + p(e_0 + \Delta)\} + r\{(1-p)x_0 + p(e_1 + \Delta)\}]_i$$
$$[(1-r)\{(1-p)x_0 + p(e_0 - \Delta)\} + r\{(1-p)x_0 + p(e_1 - \Delta)\}]_i \le [X_{max}]_i$$

(These equations correspond to the triangle B in Figure 4)

$$[X_{min}]_i \le [(1-r)\{(1-p)(e_1 + \Delta) + p\, x_0\} + r\{(1-p)(e_1 + \Delta) + p\, x_1\}]_i$$
$$[(1-r)\{(1-p)(e_1 - \Delta) + p\, x_0\} + r\{(1-p)(e_1 - \Delta) + p\, x_1\}]_i \le [X_{max}]_i$$

(These equations correspond to the triangle C in Figure 4)

where $i = x, y, z$, $\Delta = v_{max}(t_{max} - t_{min})$, $0 \le p \le 1$, $0 \le r \le 1$, $X_{min} = \langle x_{min}, y_{min}, z_{min}\rangle$, $X_{max} = \langle x_{max}, y_{max}, z_{max}\rangle$, t_{min} and t_{max} are the ranges of the hypercube. All these equations above have the same form as shown below:

$$0 \le C_{i0} + C_{i1}\, p + C_{i2}\, p\, r$$
$$0 \ge C_{i3} + C_{i4}\, p + C_{i2}\, p\, r$$

($i = x, y, z$ and C_{ij} is constant.)

Considering that RHS of equations is monotone about both variables p and r, possibility of existence of p and r is clarified by checking four points (0,0), (0,1), (1,0), (1,1) and three straight lines p=1, r=0, r=1 on pr-plane.

Algorithm 4 shows the step of triangulation of an edge trajectory.

```
inter_face4D_hypercube(4D_face, hypercube) {
        obtain 4D_face trajectory box;
        if the box does not intersect hypercube then
                                return NOT_INTERSECT;
        for all edge e in 4D_face {
                if e(tmin) or e(tmax) intersect hypercube then
                                return WILL_INTERSECT;
                <v0, v1> = e;
                if triangulation <v0(tmin), v1(tmax)> enlarge trajectory then {
                        if triangle <v0(tmin), v0(tmax), v1(tmax)>
                                intersect hypercube then
                                        return WILL_INTERSECT;
                        if triangle <v0(tmin), v1(tmin), v1(tmax)>
                                intersect hypercube then
                                        return WILL_INTERSECT;
                } else {
                        if triangle <v0(tmin), v1(tmin), v0(tmax)>
                                intersect hypercube then
                                        return WILL_INTERSECT;
                        if triangle <v1(tmin), v0(tmax), v1(tmax)>
                                intersect hypercube then
                                        return WILL_INTERSECT;
                }
        }
        for all edge e in hypercube(tmin) {
                if 4D_face(tmin) intersect e then return WILL_INTERSECT;
        }
        for all edge e in hypercube(tmax) {
                if 4D_face(tmax) intersect e then return WILL_INTERSECT;
        }
        return NOT_INTERSECT;
}
```

Algorithm 4

The main advantage of this method is that it makes the check time-continuous as shown in Figure 1 (b). Another advantages are related to the characteristics of the hexadecimal-tree. Hexadecimal-tree make time and space cost linear about the number of elements of objects. Hexadecimal-tree divides hypercube adaptively only if it is necessary to divide.

4. Experimental Results

A prototype 3D geometric modelling system was developed about three years ago [Inam90] based on a graph-based tool [Inam89]. The characteristics of this system is that the system can treat other data structures and that directed arcs can be created among all elements such as façes, edges etc. Based on this system, 4D interference checker using hexadecimal-tree is implemented.

Table 1 shows the result of a very simple example. It shows two motions with two objects. One motion causes collision, and the other is collision-free motion. In the motion which causes collision, collision is found by about 2 minutes. In the collision-free motion, it costs about 30 minuets and 1.5 Mbytes memories to authenticate collision-free. The latter costs more because the latter investigates all 4D spaces.

	collision	collicion-free
complexity of shapes & motions		
number of objects	2	2
number of components	5	5
number of faces	52	52
number of edges	120	120
number of control points	2	4
complexity of 4D spatial index		
hexadecimal tree hieght	8	6
hexadecimal tree node	289	1713
number of arcs	1068	8958
complexity of computation		
number of checks	6704	116000
number of intersections	1435	16064
time complixity (min.)	2.0	28.9
space complexity (kbytes)	369	1406

Table 1 Experimental results of check between simple two objects

Figure 5 shows 2D projection of 4D hexadecimal-tree and two moving objects at the collision position and time.

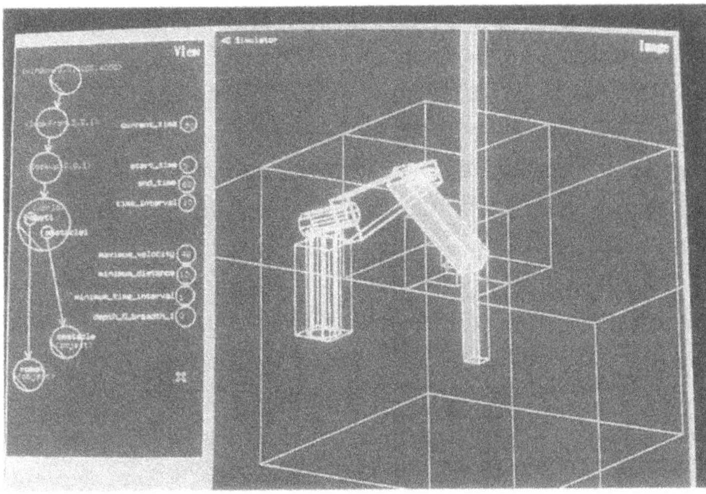

Figure 5 4D Interference position projected to a 2D plane

5. Discussion

The time-axis is not equivalent to the x,y,z-axes while the x,y,z-axes are equivalent to each other. Ratio between space width and time interval of hypercubes must be constant in a hexadecimal-tree. The current system determines this ratio according to the minimum 4D trajectory box covering all moving objects. It is considered that efficiency is the best when this ratio is almost the same with the average velocity of moving objects and when standard deviation of velocity is very small. If a very fast moving object exists in the world where movement of most objects are very slow, it is considered that efficiency of the system decreases according to the difference of velocities. This fact may be a disadvantage of the pure hexadecimal-tree.

The implemented 4D interference check system is a prototype, and have many possibilities of improvement. 1) *Maximum velocity* is constant in the current system. If maximum velocity is estimated for each object and for each time section, 4D trajectory enlarging ratio becomes small. 2) Required time is proportion to the number of faces in the current system, and the current system can treat only polyhedron. In the case that there are objects with many faces, it is better to use *simple polyhedron* covering the object instead of complex polyhedron [Dai88]. 3) There are *duplicate calculations* in the current system. For example, the interference check is performed both at the inside and at the outside of the boundary. This futility is eliminated by device of algorithms. 4) *Parallel processing* for high speed check is considered. Because divided 4D subspaces are independent, parallel processing is possible by checking interference for each subspace independently. When parallel processing is applied, upper bound of time complexity decreases from O(n) to O(log n) if each hypercube requires the same order time, where n means number of hexadecimal-tree nodes. Thus, the log n means the approximated height of hexadecimal-tree. Space subdivision is also used in ray tracing for fast check of ray intersection [Glas84, Kapl85, Fuji86]. Parallelism of such ray tracing is usually about for each ray while parallelism of the 4D interference check is about for each subspace. Of course, parallelism for each moving object is considered, however, each process depends on each other in such a case. In both cases, it is very hard to distribute tasks and data to hardware elements for realization of parallel processing [Kuni89].

In the algorithm here, only pure geometry (*kinematics*) is considered, and *dynamics* is not considered. The algorithm uses the value $V_{max} \Delta t$ (maximum velocity multiplied by time interval) as the error range size. The values obtained from force and acceleration can be used instead of Vmax Δt. Such methods are regarded as applications of dynamics and they give better approximation of the range in which moving objects exist.

In kinematics of robotics, there are concepts of C-space (configuration space) and W-space (work space) [Loza83, Hayw86]. C-space is a space of joint variables. W-space is a space of positions and orientations of an end-effecter. The current system checks the interference in the time-dependent subspace of the W-space generated by parameters of the C-space. Usually, the concept of the W-space does not depend on time. For the purpose of 4D interference check, time must be added to the W-space because it is assumed that different objects pass through the same point at the different time. In the 4D interference check algorithm here, time division is adaptively and automatically determined.

6. Conclusion

A new 4D interference check method was introduced. The characteristics of this method is that it is using hexadecimal-tree as a spatial index, and that it is a time-continuous check and reliable. A prototype system was implemented, and some experimental results were obtained.

References

Boyse, J.W. (1979) Interference Detection Among Solids and Surfaces. CACM, vol. 22, no. 1, Jan.

Cameron, S. (1989) Effective Intersection Tests for Objects Defined Constructively. the International Journal of Robotics Research, vol. 8, no. 1, Feb.

Dai, F. (1988) Collision-Free Motion of an Articulated Kinematic Chain in a Dynamic Environment. IEEE CG & A, vol.8, no.1, Jan.

Fujimura, K., Samet, H. (1989) A Hierarchical Strategy for Path Planning Among Moving Obstacles. IEEE Robotics & Automation, vol.5, no.1, pp.61-69, Feb.

Fujimoto, A., Tanaka, T., Iwata, K. (1986) ARTS: Accelerated Ray-Tracing System. IEEE CG & A, vol.6, no.4, pp.16-26, April

Fujimura, K., Kunii, T.L. (1985) A Hierarchical Space Indexing Methods. in Computer Graphics (Proc. of Computer Graphics Tokyo '85), ed. T.L. Kunii, Springer-Verlag Tokyo 1986.

Glassner, A.S. (1984) Space subdivision for fast ray tracing. IEEE CG & A, vol.4, no.10, pp.15-22, Oct.

Hayward, V. (1986) Fast Collision Detection Scheme by Recursive Decomposition of a Manipulator Work-space. IEEE International Conference on Robotics and Automation, vol.2, pp.1044-1049

Inamoto, N., Kunii, T.L. (1989) A Graph-Based Tool for Workstations. Workstations for Experiments (IFIP WG 5.10 International Working Conference, Lowell, MA, USA, July 1989), ed J.L. Encarnacao and G.G. Grinstein, Springer-Verlag 1991.

Inamoto, N. (1990) A Graph-Based Visual Tool for Workstations and its Application to 4D Geometric Modeling. PhD. thesis at the University of Tokyo, March 29, 1990.

Jacks, C.L., Tanimoto, S.L. (1980) Oct-Trees and Their Use in Representing Three-Dimensional Objects. Computer Graphics and Image Processing , vol. 14, pp. 249-270

Kambhampati, S., Davis, L.S. (1986) Multiresolution Path Planning for Mobile Robots. IEEE Robotics & Automation, vol.RA-2, no.3, pp.135-145, Sept.

Kaplan, M.R. (1985) Space tracing a constant time ray tracer. State of the Art in Image Synthesis (Siggraph '85 Course Notes), vol.11, July

Kunii, T.L., Nishimura S., Noma, T. (1989) The design of a parallel processing system for computer graphics. Parallel Processing for Computer Vision and Display, ed. P.M. Dew, R.A. Earnshaw and T.R. Heywood, 1989.

Lozano-Perez, T. (1983) Spatial Planning: A Configuration Space Approach. IEEE Trans. on Computers, vol. C-32, no. 2, Feb.

Lozano-Perez, T., Wesley, M.A. (1985) An algorithm for Planning Collision-Free Paths Among Polyhedral Obstacles. State of the Art in Image Synthesis (Siggraph '85 Course Notes), vol.11, July

Meagher, D. (1982) Geometric Modeling Using Octree Encoding. Computer Graphics and image Processing, vol. 19, pp.129-147

Moore, M., and Wilhelms, J. (1988) Collision Detection and Response for Computer Animation. Computer Graphics, vol. 22, no. 4, Aug. 1988, (proc. of SIGGRAPH '88, Atlanta, Aug. 1-5, 1988).

Noborio, H., et al. (1987) A New Interference Check Algorithm Using Octree. IEEE International Conference on Robotics and Automation, North Carolina, 1987.

Samet, H. (1984) The Quadtree and Related Hierarchical Data Structures," Computing Surveys, vol. 16, no. 19, pp.187-260, June

Singh, J.S., and Wagh, M.D. (1987) Robot Path Planning using Intersection Convex Shapes: Analysis and simulation. IEEE Robotics & Automation, vol. RA-3, no. 2, pp.101-108, April

Takahashi, O., Schilling, R.J. (1989) Motion Planning in a Plane Using Generalized Voronoi Diagrams. IEEE Robotics & Automation, vol. 5, no. 2, pp.143-150, April

Yamaguchi, K., Kunii, T.L., Fujimura, K., Toriya, H. (1984) Octree-Related Data Structures and Algorithms. IEEE CG & A, vol. 4, no. 1, pp. 53-59, Jan.

Precise Object Interactions using Solid Modeling Techniques

*Mauro Figueiredo**
*Klaus Böhm** and José Teixeira**
** Grupo de Métodos e Sistemas Gráficos, Departamento de Matemática, Universidade de Coimbra, Apartado 3008, 3000 Coimbra - Portugal, email : (mauro/teixeira)@ciuc2.uc.pt*
*** Zentrum für Graphische Datenverarbeitung e.V. (ZGDV), Wilheminenstraße 7, 6100 Darmstadt - Germany, email : boehm@igd.fhg.de*

Abstract

The great potential provided by the existing 3D hardware and software provide us the tools for modeling and displaying complete 3D physical objects in computer systems. Despite the advanced ability to create and display 3D objects, there is a lack of interaction techniques by which the user can intuitively manipulate these 3D objects and perceive information about them.

GIVEN (Gesture-driven Interactions in Virtual ENvironments) is a 3D interaction toolkit which aims at aiding in the development of new 3D interaction and dialogue techniques. The user of the GIVEN toolkit is not dealing any more with a picture of an object. He can directly manipulate 3D objects using 3D input devices, such as spaceball and dataglove, for grabbing, pushing and moving them.

With our first application, for virtual environments, we found out that very unnatural object interactions happen if the collision detection, necessary for the interaction, is made by using only bounding volumes. Precise object interactions are required to let users grab, push and position objects precisely in a 3D world.

For this purpose, a boundary representation was integrated to be used for the implementation of an advanced collision detection scheme.

This paper describes an algorithm for performing the intersection of two polyhedra. New pre-processing algorithms are explained in detail that speed up on average the overall performance of the intersection algorithm. Robustness is achieved by propagating all topological information immediately to the neighbor faces. The application of this algorithm inside GIVEN is also presented.

Keywords : Collision Detection, Intersection Algorithms, 3D Interaction Techniques, Direct Manipulation Techniques, User Interfaces, Human Computer Interaction.

1. Introduction

The recent increase of the available power of special purpose 3D hardware and software provided a new range of 3D applications.

For these applications 2D interaction techniques are no longer adequate. New interaction devices are also required. Although 2D input devices, such as mice or joysticks, can be extended to 3D, they are not intuitive and easy to use.

Present human-computer interaction for 3D applications is known to be far from optimal. Researchers are now looking for new interaction techniques (see also [FOLE87], [KRUE91]) that take full advantage of the 3D nature of these applications.

Our research in interactive computer graphics and search for better 3D interaction techniques led us to the development of GIVEN, in which 3D interaction concepts and methods are developed and evaluated.

The user or "visitor" of the GIVEN toolkit can navigate around and directly manipulate 3D objects. Via intuitive interaction techniques the user is enabled to grab, rotate, move and position 3D objects [BÖHM92]. Input devices such as dataglove and spaceball are used for controlling a virtual hand.

For the recognition of interactions between moving and static objects a collision check has to be done all the time. Our experience with GIVEN showed us that for solid modeling or molecular modeling applications it is not sufficient to do collision checks using bounding volumes aligned with the coordinate axes. Users of these applications must be able to identify, grab, push and position 3D objects very precisely.

The purpose of this paper is to describe how we realize precise interactions with 3D objects.

A boundary representation available through the Topological Data Model (TDM) toolkit [WU91] was integrated and a robustness algorithm for performing the intersection of two polyhedra was implemented. This toolkit was provided to us from FhG-IGD - Darmstadt. The algorithm for intersecting two polyhedra is well known (see also [HOFF89], [MANT88]) and we focus on new developed algorithms that can speed up on average the overall performance.

Finally, results are summarized, conclusions are drawn and directions for further research are suggested.

2. GIVEN

In this section a brief overview of the GIVEN system is presented. We will see how collision detection is important when interacting with 3D objects in virtual worlds.

The GIVEN system is a 3D interaction toolkit which aims at aiding in the development of new 3D interaction techniques.

The *visitor* of the GIVEN environment uses a small set of hand gestures to manipulate virtual worlds. Performing gestures previously defined with a functional meaning, such as "fly forward", "grab object", "release object", and others, the user is able to communicate to the computer system his intentions. In this way, (s)he is enabled to navigate around and directly manipulate 3D objects using simple and intuitive interaction techniques.

A *dataglove* is used as an input device and neural networks interpret the visitor´s gestures that are produced as different hand positions.

Behaviour is also assigned to objects in the virtual environment. Each object has its individual behaviour, that is, it knows how to react to various stimuli the environment exerts upon it. As an example, when an object is released, it falls down following the gravity laws, but it could also be like a balloon and rise in the air until it reaches the virtual room ceiling.

2.1. GIVEN´s Architecture

The main components of GIVEN are illustrated in figure 2.1. The Event Handler receives user's events from device drivers (Dataglove, Spaceball) and the conventional input devices (keyboard and mouse). According to the data received from the Event Handler the Cursor Manager controls the cursor actions. The Renderer draws the current state of world using the Silicon Graphics GL graphics language. The Collision Detection module checks if any objects are colliding in the world at any moment. Finally, the System Kernel coordinates the actions between the Cursor Manager, Renderer and Behaviour Manager.

An interaction takes place as follows. The Event Handler gets an event from a device driver. The Cursor Manager interprets the gesture information and controls the navigation. Next, the System Kernel ask the Collision Detection module if there are any collisions taking place. For objects that do collide, appropriate behaviour has to be determined. The Behaviour Manager takes care of the individual behaviour of objects. Once the behaviour evaluation is done and appropriate changes are made to the scene, a new frame can be rendered.

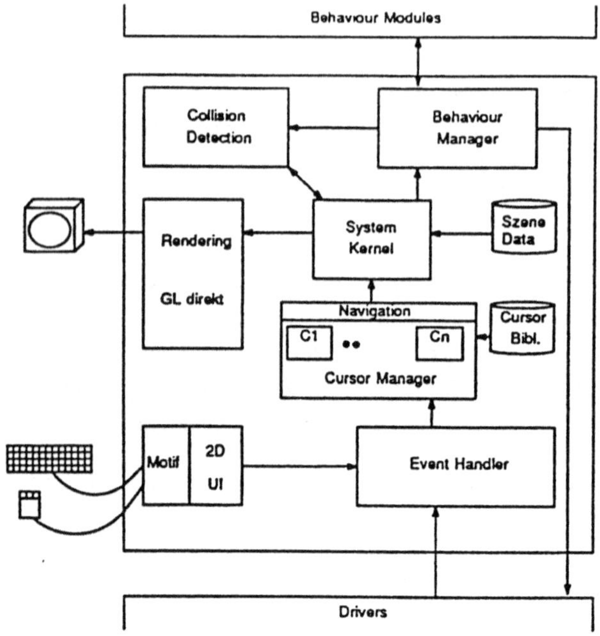

Figure 2.1 GIVEN's Architecture.

2.2. Collision Detection

Collision detection is one of the most important tasks to be realized when a *visitor* is manipulating a three-dimensional virtual world. When he comes near to an object to grab it a collision check must be done to guarantee that he is close enough. Again, when a ball is falling we must check if it is colliding with any object in the way to determine what kind of behaviour should be then executed.

Fortunately, there is no need to check all objects in the scene for collision. For instance, static objects do not require to be checked for collision against other objects in the scene. Only active objects (e.g., those that are moving like the hand cursor, a ball falling), should be checked if they are colliding with any other object in the scene.

In the first version of GIVEN, the collision detection module is based on bounding volumes (CDBV). It is implemented hierarchically with two levels of checking (figure 2.2).

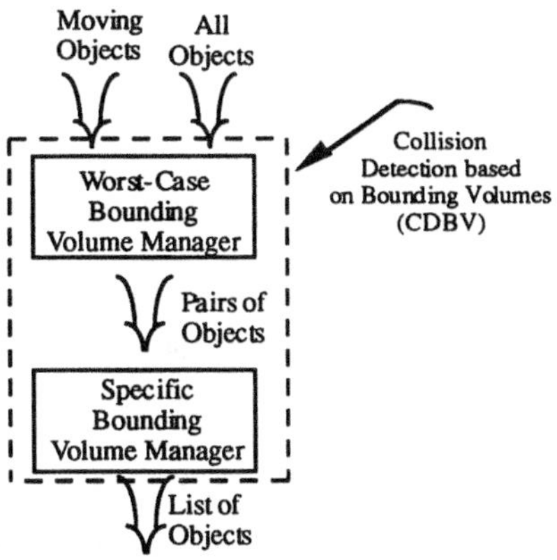

Figure 2.2 - Collision detection module's architecture.

These collision checks do not use polygon information of objects. They only use bounding volumes parallel to the coordinate axes. Therefore, we can check very fast if two objects collide.

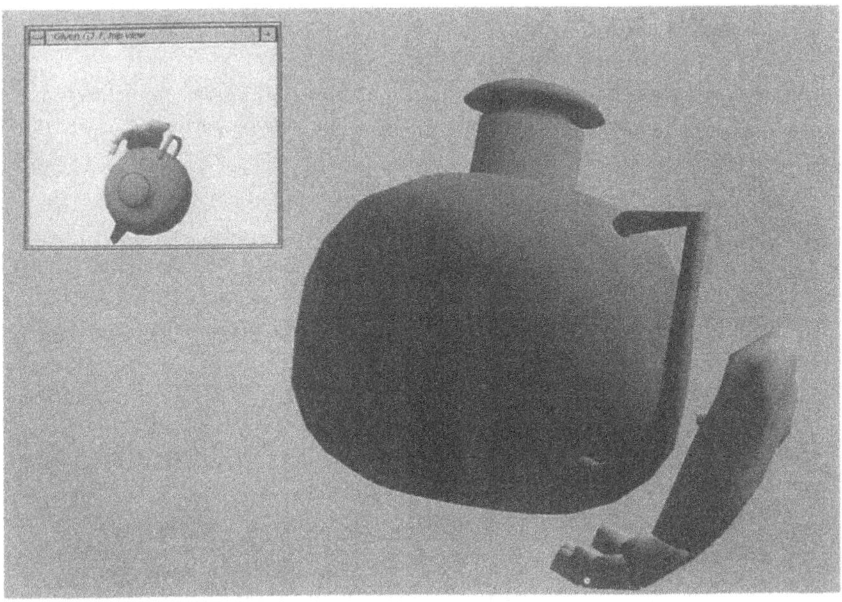

Figure 2.3 - An object is grabbed but the virtual hand is not touching the object´s surface.

Objects can be defined hierarchically in GIVEN. Performance can, therefore, be improved if we define two levels of tests using *worst-case* and *specific bounding volumes*. *Specific bounding volumes* are detailed volumes that surround each object; and *worst-case bounding volumes* include object´s specific bounding volume and the volumes of its descendents. Clearly, if there is no collision between worst-case bounding volumes of object A and B, there cannot be a intersection between the descendents of A and the descendents of B.

Using bounding volumes for collision detection is not sufficient to achieve supposed naturalness interactions in virtual worlds. The main problem stems from the fact that two objects are considered to collide if their specific bounding volumes do collide. But, the only relevant information that we could extract after the second level of detection is that objects might collide but there is no certainty. Therefore further tests should be made. For that reason, very unnatural object interactions and situations can happen. An example is illustrated in figure 2.3. Users can never get "real" close to an object because collision is detected between object and hand's bounding volumes.

3. Precise Collision Detection (PCD)

Collision detection problems and their variations are an important topic of research in computational geometry. Their importance is mainly due to the fact that two impenetrable objects cannot share a common region.

Virtual reality applications aim at creating virtual worlds with which the user interacts as if they were real. The main goal is to give the user the feeling of direct interaction with three-dimensional "real" objects as naturally as possible. For this reason, the user of such systems wants to see simulated objects acting as if they were impenetrable and sense limits to his motion and actions in the same way as when (s)he is manipulating the physical world.

For that purpose, it is necessary to extend the collision detection manager based on bounding volumes (CDBV) developed for GIVEN. Bounding volumes can be effectively used to state that two objects cannot intersect, but we cannot decide that two objects intersect just because their bounding volumes intersect.

Therefore, a precise collision detection manager was developed [FIGU93]. A boundary representation was integrated to assist in the implementation of a robustness algorithm for intersecting two polyhedra and to find out how much one object is inside another.

This section describes the key ideas and algorithms used to implement the precise collision detection manager. New developed algorithms are presented that can speed up on average the overall performance.

3.1. Boundary Representation in GIVEN

The data representation scheme first developed for the GIVEN toolkit was mainly concerned in realizing fast rendering.

Most of the shading models discussed in the literature, such as constant shading, Gouraud shading and Phong shading, implement efficient shading algorithms for surfaces defined by polygons and polygon meshes. For this reason, three-dimensional objects are modeled in GIVEN as polyhedral, faceted objects and the data model stores the polygons that make up the object´s surface. The data structure is a very simple polygon modeling scheme [MORT85] where the object is the basic entity and its geometric shape is defined by cross-referenced lists of vertices and faces that represent the object's surface.

Our desire of natural and precise interactions on virtual environments generated new ideas and therefore new questions such as the following :

- Is this moving object colliding with any other ?
- Is this object inside or outside this other one ?
- What is the weight, volume, center of gravity, etc. of the object ?

Unfortunately, the GIVEN data structure, which was designed mainly to attain fast rendering, was not able to give sufficient information for answering these questions. For this purpose a solid modeling representational scheme was required that guarantees the creation of valid *bounded* and *connected* three-dimensional objects [MANT88].

For this reason, a boundary representation was integrated into GIVEN. We used a non-manifold boundary scheme because it was the only representation available for us. It was important for us to have the power of a solid modeling system, which is adequate for answering arbitrary geometric questions algorithmically. Additionally, the extended domain of a non-manifold boundary representation would enable the designer of virtual environments that uses the GIVEN toolkit to exercise his creativity. However, this data structure was available as a toolkit. Unfortunately, using a toolkit is not as efficient as directly accessing the data structures. Therefore, this boundary representation was not efficient for rendering, and the original polygon modeling scheme was still needed.

The GIVEN toolkit is now supported by two representational schemes as illustrated in figure 3.1. The polygon modeling scheme is usually used for rendering. Only when this data structure is unable to give sufficient information for determining the geometric properties, we access this information from the boundary model.

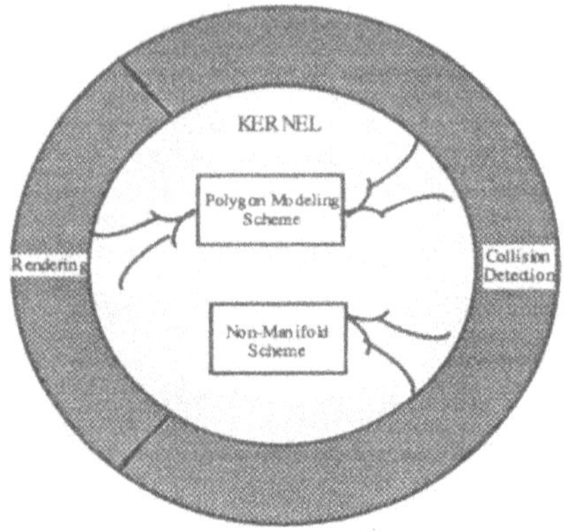

Figure 3.1 - GIVEN's representational scheme.

3.2. Realization of Precise Collision Detection

In this section we describe the precise collision detection algorithm. The main goal of this algorithm is to find out if two objects are intersecting.

3.2.1. Precise Collision Detection Architecture

The heart of a precise collision detection algorithm is a method for intersecting two polyhedra, A and B, which requires testing each face-pair for intersection. This is not efficient if it has to be done for every pair of objects in the scene. Therefore, a preceding calculation that filters out objects that cannot intersect should be done.

The aim of the collision detection manager based on bounding volumes (CDBV) (see figure 2.2) is to construct a list of objects whose bounding volumes intersect.

Using this information we can extend the old collision detection pipeline to include then a third manager, called *Polyhedral Intersection Manager* (*PIM*), which will be responsible for calculating the intersection between two polyhedra (figure 3.2). Maintaining those pre-processing steps presented in figure 3.2, allow us quickly to filter out those objects that cannot intersect, and a list is constructed for those objects whose specific bounding volumes do intersect. Thus, performance of the precise collision detection manager is improved because only a small set of pairs of objects will be tested by the *Polyhedral Intersection Manager*.

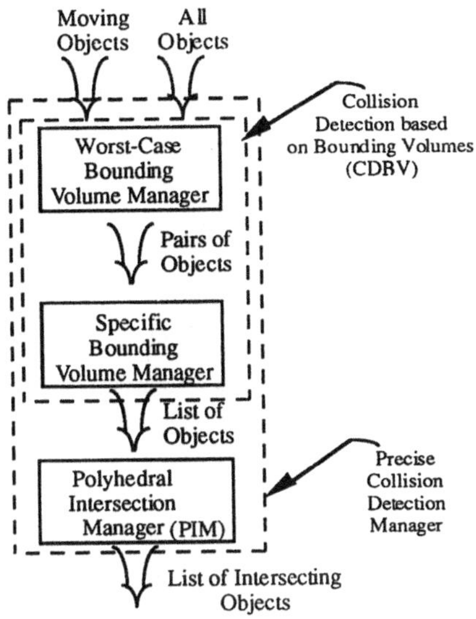

Figure 3.2 - Precise Collision Detection Manager's Architecture.

3.2.2. Intersecting Polyhedral Objects

An algorithm for intersecting two polyhedra, A and B, requires a testing for each face $f \in A$ against each face $g \in B$ for intersection. However, a straightforward implementation, which tests each pair of faces for intersection, leads to a O($\mathbf{n} \times \mathbf{m}$) computational complexity (n and m is the number of faces of polyhedra A and B, respectively). Therefore, a preceding computation that filters out face pairs that cannot intersect should be done.

These prepossessing steps cannot speed up certain cases of intersecting polyhedra. However, they do speed up the algorithm on average and therefore they were implemented.

The intersection of polyhedral objects is performed in two steps :

- 1. Filter out face pairs that cannot intersect (advanced filtering faces algorithm). If it is found that there is no pair of intersecting faces, we do only a containment test and skip the next step.
- 2. Calculate intersection between pairs of faces and construct the intersection curve (intersection curve determination).

3.2.2.1. Advanced Filtering Faces

This pre-processing step should eliminate pairs of faces from polyhedra A and B that cannot intersect.

A simple way to do this is to enclose every planar face, $f \in A$ and $g \in B$, in the smallest bounding volume that completely contains the face, whose sides are aligned with the coordinate axes.

Then, for each pair of faces, $f \in A$ and $g \in B$, we check if their bounding volumes intersect. If the bounding volumes do not intersect, then the faces inside them cannot intersect and are not further considered. For those pairs of faces whose bounding volumes intersect we cannot assume anything about their intersection and therefore they should be stored for further processement.

This straightforward algorithm for rejecting face pairs that cannot intersect uses every pair of bounding volumes to check whether they intersect or not. This leads to an algorithm with worst-case complexity $O(\mathbf{n} \times \mathbf{m})$, where n and m is the number of faces of polyhedra A and B, respectively. In situations where objects have many faces and only a few do actually intersect, this algorithm does not perform well.

To improve the average performance of the face filtering algorithm we developed an *Advanced Filtering Face* algorithm. Our approach introduces a pre-prossessing computation that reduces the set of faces of polyhedra A and B which have to be tested.

This algorithm first calculates the *intersection bounding volume* of the two polyhedra. This volume is the intersection of the bounding volumes of the two polyhedra A and B. Second, for every face, $f \in A$ and $g \in B$, we check to see if their bounding volumes intersect the *intersection bounding volume*. Those faces that actually intersect the *intersection bounding volume* are annotated and two sets of faces, $f' \in A$ and $g' \in B$, are constructed in this way. Third, only those faces, $f' \in A$ and $g' \in B$, that were selected in the previous step are candidates for intersection and now we will check to see if their bounding volumes intersect.

This additional pre-processing step introduced in the *advanced filtering faces* algorithm provides better performance on average to the overall algorithm. However, we cannot expect better performance than $O(n \times m)$ in special cases of the polyhedra intersection.

An example of the intersection between two faces in 2-dimensions (figure 3.3) shows us this method.

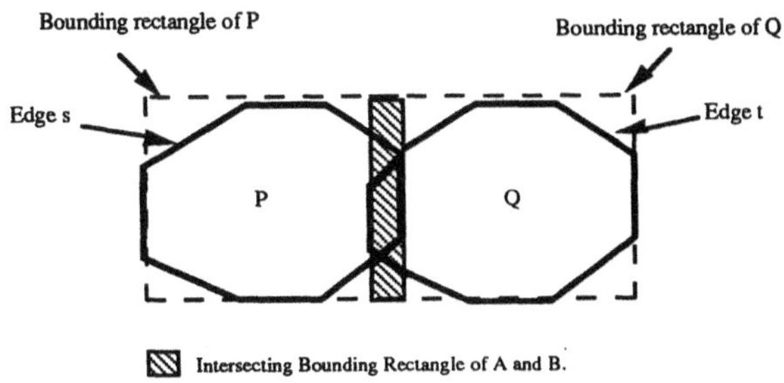

Figure 3.3 - The intersecting edges share the region defined by the common region on the face´s bounding rectangles.

The *Advanced Filtering Faces* algorithm which filters out face pairs that cannot intersect works as follows :

- 1. for every face f of A and g of B, determine the smallest bounding volume whose sides are parallel to the coordinate axis;
- 2. Calculate the *intersection bounding volume* between the two polyhedra A and B.
- 3. Construct the set X of faces, f∈A, whose bounding volume intersects the *intersection bounding volume*; symmetrically, construct the set Y of faces, g∈B, whose bounding volume intersects the intersection bounding volume;
- 4. Test every face in the set X against every face in the set Y to find out pairs of faces whose bounding volumes intersect.

This algorithm suggests that before intersecting every bounding volume of faces f∈A against every bounding volume of faces g∈B to see if they intersect, we should filter out faces of A and B which are not in the *intersecting bounding volume* and therefore cannot intersect any other faces. This additional filtering process can be done in **n** steps for one object, and for two objects it will require therefore n+m checks. On the average it will reduce the number of faces which has to be later tested, and it will improve the overall performance of the algorithm.

Therefore, this algorithm will perform much better in those situations where A and B have many faces but only a few of them actually intersect and therefore it was implemented. The worst-case running time for the bounding volumes intersection cannot be improved, but the average running time can be significantly improved.

3.2.2.2. Polyhedral Containment Test

After performing the advanced filtering algorithm, we may arrive at a situation where it is found that none of the faces´ bounding volume pairs intersect. Therefore the two polyhedra, A and B, cannot intersect. In this case, however, it can happen that one of the polyhedra is inside the other one and a polyhedral containment[1] test must be performed.

For this purpose, we have developed an extended version for three-dimensions of the Cohen-Sutherland line clipping algorithm [FOLE90]. It makes use of faces´ bounding volume and therefore it can be applied to any type of polyhedral object and the containment test can be done very quickly.

Figure 3.4 illustrates an example in two-dimensions of the two possible situations between which we want to distinguish when it is found that two objects cannot intersect.

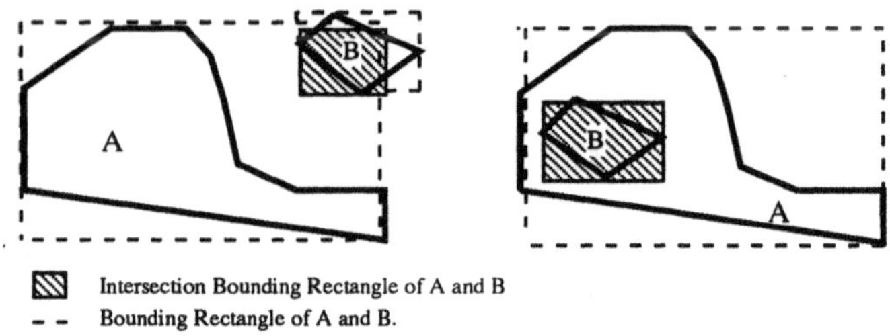

Figure 3.4 - Two distinct situations where edge´s rectangles of A and B do not intersect.

Considering that we want to perform the polyhedral containment test for polyhedra A against polyhedra B. In this case, the bounding volume of object A and the faces' bounding volumes of object B will be used. To perform this test we start by extending the planes of the bounding volume of polyhedra A to divide three-dimensional space into twenty-seven regions (figure 3.5-a).

To each of these regions in space a six bit code is assigned, determined by where the region lies with respect to the outside halfspace of the bounding volume planes. Each bit in the code is set to either 1 (true) or 0 (false). The six bits in the code are established according to the following rule :

- First bit, outside halfspace of top plane, above top plane, $y \geq y_{max}$
- Second bit, outside halfspace of bottom plane, below bottom plane, $y \leq y_{min}$
- Third bit, outside halfspace of right plane, to the right of right plane, $x \geq x_{max}$
- Fourth bit, outside halfspace of left plane, to the left of left plane, $x \leq x_{min}$
- Fifth bit, outside the halfspace of front plane, to the front of front plane, $z \geq z_{max}$
- Sixth bit, outside the halfspace of back plane, to the back of the back plane, $z \leq z_{min}$.

[1]A containment check will determine if one object is inside or outside another one.

Then every faces´ bounding volume of polyhedra B is classified according to its spatial position in relation to the bounding volume of polyhedra A. The code of the region where it lies is assigned to the two extreme points that define each face's bounding volume of B. Then, we can annotate the regions where the face's bounding volume are located.

Clearly, polyhedra A will be inside B if it is found that faces' bounding volumes of B fill all the twenty six regions in the space around the bounding volume of polyhedra A.

A further improvement can be made if we consider only the fourteen regions illustrated in figure 3.5 -b). In fact, it is sufficient to verify that the faces' bounding volumes of B lie in these regions to be sure that polyhedra A is inside polyhedra B.

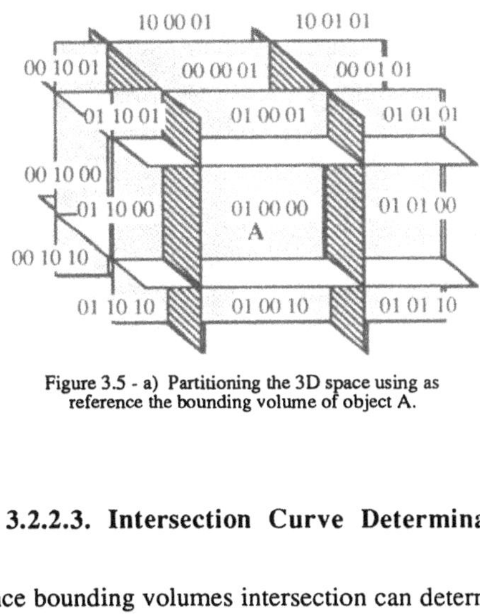

Figure 3.5 - a) Partitioning the 3D space using as reference the bounding volume of object A.

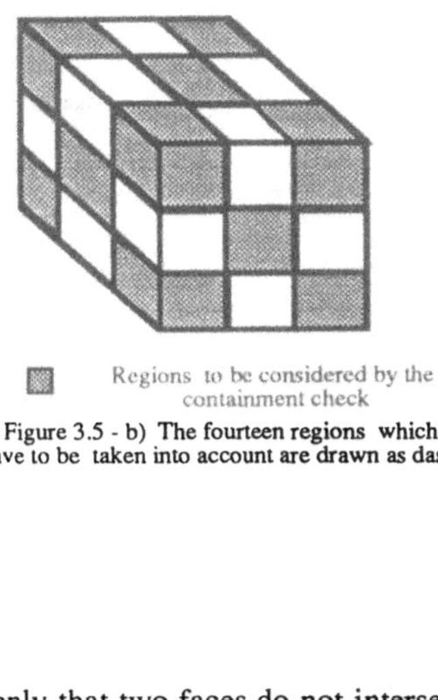

Figure 3.5 - b) The fourteen regions which have to be taken into account are drawn as dash.

3.2.2.3. Intersection Curve Determination

Since bounding volumes intersection can determine only that two faces do not intersect, we arrived at a situation where we have found all candidates of intersecting face pairs. Now we have to intersect face pairs and construct their intersection curve.

The implementation of such an algorithm should resolve possible numerical uncertainty problems rooted in floating point arithmetic. Therefore a boundary representation is used to achieve a robustness algorithm for the determination of the intersection curve between two polyhedral objects [MANT88], [HOFF89].

It is assumed that the boundary representation that was integrated provides the following topological information :

- for each vertex, the adjacent vertices, edges and faces are given;

- for each edge, the bounding vertices and the adjacents faces are specified;
- for each face, the bounding edges and vertices are given, and they are organized in a loop locally enclosing the face area to the left.

The geometric information available from the boundary model specifies the equations for the planes containing faces. The plane normal direction points locally to the solid exterior (figure 3.6). A face is a finite, non zero convex area in a plane, bounded by one loop of vertices and edges. Edges are directed such that the face area locally lies to the left, as seen from the exterior of the solid. An edge is defined geometrically as a line segment bounded by two vertices and is characterized by the line direction. A vertex is a point element defined by a position vector in $\Re^3$.

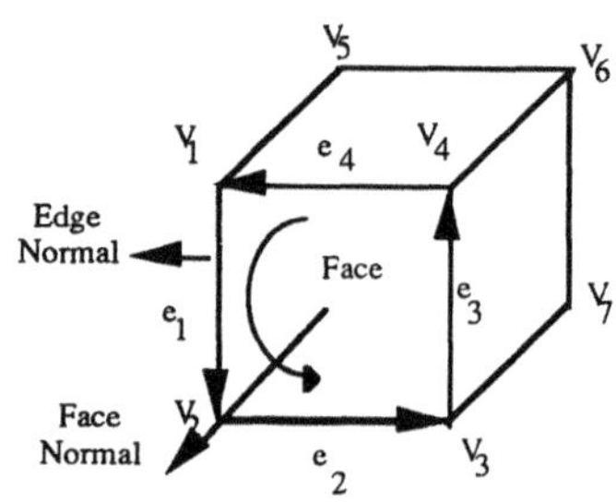

Figure 3.6 - Geometrical and topological convention.

The conceptualized algorithm for intersecting face pairs works as follows :

for each face pair f∈ A and g∈ B
    if face f and g are coplanar **then return**;
    else
        if face f do not intersect the plane α that contains face g **then return**;
        else
            if the intersection of face f with plane α is one point P1 **then**
                test if P1 is in face g;
            else
                Let r be the intersection segment of face f with plane α;
                Perform a line clipping algorithm for segment r on face g;
            Propagate topological information to neighbor faces.

In the presence of coplanar faces this algorithm does nothing. When the two polyhedral objects have some faces in common, our only interest is in determining their boundary polygon.

However, their common boundary can be determined from the intersection of non coplanar faces adjacent to them and therefore it is not necessary to consider coplanar face pairs.

For non coplanar and convex faces, $f \in A$ and $g \in B$, we intersect the bounding edges of f with the plane α containing g (figure 3.7). The intersection will yield zero, one or two intersecting points. It is important at this point to classify these intersection points and store in a data structure their classifications. Each plane α is considered to be a slab with thickness 2ε and each intersection point is then classified as either coincident to a vertice or belonging to an edge of face f.

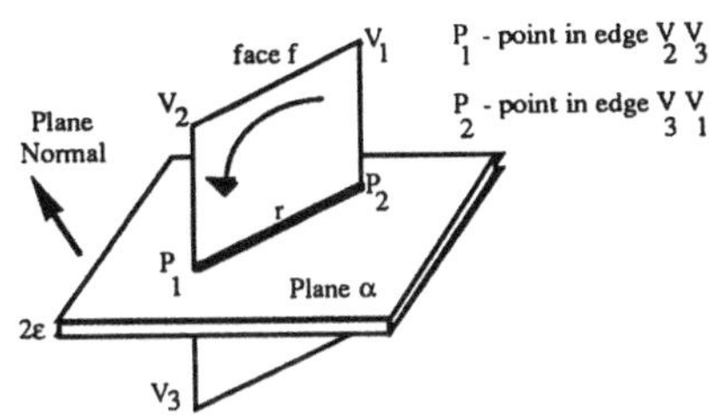

Figure 3.7 - Intersection of face f with plane α yields the segment r.

If no intersection point was found after intersecting the face f with the plane α then this face pair do not intersect. In this case, we store only if face f is inside or outside the halfspace defined by the plane α.

If f is intersecting plane α in one point, we must check if this point is in face g. Therefore, we must traverse each edge in the loop of face g and classify the point as coincident with one of the bounding vertices, with the edge interior, or if it is interior or exterior to the face g. These tests should be performed in this order. Tolerance regions must be introduced for vertex and edge elements as illustrated in figure 3.8. A vertex has a tolerance region which is a sphere with radius ε. The edge tolerance region is a cylinder with the same length as the edge and radius ε.

If the point is exterior to the loop, the pair of faces f and g do not intersect.

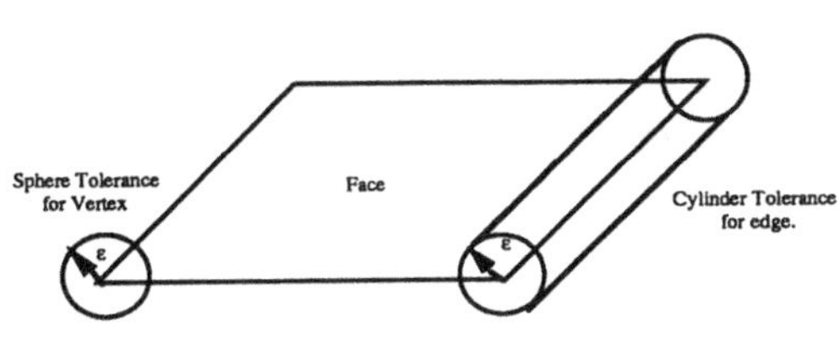

Figure 3.8 - Tolerance regions for vertex and edge elements.

The intersection of face f with plane α can also be a line segment r defined by two ending points, P_1 and P_2. In this situation, the line segment common to the face pair is calculated using a line clipping algorithm. We implemented the Cyrus-Beck [HILL91] line clipping algorithm which is efficient and can be applied to any convex polygon.

Our goal is to determine the part of segment r that lies in the interior of face g (figure 3.9). The interior of the convex face g is defined as the region in the inside half-space of every edge in the face. Therefore, segment r is tested against each edge of face g. Pieces lying in outside half-spaces are "cut". When all edges have been processed, the piece of r that remains, call it r', must lie in the interior of face g and therefore is the intersection of the two faces.

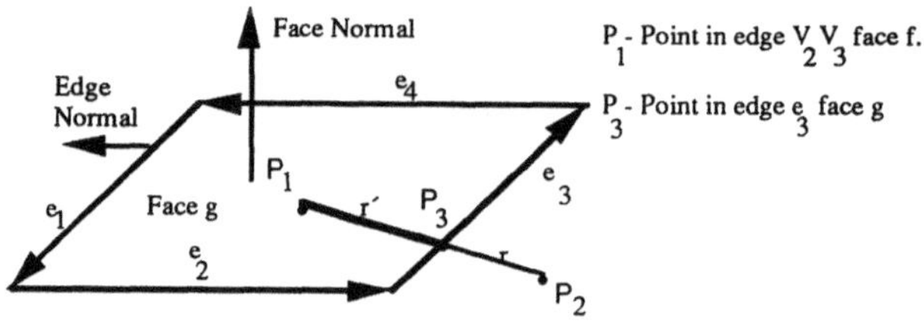

Figure 3.9 - Clipping the segment r against face g.

Once again, we must classify the bounding vertices of r' as being coincident to any vertice, in the interior of an edge or inside of face g. For that purpose, we must consider again the tolerance regions, presented in figure 3.8, for the vertice and edge elements of face g.

Finally, if it was found that the two faces f and g intersect, we must create new points and edges to propagate the topological information to the neighbor faces. During the calculation of the intersection curve every point was classified as coincident with a vertice or on an edge. For those intersecting points classified on an edge we must create a new point and split the original edge into two new edges to increase robustness. In this way, when analysing neighbor faces, the new intersecting points which have to be calculated will be "attracted" to these points.

This algorithm presented here proved to be reliable and robust. The only disadvantage that can be pointed out is the requirement to define faces of polyhedra A and B as convex. Nevertheless, if a new line clipping algorithm that deals with concave faces is implemented we have a curve intersection determination algorithm that can be applied to any type of polyhedral objects.

4. Results

The precise collision detection manager developed for GIVEN allows the users of the GIVEN environment to interact very precisely with three-dimensional objects.

Now the user is able to get close to objects and has the "feeling" of touching 3D objects. In this way, the user is directly manipulate three-dimensional objects by pushing, grabbing and releasing them only when (s)he is touching its surface and not when (s)he is touching its bounding volumes (see figure 2.3). An example is illustrated in figure 4.1 where the user is enabled to grab a cone and put it on top of a teapot very precisely.

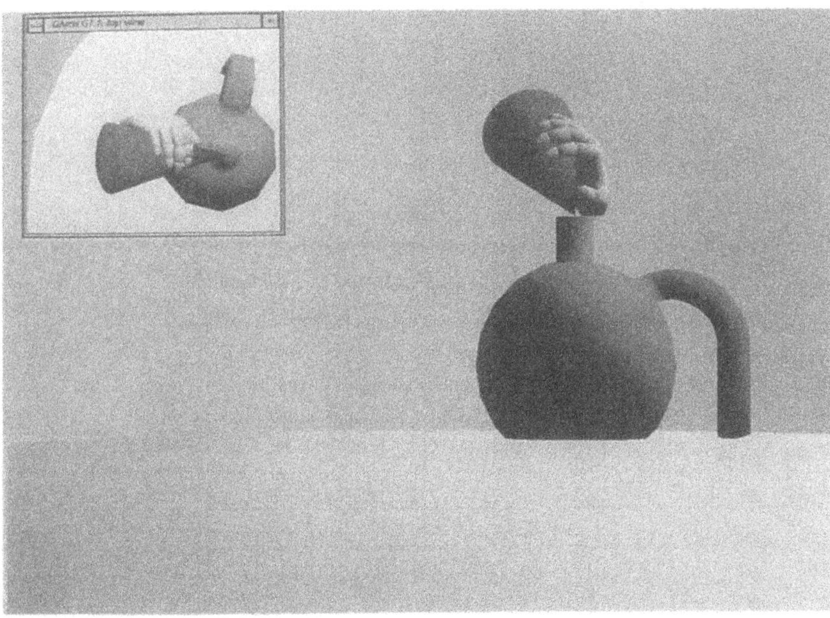

Figure 4.1 - Precise manipulation of 3D objects.

In the GIVEN toolkit the intersection curve between three-dimensional objects is used to provide additional depth perception of spatial relationships between objects in complex scenes (figure 4.2). For example, it can be particularly useful for positioning tasks where one object must be parallel to another or where adjacent objects must be positioned with their edges aligned.

Figure 4.2 - Displaying the intersection curve for attaining depth perception.

Objects	Complexity	Operation	Time
scene	700 polygons	navigation	50 msec / frame
scene	700 polygons	imprecise collision detection (specific bounding volumes)	70 msec / frame
hand & cube	162 + 6 polygons	precise collision detection	390 msec / frame
thumb#1 & cube	30 + 6 polygons	precise collision detection	270 msec / frame
cube & cylinder	6 + 22 polygons	precise collision detection	130 msec / frame

Table 4.1 - Execution speed for grabbing interactions.

Several scenes were constructed and execution time for various interaction tasks were measured on a Silicon Graphics 4D/320 VGX (table 4.1). The test scene contains 3 objects. The virtual hand which is a hierarchical object defined by the following parts : hand (162 polygons), thumb#0 (46 polygons), thumb#1 (30 polygons), index#0 (32 polygons), index#1 (32 polygons), index#2 (30 polygons), middle#0 (32 polygons), middle#1 (32 polygons), middle#2 (30 polygons), ring#0 (32 polygons), ring#1 (32 polygons), ring#2 (30 polygons), little#0 (32 polygons), little#1 (32 polygons), little#2 (30 polygons). The two remaining objects are a cube (6 polygons) and a cylinder (22 polygons).

As shown in table 4.1 acceptable speed is achieved when the moving object has a small number of polygons.

5. Conclusions and Future Work

Experience with GIVEN showed us that very unnatural and imprecise object interactions happen in virtual environments if collision detection is made by using bounding volumes aligned with the coordinate axes.

To enable the user of GIVEN to interact precisely with 3D objects, a non-manifold boundary representation toolkit, called Topological Data Model - TDM, was integrated in GIVEN to assist in the development of a precise collision detection manager.

Collision detection is now made very precisely by intersecting two polyhedral objects and determining the vertices, edges and faces where the intersection curve lies. In this way, the user of GIVEN is enabled to get "close" to objects and to have the "feeling" of touching 3D objects.

We believe that 3D interaction toolkits should be supported by solid modeling representational schemes.

In the current situation we are using a toolkit where we do not have direct access to the data structure. In this case, the inquiring of the data structure costs too much time. For this reason, we are planning to implement a solid modeling representation scheme in the GIVEN kernel.

We would like to use GIVEN in future as a testbed for developing new interaction techniques for solid modeling. With the precise collision detection manager the user is enabled to identify topological entities. In this way the user could directly construct 3D models in a complete 3D environment, using intuitive interaction techniques.

Acknowledgments

The authors would like to thank Professor Dr.-Ing. José Encarnação and Dr-Ing. Wolfgang Hübner for his support to this work. We are also grateful to Ting Wu for the permission to use the non-manifold boundary representation toolkit she wrote and for the invaluable support, suggestions and help provided. Thanks also to Rolf Fischer, Jörg Zedler and Hansgeorg Seeger for the suggestions and assistance.

Bibliography

[ALA92] Ala-Rantala, Marti; "NeuroGlove : An Interactive Test Environment for Hand Posture and Gesture Recognition Using Dataglove and Neural Networks"; Master's thesis, Technische Hochschule Darmstadt, 1992.

[BÖHM92] Böhm, Klaus; Hübner, Wolfgang; Väänänen, Kaisa; " GIVEN : Gesture Driven Interactions in Virtual Environments, a Toolkit Approach to 3D Interactions"; Proceedings of the "Interfaces to Real and Virtual Worlds" Conference, Montepelier, March 23-27, 1992.

[BRIL92] Brill, Louis M.; "Facing Interface Issues"; Computer Graphics World, April 1992.

[BRYS92] Bryson, Steve; "Survey of Virtual Environment Technologies and Techniques"; in "Implementation of Immersive Virtual Environments", Course Notes 9, Siggraph 92.

[FIGU93] Figueiredo, Mauro; "Precise Object Interactions in Virtual Environments"; Master's thesis, to be submitted, Universidade de Coimbra, Portugal, 1993.

[FOLE84] Foley, James D.; "The Human Factors of Computer Graphics Interaction Techniques"; IEEE Computer Graphics & Applications, Nov. 1984.

[FOLE87] Foley, James D.; "Interfaces for Advanced Computing"; Scientific American, 1987.

[FOLE90] Foley; van Dam; Feiner; Hughes; "Computer Graphics - Principles and Practice"; Addison-Wesley Publishing Company; 1990.

[GURS91] Gursoz, E. Levent, & al.; "Boolean Set Operations on Non-Manifold Boundary Representation Objects"; Computer Aided Design, February, 1991.

[HILL91] Hill, Jr. F. S.; "Computer Graphics"; Maxwell MacMillan International Editions; 1991.

[HOFF89] Hoffman, Cristoph M., & al.; "Robust Set Operations on Polyhedral Solids"; IEEE Computer Graphics & Applications, November 1989.

[HOFF89] Hoffmann, Cristoph M.; "Geometric and Solid Modeling - An Introduction"; Morgan Kaufmann Publishers Inc., 1989.

[KRUG91] Krueger, Myron; "Artificial Reality II", 1991.

[MANT88] Mäntylä, Martti; "An Introduction to Solid Modeling"; Computer Science Press, Inc., 1988.

[MORT85] Mortenson, Michael; "Geometric Modeling"; John Wiley & Sons Inc; 1985.

[SEEG91] Seeger, Hansgeorg; "Konzeption und Entwicklung von Interaktionstechniken für virtuelle Welten am Beispiel von Navigation und Objektverhalten für das GIVEN Toolkit"; Master's thesis, Technische Hochschule Darmstadt, 1991.

[WEIL86] Weiler, Kevin J.; "Topological Structures for Geometric Modeling", PhD Thesis, 1986.

[WU91] Wu, Shin-Ting; "Topologie von Hibriden Objekten"; PhD Dissertation; Darmstadt 91.

ON THE SPHERICAL SPLINES FOR ROBOT MODELING *

Martin Mellado, Josep Tornero
Departamento de Ingeniería de Sistemas,
Computadores y Automática (DISCA),
Universidad Politécnica de Valencia
P.O.B. 22012, E-46071 Valencia, SPAIN.
E-mail: martin@aii.upv.es. jtornero@aii.upv.es

Abstract

This paper presents a new mathematical representation for modeling robotic systems based on the use of spherical splines. They can be considered as a generalization of the spline concept with the introduction of control spheres. Very complex volumes modeled by spherical splines are described in funtion of a low number of control spheres. To modify the robot configuration, only control spheres must be recomputed. An extended hierarchical structure with different levels of accuracy including polyhedra, spherical volumes and spherical splines is explained in the paper. Distance computation for collision detection between robots results very fast when this structure is used.

Introduction

In the manufacturing and assembly processes of an integrated factory, robots are one of the main elements. To reach a completely authomatized process, robots must be intelligent enough to move independently. Therefore, they have to be able to decide its own motion to avoid any collision with objects in their workspace. To solve collision avoidance, every element of the manufacturing and assembly area, as well as robots, must be modeled.

Two aspects must be considered in the implementation of a correct collision avoidance system: the type of volumes used to model objects, usually convex polyhedra (polytopes), and distance computation procedures. Distances between polytopes and its computational complexity have been studied deeply during last years [Dobkin & Kirkpatric, 1985], [Gilbert, Johnson & Keerthi, 1988], [Lin & Canny, 1991].

The type of model chosen has an important effect on collision avoidance. It can make easier and faster the distance computation, as well as accuracy depends on it. Convex polyhedra have been the most frequently used model in collision avoidance [Canny, 1986].

*This work was partially supported by Comisión Interministerial de Ciencia y Tecnología (CICYT) under the project ROB 91-0362

Each object can be represented as a convex polyhedron, or union of convex polyhedra. Many real world objects that have curved surfaces are represented by polyhedral approximations. The accuracy of the approximations can be improved by increasing the resolution or number of vertices and edges, but also increasing computational cost.

When modeling robots for path planning, two different approximations are usually considered: transformating objects in the Configuration Space [Udupa, 1977] and working on Cartesian Space. The underlying idea of Configuration Space is to represent the robot in an appropiate space, the robot's configuration space, and to map the obstacles in this space. The robot shrink to a point by enlarging the obstacles [Lozano-Pérez & Wesley, 1979]. Some problems can arise with moving obstacles, which must be transformed into the Configuration Space after every movement.

Working in the Cartesian Space, collision is detected by intersections between geometries of robot and obstacles. Roadmap techniques [Nilsson, 1969] and cell-decomposition [Lozano-Pérez, 1981] methods have been applied firstly in Cartesian Space and latter in Configuration Space. Other modeling methods frequently used in path planning are Oct-Trees, used in [Faverjon, 1984] and generalized quad-trees with 2^n trees in [Paden, Mess & Fisher, 1989].

Although the most of research works in collision avoidance and path planning have considered polyhedrical approaches for robot and obstacle modeling, several authors have used other kind of models. [Oommen & Reichstein, 1986] used ellipses to model moving objects and obstacles. [Fink & Wend, 1991] make a distinction between static obstacles modeled in detail with polyhedra and changing obstacles described with spheres. [Khatib, 1986] model objects by envolving n-ellipses and n-cylinders for applying potencial function method. [Johnson & Gilbert, 1985] apply collision avoidance techniques on a 3 degree of freedom manipulator modeled with cylindrical elements.

A new approach has been recently presented in [Tornero, Hamlin & Kelley, 1990], where objects (and links of robot-arms) are approximated by an infinite number of spheres, producing spherical volumes. The distance computation between these models results very fast. A hierarchical structure using spherical objects is presented in [Tornero, Mellado, Hamlin & Kelley, 1992] with reduction in computational cost. Hierarchical structures are suitable to robotic systems because of their natural configuration, as for example in [Henrich, Cheng, Rembold & Dillmann, 1992].

This paper presents a new mathematical representation for modeling robotic systems based on the use of spherical splines. Firstly, hierarchical structure of robotic systems is presented. Next section introduces spherical splines described in funtion of a low number of control spheres. Last section considers an extended hierarchical structure with different levels of accuracy including polyhedra, spherical volumes and spherical splines.

Hierarchical Structure for Robot Modeling

A hierarchical structure is considered for describing the manufacturing and assembly area of the factory where static and mobile robots are working. This area is decomposed in cells, systems, subsystems and elements. Cells are the toppest level in the structure. The

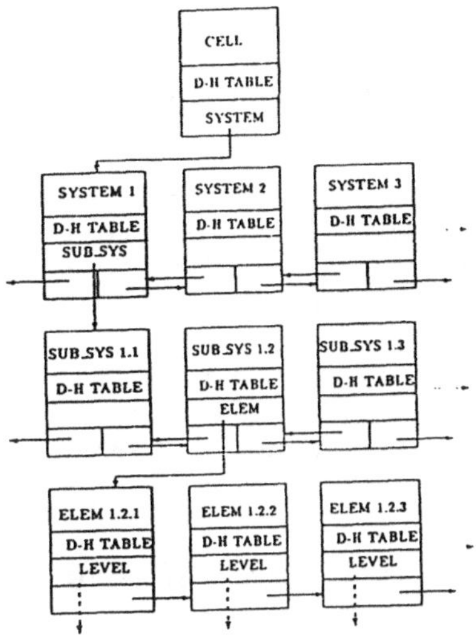

Figure 1: Multi-level hierarchical structure

following levels correspond to systems for describing mobile robots, assembly lines, etc.; subsystems for robot-arms, machine-tools, conveyors, etc.; and finally elements for the robot-links, components of machine-tools, etc. as can be seen in Figure 1.

For robot-arms, a kinematical model based on homogeneous transformation matrices using a modified form of the Denavit-Hartenberg parameters [Denavit, 1955] is used in order to determine the position of the robot links. Characteristic points in each link are described with respect to its local coordinate system. The matrices relate the position of each coordinate frame to the previous one. According to [Craig, 1986], the homogeneous transformation relating frame i to frame $i-1$ is given as follows:

$$\begin{bmatrix} C\theta & -S\theta & 0 & a_{i-1} \\ S\theta C\alpha_{-1} & C\theta C\alpha_{-1} & -S\alpha_{-1} & -S\alpha_{-1}d_i \\ S\theta S\alpha_{-1} & C\theta S\alpha_{-1} & C\alpha_{-1} & C\alpha_{-1}d_i \\ 0 & 0 & 0 & 1 \end{bmatrix} \tag{1}$$

where $C\theta$, $S\theta$, $C\alpha$ and $S\alpha$ stand for $\cos\theta_i$, $\sin\theta_i$, $\cos\alpha_i$ and $\sin\alpha_i$ respectively, $C\theta_{-1}$, $S\theta_{-1}$, $C\alpha_{-1}$ and $S\alpha_{-1}$ stand for $\cos\theta_{i-1}$, $\sin\theta_{i-1}$, $\cos\alpha_{i-1}$ and $\sin\alpha_{i-1}$ respectively and θ_i defines the angular position of joint i for a manipulator with revolute joints, and α_i, a_i, d_i are the constant D-H parameters.

Checking a robotic system for collisions consists of two steps. First, the characteristic points of the volumes in local coordinates are translated into world coordinates based on the forward kinematics. Second, distances between objects are computed using the appropriate algorithms.

For the purpose of collision-detection, the different objects in the world need to be modeled. Each object can be represented by one or several models depending on the accuracy required, giving an extension of the conventional hierarchical structure concept. Generally, the complexity of the models used is directly related to the exactness of the representation obtained. Any attempt to make the model less complex leads to some kind of approximation. There is a trade off depending on how much simplification is acceptable for the accuracy required versus the speed up in the collision detection.

In addition, several objects in one level can be modeled separately, or globally at the toper level. For example, the links of a robot can be modeled at the element level or globally at the subsystem level. Obviously, the volume of the model at a level must contain the volume of the union of models used at lower level. Ususally, elements at the lowest level are formed by means of union of convex polyhedra.

As an example, the hierarchical structure with three levels (system, subsystem and element) based on polyhedra for a robotic system compound of an ABB IRB L6 robot-arm on an ABB IRBT 6000S track motion is shown in Figure 2.

Solid Modeling with Spherical Splines

Splines are well known in Computer Aided Geometric Design [De Boor, 1978], [Bartels, Beatty & Barsky, 1987]. They have been widely used for modeling curves (and surfaces) that must pass exactly through individual points. For a set of points, $P_0, \ldots, P_n$, the spline curve $r(u), u_0 \leq u \leq u_n$ is given by a piecewise curve. Each segment, $r_i(u), u_i \leq u \leq u_{i+1}$, interpolates two of the given points: $r_i(u_i) = P_i, r_i(u_{i+1}) = P_{i+1}$. By derivative constraints, the spline is continous up to the second derivation.

Since a cubic function is the simplest twisted curve, cubic splines, (particularly, natural cubic splines), are the most often used to represent twisted spatial curves. A cubic path segment limited by P_i, P_{i+1} is given by

$$r_i(u) = \sum_{j=0}^{3} a_{ij} u^j, u_i \leq u \leq u_{i+1} \tag{2}$$

where $a_{i0}, \ldots, a_{i3}$ determine the shape, location and size of segment i. The values of a_{ij} are function of $P_0, \ldots, P_n$, which can be used as control points to modify the curve. In this paper, the complete spline is going to be represented by

$$Sp(u) = [r(u), P_0, \ldots, P_n] \tag{3}$$

As splines are parametric formulae, it can be consireded as non-dimensional, that is, when applied on 2D, 3D or d-D points, the result is on 2D, 3D or d-D space respectively.

On the other hand, the topology of the result of appliying splines on points in the Cartesian space depends on the degree of freedom (dof) considered. For example:

- For 1-dof, the result is a curve, represented by Equation (3).
- For 2-dof, the result is a surface, represented by

$$[s(u,v), P_{ij}, i = 0, \ldots, n, j = 0, \ldots, m] \tag{4}$$

- For 3-dof, a volume is obtained, represented by

$$[v(u,v,w), P_{ijk}, i = 0, \ldots, n, j = 0, \ldots, m, k = 0, \ldots, l] \tag{5}$$

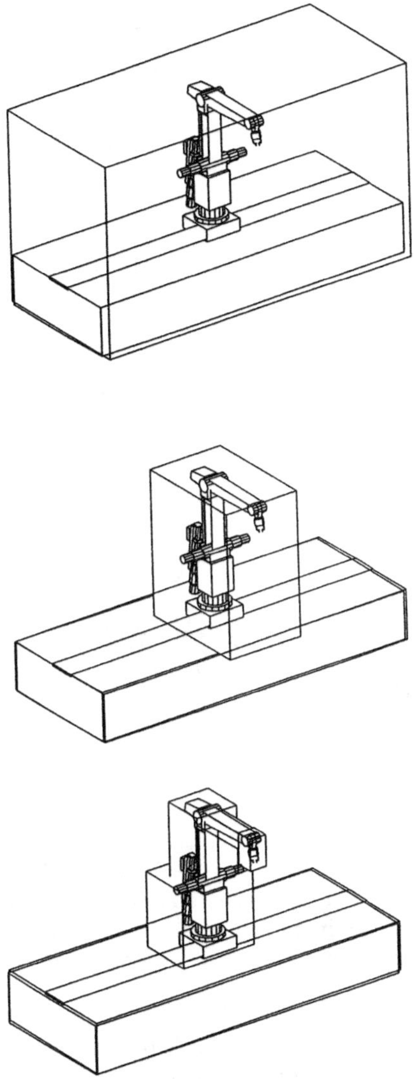

Figure 2: Hierarchical structure for an ABB IRB L6 on an ABB IRBT 6000S: a)System Level; b)Subsystem Level; c)Element Level

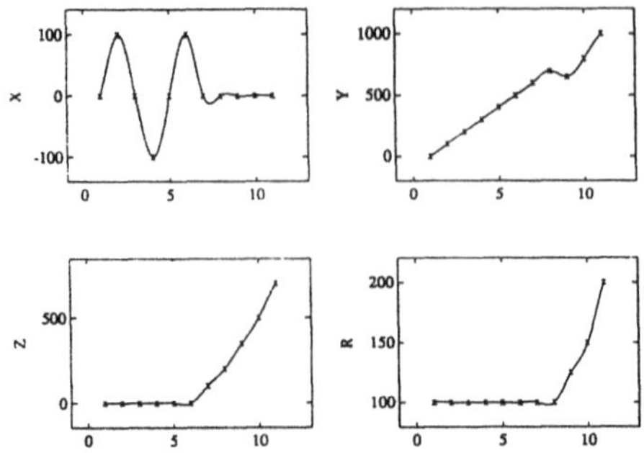

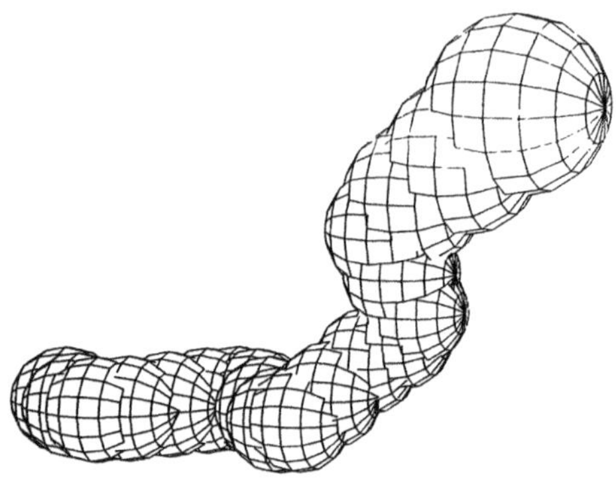

Figure 3: Spherical Spline with 1-dof: a) Center Coordinate and Radious Interpolation with the Use of Splines b) Volume of the Spherical Spline

A *spherical spline* consists on extending the concept of splines applied on points to splines applied on spheres. A sphere is represented as a four dimensional vector, $s = (x, y, z, r)$, where the first three components represent the coordinate of the center of the sphere, c, and the last one its radious r. In this way, the representation is with four dimensional vectors projected into 3D space. The formulae is an extension of Equation (3):

$$SS(u) = [v(u), s_0, \ldots, s_n] \tag{6}$$

where $s_i, i = 0, \ldots, n$ are called control spheres. The spherical spline should not be considered as a sphere whose center is moving along a spline curve, because radious is also involved in the relationship of the spline. This case can be obtained when all the radii of the control spheres are the same. The proper result is the volume of the union of a (infinte) set of spheres. It is obvious that conventional splines are particular cases of the spherical spline (control spheres with null radii). Figure 3 shows how center coordinate and radii are generated from those of the control spheres with the use of splines and the final volume obtained. The shape of a spherical spline can remind snakes, tentacles or trunks of elephants. In fact, spherical splines are specially suitable for flexible and/or deformable objects, or as will be seen below, for articulated chains such as robot-arms.

As the basic element of spherical splines is a volume, volumes are always generated, even for higher dof, opposite to conventional splines, where, as mentioned before, result depends on dof.

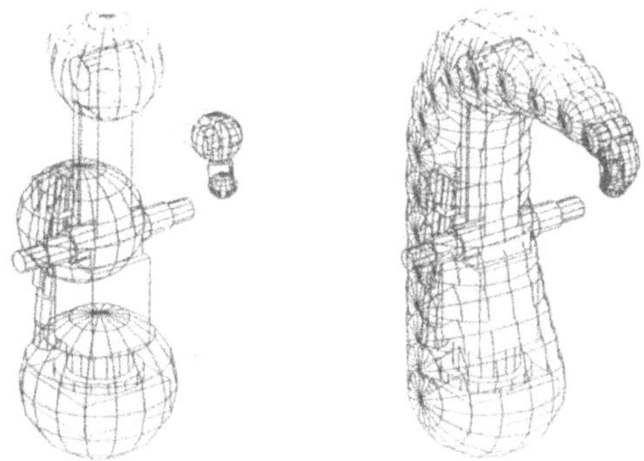

Figure 4: Control Spheres and Spherical Spline with 1-dof for an ABB IRB L6 robot-arm

In conventional splines, when the number of control points are equal to the dof plus one, particular cases are given: for 1-dof, 2 (not equal) control points give a straigh line; for 2-dof, 3 (not co-linear) control points define a plane and for 3-dof, 4 (not co-planar) control points give a tetrahedron. For spherical splines, the following particular cases are given:

- 2 (not equal) spheres define with 1-dof a *bi-sphere*, which can be considered as a spherical cone.
- 3 (not co-linear) spheres define with 2-dof a *tri-sphere*, which can be considered as a spherical plane.
- 4 (not co-planar) spheres define with 3-dof a *tetra-sphere*, which can be considered as a spherical tetrahedron.

These cases are given for linear relationship between control spheres. They have been presented in [Tornero, Hamlin & Kelley, 1990] and considered as spherically-extended polytopes in [Hamlin, Kelley & Tornero, 1992].

Robot Modeling with Spherical Splines

The use of spherical splines as a modeling technique fits adecuately to model a robot-arm at the subsystem level. Robot-arms are usually articulated chains whose joints will be used to define control spheres for defining the spherical spline. If radii are suitably choosen, links between joints will be contained in the volume generated by the spherical spline. Therefore, an enveloping volume of the robot-arm is obtained. Figure 4 shows an ABB IRB L6 robot-arm with 5 control spheres and its model using a spherical spline generated from the control spheres. Note that two robot motors have not been considered for the model. To be included, bigger radii of control spheres could be taken, or a bi-sphere with horizontal axis could be joint to the spherical spline.

When the robot-arm is moving, only new centers of the control spheres involved in the motion must be recomputed, by product of matrices defined by Equation (1), to obtain the new spherical spline.

Splines have been frequently used in robotics to define an end-effector trajectory [Wu & Jou, 1988] [Schütte, Moritz & Neumann, 1991]. Spherical splines can take advantage of this fact: a 2-dof spherical spline will give the swept volume of such a movement. Therefore, only a set of control spheres need to be determined for describing the movement. If this swept volume does not intersect with an static obstacle, the movement is free-collision.

For a system with two robot-arms, the intersection of these 2-dof spherical splines will not imply that robot-arms collide. One robot could have completely passed through the intersection area before the other one has done it, producing no collision. This is because time has not been included. To include time constrains, one additional dimension can be considered.

A *temporary spherical spline* is define as a spherical spline considering time as an additional dimension. For 1-dof spherical spline, its corresponding temporary spherical spline is represented as

$$[[r(u), s_0, \ldots, s_n], t_1, \ldots, t_m] \tag{7}$$

For a fixed t_i, a robot-arm configuration is given by the spherical spline $[r(u), s_0, \ldots, s_n]$. Forcing the robot to move according several configurations at time t_i means a spline interpolation in time space. Only intersections at fixed time t_i must be computed.

To make easier distance computation, spherical splines can be considered as union of spheres. The number of spheres to be considered will depend on the accuracy required, but usually few spheres are enough to obtain a volume which envelopes completely the robot-arm. The problem of finding the shortest distance between two robot-arms modeled with spherical splines, say SS_i and SS_j, can be stated as a minimization problem as follows,

$$d(SS_i, SS_j) = \min_{s_i \in SS_i, s_j \in SS_j} d(s_i, s_j) \tag{8}$$

with

$$d(s_i, s_j) = f\{\mid c_i - c_j \mid - r_i - r_j\} \tag{9}$$

where $f\{x\} = x$ if $x \geq 0$
$= 0$ otherwise

The problem can be expressed in terms of finding two spheres, each belonging to a distinct spherical spline, with the shortest distance between them. A set of sphere-sphere distances can be represented as a mesh where the height means distance and the other two axes mean sphere considered for each robot. Figure 5 shows an example of a mesh with its contour: The flat in the mesh represents a collision area. This mesh was obtained for two ABB IRB L6 modeled as in Figure 4. Considering 20 spheres for each robot (less spheres could be considered), there are 400 sphere-sphere distances to be computed. For an average time of 0.05ms for sphere-sphere distance computation (see [Tornero, Hamlin & Kelley, 1991]) the complete collision detection problem between the two robot-arms can be computed in 20ms.

Spherical splines could also be simplified using a lower number of bi-spheres instead of spheres. For distance computation between bi-spheres, fast geometrical algorithms presented in [Tornero, Hamlin & Kelley, 1990] can be adopted. In [Hamlin, Kelley & Tornero, 1992] this geometrical solution has been formalized as a spherical extension of the polytope model.

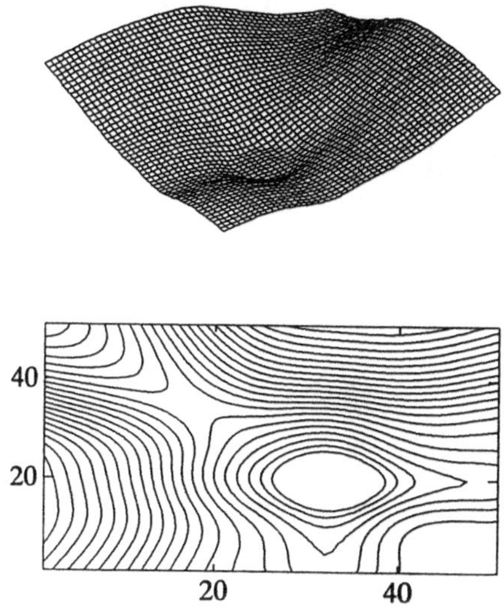

Figure 5: Distances between Spherical Splines: Mesh and its Contour of a Set of Sphere-Sphere Distances Values for two Robots Modeled with Spherical Splines

Spherical splines can be included in the hierarchical structure presented in first section. All the entities in the hierarchical structure are modeled by spherical-volumes. A given object or set of objects can be modeled by different spherical-volumes with different degree of accuracy. For entities at the element level, volumes used will depend on the shapes and dimensions of the objects. Toper entities, such as subsystems, systems and cells, will be modeled taking into account, in addition to shapes and dimensions of the objects included, the configuration at each instant.

This hierarchical structure can be extended by considering different models in accordance with the degree of accuracy required as, for example, spheres, bi-spheres, tri-spheres and spherical splines. Figure 6 shows the ABB IRB L6 robot-arm models with two different degrees of accuracy (sphere and spherical-cone) at subsystem and element levels. Spherical splines can be a model for a different degree of accuaracy in the subsystem level.

The links of the robot-arms are modeled by spherical objects described with respect to their local coordinate systems. The kinematical representation given in Equation (1) is used in order to determine the position of the robot links. Characteristic spheres (control-spheres) in each link are described with respect to its local coordinate system.

Each one of the models at the required level is obtained as a minimization problem: compute minimum volume of considered type which envelope all parts at this level.

Depending on the relative position between entities, local or global models are chosen. For example, the links of a robot can be modeled globally at the subsystem level just as one object or separately at the element level when required.

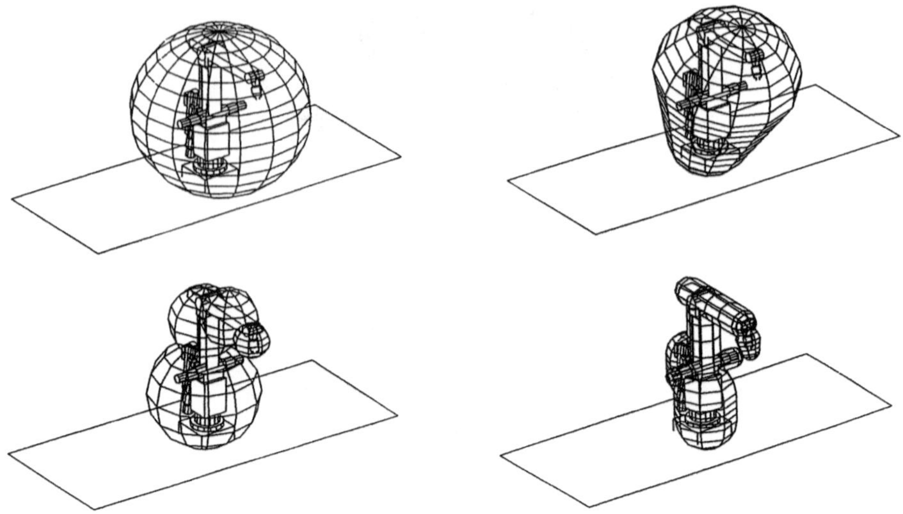

Figure 6: Models at Subsystem and Element Levels for the ABB IRB L6 with two Degrees of Accuracy: a) Spheres; b) Spherical-Cones

For the particular case commented above, the collision-detection procedure starts by checking global models for the robotic system at lowest accuracy (i.e. sphere). If collision is detected, better global models with higher accuracy are considered (i.e. spherical-cones).

When the highest level of accuracy has been reached, local models in the system, describing the subsystems, (robot-arm and motion track) are considered, starting with their lowest accurate representation. If collision is detected, repeat process for lower level, that is element level. The procedure ends when no collision occurs or when local models at highest accuracy have been checked.

The collision-detection procedure manages the multi-level hierarchical structure obtaining reductions in computational time around 90% on average as was shown in [Tornero, Mellado, Hamlin & Kelley, 1992].

Conclusions

This paper has presented an extended hierarchical structure for describing complex robotic systems, with different levels of accuracy, in connection to an efficient distance computation procedure.

A new class of models for robotic modeling, based on the use of splines applied to spheres is introduced. It can be considered as a generalization of spherical volumes. Spherical splines are described in funtion of a low number of control spheres. To modify the robot configuration, only control spheres must be recomputed. Objects based on spherical approximation make easier the development of distance computation algorithms.

The distance computation procedure based on the multi-level hierarchical structure is highly efficient when dealing with complex objects, for which different models with different accuracy can be considered. The reduced time consuming required makes this procedure useful for real-time applications.

References

- Bartels, R.H., Beatty, J.C. & Barsky, B.A., 1987
"An Introduction to Splines for Use in Computer Graphics & Geometric Modeling"
Morgan Kaufmann Publishers.

- Canny, J.F., 1986
"Collision Detection for Moving Polyhedra"
IEEE Transactions on Pattern Analysis and Machine intelligence, vol.PAMI-8, no.2, pp.200-209.

- Craig, J., 1986
"Introduction to Robotics, Mechanics and Control"
Addison-Wesley Publishing Company.

- Denavit, R.H., 1955
"A Kinematic Notation for Lower-Pair Mechanism based on Matrices"
ASME Journal Applied Mechanics., vol.1, no.22.

- De Boor, C., 1978
"A Practical Guide to Splines"
Springer-Verlag.

- Dobkin, D.P. & Kirpatrick, D.G., 1985
"A Linear Algorithm for Determining the Separation of Convex Polyhedra"
Journal of Algorithms 6, pp.381-392.

- Faverjon, B., 1984
"Obstacle Avoidance using an Octree in the Configuration Space of a Manipulator"
IEEE Int. Conf. on Robotics, Atlanta (Georgia), pp.504-512.

- Fink, B. & Wend, H.D., 1991
"Fast Collision-Free Motion-Planning for Robot Manipulators based on Parallelized Algorithms"
Preprints of Symposium on Robot Control (SYROCO), Vienna (Austria), pp.681-686.

- Gilbert, E.G., Johnson, D.W. & Keerthi, S.S., 1988
"A Fast Procedure for Computing the Distance Between Complex Objects in Three-Dimensional Space"
IEEE Journal of Robotics and Automation, vol.4, no.2 pp.193-203.

- Hamlin, G.J., Kelley, R.B., & Tornero, J., 1992
"Efficient Distance Calculation using the Spherically-Extended Polytope (S-tope) Model"
IEEE Int. Conf. on Robotics and Automation, Nice (France), vol.3, pp.2502-2507.

- Henrich, D., Chenng, X., Rembold, U. & Dillmann, R., 1992
  "Fast Distance Computation for On-Line Collision Detection with Multi-Arm Robots"

  IEEE Int. Conf. on Robotics and Automation, Nice (France), vol.3, pp.2514-2519.

- Johnson, D.W. & Gilbert, E.G., 1985
  "Minimum Time Robot Path Planning in the Presence of Obstacles"
  24th Conf. on Decision and Control, Lauderdale (FL), pp.1748-1753.

- Khatib, O. 1986
  "Real-Time Obstacle Avoidance for Manipulators and Mobile Robots"
  The International Journal of Robotics Research, vol.5, no.1, pp.90-98.

- Lin, M.C. & Canny, J.F., 1991
  "A Fast Algorithm for Incremental Distance Calculation"
  IEEE Int. Conf. on Robotics and Automation, vol.2, pp.1008-1014.

- Lozano-Pérez, T. & Wesley, M.A., 1979
  "An Algortihm for Planning Collision-Free Paths among Polyhedral Obstacles"
  Communications of the ACM, 22(10), pp.560-570.

- Lozano-Pérez, T., 1981
  "Automatic Planning of Manipulator Transfer Movements"
  IEEE Transactions on Systems, Man and Cybernetics, SMC-11(10), pp.681-698.

- Nilsson, N.J., 1969
  "A Mobile Automaton: An Application of Artificial Intelligence Techniques"
  Proc. of the 1st Int. Joint Conf. on Artificial Intelligence, Washington D.C., pp.509-520.

- Oommen, B.J. & Reichstein, I., 1986
  "On Translating Ellipses Amidst Elliptic Obstacles"
  IEEE Int. Conf. on Robotics and Automation, San Francisco (California), pp.1755-1760.

- Schütte, H., Moritz, W. & Neumann, R., 1991
  "Analytical Calculation of the Feedforwards up to their Second Derivatives and Realization of an Optimal Spatial Spline Trajectory for a 6-dof Robot"
  Preprints of Symposium on Robot Control (SYROCO), Vienna (Austria), pp.507-512.

- Tornero, J., Hamlin, G.J. & Kelley, R.B., 1990
  "Efficient Distance Functions Using Spherical-Objects and Their Application to the Two-Puma Platform System"
  Tech. Rep. CIRSSE-TR-90-64, Center for Intelligent Robotics Systems for Space Exploration, Rensselaer Polytechnic Institute, Troy (NY).

- Tornero, J., Hamlin, G.J. & Kelley, R.B., 1991
  "Spherical-Object Representation and Fast Distance Computation for Robotics Applications",
  IEEE Int. Conf. on Robotics and Automation, Sacramento (California), vol.2, pp.1602-1608.

- Tornero, J., Mellado, M., Hamlin, G.J. & Kelley, R.B., 1992
"An Extended Hierarchical Robotic System Representation for Industrial Applications"
International Symposium on Industrial Robots (ISIR), Barcelona (Spain).

- Udupa, S. 1977
"Collision Detection and Avoidance in Computer Controlled Manipulators"
Ph.D. Dissertation, Dept. of Electrical Engineering, California Institute of Technology.

- Wu, C.H. & Jou, C.C., 1988
"Design of a Controlled Spatial Curve Trajectory for Robot Manipulators"
27-th Conf. on Decision and Control, (Austin, Texas), pp.161-166.

Chapter 4

Geometric Modeling

Different Combinatorial Models based on the Map Concept for the Representation of Subsets of Cellular Complexes

Hervé Elter, Pascal Lienhardt***
**, **Centre de Recherche en Informatique, **C.N.R.S.*
Université Louis Pasteur, 7 rue René Descartes, 67084 Strasbourg Cedex, France
email : {elter,lienhardt}@dpt-info.u-strasbg.fr

Abstract. N-dimensional chains of maps, or n-chains, is a combinatorial model defined for representing the topology of cellular complexes. In this paper, we deduce from n-chains specialized combinatorial models for the representation of subsets of cellular complexes. Operations for handling these models are deduced from operations defined for handling n-chains. After generalization and systemization, we think that this study can be used in order to define the kernel of a geometric modeler, not based upon a single combinatorial model, but upon a set of combinatorial models. This can be very useful when simultaneously handling different subsets of cellular complexes.

Keywords. Geometric modeling, non-manifold modeling, topological modeling, combinatorial models, cellular complexes, cellular manifolds, chains of maps, generalized maps.

1. Introduction

During the last years, many combinatorial models have been defined for the representation of the topology of *subdivisions* of topological spaces. A subdivision is a partition of the space into cells : vertices, edges, faces, volumes... First, combinatorial models have been defined for Solid Modeling, i.e. for the representation of the topology of subdivisions of compact orientable surfaces, which define the boundaries of solids [AFF,Bau,Män,We85]. Then, other combinatorial models have been studied for the representation of subdivisions of more general spaces : orientable or not orientable surfaces [GuSt], 3-dimensional and n-dimensional manifolds [ArKo,Bri,DoLa,Ede,FePa,Li89,Sob,Spe]), 3-dimensional and n-dimensional cellular complexes, i.e. for non-manifold modeling [ElLi,GCP,LiEl,LuLu,MuHi,RoOC, We86]. Handling general cellular complexes can be very useful for Geometric Modeling constructions [RoOC].

The origins of the work presented in this paper are the two following remarks :

– A combinatorial model defined for representing the topology of general cellular complexes is *often more complex* than a combinatorial model defined for representing the topology of subsets of cellular complexes, i.e. more informations are *explicitly* represented. For instance, cells are not explicitly represented in many models used for the representation of the topology of cellular manifolds [ArKo,Bri,DoLa,GuSt,Li89,Spe]. When the topology of an object of a subset of cellular complexes is represented by a model defined for the representation of the topology of general cellular complexes, informations are often *redundantly* represented.

– Some subsets of cellular complexes are not closed under some construction operations. For instance, non-regularized boolean operations, applied to subdivisions of manifolds, do not ever produce subdivisions of manifolds. When using such operations for constructing subdivisions of manifolds, it can thus be necessary to temporary model more general cellular complexes. Either all subdivisions handled during the construction process are represented by a same general model, and redundancy is not avoided, or *several combinatorial models can be used, according to the subset of cellular complexes* to which the current subdivision belongs. This second solution is investigated in the paper.

N-dimensional chains of maps, or *n-chains*, have been defined for the representation of the topology of n-dimensional cellular complexes [ElLi,LiEl]. In this paper, we study several subsets of cellular complexes, and we *deduce from n-chains specialized models* for the representation of these subsets. This approach presents the following interests :

– There is a rigorous correspondence between each specialized model and the corresponding subset of cellular complexes, i.e. only *valid objects* can be modelled. Moreover, topological properties can be computed on the combinatorial model. Rigor and computation of properties are useful for the *control* of a construction process ;

– All models are deduced from a same general model, and use a *same formalism*. Their definitions are based upon a single type of basic elements, on which applications act. The translation of this formalism into a data structure is direct. For instance, each basic element can be implemented by a record which contains, for each application, a pointer to the record corresponding to its image by this application. Moreover, these models are deduced by applying *very simple mechanisms*. *Conversion operations* between these models are thus easily defined.

– Operations have been defined for handling n-chains. Specialized operations are here defined for handling specialized models deduced from n-chains. All operations can be expressed using the basic operations defined for constructing n-chains. Each subset of cellular complexes is closed under the related set of operations.

Cellular complexes and subsets of cellular complexes are studied in section 2, and the definition of n-chains is also recalled in this section. Specialized models deduced from n-chains are presented in section 3. We conclude in section 4.

2. Cellular complexes and n-chains

In this section, we define cellular complexes and severals subsets of cellular complexes which are considered in section 3. Then, the notion of n-dimensional chains of maps, or n-chains, and the relation between n-chains and the topology of cellular complexes are recalled, but they are not formally detailed : cf. [LiEl].

2.1. Cellular complexes and subsets of cellular complexes

Here, cellular complexes are defined as *simplicial complexes structured into cells*. A *simplicial complex* is a set of *simplices*, i.e. vertices, edges, triangles, tetrahedra..., which satisfy some properties (cf. below). This definition of cellular complexes is based on the fact that, starting from a cellular object which satisfies some properties not detailed here (cf. [Bri] for instance), we can deduce a structured simplicial complex by computing its *barycentric triangulation* : cf. Figure 1-1. This classical idea is employed in [Bri] in order to define cell-tuple structures.

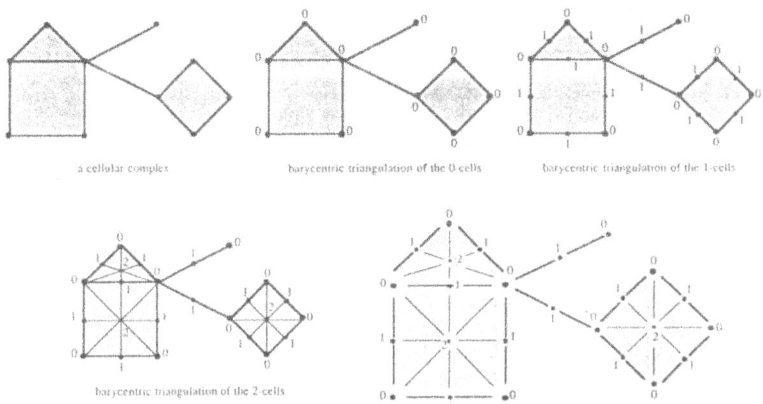

Figure 1-1. Top left, a cellular complex. Its barycentric triangulation is computed : each cell is triangulated by inserting a vertex at its barycenter, whose associated number is the dimension of the cell. Down right, a splitted view of the resulting numbered simplicial complex.

Combinatorial models for the representation of cellular complexes [Bri,Li89,LiEl] can be defined as extensions of combinatorial models defined for representing simplicial complexes [FePa,FrPi]). Though the relation between cellular combinatorial models and cellular complexes is established through simplicial complexes, these models are *cellular* ones, i.e. cells can be any cells, and not only simplices.

Here, we give combinatorial definitions of simplicial and cellular complexes. The relation between these combinatorial objects and geometric objects is not detailed here, since it is well-known in mathematics and intuitive enough [FrPi].

Let $V = \{v_0, ..., v_v\}$ be a finite set of abstract objects called *vertices*. An *n-dimensional simplex* or *n-simplex* is a set of n+1 distinct vertices, $n \geq 0$. An i-simplex $\{v_{i0}, ..., v_{ii}\}$ is an *i-face* of an n-simplex $\{v_0, ..., v_n\}$ if and only if $\{v_0, ..., v_n\} \supset \{v_{i0}, ..., v_{ii}\}$. An *n-dimensional simplicial complex* K is a finite set of 0-, 1-, ..., n-simplices, such that (Figure 1-2) :

– Any face of any simplex of K is a simplex of K ;

– The intersection of two simplices of K is either empty, or it is a simplex of K.

A simplicial complex can be constructed by *adding "closed" simplices*, i.e. a simplex and all its faces, and by *identifying* simplices : Figure 1-2. With a constructive point of view, a *simplicial manifold* can be defined as a simplicial complex constructed by adding "closed" n-simplices and by identifying (n-1)-simplices in such a way that an (n-1)-simplex belongs to the boundaries of at most two n-simplices.

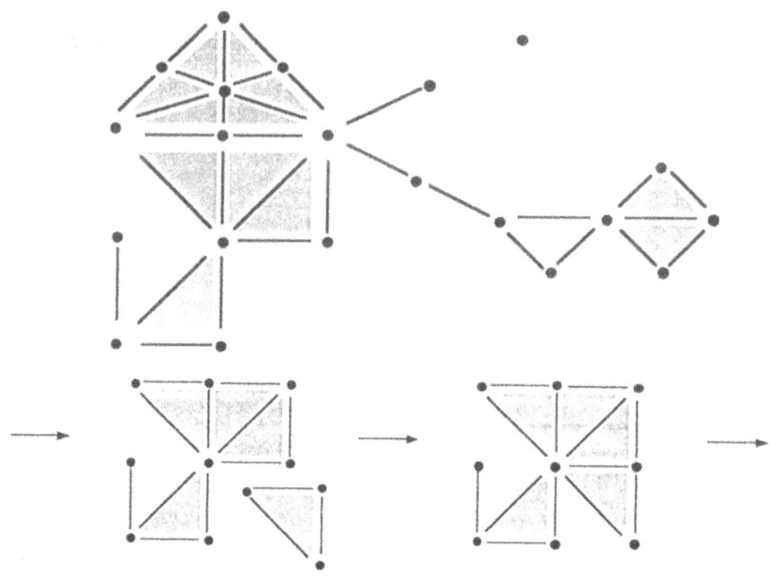

Figure 1-2. Top, a simplicial complex. Down, constructing a simplicial complex.

A *cellular complex* is a simplicial complex such that (Figure 1-1 down right and 1-3) :

- It is *structured by numbering its vertices*. A number n(v) is associated to each vertex v, such that, for any i-simplex $\sigma = \{v_0, ..., v_i\}$ which is not a face of a j-simplex, j > i, the numbers $n(v_0), ..., n(v_i)$ are all distinct, and $0 \leq n(v_0), ..., n(v_i) \leq i$. A simplex incident to vertices numbered $n_0, ..., n_p$ is denoted by $\{n_0, ..., n_p\}$, with $n_0 \leq ... \leq n_p$. An *i-dimensional cell*, or *i-cell*, is the set of all j-simplices $\{n_0, ..., n_{j-1}, i\}$ incident to a same vertex numbered $\{i\}$, $0 \leq j \leq i$;
- Each "closed" cell, i.e. a cell and its boundary, is a *cellular manifold* as defined below.

A cellular complex can be constructed by adding "closed" cells and by identifying cells : Figure 1-3. Classical notions as *boundary* or *star* of a cell, *incidence* and *adjacency* relations between cells can be easily defined on so-defined cellular complexes.

Intuitively, numbering a simplicial complex is the converse operation of barycentric triangulation. It is not possible to define such a structure on any simplicial complex, but it is always possible to subdivide it in order to get a simplicial complex which can be structured into a cellular complex.

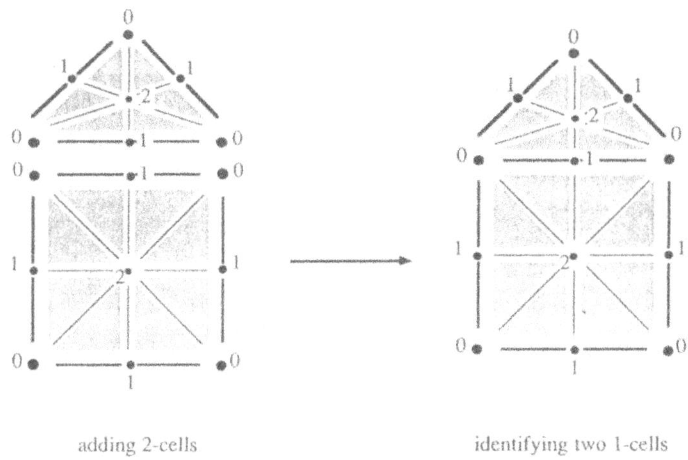

Figure 1-3. Constructing a cellular complex.

This definition of cellular complexes is now *extended* in order to include cellular objects such that *the boundary of a cell may be incomplete* [RoOC] : Figure 1-4. In terms of associated simplicial complexes, that means that simplices exist, such that all their faces do not belong to the complex. Such objects can be constructed by adding "closed" cells, by identifying cells and by removing cells.

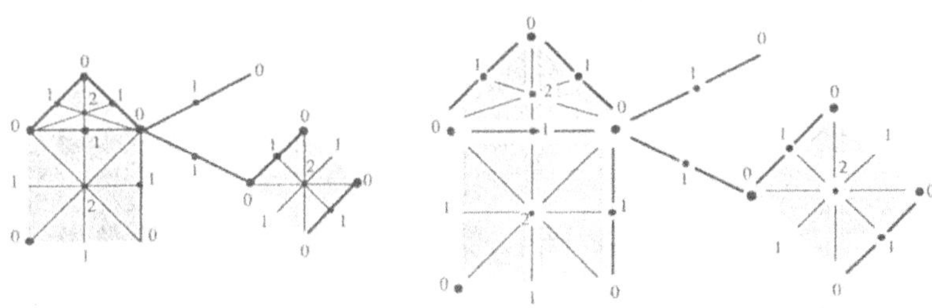

Figure 1-4. Left, a cellular complex where the boundaries of cells are incomplete. Right, a splitted view of this cellular complex.

Starting from so-defined n-dimensional cellular complexes, we study (Figure 1-5) :

- "Closed" cellular complexes, in which the boundary of each cell belongs to the cellular complex : they are cellular complexes as initially defined : Figure 1-1 down right ;
- Homogeneous cellular complexes, in which each i-cell belongs to the boundary of an n-cell, $0 \leq i < n$;
- Regular cellular complexes : with a constructive point of view, regular cellular complexes can be constructed by adding "closed" n-cells, and by identifying (n-1)-cells ;
- Cellular manifolds, which are regular cellular complexes in which an (n-1)-cell belongs to the boundaries of at most two n-cells.

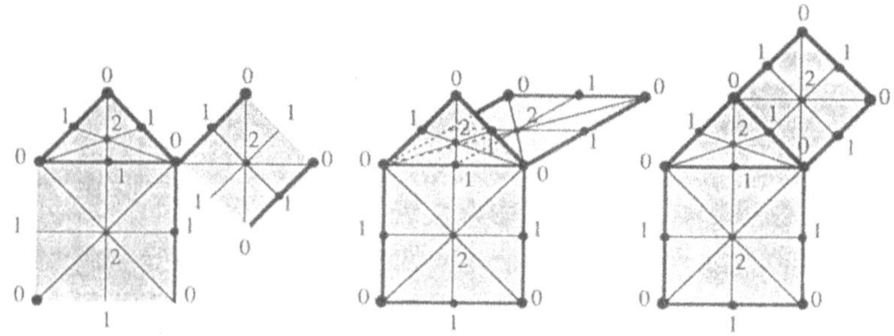

Figure 1-5. Left, an homogeneous cellular complex. Middle, a regular cellular complex. Right, a cellular manifold.

2.2. N-chains

N-chains are defined for the representation of cellular complexes as previously defined. Roughly speaking, a cellular complex is a set of 0-, 1-, ..., n-cells on which a ***boundary*** relation is defined, i.e. each i-cell is associated with the 0-, ..., (i-1)-cells of its boundary. I-cells are modelled by *i-dimensional generalized maps*, or *i-G-maps*, and the boundary relations between i-cells and j-cells are formalized by applications σ_j^i, $0 \leq j < i \leq n$.

Cells. An n-G-map $G = (D, \alpha_0, \alpha_1, ..., \alpha_n)$ is defined by [Li89] (Figure 2-1) :

- D is a finite set of *darts* ;
- α_i is an *involution*, i.e. for each dart d of D, $\alpha_i(\alpha_i(d)) = d\alpha_i\alpha_i = d$;
- For any i, j, $0 \leq i < i+2 \leq j \leq n$, $\alpha_i\alpha_j$ is an involution.

The relation between *n-G-maps and n-dimensional cellular manifolds* is the following. It is well-known that an n-dimensional simplicial manifold can be represented by *only representing n-simplices* and by *associating each n-simplex with at most n+1 n-simplices* which share with it (n-1)-simplices [FePa]. Since simplicial manifolds are here structured by numbering the vertices, an n-simplex is incident to vertices numbered from 0 to n, and an (n-1)-simplex is incident to *vertices whose set of associated numbers is {0, ..., n}-{i}*, $0 \leq i \leq n$. Moreover, a cellular manifold is not constructed by *simply identifying (n-1)-simplices, but (n-1)-cells.*

Each dart of D corresponds to an n-simplex, and conversely. Let σ and τ be two n-simplices, and d^σ, d^τ be the corresponding darts. If σ and τ share an (n-1)-simplex numbered {0, ..., n}-{i}, $d^\sigma\alpha_i = d^\tau$, and $d^\tau\alpha_i = d^\sigma$. α_i is obviously an involution. The fact that $\alpha_i\alpha_n$ is an involution for $0 \leq i < i+2 \leq n$ corresponds to the fact that *(n-1)-cells are identified* during the construction of an n-dimensional cellular manifold : cf. [Li89] and Figure 2-1.

All notions related to n-G-maps are defined through the *orbit* concept : Figure 2-2. The orbit of dart d related to involutions $\alpha_{i0}, \alpha_{i1}, ..., \alpha_{ij}$, $0 \leq i_0 < i_1 < ... < i_j \leq n$ and $j \geq -1$, is the set of all darts which can be reached by applying these involutions in any order, starting from d. If j = n, this orbit is a *connected component* of the n-G-map, since it contains all darts corresponding to n-simplices of a connected component (in its usual meaning) in the associated cellular manifold. If j < n, this orbit corresponds to a (n-j-1)-simplex, since it contains all darts corresponding to n-simplices which share an (n-j-1)-simplex numbered $\{0, ..., n\}-\{i_0, ..., i_j\}$ in the associated cellular manifold. An *i-cell* of an n-G-map is the orbit of a dart for all involutions except α_i : it contains all darts corresponding to n-simplices which share a same 0-simplex numbered $\{i\}$.

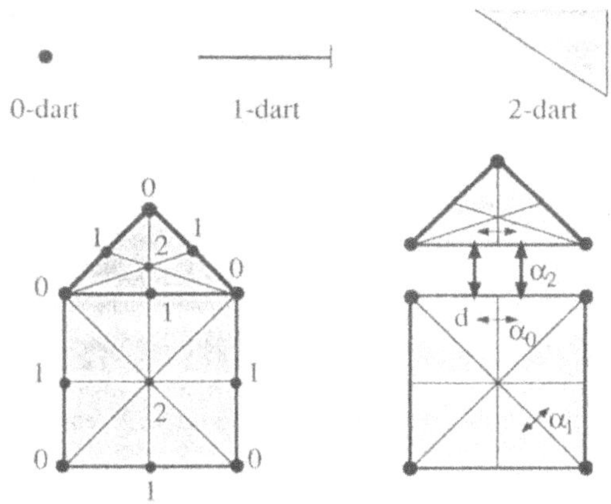

Figure 2-1. Top, graphical representation of darts. Down left, a cellular manifold. Down right, the corresponding 2-G-map (D, α_0, α_1, α_2) where the boundary of each cell is represented. Darts d, $d\alpha_0$, $d\alpha_2$, $d\alpha_0\alpha_2$ are not filled, and $d\alpha_0\alpha_2 = d\alpha_2\alpha_0$.

Let G = (D, α_0, α_1, ..., α_n) be a connected n-G-map, and let ϖ be an application on D, which value is undefined for each dart of D. If α_n is the identity on D, G models a *"closed" n-cell*, (D, α_0, α_1, ..., α_{n-1}, ϖ) models the *open n-cell*, and (D, α_0, α_1, ..., α_{n-1}) models the *boundary* of this cell : cf. Figure 2-2.

Operations. Operations have been defined for handling n-G-maps [BDFL,Duf,Li89] :

- Any traversal of an n-G-map can be performed by applying involutions α_i or compositions of these involutions. For instance, such traversals are needed for computing cells or topological properties as orientability ;
- Any n-G-map can be constructed by adding "closed" n-cells and by identifying (n-1)-cells. Due to the definition of n-cells, adding an n-cell mainly consists in constructing an (n-1)-G-map. Identifying (n-1)-cells is achieved by the sewing operation, which consists in modifying involution α_n on the darts of the (n-1)-cells which are identified, i.e. on orbits for α_0, ..., α_{n-2}.

Boundary relations and n-chains. As mentionned above, a cellular complex can be defined as a set of i-cells on which boundary relations between i-cells and j-cells are defined, for $0 \leq i \leq n$, $0 \leq j < i$. Boundary relations satisfy the properties :

– If a k-cell c_k belongs to the boundary of a j-cell c_j, and if c_j belongs to the boundary of an i-cell c_i, c_k belongs to the boundary of c_i, $0 \leq k < j < i \leq n$;
– In an i-cell, all i-simplices joined through faces opposite to vertices numbered {j+1}, ..., {i-1} share a same j-simplex numbered {0, ..., j}, $0 \leq j < i$;
– There is a correspondence between the numbering of an i-cell and the numbering of the j-cells of its boundary, $0 \leq j < i$: in other words, numbering is invariant under boundary relations.

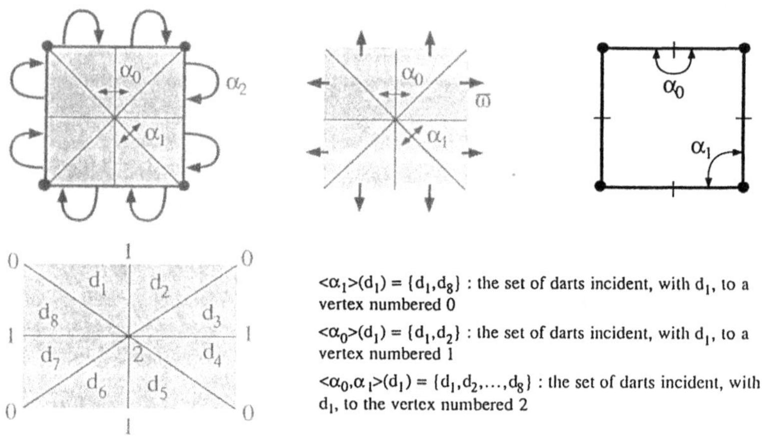

Figure 2-2. Top, 2-G-maps which represent, from left to right, a closed cell, the corresponding open cell and its boundary. Down, a 2-G-map which represents an open cell, and examples of orbits.

Formally, an n-chain $C = ((G^i)_{i=0,\dots,n}, (\sigma^i_j)_{0 \leq j < i \leq n})$ is defined by [ElLi] (Figure 2-3) :

– $G^i = (D^i, \alpha^i_0, \dots, \alpha^i_{i-1}, \alpha^i_i = \varpi)$ is an i-G-map, such that ϖ is an application on D^i which value is undefined for any dart : *G^i models open i-cells* ;

– $(\sigma^i_j)_{j=0,\dots,i-1}$ are applications from D^i to $D^j \cup \{\varepsilon\}$. *Applications σ^i_j model the boundary relation between i-cells and j-cells*. They satisfy for each dart d of D^i :

- Property 1 : if $d\sigma^i_j \neq \varepsilon$, $d\sigma^i_j\sigma^j_k = d\sigma^i_k$, $0 \leq k < j < i$;
- Property 2 : $d\alpha^i_k\sigma^i_j = d\sigma^i_j$, $j+1 \leq k \leq i-1$;
- Property 3 : $d\alpha^i_k\sigma^i_j = d\sigma^i_j$, or $d\alpha^i_k\sigma^i_j = d\sigma^i_j\alpha^j_k$, $0 \leq k < j < i$.

ε is an undefined value. Let d be a dart of D^i. If $d\sigma^i_j = \varepsilon$, the corresponding i-cell is *locally not incident* to a j-cell, else it is.

Operations. The principle of traversal operations is similar to the corresponding operations on n-G-maps : they consist in traversing darts by applying involutions α^i_k and applications σ^i_j. For instance, the boundary of an i-cell can be computed by applying applications σ^i_j to all darts of the i-cell, for $0 \leq j < i$.

Any n-chain can be constructed by applying two basic operations : adding an open i-cell, and joining an open i-cell with the j-cells of its boundary from dimension 0 to j, $0 \leq i \leq n$, $0 \leq j < i$: cf. [ElLi,Elt].

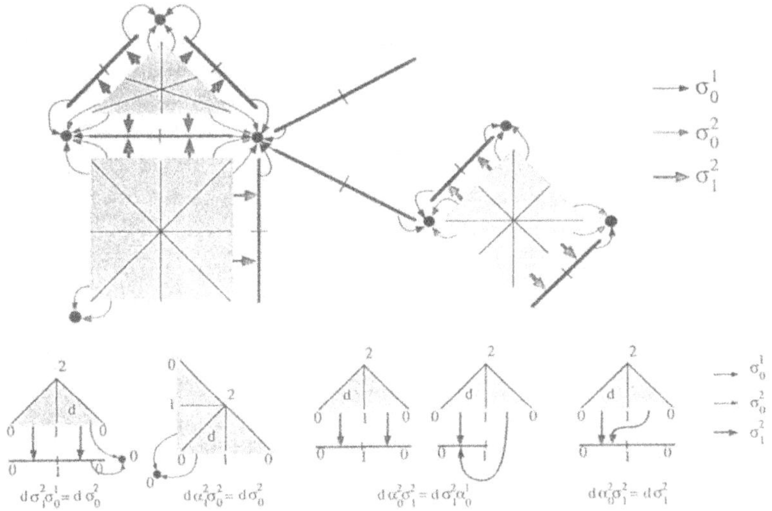

a.. b. c. d. e.

Figure 2-3. Top, a 2-chain which models the cellular complex displayed in Figure 1-4. Down : illustrations of properties : a. property 1 ; b. property 2 ; c., d. and e. property 3.

Implementation. An n-G-map can be easily implemented using records and pointers [BDFL,LI89]. Each dart is implemented by a dart record, which contains n+1 pointers to dart records. Each pointer associates the record with the dart record corresponding to the image of the dart by an involution. Constraints of consistency, necessary for such a data structure implements n-G-maps, are also easily deduced from the definition of n-G-maps. All traversals can be performed by a single algorithm, similar in spirit to a depth-first search traversal in a graph [BDFL]. Construction operations are implemented by operations which modify pointers on dart records, and they are directly deduced from the "adding cell" and sewing operations. This type of implementation can be *easily generalized for n-chains and all models deduced from n-chains* in section 3. It is clear that other types of implementation can be defined [BDFL,Duf].

3. Subsets of cellular complexes and related combinatorial models

Specialized models are deduced from n-chains for the representation of subsets of cellular complexes. In fact, properties of cellular complexes of these subsets are used in order to *reduce the amount of explicit informations* contained in the model. The mechanisms employed for deducing specialized models are classical and simple ones :

– If ϕ, γ and η are applications, such that $\eta = \gamma\phi$, the explicit representation of η can be omitted if ϕ and γ are explicitly represented ;

– If an object is such that it implicitly exists and no application is explicitly represented on it, its explicit representation can be omitted.

These mechanisms, applied to a model, produce an *equivalent* model, i.e. both models correspond to a same subset of cellular complexes. Classical consequences are the followings. It is clear that less space is required for implementing a model in which the amount of informations explicitly represented is reduced. But if implicit informations have to be explicitly handled, they have to be computed, meaning more computing time. Similarly, some operations can be less costly, since less explicit informations have to be modified. On the other hand, if arguments of these operations are implicit, it is possible that they have to be explicitly computed before applying the operation. Examples of these classical consequences are mentioned for combinatorial models deduced from n-chains.

First, these mechanisms are applied to n-G-maps and n-chains ; then, they are applied in order to deduce specialized models for the representation of "closed", homogeneous and regular cellular complexes, i.e. *"closed", homogeneous and regular n-chains.* At last, we show that n-G-maps is a specialized model which can be deduced from regular n-chains for the representation of cellular manifolds.

3.1. Generalized maps

Let $G = (D, \alpha_0, \alpha_1, ..., \alpha_n)$ be an n-G-map, and M be the associated cellular manifold. M can be constructed by adding n-cells and by identifying (n-1)-cells. This corresponds in G to the fact that α_n joins all darts corresponding to n-simplices incident to a same (n-1)-cell, i.e. $\alpha_i\alpha_n$ is an involution for $0 \leq i \leq n-2$: in other words, α_n is an *isomorphism* between two orbits for $\alpha_0, \alpha_1, ..., \alpha_{n-2}$. It is thus *useless to keep the explicit definition of α_n for all darts of these orbits* : it is sufficient to only know that two darts of these orbits are images from each other by α_n : Figure 3-1.

Let d and d' be two darts of these orbits, such that $d\alpha_n = d'$. We define A_n by $dA_n = d'$, $d'A_n = d$, and A_n is undefined for all other darts of the orbits. Conversely, it is possible to extend A_n for all other darts of the orbits in an isomorphism between these orbits, and get the definition of α_n. d and d' are called *representative* darts of the orbits.

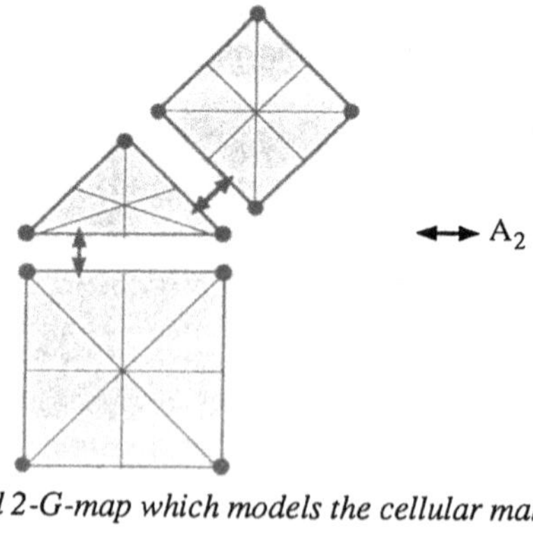

Figure 3-1. A reduced 2-G-map which models the cellular manifold of Figure 1-5.

This can be extended for all involutions α_i such that $i \geq 2$, since $\alpha_j\alpha_i$ is an involution for $0 \leq j \leq i-2$. A main drawback is the fact that *computing orbits in so-reduced n-G-maps is more complex* than in non-reduced n-G-maps [Elt].

3.2. Chains

Properties 1 and 2 satisfied by applications σ of n-chains can be used in order to reduce the amount of explicit informations contained in n-chains.

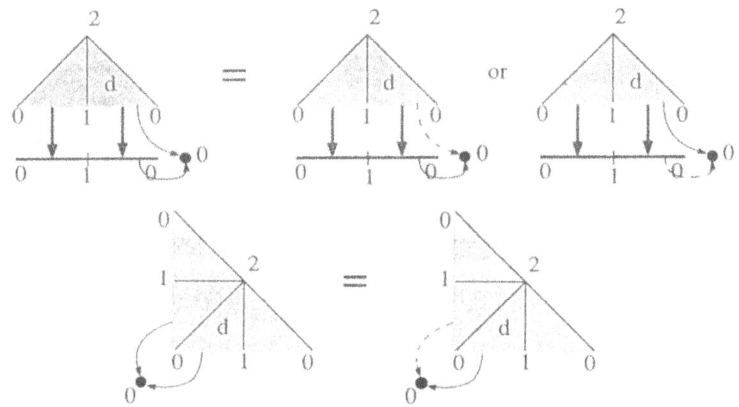

Figure 3-2. Using properties 1 (top) and 2 (down) in order to reduce the amount of explicit inter-cellular relations in 2-chains. Dashed arrows mean that the corresponding relation is not explicitly represented. These relations are not represented at all in the following figures.

Property 1 means that if a k-cell c_k belongs to the boundary of a j-cell c_j, and if c_j belongs to the boundary of an i-cell c_i, c_k belongs to the boundary of c_i, $0 \leq k < j < i \leq n$:

- If the boundary relations between c_i and c_j, c_j and c_k are explicitly represented, it is *useless to explicitly represent the boundary relation between c_i and c_k*. More formally, let d be a dart, such that $d\sigma^i_j \neq \varepsilon$: if σ^i_j and σ^j_k are explicitly represented for d and $d\sigma^i_j$, the explicit representation of σ^i_k for d is useless : Figure 3-2. This property is employed in section 3.3 in order to define a specialized model for representing "closed" cellular complexes ;
- If the boundary relations between c_i and c_j, c_i and c_k are explicitly represented, it is *useless to explicitly represent the boundary relation between c_j and c_k*. More formally, let d be a dart, such that $d\sigma^i_j \neq \varepsilon$: if σ^i_j and σ^i_k are explicitly represented for d, the explicit representation of σ^j_k for $d\sigma^i_j$ is useless : Figure 3-2. This property is employed in section 3.4 in order to define a specialized model for representing homogeneous cellular complexes.

Property 2 means that in an i-cell, all i-simplices joined through faces opposite to vertices numbered {j+1}, ..., {i-1} share a same j-simplex numbered {0, ..., j}, $0 \leq j < i$. The *explicit representation between all i-simplices and the j-simplex is useless*, since the explicit representation between *one* i-simplex and the j-simplex is sufficient. More formally, given a dart d of D^i, it is sufficient to explicitly represent σ_j^i for d, and not for all darts of the orbit of d for involutions α_{j+1}^i, α_{j+2}^i, ... α_{i-1}^i : cf. Figure 3-2. This is employed in section 3 in order to simplify the drawings.

3.3. "Closed" chains

"Closed" cellular complexes. Roughly speaking, "closed" cellular complexes are cellular complexes such that the *boundary of each cell is completely defined* and belongs to the cellular complex. Let C be a "closed" cellular complex, c_k and c_i be a k-cell and an i-cell of C, such that c_k belongs to the boundary of c_i, with $i > k+1$. An (i-1)-cell c_{i-1} of C exists, such that c_k belongs to the boundary of c_{i-1} and c_{i-1} belongs to the boundary of c_i. It is thus useless to represent all boundary relations between cells. Only the *explicit representation of boundary relations between i-cells and (i-1)-cells* is needed, $0 < i \leq n$.

"Closed" n-chains. This corresponds in n-chains to the fact that for any dart d of D^i, $d\sigma_j^i \neq \varepsilon$ for any i, j, $0 \leq j < i \leq n$. A "closed" n-chain $C = ((G^i)_{i=0,\ldots,n}, (\sigma_{i-1}^i)_{0<i\leq n})$ is defined by (Figure 3-3) :

- $G^i = (D^i, \alpha_0^i, \ldots, \alpha_{i-1}^i, \alpha_i^i = \varpi)$ is an i-G-map which models open i-cells ;
- σ_{i-1}^i is an application from D^i to D^{i-1} which satisfy, for any dart d of D^i :
  - Property 4 : $d\alpha_{i-1}^i\sigma_{i-1}^i\sigma_{i-2}^{i-1} = d\sigma_{i-1}^i\sigma_{i-2}^{i-1}$, $0 \leq i-2 < i \leq n$;
  - Property 5 : $d\alpha_k^i\sigma_{i-1}^i = d\sigma_{i-1}^i\alpha_k^{i-1}$ or $d\alpha_k^i\sigma_{i-1}^i = d\sigma_{i-1}^i$, $0 \leq k \leq i-2 < i \leq n$.

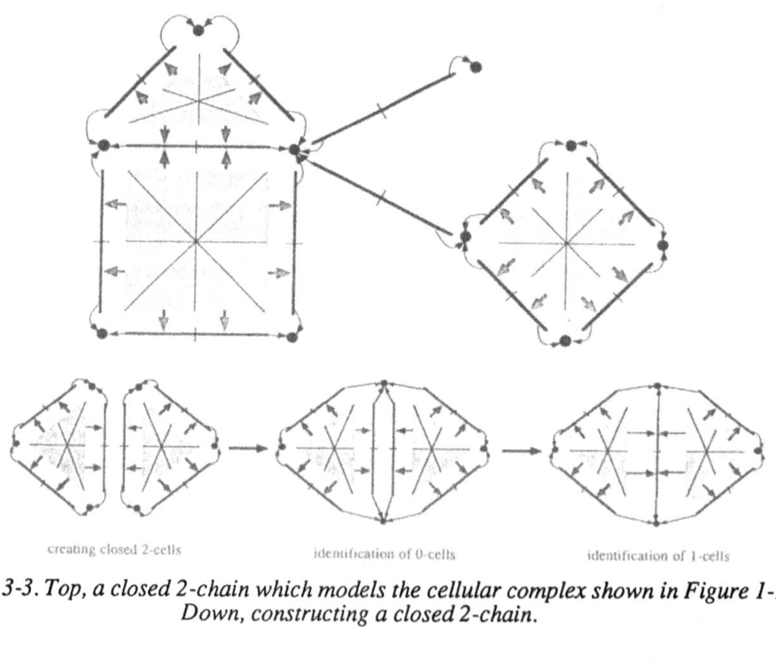

Figure 3-3. Top, a closed 2-chain which models the cellular complex shown in Figure 1-1. Down, constructing a closed 2-chain.

It is possible to compute for any dart d of D^i a dart of the incident j-cell by applying $\sigma_{i-1}^{i}...\sigma_{j}^{j+1}$. Property 4 (resp. property 5) corresponds to properties 1 and 2 (resp. property 3) of n-chains.

Operations. Traversal operations for handling "closed" n-chains are obviously deduced from the corresponding operations on n-chains. For instance, the boundary of an i-cell may be computed incrementally by computing the (i-1)-cells of its boundary by applying σ_{i-1}^{i} to all darts of the i-cell, then the (i-2)-cells of its boundary by applying σ_{i-2}^{i-1} to all darts of the computed (i-1)-cells, and so on.
Two basic operations are defined for constructing any "closed" n-chain : creating a "closed" i-cell, i.e. an i-cell and its boundary, and identifying i-cells : cf. Figure 3-3. They can be defined by the basic operations defined for constructing n-chains. For instance, creating a "closed" cell consists in creating a cell, creating the cells of its boundary, and in joining all these cells together.

3.4. Homogeneous chains

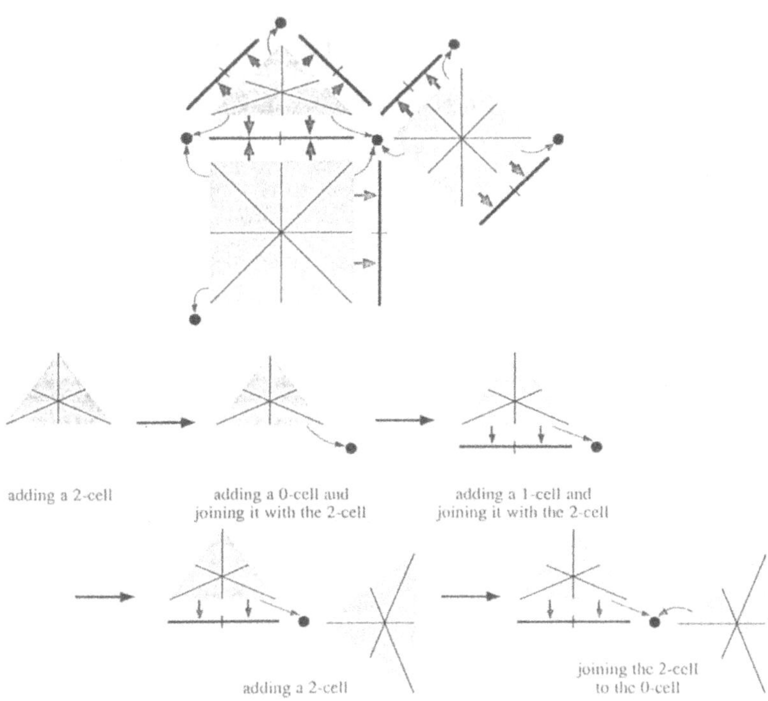

Figure 3.4. Top, an homogeneous 2-chain which models the homogeneous cellular complex drawn in Figure 1-5. Down, constructing an homogeneous 2-chain.

Homogeneous cellular complexes. An n-dimensional homogeneous cellular complex is an n-dimensional cellular complex, such that *each i-cell belongs to the boundary of an n-cell*, 0

$\leq i < n$. The *explicit representation of boundary relations between i-cells and j-cells is useless for $0 \leq j < i < n$*, since they can be deduced from the boundary relations between n-cells and i-cells, and between n-cells and j-cells.

Homogeneous n-chains. This corresponds for n-chains to the fact that for each dart d of D^i, a dart d' of D^n exists, such that $d'\sigma_i^n = d$, for $0 \leq i < n$. An homogeneous n-chain $C = ((G^i)_{i=0,...,n}, (\sigma_i^n)_{i=0,...,n-1})$ is defined by (Figure 3-4) :

- $G^i = (D^i, \alpha_0^i, ..., \alpha_{i-1}^i, \alpha_i^i = \varpi)$ is an i-G-map which models open i-cells ;
- σ_i^n is an application from D^n to $D^i \cup \{\varepsilon\}$. For sake of simplicity, properties satisfied by these applications are not detailed : cf. [Elt].

It is clear that for any dart d of D^i, it is possible to compute a dart of an incident j-cell by computing a dart d' of D^n such that $d'\sigma_i^n = d$, and by applying σ_j^n to d', for $0 \leq j < i < n$.

Operations. Traversal operations are not changed for n-cells : for instance, the boundary of an n-cell can be computed as for n-chains. But it can be necessary to compute applications σ_j^i, $0 \leq j < i < n$ for traversing the other j-cells, for instance when computing the boundary of an i-cell.

An homogeneous n-chain can be constructed by first constructing n-cells, using the operation for creating cells defined for handling n-chains, and second by constructing i-cells of their boundaries and joining the n-cells with these i-cells : cf. Figure 3-4. Note that it may be necessary to compute applications σ_j^i, $0 \leq j < i < n$, when joining an n-cell with an i-cell, in order to check the validity of the resulting n-chain.

3.5. Isomorphic chains

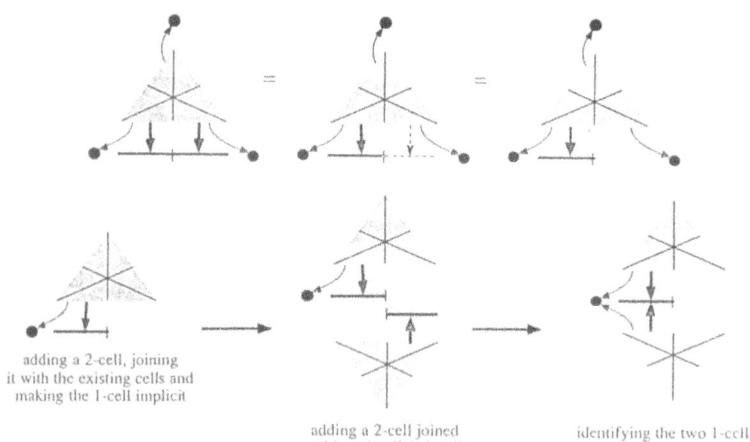

Figure 3-5. Top, making a 1-cell implicit. Down, constructing an isomorphic 2-chain.

Isomorphic cellular complexes. Isomorphic cellular complexes are cellular complexes for which property 3 of cellular complexes is *stronger*. Isomorphic cellular complexes are such that *the "subdivision" of a cell corresponds exactly to the "subdivision" of its boundary* : cf. Figure 2-3-c. Non-isomorphic cellular complexes are in fact objects which are not generally handled in Geometric Modeling : cf. Figures 2-3-d and 2-3-e.

Isomorphic n-chains. Isomorphic n-chains are such that, for each dart d of D^i and for each j, $0 \leq j < i \leq n$, $d\sigma^i_j = \varepsilon$ or σ^i_j is an *isomorphism* between the orbit of d for involutions α^i_0, ..., α^i_{j-1} and the j-cell to which $d\sigma^i_j$ belongs : cf. Figure 2-3-c. As for n-G-maps, it is useless to explicitly represent σ^i_j on all darts of the orbit of d : cf. section 3.1. d and $d\sigma^i_j$ are *representative* darts of their orbits, and we just have to *explicitly represent this "relation" between d and* $d\sigma^i_j$. Moreover, since the j-cell belongs to the boundary of the i-cell, it is *useless to explicitly represent the boundary relations between the j-cell and the k-cells of its boundary*, $0 \leq k < j$, since they can be deduced from the boundary relation between the i-cell and the k-cells. At last, the *explicit representation of all darts of the j-cell is useless*, except for $d\sigma^i_j$, since no applications are explicitly defined on them : cf. Figure 3-5.

Operations. As an example of traversal operations, the boundary of a j-cell may be computed as in n-chains if the j-cell is explicitly represented, else it is necessary to compute an explicitly represented i-cell, $0 \leq j < i \leq n$, such that its boundary contains the j-cell. Since the cells of the boundary of the j-cell belongs to the boundary of the i-cell, it is possible to easily compute the boundary of the j-cell starting from the i-cell. This is similar to the corresponding operation in homogeneous n-chains.
An isomorphic n-chain may be constructed by adding an explicitly represented i-cell, joining an explicitly or implicitly represented j-cell with an i-cell, $0 \leq j < i \leq n$, and making a cell implicit as described above: cf. the definition of isomorphic n-chains and Figure 3-5. Some "technical" problems can arise : for instance, it may be necessary to modify the representative dart of a cell. In fact, these problems can be automatically handled during an interactive construction process.

3.6. "Closed", homogeneous and isomorphic chains

"Closed" homogeneous isomorphic cellular complexes. These cellular complexes simultaneously satisfy the properties of "closed", homogeneous and isomorphic cellular complexes (cf. sections 3.3, 3.4 and 3.5). According to these properties, it is *useless to explicitly represent i-cells*, for $0 \leq i < n$. Only *n-cells are explicitly represented*, the other cells are implicitly represented. The *boundary relations are represented only between n-cells and implicit i-cells*, $0 \leq i < n$.

"Closed", homogeneous and isomorphic n-chains. An i-cell is implicitly represented by a *representative dart*. Applications σ^n_i map representative darts of orbits for α^n_0, ..., α^n_{i-1} to representative darts of i-cells. Formally, such an n-chain is defined by $((D^i)_{i=0,\dots,n-1}, G^n, (\sigma^n_i)_{i=0,\dots,n-1})$, with (Figure 3-6) :

- D^i is a set of darts ; each dart of D^i implicitly represents an i-cell ;
- G^n is an n-G-map which models open n-cells ;
- σ^n_i is an application which maps representative darts of orbits for α^n_0, ..., α^n_{i-1} onto D^i.

Properties satisfied by these applications can be easily deduced from properties 1–3 of n-chains. For instance, let d be the representative dart of an implicit i-cell, and let $d_1, ..., d_p$ be the representative darts of all explicit n-cells, such that $d_q\sigma_i^n = d$, $1 \le q \le p$; for all q, q', $1 \le q, q' \le p$, the orbits of d_q and $d_{q'}$ for $\alpha_0^n, ..., \alpha_{i-1}^n$ are isomorphic to each other.

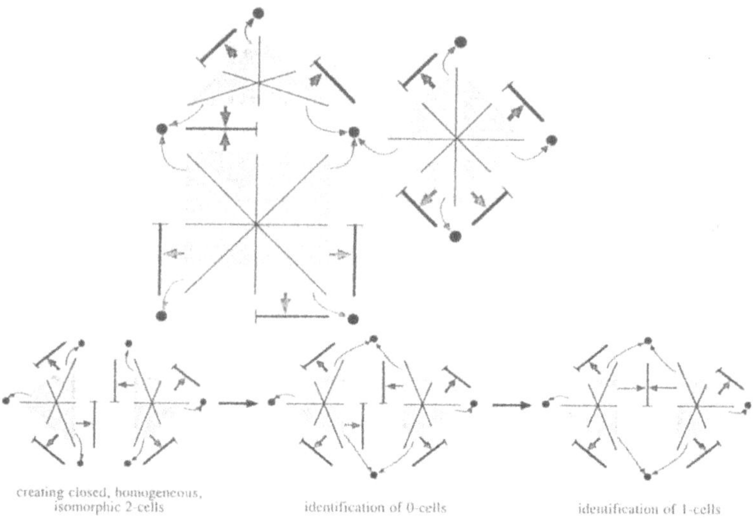

FIgure 3-6. Top, a "closed" homogeneous isomorphic 2-chain. Down, constructing such a 2-chain.

Operations. Traversal operations are similar to those defined for handling isomorphic chains. For instance, the boundary of an n-cell can be computed as in isomorphic n-chains ; the boundary of an i-cell can be computed through the incident n-cells, $0 \le i < n$.
N-chains of this type may be constructed as closed n-chains, by creating closed n-cells and by identifying implicit i-cells, $0 \le i < n$.

3.7. Regular chains

Regular cellular complexes. Regular cellular complexes are "closed" homogeneous isomorphic cellular complexes, which can be *constructed by adding "closed" n-cells and by identifying (n-1)-cells*. The *explicit definition of i-cells is useless*, for $0 \le i < n-1$. Consequently, the *explicit representation of the boundary relations between i-cells and j-cells is also useless*, $j < i$.

Regular n-chains. I-cells are not represented for $0 \le i \le n-2$. (n-1)-cells are implicitly represented by a representative dart. A regular n-chain is defined by $(D^{n-1}, G^n, \sigma_{n-1}^n)$, with (Figure 3-7) :

- D^{n-1} is a set of darts ; each dart implicitly represents an (n-1)-cell ;
- G^n is an n-G-map which models open n-cells ;

– σ_{n-1}^{n} is an application which maps representative darts of orbits for α_0^n, ..., α_{n-2}^n in G^n onto D^{n-1}.

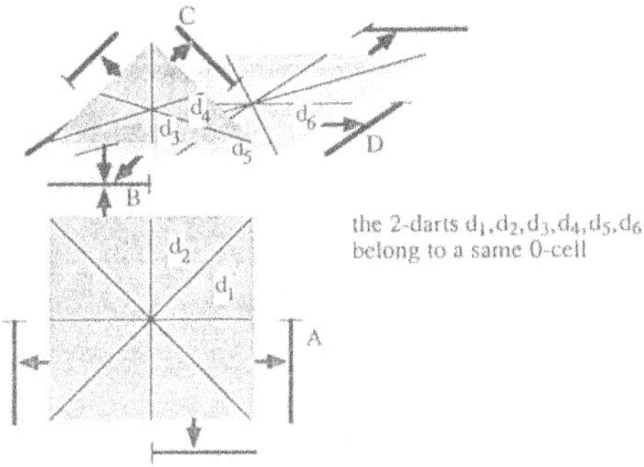

Figure 3-7. A regular 2-chain which models the regular cellular complex of Figure 1-5.

Properties 1–3 of n-chains are implicitly satisfied through the definition iself of regular n-chains. I-cells which are not represented are defined through a notion which is very close to the notion of orbit for n-G-maps. For instance, the 0-cell incident to a dart d of D^n is defined as the set of darts which are reached by applying successively involutions α_1^n, α_2^n, ..., α_{n-1}^n, application σ_{n-1}^n and its "inverse" $(\sigma_{n-1}^n)^{-1}$ in any order : cf. Figure 3-7.

Operations. Traversal operations are here quite different from the corresponding operations defined for handling closed, homogeneous and isomorphic chains, since i-cells are not represented at all for $0 \le i \le n-2$. In fact, traversal operations are closed to traversal operations defined for handling n-G-maps [Elt].
Constructing regular chains is very simple, since it consists in creating n-cells and in joining these cells through σ_{n-1}^n along implicit (n-1)-cells. It is easy to prove that this operation is thus simpler and less costly than the corresponding operation defined for handling general chains.

3.8. G-maps

Cellular manifolds. Cellular manifolds are regular cellular complexes such that each (n-1)-cell belongs to the boundary of at most two n-cells.

Manifold n-chains and n-G-maps. Let $G = (D^{n-1}, G^n, \sigma_{n-1}^n)$ be a regular n-chain which models a cellular manifold. Properties of cellular manifolds correspond to the fact that, for each dart d of D^{n-1}, at most two darts d_1 and d_2 exist in D^n such that $d_1\sigma_{n-1}^n = d_2\sigma_{n-1}^n = d$. We can thus define an application A_n such that $d_1A_n = d_2$, and $d_2A_n = d_1$. A_n is obviously an involution, and d corresponds to the orbit of d_1 or d_2 for A_n.

A manifold n-chain is defined by (G^n, A_n), where $G^n = (D^n, \alpha_0^n, ..., \alpha_{n-1}^n, \varpi)$ is an n-G-map which models open n-cells, and A_n is an involution which maps representative darts of orbits for α_0^n, ..., α_{n-2}^n onto other representative darts of such orbits. This involution can be extended in an isomorphism α_n between orbits for α_0^n, ..., α_{n-2}^n, and the manifold n-chain is obviously equivalent to the n-G-map $(D^n, \alpha_0^n, ..., \alpha_{n-1}^n, \alpha_n)$: cf. Figure 3-8.

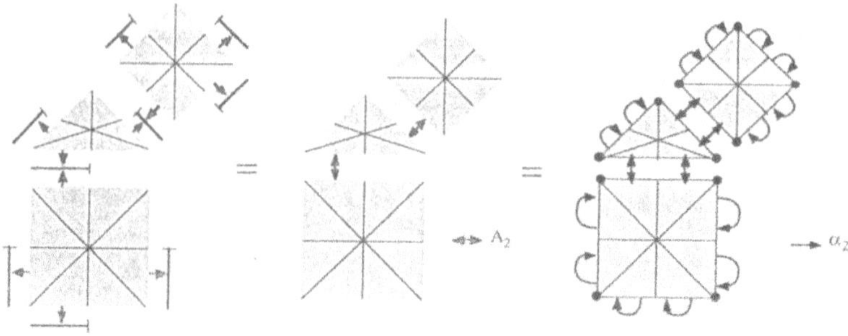

Figure 3-8. From a regular 2-chain which models a cellular manifold to a 2-G-map.

Other specialized models can be defined by a systematic study. For instance *oriented maps* have been defined for representing oriented cellular manifolds [Li89]. [Bri] has proved that *incidence graphs* as defined in [Ede,Sob] are equivalent to cell-tuple structures or n-G-maps for the representation of the topology of cellular manifolds in which no cell exists such that its boundary self-intersects.

4. Conclusion

This paper presents a set of combinatorial models, from n-chains defined for the representation of the topology of cellular complexes, to n-G-maps defined for the representation of the topology of cellular manifolds. There is an exact correspondence between each subset of cellular complexes and the related combinatorial model. Operations are defined for handling each subset of cellular complexes, and this subset is closed under the related operations. Moreover, if it is necessary to temporary model more general cellular complexes during a construction process, conversion operations exist for converting a model into a more general model, and conversely [Elt].

A specialized model corresponds to a subset of n-chains which satisfy some properties. These properties are employed in order to reduce the amount of explicit informations contained in the model. The consequences of such a process are classical and well-known. Less space is required for implementing a specialized model, but more computing time can be needed, e.g. for computing the implicit informations. Nevertheless, it is often not necessary to explicitly handle all informations ; and many construction operations are less costly on specialized models than on general n-chains, since less informations have to be modified. A complementary systemic study is now necessary in order to get precise results about the classical space/time duality in this case.

We are now studying :

– The definition of *other subsets of cellular complexes*, in order to deduce specialized models for their representations ;
– The *implementation of a set of combinatorial models* in the kernel of a geometric modeller. A possible approach is the study of the *algebraic specification* of a set of models, from n-chains to n-G-maps [BDFL,Duf] ;
– The *automatic choice of a model* according to the object which has to be represented and to space/time requirements. The use of a specialized model can be completely tranparent for a user : that means that the user knows that (s)he handles a sub-class of cellular complexes which satisfy some properties, but (s)he does not know the specialized model which is employed for the representation of these cellular complexes if (s)he does not want to ;
– The *automatic generation of combinatorial models*, given the properties of the cellular complexes which have to be represented ;
– The *automatic definition of operations* for a specialized model, according to its properties ;
– The *comparison* between these extensions of the notion of map and other non-manifold models used in Geometric Modeling. It will be an extension of the comparison between n-G-maps and combinatorial models used for the representation of cellular manifolds presented in [Li91].

Acknowledgements

This study has been realized with the financial help of the French P.R.C. Mathématique et Informatique. Great thanks to all members of the Geometric Modeling Group at Strasbourg, and special thanks to Y. Bertrand, J.-F. Dufourd, J. Françon and J.-P. Réveillès for many helpful discussions.

References

[AFF] Ansaldi, S, De Floriani, L, Falcidieno, B (1985) Geometric Modeling of Solid Objects by Using a Face Adjacency Graph Representation *Computer Graphics* 19,3:131–139

[ArKo] Arquès, D, Koch, P (1989) Modélisation de solides par les pavages *Proc. Pixim'89* Paris, France:47–61

[Bau] Baumgart, B (1975) A Polyhedron Representation for Computer Vision *AFIPS Nat. Conf.* 44:589–596

[BDFL] Bertrand, Y, Dufourd, J-F, Françon, J, Lienhardt, P (1993) Algebraic Specification and Development in Geometric Modeling *Proc. TAPSOFT'93* Orsay, France

[Bri] Brisson, E (1989) Representing Geometric Structures in D Dimensions : Topology and Order *Proc. 5th A.C.M. Symposium on Computational Geometry* Saarbrücken, F.R.G.:218–227

[DeSt] Desaulniers, H, Stewart, N.F. (1992) An extension of manifold boundary representation to the r-sets *Transactions on Graphics* 11,1:40–60

[DoLa] Dobkin, D, Laszlo, M (1987) Primitives for the Manipulation of Three-Dimensional Subdivisions *Proc. 3rd Symposium on Computational Geometry* Waterloo, Canada:86–99

[Duf] Dufourd, J-F (1991) An OBJ3 Functional Specification for the Boundary Representation *Proc. 1st ACM Symposium on Solid Modeling Foundations and CAD/CAM Applications* Austin, U.S.A.:61–72

[Ede] Edelsbrunner, H (1987) Algorithms in Computational Geometry *Springer-Verlag* New-York, U.S.A.

[ElLi] Elter, H, Lienhardt, P (1992) Extension of the Notion of Map for the Representation of the Topology of Cellular Complexes *Proc. 4th Canadian Conference on Computational Geometry* St John's, Canada

[Elt] Elter, H (in preparation) Chains of maps and cellular complexes *PhD Thesis* Department of Computer Science, Université Louis Pasteur, Strasbourg, France

[FaRa] Falcidieno, B, Ratto, O (1992) Two-manifold cell-decomposition of r-sets *Proc. Eurographics'92* Cambridge, U.K.:391–404

[FePa] Ferrucci, V, Paoluzzi, A (1991) Extrusion and Boundary Evaluation for Multidimensional Polyhedra *Computer-Aided Design* 23,1:40–50

[FrPi] Fritsch, R, Piccinini, R.A. (1990) Cellular Structures in Topology *Cambridge University Press*

[GuSt] Guibas, L, Stolfi, J (1985) Primitives for the Manipulation of General Subdivisions and the Computation of Voronoï Diagrams *Transactions on Graphics* 4,2:74–123

[GCP] Gursoz, E.L., Young Choi, Prinz, F.B. (1990)Vertex-based representation of non-manifold boundaries *in Geometric Modeling for Product Engineering* M. Wozny, J. Turner and K. Preiss eds., North-Holland

[Li89] Lienhardt, P (1989) Subdivisions of N-Dimensional Spaces and N-Dimensional Generalized Maps *Proc. 5th A.C.M. Symposium on Computational Geometry* Saarbrücken, F.R.G.:228–236

[Li91] Lienhardt, P (1991) Topological Models for Boundary Representation : a Comparison with N-Dimensional Generalized Maps *Computer-Aided Design* 23,1:59–82

[LiEl] Lienhardt, P, Elter, H (1992) Chains of maps : a combinatorial model for the representation of cellular complexes defined as structured simplicial complexes *Submitted*

[LuLu] Luo, Y, Lukacs, G (1991) A boundary representation for form-features and non-manifold solid objects *Proc. 1st ACM Symposium on Solid Modeling Foundations and CAD/CAM Applications* Austin, Texas

[Män] Mäntylä, M (1988) An Introduction to Solid Modeling *Computer Science Press* Rockville, U.S.A.

[MuHi] Murabata, S, Higashi, M (1990) Non-manifold geometric modeling for set operations and surface operations *IFIP/RPI Geometric Modeling Conference* Rensselaerville, N.Y.

[RoOC] Rossignac, J, O'Connor, M (1989) SGC : A Dimension-Independent Model for Pointsets with Internal Structures and Incomplete Boundaries *in Geometric Modeling for Product Engineering* M. Wozny, J. Turner and K. Preiss eds., North-Holland

[Sob] Sobhanpanah, C (1989) Extension of a Boundary Representation Technique for the Description of N-Dimensional Polytopes *Computer and Graphics* 13,1:17–23

[Spe] Spehner, J-C (1991) Merging in Maps and Pavings *Theoretical Computer Science* 86:205–232

[We85] Weiler, K (1985) Edge-Based Data Structures for Solid Modeling in Curved–Surface Environments *Computer Graphics and Applications* 5,1:21–40

[We86] Weiler, K (1986) The Radial-Edge Data Structure : A Topological Representation for Non-Manifold Geometric Boundary Modeling *Proc. IFIP WG 5.2 Working Conference* Rensselaerville, U.S.A., *in Geometric Modeling for CAD Applications* (1988) Elsevier Science:3–36

A Scheme for Single Instance Representation in Hierarchical Assembly Graphs

Ari Rappoport

Institute of Computer Science, The Hebrew University of Jerusalem
Jerusalem 91904, Israel. arir@cs.huji.ac.il

Abstract: The Hierarchical Assembly Graph (HAG) is a common representation method for geometric models. The HAG is a directed acyclic graph. Nodes in the graph represent objects, and arcs denote the sub-part relation between objects. Affine transformations and other instantiation parameters are attached to the arcs. An *instance* of an object in a HAG is defined as a *path* ending at its node. Information common to all instances whose paths end at a given node can be attached to this node. Data associated with a *single* instance cannot be attached to any single node or arc in the graph. Such private data can be stored in an external list, hash table, or a partial expansion of the graph into a tree, but all of these schemes have severe drawbacks in terms of storage, access efficiency, or update efficiency.

In this paper we present a scheme for representing single instances in the assembly graph itself, by identifying an instance with the last node in its path when the only way of reaching the last node is through a unique path starting at the first node of the path. We give an algorithm for *singling* an instance in the graph, i.e. transforming the graph into an equivalent one in which the instance can be identified with a node. We also show how to undo an instance's singling when its private data is no longer needed.

Keywords: Assembly, Hierarchical Assembly Graph (HAG), geometric data structures, single instance representation, singling algorithm.

1 Introduction

One of the most important activities in computer-aided design and computer graphics is the design of geometric models [Hoffmann89, Mäntylä88]. The preferred way of designing a model is hierarchically, by composing objects or parts into more complex objects. A common method of representing such a model is by a hierarchical assembly graph (HAG), a directed acyclic graph in which nodes denote objects and arcs denote the sub-part relation between objects. Geometric and other parameters related to the model can be attached to the nodes or the arcs. The most common example is attaching affine transformations to arcs to denote relative placement and scale of part and sub-part [Braid78].

An important observation regarding the HAG is that internal nodes do not represent *instances* of objects in the final model, but 'generic objects'. The generic object appears in as many instances as there are *paths* leading to it from the root of the graph. The HAG has two notable advantages: space efficiency – information common to all instances generated from the same generic object (including their sub-graphs) is stored only once; and fast update – modification of parameters or information in the generic object is instantaneously reflected in all its instances in the graph.

In many cases it is desired to attach data to a single instance. For example, saying that the color of one chair in a meeting room is different from the default color of the other chairs; or that a specific screw in a machine has a unique mark on top. In this paper we call this type of data *private instance data*, and assume that there is no special structure imposed on it, i.e., private data of one instance is independent of private data that may be attached to other instances. Note that since our graph can be instantiated as a sub-part in another graph, we actually want to associate private data with a sub-path in this other graph (a *sub-instance*).

An instance is specified by a path in the graph, therefore private data cannot be attached to a single node or arc. There are some simple methods for single instance representation, which include an external list or hash table, an expansion of the graph into a tree, and storage of a partial expanded tree having only paths leading to instances with private data. Each of these schemes has disadvantages in terms of storage, access efficiency, or update efficiency, to be described later.

We are not aware of substantial previous work on the issue of single instance representation or even on the representation of assemblies. There is a rich literature on boundary representations (see the textbooks [Hoffmann89, Mäntylä88]) and some work on hierarchical boundary models, e.g. [Floriani88]. Braid [Braid78] and Lee and Gossard [Lee85] describe assembly data structures which are essentially hierarchical assembly graphs. A more complex assembly structure, including symbolic repetitions and recursions, is described in [Emmerik91]. A modeling system using sequences of parameterized transformations is described [Rossignac89], and a method for interactive editing of a node's affine transformation is detailed in [Rossignac90]. None of these papers deals with the general problem of associating private data to single instances in geometric hierarchies. Requicha and Chan [Requicha86] briefly discuss the fact that single instances correspond to paths, in the context of representing features and tolerances in CSG. Rossignac [Rossignac86] presents a technique for storing, at any node, lists to sub-node instances, using a relative path. These references are used to override the inherited attributes for that instance during evaluation. However, usage of private instance data is done by expanding the graph into a tree.

The single instance representation issue is extremely practical, and was probably solved ad-hoc in many systems. The lack of literature may be attributed to the existence of seemingly simple and obvious solutions. However, the issue is important enough to justify a separate discussion, and its elegant and efficient solution is not as simple as first imagined.

This paper has two main contributions. First, we discuss the single instance representation issue in a general manner, defining the problem and the requirements from a solution. We describe numerous obvious solutions and show that they are not efficient in terms of time and space.

Second, we present a scheme for representing single instances in the assembly graph itself, by identifying an instance with the last node in its path when the only way of reaching it is through a unique path from the first node. We give an algorithm for *singling* instances in the graph, i.e., transforming the graph into an equivalent one in which the instance can be identified with a node. We also show how to undo an instance's singling when its private data is no longer needed. The elegance of our scheme lies in that it enables private data to be stored uniformly within the graph itself, in a similar way to storage of common data and transparently to algorithms manipulating the graph.

Section 2 defines the problem and discusses the advantages and disadvantages of the simple solutions. Section 3 presents the singling algorithm and some of its properties, and also shows how to undo the effects of the algorithm in order to delete private instance data once it is not needed.

2 Instances in Hierarchical Assembly Graphs

In this section we motivate and define the problem of representing single instances in hierarchical assembly graphs. We define the terms strict instance and sub-instance, discuss simple solutions to the problem and show that they have severe disadvantages.

2.1 The Hierarchical Assembly Graph (HAG)

A geometric model is best designed hierarchicaly, by composition of simple objects into more complex ones. The natural way of representing such a model is by a directed acyclic graph (DAG) [1]. A node in the graph represents a *generic object*. We denote objects and nodes by capital letters (A, B, N), where 'object A' means the sub-graph rooted at node A. An arc in the graph from node A to node B means that object B is one of the objects used in defining object A. We say that the meaning of the arc is an *instantiation* of the generic object B; we also refer to B as a *sub-object* of A and to A as a *parent* of B. We denote arcs by small letters (e_i, e_k). Note that it is a mistake to denote an arc by the pair of nodes it connects, since there may be several arcs connecting the same two nodes; an object can utilize another object more than once.

Figure 1(a) gives a textual specification of a simple HAG, in the notation described in [Emmerik91]. The same HAG is visualized in Figure 1(b); bold, hatched arcs denote several arcs, numbered in the range shown to their right. Figure 1(c) shows a possible object represented by the HAG.

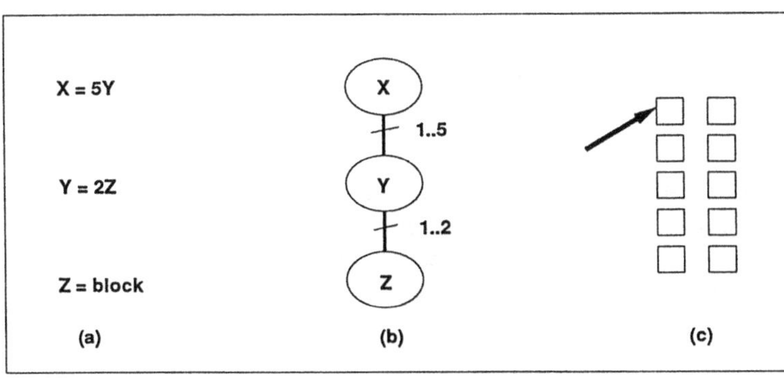

Figure 1: An example of a HAG.

Various parameters of an instantiation are attached to the corresponding arc. One such common parameter is an affine transformation expressing the placement and scale of a sub-object relative to those of its parent. There may be other parameters, for example, if the

[1] By requiring that the graph be acyclic we rule out using it for representing fractal-like objects. This is not a practical limitation. See [Emmerik91] for a description of a system allowing cyclic graphs.

```
Display (Node N) {
    UpdateCurrentColor (Color(N))
    if N is a leaf
        DisplayPrimitive (Geometry(N))
    else
        for each out-going arc e {
            PushGraphicsState()
            MultCurrentTransformation (Transformation(e))
            Display (DestinationNode (e))
            PopGraphicsState()
        }
}
```

Figure 2: A procedure for displaying a model represented by a hierarchical assembly graph.

sub-object is an object parameterized by dimensions then an instantiation can supply the desired dimensions.

As an illustrative example, Figure 2 gives pseudo-code for displaying a model represented in a HAG, assuming: (1) all children of a node are combined with the set union operator, (2) every node has a color attached to it which is inherited by its children, (3) there are display functions available for the geometric primitives in the leaves of the graph.

2.2 Instances

The HAG is a graph and not a tree since one generic object may be instantiated more than once, by different objects or even by the same object. For example, in mechanical engineering there is a large number of standard parts which are commonly utilized in many of the components of a machine. In interior design, the same chair, lamp, or tile can be used many times in a building.

We define a *strict instance* of an object A in the graph as a path in the graph starting from the root and ending in A. When the path can start in any node we say that the path is a *sub-instance*, because it corresponds to a strict instance in the sub-graph rooted at the path's first node. For simplicity, we will refer to both types as an *instance* and use sub- or strict-instance only when the differentiation is needed.

An instance I is denoted by the list of the arcs on its path: $I = (e_1, ..., e_k)$. Note again that it is wrong to denote a path by a list of its nodes since this creates an ambiguity when there is more than a single arc connecting the same two nodes. Note also that an instance's path does not have to end in a leaf.

We say that an instance *contains* another if its path contains the other instance's path. Instances *overlap* if their paths have common arcs.

2.3 Single Instance Representation

Information common to all instances of a node is attached to the node. This information may include the object's basic geometry, default color and material, and so on. It may be desired to associate *private data* to an instance. As examples, pin number 1 in a VLSI chip should be marked by a slight change in geometry; In Figure 1 the block pointed to by the arrow needs to be drawn in a different color. We call the operation of associating private data to an instance I a *singling* of I.

Private instance data cannot be attached to any specific node or arc in the graph since it is associated with a whole path in the graph. A scheme for representing single instances is needed. Note that private instance data should not be lost when the object is instantiated in another object; this is the whole point in hierarchical design. Hence, a requirement from such a scheme is that it be capable of representing sub-instances (corresponding to partial paths), not only strict instances (corresponding to paths from the root).

On the other hand, there is no reason why a single instance representation scheme should be required to represent two overlapping or containing instances. From the point of view of the design process, it is meaningless to associate different private data with two such instances; it only matters which object is instantiated and through which path from the root.

An interesting issue is the way in which instances are specified. In an interactive system, the user is obviously not expected to type in whole paths in the graph. Instead, he/she can graphically select one strict instance and be given the power to step up and down its path to narrow or widen it. An instance may also be the result of querying. For example, instances located in a specified area of space, touching a specified object, or visible from a certain location. Instance specification is an orthogonal issue to the instance representation issue discussed in this paper.

2.4 Simple Solutions: List, Hash Table, Partial Tree and Graph

A very simple scheme for single instance representation is to expand the graph into a tree, in which case private data can be attached to any node because there is only one way of reaching a node. However, this method loses the two main advantages of the graph. Storage efficiency is lost because common instance information will be duplicated. For large models this becomes prohibitive. Update efficiency is damaged because a modification of a generic object is no longer automatically reflected in all of its instances, and requires traversing the tree and performing the modification on every duplicated node.

A second scheme for single instance representation is to store the instances in a separate, external structure, in which a single entity corresponds to a path in the assembly graph. This scheme has the appealing interpretation that the graph stores the common instance information and the other structure stores the differing information.

The external structure can be a simple list whose nodes correspond to paths in the graph. This scheme requires a search in the list each time an instance is visited in the graph, in order to determine whether it has an associated private data. A hash table can be used instead of a list to make the search more efficient, but there are problems in designing efficient hash functions, especially that a key here is of varying length. Another alternative, an array indexed by an instance's serial number, consumes too much space and creates consistency problems when the numbers change as a result of a change in the HAG.

It is possible to combine both schemes by using a *partial tree.* A partial tree is an expansion of the graph into a tree having only the paths leading to instances with private data. Figure 3 shows a HAG (a) and a partial tree singling the sub-instance (5) (b). Arcs 6 and 7, which are not contained in any path leading to sub-instance (5), do not appear in the partial tree. A traversal of the graph is accompanied by a coordinated, synchronized traversal of the tree to identify the existence of private data.

The partial tree scheme is indeed attractive for representing strict instances, but not for sub-instances. Suppose that an object B with private instance data is used a large number of times in an object A, i.e., it appears in many paths in the graph of A. The partial tree will duplicate all of the instances of object B, but all the duplicates will be identical (Figure 3(b)). We see that the partial tree has the same disadvantages as the fully expanded tree in terms of storage and update efficiency.

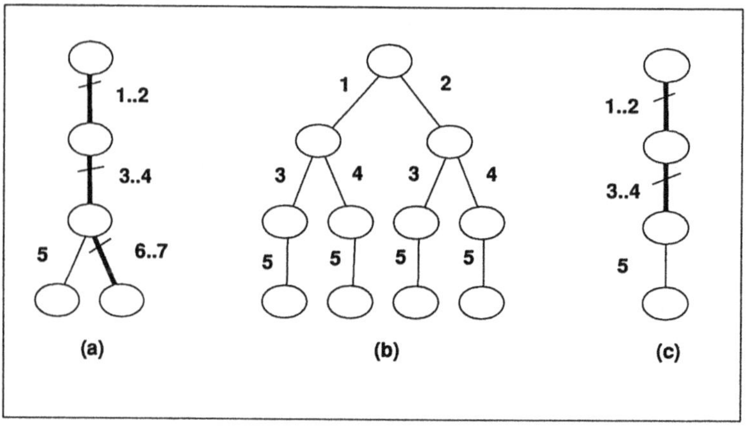

Figure 3: (a) A HAG, (b) a partial tree singling sub-instance (5), (c) a partial graph singling the same instances.

A solution may be to store a *partial graph* instead of a partial tree. In a partial graph, instances are represented by a partial tree rooted at the first node on the instance's path, and all arcs which do not lead to the first node are removed from the graph. Figure 3(c) shows a partial graph singling instance (5); arcs 6 and 7 do not appear, while parts leading to the first node of instance (5), the third node, are stored as a graph. This scheme presents a problem when an instance whose path contains the path of a singled instance is to be singled, with different data (for example, instance $(1,3,5)$ in Figure 3(c)). An algorithm is required for singling instances in partial graphs.

The singling algorithm presented in the next section singles instances in general directed acyclic graphs. As such, it can be used on the partial graph too. However, it can be used directly on the orignial graph, obviating the need for the partial graph.

3 A Scheme for Instance Singling

In this section we present a scheme for singling instances in directed acyclic graphs. The scheme stores instances as equal-status nodes in the graph. We give an algorithm for instance singling and show how to undo its effects.

3.1 General Idea

The main observation on which the scheme is based is that a *path* (hence an instance) can be *identified with its last node*, if and only if the only way of reaching the last node of the path is through a unique path starting from the first node. Another way of phrasing this condition is that there is no *upward ambiguity* when going from the last node up to the first node of the path. Note that the condition has two essential parts: that the only way way of reaching the last node of the path is from the first node, and that there is only one such way. When this condition is fulfilled, the instance's private data can be associated with this node or with the arc directly leading to it (Figure 4).

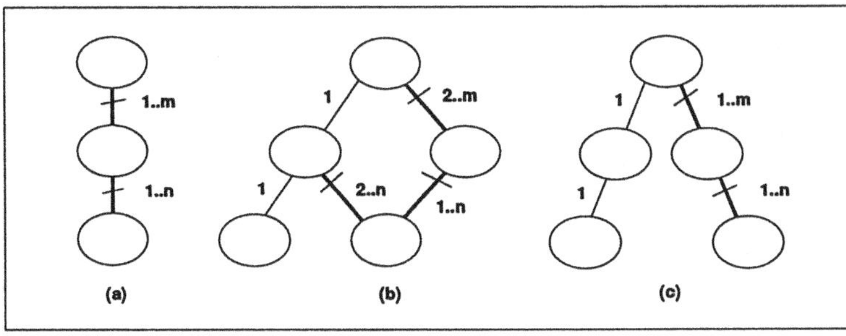

Figure 4: (a) An example of a HAG having three nodes, $m + n$ arcs, $n \times m$ strict instances, and $n \times m + m + n$ instances. No single node or arc can be identified with an instance. (b) The output of the singling algorithm when singling the path $(1,1)$. (c) An erroneous answer in which the path is duplicated.

The graph is transformed to achieve this situation. The transformation process should be careful to preserve all original paths in the graphs, not to duplicate paths, and not to add new paths. The graph in Figure 4(a) can be transformed as in (c) to single the path $(1,1)$. However, the old path still exists in the graph. A correct solution is shown in (b), where all and only original paths are present and no path is duplicated.

Our scheme has the advantage that it is completely transparent to graph traversal algorithms; they operate as they ordinarily would, not knowing or caring whether the data they find associated with a node is private or not. There is no need to search for instances in external structures or to coordinate the traversal with one on a partial tree or a partial graph. For example, in Figure 2, a node's color is used to update the current display color. The procedure is used with no change when the color belongs to a single instance.

Every operation that could be performed on the original graph can also be performed on the transformed graph. In particular, a different instance can now be singled, so that a singled graph represents the whole assembly, including private data of many single instances.

3.2 A Singling Algorithm

Denote the path of the instance I to be singled by $I = (e_j, ..., e_k), 0 < j \leq k$ and the nodes it passes through by $(N_{j-1}, ..., N_k)$. $InArcs(N), OutArcs(N)$ denote the sets of in-coming and out-going arcs of node N, respectively. C_{i+1} (C for 'children') denotes the arcs in $OutArcs(N_i)$ which connect to nodes other than N_{i+1}. P_i (P for 'parents') denotes the arcs in $InArcs(N_i)$ which arrive from nodes other than N_{i-1}. E_i denotes the set of arcs in $OutArcs(N_i)$ connecting N_{i-1} to N_i, other than e_i. Pseudo-C code of the algorithm is shown in Figure 5, and Figure 6 shows the main transformation performed.

The algorithm performs $k - j + 1$ stages, such that stage i deals with $N_i, i = k..j$. Note that the order is bottom-up. At stage i, if e_i is not the only in-coming arc to node N_i the node is split into two nodes N_i^I and N_i^O, I for 'instance' and O for 'other'. The out-going arcs of node N_i are duplicated and each new node receives a copy, except that the copy of e_{i+1} coming out of N_i^O does not connect to N_i^I but to N_{i+1}^O. The only in-coming arc of N_i^I is e_i, to assure

```
Singling (Graph G, Path I, Data data) {
    let the arcs on I be e_j, ..., e_k
    let the nodes on I be N_{j-1}, ..., N_k

    for i = k to j {
        if there is only one arc in InArcs(N_i)
            continue
        replace N_i by two nodes N_i^I and N_i^O
        OutArcs(N_i^I) = OutArcs(N_i)
        OutArcs(N_i^O) = OutArcs(N_i), with e_{i+1} connecting to N_{i+1}^O instead of N_{i+1}^I
        InArcs(N_i^I) = e_i
        InArcs(N_i^O) = InArcs(N_i) - e_i
    }
    attach data to node N_k^I or its in-coming arc
}
```

Figure 5: Pseudo-C code for the singling algorithm.

upward disambiguity (the condition necessary for identifying the new node N_k^I with the singled instance). All other in-coming arcs to N_i become in-coming arcs of N_i^O.

Note that only the arcs C_{i+1} are duplicated, not the whole sub-graph descending from them; both sets of arcs denoted by C_{i+1} in Figure 6(b) lead to the same nodes.

To prove that the algorithm is correct, we have to prove (1) instance I can be identified with node N_k^I; (2) the new graph is equivalent to the original one in terms of their instances. For (1), all we need is the following invariant, whose proof is easy:

- After stage i there is a node N_i^I which has a unique in-coming arc e_i, reaching from N_{i-1}, and (among others) an out-going arc e_{i+1}, connecting to N_{i+1}^I.

As a result, after stage i there exist two nodes N_k^I and N_{i-1} connected by a unique path $N_{i-1}, N_i^I, ..., N_k^I$. This path can be denoted by the names of its nodes because there is no ambiguity – only a single arc connects each pair of nodes. After the last stage, in which $i = j$, we can safely identify the original path $(e_j, ..., e_k)$ with node N_k^I.

Instance-equivalence of the new and original graphs means (1) all previously existing paths still exist (2) they exist not more than once (3) no new paths are added. To verify these conditions we enumerate the paths in the graphs explicitly. Before stage i there are 10 types of paths in the graph: paths that do not pass through N_i, and nine types of paths which pass through it in the following ways:

$$(e_i, e_{i+1}), (e_i, e_{i+1}^O), (e_i, c), (e_i^O, e_{i+1}), (e_i^O, e_{i+1}^O), (e_i^O, c), (p, e_{i+1}), (p, e_{i+1}^O), (p, c)$$

where $e_i^O \in E_i, e_{i+1}^O \in E_{i+1}, c \in C_{i+1}, p \in P_i$. From the formulation of the algorithm it is clear that if we identify the new nodes N_i^I and N_i^O with the original N_i for the purpose of path equivalence, the paths above are exactly those which are present in the graph after stage i, and that none of them is duplicated. We conclude that the transformed graph possesses exactly the same instances as the original graph. Hence the algorithm is correct.

The time complexity of the algorithm is $O(\sum_i |OutArcs(N_i)|)$, because the work performed at stage i is dominated by the duplication of out-going arcs. Regarding space complexity, in the worst case the graph's storage may double, because the space occupied by $\sum_i OutArcs(N_i)$ may turn out to be on the same order as that of the whole graph.

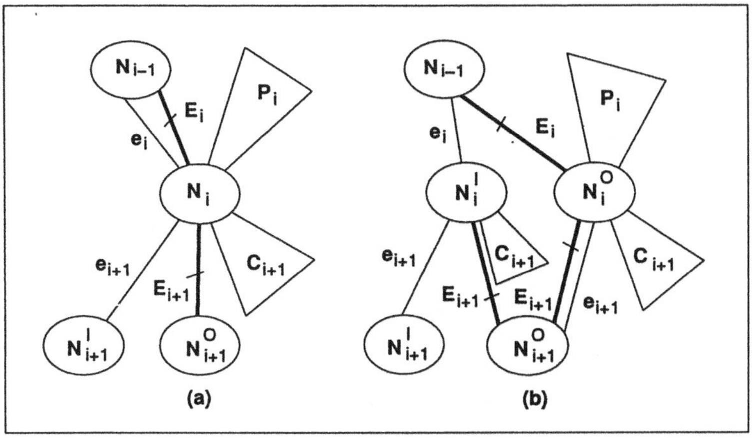

Figure 6: The situation in (a) is replaced by that in (b). Node N_i is split into two nodes, N_i^I, which belongs to the path to the singled node, and N_i^O, for all the other paths.

The algorithm is optimal in terms of the number of nodes in the transformed graph, since a node is split into two if and only if there is more than one in-coming arc, and in this case the node must be split in order to prevent upward ambiguity.

Finally, note that consecutive singling of each and every strict instance in the graph will result in an expansion of the graph into a tree, since at the end no node will have more than a single in-coming arc.

3.3 Deleting Singled Instances

In a dynamic or interactive environment it is necessary to provide a way of deleting singled instances once their private data is no longer needed, in order to optimize the graph's storage and the efficiency of graph traversal algorithms. Deleting singled instances is done by reversing the process shown in Figure 6, and it requires two small modifications to the singling algorithm: twin node connection and arc counting.

Twin node connection means linking the two nodes N_i^I and N_i^O which result from splitting node N_i at stage i. This symbolic link is essential when searching for two nodes to join to a single node.

Arc counting means keeping a counter on every arc e_i participating in a singled path. The counter counts the number of singled paths using this arc. Arc counting is necessary since singling of some instance J may utilize arcs created for singling of a previous instance I. If those arcs were to be joined automatically when deleting instance I, instance J may not be singled anymore, which would impair the equivalence of the transformed and the original graphs.

In Figure 7, singling instance (1) in the simple graph (a) results in the graph (b). Singling instance (2) does not change the graph. Suppose it is now desired to cancel the singling of instance (1). If this is done by joining the two nodes B_1^I and B_2^I, instance (2) is not singled anymore. A counter on arc 2 will show that it is used for singling some instance hence the node it leads to (B_2^I) cannot be joined to another.

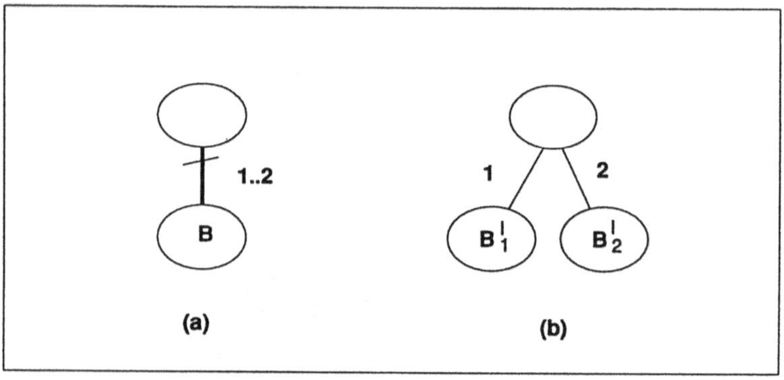

Figure 7: An example for the necessity of arc counters.

When deleting singled instances, the process of joining two twin nodes together back into one node is only done when all counters in all in-coming arcs have a value of 1. Otherwise, no joining is done and the only operation done in stage i is decrementing the counter on arc e_i.

4 Discussion

We have motivated and defined the problem of associating private data with single instances in hierarchical assembly graphs (HAGs). An algorithm for singling instances was presented. The algorithm is suited for singling instances corresponding to arbitrary paths in the graph, not necessarily paths starting at the root (strict instances) or ending at a leaf.

The singling algorithm can be used in two ways to solve the above problem. First, it can be used on the original HAG itself. Second, it can be used on a partial graph, as defined in Section 2. The latter option is appealing since the common and private data of instances are clearly separated into two structures. The former is more elegant since the whole singling process is completely transparent to algorithms manipulating the HAG. These operate with no modification since singled nodes are similar in structure and functionality to the other nodes in the graph.

In this paper we have not dealt with updating singled instances after modification of the graph itself (i.e., when adding or deleting nodes or arcs). The arc counters (Section 3) can be easily used to notify the user that an editing operation invalidates an instance's private data; meaningful automatic treatment of this case is left to future reports.

Another topic for future work is how to organize the private data when imposed on it there is a structure different from the structure of the assembly graph (for example, if color inheritance of instances depends upon their location and not upon their sub-part hierarchy). It seems that in this situation an external structure cannot be avoided.

Acknowledgements

I thank Maarten van Emmerik for an enjoyable and productive collaboration, in which the issue of single instance manipulation first arose. I thank Jarek Rossignac, Eyal Piassetsky and Martti Mäntylä for discussions and correspondence improving my understanding of the issue.

References

[Braid78] Braid, I.C., On storing and changing shape information, *Computer Graphics*, 12(3):252-256, 1978 (SIGGRAPH '78).

[Emmerik91] van Emmerik, M.J.G.M., Rappoport, A., Rossignac, J., ABCSG: a hypertext approach for interactive design of solid models, assemblies and patterns, to be published in *The Visual Computer*, 1991.

[Floriani88] de Floriani, L., Falcidieno, B., A hierarchical boundary model for solid object representation, *ACM Transactions On Graphics* 7(1):42-60, 1988.

[Hoffmann89] Hoffmann, C., Geometric and Solid Modling: an Introduction, Morgan Kaufmann, 1989.

[Lee85] Lee, K., Gossard, D.C., A hierarchical data structure for representing assemblies: part 1, *Computer-Aided Design* 17(1):15-19, 1985.

[Mäntylä88] Mäntylä, M., An Introduction to Solid Modeling, Computer Science Press, Maryland, 1988.

[Requicha86] Requicha, A.G., Chan, S.C., Representation of geometric features, tolerances, and attributes in solid modelers based on constructive geometry, *IEEE J. Robotics and Automation*, 2(3):156-166, 1986.

[Rossignac86] Rossignac, J.R., Constraints in constructive solid geometry, *ACM Symposium on Interactive 3D Graphics*, ACM Press, 1986, pp. 93-110.

[Rossignac89] Rossignac J.R., Borrel P., Nackman L.R., Interactive design with sequences of parameterized transformations, in: Intelligent CAD Systems 2: Implementational Issues, Springer-Verlag, pp. 93-125, 1989.

[Rossignac90] Rossignac, J.R., Borrel, P., Kim, J., Mastrogiulio, J., BIERPAC: basic interactive editing for the relative positions of assembly components, IBM Research report, RC 17339 (#76615), October 1990.

Towards the Integration of Solid and Surface Modeling by Means of Pseudo-Boolean Operators

Luca Mari, Cristiano Sacchi
CNR-IMU, CAD Group
Via Ampere 56, 20131 Milano, Italy

Abstract: *In geometric modeling two main technologies have been successful and are continuing their development: solid modeling and surface modeling. These techniques are still used separately while being complementary in their advantages: a solid modeler is able to describe objects with a clear distinction between inner and outer parts, whereas a surface modeler is better suited in the description of free form objects, but leaves the model validity to the user responsibility. The integration of the two technologies is therefore an important topic of the current research in the field.*
This paper presents a new technique to perform booleans with trimmed curves and surfaces; such a technique is not based on point set classification, but exploits geometry orientation; this makes it able to deal with non closed topologies, thus extending the classical concept of boolean operators. According to this approach several valid operators can be defined, which behave like booleans in the case of closed topologies but differently with non closed ones.

1. Introduction

In geometric modeling two main technologies have been successful and are continuing their development: solid modeling and surface modeling. These techniques are still used separately while being complementary in their advantages: a solid modeler is able to describe objects with a clear distinction between inner and outer parts, whereas a surface modeler is better suited in the description of free form objects, but leaves the model validity to the user responsibility. The integration of the two technologies is then an important topic of the current research in the field.
Some works have been published about non-manifold topology [WEI86, MAS90], and some others covered the topic of the integration of surfaces and solids [VAR84]. A modeler that performs booleans on solids bounded by trimmed surfaces is described in [CAS87]; another approach to the same problem is presented in [FAR87]. Both approaches are based on point set classification. This is a clear limitation when unbounded topology is allowed by the representation scheme, a typical situation in surface modelers. An interesting approach toward the integration of solids and surfaces was published by Chiyokura [CHI91], but further

research is needed to define a robust theoretical background about "open-sets". A system which handles solids and surfaces in a homogeneous way is known to the authors [XOX90]; unfortunately no detailed description of the underlying approach has ever been published.
This paper presents a new technique to perform booleans with trimmed curves and surfaces. Such operators, here called *pseudo-booleans*, are not based on point set classification, but exploit geometry orientation; this allows to deal with non closed topologies, thus extending the classical concept of boolean operators. Moreover, it is pointed out that according to this approach several valid operators can be defined, which behave as booleans in the case of closed topologies and can be applied also to non closed ones.
Since the point set classification can be here avoided in most cases, a modeler using the presented technique is faster and more robust than a classical one in computing booleans; indeed, it has to perform few vector operations, where a classification of points against solids is usually in order.
Furthermore, this approach makes easier the surface trimming; indeed, by just indicating the surface to be trimmed and the trimming surface, the modeler is able to decide which parts to retain on the basis of the surface orientation.

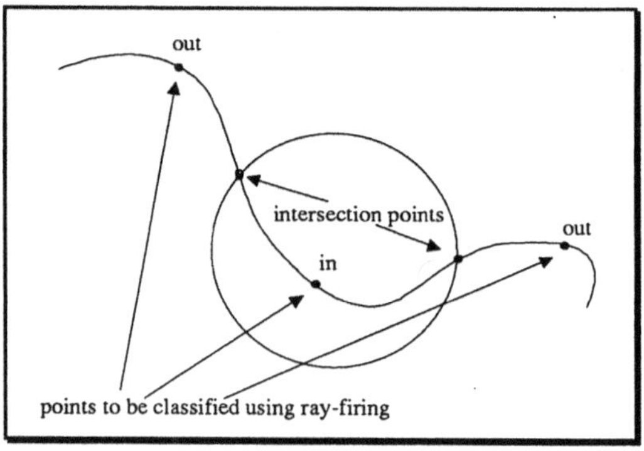

Fig. 1 - Curve classification via ray-firing.

The approach also allows to create bounded solids from sets of surfaces, no user intervention being needed during the process. Free form geometries can be used during the first phases of the design, so that solids from surfaces can be automatically generated for a more accurate analysis of the design.

2. General description

The basic assumption of point set classification is that a solid divides the space in three parts: interior, exterior, and boundary. Then a point set classification algorithm typically returns either *in*, *out*, or *on*, depending on the location of the given point with respect to the solid.

In the case of BRep models, the most effective point set classification algorithm is called *ray-firing*. A ray is fired in a random direction from the point to be classified, counting the number of intersections with the boundary of the solid. For even numbers the point is outside, and for odd ones it is inside, whereas the point is classified as *on* if lying on a face.
When the element to be classified is a curve, the traditional approach is to split the curve at any intersection with the boundary and to classify its resulting parts, such a classification simply consisting in the point set classification of a point lying on each curve part (Fig. 1).
It can be noted that a curve intersecting the solid changes its "local status" when passing from the interior of the solid to the exterior, or vice versa (Fig. 2).

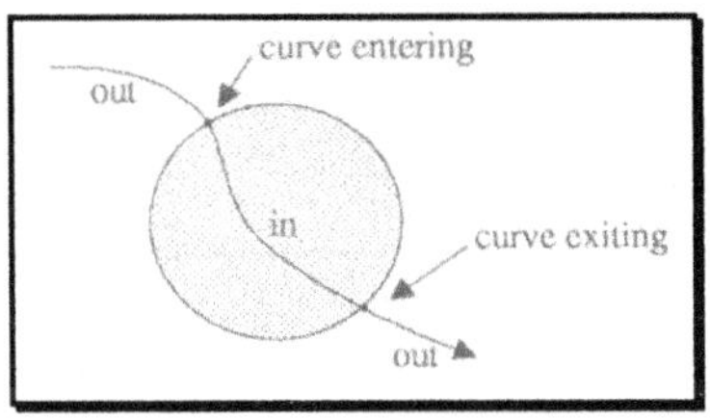

Fig. 2 - Local transitions of a curve with respect to a solid.

Therefore, in the case the local transition between interior and exterior can be computed, the curve classification might be done without ray-firing. Since the boundary of a solid is oriented, the normal to the surface being the geometric element which determines the orientation, if also the curve has an orientation the test for computing the local transition is usually simple. A transition from interior to exterior happens when the normal to the surface and the curve have the same orientation, in the other case the transition being from exterior to interior (Fig. 3).
It can be noted that the same approach has been followed by Crocker and Reinke [CRO87] to avoid expensive point set classification during boolean operators computation for BRep solids.

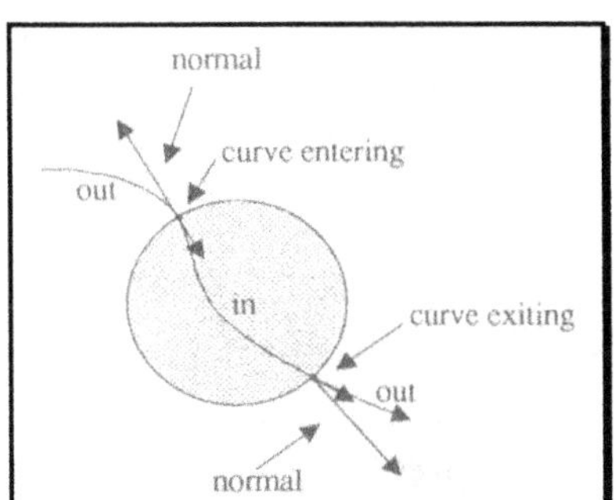

Fig. 3 - Curve orientation with respect to the solid boundary.

A classification realized by checking local transitions does not require the closeness of objects, thus resulting in an actual extension of the domain of the algorithm: with a local transition check technique, a curve can be classified with respect to an object without a complete boundary, whereas this is not possible with ray-firing algorithms which rely on the closeness of the boundary.

Since the object boundary can be non closed, the semantics of the classification should be changed here, considering that a curve may cross the boundary only once. It results in configurations where a curve "enters" the object without "leaving" it, or vice versa (Fig. 4).

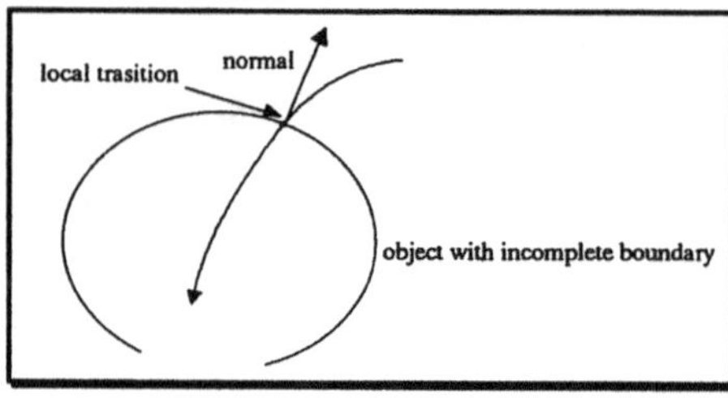

Fig. 4 - A curve "entering" an object without leaving it.

This approach to local transition evaluation is exploited by a new kind of operators, called *pseudo-booleans*. When a pseudo-boolean operator is applied to objects with closed boundary it behaves as a "regular" boolean does, but it operates also in the case of objects with open boundary, with a behavior which is predictable for a user aware of the orientation of the entities under consideration. In this sense, pseudo-booleans actually have a broader domain than "regular" booleans.

In the following the algorithm for computing pseudo-intersections is discussed; pseudo-unions and pseudo-differences are conceptually analogous, except for geometry orientation.

3. Two dimensional algorithm

In this Section, first some notation is introduced. Then the pseudo-intersection of two curves intersecting in one point is defined. Finally, the definition is extended, considering curves intersecting in more than one point and curve chains.

3.1. Notation

Consider two oriented curves $c_i=[\mathbf{a}_i,\mathbf{b}_i]$, i=1,2, defined with a trimmed parametric representation $c_i=c_i(t_i)$. Let c_1 and c_2 be G^1, non self-intersecting, and non overlapping (i.e., if $c_1 \cap c_2 \neq \emptyset$, then $\dim(c_1 \cap c_2)=0$; so that they intersect in single points).

An intersection point **p** of c_1 and c_2 is defined so that there exist the values $\bar{t}_1 \in T_1$ and $\bar{t}_2 \in T_2$ such that $c_1(\bar{t}_1)=c_2(\bar{t}_2)=\mathbf{p}$. Given such a point **p**, it can be shown that the conditions imposed on the curves imply that there exists $\varepsilon>0$ such that $N(\mathbf{p},c_1,c_2,\varepsilon)$ is a non empty neighborhood of **p** with radius ε such that:

$$c_1(\tau_1) = c_2(\tau_2) = \mathbf{q},\ \mathbf{q} \neq \mathbf{p} \quad \Rightarrow \quad \mathbf{q} \notin N(\mathbf{p},c_1,c_2,\varepsilon);$$

$$c_i(\overline{t}_i \pm \delta) \in N(\mathbf{p},c_1,c_2,\varepsilon) \quad \Rightarrow \quad c_i(\overline{t}_i \pm \delta') \in N(\mathbf{p},c_1,c_2,\varepsilon),\ \forall \delta',\ 0<\delta'<\delta,\ i=1,2.$$

The first condition (Fig. 5) expresses that **p** is the only point in the neighborhood belonging to both curves; the second condition (Fig. 6) establishes that the neighborhood contains only points of the curves defined by a connected set of values of the parameter t_i (in the following the neighborhoods will be indicated as N(**p**) whenever this cannot generate ambiguities).

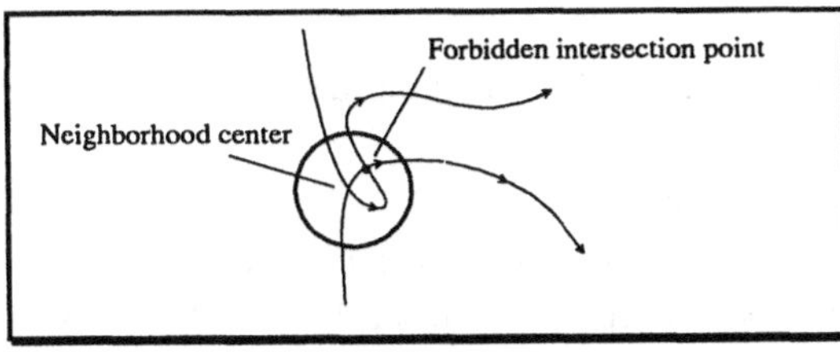

Fig. 5 - A case of violation of first condition.

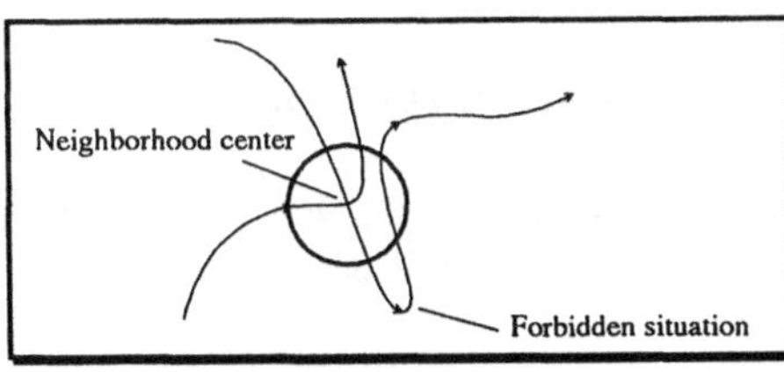

Fig. 6 - A case of violation of second condition.

A normal vector is defined for each point on c_i as the unit vector orthogonal to the first derivative to the curve in the point and right-bounded with respect to the derivative. Then each c_i splits N(**p**) in two parts: a (conventional) "local outer" part, $N_i^O(\mathbf{p})$, where the normal of the curve in **p** lies, and a "local inner" one, $N_i^I(\mathbf{p})$ (in the case **p** is the extreme point of a curve, it can be assumed that the curve is locally extended, so that $N_i^O(\mathbf{p})$ and $N_i^I(\mathbf{p})$ result however well-defined: such a case is immaterial for the algorithm).

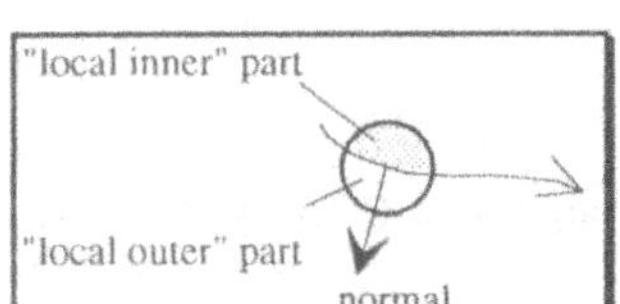

Fig. 7 - The normal of each curve in the intersection point **p** splits the neighborhood N(**p**) in two parts.

Since the curves have an orientation, the intersection point **p** splits each curve in two parts, one part "entering" the neighborhood, $\gamma_{i,1} = [\mathbf{a}_i, \mathbf{p}]$, and one part "leaving" it, $\gamma_{i,2} = [\mathbf{p}, \mathbf{b}_i]$.

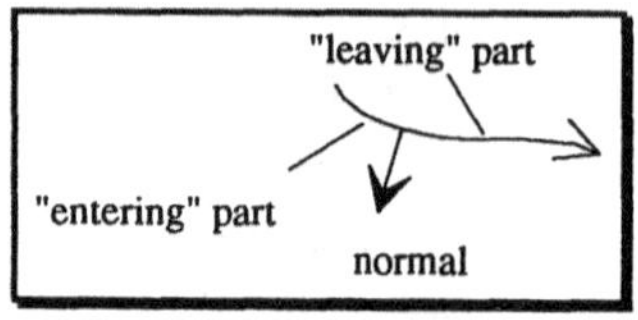

Fig. 8 - Due to its orientation, each curve has an "entering" and a "leaving" part with respect to a point.

A relation of "local containment" $\Subset$ is then defined between parts of curves and neighborhoods, such that:

$$\gamma_{i,j} \Subset N(\mathbf{p}) \quad \Leftrightarrow \quad \exists q \in \gamma_{i,j}: q \in N_{3-i}^{I}(\mathbf{p}).$$

Therefore, a part of a curve with an extreme in an intersection point is "locally contained" in the neighborhood of that point iff some of its points lie in the "local inner" part defined on the neighborhood by the other curve (note that given a curve c_i the index 3-i simply identify the other curve).

3.2. A basic definition of pseudo-intersection

Let c_1 and c_2 be oriented, G^1, non self-intersecting, and non overlapping.
The pseudo-intersection of c_1 and c_2, $c_1 \cap_+ c_2$, is defined as:

$$c_1 \cap_+ c_2 = \bigcup_{\gamma_{i,j} \Subset N(p)} \gamma_{i,j}$$

for i=1,2, j=1,2, with the further assumption that:

$$c_1 \cap_+ c_2 = c_1 \cap c_2$$

if the curves intersect in **p** but $\bigcup_{\gamma_{i,j} \Subset N(p)} \gamma_{i,j} = \varnothing$, or do not intersect (thus in the first case $c_1 \cap_+ c_2 = \{\mathbf{p}\}$, in the second one $=\varnothing$).
Therefore, the pseudo-intersection is constituted by the parts of each curve lying in the "local inner" part defined on the neighborhood of the intersection point by the other curve.

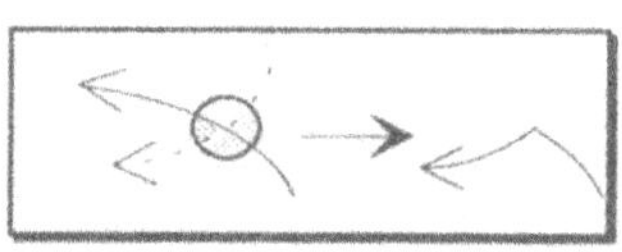

Fig. 9 - Two intersecting curves (left) and their pseudo-intersection (right).

It should be noted that when the curves are tangent in the intersection point a number of cases arises.
The given definition of $\cap_+$ can be translated to a more suitable form from a computational point of view.
Let n_i and d_i be respectively the normal and the first derivative of c_i in **p**.

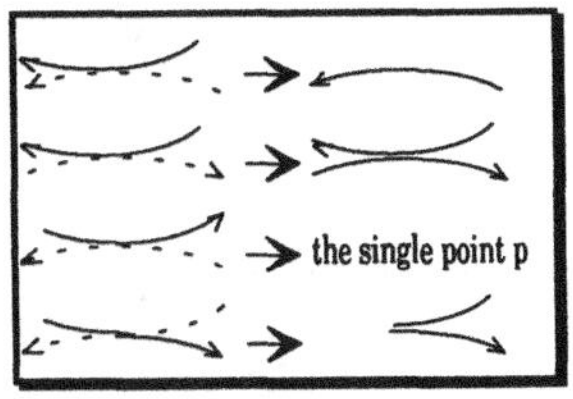

Fig. 10 - The cases of pseudo-intersections arising when the normals in the intersection point are colinear.

In the case $n_1 \neq \pm n_2$ (non local colinearity), it can be shown that the relation of local containment can be expressed in terms of n_i and d_i, as:

$$[\mathbf{a}_i, \mathbf{p}] \Subset N(\mathbf{p}) \quad \Leftrightarrow \quad d_i \bullet n_{3-i} > 0$$

$$[\mathbf{p}, \mathbf{b}_i] \Subset N(\mathbf{p}) \quad \Leftrightarrow \quad d_i \bullet n_{3-i} < 0$$

("x•y" is here the inner product of x and y). It should be noted that $d_1 \bullet n_2 > 0$ iff $d_2 \bullet n_1 < 0$, and therefore conditions $d_1 \bullet n_2 > 0$ and $d_2 \bullet n_1 > 0$ are mutually exclusive. Moreover, while the absolute value $|d_i|$ of the derivatives depends on the specific parametrization, their direction does not, so that such conditions are well defined. On the other hand, if the normals of the curves in **p** are colinear, these equivalencies cannot be applied, and a deeper analysis is in order.

In such a case the information brought by the first derivative is "too local" for discriminating which parts of which curves constitute $c_1 \cap_+ c_2$. While relying only on differential geometry would require derivatives of higher and higher order, a more effective approach, although perhaps less elegant from a theoretical point of view, allows to reach a computationally efficient definition of $\cap_+$, and can be applied also in the case of G^1 curves.

Let NB(**p**) the boundary of the neighborhood N(**p**) (in 2D a circumference centered in **p** and with radius ε). On the basis of the conditions imposed on the curves, each entering part $[\mathbf{a}_i, \mathbf{p}]$ intersects NB(**p**) in a different point $\mathbf{q}_i$. In the same way, each leaving part $[\mathbf{p}, \mathbf{b}_i]$ intersects NB(**p**) in a different point $\mathbf{r}_i$. Therefore the segments $[\mathbf{q}_i, \mathbf{p}]$ and $[\mathbf{p}, \mathbf{r}_i]$ are defined.

Then, two cases must be distinguished, on the basis the curves are defined with the same orientation (i.e., $n_1 = n_2$), or with opposite orientation (i.e., $n_1 = -n_2$).

In the first case, $n_1 = n_2$, the relation of local containment becomes:

$$[\mathbf{a}_i, \mathbf{p}] \Subset N(\mathbf{p}) \quad \Leftrightarrow \quad [\mathbf{q}_i, \mathbf{p}] \bullet n < [\mathbf{q}_{3-i}, \mathbf{p}] \bullet n$$

$$[\mathbf{p}, \mathbf{b}_i] \Subset N(\mathbf{p}) \quad \Leftrightarrow \quad [\mathbf{p}, \mathbf{r}_i] \bullet n < [\mathbf{p}, \mathbf{r}_{3-i}] \bullet n$$

(note that being $n_1 = n_2$ the subscript can be dropped), while in the second case, $n_1 = -n_2$:

$$[\mathbf{a}_i, \mathbf{p}] \Subset N(\mathbf{p}) \quad \Leftrightarrow \quad [\mathbf{q}_i, \mathbf{p}] \bullet n_i > [\mathbf{p}, \mathbf{r}_{3-i}] \bullet n_i$$

$$[\mathbf{p}, \mathbf{b}_i] \Subset N(\mathbf{p}) \quad \Leftrightarrow \quad [\mathbf{p}, \mathbf{r}_i] \bullet n_i > [\mathbf{q}_{3-i}, \mathbf{p}] \bullet n_i$$

3.3. Pseudo-intersection of curve chains

In the general case the pseudo-intersection has to be performed between curves intersecting in more than one point and curve chains.

If two curves intersect in more than one point each curve is implicitly divided in parts by intersection points (Fig. 11), so that the pseudo-intersection operator has to decide which curve parts have to be retained.

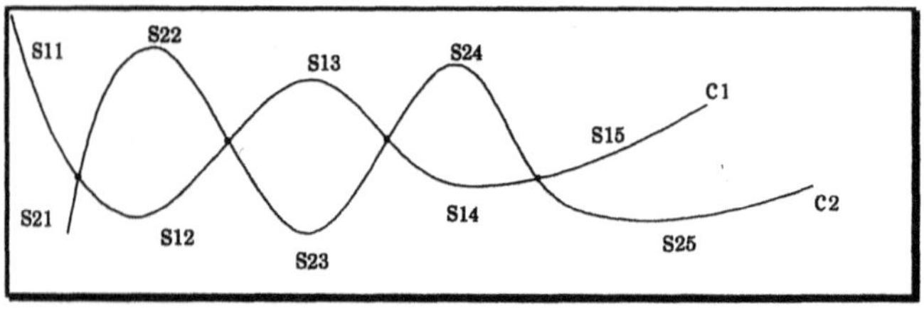

Fig. 11 - Intersection between two curves in many points.

The condition to discard a curve part is that at least one of its ends lies locally outside with respect to the other curve, the local containment relation being computed for each intersection point as discussed in the previous Section. The algorithm for the pseudo-intersection of curves intersecting in more than one point is then (Fig. 12):

1) intersect the two curves;

2) evaluate the local containment relation at the ends (intersection points) of each curve part;

3) for each curve discard all the parts having at least one end lying locally outside the other;

4) connect the remaining parts in order to create a curve chain.

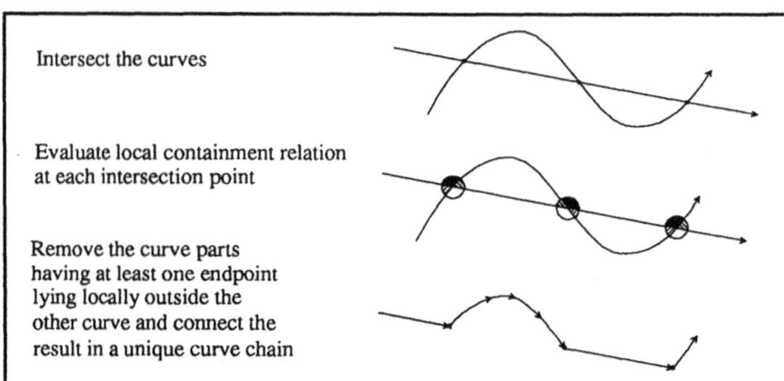

Fig. 12 - Steps for the pseudo intersection of curves intersecting in more than one point.

Also the case of intersection of curve chains can be dealt with as already presented: by considering a curve chain as a unique C^0 curve, the algorithm for curves intersecting in more than one point can be directly adopted (when curves intersect in a vertex, the local containment can be evaluated as described for intersections at curve endpoints). An example of pseudo-intersection between curve chains is shown in Fig. 13.

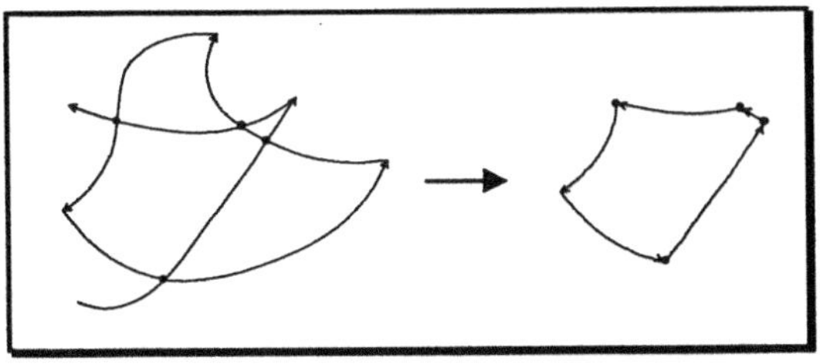

Fig. 13 - Pseudo-intersection between two curve chains.

4. Three dimensional algorithm

The approach presented in the previous Section can be extended to surfaces in a straightforward way by exploiting the 2D algorithm. The basic idea is to preprocess surfaces to orient intersection curves in parametric space, and then to use the 2D algorithm.
This Section explains the way data are preprocessed and how pseudo-booleans between sets of surfaces are performed.

4.1. Constraints

The set of surfaces on which the pseudo-intersection operator is defined must satisfy some constraints. In analogy to the 2D case, surfaces are assumed as non overlapping, so that the intersection between two surfaces is a curve, possibly reduced to single points or the empty set. The overlapping situation should be detected before the application of the operator in order to properly modify the involved surfaces. Another annoying problem arises since intersection curves are computed numerically, so that the real intersection and the computed curve could not match exactly. This problem is unavoidable while numerical computation is used. The treatment of this problem being beyond the scope of the paper, it is assumed here that the match between curves is exact; since the algorithm works on trimmed surfaces, the trims are assumed to be coincident with the boundary curves of each surface. It is also assumed that a data representation for trimmed surfaces and solids exists and that it connects the model parts in a complete way, i.e., it allows the interrogation of the relations between parts starting from any point of the data structure [WOO85].

4.2. Some preliminary concepts

A parametric surface is a mapping from R^2 to R^3. As in the case of curves, the goal is to select the parts of a surface lying locally outside with respect to the other in order to remove them during the pseudo-intersection computation. If the surface normal is defined as the unit vector orthogonal to the surface in each point and pointing outside the virtual material, the parts of a surface to be removed can be selected according to the criterion of being "on the same side" of the other surface normal. Again, this selection can be realized in a simple way by exploiting the orientation of the intersection curves.

The intersection of two parametric surfaces is a mix of points, curves and surfaces. Any point belonging to the intersection can be inversely mapped to the parametric space of the involved surfaces; then, in the case the intersection is a curve, the inverse mapping defines two curves, called "curves on surface", each one lying in the parametric space of a surface. The representation of a curve on surface is defined as follows. Let c(w) be a 2D curve in parametric space, and s(u,v) the surface which the curve lies in, being $c_x(w)$ and $c_y(w)$ the two component functions of the curve. The curve on surface $c_s(w)$ is then $c_s(w) = s(c_x(w),c_y(w))$.

4.3. The algorithm for two surfaces

The intersection of two surfaces consists of some curve branches. The typical representation of each branch consists of a curve in Cartesian space and two curves on surface (one for each surface). Since the curves in parametric space (often called "trimming curves") define the valid portion of the surface domain of a trimmed surface, the parametric space representation of the curves on surface is all is needed to perform the algorithm, and a suitable application of the 2D pseudo-intersection in parametric space is able to select the valid part.

The orientation phase proceeds as follows (Fig. 14):

1) let $n_i(u,v)$ be the normal to the i-th surface in the point (u,v), c(w) the intersection curve, and d(w) its first derivative in the point w. The normal of the 2D curve on surface s_i can be remapped in 3D, its direction being given by the cross product $d(w)\times n_i(c_x(w),c_y(w))$;
2) for each point of c(w), the direction of the mapped normal of the curve on surface s_1 has to point in the half space defined by the normal of s_2. In the general case, to correctly orient the curve it is sufficient to compute the sign of the inner product between the mapped normal and the surface normal in one point of the curve (analogously to what has been shown for curves). As previously, the special case of the colinearity of normals has to be managed in a different way;
3) when one trimming curve has been oriented, the other one simply assumes the opposite orientation.

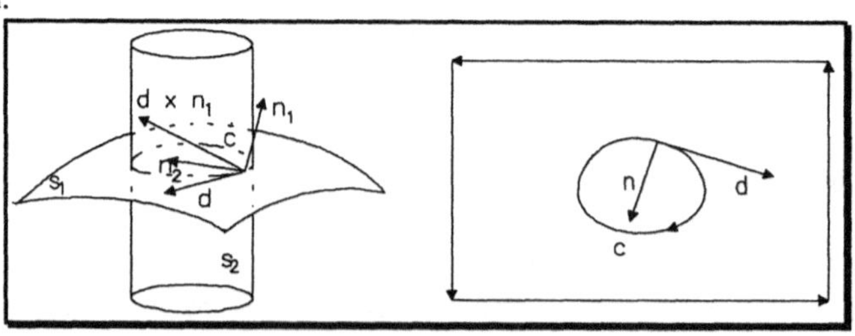

Fig. 14 - An example of orientation of curves

Once the curves have been oriented, the algorithm proceeds performing the 2D boolean as described in the previous Section.

After the orientation phase all curve normals in parametric space point in the direction of the side to be removed. Applying the 2D algorithm in the parametric space of each surface the new trim can be computed. The entire process is summarized in Fig. 15.

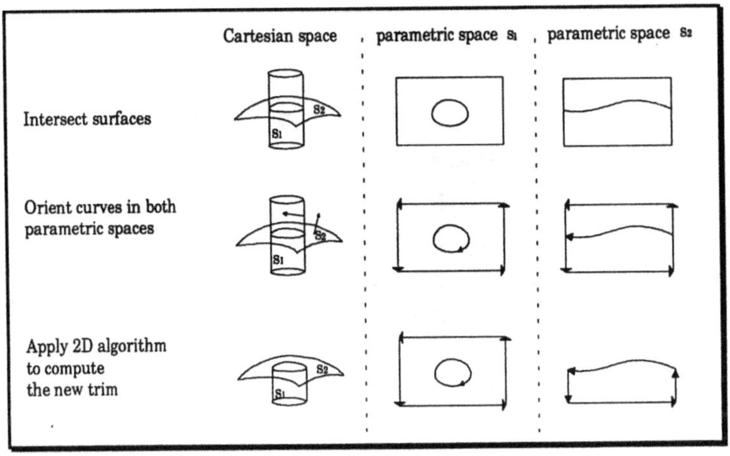

Fig. 15 - Steps for computing the pseudo-intersection between two surfaces.

4.4. Special cases

The problem of colinear normals arises also for surfaces, and it is even more common than in 2D (as an example, consider a cylinder touching a plane). The technique for selecting which part has to be retained is based again on a preprocessing for the 2D algorithm. To detect this situation, a "check plane" orthogonal to the tangent of the intersection curve is defined. Such a plane intersects both surfaces, thus generating two curves that just touch when they cross the intersection curve. The local containment test can be performed in the parametric space of the check plane, to know whether the two surfaces intersect or just touch (Fig. 16).

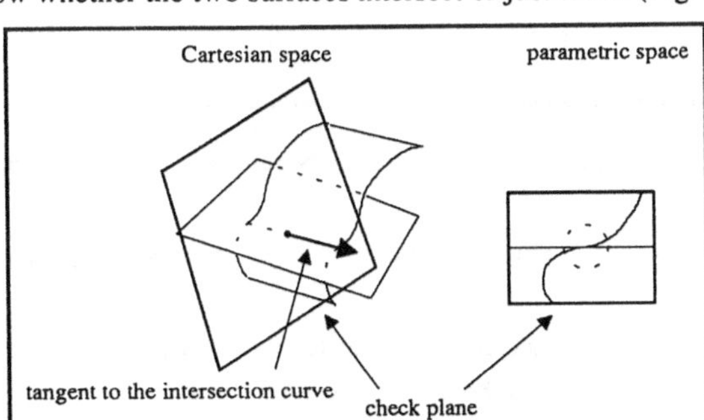

Fig. 16 - Check plane construction.

If the two surfaces intersect, curves on surfaces have to be oriented. The local containment check can provide information about curve orientation in the parametric space; indeed, the vector $d(w) \times n_i(c_X(w), c_Y(w))$ has to point in the direction of the trimmed part (Fig. 17).

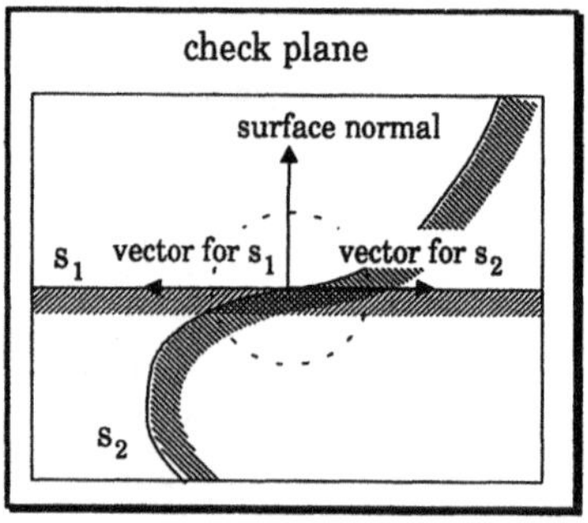

Fig. 17 - Choice of the $d(w) \times n_i(c_x(w), c_y(w))$ vector.

4.5. The algorithm for set of surfaces

If two sets of surfaces are involved the algorithm has to be slightly modified. Each surface of each set is intersected with each surface of the other set to obtain all intersection curves, and such curves are oriented in the way described in the previous Section. Then, for each surface, they are connected to generate a set of composite curves on the surface. Finally the 2D pseudo-boolean can be performed (Fig. 18).

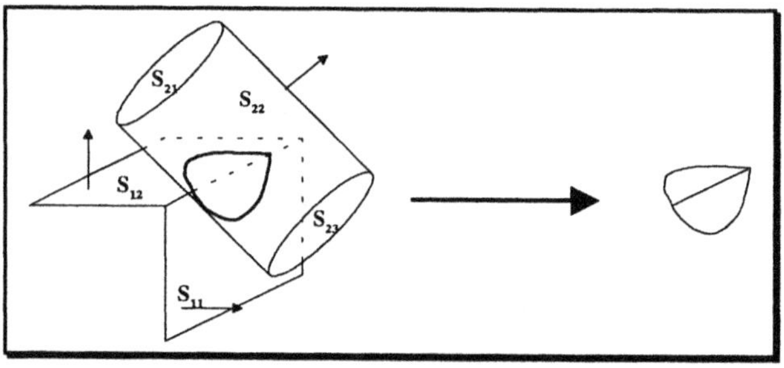

Fig. 18 - Pseudo-intersection between two sets of surfaces.

This stage can involve the problem that the curves in the parametric space could not generate a closed shape (Fig. 19).

The algorithm could recognize the problem and take some decision, the simpler one being to abort the operation and rollback to the previous status.

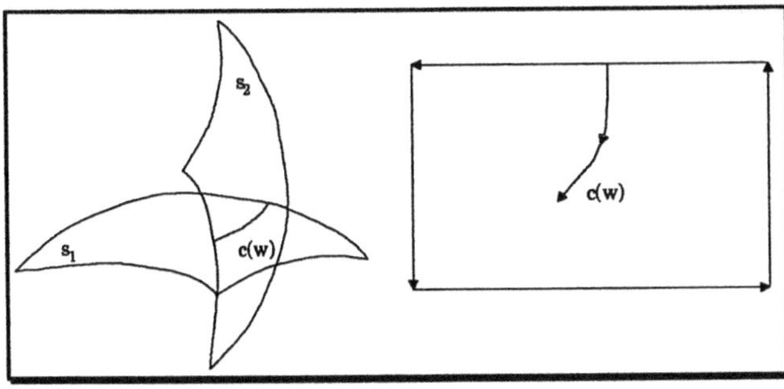

Fig. 19 - A case in which the intersection does not generate a closed shape.

5. Open Problems

To maintain model consistency is the most difficult thing in the development of geometry based algorithms. This holds in particular in the case of surfaces, since the domain is 2D and many consistency conditions are extremely difficult to be checked. An example of this is in Fig. 20.

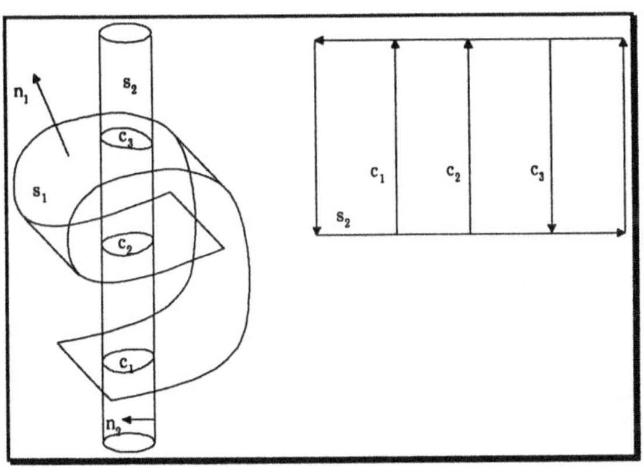

Fig. 20 - A typical example in which difficulties arise in the consistency check.

The main problem is that in some cases the trimming curves are closed but their orientation depends on the side in which the curve is analyzed. In case of curves similar situations can be easily detected because intersections consist of single points and inconsistencies between sides are evident. On the other hand, in the case of surfaces such kind of inconsistencies can lead to non trivially detectable inconsistencies, since the curves are locally correct whereas the trim is globally wrong.

6. Conclusions and future work

The paper presented a new operator, called pseudo-intersection, extending the classical concept of booleans. This operator is aimed to integrate surface and solid modelers, allowing operations between any entity in the model.

It should acknowledged that this is just a very initial step toward such an integration. While pseudo-booleans are "solid oriented" operators extended to surfaces, "surface oriented" operators should be extended to solids, and perhaps brand new operators have to be introduced.

The algorithm itself for computing pseudo-boolean requires further investigations. The Authors do not know whether pseudo-booleans can be computed exploiting local information only. Is it possible to know which part of the curve/surface has to be retained by interrogating higher order derivatives only? Furthermore, the detection of inconsistent results should be enhanced in the case of surfaces, and the management of overlapping curves and surfaces has to be addressed in future research work.

The implementation of pseudo-booleans for surfaces is on going, so that it is still impossible to perform speed tests. However, our guess is that pseudo-booleans are faster than regular ones because they do not use the ray-firing algorithm when surfaces intersect.

A straightforward extension of this algorithm can perform a pseudo-boolean among many sets of surfaces to find a pseudo-common volume. A free form geometry can be thus built by using surface based operators, converting the result into a solid by just trimming away redundant parts.

References

[CAS87] M.S.Casale, 1987: *Free-Form Solid Modeling With Trimmed Surface Patches*, IEEE Computer Graphics and Applications, 1.

[CHI91] H.Chiyokura, T.Satoh, 1991: *Boolean Operations On Sets Using Surface Data*, Proceedings of the First Symposium on Solid Modeling Foundations and CAD/CAM Applications, Austin (TX).

[CRO87] G.A. Crocker, W.F. Reinke, *Boundary Evaluation of Non-Convex Primitives to Produce Parametric Trimmed Surfaces*, Computer Graphics, Vol. 21, n. 4, 7, 1987.

[MAS90] H.Masuda et al., 1990: *A Mathematical Theory And Applications Of Non Manifold Geometric Modeling, in:* Advanced Geometric Modeling for Engineering Applications, F.L.Krause & H.Jansen editors, North-Holland.

[FAR87] R.T.Farouki, 1987: *Trimmed-Surface Algorithm For The Evaluation And Integration Of Solid Boundary Representations*, IBM J.Research and Development, 31, 3.

[VAR84] T.Varady, M.J.Pratt, 1984: *Design Techniques For The Definition Of Solid Objects With Free Form Geometry*, Computer Aided Geometric Design, 1.

[WEI86] K.J.Weiler, 1986: *Topological Structures For Geometric Modeling*, Ph.D. Thesis, Rensellaer Polytechnic Institute.

[WOO85] T.C.Woo, 1985: *A combinatorial analysis of boundary data structure schemata*, IEEE Computer Graphics and Applications, 3.

[XOX90] XOX Corporation, 1990: *SHAPES Geometry Library Reference Manual.*

Chapter 5

Surface Modeling as a Creative Tool

Interactive Axial Deformations

Francis Lazarus, Sabine Coquillart and Pierre Jancène

INRIA Rocquencourt

BP 105, 78153 Le Chesnay Cedex, FRANCE

{Francis.Lazarus,Sabine.Coquillart,Pierre.Jancene}@inria.fr

Abstract

This paper presents an interactive deformation technique. The entity employed for defining the deformation of an object is a 3D axis as well as some associated parameters.

The technique allows an easy specification and control of deformations that can be defined with that entity such as bending, twisting and scaling.

Contrary to existing techniques, the method developed is independent of both the geometric model of the object to be deformed and the creation technique used to define the object.

Moreover, it can easily be integrated into traditional interactive modeling systems.

CR Categories and Subject Descriptors: I.3.5 [Computer Graphics]:Computational Geometry and Object Modeling - Curve, surface, solid, and object representation; Geometric algorithms, languages, and systems; Hierarchy and geometric transformations; I.3.6 [Computer Graphics]: Methodology and Techniques - Interaction techniques.

Additional Keywords and Phrases: Solid geometric modeling, deformations.

1 Introduction

Today's graphics systems for producing images consist of several software components, the first one being a 3D geometric modeler with which a user can define objects geometry.

A geometric modeler often includes two classes of modeling techniques: the creation techniques such as the sweep, the loft or the extrusion and the modification techniques. Modification, or deformation, techniques may be used either for refining the shape of an object defined using creation techniques or for changing the shape of existing objects obtained by scanning a real object, for instance.

The approaches taken to deforming objects include:

- Manipulation of the geometric model.

  The deformation techniques of this class consist of direct manipulation of the geometric model representing the surface. They are often very dependent on the geometric model. For instance, one may interactively move the control points of a spline surface or of a hierarchical spline surface [FB88]. If the geometric model representing the surface is an implicit surface [WBB+90] defined by points (resp. axis), the deformation technique involves moving the points (resp. deforming the axis).

  Recent work has also shown that the trivial solution that consists of moving the control points of a spline surface can be extended to allow the user to manipulate freely any point or even a curve of the surface [BB91, WW92]. These new techniques make direct manipulation less dependent on the geometric model.

- Manipulation of a creation entity.

  In a general modeling system, it is usually preferable to use the same geometric model such as a spline or a polygonal surface, for representing each object. In this case the creation technique and thus the creation entities used for defining an object are often independent of the geometric model of the object. Creation entities may include the axis or the cross-section used for creating a surface as a sweep, or the profile curve, or angle used for the defining of a surface as a surface of revolution. A common practice for deforming objects this way consists of manipulating the entities, or the parameters, used to create the surface.

Basically, deformations of this class can be resumed as a redefinition of some of the creation entities followed by a recomputation of the surface.

- Manipulation of a deformation entity.

  Techniques for which a deformation entity is defined and used to deform the object fall into this class. The deformation entity can be compared to the creation entity, since it plays the role of an interface between the geometric model and the user. One of its consequences is to make the deformation technique independent of both the geometric model and the creation technique. Techniques such as the FFD and the EFFD [SP86, Coq90], or Cobb's region or skeletal warp [Cob84] lie in that class.

Techniques of the third class present several advantages:

- From a user point of view, the same deformation technique can be applied to any object, no matter where it comes from. Furthermore, the geometric model becomes transparent for the user.
- These techniques can be combined with one another to increase the power of the modeling system.
- The deformation is completely defined by the deformation entity. A deformation tool [Coq90] can thus be defined, permitting the reproduction of the deformation several times, on possibly different surfaces.

In order to take advantage of these benefits, one of our goals was extending some deformation techniques of the first two classes to the third one.

This paper deals with deformations defined by an axis. These deformations are simple and specific, but very useful and commonly employed. They include bending, twisting and scaling around an axis.

Several techniques exist for deforming an object with an axis.

One of them consists of defining the object as a sweep surface and then deforming the axis or modifying other parameters such as a scale factor or a twist factor defined along the axis (cf. Manipulation of a creation entity). A second solution consists of using implicit surfaces, defined by a skeleton-axis, to represent the surface (cf. Manipulation of the geometric model).

It follows that:

- The object has to be defined as either a sweep surface or an implicit surface with an axis as skeleton. The class of objects that can be defined this way is rather restricted.
- The only axis that may be used to deform such an object is the creation axis.
- Combining these deformations with other deformations is rarely possible.

Parent [Par77] uses axial deformations for deforming 2D shapes while Barr [Bar84], has proposed 3D axial deformations where the axes considered are only straight axes and the bending operations are very restricted in comparison with what we can expect from a real 3D axis.

Our purpose is thus to develop an axial deformation technique that is independent of the geometric model and valid for any creation technique and any axis.

The following section explains the principles of the Axial Deformation technique and emphasizes the computation process. Section 3 presents several extensions increasing both the generality and the power of the previously defined deformation techniques. Finally, we give some examples to illustrate our approach.

2 Axial Deformations

Our goal is to define a deformation technique that makes use of a 3D axis for deforming existing objects. This technique is called AxDf, for Axial Deformation. Suppose we have an object. From the user's point of view, the deformation process is as follows:

- First, the user defines a 3D axis, that can be positioned either inside or outside the object. This 3D axis may have any shape, depending on the deformation desired.
- Second, the user changes the shape of the axis, and the deformations so applied to the axis are automatically passed on to the object.

Figure 1 illustrates the AxDf technique by a simple example. Figure 1-left shows the sphere we wish to deform as well as the axis used for defining the deformation; a straight axis, in black has been designed. Figure 1-right shows the sphere deformed in a manner that is intuitively consistent with the motion of the axis visualized in black.

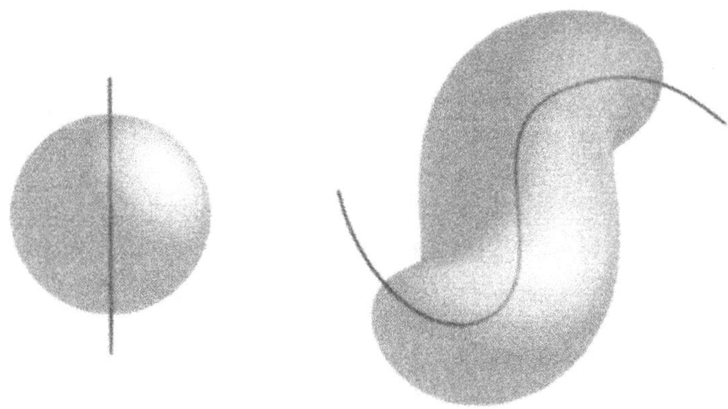

Figure 1: Deforming a sphere.

Within an interactive modeling system, the 3D axis will be represented by a 3D curve; any spline curve can be used.

To make this deformation technique practical, we must find a way to pass the axis' deformations to the object. We handle this problem using a two-step process. First, each vertex [1] V of the object is attached to one point A_V of the axis and its local coordinates (x, y, z) in the axis' local coordinate system are computed. Second, the deformed vertex is obtained by computing the associated local coordinate system at A'_V, homologous to A_V on the deformed axis, and transforming the (x, y, z) coordinates from this coordinate system to the world coordinate system.

Three problems have to be considered:

- attaching a vertex to the axis,
- defining local coordinate frames on the axis,
- computing the coordinates of the deformed vertices.

These three problems will be studied in the following paragraphs.

[1] From now on, every point of an object will be called a vertex to avoid any confusion with the points of the deformation axis.

2.1 Attaching a vertex to the axis

To compute axial deformations, each object vertex must be attached to the 3D axis. A natural association consists of attaching the vertex to the closest point of the curve. The closest point can be computed either recursively by using the convex hull property of a spline curve or by discretizing the curve. Selecting the closest point of the curve may raise some problems, namely when several points of the axis are located at equal distance from the object vertex, or when a vertex lies in two different planes normal to the axis and the best choice is not the closest axis point. Several techniques for improving that choice are under consideration. One of them consists of taking into account vertex adjacencies in order to make the association function continuous.

The attach point is represented by its parameter value on the axis curve.

2.2 Axis local coordinate frames

After attaching each object vertex to a point of the axis, we now define a local coordinate frame at each point of the axis in order to allow the computation of the (x, y, z) local coordinates of each object vertex in this coordinate system.

Several methods exist for defining coordinate frames at each point of a 3D curve. A common practice consists of considering the well known Frenet frame. For each point of a 3D curve, the Frenet frame is represented by the three orthogonal unit vectors defined by the tangent, the normal and the binormal at that point. This frame depends on the first and the second derivatives of the curve, it can thus be computed explicitly.

However, three problems exist:

- The normal is not defined on linear curve segments, nor more generally, where the curvature vanishes.
- The normal direction flips at the inflection points.
- The normal can rotate in an undesirable manner around the 3D curve.

An alternative to the Frenet frame has been proposed by Klok in [Klo86]. Klok defines a rotation minimizing orthogonal frame by the requirement that the rotation of the frame be minimized along the curve.

Assuming that $C(s)$, $s \in [0, L]$ is a regular curve, Klok defines the rotation minimizing orthogonal frame $t(s), f(s), g(s)$ along C such that

$$t(s) = C'(s)/||C'(s)||$$
$$f'(s) = -(C''(s).f(s))C'(s)/||C'(s)||^2$$
$$g'(s) = -(C''(s).g(s))C'(s)/||C'(s)||^2$$

$f(0)$ and $g(0)$ being chosen such that $t(0)$, $f(0)$ and $g(0)$ are mutually orthogonal unit vectors.

These equations guarantee that the rotation of $f(s)$ is minimal along the curve.

As a closed-form solution of the previous equations does not exist, Klok also gives a geometric construction of the rotation minimizing frame based on an approximation of the curve by a sequence of straight line segments.

This solution has been adopted for computing the frames at each point of the axis. Note that a special treatment has been added for cusps: when a cusp is detected on the axis, the orientation of the following frames is reversed.

The (x, y, z) coordinates of V are thus defined as the coordinates of V in the frame associated to A_V. Note that in most cases, x equals zero.

2.3 Deformed vertices

The process for computing the deformed position V_{AxDf} of a vertex V is as follows.

Let A'_V be the point of the deformed axis corresponding to A_V. A'_V is defined such that its parameter value on the deformed axis is equal to the previously computed parameter value of A_V.

V_{AxDf} is the vertex defined by the (x, y, z) local coordinates in the frame associated with A'_V.

3 Extensions

We have thus far proposed a basic version of the AxDf technique. The only deformations that can be controlled are the deformations obtained either by bending or stretching the axis (cf. Figure 1 for a simple example). Other parameters can be defined in order to extend the AxDf technique. Some of them are suggested in the following paragraphs.

3.1 Scale and twist

Scale and twist graphs can easily be added to the Axial Deformation technique. The twist (resp. scale) value permits the twisting (resp. scaling) of the object around the axis. The objective is to define both a twist and a scale factor at each point of the axis; these factors are then used for computing the deformed object's vertices. From the user's point of view, a twist (resp. scale) factor can be defined at any point of the axis. The value along the axis is thus obtained by interpolating the values defined by the user. Figure 2 illustrates the twist factor by a simple example. The undeformed object is composed of two rods shown in Figure 2-left; a straight axis has been positioned between the 2 rods. Figure 2-right is obtained without changing the shape of the axis, just by adding a twist factor of 0 at one end and another of 360 degrees at the other end.

Figure 2: Twisting two straight rods.

3.2 Zone of influence

In order to improve the Axial Deformation technique, a zone of influence can be introduced to define the portion of the 3D space to be deformed. In our implementation, we have taken advantage of the deformation axis to define that space. A simple solution consists of defining two zones of influence ZImin and ZImax as general cylinders around the deformation axis, ZImin being included into ZImax.

The vertices of the object lying inside ZImin (resp. outside ZImax) will be fully deformed (resp. will not be deformed at all). Vertices in-between will be partially deformed by interpolating the deformation parameters, such as twist, scale and attach point.

Each zone of influence is defined by the two radii R_{min} and R_{max} of each circular cross-section along the axis. These radii are defined in the same manner as the twist or the scale parameters.

Figure 3 illustrates the use of the zone of influence. In Figure 3-left, a planar surface is shown and the axis used to deform the surface is visualized in black. The two zones of influence are also visualized using transparencies: ZImin is the inner zone while ZImax is the outer one. Only the vertices of the object lying inside ZImax will be deformed. The deformed surface is shown in Figure 3-right where the deformed axis is shown in black.

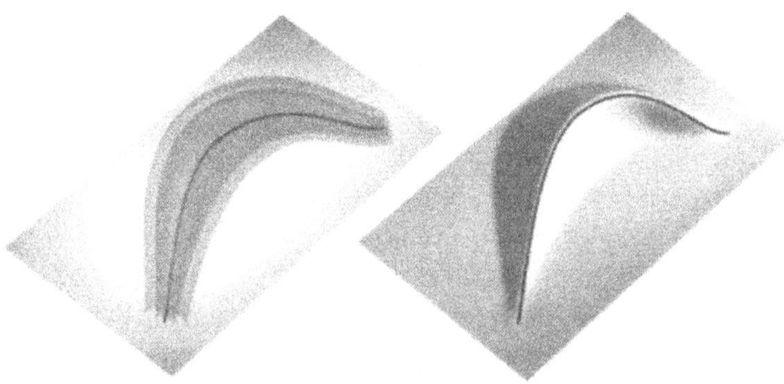

Figure 3: Zone of influence.

3.3 Deformation tool

A consequence of the independence of the AxDf technique and the geometric model is the capacity of exploiting the deformation tool paradigm. The deformation tool must fully describe the deformation. In AxDf, a deformation tool is composed of:

- two axes: the undeformed, or initial axis, and the deformed, or final one,
- two zones of influence, ZImin and ZImax,
- a twist graph and a scale graph.

Figure 4: The same deformation applied to two different objects.

As the deformation is fully described by the deformation tool, the same deformation can be applied several times to different objects, simply by using the same deformation tool. In Figure 4 the same deformation tool is applied to two different objects: a straight ribbon and the twisted rods presented in Figure 2. The initial axis is a straight line while the final axis represents a node. A twist has also been added to this deformation.

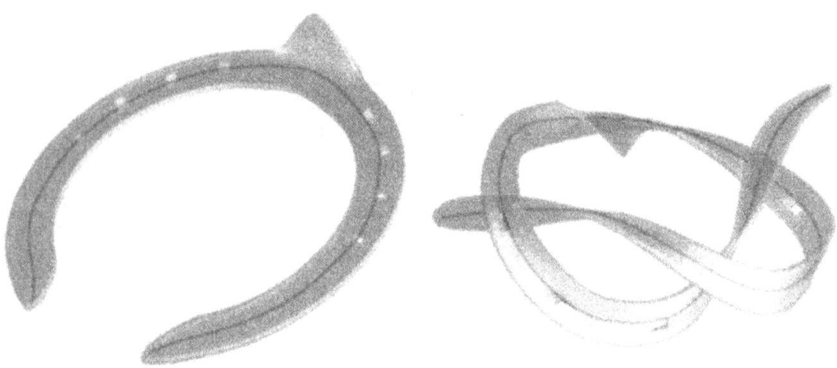

Figure 5: Adapting the deformation tool to the object.

A deformation tool can also be adapted to the object to which it will be applied. In Figure 5 we have applied the node-deformation tool to an object that is not straight, a horseshoe. This has been made possible simply by adapting the initial axis to the shape of the object. In Figure 5-left the visualized axis is the new initial one. The deformed horseshoe is shown in Figure 5-right together with the final axis.

4 Examples and Concluding Remarks

Two simple examples of deformations of well known objects by the AxDf technique are illustrated in Figure 6 and 7. Figure 6 presents two teapots. On top, an axis has been designed by the user inside the spout of the undeformed teapot. The deformed teapot presented below results from a deformation of the axis.

Figure 6: Deforming the teapot.

In Figure 7, a deformation that includes both a deformation of the axis and a modification of the scale graph is applied to the VW.

In our implementation, computing the deformation of the most detailed object (2160 vertices) takes approximatively 0.30 second on an IRIS 310 VGX.

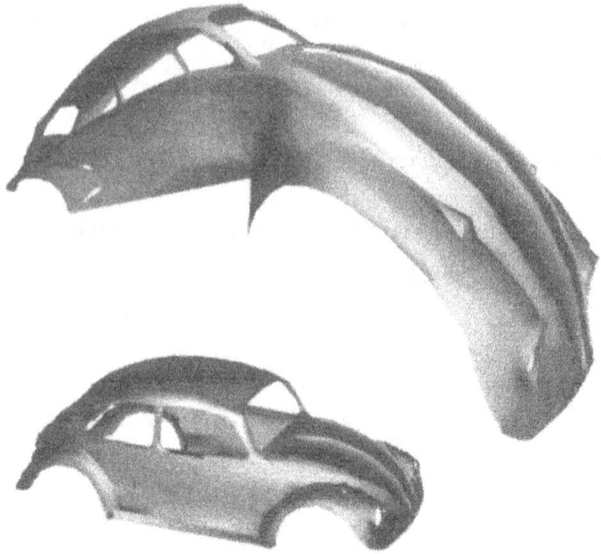

Figure 7: Deforming the VW.

Although specific and simple, the deformations that can be controlled with the AxDf technique are very common and most useful. Furthermore, AxDf offers the following advantages:

- Since the deformation is independent of the object to which it is applied, it can be re-used to deform other objects.
- Since AxDf is independent of the creation technique, it can be used to deform any existing object.
- AxDf can easily be combined with other deformation techniques, such as FFD.
- AxDf can be applied to many different geometric models such as spline surfaces, polygonal surfaces or hierarchical surfaces.
- AxDf can easily be integrated into most general and interactive modeling systems.
- AxDf is very intuitive and fully interactive.

This paper has shown that AxDf is a viable deformation technique for geometric modeling. It greatly increases the class of deformations obtained by manipulating a deformation entity and makes easier the control of some deformations usually defined using the FFD techniques. There are however a number of enhancements and extensions to AxDf that we should like to investigate. Some of them are:

- checking for self-intersection of the deformed surface,
- automatically (or semi-automatically) designing the first axis on the surface,
- implementing an adaptative subdivision technique such as that of Griessmair et al. [GP89] in order to maintain an acceptable resolution of the surface,
- allowing several axis to be used simultaneously for deforming an object.

Furthermore, due to the simplicity of the deformation entity (the axis), it seems likely that this approach would also be very attractive for animation applications.

AxDf is part of ACTION3D, a general interactive modeling system developed jointly by SOGITEC and INRIA.

References

[Bar84] A.H. Barr. Global and Local Deformations of Solid Primitives. *SIGGRAPH'84, Computer Graphics*, 18(3):21–30, July 1984.

[BB91] Paul Borrel and Dominique Bechmann. Deformation of n-Dimensional Objects. In *Symposium on Solid Modeling Foundations and CAD/CAM Applications*, pages 351–369. ACM, June 1991.

[Cob84] B.S. Cobb. *Design of Sculptured Surfaces Using the B-Spline Representation.* PhD thesis, University of Utah, June 1984.

[Coq90] Sabine Coquillart. EFFD: A Sculpturing Tool for 3d Geometric Modeling. *SIGGRAPH'90, Computer Graphics*, 24(4):187–196, August 1990.

[FB88] D.R. Forsey and R.H. Bartels. Hierarchical B-Spline Refinement. *SIGGRAPH'88, Computer Graphics*, 22(4):205–212, August 1988.

[GP89] J. Griessmair and W. Purgathofer. Deformation of Solids with Trivariate B-Splines. In *EUROGRAPHICS'89*, pages 137–148. North-Holland, 1989.

[Klo86] F. Klok. Two Moving Coordinate Frames for Sweeping along a 3d Trajectory. *Computer Aided Geometric Design*, (3):217–229, 1986.

[Par77] R.E. Parent. A System for Sculpting 3-D Data. *Computer Graphics*, 11(2):138–147, July 1977.

[SP86] T.W. Sederberg and S.R. Parry. Free-Form Deformation of Solid Geometric Models. *SIGGRAPH'86, Computer Graphics*, 20(4):151–160, August 1986.

[WBB+90] B. Wyvill, J. Bloomenthal, T. Beier, J. Blinn, A. Rockwood, and G. Wyvill. Modeling and Animating with Implicit Surfaces. *Siggraph Course Notes*, 23, 1990.

[WW92] W. Welch and A. Witkin. Variational Surface Modeling. *SIGGRAPH'92, Computer Graphics*, 26(2):157–166, July 1992.

Surface Generation from an Irregular Network of Parametric Curves

Shigeru Kuriyama
Tokyo Research Laboratory, IBM Japan, Ltd.
1623-14 Shimotsuruma Yamato-shi Kanagawa 242, Japan

Abstract

This paper proposes a method of generating surfaces from a network of curves that have arbitrary parametric forms, and that intersect in an arbitrary topology.

The surfaces generated from the network are represented by multisided patches defined on a multivariate coordinate system. An m-sided patch is generated by blending m sub-surfaces with a transfinite interpolant, and each sub-surface is generated by blending two sweep surfaces that are defined by a pair of curves intersecting with each other in the network. An advantage of the final surfaces is that they have everywhere the same order of continuity as the curves.

This method is flexible in its representation of the curve expressions and the connective topology of a network. It can implement a surface model in user-friendly and designer-oriented CAD interfaces that handle direct input of 3D curves.

Key Words: Computer-aided geometric design, Multisided patches, Sweeping, Blending, Geometric continuity, Curve network.

1 Introduction

New technologies in computational graphics, such as photo-realistic rendering, enhance the visual effect of presentations in industrial design and commercial production. The input of shapes, however, is still a time-consuming process, and needs the support of skilled CAD operators.

A new paradigm is required for current 3D-CAD systems used to design the shapes of free-form surfaces, because the systems are inadequate for quick input of shapes in the initial stage of conceptual design. 3D-CAD systems have come to use the metaphor of sketching that was used by 2D-drawing systems in order to realize a designer-oriented environment of shape input. Sketching systems aim at a user-friendly interface that is easy to use, intuitive, and good at handling complicated shapes.

In current surface modellers, free-form surfaces have a topological constraint on their control points or profile curves; they must be arranged in the topology of a regular two-dimensional mesh. This constraint is derived from the formation rule of tensor product surfaces. 3D-sketching systems based on current surface modellers therefore generate tensor product surfaces such as loft or sweep surfaces from a set of hand-drawn curves arranged in the topology of a regular mesh. This topological constraint, however, limits the expressional flexibility of designers.

On the other hand, advanced three-dimensional input devices have been proposed for CAD systems whose interface handles the input of free-form curves. For example, an MIT group (Sachs, Roberts and Stoops, 1991) has developed a CAD interface that allows users to design shapes by entering information of free-form curves directly in three dimensions, using a pair of hand-held sensors. The interface manages the input of a curve network that is free from the topological constraint of a regular mesh. We call such a network *irregular*. The network, however, represents only a wireframe model and lacks a surface model. This limitation of the representative model makes it impossible to conduct engineering evaluations and simulations such as interrogation or rendering of surfaces, or data generations for Numerical Control machine or Finite Element Method. The above example highlights the need for a method of skinning an irregular network of curves.

Multisided patches have the potential to generate smooth surfaces from an irregular network of curves, because they can have an arbitrary number (more than two) of sides corresponding to their boundary curves. The existing methods of generating multisided patches have the following common drawbacks:

- Each boundary curve of a patch must contain only one segment; it is always defined by one expression.
- It is impossible or very complicated to generate curvature-continuous surfaces.

Each boundary curve of a patch often comprises many curve segments if it is designed by sketching. Moreover, designers using surface modellers in industrial design often impose strict conditions on the continuity of surfaces so that shapes will have a smooth appearance. They claim that G^2 continuity (that is, uniqueness of surface normals and of either principal curvatures or principal directions) is necessary in order to confirm the shape from the continuous reflection curves on the surfaces. However, the existing methods are inadequate to satisfy these conditions.

For these reasons, we have improved the mathematical model of multisided patches to match data incidents to corresponding edges, and to ensure geometric continuity of arbitrary degrees.

In this paper, we propose a method of skinning a network with multisided patches. These are generated by sweeping and blending the curves corresponding to the boundaries of the patches. This method can implement a surface model in CAD interfaces that handle only a wireframe model by allowing direct sketching of curves in three-dimensional space.

In Section 2, we explain the existing methods of generating multisided patches and sweep surfaces. In Section 3, we propose a method of generating a multisided patch from curves surrounding the patch. In Section 4, the method proposed in Section 3 is modified for singular conditions on the topology of the network: patches that have multiple and T-connected intersections, and open-sided and two-sided patches are considered. In Section 5, we give examples of curve networks and surfaces generated from them by our method, and in Section 6, we offer some conclusions and discuss future work. The Appendix includes a proof of the geometric continuity of the patches defined in Section 3.

2 Previous Work

Methods of generating multisided patches have become important as a result of the need for a mathematical model that can handle complicated shapes. These methods eliminate the drawback of tensor product surfaces; namely, a constraint on the arrangement of control points or profile curves.

Catmull and Clark (1978), Doo and Sabin (1978), and Nasri (1987) proposed the recursive subdivision method, to remove the restriction on the topology of surfaces. This method, however, does not have closed-form parametrization. Hosaka and Kimura (1984), and Loop and DeRose (1989) introduced multisided patches, which are regarded as a generalization of Bézier patches for multivariate barycentric coordinates. Loop and DeRose (1990) presented a method of constructing multisided B-spline surfaces with multisided patches, called S-patches, by using Sabin nets (Sabin, 1983). However, it is hard to calculate the control points of these patches in such a way as to generate G^2 continuous surfaces.

Varady (1991) proposed a method of overlapping patches, introducing local parametrization for individual vertex patches, and Charrot and Gregory (1984) introduced multisided patches by using local parametrization of a multivariate coordinate system and a convex combination of blending functions. Nielson (1987), and Hagen and Pottmann (1989) also proposed triangular patches defined on barycentric coordinates through the use of blending functions. Their methods are similar to Charrot and Gregory's, and are extendible to multisided patches. These methods can generate G^2 surfaces by increasing the degree of constituent equations, and they have no constraints on the representation of sub-surfaces to be blended.

The above-mentioned methods of generating topologically free surfaces are still used for patches that match data incidents only to corresponding vertices. That is to say, the surfaces are defined by geometrical values assigned to corresponding corners of the patches.

On the other hand, methods of generating sweep surfaces are well known and are implemented on most surface modellers, because they allow the design of shapes to be curve-based rather than vertex-based.

Woodward (1988) proposed techniques for skinning surfaces by using interpolation based on B-splines, and Coquillart (1987) described a method based on non-uniform rational B-splines by adding a profile curve to scale the inbetween cross sections. Choi and Lee (1990) classified sweeping rules as parallel, rotational, spined, and synchronized sweeps; these sweeps are generalized by combining coordinate transformation and blending. Klok (1986) proposed a method of sweeping along a 3D trajectory by using rotation minimizing sweep that is a modification of Frenet frame sweep, and Tai, Loe and Kunii (1992) presented techniques of homotopy sweep.

Their methods are flexible in terms of shape definition, but the representations of surfaces are restricted to tensor form. That is to say, the surface expressions comprise only the product of two independent parameters for cross sectional curves and guide curves, and this property restricts the topology of surfaces.

3 Surface Model

In this section, we propose a method of generating an m-sided patch surrounded by m boundary curves by using m-variate coordinates. We first introduce generalized barycentric coordinates for the m-sided domain. Next, we generate two sweep surfaces by sweeping two cross sectional curves along the ith boundary curve; the cross sectional curves are selected from those curves sharing an intersection with the ith curve. Next, we generate a surface by blending the above two sweep surfaces, and call it the ith *sub-surface.* Finally, we generate an m-sided patch by blending the m sub-surfaces. This blending uses a transfinite interpolant that preserves the geometric continuity of the ith sub-surface on the ith boundary curve.

3.1 Generalized barycentric coordinates

Let a patch be surrounded by boundary curves $\mathbf{C}_i$, $i = 1, 2, ..., m$, and be defined over an m-lateral polygon called a *domain polygon.* Each vertex of the domain polygon p_i corresponds to an intersection of the curves, and each edge of the domain polygon e_i corresponds to a section of a curve between two intersections, as shown in Figure 1.

We embed the multivariate coordinates on the domain polygon by using the generalized barycentric coordinates proposed by Loop and DeRose (1989; 1990). The mapping from each point p on the domain polygon $P = \{p_1, p_2, ..., p_m\}$ to the generalized barycentric coordinates $\ell = \{\ell_1, \ell_2, ..., \ell_m\}$ is defined as follows:

$$\ell_i(p) = \frac{\pi_i(p)}{\sum_{i=1}^m \pi_i(p)} \quad , \qquad \pi_i(p) = \frac{\prod_{i=1}^m \alpha_i(p)}{\alpha_{i-1}(p)\alpha_i(p)} \quad ,$$

where $\alpha_i(p)$ denote the signed area of triangle $p\, p_i\, p_{i+1}$, whose sign is determined to be positive if p is inside P.

The coordinates ℓ define m-sided patches, and have the following properties:

- *Division of one:* $\sum_{i=1}^m \ell_i = 1$.
- *Vertex preservation:* p_i is mapped to $\ell_i = 1 \cap \ell_{j\neq i} = 0$.
- *Edge preservation:* e_i is mapped to $\ell_i + \ell_{i+1} = 1 \cap \ell_{j\neq i,i+1} = 0$.
- *Pseudo-affine property:* $p = \sum_{i=1}^m \ell_i(p)\, p_i$ holds if the domain polygon is regular.

3.2 Construction of sub-surfaces

In this subsection, we propose a method of constructing sub-surfaces. The ith sub-surface, denoted by $\mathbf{S}_i$, is generated from the boundary curves on e_i, e_{i-1}, and e_{i+1}. Without loss of generality, we assume that the curve $\mathbf{C}_i(t)$ on e_i spans from 0 to Δ_i, and let $\mathbf{C}_{i-1}(0)$ and $\mathbf{C}_{i+1}(0)$ coincide with the vertices p_i and p_{i+1} respectively (see Figure 1). All the curves can have arbitrary parametric forms that map the value of a parameter $t \in [0, \Delta_i]$ to a 3D point $\mathbf{C}_i(t)$; they can have arbitrary degrees and nodes of segments if they are represented by polynomial spline functions. The spans Δ_i are also arbitrarily set; however, it is desirable to make the spans be proportional to the arc length or the Euclidean distance between two intersections of the curve $\mathbf{C}_i$ in order to avoid generating unnaturally shaped surfaces.

We here consider a sweep of cross sectional curves $\mathbf{C}_{i-1}$ and $\mathbf{C}_{i+1}$ in which $\mathbf{C}_i$ is regarded as a guide curve.

First, we introduce the local parameters u_i and v_i: u_i defines the parameter space of the guide curve $\mathbf{C}_i$, and v_i defines that of the cross sectional curves $\mathbf{C}_{i-1}$ and $\mathbf{C}_{i+1}$.

$$\begin{aligned} \mu &= \left\lfloor \frac{m}{2} \right\rfloor \quad , \quad \omega_i = \begin{cases} \Delta_i & ; \ m \ \text{even} \\ \Delta_i/(1-\ell_{i+\mu+1}) & ; \ m \ \text{odd} \end{cases} \quad , \\ u_i &= \omega_i \sum_{k=1}^{\mu} \ell_{i+k} \quad , \\ v_i &= \left[\Delta_{i-1}\left(1-\frac{u_i}{\Delta_i}\right) + \Delta_{i+1}\frac{u_i}{\Delta_i}\right] \sum_{k=2}^{m-1} \ell_{i+k} \quad , \end{aligned} \tag{1}$$

where the suffix of ℓ is defined to modulus m, and $\lfloor\ \rfloor$ represents a floor function.

Let the cross directional derivative D_i about e_i be defined by partial derivatives with respect to ℓ_i , $i = 1, 2, ..., m$:

$$\begin{aligned} D_i &= (\ell_i + \ell_{i-1}) \frac{\partial}{\partial \ell_{i-1}} + (\ell_{i+1} + \ell_{i+2}) \frac{\partial}{\partial \ell_{i+2}} \\ &\quad + \sum_{k=3}^{m-2} \ell_{i+k} \frac{\partial}{\partial \ell_{i+k}} - (\Delta_i - u_i) \frac{\partial}{\partial \ell_i} - u_i \frac{\partial}{\partial \ell_{i+1}} \quad , \end{aligned}$$

then (u_i , v_i) form an orthogonal parameter space with respect to D_i:

$$\begin{aligned} D_i u_i &= 0 \, , \\ D_i v_i &= \Delta_{i-1}\left(1-\frac{u_i}{\Delta_i}\right) + \Delta_{i+1}\frac{u_i}{\Delta_i} \, . \end{aligned}$$

The sweep surface $\mathbf{T}_{i,p}$ is then represented in (u_i , v_i) coordinates by

$$\mathbf{T}_{i,p}(u_i , v_i) = \mathbf{M}_p \left[\mathbf{C}_p(v_i) - \mathbf{C}_p(0)\right] + \mathbf{C}_i(u_i) \, , \quad p = i-1, \ i+1 \, , \tag{2}$$

where $\mathbf{M}_p$ represents an affine transformation matrix whose 3×3 elements are functions depending only on the parameter u_i, and a parallel (or translational) sweep of $\mathbf{C}_p$ along $\mathbf{C}_i$ is obtained by setting $\mathbf{M}_p$ to a unit matrix. The elements of the matrix $\mathbf{M}_p$ can be also determined by calculating an orthonormal coordinate frames along the guide curve $\mathbf{C}_i$, using a method of Frenet frame or rotation minimizing sweep (Klok, 1986). This method imposes only weak restrictions on the guide curve; it must be regular and twice continuously differentiable with non-vanishing curvature.

Next, we generate the ith sub-surface $\mathbf{S}_i$ by blending the two sweep surfaces $\mathbf{T}_{i,i-1}$ and $\mathbf{T}_{i,i+1}$ with functions $g_{i-1}(u_i)$ and $g_{i+1}(u_i)$

$$\mathbf{S}_i(\ell) = g_{i-1}(u_i)\,\mathbf{T}_{i,i-1}(u_i\ ,\ v_i) + g_{i+1}(u_i)\,\mathbf{T}_{i,i+1}(u_i\ ,\ v_i)\ , \tag{3}$$

where g_{i-1} and g_{i+1} are determined in such a way as to satisfy the following constraints:

$$\begin{aligned} g_{i-1}(u_i) + g_{i+1}(u_i) &\equiv 1\ , \quad u_i \in [0, \Delta_i]\ , \\ g_{i-1}(0) = g_{i+1}(\Delta_i) &= 1\ . \end{aligned} \tag{4}$$

We here introduce weight parameters w_i for each curve $\mathbf{C}_i$, and construct the functions g_{i-1} and g_{i+1} by using w_i as

$$\begin{aligned} g_{i-1}(u_i) &= \frac{w_{i-1}(\Delta_i - u_i)}{w_{i-1}(\Delta_i - u_i) + w_{i+1}u_i}\ , \\ g_{i+1}(u_i) &= \frac{w_{i+1}u_i}{w_{i-1}(\Delta_i - u_i) + w_{i+1}u_i}\ , \end{aligned}$$

where the parameter w_i controls the influence of $\mathbf{C}_i$ on the shape of the sub-surface $\mathbf{S}_i$.

The values of the elements of the matrix $\mathbf{M}_p$ and the function g_p are uniquely determined for each pair of the intersecting curves ($\mathbf{C}_i$, $\mathbf{C}_p$). The above-mentioned methods of determining these values are effective in that they can calculate smooth and natural shaped surfaces fast and stably. We may use nonlinear optimization techniques to minimize the variation of curvature or the energy of surfaces in order to generate the fair shapes (Moreton and Séquin, 1992). Their calculation, however, is time-consuming and unstable for our surface model.

It is noteworthy that the sub-surface $\mathbf{S}_i$ defined by the above expressions has the same order of geometric continuity as the cross sectional curves $\mathbf{C}_{i-1}$ and $\mathbf{C}_{i+1}$ (see Appendix).

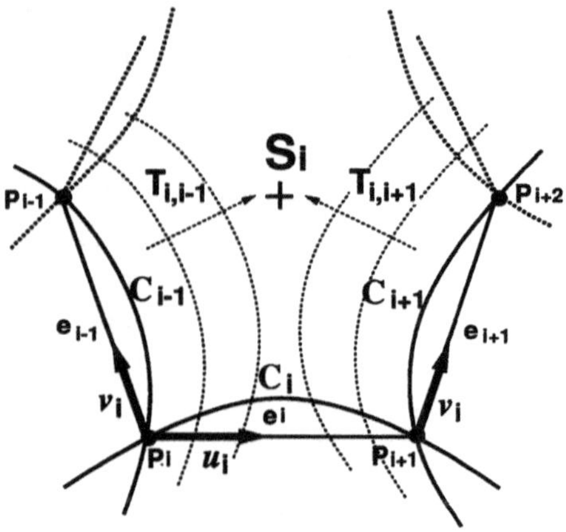

Figure 1: Sweeping of curves

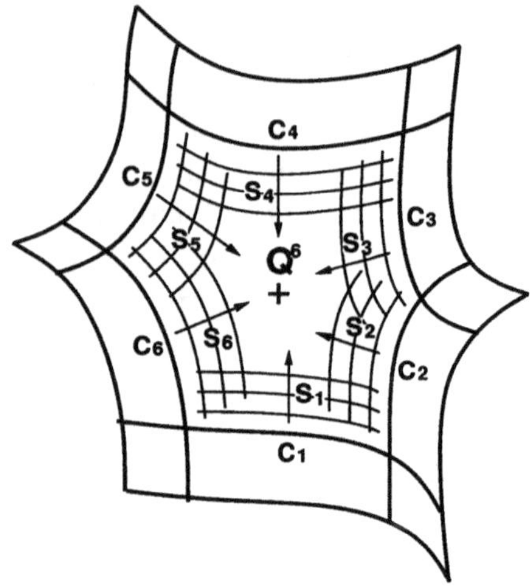

Figure 2: Blending of sub-surfaces

3.3 Blending of sub-surfaces

In this subsection, we generate an m-sided patch $\mathbf{Q}^m$ by introducing a *blending function* B_i^n of the nth-degree. The patch $\mathbf{Q}^m$ is composed by the convex combination of the m sub-surfaces $\mathbf{S}_i$, $i = 1, 2, ..., m$ as follows (see Figure 2):

$$\mathbf{Q}^m(\ell) = \sum_{i=1}^{m} \mathbf{S}_i(\ell)\, B_i^n(\ell) \ ,$$

where B_i^n is defined by

$$B_i^n(\ell) = \frac{(\ell_i \ell_{i+1})^n}{\sum_{k=1}^{m} (\ell_k \ell_{k+1})^n} \ . \tag{5}$$

Equation (5) imposes the following conditions on the edges:

$$\begin{aligned} B_i^n(\ell) &= 1 \ ; \quad \ell \in e_i \ , \\ B_i^n(\ell) &= 0 \ ; \quad \ell \in e_{j \neq i} \ , \\ \frac{\partial^h B_i^n(\ell)}{\partial {\ell_j}^h} &= 0 \ ; \quad \ell \in e_i \ , \\ & \qquad i \ , \ j = 1, 2, ..., m \ , \quad h = 1, 2, ..., n-1 \ , \end{aligned}$$

where $\ell \in e_i := \{\ell_i + \ell_{i+1} = 1 \cap \ell_{j \neq i, i+1} = 0\}$. Consequently, $\mathbf{Q}^m$ preserves the derivatives of $\mathbf{S}_i$ with respect to D_i , up to the $(n-1)^{\text{th}}$-order on e_i:

$$D_i^h \mathbf{Q}^m(\ell) = D_i^h \mathbf{S}_i(\ell) \ ; \quad \ell \in e_i \ , \ h = 0, 1, ..., n-1 \ . \tag{6}$$

Equation (6) implies that the continuity condition of $\mathbf{Q}^m$ on e_i is reduced to that of $\mathbf{S}_i$. Also, patch $\mathbf{Q}^m$ has twist compatibility at the vertices (or corners) of the domain polygon, where compatibility was introduced by Gregory (1974) for a rectangular patch.

The function B_i^n has singular points on the corners, but the singularities can be removed by adopting the limiting behavior of B_i^n near the vertices such that

$$B_i^n(\ell) = \begin{cases} 0 & ; \quad \ell \in p_{j \neq i\,,\,i+1} \\ 1/2 & ; \quad \ell \in p_{j=i\,,\,i+1} \end{cases} ,$$

where $\ell \in p_i := \{\ell_i = 1 \cap \ell_{j \neq i} = 0\}$. Note that these limiting values preserve the continuity of the generated surface.

This blending function is regarded as a generalization of the interpolant proposed by Nielson (1987) and Hagen and Pottmann (1989), whose methods concern a triangular domain. Charrot and Gregory (1984) proposed a blending function that has a similar property. Their function, however, uses a combination of three successive variables for pentagonal patches and interpolates the values on two sides, whereas our function uses a combination of two successive variables and interpolates on one side. Notice that the multivariate coordinates in the Gregory-Charrot scheme are defined by the perpendicular distances of a point from the sides of a regular polygon, and are thus not identical with the generalized barycentric coordinates.

In Figure 3, we show the equi-valued line plots of B_i^3 for domain polygons with three, four, and five sides, where each line indicates $n/10\,,\ n = 0, 1, ..., 10\,.$

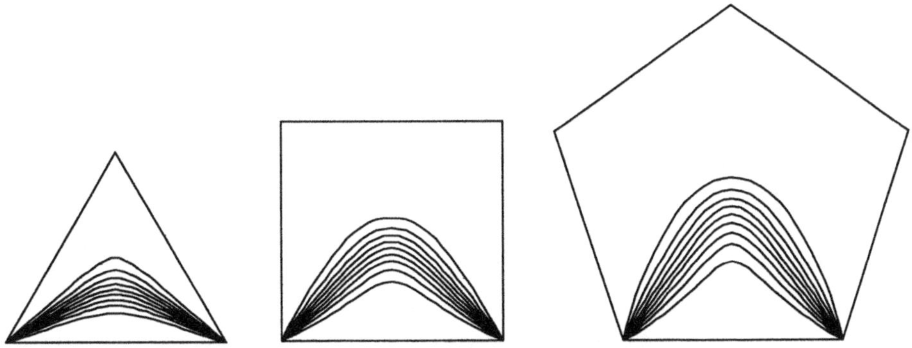

Figure 3: Equi-valued line plots of B_i^3

4 Modifications for singular topology

The sub-surface $\mathbf{S}_i$ described in Subsection 3.2 destroys the condition of geometric continuity with an adjacent sub-surface $\bar{\mathbf{S}}_i$ along the ith boundary, if the constituent cross sectional curves for $\mathbf{S}_i$ and $\bar{\mathbf{S}}_i$ are not successively parameterized.

An irregular network of curves causes such discontinuity of cross sectional curves between adjacent sub-surfaces if the following conditions on an intersection are satisfied:

- More than two boundary curves intersect at a common vertex (called, *multiple intersection*).
- The open end of a curve intersects in the middle of the other curve (called, *T-connected intersection*).

Besides, the method in Subsection 3.2 cannot deal with such conditions on a domain as

- An open set of the boundary curves defines the domain of a patch (called, an *open-sided patch*).
- Only two boundary curves enclose the domain of a patch (called, a *two-sided patch*).

We call the above four conditions *singular topology*.

We consider that a curve network of singular topology is necessary in order to design complicated shapes flexibly, and therefore modify the rules of generating and blending sub-surfaces so that they satisfy geometric continuity for singular topology. The following four subsections explain the modified methods for each condition of singular topology.

4.1 Multiple intersection

More than two curves often intersect at a common point in a network; this point may represent a pole of a sphere or the center of a symmetrical shape.

Let the guide curve $\mathbf{C}_i$ have a multiple intersection with two curves $\mathbf{C}^1_{i-1}$ and $\mathbf{C}^2_{i-1}$, as shown in Figure 4 (a). The adjacent sub-surfaces $\mathbf{S}_i$ and $\bar{\mathbf{S}}_i$ must have a boundary curve that is successively parameterized; however, two cross sectional curves $\mathbf{C}^1_{i-1}$ and $\mathbf{C}^2_{i-1}$ are independently parameterized. We therefore replace the cross sectional curve for $\mathbf{S}_i$ and $\bar{\mathbf{S}}_i$ with a common curve $\hat{\mathbf{C}}_{i-1}$ that is continuous at the multiple intersection. For example, $\hat{\mathbf{C}}_{i-1}$ is constructed by averaging the cross sectional curves such that:

$$\hat{\mathbf{C}}_{i-1}(t) = \frac{\sum_{k=1}^{\lambda} \mathbf{C}_{i-1}^{k}(t)}{\lambda} ,$$

where λ indicates the number of the curves $\mathbf{C}_{i-1}^{k}$ that intersect with $\mathbf{C}_i$ at the multiple intersection.

This modification of cross sectional curves ensures that the sub-surfaces $\mathbf{S}_i$ and $\bar{\mathbf{S}}_i$ have geometric continuity of the same order as the curves $\mathbf{C}_{i-1}^{k}$. However, the final surface does not satisfy geometric continuity at the multiple intersection, because of inconsistency of the geometric quantities at the intersections. Nevertheless, we can modify the intersecting curves in such a way that geometric continuity is satisfied at the multiple intersection. For G^1 continuity, the first-order derivatives of the curves are adjusted so that they are on a common plane at the multiple intersection. For G^2 continuity, the second-order derivatives of the curves are also modified so that the curves have a consistent principal curvature or principal direction at the multiple intersection (Miura and Wang, 1992).

4.2 T-connected intersection

Hierarchical representation of a curve network is effective for designing complicated shapes, and it is realized by using T-connected intersections in the network.

Let an open end of a curve $\mathbf{C}_T$ be connected to the middle of a boundary curve $\mathbf{C}_i(u)$ at $u = r_i\,\Delta_i$, and let the curve $\mathbf{C}_T$ split a sub-surface $\mathbf{S}_i$ into two sub-surfaces $\mathbf{S}_i^0$ and $\mathbf{S}_i^1$, as shown in Figure 4 (b).

It is obvious that the sub-surfaces $\mathbf{S}_i^0$ and $\mathbf{S}_i^1$ cannot have geometric continuity with the adjacent sub-surfaces $\bar{\mathbf{S}}_i$ if they are constructed by using $[\mathbf{C}_{i-1}^0 , \mathbf{C}_i^0 , \mathbf{C}_{i+1}^0]$ and $[\mathbf{C}_{i-1}^1 , \mathbf{C}_i^1 , \mathbf{C}_{i+1}^1]$ respectively.

We generate sub-surfaces that have geometric continuity with $\bar{\mathbf{S}}_i$ as follows:

1. Generate sub-surface $\mathbf{S}_i$ by neglecting $\mathbf{C}_T$ and using $\mathbf{C}_{i-1}^0$ and $\mathbf{C}_{i+1}^1$ as cross sectional curves and $\mathbf{C}_i := \mathbf{C}_i^0 \cup \mathbf{C}_i^1$ as a guide curve.
2. Split the sub-surface $\mathbf{S}_i(u_i , v_i)$ at $u_i = r_i\,\Delta_i$ into two sub-surfaces: $\mathbf{S}_i^0(u_i, v_i) := \mathbf{S}_i\,(r_i\,u_i , v_i)$, $\mathbf{S}_i^1(u_i, v_i) := \mathbf{S}_i\,((1 - r_i)\,u_i + r_i\,\Delta_i , v_i)$.

The curve $\mathbf{C}_T$ is used as a guide curve in constructing the sub-surfaces $\mathbf{S}_{i+1}^0$ and $\mathbf{S}_{i-1}^1$ and used as a cross sectional curve for $\mathbf{S}_{i+2}^0$ and $\mathbf{S}_{i-2}^1$. As a result, the final surfaces obtained by blending sub-surfaces have geometric continuity with $\bar{\mathbf{S}}_i$, and they exactly interpolate the curve $\mathbf{C}_T$ because the sub-surfaces $\mathbf{S}_{i+1}^0$ and $\mathbf{S}_{i-1}^1$ contain the curve $\mathbf{C}_T$.

4.3 Open-sided patch

When the shape of a surface is being designed, a transitional network of curves may contain a domain that is topologically not closed. We here consider a modification of the method described in Section 3 for generating a surface from a set of boundary curves surrounding the open domain. This technique allows designers to check the shape of the transitional network.

Assume that a virtual curve $\mathbf{C}_m$ is added to a set of boundary curves $\mathbf{C}_i$, $i = 1, 2, ..., m-1$ in order to surround an m-sided domain, as shown in Figure 4 (c).

Because sweep surfaces $\mathbf{T}_{1,m}$ and $\mathbf{T}_{m-1,m}$ cannot be defined, sub-surfaces $\mathbf{S}_1$ and $\mathbf{S}_{m-1}$ are equated to $\mathbf{T}_{1,2}$ and $\mathbf{T}_{m-1,m-2}$ respectively. We then generate the m-sided patch $\mathbf{Q}^m$ by blending the sub-surfaces as follows:

$$\mathbf{Q}^m(\ell) = \sum_{i=1}^{m-1} \mathbf{S}_i(\ell)\, \hat{B}_i^n(\ell) \ ,$$

$$\hat{B}_i^n(\ell) = \frac{(\ell_i \ell_{i+1})^n + \kappa\, (\ell_1 \ell_m)^n}{\sum_{k=1}^m (\ell_k \ell_{k+1})^n} \ , \quad \kappa = \begin{cases} u_m & ; \quad i = 1 \\ 1 - u_m & ; \quad i = m-1 \\ 0 & ; \quad i \neq 1,\ m-1 \end{cases} .$$

4.4 Two-sided patch

The definition of a domain polygon in Subsection 3.1 implies that a two-sided patch cannot be defined; however, a domain enclosed by two curves often occurs in the construction of a curve network, especially in the first stage of designing a shape. Therefore, we propose a method of skinning the two-sided domain by extending it into a quadrilateral region, as shown in Figure 4 (d).

We here split the curves $\mathbf{C}_1$ and $\mathbf{C}_2$ into two pieces as

$$\mathbf{C}_1^0(t) := \mathbf{C}_1\left(\frac{t}{2}\right) \ , \quad \mathbf{C}_1^1(t) := \mathbf{C}_1\left(\frac{\Delta_1 + t}{2}\right) \ ,$$

$$\mathbf{C}_2^0(t) := \mathbf{C}_2\left(\frac{t}{2}\right) \ , \quad \mathbf{C}_2^1(t) := \mathbf{C}_2\left(\frac{\Delta_2 + t}{2}\right) \ .$$

Then the sub-surface $\mathbf{S}_i$, $i = 1,2,3,4$ is constructed by the method proposed in Subsection 3.2 with the split curves. The sub-surface $\mathbf{S}_1$ is constructed by using $\mathbf{C}_1^0$ as a guide curve, and by using $\mathbf{C}_2^0$ and $\mathbf{C}_2^1$ as cross sectional curves, and the sub-surface $\mathbf{S}_2$ is constructed with $\mathbf{C}_1^1$, $\mathbf{C}_2^0$ and $\mathbf{C}_2^1$. The sub-surface $\mathbf{S}_3$ and $\mathbf{S}_4$ are similarly constructed by using $\mathbf{C}_2^0$ and $\mathbf{C}_2^1$ as a guide curve respectively, and by using $\mathbf{C}_1^0$ and $\mathbf{C}_1^1$ as cross sectional curves. This construction ensures the geometric continuity of the sub-surfaces $\mathbf{S}_i$ on e_i .

The final four-sided patch $\mathbf{Q}^4$ is generated by using the same blending functions B_i^n introduced in Subsection 3.3 as

$$\mathbf{Q}^4(\ell) = \sum_{i=1}^{4} \mathbf{S}_i(\ell)\, B_i^n(\ell)\,.$$

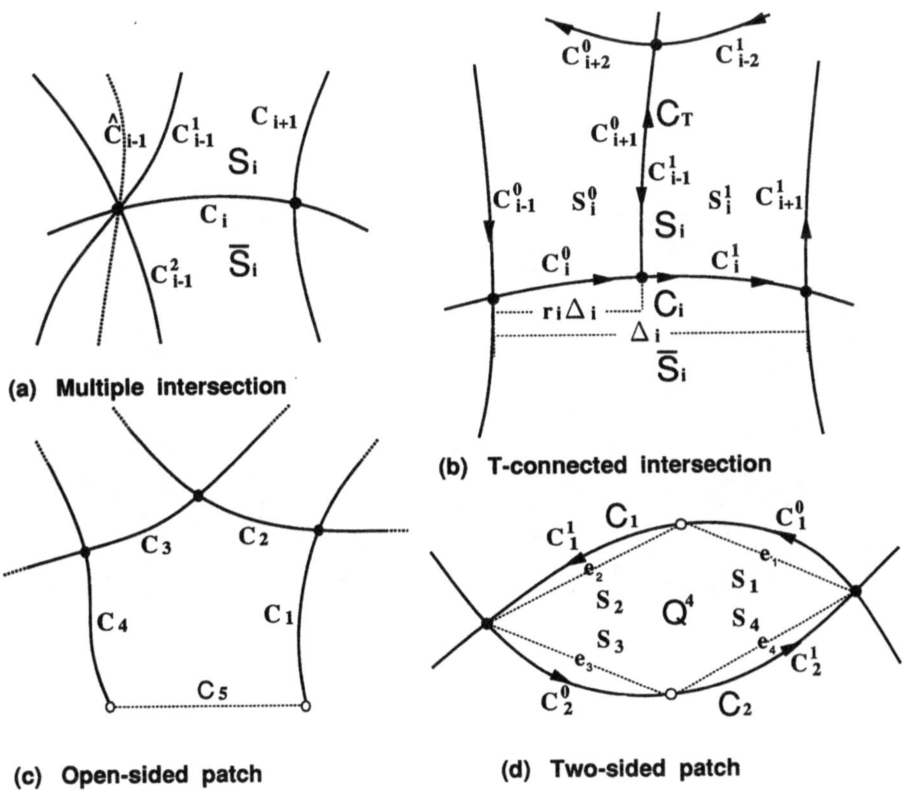

Figure 4: Singular topology

5 Examples

In this section, we present some examples of curve networks and surfaces generated from them by our method.

Figure 5 shows an example of a closed surface generated by a network that excludes the singular topology described in Section 4, where yellow balls indicate intersections of curves.

In Figure 6, we show an example of a surface defined by a curve network that contains multiple and T-connected intersections, where green balls indicate multiple intersections and red balls indicate T-connected intersections, and Figure 7 shows an example of a surface defined by a curve network that has open-sided and two-sided domains.

All surfaces are generated from curves that have C^2 continuity represented by cubic splines, where the weight parameters w_i are set to 1 for all curves, so that every pair of sweep surfaces are blended linearly. Translational sweeps are adopted for all the examples by setting $\mathbf{M}_p$ to a unit matrix. Surface data are generated by tessellating m-sided patches into triangular-stripes, and are rendered by using the Phong shading method on an IBM RISC System/6000 [1].

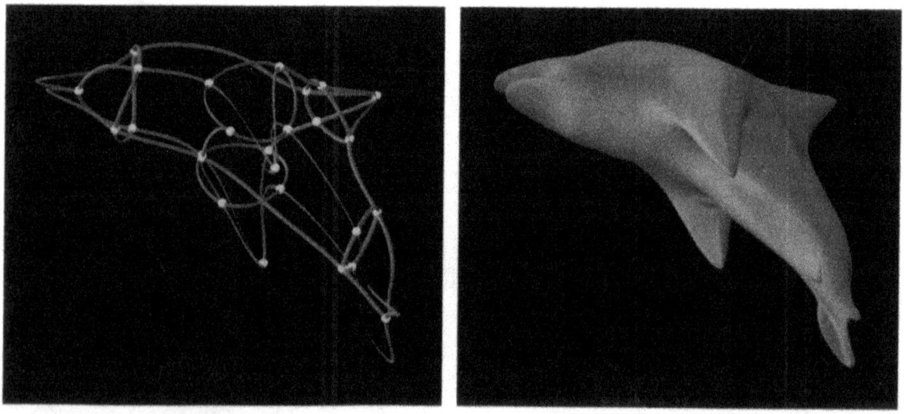

(a) A network **(b) A surface**

Figure 5: A network excluding singular topology

[1]IBM RISC System/6000 is a trademark of IBM Corp.

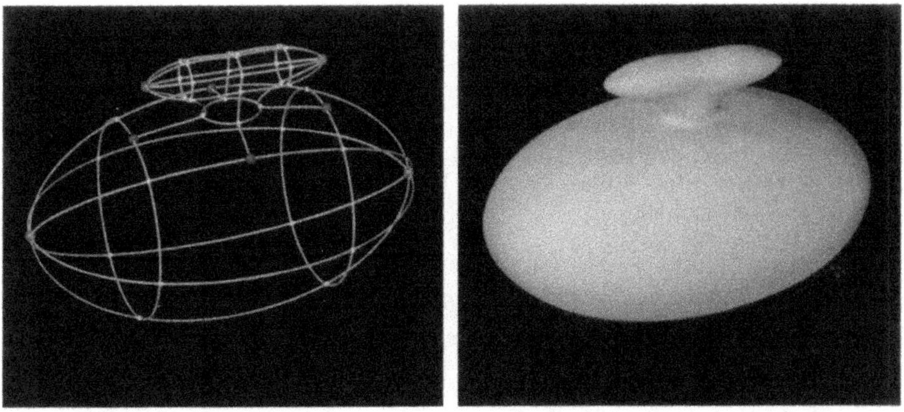

(a) A network (b) A surface

Figure 6: A network including multiple and T-connected intersections

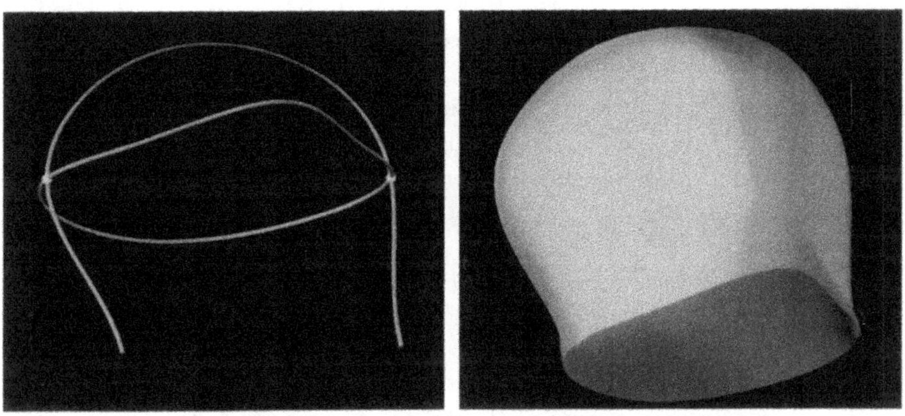

(a) A network (b) A surface

Figure 7: A network including open-sided and two-sided domains

6 Conclusions

We have presented a method of generating surfaces from a network of curves. Compared with existing methods, it has the following advantages:

- Surfaces can be defined by a network of curves that have arbitrary parametric forms.
- The network can be defined on an arbitrary connective topology, and all domains surrounded by the curves can be skinned.
- Each patch can have G^n continuity with adjacent patches if all curves surrounding it have C^n continuity.

These advantages make it possible to construct a surface model on user-friendly CAD interfaces for designing shapes by inputting 3D curves, such as (1) a sketching system with pen-input device, or (2) a virtual environment system with an advanced 3D input device such as a Spaceball or a DataGlove.

We have not considered the topological representation of a network in this paper. Our method assumes that the topological data for the network is predetermined. Because of the complexity of the topology in an irregular network, it is difficult to construct topological data automatically from curve data. The topological representation and operations (including non-manifold conditions) for the network are our next research topics.

References

Catmull, E. and Clark, J. (1978) Recursively generated B-spline surfaces on arbitrary topological meshes. *Computer Aided Design*, 10(6):350–355.

Charrot, P. and Gregory, J. A. (1984) A pentagonal surface patch for computer aided geometric design. *Computer Aided Geometric Design*, 1:87–94.

Choi, B. K. and Lee, C. S. (1990) Sweep surfaces modelling via coordinate transformations and blending. *Computer Aided Design*, 22(2):87–96.

Coquillart, S. (1987) A control-point-based sweeping technique. *IEEE Computer Graphics and Applications*, 7(11):36–45.

Doo, D. and Sabin, M. (1978) Behavior of recursive division surfaces near extraordinary points. *Computer Aided Design*, 10(6):356–360.

Gregory, J. (1974) Smooth interpolation without twist constraints. *Computer Aided Geometric Design*, pp.71–88.

Hagen, H. and Pottmann, H. (1989) Curvature continuous triangular interpolants. In Lyche, T. and Schumaker, L. editors, *Mathematical Methods in Computer Aided Geometric Design*, pp.373–384, Academic Press.

Herron, G. (1987) Techniques for visual continuity. In Farin, G. editor, *Geometric Modeling: Algorithms and New Trends*, pp.163–174, SIAM.

Hosaka, M. and Kimura, F. (1984) Non-four-sided patch expressions with control points. *Computer Aided Geometric Design*, 1:75–86.

Klok, F. (1986) Two moving coordinate frames for sweeping along a 3D trajectory. *Computer Aided Geometric Design*, 3:217–229.

Loop, C. T. and DeRose, T. D. (1989) A multisided generalization of Bézier surfaces. *ACM Transactions on Graphics*, 8(3):204–234.

Loop, C. T. and DeRose, T. D. (1990) Generalized B-spline surfaces of arbitrary topology. *Computer Graphics*, 24(4):347–356.

Miura, K. T. and Wang, K. (1992) Everywhere-G^2-continuous interpolation with C^2 Gregory patches. In Kunii, T. L. editor, *Visual Computing*, pp.497–516.

Moreton, H. P. and Séquin, C. H. (1992) Functional optimization for fair surface design. *Computer Graphics*, 26(2):167–176.

Nasri, A. H. (1987) Polyhedral subdivision method for free-form surfaces. *ACM Transactions on Graphics*, 6(1):29–73.

Nielson, G. M. (1987) A transfinite, visually continuous, triangular interpolant. In Farin, G. editor, *Geometric Modeling: Algorithms and New Trends*, pp.235–246, SIAM.

Sabin, M. (1983) Non-rectangular surface patches suitable for inclusion in a B-spline surface. In Hagen, P. editor, *Proceedings of Eurographics '83*, pp.57–69, North-Holland.

Sachs, E., Roberts, A. and Stoops, D. (1991) 3-Draw: A tool for designing 3D shapes. *IEEE Computer Graphics and Applications*, 11(6):18–26.

Tai, C., Loe, K. and Kunii, T. L. (1992) Integrated homotopy sweep technique for computer-aided geometric design. In Kunii, T. L. editor, *Visual Computing*, pp.583–595.

Varady, T. (1991) Overlap patches: A new scheme for interpolating curve networks with n-sided regions. *Computer Aided Geometric Design*, 8:7–27.

Woodward, C. D. (1988) Skinning technique for interactive B-spline surface interpolation. *Computer Aided Design*, 20(8):441–451.

Appendix

Proof of geometric continuity

The nth-order geometric continuity of surfaces, denoted by G^n, quantifies the smoothness of the connections between patches, and is independent of the parametrization of patches. Equation (6) implies that the G^n condition of $\mathbf{Q}^m$ on e_i is reduced to that of $\mathbf{S}_i$. We here prove that sub-surfaces $\mathbf{S}_i$ constructed by the method given in Subsection 3.2 have G^n continuity.

We show that $\mathbf{S}_i$ can be reparametrized to yield C^n continuity along the common boundary if cross sectional curves have C^n continuity at their intersections with a guide curve, because this property ensures G^n continuity according to Herron's definition (Herron, 1987).

Definition: *Two surface patches are said to be G^n continuous if one can be reparametrized to yield a true C^n join between the two.*

We assume the following premise without loss of generality:

[Premise]

1. Two adjacent sub-surfaces $\mathbf{S}_i$ and $\bar{\mathbf{S}}_i$ are defined on *regular* domain polygons sharing e_i.
2. The surface $\mathbf{S}_i$ (or $\bar{\mathbf{S}}_i$) is defined on u_i and v_i (or $\bar{u}_i$ and $\bar{v}_i$) formed by the barycentric coordinates ℓ (or $\bar{\ell}$) in Equation (1), and ℓ (or $\bar{\ell}$) are determined by the common two-dimensional coordinate system (x, y).
3. The coordinate system (x, y) has its origin at p_i, the direction of the x coordinate coincides with e_i, and the point (1,0) coincides with p_{i+1}.

The claim for G^n continuity is as follows:

[Claim] *There exists a reparametrization of $\tilde{x}(x,y)$ and $\tilde{y}(x,y)$ such that*

$$\frac{\partial^h \mathbf{S}_i(u_i(x,0), v_i(x,0))}{\partial x^h} = \frac{\partial^h \bar{\mathbf{S}}_i(\bar{u}_i(\tilde{x}_0,\tilde{y}_0), \bar{v}_i(\tilde{x}_0,\tilde{y}_0))}{\partial x^h}, \tag{7}$$

$$\frac{\partial^h \mathbf{S}_i(u_i(x,0), v_i(x,0))}{\partial y^h} = \frac{\partial^h \bar{\mathbf{S}}_i(\bar{u}_i(\tilde{x}_0,\tilde{y}_0), \bar{v}_i(\tilde{x}_0,\tilde{y}_0))}{\partial y^h}, \tag{8}$$

where $\tilde{x}_0 = \tilde{x}(x, 0)$, $\tilde{y}_0 = \tilde{y}(x, 0)$, $h = 0, 1, \ldots, n$, and assignment of $y = 0$ is made after the derivatives have been obtained.

From Equations (2), (3), and (4), the derivatives of $\mathbf{S}_i$ and $\bar{\mathbf{S}}_i$ with respect to x on e_i are represented by

$$\frac{\partial^h \mathbf{S}_i}{\partial x^h} = \frac{\partial^h \mathbf{C}_i(u_i)}{\partial x^h} , \quad \frac{\partial^h \bar{\mathbf{S}}_i}{\partial x^h} = \frac{\partial^h \mathbf{C}_i(\bar{u}_i)}{\partial x^h} \quad ; \quad \ell \in e_i \ , \quad h = 0, 1, ..., n \ .$$

From the premise, u_i and $\bar{u}_i$ are represented on e_i as follows:

$$\begin{aligned} u_i(x,0) &= \frac{\ell_i}{\ell_i + \ell_{i+1}} = \frac{\pi_i}{\pi_i + \pi_{i+1}} = \frac{\alpha_i}{\alpha_i + \alpha_{i+1}} = x \ , \\ \bar{u}_i(x,0) &= \frac{\bar{\ell}_i}{\bar{\ell}_i + \bar{\ell}_{i+1}} = x \ . \end{aligned}$$

Because the identical relation of $u_i(x,0) \equiv \bar{u}_i(x,0)$ holds, Equation (7) is always satisfied without reparametrizing; $\tilde{x}(x,y) = x$.

Considering $\partial u_i(x,y)/\partial y = \partial \bar{u}_i(x,y)/\partial y = 0$, we can represent the derivatives of $\mathbf{S}_i$ and $\bar{\mathbf{S}}_i$ with respect to y as follows:

$$\begin{aligned} \frac{\partial^h \mathbf{S}_i(u_i \ , \ v_i)}{\partial y^h} &= \left[\frac{\partial \mathbf{S}_i(u_i \ , \ v_i)}{\partial v_i}, \frac{\partial v_i}{\partial y} \right]^{(h)} , \\ \frac{\partial \bar{\mathbf{S}}_i(\bar{u}_i \ , \ \bar{v}_i)}{\partial y} &= \left[\frac{\partial \bar{\mathbf{S}}_i(\bar{u}_i \ , \ \bar{v}_i)}{\partial \bar{v}_i}, \frac{\partial \bar{v}_i}{\partial y} \right]^{(h)} , \end{aligned}$$

where $[\partial \mathbf{S}/\partial v, \partial v/\partial y]^{(h)}$ represents the chain rule of differentiation such as

$$\begin{aligned} \left[\frac{\partial \mathbf{S}}{\partial v}, \frac{\partial v}{\partial y} \right]^{(1)} &= \frac{\partial \mathbf{S}}{\partial v} \frac{\partial v}{\partial y} , \\ \left[\frac{\partial \mathbf{S}}{\partial v}, \frac{\partial v}{\partial y} \right]^{(2)} &= \frac{\partial^2 \mathbf{S}}{\partial v^2} \left(\frac{\partial v}{\partial y}\right)^2 + \frac{\partial \mathbf{S}}{\partial v} \frac{\partial^2 v}{\partial y^2} , \\ \left[\frac{\partial \mathbf{S}}{\partial v}, \frac{\partial v}{\partial y} \right]^{(3)} &= \cdots \ . \end{aligned}$$

If $\mathbf{C}_{i-1}$ and $\mathbf{C}_{i+1}$ satisfy C^n continuity on e_i, the derivatives of $\mathbf{S}_i$ and $\bar{\mathbf{S}}_i$ on e_i always coincide as

$$\begin{aligned} \frac{\partial^h \mathbf{S}_i(u_i, 0)}{\partial {v_i}^h} &= \frac{\partial^h \bar{\mathbf{S}}_i(\bar{u}_i, 0)}{\partial {\bar{v}_i}^h} \\ &= g_{i-1}(u_i)\, \mathbf{M}_{i-1} \frac{\partial^h \mathbf{C}_{i-1}(0)}{\partial {v_i}^h} + g_{i+1}(u_i)\, \mathbf{M}_{i+1} \frac{\partial^h \mathbf{C}_{i+1}(0)}{\partial {v_i}^h} \ . \end{aligned}$$

It is thus necessary and sufficient that

$$\lim_{y \to 0} \frac{\partial^h v_i}{\partial y^h} = \lim_{y \to 0} \frac{\partial^h \bar{v}_i}{\partial y^h} \ , \quad h = 1, 2, ..., n \ , \qquad (9)$$

holds for Equation (8) to be satisfied.

Let $\tilde{y}(x,y) = R1(x)\, y + (1/2)\, R2(x)\, y^2$,
and abbreviate $\partial v_i(x,0)/\partial y$ and $\partial^2 v_i(x,0)/\partial y^2$ as $V_y(x)$ and $V_{yy}(x)$, and similarly $\partial \bar{v}_i(x,0)/\partial \tilde{y}$ and $\partial^2 \bar{v}_i(x,0)/\partial \tilde{y}^2$ as $\bar{V}_{\tilde{y}}(x)$ and $\bar{V}_{\tilde{y}\tilde{y}}(x)$, then Equation (9) is represented by

$$\begin{aligned} V_y(x) &= R1(x)\, \bar{V}_{\tilde{y}}(x)\,, \\ V_{yy}(x) &= R1(x)^2\, \bar{V}_{\tilde{y}\tilde{y}}(x) + R2(x)\, \bar{V}_{\tilde{y}}(x)\,. \end{aligned}$$

It is clear that $\bar{V}_{\tilde{y}}(x)$ never vanishes on e_i, and thus the functions $R1(x)$ and $R2(x)$ always exist as

$$\begin{aligned} R1(x) &= \frac{V_y(x)}{\bar{V}_{\tilde{y}}(x)}\,, \\ R2(x) &= \frac{V_{yy}(x) - R1(x)^2\, \bar{V}_{\tilde{y}\tilde{y}}(x)}{\bar{V}_{\tilde{y}}(x)}\,. \end{aligned}$$

We have therefore proved that the claim is satisfied for G^2 continuity. □
For G^n, $n > 2$ continuity, we can obtain similar results by introducing $\tilde{y}(x,y) = \Sigma_{i=1}^{n}\, (1/i\,!)\, Ri(x)\, y^i$.

Hybrid Symbolic and Numeric Operators as Tools for Analysis of Freeform Surfaces*

Gershon Elber†‡ and Elaine Cohen
Computer Science Department,
University of Utah

Abstract

Freeform surfaces are commonly used in computer aided geometric design, so accurate analysis of surface properties is becoming increasingly important. In this paper, we define *surface slope* and *surface speed*, develop visualization tools, and demonstrate that they can be useful in the design process. Generally, surface properties such as curvature and twist are evaluated at a finite set of predetermined samples on the surface. This paper takes a different approach. A small set of tools is used to symbolically compute surfaces representing curvature, twist and other properties. These surfaces are then analyzed using numeric techniques.

The combination of symbolic computation to provide an exact property representation (up to machine accuracy) and numerical methods to extract data is demonstrated to be powerful and robust. This approach supports a uniform treatment once the surfaces are computed and also provides global information, so questions such as 'is a surface developable?' or 'what are the hyperbolic regions of a surface?' can be answered robustly.

Categories and Subject Descriptors: I.3.5 **[Computer Graphics]:** Computational Geometry and Object Modeling-Splines; Curve, surface, solid, and object representations.

Additional Key Words and Phrases: NURBs, Freeform surface analysis.

1 Introduction

Sculptured surface representations are fundamental forms in computer graphics and in computer aided geometric design. During different stages of modeling with sculptured surfaces, quite a few properties of the surfaces may be of interest to the designer or required for a proper design. The designer may need to isolate regions with surface slopes, defined in this paper, which are too high or too low, to detect all regions with twists larger than prespecified values, to have a visual bound on the distance traveled in the Euclidean domain while moving in the parametric domain (which we refer to as speed bound), or even to isolate all the hyperbolic (saddle) regions in the model.

Previous work directed at computing first and second order surface properties evaluated them over a discrete grid. Normals were computed and visualized by drawing them as arrows,

*This work was supported in part by DARPA (N00014-91-J-4123) and the NSF and DARPA Science and Technology Center for Computer Graphics and Scientific Visualization (ASC-89-20219). All opinions, findings, conclusions or recommendations expressed in this document are those of the authors and do not necessarily reflect the views of the sponsoring agencies.

†Appreciation is expressed to IBM for partial fellowship support of the first author.

‡Current address: Computer Science Department, Technion, Haifa 32000, Israel.

called "hedgehogs" [Schw83], over the grid. There have been attempts [Barn88, Beck86, Dill81, Forr79] to understand and compute second order surface properties such as mean and Gaussian curvatures, as well as twist, by evaluating them over the predefined grid (plate 1).

Given a surface $S(u,v)$, there is no common method to accurately subdivide S into convex, concave, and saddle regions. Using symbolic tools developed in section 2 this trichotomy becomes feasible [Elber92], as is demonstrated in section 3.

In section 2, we describe the required symbolic computation tools so properties such as Gaussian curvature, surface normal, surface slope, surface twist, and surface speed bound may be computed and represented as freeform surfaces. We call such derived surfaces *property surfaces.* We emphasize the NURBs and Bézier representations although other representations could be used, including any (piecewise) polynomial or (piecewise) rational representations. In section 3, we apply these tools to some examples and demonstrate their effectiveness. Visualization is used extensively in the section to communicate the relationship these properties have with the shape of the surface.

2 Background

Surprisingly enough the set of symbolic tools one needs for the analysis treated here is small. One needs to have representations for the derivative, sum, difference, and product of scalar curves and surfaces. Any manipulation of curves or surfaces using these tools will result in a curve or a surface of the same type. The resulting curve or surface is exact to within the accuracy of the numerical computation, since these operation have closed forms and are, in fact, symbol manipulators. Therefore, we refer to the usage of these tools as *symbolic* computation.

Contouring will also be used as a tool to extract information from the symbolically computed property surfaces.

2.1 Symbolic Tools

Given a Bézier or NURBs curve, the form of the derivative as a curve in vector space is well known (see [Farin86]),

$$\frac{dC(t)}{dt} = \frac{d\sum_{i=0}^{m-1} P_i B_i^k(t)}{dt} = (k-1)\sum_{i=0}^{m-2} \frac{(P_{i+1}-P_i)}{t_{i+k}-t_i} B_i^{k-1}(t), \tag{1}$$

and this result easily extends to tensor product surfaces.

The symbolic computation of sum and/or difference of two scalar Bézier or NURBs curves is achieved by computing the sum and/or difference of their respective control points [Elber92, Farin86, Farou88], once the two curves are in the same space. This requirement can be met by representing them as curves with the same order (using degree raising [Cohen86a, Cohen86b] on the lower order one, if necessary) and the same continuity (using refinement [Cohen80] of knot vectors for NURBs).

$$\begin{aligned} C_1(t) \pm C_2(t) &= \sum_{i=0}^{k} P_i B_{i,\tau}^k(t) \pm \sum_{i=0}^{k} Q_i B_{i,\tau}^k(t) \\ &= \sum_{i=0}^{k} \left(P_i B_{i,\tau}^k(u) \pm Q_i B_{i,\tau}^k(u)\right) \end{aligned}$$

$$= \sum_{i=0}^{k} (P_i \pm Q_i) B^k_{i,\tau}(u). \tag{2}$$

This result easily extends to tensor product surfaces as well.

Representation for product of scalar curves is the last requirement. For Bézier curves (see [Farin86, Farou88]),

$$\begin{aligned} C_1(t)C_2(t) &= \sum_{i=0}^{m} P_i B_i^m(t) \sum_{j=0}^{n} Q_j B_j^n(t) \\ &= \sum_{i=0}^{m}\sum_{j=0}^{n} P_i Q_j B_i^m(t) B_j^n(t) \\ &= \sum_{i=0}^{m}\sum_{j=0}^{n} P_i Q_j \frac{\binom{m}{i}\binom{n}{j}}{\binom{m+n}{i+j}} B_{i+j}^{m+n}(t) \\ &= \sum_{k=0}^{m+n} R_k B_k^{m+n}(t), \end{aligned} \tag{3}$$

where

$$R_k = \sum_{\substack{i,j \\ i+j=k}} P_i Q_j \frac{\binom{m}{i}\binom{n}{j}}{\binom{m+n}{k}}.$$

This result can also be extended to tensor product surfaces. It is also necessary to represent scalar products as part of representing sums and differences of rational curves and surfaces, as well as derivatives of rationals.

Finding a representation for the product of NURBs is far more difficult. A direct algorithmic approach has recently been developed [Morken] which supports symbolic computation of the coefficients of the product after finding the knot vector of the product curve. However, since it is computationally expensive and complex to implement, one might choose to exploit the B-spline representation uniqueness property and compute the coefficients of the product by solving an equivalent interpolation problem [Elber92].

2.2 Contouring operator

It is frequently useful to know the zero set of a property surface or to have all regions in which the values of the property is larger than some threshold, either for itself or to use in further analysis. Contours in the parameter space of the property surface can be used as trimming curves for the original surface [McCol88], so the trimmed surface will consist of all regions of the original surface with property values larger (or smaller) than the contouring level. The problem of computing the contours is closely related to finding surface-surface intersections and ray-surface intersections [Kaji82], problems with inherent numerical complexities and instabilities.

Let $F(u,v) = \left(\frac{x(u,v)}{w(u,v)}, \frac{y(u,v)}{w(u,v)}, \frac{z(u,v)}{w(u,v)}\right)$ and $P = Ax + By + Cz + D = 0$ be the property surface and the contouring plane, respectively. By substituting the components of $F(u,v)$ into P one can solve for all values of u and v in the parametric domain for which $F(u,v) \cap P \neq \emptyset$.

$$S(u,v) = A\frac{x(u,v)}{w(u,v)} + B\frac{y(u,v)}{w(u,v)} + C\frac{z(u,v)}{w(u,v)} + D$$

$$= \frac{Ax(u,v) + By(u,v) + Cz(u,v) + Dw(u,v)}{w(u,v)} \tag{4}$$

A single NURBs surface representation for equation 4 can be found using the operations defined in section 2.1, namely surface addition and surface multiplication. The zero set of the surface $S(u,v)$, in equation 4, is the set of parametric values for the required intersection. Since both $F(u,v)$ and $S(u,v)$ share the same parametric domain, mapping the parametric domain information back to $F(u,v)$ is trivial. $S(u,v)$ is a *scalar* surface, which leads to a simpler and faster computation. Assuming $w(u,v) \neq 0$, the zero set of $S(u,v)$ can be computed using only the numerator of $S(u,v)$. Thus, even if $F(u,v)$ is a rational surface, contouring computations can be performed on scalar polynomial surfaces.

In the following section, the tools defined in this section will be used. The four basic operations for surfaces: addition, subtraction, multiplication, and division will be combined with differentiation to define or approximate property surfaces, as necessary. Then the contouring algorithm will be used to analyze and extract useful information from them.

3 Examples

3.1 Surface slopes

The slope of a planar curve at a given point is equal to the angle between the tangent to the curve and a reference line, usually the horizontal axis. In an analogous way we define the *surface slope* at a given point, p, as the angle between the plane tangent to the surface at p and a reference plane. Without loss of generality, in the discussion below we assume that the reference plane is the xy plane.

Since the angle between two planes, is equal to the angle between their two normals, to compute surface slope, one need only compute the angle between the surface normal and the z axis. Let n be the surface unit normal and let n_z be its z component. Then, the tangent of the slope angle $\mathcal{P}$ is equal to:

$$tan(\mathcal{P}) = \frac{\sqrt{1-n_z^2}}{n_z}. \tag{5}$$

When $n_z = +1$ the surface orientation is horizontal. If $n_z = 0$ the surface is vertical, and finally if $n_z = -1$ that surface is horizontal again, but this time facing down.

Inspection of the surface unit normal equation shows that $n(u,v)$ cannot be computed directly using the symbolic tools of section 2.1 because of the need to determine the square root. However, the z component of the unnormalized normal surface, $\hat{n}$, is equal to:

$$\hat{n}_z(u,v) = \frac{\partial x(u,v)}{\partial u}\frac{\partial y(u,v)}{\partial v} - \frac{\partial y(u,v)}{\partial u}\frac{\partial x(u,v)}{\partial v}, \tag{6}$$

where $x(u,v)$ and $y(u,v)$ are the x and y components of surface $S(u,v)$.

Then, $n_z(u,v) = \hat{n}_z(u,v)/\|\hat{n}(u,v)\|$, where $\|\hat{n}(u,v)\|$ is the magnitude of $\hat{n}(u,v)$

Even though $n_z(u,v)$ contains a square root factor, it is a scalar function, and can be squared so that $n_z(u,v)^2$ can be represented.

Given a slope $\mathcal{P}$ in degrees (or radians) the conversion to the $n_z^2(u,v)$ value required is straightforward using equation 5. Therefore, given a certain slope $\mathcal{P}$, one can compute the

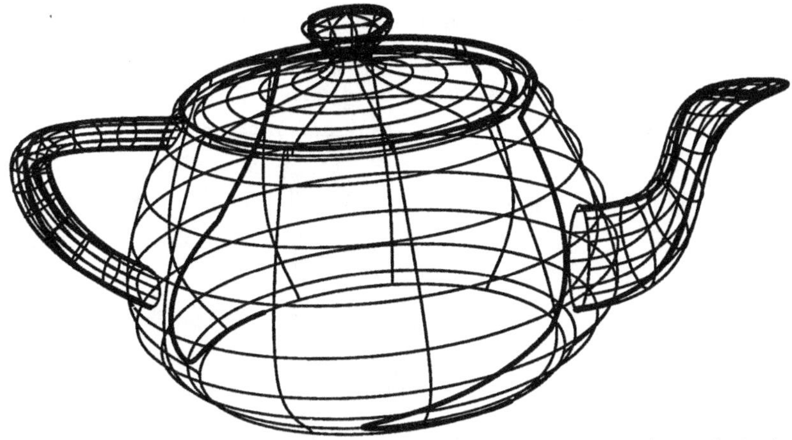

Figure 1: Silhouettes are equivalent to the zero set of equation 6 (rotated view).

required n_z and n_z^2 using equation 5. Since n_z^2 is representable using (piecewise) rationals, one can contour this surface at the required n_z^2 level. Plate 2 demonstrates this exact process for several slope levels.

Alternatively, one can use the symbolically computed property $n_z^2(u, v)$ as a scalar map designating the color of the surface at each location, much like a texture map. Plate 3 is an example for this approach, for the same surface as in plate 2.

The technique presented here has also been used to compute silhouette curves of surfaces [Elber90], and is equivalent to the zero set of equation 6. $\hat{n}_z(u, v)$ is symbolically computed and its intersection (contouring) with the plane $Z = 0$ provides the required silhouette curves in parametric space. Figure 1 shows one such example.

Slope is not an intrinsic surface property. In fact, since it is orientation dependent, it provides the designer with a measure on the planarity of the surface as well as on its orientation.

3.2 Surface Speed

The speed of a curve is defined as the distance moved in Euclidean space per unit of movement in parameter space. For a curve,

$$\begin{aligned} \mathcal{S}(t) &= \left\| \frac{dC(t)}{dt} \right\| \\ &= \sqrt{\left(\frac{dx}{dt}\right)^2 + \left(\frac{dy}{dt}\right)^2 + \left(\frac{dz}{dt}\right)^2}. \end{aligned} \tag{7}$$

We define the *speed bound* of surface $S(u, v)$ as the supremum of the speeds of all curves on the unit circle of the tangent plane using the first partials as a basis.

Let $\alpha(t)$ be a curve in the parametric domain of $S(u, v)$, that is $\alpha(t) = (u(t), v(t))$. By providing this speed bound of the surface parametrization, one can compute certain properties on $\alpha(t)$ and use the speed bound to extrapolate and provide bounds on the properties on the composed curve $S \circ \alpha = S(u(t), v(t))$.

Let $\gamma(t)$ be an auxiliary arc length parametrized curve with its image in the parametric space of $S(u,v)$, i.e. $\gamma(t) = (u(t), v(t))$, with $\sqrt{\left(\frac{du}{dt}\right)^2 + \left(\frac{dv}{dt}\right)^2} = 1$, for all t. Then

$$\begin{aligned}
\left\|\frac{dS(u(t),v(t))}{dt}\right\|^2 &= \left\|\frac{\partial S}{\partial u}\frac{du}{dt} + \frac{\partial S}{\partial v}\frac{dv}{dt}\right\|^2 \\
&= \left(\frac{\partial x}{\partial u}\frac{du}{dt} + \frac{\partial x}{\partial v}\frac{dv}{dt}\right)^2 \\
&\quad + \left(\frac{\partial y}{\partial u}\frac{du}{dt} + \frac{\partial y}{\partial v}\frac{dv}{dt}\right)^2 \\
&\quad + \left(\frac{\partial z}{\partial u}\frac{du}{dt} + \frac{\partial z}{\partial v}\frac{dv}{dt}\right)^2 \\
&\leq \left(\frac{\partial x}{\partial u}\right)^2 + \left(\frac{\partial x}{\partial v}\right)^2 + \left(\frac{\partial y}{\partial u}\right)^2 \\
&\quad + \left(\frac{\partial y}{\partial v}\right)^2 + \left(\frac{\partial z}{\partial u}\right)^2 + \left(\frac{\partial z}{\partial v}\right)^2, \qquad (8)
\end{aligned}$$

since

$$\begin{aligned}
\left(\frac{\partial x}{\partial u}\frac{du}{dt} + \frac{\partial x}{\partial v}\frac{dv}{dt}\right)^2 &= \left(\left(\frac{\partial x}{\partial u}, \frac{\partial x}{\partial v}\right) \cdot \left(\frac{du}{dt}, \frac{dv}{dt}\right)\right)^2 \\
&= \left\|\left(\frac{\partial x}{\partial u}, \frac{\partial x}{\partial v}\right) \cdot \left(\frac{du}{dt}, \frac{dv}{dt}\right)\right\|^2 \\
&\leq \left\|\left(\frac{\partial x}{\partial u}, \frac{\partial x}{\partial v}\right)\right\|^2 \left\|\left(\frac{du}{dt}, \frac{dv}{dt}\right)\right\|^2 \\
&= \left\|\left(\frac{\partial x}{\partial u}, \frac{\partial x}{\partial v}\right)\right\|^2 \\
&= \left(\frac{\partial x}{\partial u}\right)^2 + \left(\frac{\partial x}{\partial v}\right)^2. \qquad (9)
\end{aligned}$$

If $\alpha\frac{\partial S}{\partial u} = \frac{\partial S}{\partial v}$ (see figure 2 with collinear partials along the surface boundary, which implies the surface is not regular there) and $\alpha\frac{du}{dt} = \frac{dv}{dt}$, then

$$\begin{aligned}
\left\|\left(\frac{\partial x}{\partial u}, \frac{\partial x}{\partial v}\right) \cdot \left(\frac{du}{dt}, \frac{dv}{dt}\right)\right\|^2 &= \left\|\left(\frac{\partial x}{\partial u}, \alpha\frac{\partial x}{\partial u}\right) \cdot \left(\frac{du}{dt}, \frac{dv}{dt}\right)\right\|^2 \\
&= \left\|\frac{\partial x}{\partial u}(1, \alpha)\left(\frac{du}{dt}, \frac{dv}{dt}\right)\right\|^2 \\
&= \left|\frac{\partial x}{\partial u}\right|^2 (1+\alpha^2) \\
&= \left(\frac{\partial x}{\partial u}\right)^2 + \left(\frac{\partial x}{\partial v}\right)^2, \qquad (10)
\end{aligned}$$

and the upper bound established in equation 8 is reached. Therefore, this bound is minimal.

Since it is not possible to represent the square root of equation 8 as a (piecewise) rational surface, in general, we compute instead

$$\begin{aligned}
\hat{S}(u,v) &= \left(\left(\frac{\partial x}{\partial u}\right)^2 + \left(\frac{\partial y}{\partial u}\right)^2 + \left(\frac{\partial z}{\partial u}\right)^2\right. \\
&\quad \left. + \left(\frac{\partial x}{\partial v}\right)^2 + \left(\frac{\partial y}{\partial v}\right)^2 + \left(\frac{\partial z}{\partial v}\right)^2\right). \qquad (11)
\end{aligned}$$

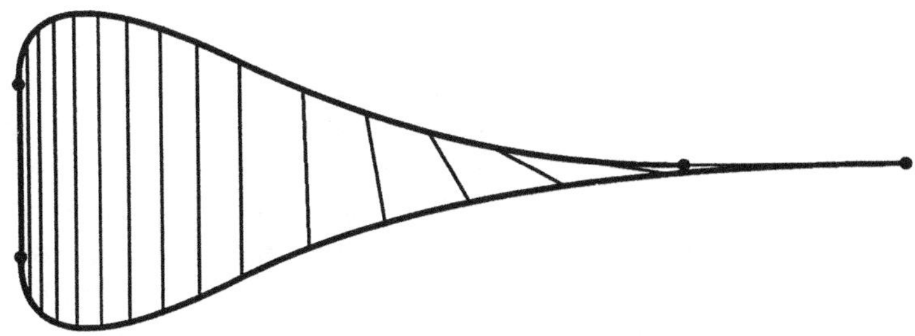

Figure 2: Degenerated boundary provides the two extremes on speed bound.

Plates 4 and 5 are two examples of using $\hat{\mathcal{S}}(u,v)$ to compute a speed bound on the surface.

The speed surface can be used to provide a measure on the quality of the parametrization. This can becomes especially important if the surface is to be evaluated (for any purpose, including rendering) at a predefined set of parameter values.

3.3 Variations on Surface Twist

Also interesting is the ability to visualize surface twist. Basically, the twist is defined as the cross derivative component:

$$\mathcal{T}(u,v) = \frac{\partial^2 S(u,v)}{\partial u \partial v}. \tag{12}$$

This equation is representable and can always be computed symbolically for (piecewise) rationals. Plates 6, 7 and 8 shows this property as a texture mapped on the surfaces.

Using equation 12 as a twist measure has a major drawback as can be seen in plate 7. Even though the surface is flat, the twist component is not zero since the speed of the parametrization is changing. In other words, the mapping from the parametric space to the Euclidean space is not isometric. It would be more helpful to use the twist component in only the surface normal direction (see [Barn88]) to eliminate the twist as a result of a non isometric mapping.

$$l_{12} = l_{21} = \left(n, \frac{\partial^2 S(u,v)}{\partial u \partial v} \right) \tag{13}$$

where l_{12}, and $= l_{21}$ are two of the components of second fundamental matrix form, L (see also [Carmo76, Mill77, Stok69]).

Obviously, this time the l_{12} component in the flat surface in plate 7 is zero showing no twist in the normal direction. Furthermore, the use of this property showed that the teapot has virtually no twist in the normal direction as well. All the twist in plate 8 was a result of the nonisometric mapping. Plate 9 shows a nonplanar surface, similar to the one in plate 7 using l_{12} as property surface mapping colors onto the surface, as texture.

Since now one can compute both the total twist (equation 12), and the twist in the normal direction (equation 13), one can consider computing the twist in the tangent plane to the surface as the difference of the two quantities. This difference would provide another measure as to the quality of the surface parametrization.

3.4 Surface Trichotomy

It is frequently desired to provide a bound on the angularity of a surface. It is also desired in some cases to detect and isolate concave or convex regions. In 5-axis NC milling, a flat end cutter is usable only for the convex part of the surface.

In [Carmo76, Elber] it is shown that one of the principal curvatures must be zero along the boundaries of convex, concave, or saddlelike regions and that this immediately necessitates that $||L|| = 0$ where $||L||$ is the determinant of the second fundamental matrix form. It is also shown in [Elber] that the zero set of $||\hat{L}||$ can be used instead where

$$\hat{L} = (l_{ij}) = \begin{bmatrix} \left(\hat{n}, \frac{\partial^2 S}{\partial u^2}\right) & \left(\hat{n}, \frac{\partial^2 S}{\partial u \partial v}\right) \\ \left(\hat{n}, \frac{\partial^2 S}{\partial u \partial v}\right) & \left(\hat{n}, \frac{\partial^2 S}{\partial v^2}\right) \end{bmatrix}, \tag{14}$$

and $\hat{n}$ is the unnormalized normal $\hat{n}(u,v) = \frac{\partial S}{\partial u} \times \frac{\partial S}{\partial v}$ to the surface.

Each element of $\hat{L}$ is representable as a NURBs, using the tools developed in section 2. The bottom of plate 10 shows the scalar surface $||\hat{L}||$ with the zero plane and their intersection. The top of plate 10 uses these intersection curves to form the surface trichotomy into convex (red), concave (green), and saddle (yellow) trimmed regions. Plate 11 demonstrates this method on a more realistic object. The teapot trichotomy degenerates into a dichotomy since no concave regions exist in the teapot model.

Finally, it is interesting to note that a sufficient condition for a surface to be developable is that its Gaussian curvature is zero everywhere, i.e. $K(u,v) \equiv 0$ [Faux79]. Since $K(u,v) = \frac{||L||}{||G||}$, where G is the first fundamental form [Carmo76, Mill77, Stok69], this condition is equivalent to the condition that $||L|| \equiv 0$, for regular surfaces when $||G|| \neq 0$. A simple practical test that can answer whether a surface is developable or not is to symbolically compute and compare each of $||L||$ coefficients to zero. Plate 12 shows two developable NURBs surfaces, one ruled along an isoparametric direction while the other is not.

3.5 Bounding the Curvature

In [Elber] it is suggested that the sum of the squares of the principal curvatures may be a relevant measure of shape and can be represented as

$$\begin{aligned} \xi &= \left(\kappa_n^1\right)^2 + \left(\kappa_n^2\right)^2 \\ &= \frac{(g_{11}\hat{l}_{22} + \hat{l}_{11}g_{22} - 2g_{12}\hat{l}_{12})^2 - 2||G||||\hat{L}||}{||G||^2||\hat{n}||^2}. \end{aligned} \tag{15}$$

ξ is bounded to be at most $\sqrt{2}$ larger than the larger absolute value of the two principal curvatures. Furthermore, ξ can be represented using the tools described in section 2. In plates 12 and 13, the ξ property has been computed for the two developable surfaces and for the Utah teapot model respectively and used as a texture mapped through a color map table.

Plate 14 shows a surface subdivided into regions based on ξ. The property surface $\xi(u,v)$ of the surface in plate 14 is contoured in figure 3 and regions with different curvature bounds are formed.

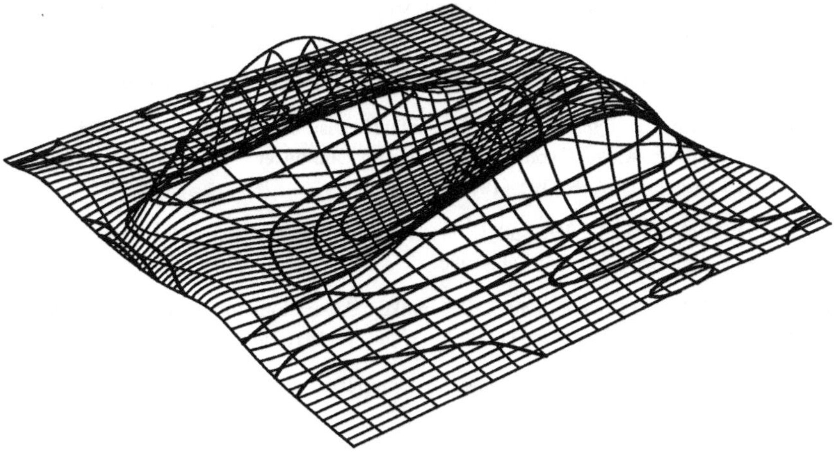

Figure 3: Curvature surface bound, ξ, of the surface in plate 14.

4 Conclusions

Surfaces derived from both first and second order analysis of sculptured surfaces are represented as NURBs surfaces using a small set of operators. We show that a combination of symbolic and numeric operators can be used to globally represent, approximate, or analyze these property surfaces. Other properties that cannot be represented as piecewise rationals have approximations that bound these properties and are representable. Further, we introduce two new derived surfaces to help visualizing and understanding surface shapes - speed and slope.

The full power of the NURBs representation can be used to analyze and to globally determine characteristics of these derived surfaces, which can then be used to visualize results or for feedback into design. For the first time the designer can guarantee that the steepness of the whole surface will be less than a specified slope or that a whole surface will have speed bound smaller than a specified value.

We show that symbolic computation supports robust computation and simplifies visualization of surface properties. Its usefulness is demonstrated in [Elber92] for applications from error bound for offset approximation to adaptive and almost optimal toolpaths for machining purposes, as well as the surface analysis discussed in this paper.

References

[Barn88] R. E. Barnhill, G. Farin, L. Fayard and H. Hagen. Twists, Curvatures and Surface Interrogation. Computer Aided Design, vol. 20, no. 6, pp 341-346, July/August 1988.

[Beck86] J. M. Beck, R. T. Farouki, and J. K. Hinds. Surface Analysis Methods. IEEE Computer Graphics and Applications, Vol. 6, No. 12, pp 18-36, December 1986.

[Dill81] J. C. Dill. An Application of Color Graphics to the Display of Surface Curvature. Siggraph 1981, pp 153-161.

[Carmo76] M. D. Carmo. Differential Geometry of Curves and Surfaces. Prentice-Hall 1976.

[Cohen80] E. Cohen, T. Lyche, and R. Riesenfeld. Discrete B-splines and subdivision Techniques in Computer-Aided Geometric Design and Computer Graphics. Computer Graphics and Image Processing, 14, 87-111 (1980).

[Cohen86a] E. Cohen, T. Lyche, and L. Schumaker. Degree Raising for Splines. Journal of Approximation Theory, Vol 46, Feb. 1986.

[Cohen86b] E. Cohen, T. Lyche, and L. Schumaker. Algorithms for Degree Raising for Splines. ACM Transactions on Graphics, Vol 4, No 3, pp.171-181, July 1986.

[Farin86] G. Farin. Curves and Surfaces for Computer Aided Geometric Design. Academic Press, Inc. Second Edition 1990.

[Farou88] R. T. Farouki and V. T. Rajan. Algorithms For Polynomials In Bernstein Form. Computer Aided Geometric Design 5, pp 1-26, 1988.

[Faux79] I. D. Faux and M. J. Pratt. Computational Geometry for Design and Manufacturing. John Wiley & Sons, 1979.

[Forr79] A. R. Forrest. On the Rendering of Surfaces. Siggraph 1979, pp 253-259.

[Elber90] G. Elber and E. Cohen. Hidden Curve Removal for Free Form Surfaces. Siggraph 90, pp 95-104.

[Elber92] G. Elber. Free Form Surface Analysis using a Hybrid of Symbolic and Numeric Computation. Ph.D. thesis, University of Utah, Computer Science Department, 1992.

[Elber] G. Elber and E. Cohen. Second Order Surface Analysis Using Hybrid Symbolic and Numeric Operators. To appear in Transaction on Graphics.

[McCol88] T. McCollough. Support for Trimmed Surfaces. M.S. thesis, University of Utah, Computer Science Department, 1988.

[Mill77] Millman and Parker. Elements of Differential Geometry. Prentice Hill Inc., 1977.

[Morken] K. Morken. Some Identities for Products and Degree Raising of Splines. To appear in the journal of Constructive Approximation.

[Kaji82] J. T. Kajiya. Ray Tracing Parametric Patches. Siggraph 1982, pp 245-256.

[Stok69] J. J. Stoker. Differential Geometry. Wiley-Interscience 1969.

[Schw83] D. L. Schwitzer. Interactive Surface Visualization Using Raster Graphics. Ph.D. dissertation, University of Utah, August 1983.

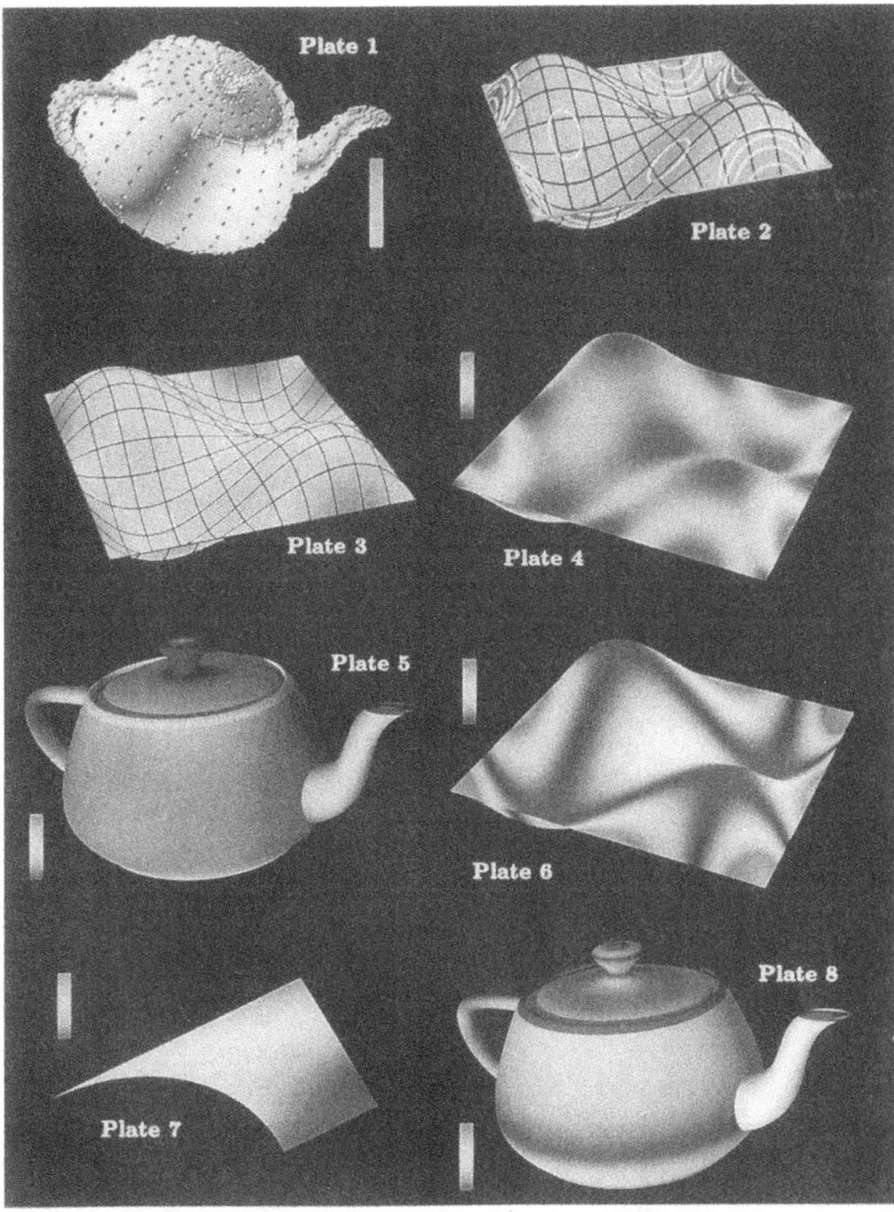
Plate 1
Plate 2
Plate 3
Plate 4
Plate 5
Plate 6
Plate 7
Plate 8

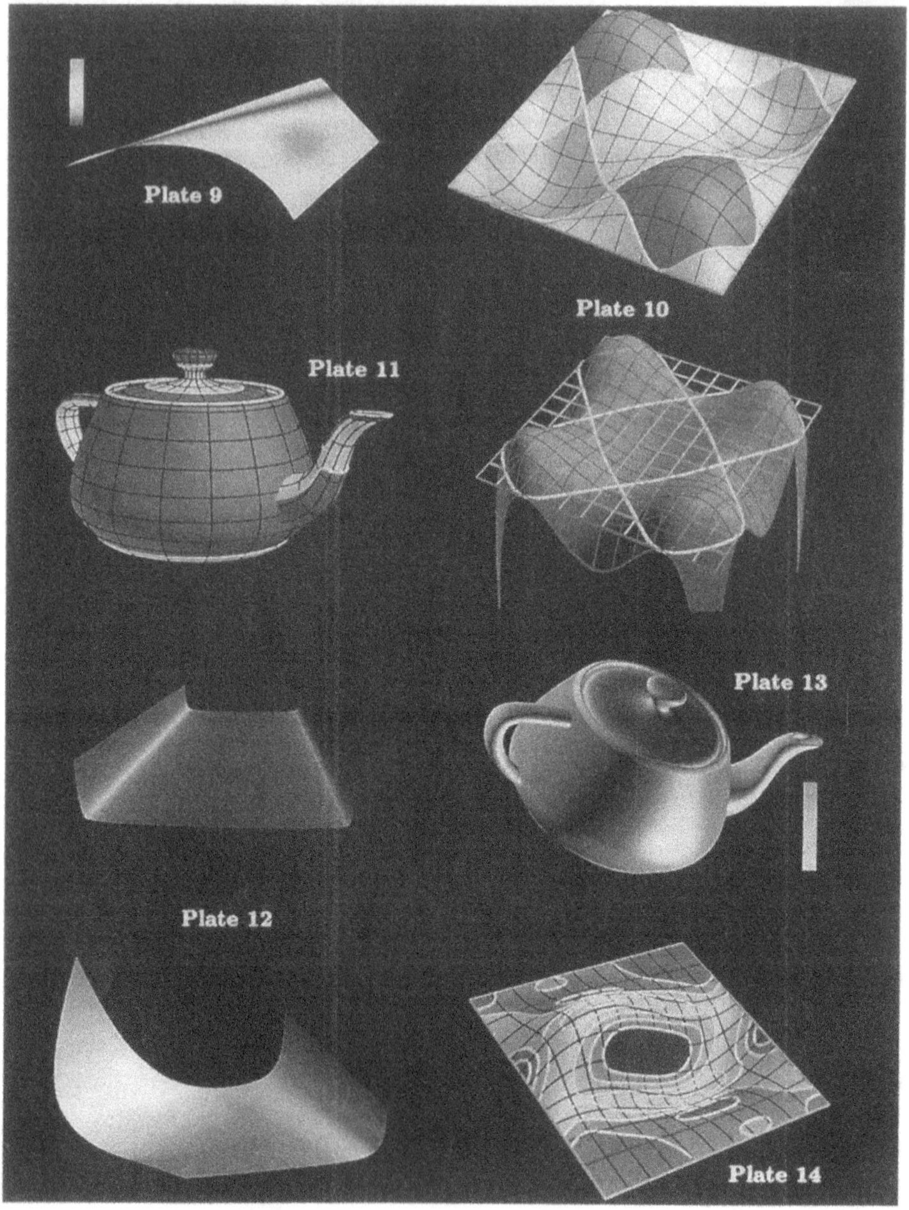
Plate 9
Plate 10
Plate 11
Plate 12
Plate 13
Plate 14

Chapter 6

Curve and Surface Modeling

Smooth Surface Interpolation with Bézier Surfaces Having Rational Bézier Points

Kenji Ueda
Ricoh Company, Ltd.
1-1-17, Koishikawa, Bunkyo-ku
Tokyo, 112, JAPAN

Abstract

The first order cross boundary derivatives of Bézier rectangles and triangles are independently derived for each boundary by putting the Bézier points in the rational Bézier form. This representation simplifies the cross boundary construction in connecting two Bézier patches. Degree elevation allows handling the Bézier rectangle and triangle in a uniform manner. The interpolating surfaces take the standard Bézier form except the control points are convex combinations of the control points defining the cross boundary derivatives. The blending functions are in the rational Bézier form of the smallest degree and have the minimum significant values to define the control points. The surfaces having rational Bézier points can be easily and economically converted to rational Bézier surfaces, however, with zero weight Bézier points at corners. A method for removing such singularities is also described.

Keywords

Bézier rectangles, Bézier triangles, radial derivatives, Gregory surfaces, convex combination surfaces, rational Bézier points, zero weights, rational Bézier surfaces.

1 Introduction

Various techniques for interpolating a mesh of curves by a smooth surface have been developed in computer aided geometric design. The Bézier surface is widely used in free-form surface modeling. Many methods have been proposed to interpolate a network of three and four-sided regions smoothly by inserting a Bézier surface in each region.

Smooth surface connection using the Bézier rectangle is reviewed in (Du and Schmitt, 1990). A local surface interpolation method with tangent plane continuity for four-sided regions is described in (Chiyokura and Kimura, 1983; 1984). This method is also used in (Shirman and Séquin, 1987; 1991) to interpolate three and four-sided regions. For Bézier triangles, some interpolation methods are presented in (Piper, 1987; Hagen, 1989). Triangular surface fitting schema are surveyed in (Mann, et al., 1992). In (Liu and Hoschek, 1989; DeRose, 1990; Wassum, 1992), geometric continuity conditions for Bézier surfaces are described.

This paper describes a general method for smoothly interpolating three and four-sided regions in a unified manner. The method constructs the Bézier rectangle and triangle control points from the cross boundary derivatives defined by using their boundary

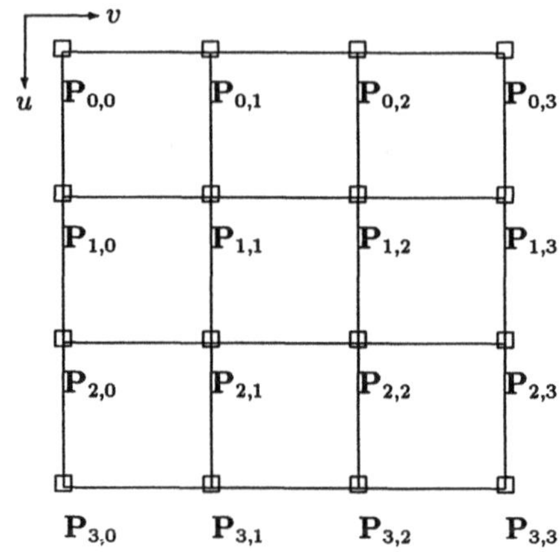

Figure 1: Bézier points of bicubic Bézier rectangle

data as the derivatives of a Bézier rectangle. The control points are blended by rational functions in the Bézier forms. Each surface patch has rational Bézier points and are easily converted to rational Bézier surfaces.

In the next section, the Bézier rectangle and triangle are defined and a property of the control points of the Bézier triangle is shown. The smooth surface connection method (Chiyokura and Kimura, 1983) of two adjacent surfaces from their common boundary's data is introduced in section 3. In section 4, smooth surface interpolation methods of three and four-sided regions by Bézier rectangles and triangles having rational Bézier points are presented. Finally, a conversion method of the interpolating surfaces to rational Bézier surfaces is shown. A technique for removing the singularities of the rational Bézier surfaces is also described.

2 Bézier Surfaces and Their Bézier Points

This section shows the definitions of Bézier rectangles and triangles and a geometric relation between a Bézier triangle and a Bézier rectangle.

2.1 Bézier rectangles and triangles

A Bézier rectangle of degree $m \times n$ is expressed by the following form:

$$\mathbf{S}(u,v) = \sum_{i=0}^{m}\sum_{j=0}^{n} \mathrm{B}_i^m(u)\mathrm{B}_j^n(v)\mathbf{P}_{i,j} \qquad (0 \le u, v \le 1), \tag{1}$$

where $\mathrm{B}_i^n(t)$ is the univariate Bernstein polynomial of degree n:

$$\mathrm{B}_i^n(t) = \binom{n}{i}(1-t)^{n-i}t^i. \tag{2}$$

Figure 1 shows the Bézier point array $\mathbf{P}_{i,j}$ when $m = n = 3$.

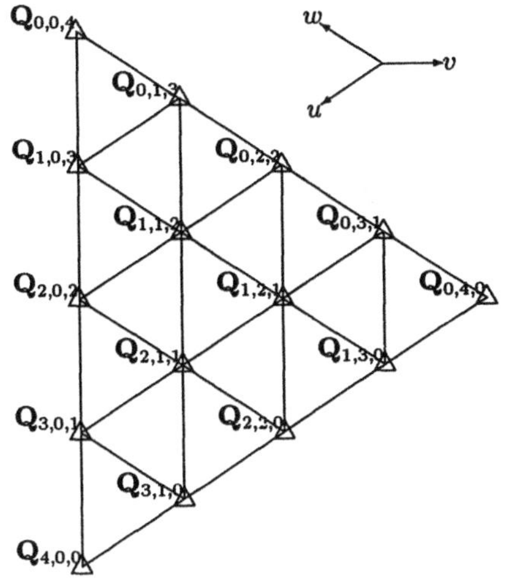

Figure 2: Bézier points of quartic Bézier triangle

A Bézier triangle of degree n is expressed by the following form:

$$\mathbf{S}(u,v,w) = \sum_{0\le i,j,k}^{i+j+k=n} \mathrm{b}^n_{i,j,k}(u,v,w)\mathbf{Q}_{i,j,k} \qquad \left(\begin{array}{c} 0 \le u,v,w \le 1 \\ u+v+w=1 \end{array}\right), \tag{3}$$

where $\mathrm{b}^n_{i,j,k}(u,v,w)$ is the bivariate Bernstein polynomial of degree n:

$$\mathrm{b}^n_{i,j,k}(u,v,w) = \frac{n!}{i!j!k!}u^i v^j w^k. \tag{4}$$

Figure 2 shows the Bézier point arrangement $\mathbf{Q}_{i,j,k}$ when $n = 4$.

2.2 Geometric properties of the Bézier triangle

The relationship between cross boundary derivatives of a Bézier rectangle of degree $n \times n$ and a Bézier triangle of degree $n+1$ is discussed in (Farin, 1982). Geometric property of Bézier triangles is shown by transforming Bézier triangles to degenerated Bézier rectangles.

A Bézier triangle of degree n is transformed to the following bivariate form by substitutions $u = t(1-v)$ and $w = (1-t)(1-v)$.

$$\begin{aligned} \mathbf{S}(u,v,w) &= \sum_{0\le i,j,k}^{i+j+k=n} \frac{n!}{i!j!k!} t^i(1-v)^i v^j (1-t)^k (1-v)^k \mathbf{Q}_{i,j,k} \\ &= \sum_{j=0}^{n} \mathrm{B}^n_j(v) \sum_{i=0}^{n-j} \mathrm{B}^{n-j}_i(t)\mathbf{Q}_{i,j,n-j-i}. \end{aligned} \tag{5}$$

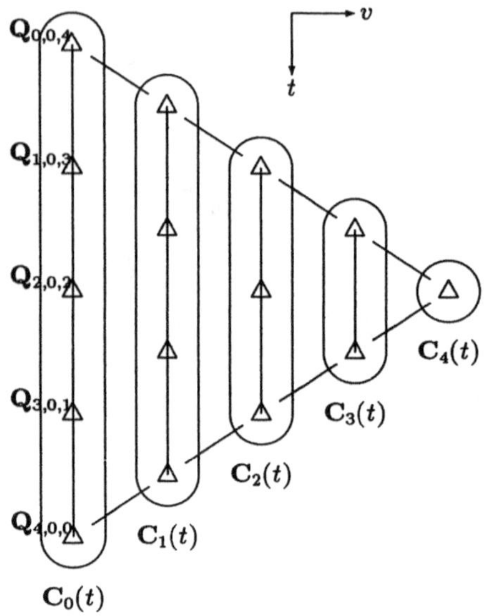

Figure 3: Interpolation of curves of varying degrees

This substitution maps barycentric coordinates (u, v, w) to Cartesian coordinates (t, v). Thus the surface $\mathbf{S}(u, v, w)$ is transformed to $\mathbf{S}(t, v)$:

$$\mathbf{S}(t, v) = \sum_{j=0}^{n} \mathrm{B}_j^n(v)\mathbf{C}_j(t), \tag{6}$$

where

$$\mathbf{C}_j(t) = \sum_{i=0}^{n-j} \mathrm{B}_i^{n-j}(t)\mathbf{Q}_{i,j,n-j-i}. \tag{7}$$

The surface $\mathbf{S}(t, v)$ is an interpolation of curves whose degrees varies from n to zero (Fig. 3). The derivatives at the boundary $v = 0$ as follows:

$$\left.\frac{\partial}{\partial v}\mathbf{S}(t, v)\right|_{v=0} = n\left(\mathbf{C}_1(t) - \mathbf{C}_0(t)\right), \qquad \left.\frac{\partial}{\partial t}\mathbf{S}(t, v)\right|_{v=0} = \frac{d}{dt}\mathbf{C}_0(t). \tag{8}$$

This surface is converted to a Bézier rectangle of degree $n \times n$ by elevating the degree of each curve to n. Each curve $\mathbf{C}_j(t)$ is converted to a curve $\mathbf{C}'_j(t)$ and the control points of all curves $\mathbf{C}'_j(t)$ form a Bézier rectangle of degree $n \times n$:

$$\mathbf{C}'_j(t) = \sum_{i=0}^{n} \mathrm{B}_i^n(t)\mathbf{Q}'_{i,j}. \tag{9}$$

The resultant Bézier rectangle has a degeneracy corresponding to the curve of degree zero as shown in Figure 4.

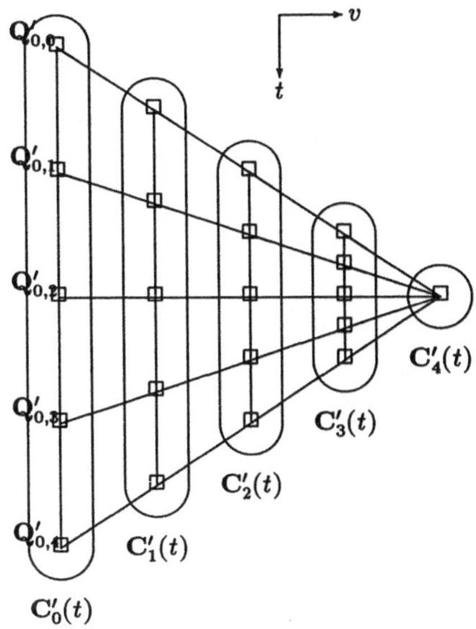

Figure 4: Degenerated Bézier rectangle

2.3 Derivatives at boundaries

The property of Bézier points of a Bézier triangle implies that it is possible to construct Bézier points of Bézier triangle of higher degree which express the cross boundary derivative of a Bézier rectangle.

For example, the Bézier points $\mathbf{Q}_{i,j,k}$ in Figure 5 are the first order derivatives of a quartic Bézier triangle constructed from the Bézier points $\mathbf{P}_{i,j}$ of a cubic Bézier rectangle that uses the following calculations:

$$\begin{aligned} \mathbf{Q}_{0,0,4} &= \mathbf{P}_{0,0}, & \mathbf{Q}_{0,1,3} &= \frac{\mathbf{P}_{0,0}+3\mathbf{P}_{0,1}}{4}, \\ \mathbf{Q}_{1,0,3} &= \frac{\mathbf{P}_{0,0}+3\mathbf{P}_{1,0}}{4}, & \mathbf{Q}_{1,1,2} &= \frac{\mathbf{P}_{1,0}+3\mathbf{P}_{1,1}}{4}, \\ \mathbf{Q}_{2,0,2} &= \frac{2\mathbf{P}_{1,0}+2\mathbf{P}_{2,0}}{4}, & \mathbf{Q}_{2,1,1} &= \frac{\mathbf{P}_{2,0}+3\mathbf{P}_{2,1}}{4}, \\ \mathbf{Q}_{3,0,1} &= \frac{3\mathbf{P}_{2,0}+\mathbf{P}_{3,0}}{4}, & \mathbf{Q}_{3,1,0} &= \frac{\mathbf{P}_{3,0}+3\mathbf{P}_{3,1}}{4}. \\ \mathbf{Q}_{4,0,0} &= \mathbf{P}_{3,0} \end{aligned} \tag{10}$$

If higher order derivative is required, the degree of a Bézier triangle is elevated according to the order.

3 Smooth Surface Connection

Various techniques to connect two Bézier surfaces at the common boundary have been developed. Although there are three combinations of a Bézier rectangle and a trian-

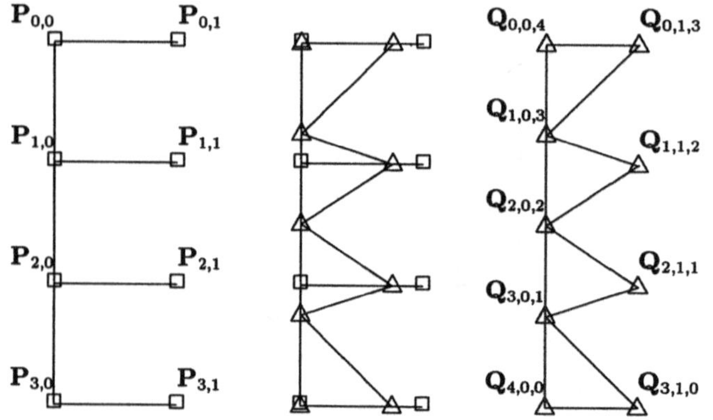

Figure 5: Derivatives of cubic Bézier rectangle and quartic triangle

gle; rectangle-rectangle, triangle-triangle and rectangle-triangle, we can get the Bézier points for Bézier rectangles and triangles from the solution for the rectangle-rectangle connection.

3.1 Smooth connection of adjacent Bézier rectangles

We introduce the technique by Chiyokura and Kimura (Chiyokura and Kimura, 1983) to connect two surfaces with tangent plane continuity along their common boundary.

Figure 6 illustrates the technique. It shows that we can obtain the inner control points, which are indicated by hollow points in the figure, satisfying the following tangent plane continuity condition:

$$\frac{\partial}{\partial v}\mathbf{S}^b(u,v)\bigg|_{v=0} = k(u)\frac{\partial}{\partial v}\mathbf{S}^a(u,v)\bigg|_{v=1} + h(u)\frac{\partial}{\partial u}\mathbf{S}^a(u,v)\bigg|_{v=1}, \tag{11}$$

where two functions $k(u)$ and $h(u)$ are assumed to have the following form:

$$k(u) = (1-u)k_0 + uk_1, \qquad h(u) = (1-u)h_0 + uh_1. \tag{12}$$

By the conditions at $u = 0$ and $u = 1$, the constants k_0, k_1, h_0 and h_1 are obtained to satisfy:

$$\mathbf{b}_0 = k_0\mathbf{a}_0 + h_0\mathbf{c}_0 \quad \text{and} \quad \mathbf{b}_3 = k_1\mathbf{a}_3 + h_1\mathbf{c}_2. \tag{13}$$

The values of $\mathbf{b}_1$ and $\mathbf{b}_2$ are obtained as the following values by solving the equations (11), (12) and (13):

$$\begin{aligned} 3\mathbf{b}_1 &= (k_1 - k_0)\mathbf{a}_0 + 3k_0\mathbf{a}_1 + 2h_0\mathbf{c}_1 + h_1\mathbf{c}_1, \\ 3\mathbf{b}_2 &= 3k_1\mathbf{a}_2 - (k_1 - k_0)\mathbf{a}_3 + h_0\mathbf{c}_2 + 2h_1\mathbf{c}_1. \end{aligned} \tag{14}$$

Although this technique was originaly for constructing the control points of Bézier rectangle, the obtained control points can be transformed to those of Bézier triangle as mentioned in section 2.3. This technique satisfies our purpose to connect any combinations of three and four-sided regions as shown in Figure 7.

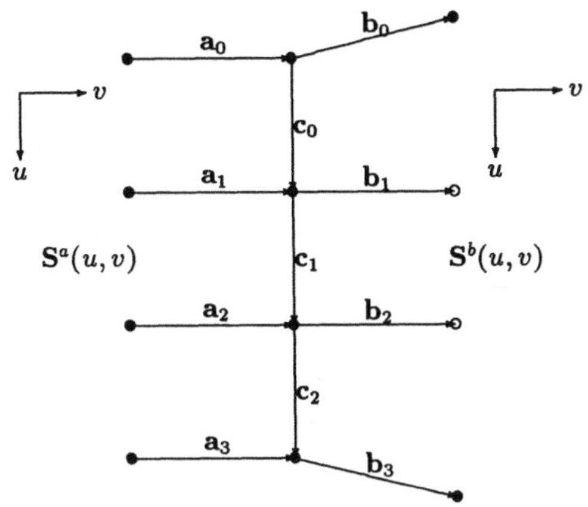

Figure 6: Connection of two Bézier rectangles

4 Smooth Surface Interpolation

In the previous section, we have obtained a technique for constructing the Bézier points which represents the cross boundary derivative at each boundary of Bézier rectangles and triangles. In this section, a method for interpolating the three and four-sided regions is presented. The interpolating surfaces are Bézier surfaces with rational Bézier control points. We also present a optimal form for the rational Bézier points.

4.1 Interpolation of four-sided regions

A Gregory patch (Chiyokura and Kimura, 1983) is a surface definition method based on the Gregory's square (Gregory, 1974) to interpolate four-sided regions. In Gregory patch, the interior control points are represented by a rational blending function of two sub-control points associated with one of the boundaries.

The bicubic Gregory patch is defined as follows:

$$\mathbf{S}(u,v)=\sum_{i=0}^{3}\sum_{j=0}^{3}\mathrm{B}_i^3(u)\mathrm{B}_j^3(v)\mathbf{P}_{i,j}(u,v), \tag{15}$$

where

$$\begin{aligned}
\mathbf{P}_{1,1}(u,v)&=\frac{u\mathbf{P}_{1,1}^v+v\mathbf{P}_{1,1}^u}{u+v},\\
\mathbf{P}_{1,2}(u,v)&=\frac{u\mathbf{P}_{1,2}^v+(1-v)\mathbf{P}_{1,2}^u}{u+(1-v)},\\
\mathbf{P}_{2,1}(u,v)&=\frac{(1-u)\mathbf{P}_{2,1}^v+v\mathbf{P}_{2,1}^u}{(1-u)+v},\\
\mathbf{P}_{2,2}(u,v)&=\frac{(1-u)\mathbf{P}_{2,2}^v+(1-v)\mathbf{P}_{2,2}^u}{(1-u)+(1-v)},
\end{aligned} \tag{16}$$

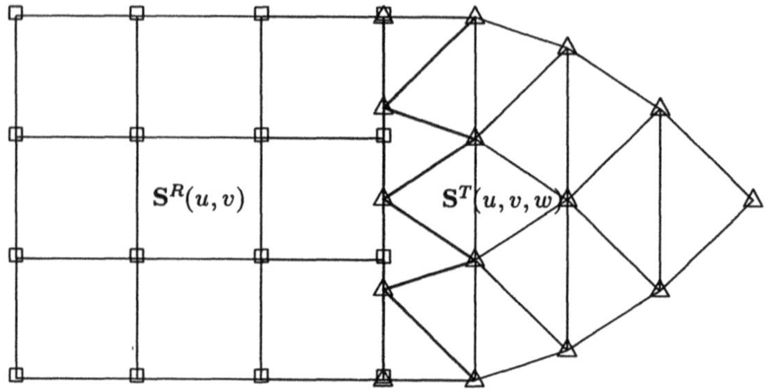

Figure 7: Connection of bicubic Bézier rectangle and quartic triangle

and $\mathbf{P}_{i,j}(u,v) = \mathbf{P}_{i,j}$ for the rest of the control points. Figure 8 illustrates the bicubic Gregory patch. The four internal control points move along line segments; the end points of each line segment are the sub-control points defining the cross boundary derivatives.

Different functions are allowable for each control points in (16) to blend the sub-control points as in (Gregory, 1983). However, those blending functions are required to satisfy at least the following conditions:

$$\begin{aligned} \mathbf{P}_{1,1}(0,v) &= \mathbf{P}^u_{1,1}, & \mathbf{P}_{1,1}(u,0) &= \mathbf{P}^v_{1,1}, \\ \mathbf{P}_{1,2}(0,v) &= \mathbf{P}^u_{1,2}, & \mathbf{P}_{1,2}(u,1) &= \mathbf{P}^v_{1,2}, \\ \mathbf{P}_{2,1}(1,v) &= \mathbf{P}^u_{2,1}, & \mathbf{P}_{2,1}(u,0) &= \mathbf{P}^v_{2,1}, \\ \mathbf{P}_{2,2}(1,v) &= \mathbf{P}^u_{2,2}, & \mathbf{P}_{2,2}(u,1) &= \mathbf{P}^v_{2,2}. \end{aligned} \tag{17}$$

Further requirements for blending functions are mentioned in section 4.3.

4.2 Interpolation of three-sided regions

The method for interpolating four-sided regions can be easily adapted to interpolate three-sided regions. Quartic Greogory triangle, for example, is defined as follows:

$$\mathbf{S}(u,v,w) = \sum_{0 \le i,j,k}^{i+j+k=4} \mathrm{b}^4_{i,j,k}(u,v,w)\mathbf{Q}_{i,j,k}(u,v,w), \tag{18}$$

where

$$\begin{aligned} \mathbf{Q}_{1,1,2}(u,v,w) &= \frac{u\mathbf{Q}^v_{1,1,2} + v\mathbf{Q}^u_{1,1,2}}{u+v}, \\ \mathbf{Q}_{2,1,1}(u,v,w) &= \frac{v\mathbf{Q}^w_{2,1,1} + w\mathbf{Q}^v_{2,1,1}}{v+w}, \\ \mathbf{Q}_{1,2,1}(u,v,w) &= \frac{w\mathbf{Q}^u_{1,2,1} + u\mathbf{Q}^w_{1,2,1}}{w+u}, \end{aligned} \tag{19}$$

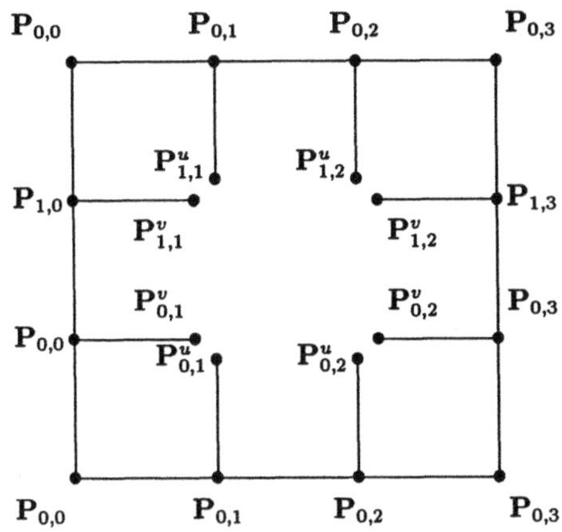

Figure 8: Bicubic rectangular Gregory patch

and $\mathbf{Q}_{i,j,k}(u,v,w) = \mathbf{Q}_{i,j,k}$ for the rest of the control points. Figure 9 illustrates a quintic triangular Gregory patch. This surface is equivalent to the tGB patch of (Schmitt, Chen and Du 1991). Another expressions for the inner control points of triangular Gregory patch are presented in (Mann, et al., 1992).

It is clear that functions to blend sub-control points must satisfy the following conditions:

$$\begin{aligned} \mathbf{Q}_{1,1,2}(0,v,w) &= \mathbf{Q}^u_{1,1,2}, & \mathbf{Q}_{1,1,2}(u,0,w) &= \mathbf{Q}^v_{1,1,2}, \\ \mathbf{Q}_{2,1,1}(u,0,w) &= \mathbf{Q}^v_{2,1,1}, & \mathbf{Q}_{2,1,1}(u,v,0) &= \mathbf{Q}^w_{2,1,1}, \\ \mathbf{Q}_{1,2,1}(u,v,0) &= \mathbf{Q}^w_{1,2,1}, & \mathbf{Q}_{1,2,1}(0,v,w) &= \mathbf{Q}^u_{1,2,1}. \end{aligned} \tag{20}$$

4.3 Rational Bézier points

The interior control points of interpolating surfaces are represented by rational functions. In other words, the surfaces are recognized as Bézier surfaces having rational Bézier points. While these surfaces interpolate three and four-sided regions well, they have special mathematical forms to define their shape. Here, we propose optimal forms for their blending function, in consideration of conversion to rational Bézier surface.

It has been mentioned that the blending function must satisfy the condition (17) or (20). It is desirable that the all functions appeared in a surface have a uniform expression. If all rational control points in a surface have a uniform expression, the surface is represented as a convex combination surface. This property minimizes the rate of degree elevation, when the surface is converted to a rational Bézier surface (Ueda, 1991).

The function $f(u,v)$ is the proposed blending function for Bézier points of a Bézier rectangle and it is defined as follows:

$$f(u,v) \;=\; \frac{(1-u)u\{(1-v)^2V_0+v^2V_1\}+(1-v)v\{(1-u)^2U_0+u^2U_1\}}{(1-u)u\{(1-v)^2+v^2\}+(1-v)v\{(1-u)^2+u^2\}}$$

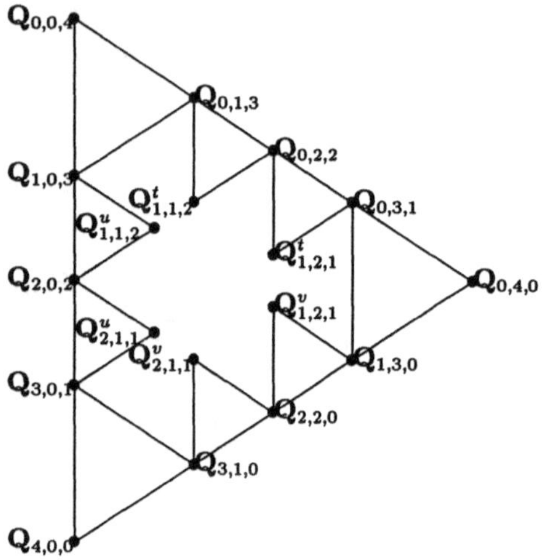

Figure 9: Quartic triangular Gregory patch

$$= \frac{\begin{bmatrix} (1-u)^2 \\ 2(1-u)u \\ u^2 \end{bmatrix}^T \begin{bmatrix} 0 & U_0 & 0 \\ V_0 & 0 & V_1 \\ 0 & U_1 & 0 \end{bmatrix} \begin{bmatrix} (1-v)^2 \\ 2(1-v)v \\ v^2 \end{bmatrix}}{\begin{bmatrix} (1-u)^2 \\ 2(1-u)u \\ u^2 \end{bmatrix}^T \begin{bmatrix} 0 & 1 & 0 \\ 1 & 0 & 1 \\ 0 & 1 & 0 \end{bmatrix} \begin{bmatrix} (1-v)^2 \\ 2(1-v)v \\ v^2 \end{bmatrix}}. \tag{21}$$

This function $f(u,v)$ is represented by the rational Bézier form, illustrated in Figure 10, and can smoothly blend the four values, V_0, V_1, U_0 and U_1. The hollow control points in the figure indicate that the weights of these control points are zero.

The function has the following properties:

$$\begin{aligned} f(u,0) &= V_0, \qquad & f(u,1) &= V_1, \\ f(0,v) &= U_0, \qquad & f(1,v) &= U_1. \end{aligned} \tag{22}$$

$$f(u,v) = \begin{cases} \dfrac{(1-u)(1-v)V_0 + uvV_1}{(1-u)(1-v) + uv} & \text{if } V_0 = U_0, V_1 = U_1, \\[2ex] \dfrac{u(1-v)V_0 + (1-u)vV_1}{u(1-v) + (1-u)v} & \text{if } V_0 = U_1, V_1 = U_0. \end{cases} \tag{23}$$

It is obvious that $f(u,v)$ can satisfy the condition (17). Using the function $f(u,v)$,

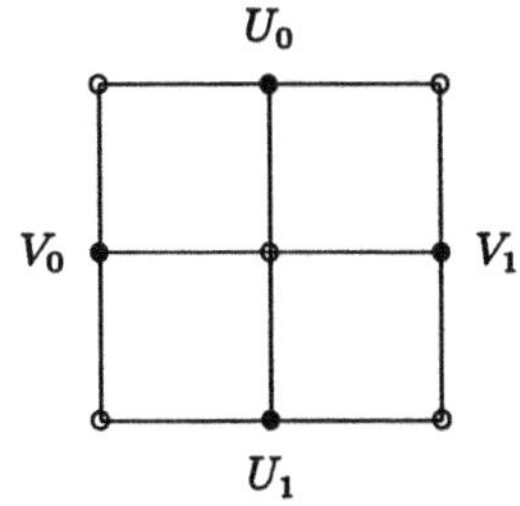

Figure 10: $f(u,v)$

the Bézier points in (16) can be replaced by the following rational Bézier points:

$$\begin{aligned}
\mathbf{P}_{1,1}(u,v) &= \frac{u(1-v)\mathbf{P}^v_{1,1} + (1-u)v\mathbf{P}^u_{1,1}}{u(1-v)+(1-u)v},\\
\mathbf{P}_{1,2}(u,v) &= \frac{uv\mathbf{P}^v_{1,2} + (1-u)(1-v)\mathbf{P}^u_{1,2}}{uv+(1-u)(1-v)},\\
\mathbf{P}_{2,1}(u,v) &= \frac{(1-u)(1-v)\mathbf{P}^v_{2,1} + uv\mathbf{P}^u_{2,1}}{(1-u)(1-v)+uv},\\
\mathbf{P}_{2,2}(u,v) &= \frac{(1-u)v\mathbf{P}^v_{2,2} + u(1-v)\mathbf{P}^u_{2,2}}{(1-u)v+u(1-v)}.
\end{aligned} \tag{24}$$

While the function $f(u,v)$ is suitable for the blending function of the rational Bézier points explained earlier, $f(u,v)$ is inadequate in some cases such as (Chiyokura, Takamura, Konno and Harada 1991; Miura and Wang 1991).

The reason of the inadequateness is related to the derivative of the Bézier surface having rational Bézier points. The derivative of the surface $\mathbf{S}(u,v)$ and the derivative at the boundary $v=0$ are as follows:

$$\frac{\partial}{\partial v}\mathbf{S}(u,v) = \sum_{i=0}^{m} \mathrm{B}_i^m(u)\left\{\sum_{j=0}^{n}\frac{d}{dv}\mathrm{B}_j^n(v)\mathbf{P}_{i,j}(u,v) + \sum_{j=0}^{n}\mathrm{B}_j^n(v)\frac{\partial}{\partial v}\mathbf{P}_{i,j}(u,v)\right\}, \tag{25}$$

$$\left.\frac{\partial}{\partial v}\mathbf{S}(u,v)\right|_{v=0} = \sum_{i=0}^{m}\mathrm{B}_i^m(u)\left\{n\left(\mathbf{P}_{i,1}(u,0)-\mathbf{P}_{i,0}(u,0)\right) + \left.\frac{\partial}{\partial v}\mathbf{P}_{i,0}(u,v)\right|_{v=0}\right\}. \tag{26}$$

To define its four cross boundary derivatives independently, the derivatives of the Bézier points must also be considered. This means the value of the derivatives of the Bézier points are zero at the four boundaries.

In the case of section 4.1, $\mathbf{P}_{i,0}$, which are not rational Bézier points, satisfy the following conditions for $i = 1, \cdots, 3$:

$$\left.\frac{\partial}{\partial v}\mathbf{P}_{i,0}(u,v)\right|_{v=0} = \mathbf{0}. \tag{27}$$

When a function of higher degree is necessary to make derivatives of the rational Bézier points to zero at the boundaries, one of the following general forms of the function $f(u,v)$ must be used.

$$f(u,v) = \frac{B^{2d}_d(u)\{B^{2d}_0(v)V_0 + B^{2d}_{2d}(v)V_1\} + B^{2d}_d(v)\{B^{2d}_0(u)U_0 + B^{2d}_{2d}(u)U_1\}}{B^{2d}_d(u)\{B^{2d}_0(v) + B^{2d}_{2d}(v)\} + B^{2d}_d(v)\{B^{2d}_0(u) + B^{2d}_{2d}(u)\}}$$
$$= \frac{(1-u)^d u^d\{(1-v)^{2d}V_0 + v^{2d}V_1\} + (1-v)^d v^d\{(1-u)^{2d}U_0 + u^{2d}U_1\}}{(1-u)^d u^d\{(1-v)^{2d} + v^{2d}\} + (1-v)^d v^d\{(1-u)^{2d} + u^{2d}\}}. \tag{28}$$

The general function $f(u,v)$ can be expressed in the following matrix form:

$$\frac{\begin{bmatrix} B^{2d}_0(u) \\ B^{2d}_1(u) \\ \vdots \\ B^{2d}_{d-1}(u) \\ B^{2d}_d(u) \\ B^{2d}_{d+1}(u) \\ \vdots \\ B^{2d}_{2d-1}(u) \\ B^{2d}_{2d}(u) \end{bmatrix}^T \begin{bmatrix} 0 & 0 & \cdots & 0 & U_0 & 0 & \cdots & 0 & 0 \\ 0 & 0 & \cdots & 0 & 0 & 0 & \cdots & 0 & 0 \\ \vdots & \vdots & \ddots & \vdots & \vdots & \vdots & \ddots & \vdots & \vdots \\ 0 & 0 & \cdots & 0 & 0 & 0 & \cdots & 0 & 0 \\ V_0 & 0 & \cdots & 0 & 0 & 0 & \cdots & 0 & V_1 \\ 0 & 0 & \cdots & 0 & 0 & 0 & \cdots & 0 & 0 \\ \vdots & \vdots & \ddots & \vdots & \vdots & \vdots & \ddots & \vdots & \vdots \\ 0 & 0 & \cdots & 0 & 0 & 0 & \cdots & 0 & 0 \\ 0 & 0 & \cdots & 0 & U_1 & 0 & \cdots & 0 & 0 \end{bmatrix} \begin{bmatrix} B^{2d}_0(v) \\ B^{2d}_1(v) \\ \vdots \\ B^{2d}_{d-1}(v) \\ B^{2d}_d(v) \\ B^{2d}_{d+1}(v) \\ \vdots \\ B^{2d}_{2d-1}(v) \\ B^{2d}_{2d}(v) \end{bmatrix}}{\begin{bmatrix} B^{2d}_0(u) \\ B^{2d}_1(u) \\ \vdots \\ B^{2d}_{d-1}(u) \\ B^{2d}_d(u) \\ B^{2d}_{d+1}(u) \\ \vdots \\ B^{2d}_{2d-1}(u) \\ B^{2d}_{2d}(u) \end{bmatrix}^T \begin{bmatrix} 0 & 0 & \cdots & 0 & 1 & 0 & \cdots & 0 & 0 \\ 0 & 0 & \cdots & 0 & 0 & 0 & \cdots & 0 & 0 \\ \vdots & \vdots & \ddots & \vdots & \vdots & \vdots & \ddots & \vdots & \vdots \\ 0 & 0 & \cdots & 0 & 0 & 0 & \cdots & 0 & 0 \\ 1 & 0 & \cdots & 0 & 0 & 0 & \cdots & 0 & 1 \\ 0 & 0 & \cdots & 0 & 0 & 0 & \cdots & 0 & 0 \\ \vdots & \vdots & \ddots & \vdots & \vdots & \vdots & \ddots & \vdots & \vdots \\ 0 & 0 & \cdots & 0 & 0 & 0 & \cdots & 0 & 0 \\ 0 & 0 & \cdots & 0 & 1 & 0 & \cdots & 0 & 0 \end{bmatrix} \begin{bmatrix} B^{2d}_0(v) \\ B^{2d}_1(v) \\ \vdots \\ B^{2d}_{d-1}(v) \\ B^{2d}_d(v) \\ B^{2d}_{d+1}(v) \\ \vdots \\ B^{2d}_{2d-1}(v) \\ B^{2d}_{2d}(v) \end{bmatrix}}. \tag{29}$$

It is apparent that $f(u,v)$ of the rational Bézier form has only one non-zero control point at each side. This property of rational Bézier points decreases the amount of computation in conversion of the surface to the one of the rational Bézier form.

This general form of the $f(u,v)$ has not only the property (22), but also the following properties :

$$\left.\frac{\partial^i}{\partial u^i}f(u,v)\right|_{u=0} = \left.\frac{\partial^i}{\partial u^i}f(u,v)\right|_{u=1} = \left.\frac{\partial^i}{\partial v^i}f(u,v)\right|_{v=0} = \left.\frac{\partial^i}{\partial v^i}f(u,v)\right|_{v=1} = 0, \tag{30}$$

where $i = 1, 2, \cdots, d-1$.

For the rational Bézier points of Bézier triangles, there is a function $g(u,v,w)$ that blends the sub-control points:

$$g(u,v,w) = \frac{vwU_0 + wuV_0 + uvW_0}{vw + wu + uv}. \tag{31}$$

The function smoothly blend three values, U_0, V_0 and W_0, and has the following properties:

$$\begin{aligned} g(0,v,w) &= U_0, \\ g(u,0,w) &= V_0, \\ g(u,v,0) &= W_0. \end{aligned} \tag{32}$$

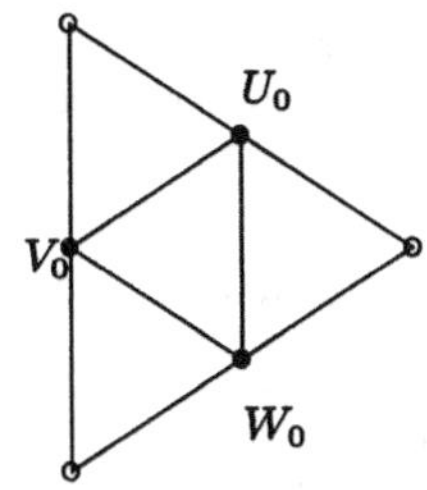

Figure 11: $g(u, v, w)$

The function $g(u, v, w)$ has its general form as well as the function $f(u, v)$, as follows:

$$\begin{aligned} g(u,v,w) &= \frac{v^d w^d U_0 + w^d u^d V_0 + u^d v^d W_0}{v^d w^d + w^d u^d + u^d v^d} \\ &= \frac{\mathrm{b}^{2d}_{0,d,d}(u,v,w)U_0 + \mathrm{b}^{2d}_{d,0,d}(u,v,w)V_0 + \mathrm{b}^{2d}_{d,d,0}(u,v,w)W_0}{\mathrm{b}^{2d}_{0,d,d}(u,v,w) + \mathrm{b}^{2d}_{d,0,d}(u,v,w) + \mathrm{b}^{2d}_{d,d,0}(u,v,w)}. \end{aligned} \tag{33}$$

This function has only one value at each side as well as $f(u, v)$, when it is expressed by the rational Bézier form. The general form of the $g(u, v, w)$ has not only the property (32), but also the following properties:

$$\left.\frac{\partial^i}{\partial u^i} g(u,v,w)\right|_{u=0} = \left.\frac{\partial^i}{\partial v^i} g(u,v,w)\right|_{v=0} = \left.\frac{\partial^i}{\partial w^i} g(u,v,w)\right|_{w=0} = 0, \tag{34}$$

where $i = 1, 2, \cdots, d-1$. The function $g(u, v, w)$ is often used in the area of interpolating three-sided region (Hagen, 1989; Foley and Opitz 1992).

Using $g(u, v, w)$, the Bézier points in (19) can be replaced by the following rational Bézier points:

$$\mathbf{Q}_{i,j,k}(u,v,w) = \frac{vw\mathbf{Q}^u_{i,j,k} + wu\mathbf{Q}^v_{i,j,k} + uv\mathbf{Q}^w_{i,j,k}}{vw + wu + uv}, \tag{35}$$

where

$$\begin{aligned} \mathbf{Q}^v_{1,2,1} &= \frac{\mathbf{Q}^w_{1,2,1} + \mathbf{Q}^u_{1,2,1}}{2}, \\ \mathbf{Q}^w_{1,1,2} &= \frac{\mathbf{Q}^u_{1,1,2} + \mathbf{Q}^v_{1,1,2}}{2}, \\ \mathbf{Q}^u_{2,1,1} &= \frac{\mathbf{Q}^v_{2,1,1} + \mathbf{Q}^w_{2,1,1}}{2}. \end{aligned} \tag{36}$$

5 Conversion to Rational Bézier Surfaces

A Bézier surface having rational Bézier points can be converted to rational Bézier surfaces. If the rational Bézier points do not have the common denominator, these points must be transformed to have their common denominator. Since the rational Bézier points, which are introduced in the previous section, have the common denominator and each control point has only three or four non-zero values, the cost of conversion and the degree of converted surface are minimum.

5.1 Bézier rectangle with rational Bézier points

A Bézier rectangle with rational Bézier points has the following form:

$$\mathbf{S}(u,v)=\sum_{i=0}^{m}\sum_{j=0}^{n}\mathrm{B}_i^m(u)\mathrm{B}_j^n(v)\mathbf{P}_{i,j}(u,v), \tag{37}$$

where

$$\mathbf{P}_{i,j}(u,v)=\frac{\sum_{k=0}^{p}\sum_{l=0}^{q}\mathrm{B}_k^p(u)\mathrm{B}_l^q(v)\mathrm{w}_{k,l}\mathbf{P}_{k,l}^{i,j}}{\sum_{k=0}^{p}\sum_{l=0}^{q}\mathrm{B}_k^p(u)\mathrm{B}_l^q(v)\mathrm{w}_{k,l}}. \tag{38}$$

Using an identity of the univariate Bernstein polynomials:

$$\mathrm{B}_i^p(t)\mathrm{B}_j^q(t)=\frac{\binom{p}{i}\binom{q}{j}}{\binom{p+q}{i+j}}\mathrm{B}_{i+j}^{p+q}(t), \tag{39}$$

the surface $\mathbf{S}(u,v)$ is converted to the following rational Bézier rectangle (Ueda, 1992):

$$\mathbf{S}(u,v)=\frac{\sum_{i=0}^{m+p}\sum_{j=0}^{n+q}\mathrm{B}_i^{m+p}(u)\mathrm{B}_j^{n+q}(v)\mathrm{w}'_{i,j}\mathbf{P}'_{i,j}}{\sum_{i=0}^{m+p}\sum_{j=0}^{n+q}\mathrm{B}_i^{m+p}(u)\mathrm{B}_j^{n+q}(v)\mathrm{w}'_{i,j}}. \tag{40}$$

In this process of conversion, computations with the zero elements are not necessary. The number of non-zero elements of rational Bézier points is always four, which is the number of the sides of a four-sided region.

For example, the surface of (15) with the control points (24) is converted to a rational biquintic Bézier rectangle. The control points $\mathbf{P}'_{i,j}$ of the rational Bézier rectangle are illustrated in Figure 12. This figure shows the control points at four corners have zero weights. The zero weights are due to the zero weights of their rational blending functions. Actually the control points near the corners have the following characteristics:

$$\begin{aligned}\mathrm{w}'_{0,0}&=0, & \mathbf{P}'_{0,1}&=\mathbf{P}'_{1,0},\\ \mathrm{w}'_{0,5}&=0, & \mathbf{P}'_{0,4}&=\mathbf{P}'_{1,5},\\ \mathrm{w}'_{5,0}&=0, & \mathbf{P}'_{5,1}&=\mathbf{P}'_{4,0},\\ \mathrm{w}'_{5,5}&=0, & \mathbf{P}'_{5,4}&=\mathbf{P}'_{4,5}.\end{aligned} \tag{41}$$

These characteristics are considered in Figure 13.

If $f(u,v)$ of higher degree, such as:

$$f(u,v)=\frac{(1-u)^2u^2\{(1-v)^4V_0+v^4V_1\}+(1-v)^2v^2\{(1-u)^4U_0+u^4U_1\}}{(1-u)^2u^2\{(1-v)^4+v^4\}+(1-v)^2v^2\{(1-u)^4+u^4\}}, \tag{42}$$

is used as a blending function, the number of control points with zero weights at the corners increases.

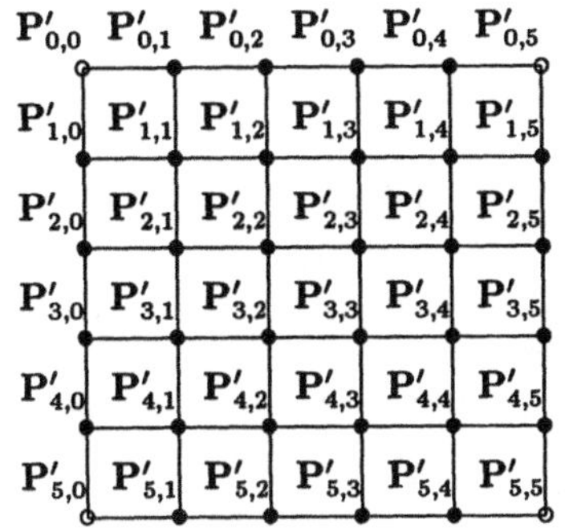

Figure 12: Rational Bézier rectangle with zero weight Bézier points

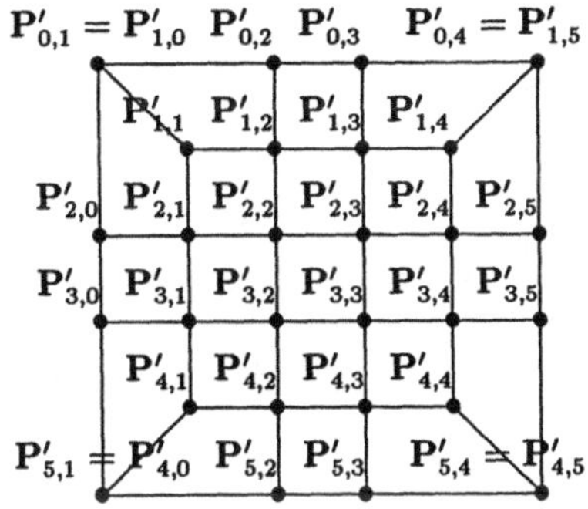

Figure 13: Geometric arrangement of rational Bézier rectangle

5.2 Bézier Triangle with rational Bézier points

A Bézier triangle with rational Bézier points has the following form:

$$\mathbf{S}(u,v,w) = \sum_{0\le i,j,k}^{i+j+k=n} \mathrm{b}^n_{i,j,k}(u,v,w)\mathbf{Q}_{i,j,k}(u,v,w), \tag{43}$$

where

$$\mathbf{Q}_{i,j,k}(u,v,w) = \frac{\sum\limits_{0\le l,m,n}^{l+m+n=p} \mathrm{b}^p_{l,m,n}(u,v,w)\mathrm{w}_{l,m,n}\mathbf{Q}^{i,j,k}_{l,m,n}}{\sum\limits_{0\le l,m,n}^{l+m+n=p} \mathrm{b}^p_{l,m,n}(u,v,w)\mathrm{w}_{l,m,n}}. \tag{44}$$

Using an identity of the bivariate Bernstein polynomials:

$$\mathrm{b}^p_{i,j,k}(u,v,w)\mathrm{b}^q_{l,m,n}(u,v,w) = \frac{\dfrac{p!}{i!j!k!}\;\dfrac{q!}{l!m!n!}}{\dfrac{(p+q)!}{(i+l)!(j+m)!(k+n)!}}\mathrm{b}^{p+q}_{i+l,j+m,k+n}(u,v,w), \tag{45}$$

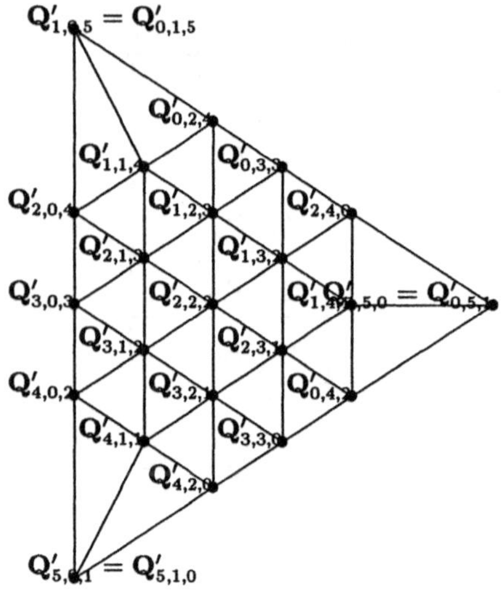

Figure 14: Geometric arrangement of rational Bézier triangle

the surface $\mathbf{S}(u,v,w)$ is converted to the following rational Bézier triangle:

$$\mathbf{S}(u,v,w) = \frac{\sum\limits_{0\le i,j,k}^{i+j+k=n+p} \mathrm{b}_{i,j,k}^{n+p}(u,v,w)\mathrm{w}'_{i,j,k}\mathbf{Q}'_{i,j,k}}{\sum\limits_{0\le i,j,k}^{i+j+k=n+p} \mathrm{b}_{i,j,k}^{n+p}(u,v,w)\mathrm{w}'_{i,j,k}}. \tag{46}$$

In this process of conversion, computations with the zero elements are not necessary as well as the Bézier rectangle. The number of non-zero elements of rational Bézier points is always three, which is the number of the sides of a three-sided region.

For example, the surface of (18) with the control points (36) is converted to a rational Bézier triangle of degree 6. The control points near the corners has the following characteristics:

$$\begin{aligned} \mathrm{w}'_{0,0,6} &= 0, \qquad \mathbf{Q}'_{1,0,5} = \mathbf{Q}'_{0,1,5}, \\ \mathrm{w}'_{0,6,0} &= 0, \qquad \mathbf{Q}'_{1,5,0} = \mathbf{Q}'_{0,5,1}, \\ \mathrm{w}'_{6,0,0} &= 0, \qquad \mathbf{Q}'_{5,0,1} = \mathbf{Q}'_{5,1,0}. \end{aligned} \tag{47}$$

The control points $\mathbf{Q}'_{i,j,k}$ of the rational Bézier triangle in consideration of the above characteristics are illustrated in Figure 14.

5.3 Removing the singularities at the corners

A rational Bézier surface converted from a Bézier surface having rational Bézier points has singularities at their corners. This singularities are usually inconvenient, because control points with zero weight are generally prohibited.

The corners are the base points (Warren, 1992) of the surface and the base points can be removed by using surface subdivision techniques (Goldman and Filip, 1987; Iino and Wilde, 1991). While this method can remove the singularities of the surfaces, it produces several degenerated surfaces from one surface.

In this section, another method for removing singularities from the surfaces is presented. Since this method (Ueda, 1992) is mathematically an approximation rather than a conversion, it is practical to use and generate only one surface. In the method, the blending function is approximated. The function $f(u,v)$ is replaced by its approximation function $f^{\epsilon}(u,v)$ and $g(u,v,w)$ by $g^{\epsilon}(u,v,w)$.

The function $f^{\epsilon}(u,v)$ is expressed by the matrix form of the following rational Bézier function:

$$\frac{\begin{bmatrix} B_0^{2d}(u) \\ B_1^{2d}(u) \\ \vdots \\ B_{d-1}^{2d}(u) \\ B_d^{2d}(u) \\ B_{d+1}^{2d}(u) \\ \vdots \\ B_{2d-1}^{2d}(u) \\ B_{2d}^{2d}(u) \end{bmatrix}^T \begin{bmatrix} (U_0+V_0)\epsilon & 0 & \cdots & 0 & U_0 & 0 & \cdots & 0 & (U_0+V_1)\epsilon \\ 0 & 0 & \cdots & 0 & 0 & 0 & \cdots & 0 & 0 \\ \vdots & \vdots & \ddots & \vdots & \vdots & \vdots & \ddots & \vdots & \vdots \\ 0 & 0 & \cdots & 0 & 0 & 0 & \cdots & 0 & 0 \\ V_0 & 0 & \cdots & 0 & 0 & 0 & \cdots & 0 & V_1 \\ 0 & 0 & \cdots & 0 & 0 & 0 & \cdots & 0 & 0 \\ \vdots & \vdots & \ddots & \vdots & \vdots & \vdots & \ddots & \vdots & \vdots \\ 0 & 0 & \cdots & 0 & 0 & 0 & \cdots & 0 & 0 \\ (U_1+V_0)\epsilon & 0 & \cdots & 0 & U_1 & 0 & \cdots & 0 & (U_1+V_1)\epsilon \end{bmatrix} \begin{bmatrix} B_0^{2d}(v) \\ B_1^{2d}(v) \\ \vdots \\ B_{d-1}^{2d}(v) \\ B_d^{2d}(v) \\ B_{d+1}^{2d}(v) \\ \vdots \\ B_{2d-1}^{2d}(v) \\ B_{2d}^{2d}(v) \end{bmatrix}}{\begin{bmatrix} B_0^{2d}(u) \\ B_1^{2d}(u) \\ \vdots \\ B_{d-1}^{2d}(u) \\ B_d^{2d}(u) \\ B_{d+1}^{2d}(u) \\ \vdots \\ B_{2d-1}^{2d}(u) \\ B_{2d}^{2d}(u) \end{bmatrix}^T \begin{bmatrix} 2\epsilon & 0 & \cdots & 0 & 1 & 0 & \cdots & 0 & 2\epsilon \\ 0 & 0 & \cdots & 0 & 0 & 0 & \cdots & 0 & 0 \\ \vdots & \vdots & \ddots & \vdots & \vdots & \vdots & \ddots & \vdots & \vdots \\ 0 & 0 & \cdots & 0 & 0 & 0 & \cdots & 0 & 0 \\ 1 & 0 & \cdots & 0 & 0 & 0 & \cdots & 0 & 1 \\ 0 & 0 & \cdots & 0 & 0 & 0 & \cdots & 0 & 0 \\ \vdots & \vdots & \ddots & \vdots & \vdots & \vdots & \ddots & \vdots & \vdots \\ 0 & 0 & \cdots & 0 & 0 & 0 & \cdots & 0 & 0 \\ 2\epsilon & 0 & \cdots & 0 & 1 & 0 & \cdots & 0 & 2\epsilon \end{bmatrix} \begin{bmatrix} B_0^{2d}(v) \\ B_1^{2d}(v) \\ \vdots \\ B_{d-1}^{2d}(v) \\ B_d^{2d}(v) \\ B_{d+1}^{2d}(v) \\ \vdots \\ B_{2d-1}^{2d}(v) \\ B_{2d}^{2d}(v) \end{bmatrix}} \tag{48}$$

The function $f^{\epsilon}(u,v)$ is obtained by putting the minute values at the four corners of (29). By this approximation the singularity at the four corners of the function $f(u,v)$ is removed. In other words, the values $f(0,0)$, $f(0,1)$, $f(1,0)$ and $f(1,1)$, which have been undefined, are fixed with the following values:

$$f^{\epsilon}(0,0) = \frac{U_0+V_0}{2}, \quad f^{\epsilon}(0,1) = \frac{U_0+V_1}{2}, \quad f^{\epsilon}(1,0) = \frac{U_1+V_0}{2}, \quad f^{\epsilon}(1,1) = \frac{U_1+V_1}{2}. \tag{49}$$

The properties of the derivatives (30) of the function $f(u,v)$, however, are inherited to the function $f^{\epsilon}(u,v)$:

$$\left.\frac{\partial^i}{\partial u^i} f^{\epsilon}(u,v)\right|_{u=0} = \left.\frac{\partial^i}{\partial u^i} f^{\epsilon}(u,v)\right|_{u=1} = \left.\frac{\partial^i}{\partial v^i} f^{\epsilon}(u,v)\right|_{v=0} = \left.\frac{\partial^i}{\partial v^i} f^{\epsilon}(u,v)\right|_{v=1} = 0, \tag{50}$$

where $i = 1, 2, \cdots, d-1$.

The approximated function of $g(u,v,w)$ is $g^\epsilon(u,v,w)$ and is defined as follows:

$$g^\epsilon(u,v,w) = \frac{\left(\begin{array}{c} \binom{2d}{d}v^dw^dU_0 + \binom{2d}{d}w^du^dV_0 + \binom{2d}{d}u^dv^dW_0 \\ + \\ v^{2d}(W_0+U_0)\epsilon + w^{2d}(U_0+V_0)\epsilon + u^{2d}(V_0+W_0)\epsilon \end{array}\right)}{\binom{2d}{d}v^dw^d + \binom{2d}{d}w^du^d + \binom{2d}{d}u^dv^d + v^{2d}2\epsilon + w^{2d}2\epsilon + u^{2d}2\epsilon}. \tag{51}$$

The function $g(u,v,w)$ is approximated by putting the minute values at the three corners of (34) as well as $f(u,v)$.

This function also fixes the undefined values of $g(u,v,w)$:

$$g(1,0,0) = \frac{V+W}{2}, \qquad g(0,1,0) = \frac{U+W}{2}, \qquad g(0,0,1) = \frac{U+V}{2}, \tag{52}$$

and it preserves the properties of its derivatives at the boundaries:

$$\left.\frac{\partial^i}{\partial u^i}g^\epsilon(u,v,w)\right|_{u=0} = \left.\frac{\partial^i}{\partial v^i}g^\epsilon(u,v,w)\right|_{v=0} = \left.\frac{\partial^i}{\partial w^i}g^\epsilon(u,v,w)\right|_{w=0} = 0, \tag{53}$$

where $i = 1, 2, \cdots, d-1$.

Both of the approximated function $f^\epsilon(u,v)$ and $g^\epsilon(u,v,w)$ affect the conversion cost of surfaces to rational Bézier surfaces. This is because the number of non-zero elements in the rational Bézier points is increased. Even if any form of the functions $f(u,v)$ or $g(u,v,w)$ is used, the number of non-zero values is merely changed from four to eight about the function $f(u,v)$, or from three to six about the function $g(u,v,w)$.

6 Conclusion

This paper describes a smooth interpolation method for three and four-sided regions in a unified manner, given an independent cross boundary derivative along each boundary curve. The Bézier triangle construction from a Bézier rectangle cross boundary derivative proves that the connection problem of two adjacent three or four-sided surfaces can always be reduced to that seen between two four-sided surfaces.

The interpolating surface is a Bézier rectangle or triangle having rational Bézier points, and the surface can be converted to a rational Bézier surface. The proposed blending functions have the smallest degree and the minimum significant values to define the control points, when the functions are represented in the rational Bézier form. These properties suppress the increase of computational cost of converting these surfaces to rational Bézier surfaces.

The interpolating surface has singularities at the corners. Introducing a small scalar deviation in the formulation removes these singularities without significantly affecting the surface shape. This approximation allows converting Bézier surface with rational Bézier points into standard rational Bézier surface and NURBs.

Acknowledgement

The author wishes to thank Dr. K. Iino for his comments which has helped to improve the paper.

REFERENCES

Chiyokura, H. and Kimura, F. (1983) Design of solids with free-form surfaces, *Computer Graphics*, Vol. 17, No. 3, pp. 289-298.

Chiyokura, H. and Kimura, F. (1984) A new surface interpolation method for irregular curve models, *Computer Graphics Forum*, Vol. 3, pp. 209-218.

Chiyokura, H., Takamura, T., Konno, K. and Harada, T. (1991) G^1 surface interpolation over irregular mashes with rational curves, *NURBS for Curve and Surface Design* , G. Farin (ed.), pp. 15-34, SIAM.

DeRose, T. D. (1990) Necessary and sufficient conditions for tangent plane continuity of Bézier Surfaces, *Computer Aided Geometric Design*, Vol. 7, pp. 169-179.

Du, W.-H. and Schmitt, F. (1990) On the G^1 continuity of piecewise Bézier surfaces: a review with new results, *Computer Aided Design*, Vol. 22, No. 4, pp. 556-573.

Farin, G. (1982) A construction for visual C^1 continuity of polynomial surface patches, *Computer Graphics and Image Processing*, Vol. 20, pp. 272-282.

Foley, T. A. and Opitz, K. (1992) Hybrid cubic Bézier triangle patches, *Mathematical Methods in Computer Aided Geometric Design II*, T. Lyche and L. l. Schumaker (eds.), pp. 275-286, Academic Press.

Goldman, R. N. and Filip, D. (1987) Conversion from Bézier rectangles to Bézier triangles, *Computer Aided Design*, Vol. 19, No. 1, pp. 25-27.

Gregory, J. A. (1974) Smooth interpolation without twist constraints, *Computer Aided Geometric Design*, pp. 71-87, Academic Press.

Gregory, J. A. (1983) C^1 rectangular and non-rectangular surface patches, *Surfaces in Computer Aided Geometric Design*, pp. 25-33, North-Holland.

Hagen, H. (1989) Geometric modeling of smooth surfaces using triangular patches, *Theory and Practice of Geometric Modeling*, H. Hagen (ed.), pp. 55-64, Springer-Verlag.

Iino, K. and Wilde, D. J. (1991) Subdivision of triangular Bézier patches into rectangular Bézier patches, *Advances in Design Automation* Vol. 2, F. H. Post and W. Bath (eds.), DE-Vol. 32-2, pp. 1-6, ASME.

Liu, D. and Hoschek, J. (1989) GC^1 continuity conditions between adjacent rectangular and triangular Bézier surface patches, *Computer Aided Design*, Vol. 21, No. 4, pp. 194-200.

Mann, S., Loop, C., Lounsbery, M., Meyers, D., Painter, J., DeRose, T. and Sloan, K. (1992) A survey of parametric scattered data fitting using triangular interpolants, *Curve and Surface design*, H. Hagen (ed.), pp. 145-172, SIAM.

Miura, K. T. and Wang, K.-K. (1991) C^2 Gregory patch, *Eurographics '91*, F. H. Post and W. Barth (eds.), pp. 481-492, North-Holland.

Piper, B. R. (1987) Visually smooth interpolation with triangular Bézier patches, *Geometric Modeling: Algorithms and New Trends*, G. Farin (ed.), pp. 221-234, SIAM.

Schmitt, F., Chen, X. and Du, W.-H. (1991) Geometric modeling from range image data, *Eurographics '91*, F. H. Post and W. Barth (eds.), pp. 317-328, North-Holland.

Shirman, L. A. and Séquin, C. H. (1987) Local surface interpolation with Bézier patches, *Computer Aided Geometric Design*, Vol. 4, pp. 279-295.

Shirman, L. A. and Séquin, C. H. (1991) Local surface interpolation with Bézier patches: errata and improvements, *Computer Aided Geometric Design*, Vol. 8, pp. 217-221.

Ueda, K. (1991) Generalization of a family of Gregory surfaces, *Scientific Visualization of Physical Phenomena*, N. M. Patrikarakis (ed.), pp. 417-434, Springer-Verlag.

Ueda, K. (1992) A method for removing the singularities from Gregory surfaces. *Mathematical Methods in Computer Aided Geometric Design II*, T. Lyche and L. L. Schumaker (eds.), pp. 597-606, Academic Press.

Warren, J. (1992) Creating multisided rational Bézier surfaces using base points, *ACM Transactions on Graphics*, Vol. 11, No. 2, pp. 127-139.

Wassum, P. (1992) Conditions and constructions for GC^1 and GC^2 continuity between adjacent integral Bézier surface patches, *Topics in Surface Modeling*, pp. 187-218, SIAM.

Curvature continuous blend surfaces

Günther Greiner and Hans–Peter Seidel
Universität Erlangen, IMMD IX
Graphische Datenverarbeitung, Am Weichselgarten 9
8520 Erlangen, Germany

ABSTRACT. We describe a method to generate blend surfaces which fit with continuous curvature to the primary surfaces. This blend surface is obtained as the bicubic tensor spline minimizing a variational problem. Among all the bicubic tensor splines which give a curvature continuous blend surface, the one is chosen which minimizes a bilinear functional. In Section 2 we summarize and extend the results of a previous paper in such a way that they are applicable to our problem. In Section 3 we outline in detail the procedure how to generate a blend surface based on these results.

1. INTRODUCTION

The problem is to find a "blend surface" which either connects two "primary surfaces" or closes a hole in a single surface. In any case one would like that the composition of these surfaces is a rather smooth object (see [12]). There are severable methods to achieve this task, rolling ball method, potential method, PDE—methods and others (see [2, 6, 9]). In [5] we presented a method based on variational principles. There we described how to obtain blend surfaces which are "geometrically smooth", briefly CG^1 (or just G^1). That is, the normal vector varies continuously (across the boundaries with the primary surfaces). However, for visual reasons as well as enginering applications, one often wants to have stronger smoothness conditions. It is known, e. g., that in general G^1–surfaces do not give smooth reflection curves.

The authors would like to thank the reviewers for their many helpful comments on this paper.

2. BLENDING TECHNIQUES BASED ON VARIATIONAL PRINCIPLES

Geometric properties of a parametrized surface $F : \Omega \to \mathbb{R}^3$ such as area, arc length, curvature, etc. can be expressed as functionals of the partial derivatives of the components F_i of F . Thus to find a blend surface it seems reasonable to look for a parametrization F which has prescribed boundary data and minimizes a functional depending on the partial derivatives of the F_i's. For example, to obtain the surface of minimal area, one has to minimize

$$J_1(F) := \int_\Omega \left\| \frac{\partial F}{\partial u_1}(u) \times \frac{\partial F}{\partial u_2}(u) \right\|_2 du \ ,$$

where $\|\cdot\|_2$ denotes Euclidean length, and $\frac{\partial F}{\partial u_1}(u) \times \frac{\partial F}{\partial u_2}(u)$ is the vector product of the tangent vectors $\frac{\partial F}{\partial u_1}(u)$ and $\frac{\partial F}{\partial u_2}(u)$ of the surface $F(u)$. In this case, one can only prescribe the boundary values not the normal or even the curvature. Thus, generating blend surfaces by this method will only yield continuous surfaces. The normal vector or the tangent plane will be discontinuous along the boundary between primary surface and blend surface. This becomes clearly looking at the one–dimensional analogue: There is no curve of minimal length, connecting two points P_1 and P_2 and having a tangent at the endpoints not parallel to $\overline{P_1P_2}$.

Minimizing one of the functionals

$$J_2(F) := \int_\Omega H_F(u)^2 \, du \ ,$$

and

$$J_3(F) := \int_\Omega (\Delta F(u)|\Delta F(u)) \, du$$

respectively, where $H_F(u)$ denotes the mean curvature of the surface F in $F(u)$ and ΔF denotes the Laplacian of F , one can prescribe boundary values and normal vectors at the boundary. By this method one can generate smooth blend surfaces, i. e. G^1–continuity at the boundary. The procedure based on functional J_3 is described in detail in [5]. A similar idea is used in [11] to construct surfaces satisfying interpolation conditions or more general linear constraints. A completely different approach, also based on a variational concept, is the *minimal norm network* chosen by [8], [7] and others. In citegre93,wel92 one cannot achieve G^2–continuity, i. e. the curvature will not be continuous (along the boundary of primary and blend surface). In order to achieve this, one has to consider functionals where partial derivatives of order 3 enter in an essential way. A possible choice is the following:

$$J_4(F) := \int_\Omega (\nabla(\Delta F)(u)|\nabla(\Delta F)(u)) + a(\Delta F(u)|\Delta F(u)) + b(\nabla F(u)|\nabla F(u)) \, du \qquad (1)$$

where (as above) "Δ" denotes the Laplacian and "∇" the gradient.

Thus

$$(\nabla F(u)|\nabla F(u)) = \textstyle\sum_{i=1}^3 \sum_{j=1}^2 \left(\frac{\partial F_i}{\partial u_j}(u)\right)^2$$

$$(\Delta F(u)|\Delta F(u)) = \textstyle\sum_{i=1}^3 \left(\sum_{j=1}^2 \frac{\partial^2 F_i}{\partial u_j^2}(u)\right)^2$$

$$(\nabla(\Delta F)(u)|\nabla(\Delta F)(u)) = \textstyle\sum_{i=1}^3 \sum_{j=1}^2 \left(\frac{\partial \Delta F_i}{\partial u_j}(u)\right)^2$$

a and b are positive constants, which later on may serve as design parameters.

Let us briefly explain the different parts of the functionals. In case the parametrization is isometric, i. e. $\frac{\partial F}{\partial u_1}$ and $\frac{\partial F}{\partial u_2}$ are orthonormal at every point, $\sqrt{(\nabla F(u)|\nabla F(u))}\,du$ is the surface element, hence $\int_\Omega(\nabla F(u)|\nabla F(u))\,du$ is the mean square of the area of the parametrized surface. $\frac{1}{4}(\Delta F(u)|\Delta F(u))$ is the square of the mean curvature $H_F(u)$ of the surface at $F(u)$. Thus the term $\int_\Omega(\Delta F(u)|\Delta F(u))\,du$ measures somehow the total mean curvature. Finally, $\nabla(\Delta F(u))$ tells how the mean curvature varies. Thus, $\int_\Omega(\nabla(\Delta F)(u)|\nabla(\Delta F)(u))\,du$ will be small if the curvature does not change much. The second and third term also allow a physical interpretation (see [3]). In case the parametrization is nearly isometric, the second and third term represent the energy due to bending and stretching respectively.

While for curves it is always possible to find an isometric parametrization (parametrize by arc length), for surfaces this is impossible in general. In fact this can be achieved if and only if the Gaussian curvature is 0 . Nonetheless, by choosing the parameter space according to the geometry of the surface, one can achieve that the interpretation of the three terms in (1) given above is true in an approximate manner.

The choice of an appropriate parameter space on the one hand and the need to give a representation of the surface by bicubic tensor splines makes it necessary, to consider more general functionals than the one given in (1). In fact, one has to consider those, which are induced by (1) via a transformation of variables. The formulation will be easier to understand, if we start with an slightly more general approach.

Since partial derivatives up to order 3 may enter the functional, we choose as the space of all possible parametrizations the Sobolov space $H^3(\Omega, \mathbb{R}^3)$. It consists of all (continuous) parametrizations $F : \Omega \to \mathbb{R}^3$, $F(u_1, u_2) = (F_1(u_1, u_2), F_2(u_1, u_2), F_3(u_1, u_2))$, such that each component F_i , $(i = 1, 2, 3)$ has square integrable partial derivatives of order ≤ 3 . For a precise definition of $H^3(R, \mathbb{R}^3)$ see [1]. $H^3 = H^3(R, \mathbb{R}^3)$ is equipped with an inner product given by

$$(F|G)_{H^3} := \int_\Omega \sum_{|\alpha| \leq 3} \left(\tfrac{\partial^{|\alpha|} F}{\partial u^\alpha}(u) \,\middle|\, \tfrac{\partial^{|\alpha|} G}{\partial u^\alpha}(u) \right) du$$

Here we used multi-index notation. That is, the sum is taken over all pairs of nonnegative integers $\alpha = (\alpha_1, \alpha_2)$ such that $|\alpha| = \alpha_1 + \alpha_2 \leq 3$. For $\alpha = (\alpha_1, \alpha_2)$: $\frac{\partial^{|\alpha|} F}{\partial u^\alpha}(u) := \frac{\partial^{\alpha_1 + \alpha_2} F}{\partial u_1^{\alpha_1} \partial u_2^{\alpha_2}}(u)$. $H^3(\Omega, \mathbb{R}^3)$ is complete for the norm $\| \cdot \|_{H^3} := \sqrt{(\cdot, \cdot)_{H^3}}$ induced by the inner product, i. e. it is a Hilbert space.

On H^3 we consider functionals B of the following form

$$B(F, G) := \int_\Omega \sum_{i,j,\alpha,\beta} w_{ij\alpha\beta}(u) \frac{\partial^{|\alpha|} F_i}{\partial u^\alpha}(u) \frac{\partial^{|\beta|} G_j}{\partial u^\beta}(u) \, du \ . \tag{2}$$

The summation taken is over all $i, j \in \{1, 2, 3\}$ and all multiindizes α, β of order ≤ 3 . $w_{ij\alpha\beta} : \Omega \to \mathbb{R}$ are bounded weight functions. B is bilinear and continuous with respect to the H^3–norm. Moreover, we assume that B is symmetric, positive semi–definite, and definite on the linear subspace H_0^3 which consists of those $F \in H^3$ which vanish together with all the partial derivatives of order ≤ 2 on the boundary $\partial\Omega$ of Ω . That is we require

$$B(F, G) = B(G, F) \quad \text{for all} \quad F, G \in H^3 \ , \tag{3}$$

$$B(F, F) \geq 0 \quad \text{for all} \quad F \in H^3 \ , \tag{4}$$

$$\text{there exists} \quad \gamma > 0 \quad \text{such that} \quad B(F, F) \geq \gamma (F|F)_{H^3} \quad \text{for all} \quad F \in H_0^3 \ . \tag{5}$$

Let us consider a concrete example.

$$B_4(F, G) := \int_\Omega (\nabla(\Delta F)(u) | \nabla(\Delta G)(u)) + a(\Delta F(u) | \Delta G(u)) + b(\nabla F(u) | \nabla F(u)) \, du \tag{6}$$

where $a \geq 0$ and $b > 0$ constants. The functional J_4 defined in (1) is precisely the quadratic form corresponding to B_4 , that is, $J_4(F) = B_4(F, F)$.

2.1 Lemma The functional B_4 satisfies the conditions (2)–(5). So does every functional, which is induced by B_4 via a (three times differentiable) transformation of variables.

Proof. Obviously, B_4 satisfies (2)–(4). It remains to verify condition (5).

By Friedrich's inequality (see [1]) there exist a constant γ_1, depending only on Ω, such that

$$\int_\Omega (G(u)|G(u))\,du \le \gamma_1 \int_\Omega (\nabla G(u)|\nabla G(u))\,du$$

provided that G vanishes on the boundary! Thus, if $F \in H_0^3$, then we can apply this to the function $G = F + \Delta F$ and obtain

$$\int_\Omega (F(u)+\Delta F(u)|F(u)+\Delta F(u))\,du \le \gamma_1 \int_\Omega (\nabla(\Delta F)(u)+\nabla F(u)|\nabla(\Delta F)(u)+\nabla F(u))\,du$$

Furthermore, since $id+\Delta$ is an isomorphism from H^k to H^{k-2} there are constants γ_2, $\gamma_3 > 0$ such that

$$\gamma_2(F|F)_{H^3} \le (F+\Delta F|F+\Delta F)_{H^1} \le \gamma_3(F|F)_{H^3} \quad \text{for} \quad F \in H^3 .$$

Then we have

$$\begin{aligned}
&\gamma_2(F|F)_{H^3} \le (F+\Delta F|F+\Delta F)_{H^1} = \\
&= \textstyle\int_\Omega (F(u)+\Delta F(u)|F(u)+\Delta F(u))\,du + \int_\Omega (\nabla F(u)+\nabla(\Delta F)(u)|\nabla F(u)+\nabla(\Delta F)(u))\,du \le \\
&\qquad \le (1+\gamma_1) \textstyle\int_\Omega (\nabla F(u)+\nabla(\Delta F)(u)|\nabla F(u)+\nabla(\Delta F)(u))\,du = \\
&= (1+\gamma_1) \textstyle\int_\Omega (\nabla(\Delta F)(u)|\nabla(\Delta F)(u)) + 2(\nabla F(u)|\nabla(\Delta F)(u)) + (\nabla F(u)|\nabla F(u))\,du
\end{aligned}$$

Since ∇F vanishes on the boundary ($F \in H_0^3$!), partial integration (more precisely Green's formula) yields $\int_\Omega (\nabla F(u)|\nabla(\Delta F)(u))\,du = -\int_\Omega (\Delta F(u)|\Delta F(u))\,du \le 0$. Thus the estimate given above in combination with the assumption $b > 0$ implies that there is $\gamma > 0$ such that

$$B_4(F,F) \ge \gamma(F|F)_{H^3} \quad \text{for} \quad F \in H_0^3 .$$

Given a transformation of variables $\Phi : \tilde{\Omega} \to \Omega$, and considering the induced bilinear functional B, i. e. $B(F,G) := B_4(F\circ\Phi, G\circ\Phi)$, then obviously B satisfies (2)-(4). That also (5) is fulfilled follows readily from the fact that under a transformation of variables H_0^3 is mapped onto H_0^3, i. e., $F \in H_0^3(\tilde{\Omega},\mathbb{R}^3) \Longleftrightarrow F\circ\Phi \in H_0^3(\Omega,\mathbb{R}^3)$. This is a consequence of the chain rule for differentiation. □

The problem we want to investigate is the following:

> Given a parametrized surface $F_0 \in H^3$ and a bilinear functional B satisfying (2)-(5) find in the affine subspace $F_0 + H_0^3 \subset H^3$ a parametrized surface F that minimizes the corresponding quadratic form $Q(\cdot) = B(\cdot,\cdot)$ i. e.
>
> $$F \in F_0 + H_0^3 \quad \text{and} \quad B(F,F) \le B(G,G) \quad \text{for all} \quad G \in F_0 + H_0^3 . \qquad (7)$$

The condition $F \in F_0 + H_0^3$ ensures that F and F_0 as well as their partial derivatives of order ≤ 2 agree on the boundary of Ω. This means, that the surfaces represented by F_0 and F respectively, have the same normal vector (or tangent plane) and the same Dupin indicatrix, in particular, the same curvature at each point of the boundary $\partial\Omega$.

Problem (7) has a unique solution, and the solution can characterized by a linear equation. In fact, the following result can be proven (compare with Proposition 2.2 in [5]).

2.2 Proposition. Given $F_0 \in H^3$ and a bilinear functional B satisfying (2)–(5), then (7) has a unique solution $F \in H^3$. Moreover, the solution is characterized by the following condition

$$B(F,G) = 0 \text{ for all } G \in H_0^3 .$$

Proof. From (2)–(5) it follows that B satisfies the parallelogramm law

$$\tfrac{1}{2}(B(F,F)+B(G,G)) = B(\tfrac{F-G}{2},\tfrac{F-G}{2}) + B(\tfrac{F+G}{2},\tfrac{F+G}{2}) \quad \text{for all} \quad F,G \in H^3 . \tag{8}$$

To prove existence, we choose a minimizing sequence $(F_n) \subset F_0 + H_0^3$. That is we have $\lim_{n\to\infty} B(F_n,F_n) = q := \inf\{B(G,G) : G \in F_0 + H_0^3\}$. From (8) we conclude that $B(\frac{F_n-F_m}{2},\frac{F_n-F_m}{2}) = \frac{1}{2}B(F_n,F_n) + \frac{1}{2}B(F_m,F_m) - B(\frac{F_n+F_m}{2},\frac{F_n+F_m}{2}) \le \frac{1}{2}B(F_n,F_n) + \frac{1}{2}B(F_m,F_m) - q \to 0$ as $n,m \to \infty$. Then (7) implies $\|F_n - F_m\|_{H^3}^2 = (F_n - F_m|F_n - F_m)_{H^3} \to 0$ as $n,m \to \infty$, which shows that (F_n) is a Cauchy sequence in the complete space H^3 . Thus $F := \lim_{n\to\infty} F_n$ exists and, since H_0^3 is a closed subspace, $F \in F_0 + H_0^3$. Moreover, since B is continuous with respect to the H^3–norm we obtain $B(F,F) = \lim_{n\to\infty} B(F_n,F_n) = q$.

Let us prove uniqueness next. Given $F,G \in F_0 + H_0^3$, $F \neq G$ and $B(F,F) = B(G,G)$, then $0 \neq F - G \in H_0^3$. Hence by (5) $B(\frac{F-G}{2},\frac{F-G}{2}) > 0$. From (8) it follows that $B(\frac{F+G}{2},\frac{F+G}{2}) < B(F,F) = B(G,G)$. Since $\frac{F+G}{2} \in F_0 + H_0^3$, neither F nor G minimizes $B(\cdot,\cdot)$.

It remains to show the characterization of the minimum. If F is a solution to (7) and $G \in H_0^3$ then for $t \in \mathbb{R}$ $F+tG \in F_0+H_0^3$, hence $B(F,F) \le B(F+tG,F+tG) = B(F,F) + 2tB(F,G) + t^2B(G,G)$. Thus the real function $f : t \mapsto B(F,F) + 2tB(F,G) + t^2B(G,G)$ has a minimum at $t = 0$. Hence $2B(F,G) = f'(0) = 0$. □

It follows from the proposition, that (7) can be solved by solving an infinite dimensional linear system. Of course, this can be done only in an approximate way, one has to consider a finite dimensional problem. In fact, one determines the minimum in an appropriate finite dimensional subspace. Let us briefly describe the procedure:

- Choose a (sufficiently large) finite dimensional subspace S_0 of H_0^3 and a basis $\{e_1, \dots, e_N\}$ of S_0 .
- Determine the coefficients $a_{ij} := B(e_i,e_j)$, $1 \le i \le j \le N$, $a_{ij} := a_{ji}$, $i > j$ and $b_i := B(F_0,e_i)$.
- Solve the $N \times N$ linear system $Ax + b = 0$, where $A = (a_{ij})$, $b = (b_i)$.
- Then $F : F_0 + \sum_{i=1}^N x_i e_i$ is the (approximate) solution.

In case the parameter space is a rectangle, as finite dimensional subspace one can choose a space of tensor spline surfaces. In fact, if n and m are the degrees with respect to first and second variable, then $S^{n,m} \subset H^3$ provided that $n \ge 3$ and $m \ge 3$. Thus for example bicubic tensor spline surfaces ($n = m = 3$) can be chosen for this purpose.

3. GENERATING BLEND SURFACES

In the following we want to outline how the results of the previous section can be applied to generate blend surfaces. We assume that the primary surfaces are given as cubic spline surfaces and we are going to construct a bicubic tensor spline surface which acts as a blend.

We consider the problem of connecting two given primary surfaces S_A and S_B each having a circular hole. Then (locally) we have parametrizations F_A and F_B of the primary surfaces. F_A , $F_B : [0, 2\pi] \times [0, 1] \to \mathbb{R}^3$ are periodic with respect to the first variable. $\Gamma_{A0}(t) := F_A(t, 1)$ and $\Gamma_{B0}(t) := F_B(t, 0)$ represent the boundary curves at the holes. $\Gamma_{A1}(t) := \frac{\partial F_A}{\partial u_2}(t, 1)$ and $\Gamma_{B1}(t) := \frac{\partial F_B}{\partial u_2}(t, 0)$ respectively are tangential fields to the surfaces at the boundary. Finally, in order to get curvature continuity, we have to consider second order derivatives, $\Gamma_{A2}(t) := \frac{\partial^2 F_A}{\partial {u_2}^2}(t, 1)$ and $\Gamma_{B2}(t) := \frac{\partial^2 F_B}{\partial {u_2}^2}(t, 0)$ respectively as well.

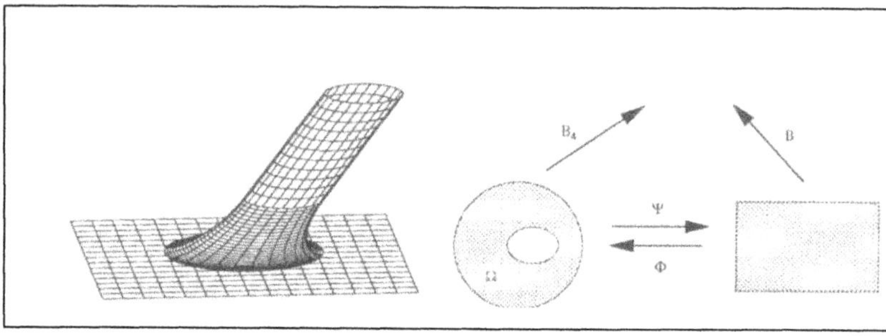

In the following we assume that the three curves $\Gamma_{A0}, \Gamma_{A1}, \Gamma_{A2}$ are periodic cubic splines over a commen grid. The same is assumed to be true for $\Gamma_{B0}, \Gamma_{B1}, \Gamma_{B2}$ This is justified by the assumption that the primary surfaces are given as cubic spline surfaces.

The need to work with tensor splines makes it necessary, that the parameter space is a rectangle (more precisely a flat cylinder, due to the periodictiy with respect to the first variable). On the other hand, the functional J_4 has the geometric interpretation given in Section 2 only if the parametrization is "nearly" isometric. This forces the parameter space to be of a similar shape than the hole which has to be closed by the blend surface. Both tasks can be accomplished, by considering a transformation of variables. Thus one has to perform the following steps:

1. Choose a primary parameter space $\Omega \subset \mathbb{R}^2$ whose boundary consists of two closed curves γ_a and γ_b and map γ_a to Γ_{A0} and γ_b to Γ_{B0} respectively. This should be done in such a way, that it fits the geometry of the hole which has to be blended best possible.

2. Find a parameter transformation $\Phi : [0, 2\pi] \times [0, 1] \to \Omega$, periodic with respect to the first variable such that $\Phi(\cdot, 0)$ is a parametrization of γ_a and $\Phi(\cdot, 1)$ is a parametrization of γ_b .

3. Choose a grid (set of knots) $0 = t_0 < t_1 < \ \ldots \ < t_N = 2\pi$ in $[0, 2\pi]$ such that $\{\Phi(t_j, 0) : 0 \leq j \leq N\}$ contains all knots of Γ_{Ai} and $\{\Phi(t_j, 1) : 0 \leq j \leq N\}$ contains

all knots of Γ_{Bi} . Choose an equidistant grid of $[0,1]$ consisting of $M+1$ points, $M \geq 3$. That is, $s_j := \frac{j}{M}$, $j = 0, 1, \ldots, M$. Then determine the canonical B–spline basis $\{b_i \otimes d_j : 1 \leq i \leq N, -1 \leq j \leq M+1\}$ of the set of all scalar-valued bicubic tensor splines subordinated to the grid $(t_i, s_j)_{0 \leq i \leq N, 0 \leq j \leq M}$ which are periodic with respect to the first variable.

4. On $H^3(\Omega, \mathbb{R}^3)$ consider the bilinear functional B_4 defined by (6) and determine the bilinear functional B on $H^3([0,2\pi] \times [0,1], \mathbb{R}^3)$ induced by B_4 via Φ .

5. Define a bicubic tensor spline surface $F_0 : [0,2\pi] \times [0,1] \to \mathbb{R}^3$, which is subordinated to the grid $(t_i, s_j)_{0 \leq i \leq N, 0 \leq j \leq M}$ and fulfils the boundary data in the following way:

$$
\begin{aligned}
&F_0(u_1,u_2) = \\
&\Gamma_{A0}(u_1)(d_{-1}(u_2) + d_0(u_2) + d_1(u_2)) + \tfrac{1}{M}\Gamma_{A1}(u_1)(d_1(u_2) - d_{-1}(u_2)) + \\
&+\tfrac{1}{M^2}\Gamma_{A2}(u_1)(\tfrac{1}{3}d_{-1}(u_2) - \tfrac{1}{6}d_0(u_2) + \tfrac{1}{3}d_1(u_2)) + \\
&+\Gamma_{B0}(u_1)(d_{M-1}(u_2) + d_M(u_2) + d_{M+1}(u_2)) + \tfrac{1}{M}\Gamma_{B1}(u_1)(d_{M+1}(u_2) - d_{M-1}(u_2)) + \\
&+\tfrac{1}{M^2}\Gamma_{B2}(u_1)(\tfrac{1}{3}d_{M-1}(u_2) - \tfrac{1}{6}d_M(u_2) + \tfrac{1}{3}d_{M+1}(u_2)) \ .
\end{aligned}
$$

Here (as in step 3) $\{d_j : -1 \leq j \leq M+1\}$ is the canonical cubic B–spline basis on the unit interval $[0,1]$ corresponding to the grid $\{\frac{j}{M} : 0 \leq j \leq M\}$

6. Determine the coefficients $c_{kij} := B(F_0, e_k(b_i \otimes d_j))$ for $1 \leq i \leq N$, $2 \leq j \leq M-2$, $k = 1,2,3$ and $a_{ij,rs} := B(e_1(b_i \otimes d_j), e_1(b_s \otimes d_t))$ for $1 \leq i,r \leq N$, $2 \leq j,s \leq M-2$. Here e_1, e_2, e_3 denotes the canonical basis in $\mathbb{R}^3$. Then solve for $k = 1,2,3$ the $N(M-3) \times N(M-3)$ the linear system $Ax_k + c_k = 0$.

7. Defining $x_{ij} := (x_{1ij}, x_{2ij}, x_{3ij})$, $1 \leq i \leq N$, $2 \leq j \leq M-2$ then $F := F_0 + \sum_{i=1}^{N} \sum_{j=2}^{M-2} x_{ij}(b_i \otimes d_j)$ is the blend surface we are looking for.

Let us comment in more detail on some of the seven steps.

ad 1) The choice of the parameter space depends on the geometry of the problem. There is no general rule for choosing Ω . Note that also the identifications of γ_a with Γ_{A0} and γ_b with Γ_{B0} should be done in a compatible way.

ad 2) Any parameter transformation that satisfies the conditions can be chosen here.

ad 3) The indentification of the spline Γ_{A0} with γ_a and finally via Φ with $[0,2\pi] \times \{0\}$ yields a set of knots in $[0,2\pi]$. In the same way one has knots induced by the spline Γ_{B0} . As grid $0 = t_0 < t_1 < \ldots < t_N = 2\pi$ one chooses the refinement of these sets of knots. Defining $t_{-k} := 2\pi - t_{N-k}$ and $t_{N+k} := 2\pi + t_k$ for $k \geq 0$ one obtains a grid on $\mathbb{R}$. Let $\tilde{b}_i$ be the B–spline vanishing outside the interval (t_{i-2}, t_{i+2}) , normalized such that $\sum_i \tilde{b}_i(u) = 1$ for all $u \in \mathbb{R}$. Then the periodic B–spline basis function b_i , $i = 1, 2, \ldots, N$ are given by $b_i := \ldots + \tilde{b}_{i-N} + \tilde{b}_i + \tilde{b}_{i+N} + \ldots$. The grid with respect to the second variable is chosen equidistant only to keep things as simple as possible. In general a few points will suffice $3 < M < 10$ should yield satisfactory results. d_j is the spline vanishing outside the interval $(\frac{j-2}{M}, \frac{j+2}{M})$, normalized such that $\sum_j d_j = 1$. Finally, $b_i \otimes d_j(u_1,u_2) := b_i(u_1)d_j(u_2)$.

ad 4) If $\Psi : \Omega \to R$ is the inverse of parameter transformation Φ then the bilinear functional B induced by B_4 via Φ is defined as follows: $B(F,G) := B_4(F \circ \Psi, G \circ \Psi)$. Differentiation of the integrand using the chain rule and then substitution of the variable $u = \Phi(\tilde{u})$ will finally lead to representation of B of the form (2) (see Example 3.2 in [5]).

ad 5). Below, in the proof of Proposition 3.1 it is shown, that F_0 actually satisfies the desired boundary conditions. Thus F_0 may be considered as a "curvature continuous" blend function. However, this will (if at all) be a reasonable blend surface only in case M is small, $M = 3, 4, 5$. Note that in the case $M = 3$, we have $H_0^3 = \{0\}$ hence $F = F_0$.

ad 6) To determine the coefficients c_{kij} , one may first of all give the representation of F_0 as linear combination the basis functions $b_i \otimes d_j$, $i = 1, \ldots, N$, $j = -1, 0, 1, M - 1, M, M + 1$. This can be easily achieved in case the boundary data Γ_{Ai} and Γ_{Bi} are given by their control points. One has to determine $B(e_k(b_r \otimes d_s), e_k(b_i \otimes d_j))$ for $i, r = 1, \ldots N$, $s = -1, 0, 1, M - 1, M, M + 1$ and $j = 2, \ldots, M - 2$. Then the coefficients c_{kij} can be easily obtained as linear combination of these quantities. Note also that $B(e_k(b_r \otimes d_s), e_k(b_i \otimes d_j)) \neq 0$ only if $|r - i| \leq 3$ and $|s - j| \leq 3$. This also shows, that the matrix A of the linear equations which finally has to be solved contains many zeros (provided that N and/or M is large).

ad 7) We have mentioned in the previous remark, that the control points of F_0 can be obtained easily, provided that the boundary data are given by their control points. The control points of F then are obtained by adding to the control points of F_0 the quantities x_{ij} .

3.1 Proposition. The procedure described above yields a curvature continuous blend surface.

Proof. We have

$$\begin{array}{lll} d_{-1}(0) = \frac{1}{6} & d'_{-1}(0) = -\frac{M}{2} & d''_{-1}(0) = M^2 \\ d_0(0) = \frac{2}{3} & d'_0(0) = 0 & d''_0(0) = -2M^2 \\ d_1(0) = \frac{1}{6} & d'_1(0) = \frac{M}{2} & d''_1(0) = M^2 \end{array}$$

$$d_j(0) = d'_j(0) = d''_j(0) = 0 \quad \text{for} \quad j > 1$$

Thus by the definition of F_0 we have at $u_2 = 0$:

$$F_0(u_1, 0) = \Gamma_{A0}(u_1) = F_A(u_1, 1) \quad , \quad \frac{\partial F_0}{\partial u_2}(u_1, 0) = \Gamma_{A1}(u_1) = \frac{\partial F_A}{\partial u_2}(u_1, 1) \, ,$$

$$\frac{\partial^2 F_0}{\partial {u_2}^2}(u_1, 0) = \Gamma_{A2}(u_1) = \frac{\partial^2 F_A}{\partial {u_2}^2}(u_1, 1) \quad , \quad \frac{\partial F_0}{\partial u_1}(u_1, 0) = \Gamma'_{A0}(u_1) = \frac{\partial F_A}{\partial u_1}(u_1, 1) \, ,$$

$$\frac{\partial^2 F_0}{\partial {u_1}^2}(u_1, 0) = \Gamma''_{A0}(u_1) = \frac{\partial^2 F_A}{\partial {u_1}^2}(u_1, 1) \quad , \quad \frac{\partial^2 F_0}{\partial u_1 \partial u_2}(u_1, 0) = \Gamma'_{A1}(u_1) = \frac{\partial^2 F_A}{\partial u_1 \partial u_2}(u_1, 1) \, .$$

Thus the partial derivatives of F_0 and F_A of order ≤ 2 agree at the common boundary. Of cousrse the same argument applies to the common boundary of F_0 and F_B .

Since $F - F_0 \in H_0^3$, the partial derivatives of F and F_0 up to order 2 agree along the boundaries $u_2 = 0$ and $u_2 = 1$. Thus the surface composed of the primary surfaces S_A , S_B and the blend surface F is C^2 as well. □

CONCLUSION. The method to generate blend surfaces by minimizing a suitable functional as described above is rather general. There are no restrictions on the geometry of the primary surfaces. It always yields a curvature continuous object. Even the assumption that the primary surfaces are given as cubic spline surfaces is not essential.

Then the final solution will not be a tensor spline surface (due to the fact, that in this case F_0 as defined in step 5 will not be a tensor spline surface).

In comparison to other existing methods, there is some relation to the PDE–method introduced by Bloor and Wilson in [2].

The relation stems from the fact that to a variational problem there corresponds an "Euler equation". Under suitable regularity assumptions, the solution of this partial equation is a solution to the variational problem. In order to obtain the same degree of smoothness by the PDE method one has to deal with (at least) sixth order pde's, which numerically by far cannot so easily be solved like, for example, second order elliptic equations.

In case the boundary data are given by splines, the method described above yields as a final result the control points of a tensor spline surface. Thus the surface can be drawn easily using these data, no additional interpolation is necessary.

References

[1] R. A. Adams, *Sobolev spaces,* Academic Press 1975

[2] M. I. G. Bloor, M. J. Wilson, Generating blend surfaces using partial differential equations. CAD 1989, pp. 165–171

[3] R. Courant, D. Hilbert, *Methoden der Mathematischen Physik,* Springer–Verlag, Berlin Heidelberg 1968.

[4] A. Friedman, *Partial Differential Equations*, Holt, Rinehart and Winston, New York 1969.

[5] G. Greiner, Blending techniques based on variational principles, *to appear*

[6] C. Hoffmann, J. Hopcroft, The potential method for blending surfaces, in G. Farin (ed.), Geometric modelling: algorithms and new trends, SIAM, Philadelphia 1987, pp. 347–364.

[7] H. P. Moreton, C. H. Séquin, Functional Optimization for fair surface design, Siggraph '92, pp. 167–176

[8] H. Pottmann, Scattered data interpolation based upon generalized minimum norm networks, Preprint Nr. 1232, TH Darmstadt, May 1989

[9] J. R. Rossignac, A. A. G. Requicha, Constant–radius blending in solid modelling, Compu. Mech. Eng. **3** (1984), pp. 65–73.

[10] G. Strang, G. J. Fix, An analysis of the finite element method, Prentic Hall, Englewood Cliffs 1973.

[11] W. Welch, A. Witkin, Variational surface modeling, Siggraph '92, pp. 157–166

[12] J. R. Woodwark, Blends in geometric modelling, in R. R. Martin (ed.), The mathematics of surfaces II, Oxford University Press, Oxford 1987, pp. 255-297.

Filling N-sided Holes

Suresh Lodha
Department of Computer and Information Sciences
University of California, Santa Cruz
CA 95064, USA

Abstract

Smooth surface patches, such as Gregory patch, Brown's square and Nielson-Foley patch, which interpolate a given function and its derivatives on the boundary of a rectangle or a triangle, with incompatible twist terms, have been constructed with rational parametric representation by using boolean sum techniques, convex combination methods and procedural methods to fill N-sided holes. Chiyokura and Kimura proposed a representation of Gregory patch in Bernstein-Bezier form, where interior control points are expressed as convex combinations of incompatible control points via rational blending functions. No such representation is known for solutions to the above problem over pentagonal domains. We construct smooth rational surface patches which interpolate a given function and its cross-boundary C^k derivatives on the boundary of any convex polygonal domain with incompatible twist data. These patches are represented in S-patch form, where control points are expressed as convex combinations of incompatible control points via rational blending functions. This constructive rational technique provides novel solutions for blending incompatible C^k data over polygonal domains. In particular, new solutions are constructed for rectangular and triangular patches as well.

Keywords: N-sided hole, rational surface patch, blending functions, S-patch, Gregory patch, Brown's square, convex polygonal domain, twist, cross-boundary derivatives.

1 Introduction

The n-sided hole problem arises when n patches surround a hole. The objective is to construct a surface patch that fills the hole and meets the surrounding surface patches smoothly. We shall restrict our attention to the case where the surrounding patches have polynomial or rational parametric representations. Thus, the problem is to construct a smooth interpolant for a parametrically defined vector-valued function and its derivatives on the boundary of a polygonal domain. These interpolants on a fixed domain generate a surface patch, which then can be fitted together with adjacent patches to create a smooth surface.

The problem of filling an n-sided hole is an important problem and has been studied by various researchers over the last thirty years. In its earliest form, the n-sided hole arose as a problem of filling wire-frame meshes of curves by surface patches. Given a user-defined network of curves and cross-boundary derivatives, a solution to the n-sided hole problem creates a smooth surface which interpolates the user-specified data.

Coons [Coo64] pioneered this study by solving the problem of interpolation to position and derivative information for networks of curves with a rectilinear structure by constructing what are known today as Coons patches. His scheme involves *side-side* interpolants, which interpolate the data and its derivatives on the two opposite sides of a rectangle. The final solution is created by taking boolean sums of these *lofting* interpolants. These patches are then fitted together over a net of rectangles to form a smooth surface. Gordon [Gor69] recognized the boolean structure of these patches, and Gordon [Gor69] and Forrest [For72] explicated these methods in detail. Barnhill, Birkhoff, and Gordon [BBG73] extended Coons patches from rectangular domains to standard triangular domains. This construction was then generalized by Little [Bar91] to arbitrary triangular domains via barycentric coordinates.

One of the difficulties associated with this problem is the incompatibility of the cross-derivatives or the twist terms at the corners of the domain. The schemes, described above require that the cross-derivatives or the *twist* terms be compatible at the vertices of the domain. However, in general, one cannot expect the twist terms to be compatible. If the twist terms are incompatible, it is well-known that a parametric polynomial patch cannot fill the hole [Pet90]. Therefore, solutions using parametric rational patches were proposed. Gregory [Gre74] proposed alternative solutions for both rectangular and triangular domains with incompatible twist terms. These schemes involve using rational blending functions to take care of the incompatible twist terms at the corners. Gregory's solution for rectangular domains, known as the Gregory patch, was represented in Bézier form by Chiyokura and Kimura [CK83]. Here interior control points are represented no longer as constants, but as rational combinations of user-specified incompatible control points. We shall refer to this representation as a *rationally controlled Bézier representation.* This representation is compact and very suitable for computation. For example, various algorithms, such as the deCasteljau algorithm for evaluation and subdivision of Bézier surface patches, can also be applied to surface patches with a rationally controlled Bézier representation. Moreover, since this representation is expressed in terms of the user-specified control points via rational blending functions, it provides some geometric intuition for understanding the patch. Nielson [Nie79] proposed an alternative solution for triangular domains by using a *side-vertex* method. Foley [Fol91] noted that the discretized version of Nielson's solution for the cubic triangular case has a rationally controlled Bézier representation. Alternative solutions for the rectangular domain were also proposed by Brown using convex combination methods [Lit83]. Brown's square [Gre83a] is another example of a solution with a rationally controlled Bézier representation. The generalization of a family of Gregory patches proposed by Ueda and Harada [UH91] also have rationally controlled Bézier representations.

Extensions of these methods to pentagonal domains and the underlying difficulties which are encountered have been studied by Gregory, Charrot, and Hahn [CG84, GH89, GH87, Gre83b, GC80]. These schemes, however, are procedural. The resulting surface patches, which fill 5-sided holes, do not have any compact representation in terms of user-specified control points. Hosaka and Kimura [HK84] derived expressions for non-rectangular patches in terms of control points, but in general they are quite complicated. The n-sided patches developed by Sabin [Sab83] are restricted to 5 and 6 sides. Other n-sided patch representations have been proposed by Herron [Her79], Varady [Var91, Var87], and Loop and DeRose [LD90].

Attempts have also been made to generalize these results, when the hole-filling surface patch meets the surrounding surface patches, not just with C^1 continuity as in the above cases, but with higher order of continuity, such as C^2 or C^3. A generalization to smooth interpolants, which match the value of the function and C^2 cross-boundary derivatives for the case of rectangular domains is described by Barnhill [Bar83] and Worsey [Wor84]. Extensions to higher dimensions have also been studied. Interpolation to boundary data on a hypercube has been investigated by Barnhill and Worsey [BW84, Wor85, BS84]; interpolation to boundary data on a simplex is described by Gregory [Gre85].

This work introduces a new solution in a compact form, suitable for computation, which works for any number of sides, any number of derivatives, and any number of dimensions. We construct these surface patches in rationally controlled S-patch representation, where the interior control points are expressed as convex combinations of user-specified incompatible control points using rational blending functions. This representation arises naturally in solving the n-sided hole filling problem, and provides good geometric intuition for the proposed solution. The S-patch representation [LD89] is itself a natural generalization of the Bézier representation. Our construction unifies the myriad solutions, proposed for filling n-sided holes, including the Gregory patch, the Brown's square and the Nielson-Foley patch.

After a review of Bézier simplexes in Section 2, of barycentric coordinates for a convex polygon in Section 3, and of the basic properties of S-patches in Section 4, the n-sided hole problem is described in Section 5. Sections 6 and 8 introduce the rationally controlled Bézier representation and rational blending functions, which are used to describe the general solution presented in Section 9. Section 7 motivates the proposed solution by giving an example of a 2-sided hole problem from the curve case. Finally, Section 10 presents many examples of filling n-sided holes using the techniques described in this paper including the Gregory patch, Nielson-Foley patch, Barnhill-Worsey patch and Brown's square.

2 Bézier Simplexes

This section describes the multi-index notation, and reviews the definition of a Bézier simplex. A detailed treatment of these topics is given in [dB87, LD89]. A multi-index will be denoted by an italic character with a diacritical arrow at the top, as in $\vec{i}$. A multi-index is a tuple of non-negative integers, for instance, $\vec{i} = (i_0, \ldots, i_n)$. The norm of a multi-index $\vec{i}$, denoted by $|\vec{i}|$ is defined to be the sum of the components of $\vec{i}$. By setting $\vec{i} = (i_0, \ldots, i_n)$ and requiring that $|\vec{i}| = d$, the n-variate Bernstein polynomials of degree d can be defined by

$$B^d_{\vec{i}}(\alpha_0, \ldots, \alpha_n) = \begin{pmatrix} d \\ \vec{i} \end{pmatrix} \alpha_0^{i_0} \cdots \alpha_n^{i_n}$$

where $\begin{pmatrix} d \\ \vec{i} \end{pmatrix}$ is the multinomial coefficient defined by

$$\begin{pmatrix} d \\ \vec{i} \end{pmatrix} = \frac{d!}{i_0! \cdots i_n!}$$

and $\alpha_0, \ldots, \alpha_n$ are non-negative real numbers that sum to one. A Bézier simplex is a polynomial map B of degree d from an affine space A_1 of dimension n to an affine space A_2 of arbitrary dimension s, and is represented in the Bernstein-Bézier basis with respect to a domain simplex Δ in A_1 as follows:

$$B(v) = \sum_{\vec{i}} C_{\vec{i}} B^d_{\vec{i}}(\alpha_0(v), \ldots, \alpha_n(v)) \tag{1}$$

where $\alpha_0, \ldots, \alpha_n$ are the barycentric coordinates of a point v relative to the domain simplex Δ. The summation in equation (1) is taken over all multi-indexes where the norm is equal to the degree of the Bernstein polynomials, viz. $|\vec{i}| = d$. It is well-known that such a representation for a polynomial map is unique. The points $C_{\vec{i}}$ are individually referred to as Bézier control points and collectively referred to as the Bézier control net for B relative to Δ. Note that for $n = 1$, $s = 3$, Bézier simplexes are Bézier curves in 3-space and for $n = 2$, $s = 3$, they are triangular Bézier patches.

3 Barycentric Coordinates

This section reviews the definition of barycentric coordinates for a regular convex polygon. Let P be a convex n-gon, defined by the intersection of n halfspaces, so that

$$P = \bigcap_{k=1}^{n} (u_k \geq 0)$$

Let $p_1, \cdots, p_n$ denote the vertices and $E_1, \cdots, E_n$ denote the edges of the polygon P. Let $u_k = 0$ be the equation of the edge E_k, which goes from the vertex p_k to the vertex p_{k+1}. In the previous statement and in what follows, all indexes are to be interpreted in a cyclic fashion, so that every index k is mapped into the range $1, \cdots, n$ by the formula $[(k-1) \ mod \ n] + 1$.

Let $\sigma_k(p)$ denote the signed area of the triangle pp_kp_{k+1} as shown in Figure 1, where the sign is chosen to be positive for points inside the polygon P. Since $\sigma_k(p)$ and $u_k(p)$ are both linear functions, both vanish at p_k and p_{k+1}, and both are positive inside the polygon P, they must differ only by a positive multiplicative constant. Therefore, $\sigma_k(p) = \xi_k u_k(p)$. Let $\pi_k(p)$ denote the product of all σ's except for $\sigma_{k-1}(p)$ and $\sigma_k(p)$; that is,

$$\pi_k(p) = \sigma_1(p) \cdots \sigma_{k-2}(p)\sigma_{k+1}(p) \cdots \sigma_n(p), k = 1, \cdots, n$$

and therefore,

$$\pi_k(p) = \rho_k u_1(p) \cdots u_{k-2}(p)u_{k+1}(p) \cdots u_n(p), k = 1, \cdots, n \tag{2}$$

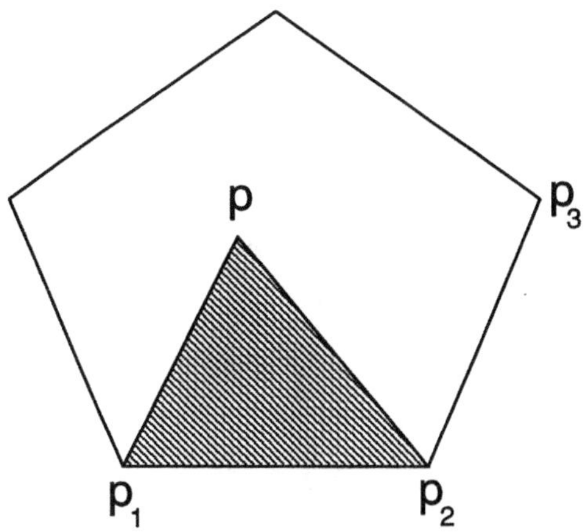

Figure 1 Geometry of the functions σ_i used to construct barycentric coordinates

where $\rho_k = \xi_1 \cdots \xi_{k-2}\xi_{k+1} \cdots \xi_n$. Let

$$\gamma_k(p) = \frac{\pi_k(p)}{\sum_{k=1}^{n} \pi_k(p)} \tag{3}$$

Theorem[LD89]: The functions $\gamma_k(p)$ for a regular convex n-gon satisfy the following properties:

1. The functions $\gamma_k(p)$ are nonnegative whenever p is inside the polygon P, that is, $\gamma_k(p) \geq 0 \;\; \forall \;\; p \epsilon P, \; k = 1, \cdots, n$.
2. The functions $\gamma_k(p)$ form a partition of unity, that is, $\sum_{k=1}^{n} \gamma_k(p) = 1 \;\; \forall \;\; p \epsilon P$.
3. $p = \sum_{i=1}^{n} \gamma_i(p) p_i$.

Remarks: The first two properties follow easily from the definition of the $\gamma_k(p)$. The third property generalizes a property satisfied by the barycentric coordinates for the triangles, and is referred to as the pseudo-affine property by Loop and DeRose [LD89]. The functions $\gamma_k(p)$ will be referred to as barycentric coordinates for the convex polygon P. More generally, any set of functions satisfying properties 1 to 3 above for a fixed domain will be referred to as barycentric coordinates for that domain.

4 S-patches

S-patches build on the theory of Bézier simplexes and barycentric coordinates. A regular n-sided S-patch is a mapping from a regular convex n-gon P and is constructed conceptually in two phases: first, the polygon P is embedded into an intermediate domain simplex $\Delta = v_1, \cdots, v_n$ in an affine space of dimension $n-1$; next, a Bézier simplex is created using Δ as its domain; finally, S is defined as the composition of the embedding and the Bézier simplex. That is, if $L : P \rightarrow \Delta$ represents the embedding, and if $B : \Delta \rightarrow R^3$ is the Bézier simplex, then

$$S(p) = B \odot L(p), \quad p \epsilon P,$$

as indicated in Figure 2.

Given the barycentric coordinates $\gamma_k(p)$ of a point p inside the regular convex n-gon P, the embedding L is defined as

$$L(p) = \sum_{k=1}^{n} \gamma_k(p) v_k.$$

If $C_{\vec{i}}$ denotes the control net of a Bézier simplex B, then an S-patch is defined as

$$S(p) = B \odot L(p) = \sum_{\vec{i}} C_{\vec{i}} B_{\vec{i}}^{d}(\gamma_1(p), \cdots, \gamma_n(p)).$$

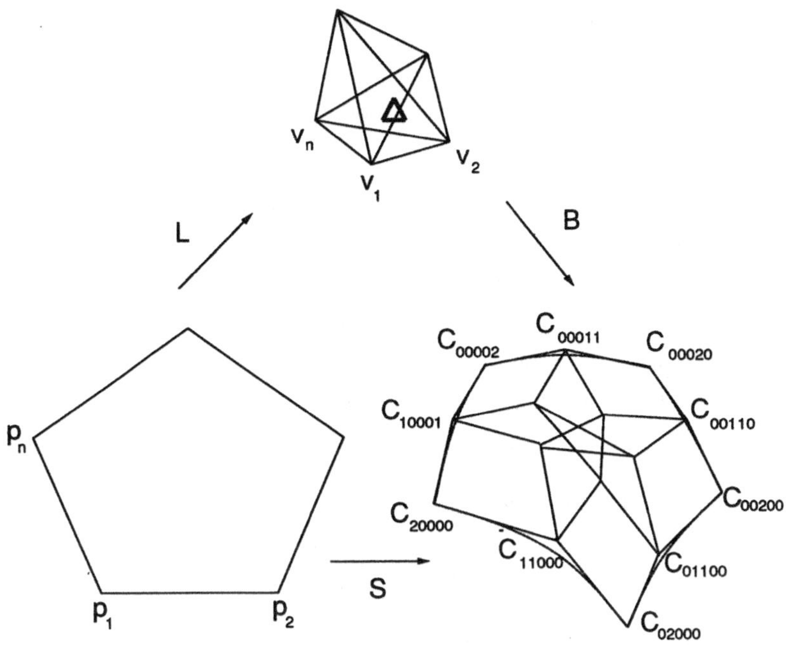

Figure 2 Schematic representation of S-patches

A rational S-patch is defined as

$$S(p) = \frac{\sum_{\vec{i}} w_{\vec{i}} C_{\vec{i}} B_{\vec{i}}^{d}(\gamma_1(p), \cdots, \gamma_n(p))}{\sum_{\vec{i}} w_{\vec{i}} B_{\vec{i}}^{d}(\gamma_1(p), \cdots, \gamma_n(p))}$$

where the weights $w_{\vec{i}}$ associated with the control points $C_{\vec{i}}$ are generally chosen to be positive.

The integer d in the above equation is known as the depth of the S-patch. Since the barycentric coordinates $\gamma_k(p)$ are rational functions of degree $n-2$, the S-patch is a rational parametric patch of degree $d(n-2)$. The control net $C_{\vec{i}}$ is referred to as the control net of S, an example of which is shown in Figure 2. The S-patch representation has the following useful properties:

- S-patches can be evaluated by first evaluating L, and then evaluating B using the deCasteljau algorithm.
- S-patches lie within the convex hull of their control nets.
- An S-patch of depth d can be described as an S-patch of depth $d+1$ using a depth elevation algorithm.

- Boundary curves are in Bézier form. For example, the boundary curve corresponding to the bottom boundary of the control net is a quadratic Bézier curve whose control points are C_{20000}, C_{11000}, and C_{02000}. Control points such as these are called *boundary control points.*

- The tangent plane variation along a boundary curve is determined entirely by the control points, which are at unit distance or less from that boundary. The distance $g_k(\vec{i})$ of a control point $C_{\vec{i}}$ from the k-th boundary is defined to be $d - (i_k + i_{k+1})$. Referring to Figure 2, the tangent plane along the bottom boundary ($k = 1$) of the control net is entirely determined by the boundary control points, which are at distance 0 from the boundary, and by the control points C_{10001}, C_{10010}, C_{10100}, C_{01001}, C_{01010}, and C_{01100}, which are at unit distance from the boundary.

- The h-th cross-boundary derivative along the k-th boundary curve is determined entirely by the control points, which are at a distance h units or less from that boundary, that is, $g_k(\vec{i}) \leq h$. These control points will be referred to as the first h *layers* of control points across the k-th boundary. Therefore, in what follows, the user will be required to prescribe the first h cross-boundary derivatives along a boundary curve in terms of the S-patch control points, which are at a distance h units or less from that boundary. If the first h cross-boundary derivatives across a boundary arise from an adjacent Bézier triangle, an algorithm to compute the regular S-patch control points at a distance h units or less from the boundary is described in Loop and DeRose[LD89]. It is only in this algorithm that the properties of the barycentric coordinates of the regular convex polygon are used. Since barycentric coordinates have now been developed for any convex polytope in arbitrary dimension [War92], the construction described later in this chapter is generalizable to higher dimensions.

- When $n = 3$, that is, for triangular domains, an S-patch is simply a triangular Bézier surface patch. In other words, regular S-patches generalize triangular Bézier surface patches. When $n = 4$, that is, for rectangular domains, an S-patch is simply a bi-d-ic tensor product Bézier surface patch. In other words, S-patches also generalize rectangular tensor product Bézier surface patches.

- More significantly, there exists an algorithm for representing an n-sided regular S-patch as m-sided regular S-patch using multiprojective blossoming [LD89, DeR88, DGHM92]. In particular, an n-sided regular S-patch can be represented as a collection of triangular Bézier surface patches.

5 The N-sided Hole Problem

The n-sided hole problem arises in situations as the one shown in Figure 3, where polynomial patches surround an n-sided hole. The objective is to construct a surface patch that fills the hole and meets the surrounding patches with C^h continuity. We shall consider the more general case where the surface patch meets the surrounding k-th patch with C^{a_k} continuity. In other words, the surface patch meets different surrounding patches with different orders of continuity.

Referring to Figure 3, the hole to be filled is assumed to be surrounded by n patches $F_1, \cdots, F_n$. The domain polygon P of H is a regular convex n-gon. Let $\vec{N_k}$ be a unit vector normal to the edge E_k. The following information is prescribed in the n-sided hole problem:

- The C^{a_k} cross-boundary derivatives of the hole across the kth boundary are given by the S-patch control points $C^k_{\vec{i}}$, which are at a distance a_k units or less from the k-th boundary, that is, $g_k(\vec{i}) \leq a_k$.

6 Rationally Controlled Bézier Representation

This chapter describes a solution which fills the hole with a single rationally controlled S-patch. The rationally controlled representation is compact and is particularly suitable for efficient computation. This section introduces the rationally controlled Bézier representation. Any parametric polynomial curve $S(p)$ of degree d can be represented in Bézier form as

$$S(p) = \sum_{\vec{i}} C_{\vec{i}} B^d_{\vec{i}}(\gamma_1(p), \gamma_2(p))$$

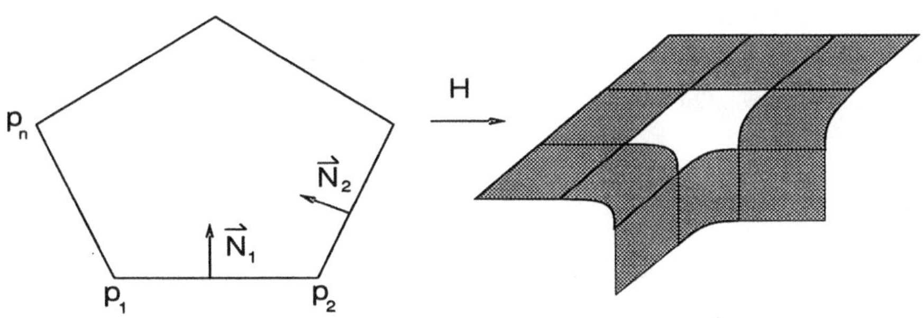

Figure 3 The n-sided hole problem

where $\vec{i} = (i_1, i_2)$ with $|\vec{i}| = d$, and $\gamma_1(p)$ and $\gamma_2(p)$ are the barycentric coordinates of a point p belonging to the domain interval Δ, so that $\gamma_1(p), \gamma_2(p) \geq 0$, and $\gamma_1(p)+\gamma_2(p) = 1$. If the domain interval is the standard unit interval $[0,1]$ and the point p on the interval has the coordinates t, then $\gamma_1(p) = t$, and $\gamma_2(p) = 1 - t$.

Any rational parametric curve $S(p)$ of degree d can be represented in rational Bézier form as

$$S(p) = \frac{\sum_{\vec{i}} C_{\vec{i}} w_{\vec{i}} B^d_{\vec{i}}(\gamma_1(p), \gamma_2(p))}{\sum_{\vec{i}} w_{\vec{i}} B^d_{\vec{i}}(\gamma_1(p), \gamma_2(p))}$$

where w_i are the weights associated with the control points.

A rational parametric curve $S(p)$ admits a *rationally controlled Bézier representation of degree d*, if it can be represented in the following form:

$$S(p) = \sum_{\vec{i}} C_{\vec{i}}(p) B^d_{\vec{i}}(\gamma_1(p), \gamma_2(p))$$

where the control points $C_{\vec{i}}(p)$ are rational functions of p. Similarly, an S-patch admits a rationally controlled S-patch representation of degree d, if it can be represented in the following form:

$$S(p) = \sum_{\vec{i}} C_{\vec{i}}(p) B^d_{\vec{i}}(\gamma_1(p), \cdots, \gamma_n(p))$$

where $C_{\vec{i}}(p)$ are rational functions of p. In this chapter, we will be interested in a very specific form for $C_{\vec{i}}(p)$, where $C_{\vec{i}}(p) = \sum_k f^k_{\vec{i}}(p) C^k_{\vec{i}}$. The control points $C^k_{\vec{i}}$ are the user-specified control points across the k-th boundary and the functions $f^k_{\vec{i}}(p)$ are rational blending functions.

Remark: It is clear that any rational parametric curve $S(p)$ (resp. S-patch) of degree d admits a rationally controlled Bézier representation of degree d. In general, a rationally controlled Bézier curve (resp. S-patch) of degree d is a rational curve (S-patch) of higher degree, which depends upon the degree of $C_{\vec{i}}(p)$. The advantage of this representation is precisely to represent curves (S-patches) of high rational degrees in terms of a compact, low degree, rationally controlled Bézier representation. Moreover, this representation arises naturally in the n-sided hole filling problem, and it provides some good intuition for the proposed solution.

7 Motivation

This section describes the motivation for introducing the rationally controlled Bézier representation by presenting an example from the curve case. The objective is to construct a curve that fills an interval, also referred to as a 2-sided hole, and meets the surrounding curves F_1 and F_2 with C^h continuity. We demonstrate how a rationally controlled Bézier curve can provide a naturally elegant solution to this problem. Section 9 generalizes these results to n-sided holes.

First, we consider the case $h = 1$, which is well-known as the Hermite interpolation problem. As a first solution, we seek a parametric curve of degree 3, which solves this problem. We assume that the user specifies the position and the derivative data at both ends of the curve in terms of the control points of the interval filling curve $H(t)$ of degree 3, as shown in Figure 4. In other words,

$$\begin{aligned} F_1(1) &= C^1_{30} \\ F_1'(1) &= 3(C^1_{21} - C^1_{30}) \\ F_2(0) &= C^2_{03} \\ F_2'(0) &= -3(C^2_{12} - C^2_{03}) \end{aligned}$$

The superscript k in $C^k_{\vec{i}}$ denotes the control point specified from the k-th end point. In this case, a well-known solution [Far88] to the 2-sided hole problem is given by the following parametric polynomial Bézier curve of degree 3:

$$H(t) = \sum_{|\vec{i}|=3} C_{\vec{i}} B^3_{\vec{i}}$$

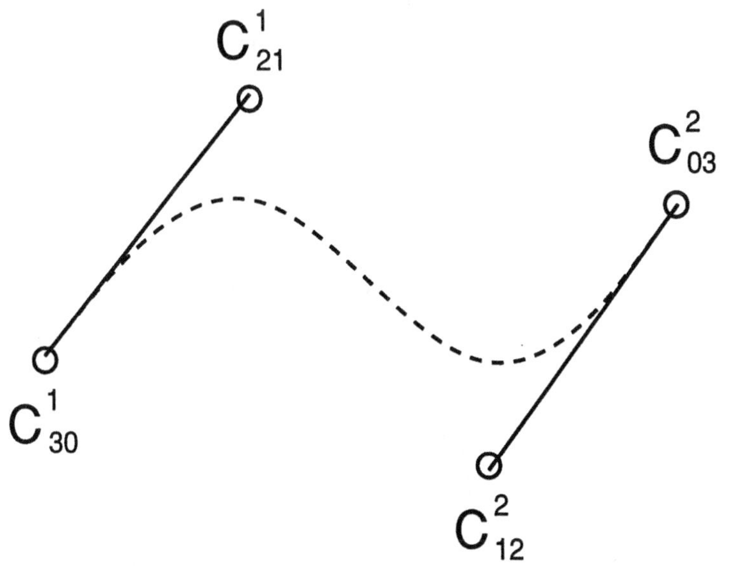

Figure 4 The 2-sided hole problem: C^1 cubic case

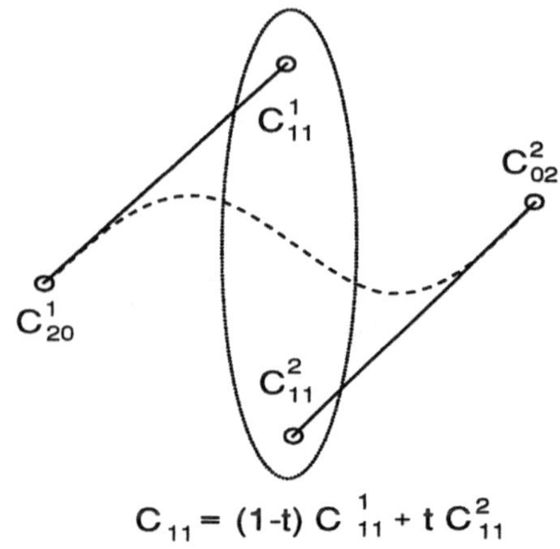

Figure 5 The 2-sided hole problem: C^1 quadratic case

where $C_{30} = C^1_{30}, C_{21} = C^1_{21}, C_{12} = C^2_{12}$, and $C_{03} = C^2_{03}$.

Now let us consider the case when the desired interval filling curve $H(t)$ of degree 2 is sought. In general, there does not exist a parametric polynomial curve of degree 2, which solves the Hermite interpolation problem. Therefore, what we seek is a rationally controlled Bézier curve of degree 2. Again, let us assume that the user specifies the position and the derivative data at the end points in terms of the control points of a curve of degree 2, as shown in Figure 5, so that the following equations hold:

$$\begin{aligned} F_1(1) &= C^1_{20} \\ F_1'(1) &= 2(C^1_{11} - C^1_{20}) \\ F_2(0) &= C^2_{02} \\ F_2'(0) &= -2(C^2_{11} - C^2_{02}) \end{aligned}$$

The following rationally controlled Bézier curve of degree 2 solves the interval filling problem:

$$H(t) = \sum_{|\vec{i}|=2} C_{\vec{i}} B^2_{\vec{i}}$$

where $C_{20} = C^1_{20}$, $C_{11} = \frac{(1-t)C^1_{11} + tC^2_{11}}{(1-t)+t}$, and $C^2_{02} = C_{02}$. In the preceding expression for C_{11}, even though the denominator sums to 1, we have written it this way to emphasize the structural similarity of this solution to the solution in the general case, presented in Section 9. A simple calculation and comparison with the first solution shows that the second solution is in fact identical to the first solution. Thus, the second solution, even though it is a rationally controlled Bézier curve of degree 2, it is in fact a parametric polynomial Bézier curve of degree 3. The control points in the rationally controlled representation are convex combinations of the user-specified control points from the two ends. Moreover, the rational blending functions, in this case simply $1-t$ and t, provide an intuitive way to blend the incompatible control points specified by the user.

In the general case of the interval filling problem, where the interval filling curve meets the surrounding curves with C^{a_k} continuity from the two ends for $k = 1,2$, a rationally controlled Bézier curve of degree $d \geq max(a_1, a_2)$ can be constructed.

Theorem 1 *Let the control points $C^k_{\vec{i}}$ with the distance $g_k(\vec{i}) \leq a_k$ for $k = 1,2$ of a Bézier curve of degree $d \geq max(a_1, a_2)$ be prescribed at both ends. Then there exists a rationally controlled Bézier curve of degree d, which solves the interval filling problem; that is, it meets the surrounding curves with C^{a_k} continuity.*

Proof: This is an immediate consequence of the more general Theorem 2, proved in Section 9. An explicit solution is given in Section 10. □

8 Rational Blending Functions

This section describes certain rational blending functions, which play a crucial role in constructing a solution to the problem of filling n-sided holes. We shall consider the general case where the n-sided hole, surrounded by polynomial patches as shown in Figure 3, meets the surrounding k-th patch with C^{a_k} order of continuity. Thus, the user will be required to prescribe a_k layers of control points across the k-th boundary. Given an edge k and a multi-index $\vec{i}$, we associate rational blending functions $f^k_{\vec{i}}(p)$, which are then used to blend the user-specified control points $C^k_{\vec{i}}$ as follows:

$$C_{\vec{i}}(p) = \sum_{k=1}^{n} f^k_{\vec{i}}(p) C^k_{\vec{i}} \tag{4}$$

Let us introduce the set $S(\vec{i}) = \{k | g_k(\vec{i}) \leq a_k\}$. In other words, $S(\vec{i})$ is the collection of indices of those edges across which the user has prescribed control points associated with the multi-index $\vec{i}$. Also, let $h^k_{\vec{i}}(p) = u_k^{a_k+1-g_k(\vec{i})}(p)$. Recall that $u_k = 0$ is the equation of the edge E_k. Therefore, the functions $h^k_{\vec{i}}$ are chosen to be suitable powers of the equations of the edges, where the power depends upon a_k, the prescribed number of cross-boundary derivatives across the k-th boundary and $g_k(\vec{i})$, the distance of the $\vec{i}$-th control point from the k-th boundary. We define the rational blending functions for $k \epsilon S(\vec{i})$ as follows:

$$f^k_{\vec{i}}(p) \quad = \quad \frac{\hat{f}^k_{\vec{i}}(p)}{\sum_{j \epsilon S(\vec{i})} \hat{f}^j_{\vec{i}}(p)} \tag{5}$$

$$\hat{f}_{\vec{i}}^{k}(p) = z_{\vec{i}}^{k}(p) \prod_{j \epsilon S(\vec{i})-k} h_{\vec{i}}^{j}(p) \tag{6}$$

where the weights $z_{\vec{i}}^{k}(p)$ are chosen to be user-specified positive functions.

Let us consider the example of a 3-sided hole, which is required to meet the surrounding patches with C^2 continuity on all the three sides, as shown in Figure 9. The objective is to construct a rationally controlled quartic triangular Bézier surface patch. Since $g_1(211) = 1$, $g_2(211) = 2$, $g_3(211) = 1$, and $a_k = 2$ for $k = 1, \cdots, 3$, $h_{211}^1 = u_1^2$, $h_{211}^2 = u_2$, and $h_{211}^3 = u_3^2$. Moreover, $S(211) = \{1, 2, 3\}$. If the weight functions $z_{\vec{i}}^{k}(p)$ are chosen to be constant unit functions, then $\hat{f}_{211}^1 = u_2 u_3^2$, $\hat{f}_{211}^2 = u_3^2 u_1^2$, and $\hat{f}_{211}^3 = u_1^2 u_2$. Therefore, the rational blending functions are:

$$f_{211}^1 = \frac{u_2 u_3^2}{u_2 u_3^2 + u_3^2 u_1^2 + u_1^2 u_2} \tag{7}$$

$$f_{211}^2 = \frac{u_3^2 u_1^2}{u_2 u_3^2 + u_3^2 u_1^2 + u_1^2 u_2} \tag{8}$$

$$f_{211}^3 = \frac{u_1^2 u_2}{u_2 u_3^2 + u_3^2 u_1^2 + u_1^2 u_2} \tag{9}$$

Remark: Note that when $g_k(\vec{i}) > a_k$ for all $k = 1, \cdots, n$, then the control point $C_{\vec{i}}^{k}$ associated with the multi-index $\vec{i}$ has not been specified for any k between 1 to n. In this case, the set $S(\vec{i})$ is empty, and we do not define any rational blending functions. In the next section, we will see that the choice of the control points associated with these multi-indices does not affect the solution of the n-sided hole problem.

We introduce the following notation. Given any function $f(p)$, let $D_k^j(f(p))$ denote the jth derivative of the function $f(p)$ in the direction $\vec{N}_k$, which is normal to the edge E_k. In other words, $D_k^j(f(p))$ denotes the j-th cross-boundary derivative of the function $f(p)$ across the k-th boundary. Also, let $f(p)|_{E_k}$ denote the value of the function $f(p)$ evaluated along the edge E_k.

Lemma 1 *The rational blending functions defined above satisfy the following properties:*

1. $f_{\vec{i}}^{k}(p) \geq 0 \;\; \forall \;\; p \epsilon P$.

2. $\sum_{k \epsilon S(\vec{i})} f_{\vec{i}}^{k}(p) = 1$.

3. $f_{\vec{i}}^{k}(p)|_{E_k} = 1$.

4. $D_k^j(f_{\vec{i}}^{l}(p))|_{E_k} = 0$ *for* $1 \leq j \leq a_k - g_k(\vec{i})$, *and* $1 \leq l \leq n$.

Proof: (1) and (2) follow immediately from the definition of the blending functions above.

(3) follows from the observation that $\hat{f}_{\vec{i}}^{j}|E_k = 0$ for $j \epsilon S(\vec{i}) - k$.

(4) follows from the observation that for $k \neq l$, $f_{\vec{i}}^{l}(p)$ contains the factor $h_{\vec{i}}^{k}$, that is, $u_k^{a_k+1-g_k(\vec{i})}$. Since, by assumption, $a_k - g_k(\vec{i}) \geq j$, $f_{\vec{i}}^{l}(p)$ contains at least the factor u_k^{j+1}. Therefore, by differentiating $f_{\vec{i}}^{l}(p)$ only j times, there still remains at least a linear factor of u_k, which vanishes along E_k.

For $k = l$, observe that $f_{\vec{i}}^{k}(p)$ is of the form $\frac{A(p)}{A(p)+u_k^{a_k+1-g_k(\vec{i})}B(p)}$, where $A(p)$ and $B(p)$ are functions of p. A simple calculation shows that the first cross-boundary derivative of $f_{\vec{i}}^{k}(p)$ contains a factor of $u_k^{a_k-g_k(\vec{i})}$. Therefore, by differentiating the blending function $f_{\vec{i}}^{k}(p)$ at most j times, where $j \leq a_k - g_k(\vec{i})$, there still remains at least a linear factor of u_k, which vanishes along E_k. □

The first property states that the rational blending functions are positive inside the polygon. The second property states that they sum to unity. These two properties together guarantee that the rationally blended control points in equation 4 are formed by taking convex combinations of the user-specified control points. The third property states that the k-th blending function is 1 on the k-th boundary. The fourth property states that the j-th cross-boundary derivatives of the rational blending function $f_{\vec{i}}^{k}$ vanish along the k-th boundary, whenever $g_k(\vec{i}) \leq a_k - j$. The third and the fourth property together ensure that the hole-filling patch meets the surrounding patches smoothly across the boundary, as proved in the next section.

Lemma 2 *The rationally blended control points $C_{\vec{i}}(p)$ in equation 4 satisfy the following properties:*

1. $C_{\vec{i}}(p)|_{E_k} = C_{\vec{i}}^{k}$ *for* $g_k(\vec{i}) \leq a_k$.
2. $D_k^j(C_{\vec{i}}(p))|_{E_k} = 0$ *for* $1 \leq j \leq a_k - g_k(\vec{i})$.

Proof: This is an immediate consequence of the lemma above and the definition of the rationally blended control points as given in equation 4. □

Referring to the example, discussed in this section earlier, the rationally blended control point C_{211} is given by $C_{211} = \frac{u_2u_3^2C_{211}^1+u_3^2u_1^2C_{211}^2+u_1^2u_2C_{211}^3}{u_2u_3^2+u_3^2u_1^2+u_1^2u_2}$, where the rational blending functions f_{211}^1, f_{211}^2, and f_{211}^3 are described in Equations 7 to 9. It is clear that these blending functions satisfy the properties (1) and (2) of Lemma 1. Moreover, $f_{211}^1|_{E_1} = 1$, $f_{211}^2|_{E_2} = 1$, and $f_{211}^3|_{E_3} = 1$, so that they satisfy the third property of Lemma 1. This in turn implies the first statement of Lemma 2. For $k = 1$ and $k = 3$, the fourth property of Lemma 1 states that $D_1^1(f_{211}^l)|_{E_1} = 0$ and $D_1^3(f_{211}^l)|_{E_3} = 0$ for $l = 1, \cdots, 3$. This is easily verified. For $k = 2$, since $a_2 - g_2(211) = 0$, the fourth property of Lemma 1 is vacuously true. This in turn implies the second statement of Lemma 2.

9 General Solution

This section presents a solution to the problem of filling n-sided holes by a single rationally controlled S-patch using the rationally blended control points, defined in the previous section. Let a_k layers of control points, that is the control points $C^k_{\vec{i}}$ with the distance $g_k(\vec{i}) \leq a_k$, of an S-patch of depth d be prescribed across its kth boundary for $k = 1, \cdots, n$, where $a_k \geq 0$, and $d \geq max^n_{k=1} a_k$. We prove the theorem that there exists a rationally controlled S-patch H of depth d which solves the n-sided hole problem; that is, the first a_k cross-boundary derivatives of the patch H across the k-th boundary are the same as those given by the prescribed a_k layers of control points across that boundary.

Theorem 2 *Let the hole-filling patch $H(p)$ be defined as follows:*

$$H(p) = \sum_{\vec{i}} C_{\vec{i}}(p) B^d_{\vec{i}}(\gamma_1(p), \cdots, \gamma_n(p)) \tag{10}$$

$$C_{\vec{i}}(p) = \sum_{k \epsilon S(\vec{i})} f^k_{\vec{i}}(p) C^k_{\vec{i}} \tag{11}$$

In equation 10, the summation is to be taken over only those multi-indices $\vec{i}$ for which there exists at least one k such that $g_k(\vec{i}) \leq a_k$. In equation 11, the rational blending functions satisfy properties 1 to 4 stated in Lemma 1. Then, for $k = 1, \cdots, n$ and for $j = 0, \cdots, a_k$,

$$D^j_k(H(p))|_{E_k} = \sum_{g_k(\vec{i}) \leq j} C^k_{\vec{i}} D^j_k(B^d_{\vec{i}}(\gamma_1(p), \cdots, \gamma_n(p)))|_{E_k} \tag{12}$$

Proof: The proof depends upon the following lemma:

Lemma 3 *The j-th cross-boundary derivative of the $\vec{i}$-th Bernstein polynomial evaluated at $(\gamma_1(p), \cdots, \gamma_n(p))$ is 0 if the distance of the $\vec{i}$-th control point from that boundary is greater than j. In other words,*

$$D^j_k B^d_{\vec{i}}(\gamma_1(p), \cdots, \gamma_n(p))|_{E_k} = 0 \quad for \quad g_k(\vec{i}) > j. \tag{13}$$

Proof: By the definition of $\gamma_i(p)$ as given in equations 2 and 3, every $\gamma_i(p)$ except $\gamma_k(p)$ and $\gamma_{k+1}(p)$ contains a factor of $u_k(p)$. Therefore, it follows from the definition of $B^d_{\vec{i}}(\gamma_1(p), \cdots, \gamma_n(p))$ that this Bernstein polynomial contains a factor of $u_k^{g_k(\vec{i})}$. After differentiating $B^d_{\vec{i}}$ j times, there still remains at least one factor of u_k common to every term, because $g_k(\vec{i}) > j$. However, $u_k = 0$ along E_k; hence the result follows. □

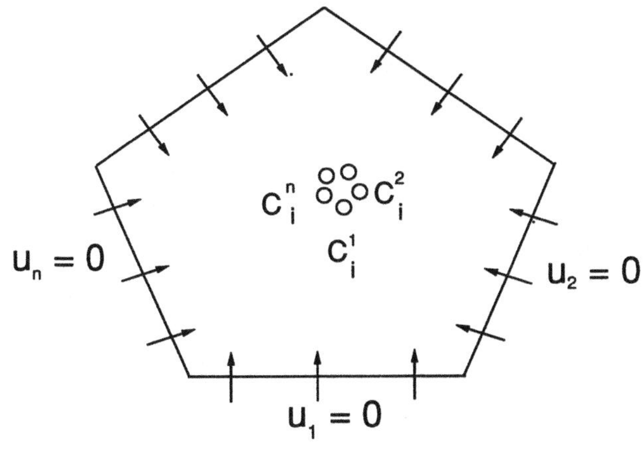

Figure 6 The n-sided hole problem: general case

The proof of Theorem 2 is as follows:

$$\begin{aligned} D_k^j(H(p))|_{E_k} &= D_k^j(\sum_{\vec{i}} C_{\vec{i}}(p) B_{\vec{i}}^d(\gamma_1(p),\cdots,\gamma_n(p)))|_{E_k} \\ &= D_k^j(\sum_{g_k(\vec{i})\le j} C_{\vec{i}}(p) B_{\vec{i}}^d(\gamma_1(p),\cdots,\gamma_n(p)))|_{E_k} \quad \textit{by Lemma } 3 \\ &= \sum_{g_k(\vec{i})\le j} \sum_{l=0}^{j} \begin{pmatrix} j \\ l \end{pmatrix} D_k^l(C_{\vec{i}}(p))|_{E_k} D_k^{j-l}(B_{\vec{i}}^d(p))|_{E_k} \end{aligned}$$

For $1 \le l \le a_k - g_k(\vec{i})$, it follows from Lemma 2 that the first term $D_k^l(C_{\vec{i}}(p))|_{E_k}$ on the right hand side vanishes. On the other hand, for $a_k - g_k(\vec{i}) < l \le j$, which implies that, $g_k(\vec{i}) > a_k - l \ge j - l$, it follows from Lemma 3 that the second term $D_k^{j-l}(B_{\vec{i}}^d(p))|_{E_k}$ on the right hand side vanishes. Therefore, the only contribution on the right hand side comes from the terms when $l = 0$. However, for $l = 0$, the first term on the right reduces to $C_{\vec{i}}^k$ by Lemma 2. Hence the following desired result is obtained:

$$D_k^j(H(p))|_{E_k} = \sum_{g_k(\vec{i})\le j} C_{\vec{i}}^k D_k^j(B_{\vec{i}}^d(\gamma_1(p),\cdots,\gamma_n(p)))|_{E_k} \quad for \;\; j = 0,\cdots,a_k. \tag{14}$$

This concludes the proof of the theorem. □

Remarks:

- We have not assumed any compatibility conditions whatsoever on the position or derivative information of the surrounding patches. However, it is inherent in the n-sided hole filling problem that the surrounding patches meet at corners. This ensures that there are no cracks between the surrounding patches. These corner compatibility condition can be expressed as

$$C^{k-1}_{n\vec{e_k}} = C^{k}_{n\vec{e_k}} \quad for \quad k = 1, \cdots, n$$

Also, in most practical situations, one assumes the derivative compatibility conditions along the boundary of the curve. In other words, the boundary control points are the same irrespective of the side from which they have been prescribed, that is,

$$C_{\vec{i}} = C^{k}_{\vec{i}} \;\; if \;\; g_k(\vec{i}) = 0 \;\; for \;\; any \;\; k = 1, \cdots, n$$

However, we certainly do *not* assume any twist compatibility conditions, such as $C^{k-1}_{\vec{i}} = C^{k}_{\vec{i}}$ if $g_{k-1}(\vec{i}) * g_k(\vec{i}) \neq 0$.

- By Lemma 3, the control points $C^k_{\vec{i}}$, where $g_k(\vec{i}) > a_k$ for every k, do not affect the desired C^{a_k} continuity with the surrounding patches. Therefore, these control points can be chosen completely arbitrarily. Moreover, the weights $z^k_{\vec{i}}$ appearing in expression 6 provide additional flexibility in constructing these patches.

- The proposed solution solves the n-sided hole filling problem, for any number of prescribed cross-boundary derivatives when the domain is a regular convex n-gon in R^2. Using generalized barycentric coordinates [War92], the solution is easily generalizable for any number of prescribed cross-boundary derivatives when the domain is a convex polytope in arbitrary dimension.

10 Examples

This section presents several applications of Theorem 2 for the case of 2-, 3-, 4- , and 5-sided hole filling problems.

1. 2-sided Hole Problem:

   (a) General Case:

   An explicit solution for the 2-sided hole problem, described in Theorem 1, can be given as follows:

$$\begin{aligned} H(t) &= \sum_{\vec{i}} C_{\vec{i}}(t) B^d_{\vec{i}}(t, 1-t) \\ C_{\vec{i}}(t) &= \frac{(1-t)^{a_2+1-g_2(\vec{i})} C^1_{\vec{i}} + t^{a_1+1-g_1(\vec{i})} C^2_{\vec{i}}}{(1-t)^{a_2+1-g_2(\vec{i})} + t^{a_1+1-g_1(\vec{i})}} \end{aligned}$$

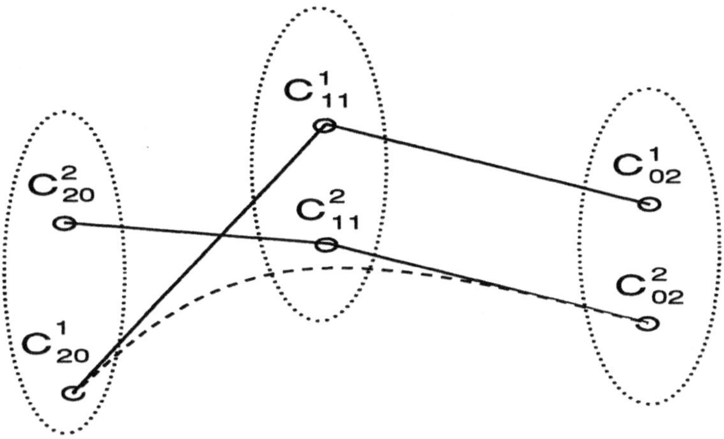

Figure 7 The 2-sided hole problem: C^2 quadratic case

The particular case of a solution with C^2 continuity from both ends by a rationally controlled quadratic Bézier curve is illustrated in Figure 7. In this case $a_1 = a_2 = 2$ and $g_1(20) = 0$, $g_1(11) = 1$, $g_1(02) = 2$, $g_2(20) = 2$, $g_2(11) = 1$, and $g_2(02) = 0$. Therefore, an explicit solution is given by

$$H(t) = \sum_{|\vec{i}|=2} C_{\vec{i}} B^2_{\vec{i}}$$

where $C_{20} = \frac{(1-t)C^1_{20}+t^3C^2_{20}}{(1-t)+t^3}$, $C_{11} = \frac{(1-t)^2C^1_{11}+t^2C^2_{11}}{(1-t)^2+t^2}$, and $C_{02} = \frac{(1-t)^3C^1_{02}+tC^2_{02}}{(1-t)+t^3}$.

(b) Particular Case:

The objective is to construct a rationally controlled Bézier curve of degree 3, which meets the surrounding curves with C^2 continuity. An explicit solution is given by

$$H(t) = \sum_{|\vec{i}|=3} C_{\vec{i}} B^3_{\vec{i}}$$

where $C_{30} = C^1_{30}$, $C_{21} = \frac{(1-t)C^1_{21}+t^2C^2_{21}}{(1-t)+t^2}$, $C_{12} = \frac{(1-t)^2C^1_{12}+tC^2_{12}}{(1-t)^2+t}$, and $C_{03} = C^2_{03}$. Note that in the above solution, since the denominators of the expressions for C_{21} and C_{12} are different, the solution after expansion is a rational curve given by a ratio of polynomial of degree 7 to a polynomial of degree 4.

An alternative representation can be obtained by choosing the weights $z^1_{21} = 1-t$, $z^2_{21} = 1$, $z^1_{12} = 1$, and $z^2_{12} = t$. The solution is now described as follows: $C_{30} = C^1_{30}$, $C_{21} = \frac{(1-t)^2C^1_{21}+t^2C^2_{21}}{(1-t)^2+t^2}$, $C_{12} = \frac{(1-t)^2C^1_{12}+t^2C^2_{12}}{(1-t)^2+t^2}$, and $C_{03} = C^2_{03}$. Since the denominators for the expressions C_{21} and C_{12} are the same, this solution has the advantage that it represents a rational curve given by a ratio of polynomial of degree 5 to a polynomial of degree 2. We shall refer to this technique of choosing weights to make the denominator common as the common denominator technique.

2. 3-sided Hole Problem:

   (a) C^1 Cubic Case (Nielson-Foley Patch):
   The objective is to construct a rationally controlled cubic triangular Bézier surface patch which meets with the surrounding patches with C^1 continuity. The nine boundary control points are prescribed to be compatible. The only remaining interior control point is prescribed from each of the three sides, as shown in Figure 8. Since $a_k = 1$ and $g_k(111) = 1$ for $k = 1, \cdots, 3$, an explicit solution by Theorem 2 is given as follows: $C_{111} = \frac{u_2 u_3 C^1_{111} + u_3 u_1 C^2_{111} + u_1 u_2 C^3_{111}}{u_2 u_3 + u_3 u_1 + u_1 u_2}$, which agrees with the solution proposed by Nielson [Nie87] and Foley [Fol91].

   (b) C^2 Quartic Case:
   The objective is to construct a rationally controlled quartic triangular Bézier surface patch, which meets with the surrounding patches with C^2 continuity. The twelve boundary control points are prescribed to be compatible. The remaining three interior control points are prescribed from each of the three sides, as shown in Figure 9. Following Theorem 2, an explicit solution is given by setting: $C_{211} = \frac{u_2 u_3^2 C^1_{211} + u_3^2 u_1^2 C^2_{211} + u_1^2 u_2 C^3_{211}}{u_2 u_3^2 + u_3^2 u_1^2 + u_1^2 u_2}$. The expressions for the

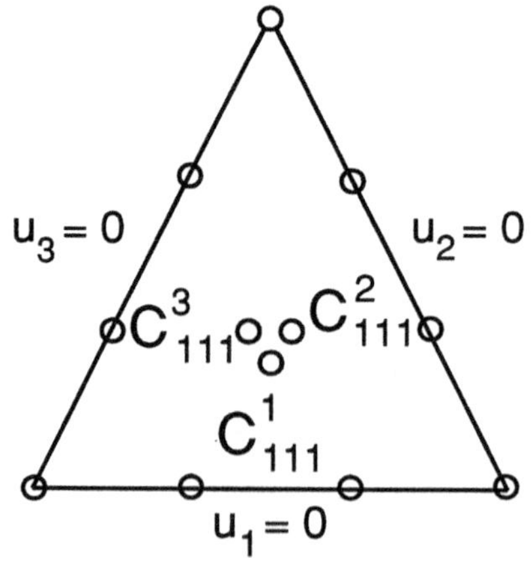

Figure 8 The 3-sided hole problem: Nielson-Foley patch

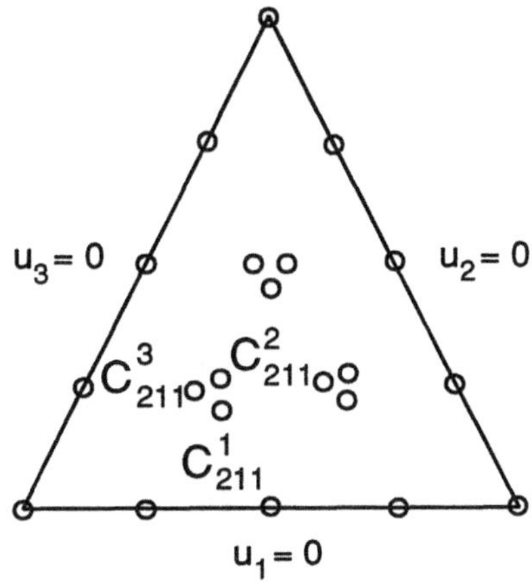

Figure 9 The 3-sided hole problem: C^2 quartic Case

other two interior control points can be derived by symmetry. An alternative new solution using the common denominator technique is given by setting $C_{211} = \frac{u_2^2 u_3^2 C^1_{211} + u_3^2 u_1^2 C^2_{211} + u_1^2 u_2^2 C^3_{211}}{u_2^2 u_3^2 + u_3^2 u_1^2 + u_1^2 u_2^2}$. In this case, the weight functions have been chosen as follows: $z^1_{211} = u_2$, $z^2_{211} = 1$, and $z^3_{211} = u_2$.

3. 4-sided Hole Problem: A 4-sided hole is filled with a rationally controlled 4-sided S-patch. Since 4-sided S-patches are generalizations of tensor product Bézier surface patches, we will use the notation for rationally controlled tensor product Bézier

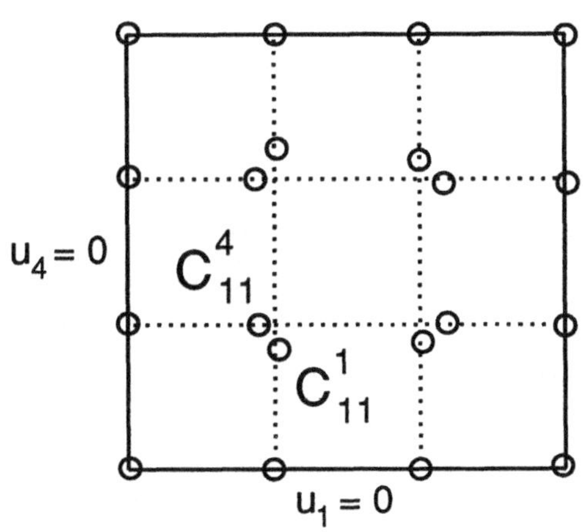

Figure 10 The 4-sided hole problem: Gregory patch

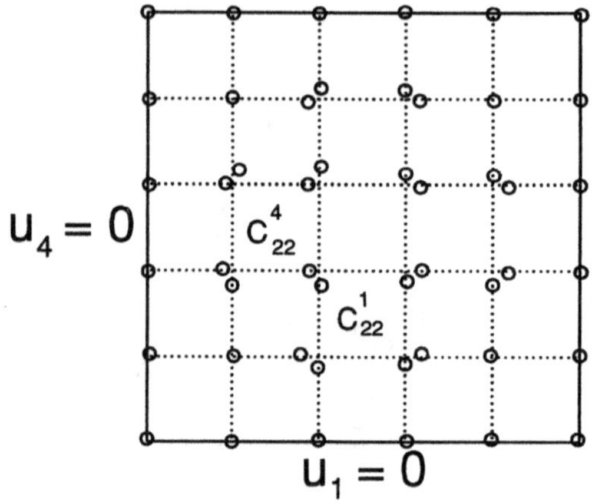

Figure 11 The 4-sided hole problem: Barnhill-Worsey patch

surface patches to describe the solution to the 4-sided hole problem. A rational tensor product Bézier surface patch of bidegree (s, t) is represented as follows:

$$S(p) = \frac{\sum_{i=0}^{i=s} \sum_{j=0}^{j=t} w_{ij} C_{ij} B_i^s(u_1) B_j^t(u_4)}{\sum_{i=0}^{i=s} \sum_{j=0}^{j=t} w_{ij} B_i^s(u_1) B_j^t(u_4)}$$

where C_{ij} are control points, w_{ij} are weights, $B_i^s(u_1) = \binom{s}{i} u_1^i (1 - u_1)^{s-i}$ are the univariate Bernstein polynomials, and (u_1, u_4) are the coordinates of the point p inside the domain rectangle $0 \leq u_1, u_4 \leq 1$. A tensor product Bézier surface patch has a rationally controlled representation of bidegree (s, t), when the coefficients C_{ij} are rational functions of p instead of constants.

(a) C^1 Cubic Case (Gregory Patch:) The objective is to construct a rationally controlled bicubic tensor product Bézier surface patch which meets the surrounding patches with C^1 continuity. The twelve boundary control points are prescribed to be compatible. Each of the remaining four interior control points are prescribed from only two sides as shown in Figure 9. Following Theorem 2, an explicit solution is given by setting: $C_{11} = \frac{u_4 C_{11}^1 + u_1 C_{11}^4}{u_4 + u_1}$, which agrees with the solution described by Chiyokura and Kimura [CK83] for the Gregory patch [Gre83a]. The expressions for the remaining three interior control points can be derived by symmetry.

(b) C^1 Cubic Case (Brown's Square:) An alternative solution for the same problem can be obtained using the common denominator technique. This gives the solution: $C_{11} = \frac{u_4^2 u_2^2 C_{11}^1 + u_3^2 u_1^2 C_{11}^4}{u_4^2 u_2^2 + u_3^2 u_1^2}$, which is known as Brown's square [Gre83a]. Note that in this case, all the interior control points have the same common denominator.

(c) C^2 Quintic Case (Barnhill-Worsey Patch:) The objective is to construct a rationally controlled biquintic tensor product Bézier surface patch, which meets with the surrounding patches with C^2 continuity. The twenty boundary control points are prescribed to be compatible. Moreover the first order twists are prescribed to be compatible, so that the four control points diagonal to the corner control points are also also uniquely determined by the user-specified control points. The remaining eight control points on the first layer can be derived using Theorem 2, which agrees with the solution proposed by Barnhill [Bar83]. Each of the remaining four interior control points are prescribed from only two sides as shown in Figure 11. Following Theorem 2, an explicit solution is given by setting: $C_{22} = \frac{u_4 C_{22}^1 + u_1 C_{22}^4}{u_4 + u_1}$, which agrees with the solution

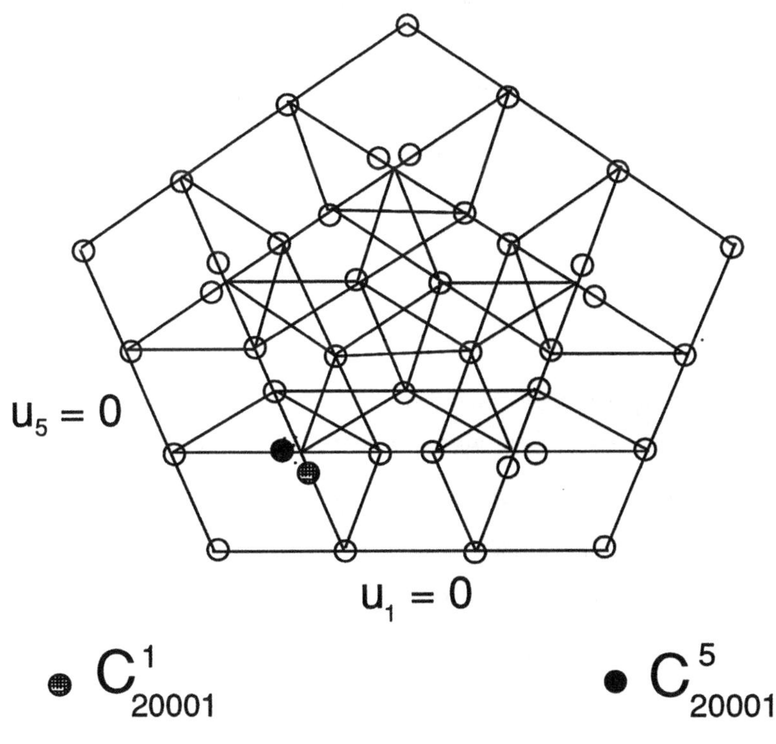

Figure 12 The 5-sided hole problem

described by Worsey [Wor84] and is an improvement over the original solution proposed by Barnhill [Bar83]. The expressions for the remaining three interior control points can be derived by symmetry.

4. 5-sided Hole Problem: The objective is to construct a rationally controlled 5-sided S-patch of depth 3, which meets the surrounding patches with C^1 continuity. All the boundary control points are prescribed to be compatible. Moreover, the tangent plane compatibility from the two sides at each corner forces the remaining control points to be uniquely determined except for the five control points C_{20001}, C_{12000}, C_{01200}, C_{00120}, and C_{00012} as shown in Figure 12. Following Theorem 2, an explicit solution is given by setting: $C_{20001} = \frac{u_5 C^1_{20001} + u_1 C^5_{20001}}{u_5 + u_1}$. The expressions for the remaining four interior control points can be derived by symmetry.

11 Conclusions

This paper described a novel mathematical technique for filling an n-sided hole by a single rationally controlled S-patch. This compact representation is constructed by taking the convex combination of user-specified control points using a judicious choice of rational blending functions. This representation can be used for efficient computation including the deCasteljau algorithm for evaluation, the depth elevation algorithm, and the representation conversion algorithm. The technique unifies several known solutions and provides some insight into the construction of the solution to the problem of filling n-sided holes.

References

[Bar83] R. E. Barnhill. Computer aided surface representation and design. In R. E. Barnhill and W. Boehm, editors, *Surfaces in CAGD*. North-Holland, 1983.

[Bar91] R. E. Barnhill. Coons patches and convex combinations. Manuscript, 1991.

[BBG73] R. E. Barnhill, G. Birkhoff, and W. J. Gordon. Smooth interpolation in triangles. *Journal of Approximation Theory*, 8(2):114–128, 1973.

[BS84] R. E. Barnhill and S. E. Stead. Multistage trivariate surfaces. *Rocky Mountain Journal of Mathematics*, 14:103–118, 1984.

[BW84] R. E. Barnhill and A. J. Worsey. Smooth interpolation over hypercubes. *Computer Aided Geometric Design*, 1:101–113, 1984.

[CG84] P. Charrot and J. A. Gregory. A pentagonal surface patch for computer aided geomteric design. *Computer Aided Geometric Design*, 1:87–94, 1984.

[CK83] H. Chiyokura and F. Kimura. Design of solids with free-form surfaces. *Computer Graphics*, 17(3):289–298, 1983.

[Coo64] S. A. Coons. Surfaces for computer aided design. Technical report, MIT, Department of Mechanical Engineering, 1964. Revised 1967, available as AD 663 504 from the National Technical Information Service, Springfield, VA 22161.

[dB87] C. de Boor. B-form basics. In G. Farin, editor, *Geometric Modeling: Algorithms and New Trends*, pages 131–148. SIAM, 1987.

[DeR88] T. DeRose. Composing Bézier simplexes. *ACM Transactions on Graphics*, 7(3):198–221, July 1988.

[DGHM92] T. DeRose, R.N. Goldman, H. Hagen, and S. Mann. Composition algorithms via blossoming: Theory, applications and implementation. *ACM Transactions on Graphics*, 1992. to appear.

[Far88] G. Farin. *Curves and Surfaces for Computer Aided Geometric Design: A Practical Guide.* Academic Press Inc., New York, 1988.

[Fol91] T. A. Foley. The cubic side-vertex method as a modified cubic triangular Bézier patch. abstract, 1991.

[For72] A. R. Forrest. On Coons and other methods for the representation of curved surfaces. *Computer Graphics and Image Processing*, 1:341–359, 1972.

[GC80] J. A. Gregory and P. Charrot. A C^1 triangular interpolation patch for computer aided geomteric design. *Computer Graphics and Image Processing*, 13:80–87, 1980.

[GH87] J. A. Gregory and J. M. Hahn. Geometric continuity and convex combination patches. *Computer Aided Geometric Design*, 4(1–2):79–89, 1987.

[GH89] J. A. Gregory and J. M. Hahn. A C^2 polygonal surface patch. *Computer Aided Geometric Design*, 6(1):69–75, 1989.

[Gor69] W. J. Gordon. Distributive lattices and the approximation of multivariate functions. In I. J. Schoenberg, editor, *Approximations with Special Emphasis on Splines.* University of Wisconsin Press, Madison, 1969.

[Gre74] J. A. Gregory. Smooth interpolation without twist constraints. In R. E. Barnhill and R. F .Riesenfeld, editors, *Computer Aided Geometric Design*, pages 71–88. Academic Press, New York, 1974.

[Gre83a] J. A. Gregory. C^1 rectangular and non-rectangular surface patches. In R. E. Barnhill and W. Boehm, editors, *Surfaces in CAGD*, pages 25–33. North-Holland, 1983.

[Gre83b] J. A. Gregory. n-sided surface patches. In J. A. Gregory, editor, *Mathematics of Surfaces*, pages 217–232. Clarendon Press, Oxford, 1983.

[Gre85] J. A. Gregory. Interpolation to boundary data on the simplex. *Computer Aided Geometric Design*, 2:43–52, 1985.

[Her79] G. Herron. *Triangular and Multisided Patch Schemes.* PhD thesis, University of Utah, Salt Lake City, Department of Mathematics, 1979.

[HK84] M. Hosaka and F. Kimura. Non-four-sided patch expressions with control points. *Computer Aided Geometric Design*, 1(1):75–86, 1984.

[LD89] C. Loop and T. DeRose. A multisided generalization of Bézier surfaces. *ACM Transactions on Graphics*, 8(3), 1989.

[LD90] C. Loop and T. DeRose. Generalized B-spline surfaces of arbitrary topology. *Computer Graphics*, 24(4):347–356, 1990.

[Lit83] F. F. Little. Convex combination surfaces. In R. E. Barnhill and W. Boehm, editors, *Surfaces in CAGD*. North-Holland, 1983.

[Nie79] G. M. Nielson. The side-vertex method for interpolation in triangles. *Journal of Approximation Theory*, 25:318–336, 1979.

[Nie87] G. M. Nielson. A transinite visually continuous triangular interpolant. In G. Farin, editor, *Geometric Modeling: Algorithms and New Trends*, pages 235–246. Siam, 1987.

[Pet90] J. Peters. *Fitting smooth parametric surfaces to 3D data.* PhD thesis, University of Wisconsin, Madison, Center for the Mathematical Sciences, 1990.

[Sab83] M. Sabin. Non-rectangular surface patches suitable for inclusion in a B-spline surface. In P. ten Hagen, editor, *Proceedings of Eurographics 1983*, pages 57–69, Amsterdam, 1983. North-Holland.

[UH91] K. Ueda and T. Harada. Generalization of a family of gregory surfaces. In N. M. Patrikalakis, editor, *Volume Visualization*, pages 417–434. 1991.

[Var87] T. Varady. Survey and new results in n-sided patch generation. In R. Martin, editor, *The Mathematics of Surfaces II*, pages 203–236. Oxford University Press, 1987.

[Var91] T. Varady. Overlap patches: A new scheme for interpolating curve networks with n-sided regions. *Computer Aided Geometric Design*, 8:7–27, 1991.

[War92] J. Warren. Barycentric coordinates for convex polytopes. private communication, 1992.

[Wor84] A. J. Worsey. A modified C^2 Coons' patch. *Computer Aided Geometric Design*, 1:357–360, 1984.

[Wor85] A. J. Worsey. C^2 interpolation over hypercubes. In R. E. Barnhill and W. Boehm, editors, *Surfaces in CAGD '84*. North-Holland, 1985.

Finite Representations of Real Parametric Curves and Surfaces

Chandrajit L. Bajaj *
Andrew V. Royappa **
* Department of Computer Sciences
Purdue University
West Lafayette, IN 47907 USA
** Computer Science Department
University of New Hampshire
Durham, NH 03824 USA

1 Introduction

Algebraic curves and surfaces are commonly used in geometric modeling. *Parametric* curves and surfaces are those that can be represented using rational parametric equations, and are particularly important. In geometric modeling applications, the parametric equations are restricted to some bounded portion of the domain, yielding a segment of a curve or a patch of a surface. However, the algebraic curve or surface is an image of the entire infinite parameter domain. Attempting to map the entire curve or surface using very large regions of the parameter domain is not a solution because some finite points may be images of infinite parameter values.

Thus a natural question arises: can one cover an entire curve or surface, using only a finite number of bounded regions of the parameter domain ? This is indeed possible, and two methods are described in this paper.

In the first method, a given rational parameterization is replaced by several bounded parameterizations that together generate all the points that the original one did, including points that correspond to infinite parameter values. Projective linear domain transformations (reparameterizations) are applied that map the unit simplex of each parameter domain onto an entire octant of the original parameter domain space in turn. This approach for the special case of real parametric curves and surfaces in the Bernstein-Bezier form, is similar to the technique called homogeneous sampling (DeRose, 1991) used to sample finite and infinite domain points of a parameterization equally. One application of our work is displaying entire real parametric curves and surfaces. Another application is the first step towards representing an entire real parametric curve (surface) by a collection of curves (surfaces) in Bernstein-Bezier form, each with positive weights (Farin, 1991; Lucian, 1991).

In the second approach, it is shown that a *single* projective reparameterization suffices to map all finite and infinite parameter values of the old parameterization, using only finite values of the new parameter domain. In this case the reparameterization is quadratic and the region of the domain space that suffices is the unit hypersphere of the new domain space. Because of the higher degree and the non-linear boundary of the domain region, this approach is less practical, but it can be used to compute *normal parameterizations* of curves and surfaces – that is, parameterizations that map all points of the curve or surface, without "missing" any (Gao and Chou, 1991). Normal parameterizations for conic curves and some quadric surfaces have been given (Gao and Chou, 1991); the problem of computing normal parameterizations for three important quadric surfaces was open, and we shall give the solutions here.

Since the results generalize to higher dimensions, our discussion will be in terms of real parametric varieties of any dimension. The problem can be stated as follows. Given a real parameterization of a parametric variety, we would like to compute an alternate set of bounded parameterizations that together generate all the real points of the variety: those that correspond to finite parameter values, and those that correspond to infinite parameter values (in the original parameterization).

This paper is organized as follows. In the next section some preliminary definitions and terminology are given, and the issue of "missing points" is discussed in some detail. In section 3, we show how to finitely represent a real parametric variety of dimension n using 2^n pieces. In section 4 it is shown that a single reparameterization is sufficient, and in section 5 we make some concluding remarks and indicate directions for future work.

2 Finite parametric representations

The set of solutions of a set of polynomial equations with real coefficients in m variables forms a real algebraic set in $\mathcal{R}^m$, where $\mathcal{R}$ is the field of real numbers. A real algebraic set that cannot be properly represented as the union of two real algebraic sets is called a real *variety*. A *parametric* variety is one whose points can be given as the image of a map over some domain space. We restrict our attention to maps defined by rational functions.

Let the points of a variety V of dimension n in R^m $(n < m)$ be given by a rational-function map in n parameters:

$$V(\mathbf{s}) = \begin{pmatrix} x_1(s_1, \ldots, s_n) \\ \vdots \\ x_m(s_1, \ldots, s_n) \end{pmatrix}, \qquad s_i \in (-\infty, +\infty)$$

The rational functions $x_i(s_1, \ldots, s_n)$ constitute a *parameterization* of the variety and are assumed to have a common denominator. Methods exist for computing rational parameterizations of various classes of varieties (Abhyankar and Bajaj, 1987ab,1988,1989; Golub and Van Loan, 1983; Levin, 1979; Schicho and Sendra, 1991; Sendra and Winkler, 1991; Sederberg and Snively, 1987). All these algorithms generate parameterizations of curves and surfaces over infinite domains.

We view the map as one from the real projective space of n dimensions to the real affine space of m dimensions, i.e. $V(\mathbf{s}) : \mathcal{RP}^n \rightarrow \mathcal{R}^m$. By doing so, we allow each parameter s_i to take on any value in $\mathcal{R}$ as well as the value ∞. It is often the case that a finite point (one in $\mathcal{R}^m$) of the variety given by rational functions is mapped by an infinite parameter value in $\mathcal{RP}^n$.

For example, a 1-dimensional real variety in $\mathcal{R}^2$ is defined by the bivariate polynomial equation $x^2 + y^2 - 1 = 0$. The points are in the image of the univariate rational functions

$$x(s) = \frac{2s}{s^2+1}, \qquad y(s) = \frac{s^2-1}{s^2+1}, \qquad s \in (-\infty, +\infty) \tag{1}$$

Notice that the point $(0,1) \in \mathcal{R}^2$ of the variety is the image of the parameter value $s = \infty \in \mathcal{RP}$.

2.1 Missing points of parameterizations

There are two categories of potential *missing points* of a real parametric representation of a variety.

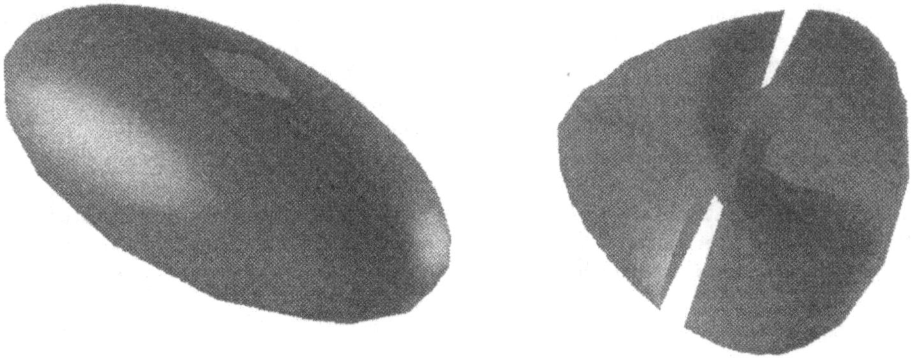

Figure 1: Missing points due to infinite parameter values

First, a parametric variety may have finite points that correspond to infinite parameter values. There are methods, though computation intensive, for proving whether or not a given parameterization has such missing points and to compute them (Gao and Chou, 1991; Wu, 1984). Two different solutions are provided in this paper for dealing with missing points and generating new parameterizations which do not have missing points.

Examples. A simple case is the unit circle, whose parameterization (1) and missing point were given earlier. Figure 1 shows two surfaces, an ellipsoid and a Steiner surface. A point is missing on the ellipsoid, and a curve from the Steiner surface. The parameterizations of the ellipsoid and the Steiner surface are given in Table 1. For each parameterization we show the image of a rectangular domain region centered at the origin. All such images show a "hole" or gap (the clover-leaf on the ellipsoid is a hole).

Increasing the area of the domain region will shrink the gap but never close it. Furthermore, if the domain region is discretized uniformly to generate a piecewise-linear mesh approximating the surface, the pieces tend to be large away from the gap, but small and dense near the gap; curvature-sensitive approximation techniques are necessary.

Second, parametric varieties of dimension greater than 1 can have *base points*, which are points in the parameter domain at which all numerators and (common) denominator of a parameterization vanish. For surfaces it has been shown that a domain base point corresponds to an entire curve on the surface (Hartshorne, 1977). For example, consider the variety defined by $x^2 + y^2 - z^2 - 1 = 0$. A parameterization for it is

$$(x(u,v), y(u,v), z(u,v)) = \left(\frac{u^2 - v^2 + 1}{u^2 + v^2 - 1}, \quad \frac{2uv}{u^2 + v^2 - 1}, \quad \frac{2u}{u^2 + v^2 - 1}\right)$$

which has the base points $(u, v) = (0, \pm 1)$; it can be shown that these points map onto the lines $(x(s), y(s), z(s)) = (-1, s, s)$ and $(x(t), y(t), z(t)) = (-1, t, -t)$ on the surface. Essentially, approaching the domain base point from two different directions leads to different surface points, in the limit.

Domain base points cause "pseudo" missing points on the variety that are the image of finite parameter values. These points on the variety are only missing in that the rational map itself is ill-defined, when specialized to the domain base points. We don't present a reparameterization solution to this problem but leave it open for future research.

One way for surfaces is as follows: besides reparameterization, one may augment the existing parameterization with parameterizations of the image points corresponding to base points (Chionh, 1990). Such space curves on the surface are called *seam curves*, and are known to be rational. Algorithms for computing rational-map parameterizations of these curves have been given but they are not practical at this time (Manocha, 1992). A more practical approach might be to numerically approximate the seam curves.

2.2 Problem statement

We wish to replace a parameterization over an infinite parameter domain with a finite number of parameterizations, each over a fixed, bounded parameter domain. Suppose we are given a parameterization $V(\mathbf{s}) : \mathcal{RP}^n \rightarrow \mathcal{R}^m$ of a variety. We wish to compute maps $Q_1, \ldots, Q_k$, with $Q_i : \mathcal{R}^n \rightarrow \mathcal{R}^m$, such that $\cup_{i=1}^k Q_i(\mathcal{R}^n) = V(\mathcal{RP}^n)$. That is, the new maps restricted to finite values together yield the same set of points that the given one does, even though the latter maps both finite and infinite domain values. To derive a *finite representation* we also find a bounded region $D \subset \mathcal{R}^n$ to which the Q_i can be be restricted, i.e., $\cup_{i=1}^k Q_i(D) = V(\mathcal{RP}^n)$.

2.3 Main results

Given one parameterization of V, it is possible to compute a finite representation of it, and we show two ways below.

In the first way, an affine variety of dimension n is finitely represented using 2^n parameterizations, with the bounded domain D being the unit simplex in $\mathcal{R}^n$. In the second way, only one parameterization suffices, but its degree is twice that of the original, and the bounded domain D is the unit hypersphere in $\mathcal{R}^n$. The second approach can be used to compute parameterizations of real parametric varieties that are free of *missing points.*

3 Piecewise finite representation

Suppose we are given a real parametric variety V of dimension n and a parameterization $V(\mathbf{s})$ for it. We compute 2^n parameterizations, each restricted to the unit simplex of the parameter domain $\mathcal{R}^n$, that together give all the points that $V(\mathbf{s})$ did for $\mathbf{s} \in \mathcal{RP}^n$.

We use linear projective domain transformations (reparameterizations) to map, in turn, the unit simplex D of the new parameter domain space onto an entire octant of the original parameter domain space. The reparameterizations are specified in affine fractional form for convenience, but in practice they would be applied by homogenizing a parameterization and then substituting polynomials.

These particular linear reparameterizations are chosen to ensure that the piecewise representation is not an overlapping: the pieces meet along sets that are of lower dimension than the variety itself. This is useful for certain applications such as surface display, in which overlappings can cause unsightly artifacts due to aliasing.

Figure 2: Piecewise finite representations

THEOREM 1 *Consider a real parametric variety in $\mathcal{R}^m$ of dimension n, $n < m$, which is parameterized by the equations*

$$V(\mathbf{s}) = \begin{pmatrix} x_1(s_1,\ldots,s_n) \\ \vdots \\ x_m(s_1,\ldots,s_n) \end{pmatrix}, \qquad s_i \in (-\infty,+\infty)$$

Let the 2^n octant cells in the parameter domain $\mathcal{R}^n$ be labelled by the tuples $< \sigma_1,\ldots\sigma_n >$ with $\sigma_i \in \{-1,1\}$. Then the 2^n projective reparameterizations $V(\mathbf{t}_{<\sigma_1,\ldots,\sigma_n>})$ given by

$$s_i = \sigma_i \frac{t_i}{1-t_1-t_2-\ldots-t_n}, \qquad i = 1,\ldots,n \tag{2}$$

together map all the points of the variety $V(\mathbf{s}), s_i \in (-\infty,+\infty)$, using only parameter values satisfying $t_i \geq 0$ and $t_1+t_2+\ldots+t_n \leq 1$.

PROOF. We must show that every point in the old domain $\mathcal{RP}^n$ is the image of some point in the new domain $\mathcal{R}^n$. In particular, we show that the hyperplane $t_1+\ldots+t_n = 1$ bordering the unit simplex in $\mathcal{R}^n$ maps onto the hyperplane at infinity in $\mathcal{RP}^n$, and the rest of the points of the unit simplex are mapped onto a particular octant of the original domain space, depending on the signs of the σ_i.

Let $\mathbf{s} = (cs_1,\ldots,cs_n,cs_{n+1}) \in \mathcal{RP}^n$, where $c \in \mathcal{R}$ is a non-zero constant of proportionality and $s_{n+1} = 0$ is the equation of the hyperplane at infinity in $\mathcal{RP}^n$. Let $\mathbf{t} = (t_1,\ldots,t_n) \in \mathcal{R}^n$. Since (2) is a map from $\mathcal{R}^n \to \mathcal{RP}^n$, the following relationship holds between the s_i and t_j, under one of the 2^n transformations $< \sigma_1,\ldots,\sigma_n >$:

$$\begin{aligned} cs_1 &= \sigma_1 t_1 \\ &\vdots \\ cs_n &= \sigma_n t_n \\ cs_{n+1} &= 1-(t_1+\ldots+t_n) \end{aligned}$$

Let $\operatorname{sign}(\alpha), \alpha \in \mathcal{R}$ be -1 or $+1$ according to whether $\alpha < 0$ or $\alpha \geq 0$, respectively.

First we show that every $\mathbf{s} \in \mathcal{RP}^n$ on the hyperplane at infinity is the image of some point $\mathbf{t} = (t_1,\ldots,t_n) \in \mathcal{R}^n$ under one of the transformations, and additionally that $t_i \geq 0$ and $t_1+\ldots+t_n = 1$.

Since $\mathbf{s}$ is on the hyperplane at infinity, $s_{n+1} = 0$, and hence

$$\begin{aligned} cs_i &= \sigma_i t_i & i = 1,\ldots,n \\ 0 &= 1-(t_1+\ldots+t_n) \end{aligned}$$

Then a solution $(t_1,\ldots,t_n)$ is derived by setting

$$\begin{aligned} \sigma_i &= \operatorname{sign}(s_i) \\ c &= \frac{1}{\sum_{i=1}^n \sigma_i s_i} \\ t_i &= \frac{\sigma_i s_i}{\sum_{i=1}^n \sigma_i s_i} \end{aligned}$$

Noting that $\sigma_i s_i \geq 0$ and not all of the $s_i, i = 1,\ldots n$ can be zero, it follows that $t_i \geq 0$ and $\sum_{i=1}^n t_i = 1$.

Second, let $\mathbf{s} \in \mathcal{R}^n \subset \mathcal{RP}^n$, i.e. $s_{n+1} \neq 0$. We show that $\mathbf{s}$ is the image of some $\mathbf{t} \in \mathcal{R}^n$ under one of the transformations, and additionally $\mathbf{t}$ lies in the unit simplex of $\mathcal{R}^n$.

We can set $s_{n+1} = 1$ w.l.o.g. and the following system of equations for the t_i is derived:

$$\begin{aligned} cs_i &= \sigma_i t_i \qquad\qquad i = 1, \ldots, n \\ c &= 1 - (t_1 + \ldots + t_n) \end{aligned}$$

We can solve this linear system by setting

$$\begin{aligned} \sigma_i &= \text{sign}(s_i) \\ c &= \frac{1}{1 + \sum_{i=1}^{n} \sigma_i s_i} \\ t_i &= \frac{\sigma_i s_i}{1 + \sum_{i=1}^{n} \sigma_i s_i} \end{aligned}$$

and since $\sigma_i s_i \geq 0$ it follows that $t_i \geq 0$ and $t_1 + \ldots + t_n < 1$, hence this point $\mathbf{t}$ is in the unit simplex in $\mathcal{R}^n$, but not on the hyperplane $t_1 + \ldots + t_n = 1$.

We have thus proved that all of $\mathcal{RP}^n$ is mapped by the transformations (2), restricting each to the unit simplex of $\mathcal{R}^n$. □

COROLLARY 1 *Rational curves given by a parameterization* $C(s) = (x_1(s), \ldots, x_m(s))^T$, $s \in (-\infty, +\infty)$ *can be finitely represented by* $C(\frac{t}{1-t})$, $C(\frac{-t}{1-t})$, *using only* $0 \leq t \leq 1$.

COROLLARY 2 *Rational parametric surfaces* $S(s_1, s_2) = (x_1(s_1, s_2), \ldots, x_m(s_1, s_2))^T$, $s_1, s_2 \in (-\infty, +\infty)$ *can be finitely represented by*

$$\begin{array}{ll} S(\frac{t_1}{1-t_1-t_2}, \frac{t_2}{1-t_1-t_2}) & S(\frac{-t_1}{1-t_1-t_2}, \frac{t_2}{1-t_1-t_2}) \\ S(\frac{-t_1}{1-t_1-t_2}, \frac{-t_2}{1-t_1-t_2}) & S(\frac{t_1}{1-t_1-t_2}, \frac{-t_2}{1-t_1-t_2}) \end{array} .$$

using only $t_1, t_2 \geq 0 \wedge t_1 + t_2 \leq 1$.

Examples. Figure 2 shows several piecewise representations of surfaces using corollary 2. Points on a surface that are correspond to a particular quadrant of the parameter domain space $\mathcal{RP}^2$ are given a color unique to that quadrant, and the entire surface is trimmed to some bounding box of $\mathcal{R}^3$. The upper left shows a Steiner quartic variety, whose quadratic parameterization is given in Table 1. In the upper right is an "elbow" cubic variety, whose parameterization is

$$\left(\frac{4t^2 + (s^2 + 6s + 4)t - 4s - 8}{2t^2 - 4t + s^2 + 4s + 8}, \frac{4t^2 + (-s^2 - 6s - 20)t + 2s^2 + 8s + 16}{2t^2 - 4t + s^2 + 4s + 8}, \frac{(2s + 6)t^2 + (-4s - 12)t - s^2 - 4s}{2t^2 - 4t + s^2 + 4s + 8} \right)$$

A singular cubic surface appears in the lower left; its parameterization is

$$\left(\frac{t^3 + 2t + s^3 - 7s^2 + 1}{t^3 + s^3 + 1}, \frac{2t^3 + 2t^2 - 7s^2 t + 2s^3 + 2}{t^3 + s^3 + 1}, \frac{2st - 7s^3}{t^3 + s^3 + 1} \right)$$

An arbitrary quartic variety whose parameterization is quadratic is given in the lower right; its parametric equations are

$$\left(\frac{2s}{s^2 + t^2 - 2}, \frac{4ts}{s^2 + t^2 - 2}, \frac{1 - s^2 - t^2}{s^2 + t^2 - 2} \right)$$

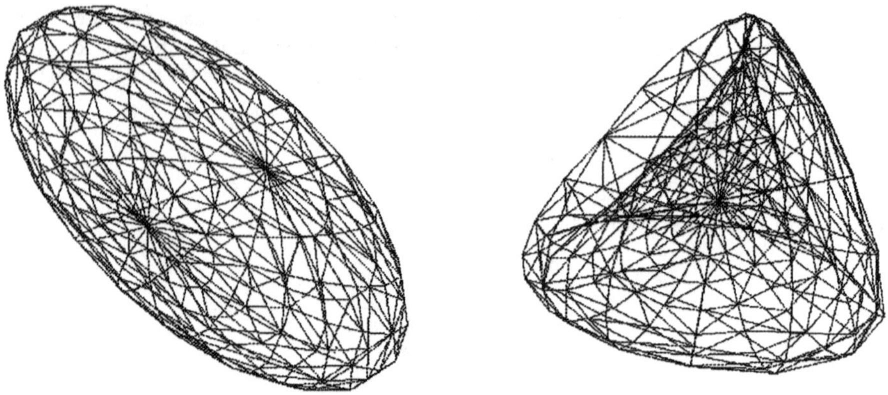

Figure 3: Single finite representations

4 Single finite representation

We now consider the problem of finitely representing a real parametric variety using only one parameterization. Put another way, can we find parameterizations of varieties that have no missing points ? Such *normal parameterizations* have been given for ellipses and some quadric surfaces (Gao and Chou, 1991); the method for proving a parameterization normal involves elimination-theoretic computations based on the method of characteristic sets developed for geometric theorem proving (Wu, 1984). The method is general, but lengthy machine computations are involved and the authors were unable to find normal parameterizations for three important quadrics, namely the ellipsoid, hyperboloid of one sheet, and hyperboloid of two sheets; they pose it as an open problem to either find such normal parameterizations or to prove they don't exist. It is also shown that the lowest-degree normal parameterization of an ellipse is of degree 4, which hints that normal parameterizations for the above quadrics will also need to be of degree 4, at least.

We can achieve the same results simply by using projective reparameterizations to bring points at infinity in the parameter domain to finite distances. Instead of using linear projective reparameterizations, however, we now use quadratic projective reparameterizations to solve this problem.

THEOREM 2 *Consider a real parametric variety of dimension n in $\mathcal{R}^m$, $n < m$, which is parameterized by the equations*

$$V(\mathbf{s}) = \begin{pmatrix} x_1(s_1, \ldots, s_n) \\ \vdots \\ x_m(s_1, \ldots, s_n) \end{pmatrix}, \qquad s_i \in (-\infty, +\infty)$$

The single projective quadratic reparameterization given in fractional affine form as

$$s_i = \frac{t_i}{1 - t_1^2 - t_2^2 - \ldots - t_n^2}, \qquad i = 1, \ldots, n \tag{3}$$

yields a finite representation $V(\mathbf{t})$ *of the rational variety* $V(\mathbf{s})$*, restricting* $t_1^2 + \ldots + t_n^2 \leq 1$.

PROOF. In this case, the proof consists of showing every point in the old domain $\mathcal{RP}^n$ is the image of some point in the new domain $\mathcal{R}^n$, using only the single transformation (3). We will show that the unit hypersphere in the new domain space maps onto the hyperplane at infinity of the old domain space, and every other point in the old parameter domain space is the image of a corresponding point in the new domain, which lies in the interior of the unit hypersphere.

Once again let $\mathbf{s} = (cs_1, \ldots, cs_{n+1}) \in \mathcal{RP}^n$, $c \in \mathcal{R}$, $c \neq 0$ and we fix $s_{n+1} = 0$ as the hyperplane at infinity. Let $\mathbf{t} \in \mathcal{R}^n$. The equations (3) are a map from $\mathcal{R}^n \to \mathcal{RP}^n$:

$$\begin{aligned} cs_i &= t_i \\ &\vdots \\ cs_n &= t_n \\ cs_{n+1} &= 1 - (t_1^2 + \ldots + t_n^2) \end{aligned}$$

First, consider points $\mathbf{s}$ on the hyperplane at infinity, i.e. $s_{n+1} = 0$. Then (3) yields a system of equations

$$\begin{aligned} cs_i &= t_i & \qquad i = 1, \ldots, n \\ 0 &= 1 - (t_1^2 + \ldots + t_n^2) \end{aligned}$$

which has two real solutions, given below:

$$\begin{aligned} c &= \pm\frac{1}{\sqrt{\sum_{i=1}^n s_i^2}} \\ t_i &= cs_i = \pm\frac{s_1}{\sqrt{\sum_{i=1}^n s_i^2}} \end{aligned}$$

For either solution, $t_1^2 + \ldots + t_n^2 = 1$, showing that $\mathbf{t}$ lies on the unit hypersphere in $\mathcal{R}^n$.

Second, consider affine points $\mathbf{s} \in \mathcal{R}^n \subset \mathcal{RP}^n$. We can set $s_{n+1} = 1$, w.l.o.g., and then (3) yields the system of equations

$$\begin{aligned} cs_i &= t_i & \qquad i = 1, \ldots, n \\ c &= 1 - (t_1^2 + \ldots + t_n^2) \end{aligned}$$

This system also has two real solutions, given by

$$\begin{aligned} c &= \frac{-1 \pm \sqrt{1 + 4\sum_{i=1}^n s_i^2}}{2\sum_{i=1}^n s_i^2} \\ t_i &= cs_i \end{aligned}$$

Choosing $c = \frac{-1+\sqrt{1+4\sum_{i=1}^n s_i^2}}{2\sum_{i=1}^n s_i^2}$, some simple algebra shows that $t_1^2 + \ldots t_n^2 < 1$.

Thus if $\mathbf{s}$ is on the hyperplane at infinity, there is a point $\mathbf{t}$ on the unit hypersphere that maps it; otherwise, there is a point $\mathbf{t}$ in the interior of the unit hypersphere that maps it. Only the single map (3) is necessary. □

Variety	Equation	Parameterization and Missing Points
Ellipse	$\frac{x^2}{a^2}+\frac{y^2}{b^2}-1=0$	$\left(\frac{a(s^2-1)}{s^2+1}, \frac{2bs}{a^2+1}\right)$ Missing: $(a,0)$
Ellipsoid	$\frac{x^2}{a^2}+\frac{y^2}{b^2}+\frac{z^2}{c^2}-1=0$	$\left(\frac{2as}{s^2+t^2+1}, \frac{2bt}{s^2+t^2+1}, \frac{c(s^2+t^2-1)}{s^2+t^2+1}\right)$ Missing: $(0,0,c)$
Hyp/1S	$\frac{x^2}{a^2}+\frac{y^2}{b^2}-\frac{z^2}{c^2}-1=0$	$\left(\frac{a(s^2-t^2+1)}{s^2+t^2-1}, \frac{2bts}{s^2+t^2-1}, \frac{2cs}{s^2+t^2-1}\right)$ Missing: $\left\{\frac{x^2}{a^2}+\frac{y^2}{b^2}-1=0, z=0\right\} \setminus \{(-a,0,0)\}$
Hyp/2S	$\frac{x^2}{a^2}+\frac{y^2}{b^2}-\frac{z^2}{c^2}+1=0$	$\left(\frac{2as}{s^2+t^2-1}, \frac{2bt}{s^2+t^2-1}, \frac{c(s^2+t^2+1)}{s^2+t^2-1}\right)$ Missing: $(0,0,c)$
Steiner	$x^2y^2+y^2z^2+x^2z^2-2xyz=0$	$\left(\frac{2s}{s^2+t^2+1}, \frac{2t}{s^2+t^2+1} \frac{2st}{s^2+t^2+1}\right)$ Missing: $(0,0,r), r \in (-1,1), r \neq 0$

Table 1: Real parametric varieties and their missing points

Given a parameterization of a variety, an application of theorem 2 yields a normal parameterization of the corresponding variety. Thus we can compute normal parameterizations of the ellipsoid and one- and two-sheeted hyperboloids, settling the open issue (Gao and Chou, 1991) of whether normal parameterizations for these varieties exist.

COROLLARY 3 *Using theorem 2, we can compute normal parameterizations for the ellipse, ellipsoid, hyperboloid of one sheet, and hyperboloid of two sheets.*

The equations of several varieties are given in Table 1. A rational parameterization for each variety is listed, as well as the missing points of each parameterization. The missing points can be computed either using general machine computations (Gao and Chou, 1991), but for these particular varieties direct, elementary arguments suffice (Royappa, 1992).

In Table 2, normal parameterizations of these varieties are given. That of the ellipse has already been found (Gao and Chou, 1991); all those for surfaces are new. For the ellipse, the parameters can be restricted to $|u| \leq 1$, and for the quadric surfaces they can be restricted to $u^2+v^2 \leq 1$. The parameterizations map these bounded domain regions onto the entire variety, without missing any points.

Examples. The left half of Figure 3 shows a normal ellipsoid parameterization graphed over the parameter region $u^2+v^2 \leq 1$. Likewise, the right half shows a normal Steiner surface parameterization. The parameters of both are restricted to the unit disk in $\mathcal{R}^2$. Each figure is unshaded to emphasize that no parts of the surface are missing (compare these to Figure 1).

Variety	Normal Parameterization
Ellipse	$\dfrac{(-a(u^4-3u^2+1),2b(u-u^3))}{u^4-u^2+1}$
Ellipsoid	$\dfrac{(2au(1-u^2-v^2),2bv(1-u^2-v^2),-c(v^4+2u^2v^2-3v^2+u^4-3u^2+1))}{v^4+2u^2v^2-v^2+u^4-u^2+1}$
Hyp/1S	$\dfrac{(a(v^4+2u^2v^2-3v^2+u^4-u^2+1),2buv,2cu(1-u^2-v^2))}{-(v^4+2u^2v^2-3v^2+u^4-3u^2+1)}$
Hyp/2S	$\dfrac{(2au(1-u^2-v^2),2bv(1-u^2-v^2),c(v^4+2u^2v^2-v^2+u^4-u^2+1))}{-(v^4+2u^2v^2-3v^2+u^4-3u^2+1)}$
Steiner	$\dfrac{(2u(1-u^2-v^2),2v(1-u^2-v^2),2uv)}{v^4+2u^2v^2-v^2+u^4-u^2+1}$

Table 2: Normal parameterizations of some varieties

5 Conclusions and future work

In this paper we have presented two ways by which infinite parameter values can be avoided when dealing with parametric curves and surfaces. The results were presented for parametric varieties of any dimension, and were used to solve the open problem of computing quadric surface parameterizations that do not have any missing points.

These results have been applied as a first step in the robust display of arbitrary real parametric curves and surface (Bajaj and Royappa, 1992). Another application is a first step towards exactly representing a arbitrary real parametric curve or surface in piecewise rational Bernstein-Bezier form, with positive weights.

Future directions for research include examining the other "missing points" problem (due to domain base points) in more detail, and also considering the issue of computing those real points on a real parametric variety that do not correspond to any real parameter value, but to a complex parameter value.

Acknowledgment

Supported in part by NSF grants CCR 90-02228, DMS 91-01424, AFOSR contract 91-0276 and a grant from AT & T.

References

Abhyankar, S. S., and Bajaj, C., (1987a), Automatic Parameterization of Rational Curves and Surfaces I: Conics and Conicoids, *Computer Aided Design*, 19, 1, 11 - 14.

Abhyankar, S. S., and Bajaj, C., (1987b), Automatic Parameterization of Rational Curves and Surfaces II: Cubics and Cubicoids, *Computer Aided Design*, 19, 9, 499 - 502.

Abhyankar, S. S., and Bajaj, C., (1988), Automatic Parameterization of Rational Curves and Surfaces III: Algebraic Plane Curves, *Computer Aided Geometric Design*, 5, 309 - 321.

Abhyankar, S., and Bajaj, C., (1989), Automatic Rational Parameterization of Curves and Surfaces IV: Algebraic Space Curves, *ACM Transactions on Graphics*, 8, 4, 325-334.

Bajaj, C., and Royappa, A., (1992), "Robust Display of Rational Parametric Curves and Surfaces," in Proceedings of *Curves and Surfaces in Computer Vision and Graphics III*, 70–80, Boston, November 15-20.

Bajaj, C., and Royappa, A., (1990), The GANITH Algebraic Geometry Toolkit V1.0, Extended abstract in Proceedings of the *First International Symposium on the Design and Implementation of Symbolic Computation Systems*, *Lecture Notes in Computer Science*, No. 429, 268–269, Capri, Italy, (Springer-Verlag), 1990.

Buchberger, B., (1985) Gröbner Bases: An Algorithmic Method in Polynomial Ideal Theory, in *Multidimensional Systems Theory*, Chapter 6, N. Bose (eds). Reidel Publishing Co.

Chionh, E., (1990), Base Points, Resultants, and the Implicit Representation of Parametric Surfaces. Ph.D. Thesis, University of Waterloo.

DeRose, T., (1991), Rational Bezier Curves and Surfaces on Projective Domains, in *NURBS for Curve and Surface Design*, G. Farin, Ed., 1-14.

Farin, G., (1991) *NURBS for Curve and Surface Design*, (Editor), SIAM Press.

Gao, X.S., and Chou, S.C., (1991) Normal Parameterizations of Curves and Surfaces, *International Journal of Computational Geometry and Its Applications*, 1, 2, 125-136.

Golub, G., and van Loan, C. (1983), *Matrix Computations*, Johns Hopkins Press, 444-448.

Hartshorne, R., (1977), *Algebraic Geometry*, Springer-Verlag.

Levin, J., (1979), Mathematical Models for Determining the Intersection of Quadric Surfaces, *Computer Graphics and Image Processing*, 11, 73 - 87.

Lucian, M., (1991), Linear Fractional Transformations of Rational Bezier Curves, in *NURBS for Curve and Surface Design*, G. Farin, Ed., 131-139.

Manocha, D., (1992), *Algebraic and Numeric Techniques in Modeling and Robotics*, Ph.D. Thesis, University of California at Berkeley, 1992.

Patterson, R., (1986), Projective Transformations of the Parameter of a Rational Bernstein Bezier Curve, in *ACM Transactions on Graphics*, 4, 276-290.

Royappa, A., (1992), *Symbolic Methods in Computer Graphics and Geometric Modeling*, Ph.D. Thesis, Purdue University.

Schicho, J., and Sendra, J. R., (1991), On the Choice of Pencils in the Parameterization of Curves, Technical Report 91-01.0, Research Institute for Symbolic Computation, Linz, Johannes Kepler University, Austria.

Sendra, J. R., and Winkler, F. (1991), Symbolic Parameterization of Curves, *J. Symbolic Computation*, 12, 6, 607-631.

Sederberg, T., and Snively, J., (1987), Parameterization of Cubic Algebraic Surfaces, *The Mathematics of Surfaces II*, ed. R. Martin, Oxford University Press, 299-321.

Sommerville, D.M.Y., (1951), *Analytical Geometry of Three Dimensions*, G. Bell and Sons, Cambridge University Press.

Wu, W., (1984), Basic Principles of Mechanical Theorem Proving in Elementary Geometries, *J. Sys. Sci. & Math. Scis.*, 4, 207-235.

Interproximation using Cubic B-Spline Curves

Fuhua Cheng[*] and *Brian A. Barsky*[**]

[*] *Department of Computer Science, University of Kentucky, Lexington, KY 40506*

[**] *Computer Science Division-EECS Department, University of California, Berkeley, CA 94720*

ABSTRACT. An algorithm for the construction of a non-uniform cubic B-spline curve that interpolates a set of 2D data $\{ \mathbf{D}_i \}$ is presented. Each $\mathbf{D}_i$ is either a point or a region. If $\mathbf{D}_i$ is a point, the curve interpolates it. Otherwise, the curve passes through the region specified by $\mathbf{D}_i$. The curve is constructed based on minimizing the energy of each of its components. The parametric knots of the curve are parametrized using the centripetal model. These processes facilitate the geometric smoothness and fairness of the curve. The new technique allows a user to design a curve with more flexibility and fewer trial-and-error iterations than conventional approach. This work is a continuation of the paper "Interproximation: Interpolation and Approximation Using Cubic Spline Curves" published in 1991.

Keywords and phrases. B-splines, interpolation, approximation, uncertain data, interproximation

1. Introduction

Modeling the shape of an image or an object usually requires the technique of parametric curve and surface interpolation, i.e., constructing a parametric curve or surface that interpolates, or passes through, a given set of points, called *interpolation points* or *data points*. The result of the interpolation process depends on two factors: the *interpolation points* and the *interpolation method*.

A good interpolation method should generate a curve or surface that faithfully reflects the shape of the desired image or object using a relatively small number of interpolation points. Given the interpolation points, this is usually achieved through the selection of an appropriate *curve/surface representation* and *interpolating parametric knots (parameter spacing)*. Spline curves and surfaces are frequently used in the interpolation process due to their *local control property*,[3-5] small *energy*,[7] and *numerical stability*.[3,5] The first property enables local modification of the resulting curve or surface while the second one facilitates its geometric smoothness. Actually, the geometric smoothness of the resulting interpolating curve and surface depends on the parameter spacing as well. Appropriately spaced parametric knots not only reduce the energy of the resulting curve or surface, but also avoid the occurrence of "oscillations" and "loops". It is generally believed that the knots should be chosen as proportional to the cumulative chord lengths of the *data polygon*.[1] However, according to a recent paper by E. T. Y. Lee,[9] a more appropriate way would be to use the so-called "centripetal model" to define the knots. The resulting interpolating curves usually are "fairer" (closer to the data polygon) than those obtained with the uniform or the chord length parametrization, see Figure 1.

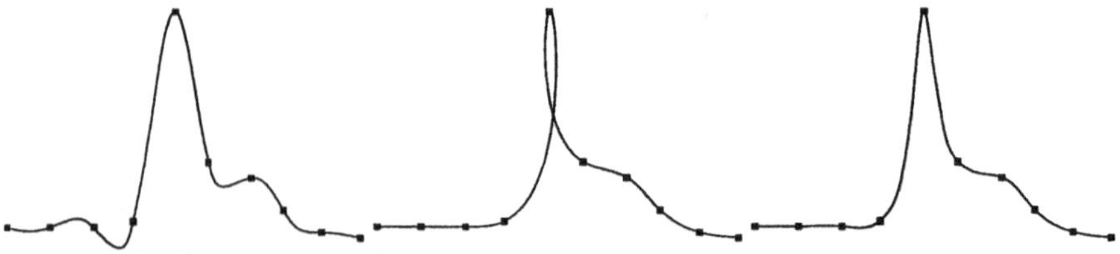

Figure 1. Cubic B-spline interpolating curves obtained with (a) uniform, (b) chord length, and (c) centripetal parametrization.

Interpolation points also have a major impact on the *shape* of the resulting curves and surfaces. These points, either sampled from existing objects or determined by some design criteria, should be selected so that shape of the data polygon would be close to the shape of the desired image or object. On the other hand, the number of interpolation points should be kept low to avoid extensive computation cost. A rule of thumb is to choose more points in regions with large curvature and fewer points in regions with small curvature. Unfortunately, no precise criterion has yet been given on this particular issue.

A problem commonly encountered in the selection of interpolation points is *uncertainty*.[6] This is especially true in the reconstruction of natural phenomena or digitized images, motion detection, and CAD applications. For instance, in sampling data from a digitized picture, one usually gets only a range of the data points, instead of the exact *locations* and *numerical values*. In the design process (using fitting techniques) of 2D and 3D shapes, it is also quite common that the designer knows the location of only a few critical points with just a rough idea about the possible range of the remaining points — a process that is usually accomplished through trial-and-error. Consequently, the fitting data appear in two forms: *points* and *regions*. The regions specify the possible ranges of the uncertain data.

Typical curve and surface interpolation techniques are not appropriate for these applications because they only deal with exact data points. Data fitting methods such as least-squares approximation may be used to approximate uncertain data points (or, interpolate perturbed data points, by backward error analysis). However, these methods do not guarantee that the resulting curve or surface would pass through specific data points, nor would the curve or surface pass through specific regions. What is desirable here is a method that will interpolate the exact data points and approximate the uncertain ones by passing through the regions that specify the range of the uncertain data points, see Figure 2. We call such a process as *interproximation* because it is a cross between interpolation and approximation.[6] The resulting curves or surfaces of the interproximation process should be relatively smooth so that not too many trial-and-error iterations are required to generate an expected shape.

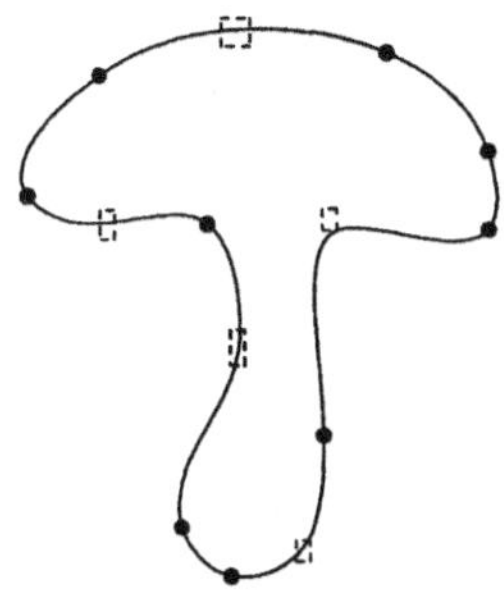

Figure 2. A curve that interproximates the given data.

Previous work in this area has been done by Ritter,[13] who presented a solution to the generalized Hermite-Birkhoff interpolation problem in Sobolev space for spline functions. Simply stated, his solution allows both the function itself and its derivatives to interproximate the given data at the given knots. Ritter's solution is general. However, for applications in computer-aided geometric design and related areas, fitting derivatives to given data usually is not required. We recently presented a more specific algorithm for the construction of a cubic spline curve that interproximates the given data.[6] The curve is generated based on minimizing the *energy* on both the x and y components of the possible interproximating curves, which is then converted to a *minimization problem* for some *quadratic form*. Therefore, geometric smoothness of the curve is guaranteed. One advantage of the algorithm over the ordinary curve interpolating techniques is that it can be used to design a curve with desired shape in fewer steps. It can also be used to remove undesired oscillations generated on an ordinary interpolating curve.[6] This is achieved by specifying a few extra regions between consecutive interpolation points to bound the behavior of the interpolating curve.

In this paper, we study the interproximation problem for B-spline curves and present an algorithm for the construction of a non-uniform cubic B-spline curve that interproximates a given data set. The new technique improves our previous work[6] in several aspects: (1) better parameter spacing technique, (2) more efficient and numerically stable computation process, (3) requiring no input on boundary conditions, and (4) allowing more flexibility in shape modification. The new technique is also easier to be integrated with other modeling systems. Details of the work will be given in the subsequent sections. We will start our work with a formal definition of the problem.

2. Definitions and Problem Formulation

Let $\{ \mathbf{D}_i \mid i=1,2,...,n+m \}$ be a set of 2D data. $\mathbf{D}_i$ could either be a point or a region. Say, $\mathbf{D}_{i_j} = \mathbf{P}_j = (x_j, y_j)$ for $j=1,2,...,n$ and $\mathbf{D}_{i_k} = \mathbf{A}_k \times \mathbf{B}_k = [a_k, b_k] \times [c_k, d_k]$ for $k=1,2,...,m$. Our goal is to construct a cubic B-spline curve to fit $\mathbf{D}_i$ in the order indicated. The fitting process is performed in the following fashion: The curve should interpolate $\mathbf{D}_i$ if it is a point. Otherwise, it is required to pass through the specified region only. In addition, the curve should have the smallest energy (smoothest shape) among all the cubic B-spline curves that satisfy the above fitting condition.

We will follow the ordinary case to construct such a cubic B-spline curve, i.e., representing it as a piecewise curve of $n+m-1$ cubic B-spline segments and using the $n+m$ endpoints of the segments to fit the given data. The representation of a cubic B-spline curve with $n+m-1$ segments requires $n+m+2$ cubic B-splines and, consequently, $n+m+6$ interpolating parametric knots. The $n+m+6$ knots are denoted by $\tau = \{\tau_{-2}, \tau_{-1}, \cdots, \tau_{n+m+3}\}$ with parameter range $\tau_1 \le u \le \tau_{n+m}$. The knots are defined as follows: $\tau_{-2} = \tau_{-1} = \tau_0 = \tau_1 = 0$

$$\tau_i - \tau_{i-1} = \frac{|\mathbf{Q}_i - \mathbf{Q}_{i-1}|^{1/2}}{\sum_{j=2}^{n+m} |\mathbf{Q}_j - \mathbf{Q}_{j-1}|^{1/2}}, \qquad 2 \le i \le n+m-1 \tag{2.1}$$

and $\tau_{n+m} = \tau_{n+m+1} = \tau_{n+m+2} = \tau_{n+m+3} = 1$ where $\mathbf{Q}_i$ equals $\mathbf{P}_j$ if $i = i_j$ for some $1 \le j \le n$ and $\mathbf{Q}_i$ equals the center of $\mathbf{A}_k \times \mathbf{B}_k$ if $i = i_k$ for some $1 \le k \le m$. Equation (2.1) is based on the *centripetal model* developed by Lee.[9] A knot sequence constructed this way has the advantage of bringing the resulting interpolating curve closer to the data polygon, and it generally produces curves that are fairer than those obtained with the uniform or the chord length parametrization.[11] A 2D cubic B-spline curve defined on [0, 1] with respect to the knot sequence τ can be represented as

$$\mathbf{S}(u) = \sum_{i=-2}^{n+m-1} \mathbf{C}_{i+2} N_{i,3}(u), \qquad u \in [0, 1] \tag{2.2}$$

where $\mathbf{C}_i$ are 2D control points and $N_{i,3}(u)$ are B-splines of degree 3 (order 4) defined by the following recurrence relation.

$$N_{i,0}(u) = \begin{cases} 1, & \tau_i \le u < \tau_{i+1} \\ 0, & \textit{otherwise} \end{cases}$$

and

$$N_{i,k}(u) = \frac{u - \tau_i}{\tau_{i+k} - \tau_i} N_{i,k-1}(u) + \frac{\tau_{i+k+1} - u}{\tau_{i+k+1} - \tau_{i+1}} N_{i+1,k-1}(u)$$

for $k \ge 1$.

If we set H to be the set of all cubic B-spline curves defined by (2.2) and, for each $\mathbf{S} \in H$, define the *energy*** of $\mathbf{S}$ to be

** The energy definition used here follows that of Kjellander.[8] More discussions on the definition of energy can be found in Lee.[10]

$$||\mathbf{S}|| \equiv \int_0^1 [(\frac{d^2\,\mathbf{S}_x(u)}{du^2})^2 + (\frac{d^2\,\mathbf{S}_y(u)}{du^2})^2]\,du \tag{2.3}$$

where $\mathbf{S}_x$ and $\mathbf{S}_y$ are the x- and y-components of $\mathbf{S}$, then our problem can be formulated as follows.

Problem 1. Find $\hat{\mathbf{S}} \in H$ such that

$$\begin{aligned} \hat{\mathbf{S}}(\tau_{i_j}) &= \mathbf{P}_j, \qquad j=1,2,\ldots,n \\ \hat{\mathbf{S}}(\tau_{i_k}) &\in \mathbf{A}_k \times \mathbf{B}_k, \qquad k=1,2,\ldots,m \end{aligned} \tag{2.4}$$

and

$$||\hat{\mathbf{S}}|| = \min\left\{ ||\mathbf{S}|| \;\middle|\; \mathbf{S} \in H, \mathbf{S} \textit{ satisfies } (2.4) \right\} \quad \square$$

Since our work will be performed on the basis of individual components and the technique involved for each component is the same, it is sufficient to consider this problem for the first component only, i.e., cubic spline functions. A B-spline function defined on [0, 1] with respect to τ can be expressed as

$$f(u) = \sum_{i=-2}^{n+m-1} e_{i+2} N_{i,3}(u), \qquad u \in [0, 1] \tag{2.5}$$

where e_i are real numbers. By defining F to be the set of cubic B-spline functions defined by (2.5) and, for each $f \in F$, defining the energy of f to be

$$||f|| \equiv \int_0^1 [f^{(2)}(u)]^2 du$$

where $f^{(2)}$ is the second derivative of f with respect to u, we can rewrite our problem as follows:

Problem 1′. Find $\hat{f} \in F$ such that

$$\begin{aligned} \hat{f}(\tau_{i_j}) &= x_j, \qquad j=1,2,\ldots,n \\ \hat{f}(\tau_{i_k}) &\in A_k, \qquad k=1,2,\ldots,m \end{aligned} \tag{2.6}$$

and

$$||\hat{f}|| = \min\left\{ ||f|| \;\middle|\; f \in F, f \textit{ satisfies } (2.6) \right\} \quad \square$$

The dimension of F is $n+m+2$ and we have only $n+m$ fitting conditions. As in the ordinary case where two extra *end conditions* are added to solve for a cubic B-spline curve interpolating $n+m$ points, we shall also impose two extra end conditions on the B-spline function defined by (2.5). We adopt the "natural" conditions. Namely, the second derivatives of f at the endpoints of the parameter range are set to zero.

$$f^{(2)}(\tau_1)=0, \quad f^{(2)}(\tau_{n+m})=0 \tag{2.7}$$

Note that

$$\begin{aligned}
N_{-2,3}(u) &= \frac{(\tau_2-u)^3}{(\tau_2-\tau_1)^3}, \quad \tau_1 \le u < \tau_2 \\
&= 0, \quad \textit{elsewhere}
\end{aligned}$$

$$\begin{aligned}
N_{-1,3}(u) &= (u-\tau_1)\left[\frac{(\tau_2-u)^2}{(\tau_2-\tau_1)^3}+\frac{(\tau_3-u)(\tau_2-u)}{(\tau_3-\tau_1)(\tau_2-\tau_1)^2}+\frac{(\tau_3-u)^2}{(\tau_3-\tau_1)^2(\tau_2-\tau_1)}\right], \quad \tau_1 \le u < \tau_2 \\
&= \frac{(\tau_3-u)^3}{(\tau_3-\tau_1)^2(\tau_3-\tau_2)}, \quad \tau_2 \le u < \tau_3 \\
&= 0, \quad \textit{elsewhere}
\end{aligned}$$

$$\begin{aligned}
N_{0,3}(u) &= \frac{(\tau_2-u)(u-\tau_1)^2}{(\tau_3-\tau_1)(\tau_2-\tau_1)^2}+\frac{(\tau_3-u)(u-\tau_1)^2}{(\tau_3-\tau_1)^2(\tau_2-\tau_1)}+\frac{(\tau_4-u)(u-\tau_1)^2}{(\tau_4-\tau_1)(\tau_3-\tau_1)(\tau_2-\tau_1)}, \quad \tau_1 \le u < \tau_2 \\
&= \frac{(\tau_3-u)^2(u-\tau_1)}{(\tau_3-\tau_1)^2(\tau_3-\tau_2)}+\frac{(\tau_4-u)(u-\tau_1)(\tau_3-u)}{(\tau_4-\tau_1)(\tau_3-\tau_1)(\tau_3-\tau_2)}+\frac{(\tau_4-u)^2(u-\tau_2)}{(\tau_4-\tau_1)(\tau_4-\tau_2)(\tau_3-\tau_2)}, \quad \tau_2 \le u < \tau_3 \\
&= \frac{(\tau_4-u)^3}{(\tau_4-\tau_1)(\tau_4-\tau_2)(\tau_4-\tau_3)}, \quad \tau_3 \le u < \tau_4 \\
&= 0, \quad \textit{elsewhere}
\end{aligned}$$

and, for $1 \le i \le n+m-4$,

$$\begin{aligned}
N_{i,3}(u) &= \frac{(u-\tau_i)^3}{(\tau_{i+3}-\tau_i)(\tau_{i+2}-\tau_i)(\tau_{i+1}-\tau_i)}, \quad \tau_i \le u < \tau_{i+1} \\
&= \frac{(u-\tau_i)^2(\tau_{i+2}-u)}{(\tau_{i+3}-\tau_i)(\tau_{i+2}-\tau_i)(\tau_{i+2}-\tau_{i+1})}+\frac{(u-\tau_i)(\tau_{i+3}-u)(u-\tau_{i+1})}{(\tau_{i+3}-\tau_i)(\tau_{i+3}-\tau_{i+1})(\tau_{i+2}-\tau_{i+1})} \\
&\quad +\frac{(\tau_{i+4}-u)(u-\tau_{i+1})^2}{(\tau_{i+4}-\tau_{i+1})(\tau_{i+3}-\tau_{i+1})(\tau_{i+2}-\tau_{i+1})}, \quad \tau_{i+1} \le u < \tau_{i+2} \\
&= \frac{(u-\tau_i)(\tau_{i+3}-u)^2}{(\tau_{i+3}-\tau_i)(\tau_{i+3}-\tau_{i+1})(\tau_{i+3}-\tau_{i+2})}+\frac{(\tau_{i+4}-u)(u-\tau_{i+1})(\tau_{i+3}-u)}{(\tau_{i+4}-\tau_{i+1})(\tau_{i+3}-\tau_{i+1})(\tau_{i+3}-\tau_{i+2})}
\end{aligned}$$

$$+\frac{(\tau_{i+4}-u)^2(u-\tau_{i+2})}{(\tau_{i+4}-\tau_{i+1})(\tau_{i+4}-\tau_{i+2})(\tau_{i+3}-\tau_{i+2})}, \quad \tau_{i+2} \le u < \tau_{i+3}$$

$$=\frac{(\tau_{i+4}-u)^3}{(\tau_{i+4}-\tau_{i+1})(\tau_{i+4}-\tau_{i+2})(\tau_{i+4}-\tau_{i+3})}, \quad \tau_{i+3} \le u < \tau_{i+4}$$

$$=0, \quad \textit{elsewhere}$$

Since $N_{i,3}^{(2)}(\tau_1)=0$ for $i \ge 1$, it is easy to check that

$$f^{(2)}(\tau_1)=e_0 N_{-2,3}^{(2)}(\tau_1)+e_1 N_{-1,3}^{(2)}(\tau_1)+e_2 N_{0,3}^{(2)}(\tau_1)$$
$$=\frac{6}{(\tau_2-\tau_1)^2}(e_0-\frac{\tau_3+\tau_2-2\tau_1}{\tau_3-\tau_1}e_1+\frac{\tau_2-\tau_1}{\tau_3-\tau_1}e_2)$$

Hence, the first condition in (2.7) gives that

$$e_0=(\frac{\tau_3+\tau_2-2\tau_1}{\tau_3-\tau_1})\,e_1-(\frac{\tau_2-\tau_1}{\tau_3-\tau_1})\,e_2 \tag{2.8}$$

Similarly, the second condition in (2.7) gives that

$$e_{n+m+1}=(\frac{\tau_{n+m-2}+\tau_{n+m-1}-2\tau_{n+m}}{\tau_{n+m-2}-\tau_{n+m}})\,e_{n+m}-(\frac{\tau_{n+m-1}-\tau_{n+m}}{\tau_{n+m-2}-\tau_{n+m}})\,e_{n+m-1} \tag{2.9}$$

Based on (2.8) and (2.9), a cubic B-spline function defined by (2.5) and satisfying the natural conditions (2.7) can be expressed as

$$f(u)=\sum_{i=1}^{n+m} e_i\, w_i(u) \tag{2.10}$$

where

$$w_1(u)=\frac{\tau_3+\tau_2-2\tau_1}{\tau_3-\tau_1}N_{-2,3}(u)+N_{-1,3}(u) \tag{2.11}$$

$$w_2(u)=-\frac{\tau_2-\tau_1}{\tau_3-\tau_1}N_{-2,3}(u)+N_{0,3}(u) \tag{2.12}$$

$$w_i(u)=N_{i-2,3}(u), \quad 3 \le i \le n+m-2 \tag{2.13}$$

$$w_{n+m-1}(u)=-\frac{\tau_{n+m-1}-\tau_{n+m}}{\tau_{n+m-2}-\tau_{n+m}}N_{n+m-1,3}(u)+N_{n+m-3,3}(u) \tag{2.14}$$

$$w_{n+m}(u) = \frac{\tau_{n+m-2}+\tau_{n+m-1}-2\tau_{n+m}}{\tau_{n+m-2}-\tau_{n+m}} N_{n+m-1,3}(u) + N_{n+m-2,3}(u) \tag{2.15}$$

If we define $\hat{F}$ as the set of all cubic B-spline functions defined by (2.10) then the problem that we are in a position to solve is

Problem 1″. Find $\hat{f} \in \hat{F}$ such that (2.6) is satisfied and

$$\|\hat{f}\| = \min\left\{ \|f\| \;\middle|\; f \in \hat{F}, f \textit{ satisfies } (2.6) \right\}. \quad \square$$

This formulation has a major problem, i.e., the indexing of the fitting condition (2.6) would lead to sparse matrices which are not numerically stable and efficient when performing Gaussian elimination in the computation process (this point will become clear when we present the solution in the next section). We shall rename τ to be $\{u_1, u_2, \cdots, u_n, v_1, v_2, \cdots, v_m\}$ where

$$u_j = \tau_{i_j}, \qquad \textit{for } j=1,2,\ldots,n$$

and

$$v_k = \tau_{i_k}, \qquad \textit{for } k=1,2,\ldots,m.$$

We also rename $\{w_i(u)\}$ defined by (2.11) through (2.15) to be $\{g_1(u), \cdots, g_n(u), h_1(u), \cdots, h_m(u)\}$ with

$$g_j(u) = w_{i_j}(u), \qquad j=1,2,\ldots,n$$

and

$$h_k(u) = w_{i_k}(u), \qquad k=1,2,\ldots,m$$

If we rewrite (2.10) as

$$f(u) = \sum_{j=1}^{n} \alpha_j\, g_j(u) + \sum_{k=1}^{m} \beta_k\, h_k(u) \tag{2.16}$$

and define $\hat{F}$ to be the set of cubic B-spline functions defined by (2.16) then **Problem 1″** is equivalent to

problem 1‴. Find $\hat{f} \in \hat{F}$ such that

$$\hat{f}(u_j) = x_j, \qquad j=1,2,\ldots,n \tag{2.17}$$

$$\hat{f}(v_k) \in A_k, \qquad k=1,2,\ldots,m \tag{2.18}$$

and

$$\|\hat{f}\| = \min\left\{ \|f\| \;\middle|\; f \in \hat{F}, f \text{ satisfies (2.17) and (2.18)} \right\}. \quad \square$$

It is this problem that we intend to solve in this paper. The solution to this problem will be presented in the next section.

3. The Solution

We will first convert the fitting conditions in (2.17) and (2.18) into matrix form. Define $\alpha \equiv (\alpha_1, \alpha_2, .., \alpha_n)^t$, $\beta \equiv (\beta_1, \beta_2, .., \beta_m)^t$, $\mathbf{x} \equiv (x_1, x_2, .., x_n)^t$,

$$A \equiv \prod_{k=1}^{m} A_k \qquad \text{and} \qquad N \equiv \begin{bmatrix} N_1 & M_1 \\ M_2 & N_2 \end{bmatrix}_{(n+m)\times(n+m)}$$

where

$$N_1 \equiv \left[a_{i,j} \right]_{n\times n}, \quad a_{i,j} = g_j(u_i) \quad 1 \le i, \, \le n \tag{3.1}$$

$$M_1 \equiv \left[b_{i,j} \right]_{n\times m}, \quad b_{i,j} = h_j(u_i) \quad 1 \le i \le n, \; 1 \le j \le m \tag{3.2}$$

$$M_2 \equiv \left[c_{i,j} \right]_{m\times n}, \quad c_{i,j} = g_j(v_i) \quad 1 \le i \le m, \; 1 \le j \le n \tag{3.3}$$

$$N_2 \equiv \left[d_{i,j} \right]_{m\times m}, \quad d_{i,j} = h_j(v_i) \quad 1 \le i, j \le m \tag{3.4}$$

The fitting conditions in (2.17) imply that

$$N_1\alpha + M_1\beta = \mathbf{x}$$

or

$$\alpha = N_1^{-1}\mathbf{x} - N_1^{-1}M_1\beta \tag{3.5}$$

while those in (2.18) imply that

$$M_2\alpha + N_2\beta \in \mathbf{A}$$

or

$$(N_2 - M_2N_1^{-1}M_1)\beta \in \mathbf{A} - M_2N_1^{-1}\mathbf{x} \tag{3.6}$$

(3.5) shows that the value of α depends on β. Therefore, the essential work is to find β such that $\|\hat{f}\|$ is minimum subject to constraint (3.6).

Define

$$G_1 = \left[g_{i,j} \right]_{n \times n}, \quad g_{i,j} = \int_0^1 g_i^{(2)}(u)\, g_j^{(2)}(u)du, \quad 1 \le i, j \le n \tag{3.7}$$

$$G_2 = \left[h_{i,j} \right]_{m \times m}, \quad h_{i,j} = \int_0^1 h_i^{(2)}(u)\, h_j^{(2)}(u)du, \quad 1 \le i, j \le m \tag{3.8}$$

$$Q = \left[q_{i,j} \right]_{n \times m}, \quad q_{i,j} = \int_0^1 g_i^{(2)}(u)\, h_j^{(2)}(u)du, \quad 1 \le i \le n,\ 1 \le j \le m \tag{3.9}$$

Note that G_1 and G_2 are symmetric. According to the definition of $||\hat{f}||$, we have

$$\begin{aligned}
||\hat{f}|| &= \int_0^1 (\sum_{i=1}^{n} \alpha_i g_i^{(2)}(u) + \sum_{i=1}^{m} \beta_i h_i^{(2)}(u))^2 du \\
&= \int_0^1 (\sum_{i=1}^{n} \alpha_i g_i^{(2)}(u))^2 du + \int_0^1 (\sum_{i=1}^{m} \beta_i h_i^{(2)}(u))^2 du \\
&\qquad + 2\int_0^1 (\sum_{i=1}^{n} \alpha_i g_i^{(2)}(u))\, (\sum_{i=1}^{m} \beta_i h_i^{(2)}(u)) du \\
&= \sum_{i=1}^{n}\sum_{j=1}^{n} \alpha_i \alpha_j g_{i,j} + \sum_{i=1}^{m}\sum_{j=1}^{m} \beta_i \beta_j h_{i,j} + 2\sum_{i=1}^{n}\sum_{j=1}^{m} \alpha_i \beta_j q_{i,j} \\
&= \alpha^t G_1 \alpha + \beta^t G_2 \beta + 2\alpha^t Q \beta
\end{aligned} \tag{3.10}$$

Combining (3.10) with (3.5), we get

$$||\hat{f}|| = (N_1^{-1}\mathbf{x} - T\beta)^t G_1 (N_1^{-1}\mathbf{x} - T\beta) + \beta^t G_2 \beta + 2(N_1^{-1}\mathbf{x} - T\beta)^t Q \beta$$

where $T = N_1^{-1} M_1$. Through simple algebra it can be shown that

$$||\hat{f}|| = C + \beta^t (G_2 - 2Q^t T + T^t G_1 T)\beta + 2(N_1^{-1}\mathbf{x})^t (Q - G_1 T)\beta$$

where $C = (N_1^{-1}\mathbf{x})^t G_1 (N_1^{-1}\mathbf{x})$ is a constant. The fact that G_1 being symmetric has been used in the above derivation. Therefore, to minimize $||\hat{f}||$ it is sufficient to minimize

$$\Gamma(\beta) = \beta^t W \beta + 2(N_1^{-1}\mathbf{x})^t Z \beta \tag{3.11}$$

where

$$W = G_2 - 2Q^t T + T^t G_1 T \tag{3.12}$$

$$Z = Q - G_1 T \tag{3.13}$$

with constraint (3.6). This is the well-known quadratic programming problem in nonlinear programming.[2] Standard optimization routine can be used to solve this problem.

The matrix $T = N_1^{-1} M_1$ can be computed easily. Indeed, if we perform block Gaussian elimination on

$$N^t = \begin{bmatrix} N_1^t & M_2^t \\ M_1^t & N_2^t \end{bmatrix}$$

to get

$$\begin{bmatrix} N_1^t & M_2^t \\ 0 & U^t \end{bmatrix}$$

which corresponds to

$$\begin{bmatrix} I & 0 \\ L & I \end{bmatrix} N^t = \begin{bmatrix} N_1^t & M_2^t \\ 0 & U^t \end{bmatrix} \tag{3.14}$$

with L containing the multipliers, then since $LN_1^t + M_1^t = 0$, it follows that

$$N_1^{-1} M_1 = -L^t .$$

The block Gaussian elimination process also gives us the value of $N_2 - M_2 N_1^{-1} M_1$ in (3.6) as it is easy to see now that its value is equal to the submatrix U contained in (3.14).

The block Gaussian elimination process can be performed in a very efficient and stable manner since N_1 and N_2 are both banded square matrices and M_1 and M_2 are sparse matrices with the non-zero entries concentrated on a banded neighborhood of the diagonal line (the number of non-zero entries within each row of these matrices is at most 3).

Based on the above observation, the solution to **Problem 1‴** can be computed as follows:

1. Compute $N_1, M_1, M_2, N_2, G_1, G_2$ and Q defined by (3.1), (3.2), (3.3), (3.4), (3.7), (3.8) and (3.9), respectively.
2. Solve $N_1 \gamma = \mathbf{x}$ to get $\gamma = N_1^{-1} \mathbf{x}$.
3. Perform block Gaussian elimination on

$$N^t = \begin{bmatrix} N_1^t & M_2^t \\ M_1^t & N_2^t \end{bmatrix}$$

to determine $T = N_1^{-1} M_1$ and $U = N_2 - M_2 N_1^{-1} M_1$.

4. Compute W and Z defined by (3.12) and (3.13), respectively.
5. Minimize

$$\Gamma(\beta) = \beta^t W \beta + 2\gamma^t Z \beta$$

subject to

$$U\beta \in \mathbf{A} - M_2\gamma$$

6. Compute α defined by (3.5).

4. Implementation

The algorithm has been implemented in C on a Sequent multiprocessing machine, Balance 20000. Input and output are performed in an interactive X Window Systems environment. A Postscript file has also been generated for each test case so that the results can be output in hard copy as well.

The construction of the matrices N_1, M_1, N_2 and M_2 may be performed by using the corresponding expressions of w_i in (2.11) - (2.15) to find the values of g_j or h_j at the given knots. These matrices are all banded matrices with a band width of at most 3. The construction of the matrices G_1, G_2 and Q may be performed by first applying the technique of *integration by parts* to the expressions in (3.7) - (3.9) to find the following expressions:

$$g_{i,j} = g_i^{(2)}(1)g_j^{(1)}(1) - g_i^{(3)}(1)g_j(1) - g_i^{(2)}(0)g_j^{(1)}(0) - g_i^{(3)}(0)g_j(0)$$
$$h_{i,j} = h_i^{(2)}(1)h_j^{(1)}(1) - h_i^{(3)}(1)h_j(1) - h_i^{(2)}(0)h_j^{(1)}(0) - h_i^{(3)}(0)h_j(0)$$
$$q_{i,j} = g_i^{(2)}(1)h_j^{(1)}(1) - g_i^{(3)}(1)h_j(1) - g_i^{(2)}(0)h_j^{(1)}(0) - g_i^{(3)}(0)h_j(0)$$

and then computing their values at the given knots. G_1 and G_2 are also banded matrices. Since the values of g_i, h_j and their first, second and third derivatives at the knots will be used several times in the construction of these matrices, one should build a look-up table for these values and reference appropriate entries of the table to construct these matrices.

The Gaussian elimination process required in Steps 2 and 3 is performed by exploiting the fact that N_1, M_1, N_2 and M_2 are banded matrices. This fact allows us to perform the Gaussian elimination process in linear time.

The minimization problem of the quadratic form (3.11) with constraint (3.6) is carried out by calling the NAG FORTRAN Library Routine, E04NAF.[12] This routine requires 29 parameters as input. In our algorithm, however, only 8 of them are variables; the remaining ones are constants.

The program has been tested on several data sets; some of the test results are shown in Figures 3 and 4. In Figure 3, the data sets used in Figures 3b, 3c and 3d of our previous work[6] are used to generate the profile of a human head (Figure 3a). A non-uniform cubic B-spline curve whose parametric knots are parametrized using the centripetal model is first constructed to interpolate 22 points (Figure 3b) taken from the profile shown in 3a. The shape of the curve is then improved by adding a few regions between some of the interpolation points (Figure 3c) and further confined by reducing the sizes of and adjusting some of the regions (Figure 3d). The new algorithm is used in all three cases with the number of regions in case 3b being zero. The resulting non-uniform cubic B-spline curves in all three cases are fairer than the previous examples. But they do not faithfully reflect the shape of the original profile in areas such as the nose, the lips, area around the chin, and area around point A (Figure 3d). This is because in our previous work[6] the interpolation points were not selected to completely reflect the shape of these areas. Rather, they were selected to accommodate the possible oscillation of an interpolating uniform spline curve so that the resulting curve would match the shape of the original profile (otherwise, one would have to select more interpolation points in these areas). For a non-uniform B-spline curve whose knots are parametrized using the centripetal model, since the shape will closely reflect the shape of the data polygon, one should choose interpolation points and regions from areas with high curvature.

The improvement process of these areas is shown in Figure 4. By removing the point at B (Figure 3d) and putting a region C at the tip of the nose, one immediately gets a good approximation of the original shape of the nose (Figure 4a). The improvement of the lips, the chin and the area around point A is then performed by replacing the interpolation points at E and F with two small regions, G and H, adding one region below F, and putting a region below A. These were the areas of the original profile with high curvature. A point in region C has been selected as interpolation point to fix the shape of the curve in this area. The result is shown in Figure 4b.

5. Conclusions

The problem of interproximating uncertain data using non-uniform cubic B-spline curves has been studied. An algorithm is presented for the construction of a non-uniform cubic B-spline curve that interpolates specific data points at some parametric knots and passes through specific rectangular regions at some other parametric knots, with minimum energy at each of its components. This approach allows a user to design a curve with more flexibility and fewer trial-and-error iterations than conventional approach.

The algorithm presented in this paper improves our previous work[6] in four aspects. (1) The parametric knots are parametrized using the centripetal model[9] instead of uniform parametrization. This approach gives fairer interproximating curve than those obtained with the uniform or the chord length parametrization. (2) B-splines, instead of reproducing kernels, are used in the computation process. The construction of the matrices and the Gaussian elimination process, hence, can be performed more efficiently and numerically stably, since all the involved matrices are banded. (3) The new approach does not require user input of boundary conditions. (4) The new approach allows the user to make local modification by adjusting the control points of the curve and can easily be integrated with any B-spline or NURB based modeling systems.

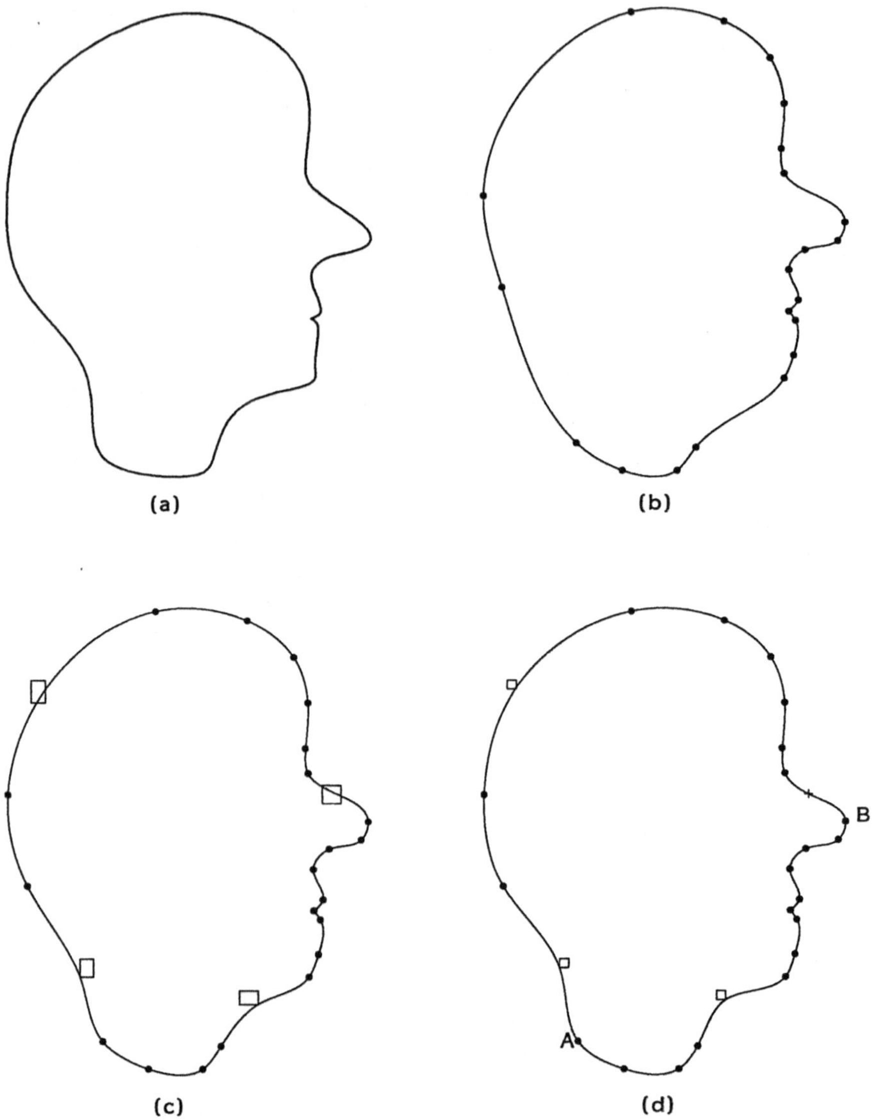

Figure 3. Shape modeling I.

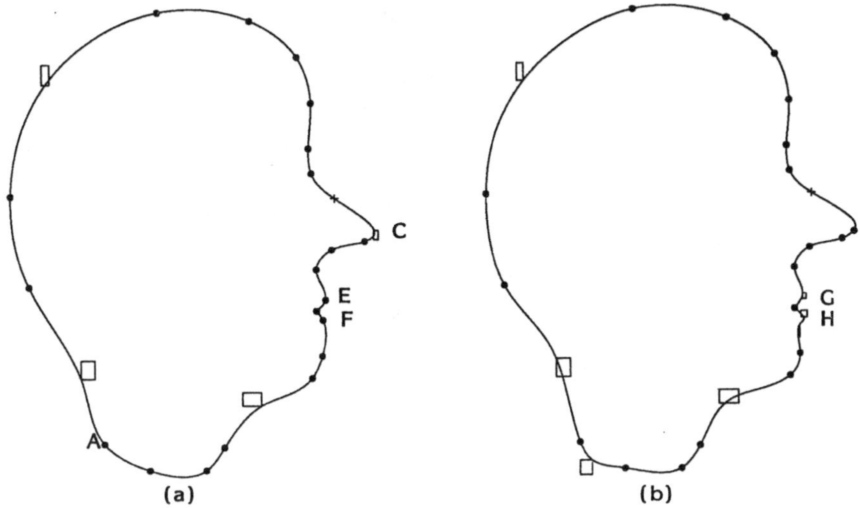

Figure 4. Shape modeling II.

Acknowledgements. The authors wish to thank W.H. Li for implementing the algorithm presented in this paper. The work of the first author was supported in part by IBM.

References

1. J.H. Ahlberg, E.N. Nilson, and J.L. Walsh, in *The Theory of Splines and Their Applications*, Academic Press, New York, 1967.
2. M. Avriel, *NONLINEAR PROGRAMMING: Analysis and Methods*, Prentice-Hall, Englewood Cliffs, New Jersey, 1976.
3. R. H. Bartels, J. C. Beatty, and B. A. Barsky, *An Introduction to Splines for Use in Computer Graphics and Geometric Modeling*, Morgan Kaufmann Publishers, Inc., San Mateo, California, 1987.
4. W. Boehm, G. Farin, and J. Kahmann, ''A survey of curve and surface methods in CAGD,'' *Computer Aided Geometric Design*, vol. 1, no. 1, pp. 1-60, July 1984.
5. C. de Boor, *A Practical Guide to Splines*, Springer-Verlag, New York, 1978.
6. F. Cheng and B. A. Barsky, ''Interproximation: Interpolation and Approximation Using Cubic Spline Curves,'' *Computer Aided Design*, vol. 23, no. 10, pp. 700-706, December 1991.
7. J.C. Holladay, ''Smoothest curve approximation,'' *Math. Tables Aids Computation*, vol. 11, pp. 233-243, 1957.

8. J.A.P. Kjellander, "Smoothing of cubic parametric splines," *Computer-Aided Design*, vol. 15, no. 5, pp. 175-179, 1983.

9. E.T.Y. Lee, "On choosing nodes in parametric curve interpolation," *Computer Aided Design*, vol. 21, no. 6, pp. 363-370, July/August, 1989.

10. E.T.Y. Lee, "Energy, Fairness and a Counterexample," *Computer-Aided Design*, vol. 22, no. 1, pp. 37-40, January/February 1990.

11. E.T.Y. Lee, "Corners, Cusps, and Parametrization: Variation on a Theorem of Epstein," *SIAM J. of Numerical Analysis*, to appear.

12. NAGFLIB, *NAG FORTRAN Library Routine Document*, (November 1983).

13. K. Ritter, "Generalized Spline Interpolation and Nonlinear Programming," in *Approximation with Special Emphasis on Spline Functions*, ed. I.J. Schoenberg, pp. 75-118, Academic Press, London, 1969.

PART 2

Modeling for Applications

Chapter 7

Modeling for Animation

Animated Parameter Space

Miroslav M. Novak

School of Physics, Kingston University, Kingston-upon-Thames, Surrey KT1 2EE, UK

Abstract

Description of an interaction of a charged particle with fields is well known, in principle. Under some conditions, this system undergoes a very complicated behaviour. Two challenging tasks must be met, before the deeper insight into and understanding of the dynamics of such a system can be retrieved from the modelling: numerical and representational. The former is due to the excessive computer processing times, the latter deals with a way to display the large amount of data in a useful way. In this paper, we concentrate on the latter and describe some aspects of producing an animated display, within the tight budgetary constraints.

1 Introduction

Most frequently, the description of a dynamical system is given in terms of differential equations. These equations are set up using the governing physical principles, and then solved numerically. A number of algorithms is available, and their adoption depends on the stability considerations as well as efficiency demands. When dealing with dynamical systems, which may give rise to chaotic motion, a particular attention must be paid to the chosen integration scheme. Data used for this presentation were obtained with the fourth order Runge-Kutta method and checked for consistency with the Bulirsch-Stoer method [Press et al, 1986].

Problems begin to arise, when one attempts to interpret the large sets of data, obtained in such simulation. In practice, the number of dimensions describing all but the very simplest of systems require well above 3 dimensions - a case that is not readily handled by display devices. A number of approaches exist that implement various ways to display higher dimensional entities on a screen. Currently very prominent in this area of research is volume visualization [Kaufman, 1991]. In this paper, an affordable way to represent additional dimension is described, by the use of animation.

There are a number of computer installations, with large budgets and personnel assigned to video productions, mainly in the entertainment industry. The need for dedicated supercomputers, professional frame-by-frame video recorders and large storage devices soon exceed the budget of many academic departments. With the emergence of fast networks, the use of national academic centres may provide the services required for the motion displays, however, a number of logistic problems makes this option not always the most convenient. It is shown below that an acceptable animated display can be produced on a modest departmental budget. Although the resulting motion video is somewhat inferior to that produced by the top installations, nevertheless, such a recording still fulfils most needs of a working scientist as it provides additional and very important insight into the nature and evolution of the system under observation. In addition to helping with the research, such a video provides excellent pedagogical material.

This contribution is divided into several distinct sections. We begin by setting up a physical system, in section 2, data from which are then used to create the animation. In section 3 some details of the associated image generation are presented, together with the main steps needed for successful video production. Section 4 briefly comments on some findings. In concluding part, the main results are listed.

2 Description of a dynamical system

The dynamical system that is considered in this paper deals with the charged elementary particle, such as electron, placed inside a static magnetic field, **B**. This system is further influenced by a plane electromagnetic wave that travels in the direction perpendicular to the **B**-field, with its magnetic field parallel to the direction of the **B**-field. The mutual orientation of static and travelling fields is important and greatly affects the final outcome. For the sake of clarity, the static **B**-field points in the z-direction, the polarization vector of the travelling wave is parallel to the y-direction, while the wave travels in the x-direction. Several different approaches to describe such a system are possible - here we select the Hamiltonian formalism [Barut, 1980] that naturally lends itself to the relativistic generalization.

The interaction is described using the vector potential **A**, which is assumed to be of the form

$$\mathbf{A} = (By,\ f\ \sin(kx - \omega t),\ 0) \tag{1}$$

where f is the amplitude of the travelling wave, k and ω are the wave vector and frequency, respectively. The associated magnetic field contains z-components only, while the electric field vector has only a single nonvanishing component, along the y-axis. The Hamiltonian H describing the dynamics of this systems is given by

$$H = (m^2c^4 + (\mathbf{P} - e\mathbf{A})^2)^{0.5} \tag{2}$$

where **P** is the generalized momentum, m the mass of the particle, e is its charge, and c is the velocity of light. The canonical equations of motion can now be written in the form

$$\dot{r} = \frac{c}{H}(P-eA)$$
$$\dot{P} = \frac{e}{c}\dot{r}\frac{\partial A}{\partial r}$$

(3)

where the dot above the letters denotes the time derivative, and r is the generalized position vector. As there is no z-dependence in the vector potential (1), the z-component of the generalized momentum is constant, here conveniently set to zero. The x and y components of equations of motion then have the form

(4)

$$\dot{x}=\frac{c}{H}(P_x-eBy)$$
$$\dot{y}=\frac{c}{H}(P_y-ef\sin(kx-\omega t)$$
$$\dot{P}_x=\frac{c}{H}(efkP_y-e^2f^2k\sin(kx-\omega t))\cos(kx-\omega t)$$
$$\dot{P}_y=-\frac{ceB}{H}(eBy-P_x)$$

In the absence of the travelling wave, f=0 in (1), the particle moves in a circle with the radius proportional to the ratio of momentum and the static magnetic field. When f is nonvanishing, the interaction between the rotational motion (due to the static magnetic field) and translational motion (due to the travelling wave) gives rise to the complicated dynamics. In this paper we look at the effect of initial conditions, for a given set of values for x, P_x, and P_y, on the final particle's momentum. It is found that at low energies particle executes regular motion, represented by elliptical regions in the phase space. Slight changes in the initial conditions have virtually no effect on the final momentum. As the energy of the particle increases, the regions of regular motion get distorted and soon disintegrate, giving rise to new division of the phase space. In the relativistic domain, the sensitive dependence on the initial conditions indicates that the dynamics has become chaotic. The transition boundary is not smooth and displays self-similarity, typical of fractal objects. In the realm of higher energies, the particles momentum increases stochastically, almost without a bound. Similar situation for stochastic heating is observed, when the amplitude of the travelling wave is large. Then, regular motion is largely suppressed, even in the domain of small energies.

This relatively simple system displays intricate behaviour that is difficult to infer from static display. The situation gets even further complicated as the need for the inclusion of more dimensions increases. To provide the tool to analyze the formation of patterns in the parameter space, thereby allowing for a direct increase in the display dimensionality, the use of simple animation techniques is adopted.

3 Data generation and video production

Bearing in mind the assumption of this paper, the set (4) is represented by four coupled differential equations. In order to increase the numerical efficiency, the trigonometric functions occurring in (4) are replaced by the difference equations, resulting in noticeable decrease of the processing time. In order to establish the stability of patterns, several runs were needed. These used different step sizes, until an optimal value was determined. In order to avoid transients, integration over 100 periods was performed, before accumulation of results began. This apparently short time interval was sufficient, as all the values have by now settled, as was established through numerous simulations. Integrations were performed on a regular 128 x 128 grid, representing the values of the initial x-position and P_x momentum. At a specified time, the value of the resultant momentum is stored for further processing. On completion of the calculation, a large number of datasets (575), one for each initial value of P_y, contain encoded information that reflect the relation between the initial conditions and the final value of the momentum. As already indicated, two different integration schemes were used to ascertain the validity of the calculations. These are very computationally intensive, with processing times of the order of days on Unix workstations. For regular production runs, access to supercomputers is mandatory.

Having accumulated the data from integration of the set (4), graphical rendering and animation are performed next. For more sophisticated images, this step was performed on the workstation, using the PHIGS [ISO, 1987] library with extensions. However, in the production of the accompanying video, relatively simple images were used, which were well suited for processing on a PC equipped with a 486 processor. Restriction to somewhat low resolution of 128x128 grid cells was justified in view of the production of a moving display. The gradual changes in the pattern formation take over and the eye inertia makes the resultant movement quite acceptable.

Each of the files produced on a workstation is character encoded and occupies about 16K. Its content reflects the values of the final momentum of the electron. Each of the characters corresponds to one of the 64 colours, selected for this video production from a range of 255 that were available. Each of the files contains the results of the calculations for different values of the initial momentum P_y. The static analysis of the structures embedded in the data is performed using in-house developed visualization tools. These allow for a direct viewing of each file separately as well as the ability to construct 3D solid objects. Various operations can then be performed, such as arbitrary dissection, contours, thresholding, volume extraction, and others.

Numerical work is done on Unix workstation and sent to the recording site via a local area network. This step is needed as, at present, the workstation cannot generate PAL compatible signal, required for the video recorder. Once on a 486 hard disk, each file is individually processed and compressed using a board specific run length encoding algorithm. For complicated images with low coherence, this step generates larger files than the original, however, the speed of subsequent display is dramatically increased - and this is clearly of paramount importance in animation.

The graphics SVGA card, used to generate the display, was based on VESA protocol and could produce 256 colours in 640x480 resolution. This is more that ample, as the video is recorded in the VHS format, which stores only 240 lines per frame. Although the image deterioration of individual frames is quite noticeable during this stage, the overall motion retains all the essential features of the dynamics. The recording format was selected in view of the available resources. The scan converter, required to transform monitor image into the form suitable for recording is able to handle also the better SVHS format, that would be used in the future. Although, ideally, a frame editing video recorder is needed to produce smooth animations, such an equipment was not available. The video recording was done in real time, by replaying the prerecorded images and achieved about 11 frames per second. This rate is far below the 25 frames/sec needed to convey the continuous motion. In spite of this weakness, the resultant animation is acceptable, does not require days of video production and is readily accessible.

4 Evaluation of the results

The length of the animation depends on the number of files that is available from the simulation and on the display rate. Each file representing a fixed value of P_y has to be encoded initially, to speed up the display process. This step requires approximately 3 seconds per frame. Prior to the recording, all the processed frames can be previewed on the computer monitor, in sequence and individually. Unlike the first, compressing stage, the final display runs in real time. The overall quality of the animation depends on the access time of the hard disk and the speed of the graphics card. In the current production no blending between the frames has been used, although currently, the Utah raster toolkit [Petersen et al] is being investigated. If successful, only the key frames would have to be computed, thus yielding substantial saving in the generation of data.

When viewing the animation, a realization of the mixing in the phase space is vividly demonstrated. Low energy particles experience regular and coherent motion, represented by colour homogeneity, when the amplitude of the travelling wave is small. As the initial energy increases, regions of the phase space become fragmented, and adjacent points display very different behaviour. This is the clearest indication that the system has undergone a transition to the chaotic state.

5 Conclusion

Numerical modelling of the parameter space requires excessive processing times. Unfortunately, faster but less accurate methods cannot be used, as these would introduce numerical artifacts. The nature of this problem is such that it is ideally suited for parallel computation. On sequential computers, faster algorithms exploiting the coherence properties should yield considerably improved processing times.

Animation results are acceptable, particularly as the motion involves unreal, mathematical objects propagating in the parameter space. The purpose of the video presented here is to show the valuable technique that can be readily exploited even on a modest budget.

Acknowledgements

This work would not have been realized without the generous support of the Sun Microsystems Inc. Scan conversion was made possible by support from VideoLogic Ltd.

References

Barut, A. O. (1980) Electrodynamics and Classical Theory of Fields and Particles, Dover Publications

ISO Programmer's Hierarchical Interactive Graphics System (1987) International Standards Organization, Geneva

Kaufman, A. (1991) Volume Visualization, IEEE Computer Society Press, Los Alamitos

Petersen, J. W., Bogart, R. G., Thomas, S. W. The Utah Raster Toolkit, University of Utah, Department of Computer Science, Salt Lake City, Utah

Press, W. H., Flannery, B. P., Teukolsky, S. A., Vetterling W. T. (1986) Numerical Recipes, Cambridge University Press

Modelling Facial Communication Between an Animator and a Synthetic Actor in Real Time

Nadia Magnenat Thalmann[*] [**]
Antoine Cazedevals [**] and Daniel Thalmann[***] [**]

[*] MIRALab, CUI, University of Geneva
24 rue du Général-Dufour, CH 1205 Geneva, Switzerland
Email: thalmann@uni2a.unige.ch

[**] MIRALab, HEC, University of Montreal, Canada

[***] Computer Graphics Lab
Swiss Federal Institute of Technology
CH 1015 Lausanne, Switzerland
Email: thalmann@eldi.epfl.ch

Abstract

This paper describes methods for acquiring and analyzing in real-time the motion of human faces. It proposes a model based on the use of snakes and image processing techniques. It explains how to generate real-time facial animation corresponding to the recorded motion. It also proposed a strategy for the communication between animators and synthetic actors.

Keywords: facial analysis, facial animation, snake, muscles

1. Introduction

There has been extensive research done on basic facial animation and several models have been proposed. Early methods proposed by Parke (1975, 1982) are based on ad-hoc parameterized models. Platt and Badler (1981) introduced facial expressions manipulated by applying forces to the elastically connected skin mesh via underlying simplified muscles. Their system is based on the Facial Action Coding System (FACS) developed by Ekman and Friesen (1975). Waters (1987) developed a face model which includes two types of muscles: linear/parallel muscles that pull, and sphincter muscles that squeeze. Nahas et al. (1988) proposed a method based on B-splines; motion of the face is obtained by moving the control points. Magnenat-Thalmann et al. (1988) provided another approach to simulate a muscle action by using a procedure called an Abstract Muscle Action (AMA) procedure.

Terzopoulos and Waters (1990) proposed a physics-based model three layered deformable lattice structures for facial tissues: skin, subcutaneous fatty tissue, and muscles. Parke (1991) reviews different parameterization mechanism used in different previously proposed models and introduces the future guidelines for ideal control parameterization and interface. Kalra et al. (1991) introduced a multi-layer approach where, at each level, the degree of abstraction increases. They also described another approach to deform the facial skin surface using rational free form deformations (Kalra et al. 1992). DiPaola (1991) proposed a facial animation system allowing the extension of the range of facial types. We may also mention efforts for lip synchronization and speech automation by several authors (Lewis and Parke; 1987; Hill et al. 1988; Magnenat-Thalmann et al. 1987; Lewis 1991) .

Recently several authors have proposed new facial animation techniques which are based on the information derived from human performances. The information extracted is used for controlling the facial animation. These performance driven techniques provide a very realistic rendering and motion of the face. Williams (1990) used a texture map based technique with points on the surface of the real face. Mase and Pentland (1990) apply optical flow and principal direction analysis for lip reading. Terzopoulos and Waters (1991) reported on techniques for estimating face muscle contraction parameters from video sequences. Kurihara and Arai (1991) introduced a new transformation method for modeling and animating the face using photographs of an individual face. Waters and Terzopoulos (1991) modeled and animated faces using scanned data obtained from a radial laser scanner. Saji et al. (1992) introduced a new method called "Lighting Switch Photometry" to extract 3D shapes from the moving human face. Kato et al (1992) use isodensity maps for the description and the synthesis of facial expressions. These techniques do not process the information extraction in real-time. However, real-time facial animation driven by an interactive input device was reported by DeGraf (1989).

This paper describes a model for real-time analysis and synthesis of facial expression and emotion recognition. Section 2 explains the basic principles of the real-time analysis based on snakes and image processing techniques. Section 3 describes the way of recognizing simple expressions and emotions. The synthesis of facial animation from information extracted during the analysis phase is developed in Section 4. Section 5 proposed the use of our approach for the communication between an animator and synthetic actors. Finally implementation issues are discussed in Section 6.

2. The analysis method

2.1 The use of snakes

Our recognition method is based on snakes as introduced by Terzopoulos and Waters (1991). A snake is a dynamic deformable 2D contour in the x-y plane. A discrete snake is a set of nodes with time varying positions. The nodes are coupled by internal forces making the snake acting like a series of springs resisting compression and a thin wire resisting bending. To create an interactive discrete snake, nodal masses are set to zero and the expression forces are introduced into the equations of motion for dynamic node/spring system. The resulting equation for a node i (1 = 1,...,N) is as follows

$$\gamma_i \frac{dx_i}{dt} + \alpha_i + \beta_i = f_i$$

where γ_i is a velocity-dependent damping constant, α_i are forces resisiting compression, β_i are forces resisting bending and f_i are external forces. To turn the deformable contour into a discrete snake, Terzopoulos and Waters make it responsive to a force field derived from the image. They express the force field which influences the snake's shape and motion through a time-varying potential function. To compute the potential, they apply a discrete smoothing filter consisting of 4-neighbor local averaging of the pixel intensities allowed by the application of a discrete approximation.

Our approach is different from Terzopoulos-Waters approach because we need to analyze the emotion in real-time. Instead of using a filter which globally transforms the image into a planar force field, we apply the filter in the neighborhood of the nodes of the snake. We only use a snake for the mouth; the rest of the information (jaw, eyebrows, eyes) is obtained by fast image-processing techniques.

For the mouth snake, we use the method illustrated by Fig.1. On this figure, we may see the snake working around the mouth. The small lines starting from the nodes show the direction of the forces generated. Because of the elasticity of the snake, if there is no force, the snake tends to contract and becomes a single point.

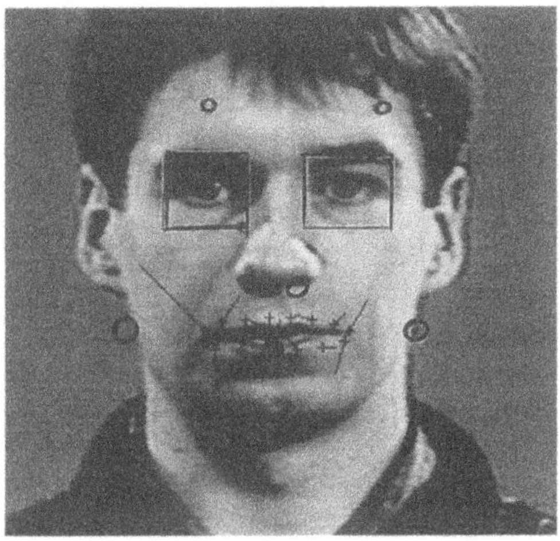

Fig.1 Visualization of the recognition system

To generate the forces, we extract a 6x6 matrix M_1 around the node P as shown in Fig.2. The node's coordinates are converted into integer values.

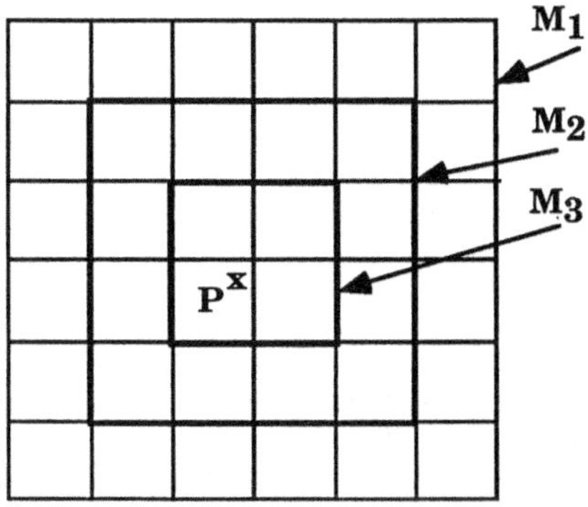

Fig.2. Computation of the filter

To compute the potential, we first transform the RGB information into intensity information; for example, red contributes 30%, green 59% and blue 11%. Secondly, we apply on the matrix a discrete smoothing filter followed by a discrete approximation to the gradient operator. The first filter is applied on the 4x4 square matrix M_2 included in M1. The second filter is applied on the 2x2 square matrix M_3 at the center of the matrix. With these 4 points, we can interpolate bilinearly the force vector.

The snake we used has the same tension constant for all the springs. The rigidity constant is less at the corners of the mouth.

Because of real-time constraints, the snake can have some difficulties following the mouth's edges with good accuracy. The main problem is guiding the snake on the x-axis because the mouth has no strong vertical edge.

In our system, the snake is forced to stay at the center of the head. On Fig.1, we may see two circles near the edges of the neck. These two circles have the same y positions as the endpoints of the snake.

As shown in Fig.3, to determine the x position for the left circle (abscissa of T), we start at the left of the image (S) and scan to the right until an edge is detected. To detect the edge, we first calculate an average of the intensity of the right point and its 4 neighbors:

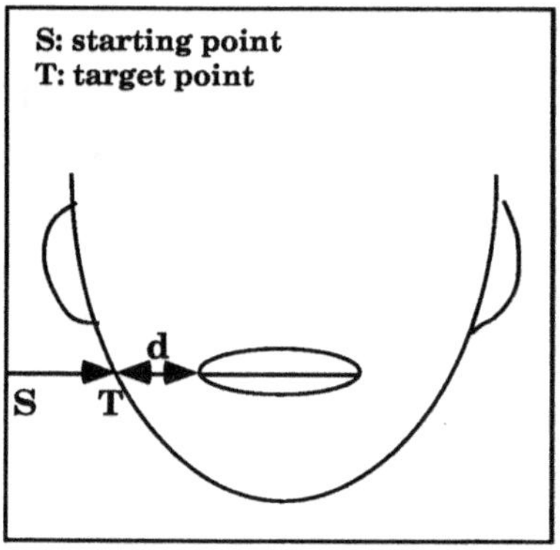

Fig.3. Computation of distance d

Secondly, we compare the result with the point where we are, and if there is not an important difference of intensity, we go right of 1 point.

We then use the information provided by the snake to find the distance d.

We perform the same processing for the right side. We then compare the distance d with the same distance d_0 stored during the initial procedure described later on. If d is less than d_0, we apply some forces to the extremum of the snake and reduce the difference. The magnitude of the generated force is computed as follows:

$$F = k \mid d - d_0 \mid^3$$

2.2. Image processing methods

For the **jaw**, we consider that the lower part of the lower lip (using information given by the snake) is moving with the jaw i.e. if the law opens, the lower part goes down with the jaw. On Fig.1, we may see a circle which uses its y coordinate to find the position of the jaw.

For the **nose**, we use the center point of the upper part of the mouth (also using the snake) and we scan upwards until an edge is detected. As we assume that the illumination is very strong, the edge should belong to the shadow of the nose. The circle on the nose on Fig.1 indicates the position found by the program.

For the **eyebrows**, we use the same principles as the nose. We start from the forehead and scan downwards until we detect an edge. This should be the eyebrow. On Fig.1, we show two circles on the forehead (the starting points) and under them, the two circles indicating the positions for the eyebrows.

For the **eyes**, we define a rectangular region around the eyes (using the position of the nose and eyebrows) and we count the number of white points in the region. If the number of white points is under a threshold value, we consider the eye as closed. On Fig. 1, we show rectangles defining the region. In order to process the analysis in real-time, we only consider one point out of two.

A first step is always necessary to store information when the person has a neutral expression. To determine the intensity of an expression, we compare the information of the current frame with the corresponding information for the neutral expression. For example, if the distance between one eyebrow and the nose is larger than the initial distance, we know that this eyebrow has a higher position. A more general methodology for expression and emotion recognition is explained in the next section.

3. Emotion recognition

In order to recognize expressions and emotions for a new person, the system first needs to know the values of parameters corresponding to the neutral expression. This reference data capture is performed using the snake technique; the person should keep his/her face very quiet and then push the INIT button on the control panel of the program to record these reference parameters. Typical reference parameters are:

the reference left eyebrow height: le_0

the reference right eyebrow height: re_0

the reference mouth width: mw_0

the reference mouth height: mh_0

Fig.4 shows the extracted information.

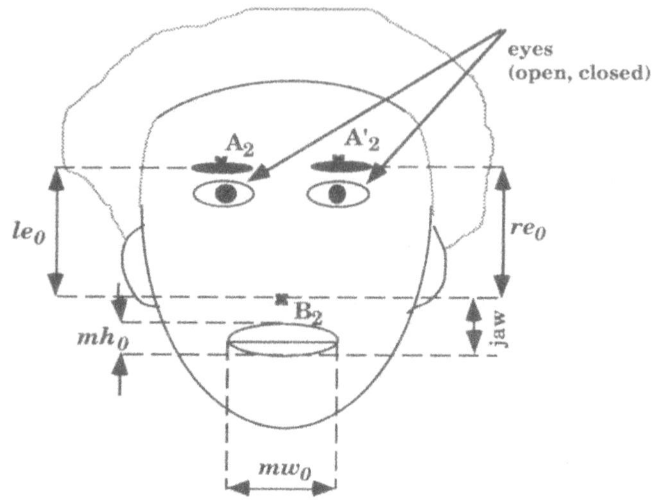

Fig.4. The extracted information

The expression/emotion recognizer compares values obtained in real-time to the reference values to decide the type of expression/emotion. The rules are generally too simple but they may be easily changed. For example, we give six rules using the following notations for the current parameter values:

the reference left eyebrow height: le
the reference right eyebrow height: re
the reference mouth width: mw
the reference mouth height: mh

examples of rules:

1) open mouth:
   if $mw/mh < 2$ then "mouth in O"

2) lowered eyebrows:
   if $le < 0.9*le_0$ and $re < 0.9*re_0$ then "not happy"

3) open mouth but especially horizontally
   if $mw*mh > 2*mw_0*mh_0$ and $2 < mw/mh < 2.5$ then "laugh"

4) open mouth but not circular and eyebrows lightly raised:
   if $mw*mh > 2*mw_0*mh_0$ and $mw/mh < 2$ and $0.9*le_0 < le < 1.1*le_0$ and $0.9*re_0 < re < 1.1*re_0$ then "strong laugh"

5) mouth in O and high eyebrows:
   if $mw*mh > 2*mw_0*mh_0$ and $mw/mh < 1.8$ and $le > 1.1*le_0$ and $re > 1.1*re_0$ then "afraid"

6) half open mouth and high eyebrows:
   if $mw*mh > 1.5*mw_0*mh_0$ and $mw*mh < 2*mw_0*mh_0$ and $mw/mh < 1.8$ and $le > 1.1*le_0$ and $re > 1.1*re_0$ then "surprised"

4. Synthesis of facial animation

One of the first application of the face analysis is the generation of the same expressions on a synthetic actor (see Fig. 5). For this purpose, we work at the low level of minimal perceptible actions as defined in our multilayered Facial Animation system SMILE (Kalra et al. 1991). Only 8 minimal perceptible actions are used:

open_jaw
raise_left_eye, raise_right_eye
close_left_eyelid, close_right_eyelid
raise_upper_lip, raise_lower_lip
pull_mid_lips

This is enough to control the main changes of the face, but not to copy exactly the expression of the real face, but again, our purpose is real-time processing more than accuracy. The facial deformations are performed using Rational Free-Form Deformations as defined by Kalra et al. (1992).

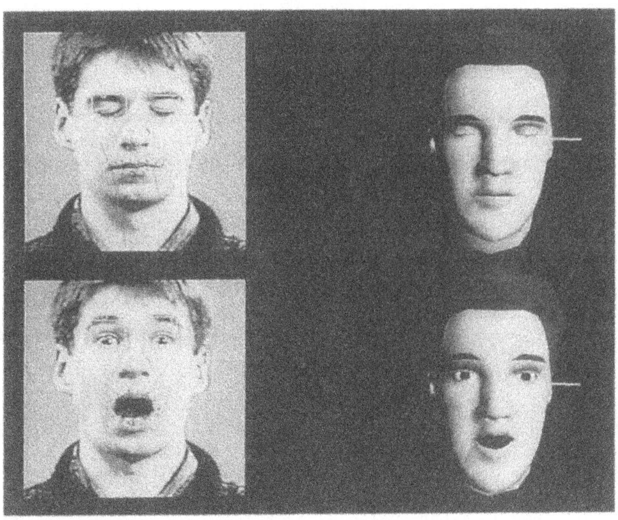

Fig.5. Example of real time recognition/synthesis process

5. Communication actor-animator

Based on the model described in this paper, we are developing an animator-actor communication as described in Magnenat Thalmann- Thalmann (1991).

As shown in Fig. 6, the system is mainly an inference system with facial and gesture data as input channels and face and hand animation sequences as output channels. The input data is captured in two ways: the methodology described previously for face expressions and datagloves for hand motions.

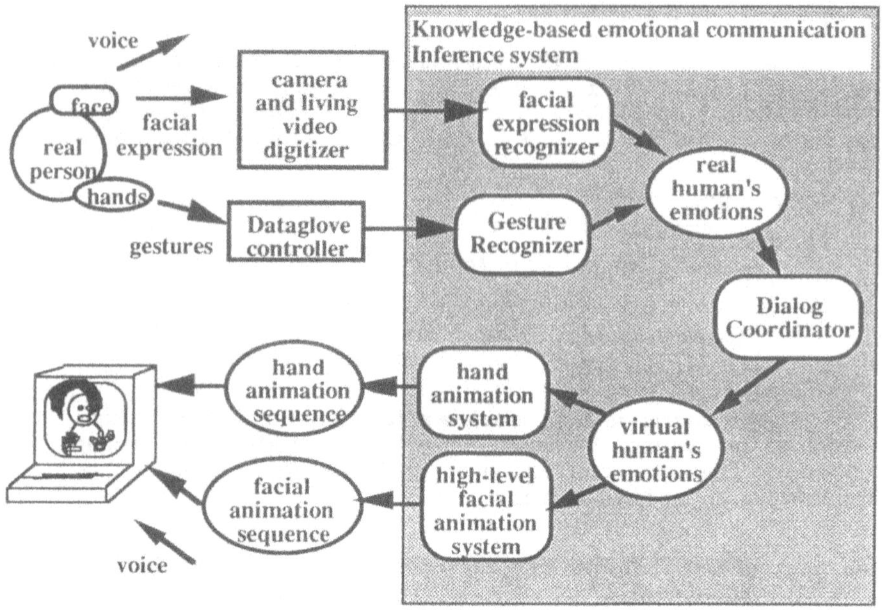

Fig.6 Organization of the proposed system

The development of the inference system is divided into three subsystems:

i) a subsystem for the recognition of emotions from facial expressions, head-and-shoulder gestures, hand gestures and possibly speech

ii) a subsystem for the synthesis of facial expressions and hand motions for a given emotion and speech

iii) a subsystem for the dialog coordination between input and output emotions

This last subsystem is a rule-based system: it should decide how the virtual actor will behave based on the behavior of the real human. The dialog coordinator analyzes the humor and behavior of the user based on the facial expressions and gestures. It then decides which emotions (sequences of expressions) and gestures (sequence of postures) should be generated by the animation system. For the design of correspondence rules, our approach is based on existing work in applied psychology, in particular in the area of non-verbal communication.

6. Implementation

The recognition program is working on any SG IRIS workstation, but real-time (about 10 frames/sec) is obtained on the 4D/440 VGX for simple emotions as discribed here. The video input is obtained using a professional camera connected to the SG Living Video Digitizer. The program has been developed in C using the Fifth Dimension object-oriented toolkit (Turner et al. 1990). The program interface only uses buttons and panels.

The SMILE system and the recognition program work on different UNIX processes. As the animation of the virtual face should be done at the same time as the recognition, both programs should exchange information. We use the UNIX inter-process communication protocol (ipc) which allows processes to send and receive messages.

7. Conclusion

This paper has shown that recognition of emotions in real-time is possible. This recognition may be used for generation of expressions by synthetic actors with same expressions or for truly communication between animators and synthetic actors. The main weakness of our program is that it uses techniques which require information from the previous frame to analyze the next one. This means that if the program does not succeed in extracting information from one frame, it cannot later extract information from the next ones. Only a tool analyzing frames independently could solve this problem, but in this case, real-time processing could not be possible any longer.

Acknowledgment

The authors are grateful to Prem Kalra for his help with the facial animation system. The project was sponsored by the Fonds National Suisse pour la Recherche Scientifique and the Natural Sciences and Engineering Council of Canada.

References

deGraf B (1989) in State of the Art in Facial Animation, SIGGRAPH '89 Course Notes No. 26, pp. 10-20.

DiPaola S (1991) Extending the Range of Facial Types, Journal of Visualization and Computer Animation, Vol.2, No4, pp.129-131.

Ekman P, Friesen WV (1975), Unmasking the Face: A Guide to Recognizing Emotions from Facial Clues, Printice-Hall

Hill DR, Pearce A, Wyvill B (1988), Animating Speech: An Automated Approach Using Speech Synthesised by Rules, The Visual Computer, Vol. 3, No. 5, pp. 277-289.

Kalra P, Mangili A, Magnenat-Thalmann N, Thalmann D (1991) SMILE : A Multilayered Facial Animation System, Proc IFIP WG 5.10, Tokyo, Japan (Ed Kunii Tosiyasu L) pp. 189-198.

Kalra P, Mangili A, Magnenat Thalmann N, Thalmann D (1992) Simulation of Facial Muscle Actions Based on Rational Free Form Deformations, Proc. Eurographics '92, pp.59-69.

Kato M, So I, Hishinuma Y, Nakamura O, Minami T (1992) Description and Synthesis of Facial Expression based on Isodensity Maps, in: Tosiyasu L (ed): Visual Computing, Springer-Verlag, Tokyo, pp.39-56.

Kurihara T, Arai K (1991), A Transformation Method for Modeling and Animation of the Human Face from Photographs, Proc. Computer Animation '91 Geneva, Switzerland, Springer-Verlag, Tokyo, pp. 45-57.

Lewis JP, Parke FI (1987), Automated Lipsync and Speech Synthesis for Character Animation, Proc. CHI '87 and Graphics Interface '87, Toronto, pp. 143-147.

Lewis J (1991) Automated Lip-sync: Background and Techniques, Journal of Visualization and Computer Animation, Vol.2, No4, pp.117-122.

Magnenat-Thalmann N, Primeau E, Thalmann D (1988), Abstract Muscle Action Procedures for Human Face Animation, The Visual Computer, Vol. 3, No. 5, pp. 290-297.

Magnenat-Thalmann N, Thalmann D (1987), The Direction of Synthetic Actors in the film Rendez-vous à Montréal, IEEE Computer Graphics and Applications, Vol. 7, No. 12, pp. 9-19.

Magnenat-Thalmann N, Thalmann D (1991), Complex Models for Visualizing Synthetic Actors, IEEE Computer Graphics and Applications, Vol. 11, No. 6.

Mase K, Pentland A (1990) Automatic Lipreading by Computer, Trans. Inst. Elec. Info. and Comm. Eng.,vol. J73-D-II, No. 6, pp. 796-803.

Nahas M, Huitric H, Saintourens M (1988), Animation of a B-Spline Figure, The Visual Computer, Vol. 3, No. 5, pp. 272-276.

Parke FI (1975), A Model for Human Faces that allows Speech Synchronized Animation, Computer and Graphics, Pregamon Press, Vol. 1, No. 1, pp. 1-4.

Parke FI (1982), Parametrized Models for Facial Animation, IEEE Computer Graphics and Applications, Vol. 2, No. 9, pp. 61-68.

Parke FI (1991), Control Parameterization for Facial Animation, Proc. Computer Animation '91, Geneva, Switzerland, Springer-Verlag, Tokyo, pp. 3-13.

Platt S, Badler N (1981), Animating Facial Expressions, Proc SIGGRAPH '81, pp. 245-252.

Saji H, Hioki H, Shinagawa Y, Yoshida K, Kunii TL (1992) Extraction of 3D Shapes from the Moving Human face Using Lighting Switch Photometry, in Magnenat Thalmann N , Thalmann D (eds) Creating and Animating the Virtual World, Springer-Verlag Tokyo, pp. 69-86.

Terzopoulos D, Waters K (1990) Physically Based Facial Modeling, Analysis, and Animation, Journal of Visualization and Computer Animation, Vol. 1, No. 2, pp. 73-80.

Terzopoulos and Waters (1991) Techniques for Realistic Facial Modeling and Animation, Proc. Computer Animation '91, Geneva, Switzerland, Springer-Verlag, Tokyo, pp. 59-74.

Turner R, Gobbetti E, Balaguer F, Mangili A, Thalmann D, Magnenat-Thalmann N, An Object-Oriented Methodology Using Dynamic Variables for Animation and Scientific Visualization, CG International '90, Springer Verlag, pp. 317-328.

Waters K (1987), A Muscle Model for Animating Three Dimensional Facial Expression, Proc SIGGRAPH '87, Vol. 21, No. 4, pp. 17-24.

Waters K, Terzopoulos D (1991) Modelling and Animating Faces using Scanned Data, Journal of Visualization and Computer Animation, Vol. 2, No. 4, pp. 123-128.

Williams L (1990), Performance Driven Facial Animation, Proc SIGGRAPH '90, pp. 235-242.

Synthesis and animation of human faces: artificial reality in interpersonal video communication

S. Curinga, A. Grattarola and F. Lavagetto
DIST, Department of Communication, Computer and Systems Science
University of Genova - Via Opera Pia 11a, Genova, I-16145, Italy

Abstract

This paper describes an approach to use artificial reality techniques for real-time interpersonal visual communication at very low bitrate. A flexible structure is suitably adapted to the specific characteristics of the speaker's head by means of few parameters estimated from the analysis of the real image sequence, while head motion and facial mimics are synthesized on the model by means of knowledge-based deformation rules acting on a simplified muscle structure. The analysis algorithms performed at the transmitter to estimate the model parameters are based on feature-oriented operators aimed at segmenting the real incoming frames and at the extraction of the primary facial descriptors. The system performances have been evaluated on different "head-and-shoulder" sequences and the precision, robustness and complexity of the employed analysis/synthesis algorithms have been tested. Promising results have been achieved for applications both in videophone coding and in picture animation where the facial mimics of a synthetic actor is reproduced according to the parameters extracted from a real speaking face.

1 Introduction

The idea of using object-oriented approaches for efficient coding of images and sequences has inspired almost all the so-called "second generation" techniques (Gilge, Engelhardt and Melhan, 1989; Hoetter and Thoma, 1988; Musmann, Hoetter and Ostermann, 1989; Kunt, Benard and Leonardi, 1987; Kunt, Ikonomopoulos and Kocher, 1985; Musmann, Pirsh and Grallert, 1985) based on the shared opinion that any effective video compression necessarily relies on a preliminary good image segmentation. The standardization process, both in real-time (CCITT, 1990) and interactive (MPEG, 1990) visual communication, has strongly recommended the universality of the proposed techniques leading to block-oriented DCT-based schemes where the intrinsic characteristics of the scene (real edges, 3D objects structure, texture-homogeneous regions, etc.) are substantially ignored.

On the other hand, application-oriented approaches are drawing more and more attention to very low bitrate communications where the specific visual information can be efficiently formalized, modelled and predicted. Videophone sequences, in particular, identify an easy-to-model class of images, suitable to object-oriented processing for high compression coding. Different methodologies have been proposed to exploit the a priori knowledge and to design the appropriate scene model, depending on the aimed compression, complexity and quality. These methodologies include image classification into high and low priority blocks within conventional schemes (Badique', 1990; Pereira and Masera, 1990), to complex object-oriented approaches (Buck and Diehl, 1990; Buck, 1990) and highly sophisticated 3D models (Aizawa, Harashima and Saito, 1989; Nakaya, Chuah and Harashima, 1991; Parke, 1982).

Modelling a videophone scene basically means modelling a human head, that of the speaker, paying particular accuracy to the reproduction of the time-varying somatic details of the face (Magnenat-Thalmann, Primeau and Thalmann, 1988; Waters, 1987) and to the synchronization of the lip movements with speech (Morishima, Aizawa and Harashima, 1988; Yuhas, Goldstein Jr. and Sejnowski, 1989). Different data structures and algorithms have been proposed both for what concerns head modelling and analysis-synthesis coding techniques. Among the many approaches, those based on flexible structures (Choi, Harashima and Takebe, 1991; Forchheimer and Kronander, 1989; Lavagetto, Grattarola, Curinga and Braccini, 1992; Terzopoulos and Waters, 1990) have yielded the most promising results in terms of computational complexity and rate-distortion performances.

The approach described in this paper is based on a flexible wire-frame structure suitably adapated to the face of the speaker (Lavagetto, Grattarola, Curinga and Braccini, 1992), capable to reproduce mimic expressions by means of knowledge-based rules (Ekman and Friesen, 1977). The wire-frame structure can be animated either by means of synthetic parameters or, conversely, through true parameters estimated by analyzing a real videophone sequence. On the other hand, these true parameters can be employed to actually animate the modelled speaker's face or, alternatively, to animate the generic face of a synthetic actor.

In the next Section a brief description of the modelling-synthesis procedures is presented while the analysis algorithms, performed at the transmitter to estimate the model parameters, and the achieved experimental results are discussed in details in Sections 3 and 4, respectively.

2 Image modelling and synthesis

Human faces are modelled, as shown in the example in Figure 1, through a flexible wire-frame structure suitably adapted to their somatic characteristics with increasing resolution in correspondence of high detail features like eyes and mouth. The wire-frame structure is organized in a set of subregions, each of them affected by predefined deformation rules producing time-varying variations to simulate muscle contraction.

The human face is modelled as a system whose internal variables, called status or synthesis parameters, express the strength of the contraction stimula actually applied to its muscles: with reference to the wire-frame model, this corresponds to the deformation rules which are applied to each specific subregion. The system observable variables, called output or analysis parameters, are conversely associated to the external face appearing and are basically linked to facial primary somatics as described in Figure 2.

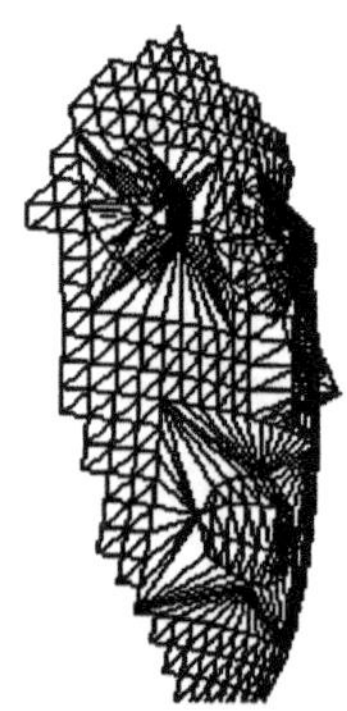

Figure 1: Flexible wire-frame structure adapted to "Miss America".

Differently from a previous approach (Lavagetto, Grattarola, Curinga and Braccini, 1992), where synthesis parameters were estimated through iterative procedures, a straightforward estimation is here obtained by means of an inverse outputs-to-status mapping function.

As the modelled object is a human face, the key problem of translating the observable variables, estimated through the analysis of the input image, into suitable synthesis parameters, can be performed efficiently by taking into account a priori knowledge concerning facial muscles and facial mimics. Through a learning procedure applied to a representative set of facial image sequences the system has been suitably trained and a lookup table has been constructed for the straightforward conversion from the vector of the analysis parameters, used to address the lookup table, to synthesis parameters used for the model adaptation. The mapping function is implemented by means of a codebook obtained by clustering a training set of analysis and synthesis vectors collected from different sources (i.e. from different facial image sequences).

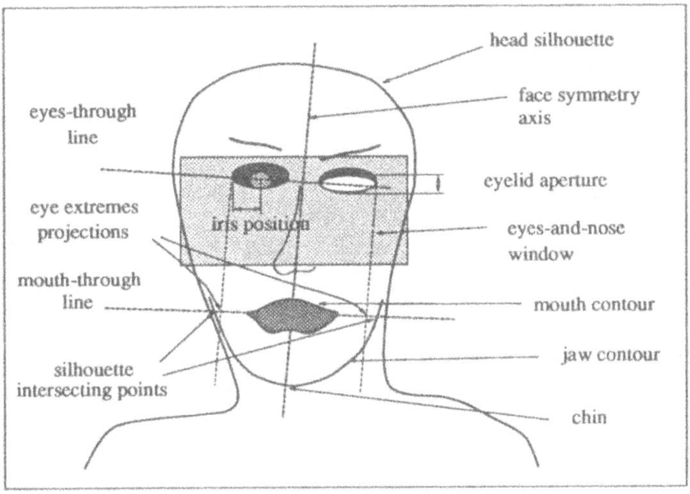

Figure 2: Description of the output or analysis parameters.

The definition of the deformation rules acting on the wire-frame structure and the characteristics of the affected model subregions depend on the specific image class. Full-screen facial images are usually rather easy to be analyzed as somatic features extend over an appreciable image area and can be successfully extracted: in this case facial mimics can be effectively reproduced by means of the full set of deformation rules. On the other hand, within different image classes where the face region extends over a small area, only coarse mimics can be reproduced as only a few analysis parameters can be reliably extracted: in this case a basic set of deformation rules is used, capable to synthesize only eyes and mouth opening/closing.

3 Image analysis and model parameter estimation

The estimation of the analysis parameters is performed through the following steps:

1. estimation of the face symmetry axis;
2. eyes detection;
3. mouth contour detection;
4. chin and jaw contour detection.

The face symmetry axis is estimated by minimizing a suitable functional within an image window internal to the head silhouette extracted through interframe segmentation. The symmetry functional is computed, for each column k of the window, as follows:

$$S(k) = \frac{2}{XY}\sum_{j=0}^{Y}\sum_{i=1}^{X/2} ||x(j,k-i) - x(j,k+i)|| \tag{1}$$

where $x(j,i)$ is the luminance value of the pixel corresponding to the j-th raw and i-th column within the $X \cdot Y$ pixel window.

The estimation of the face symmetry axis is rather sensitive to the particular image window used for the computation of the functional $S(k)$: as shown in Figure 3, the eyes-and-nose region usually exhibits more axial symmetry than other face regions where less somatic morphology is available. Depending on the image format and typology, also the window size represents a rather critical parameter as shown by the plots in Figure 4.

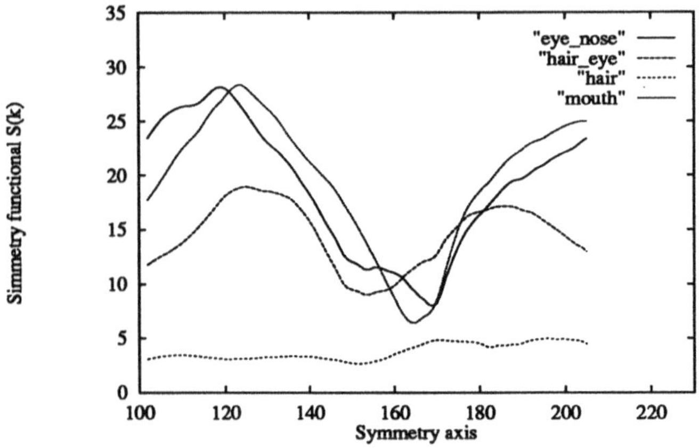

Figure 3: Symmetry axis estimation computed within different image subregions: the correct estimation is evaluated within the eye-nose region. Simulation results are referred to the sequence "Miss America", frame n. 20.

The luminance distribution is then analyzed orthogonally to the face symmetry axis in order to detect the presence of eye-patterns modelled as "dark-bright-dark-bright-dark" transitions. Each matching eye-pattern, as shown in Figure 5, is then weighted by means of a reliability coefficient proportional to the luminance activity (gradient) integrated along the cross-line in correspondence of the pattern itself. The most reliable matching pattern is consequently chosen and the central bright-dark-bright transition is used as estimation of the iris position, as shown in Figure 7.

The mouth is then sought within an image window located under the eyes and crossing the symmetry axis. The plot in Figure 6 represents the error between the predicted position of the mouth and its actual position. The luminance distribution is filtered internally to the mouth search window, by means of the following operator H defined over a 5x5 pixel matrix:

$$H(m,n) \;=\; H'[x(m,n)] \;=\; \frac{\sigma^2_{(m,n)} \cdot [255 \;-\; x(m,n)]^2}{255^2} \tag{2}$$

where 255 is the highest representable luminance value and $\sigma^2_{(m,n)}$ is the local luminance variance evaluated over the 5x5 pixel matrix. The filter response is therefore maximum in correspondence of dark pixels surrounded by highly varying luminance regions corresponding, as far as the mouth area is concerned, to the external lip contour.

The cumulative pixel difference of the $H(m,n)$ filtered signal is computed in correspondence of the k-th raw or column as:

$$\begin{aligned} D_{raw}(k) &= \textstyle\sum_{i=0}^{R} \|H(i,k) \;-\; H(i-1,k)\| \\ D_{col}(k) &= \textstyle\sum_{i=0}^{C} \|H(k,i) \;-\; H(k,i-1)\| \end{aligned} \tag{3}$$

where D_{raw} and D_{col} are the cumulative pixel differences evaluated on the k-th raw or column, respectively, inside the mouth window of size $R \cdot C$ pixels.

The mouth search window is resized to the subwindow where $D_{raw}(k)$ and $D_{col}(k)$ exhibit the highest cumulative values (see Figure 7), yielding the result shown in the picture of Figure 8.

Further processing is then performed inside the resized window to detect the mouth contour modelled as the closed curve maximizing the $H(m,n)$ contrast along its boundary. This result is obtained by analyzing the $H(m,n)$ distribution along each column, bottom-up and top-down, marking the first pixel where it exceeds a given threshold T. Marked

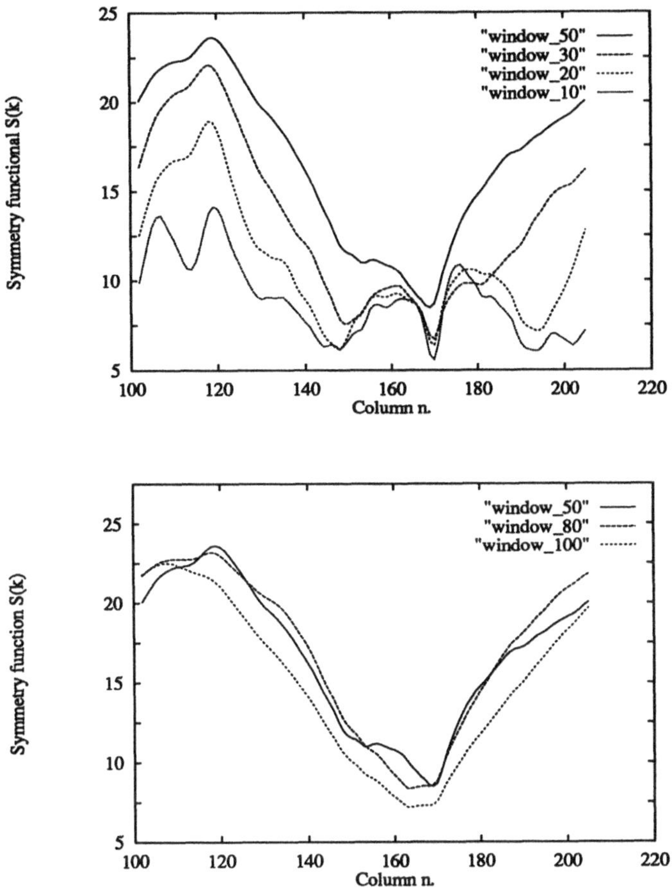

Figure 4: Effects produced by incorrectly sizing the subregion for the estimation of the symmetry axis: undersizing (top) and oversizing (bottom). The correct size is 50 pixels where the functional presents a single sharp minimum. Simulation results are referred to the sequence "Miss America", frame n. 20.

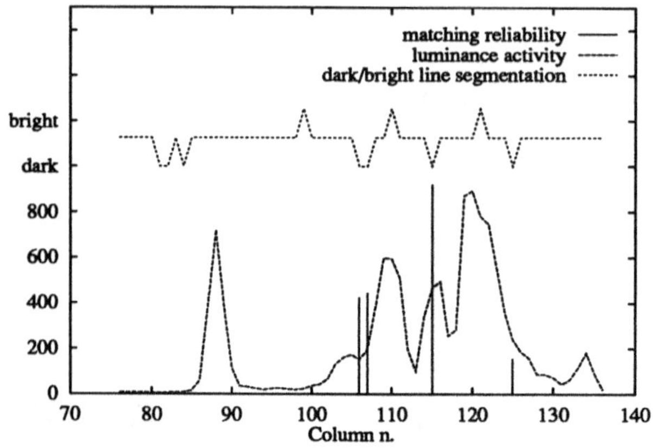

Figure 5: (Top) Segmentation of the eyes-through-line into dark-and-bright patterns. (Bottom) Estimation of the eye position: each matching eye-pattern is weighted by means of a reliability coefficient proportional to the activity of the luminance distribution in correspondence of the pattern. Simulation performed on the sequence "Miss America", frame n.20

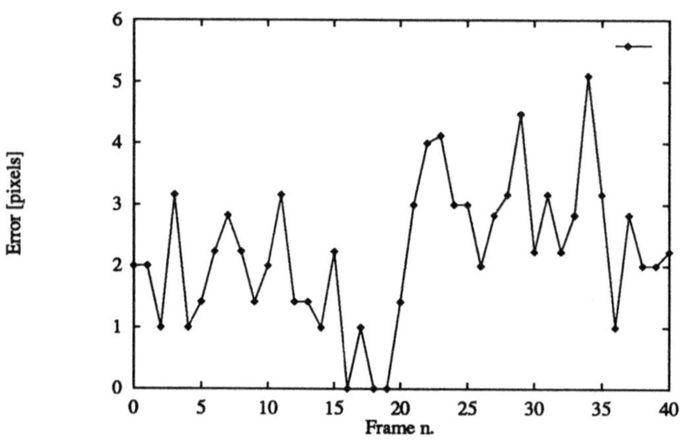

Figure 6: Simulation performed on the sequence "Miss America". Plot of the error, expressed in pixels, between the actual position of the mouth centroid and its prediction based on eyes position and face symmetry axis.

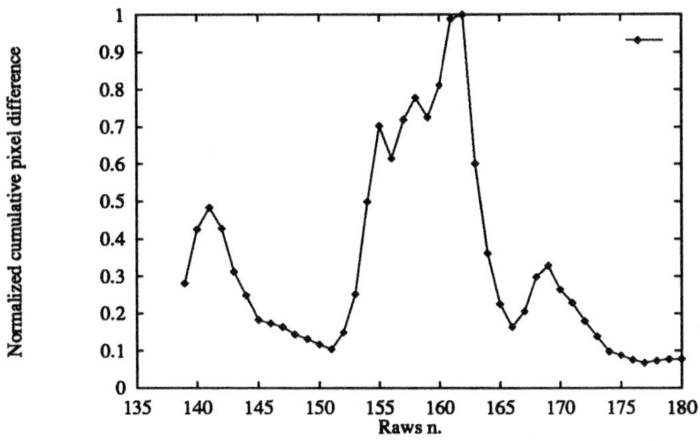

Figure 7: Normalized cumulative pixel difference $D_{raw}(k)$. The window is resized to the raws having high $D_{raw}(k)$ values. Simulation performed on the sequence "Miss America", frame n. 20.

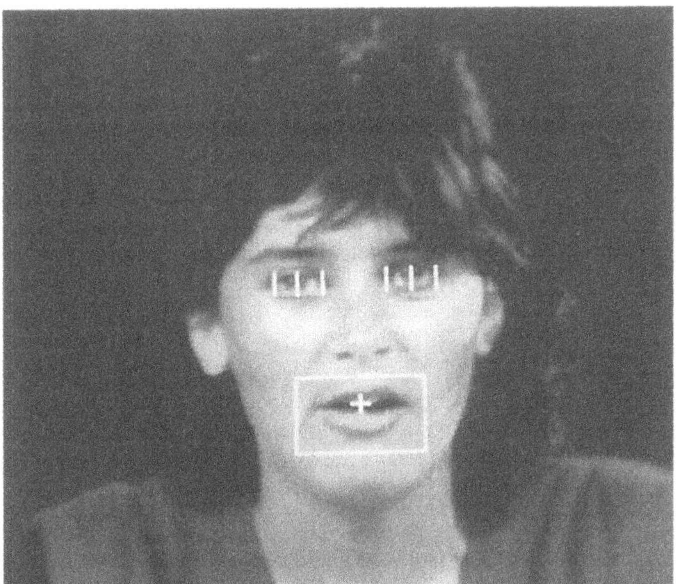

Figure 8: The window is suitably resized around the mouth.

pixels are then connected to each other to form a closed curve $c(T)$ and the contrast functional $F[c(T)]$ is computed along its boundary as:

$$F[c(T)] = \frac{1}{L(T)} \sum_{\forall(m,n)\in c(T)} [H(m_o,n) - H(m_i,n)] \quad (4)$$

where $L(T)$ is the length of the curve $c(T)$ expressed in pixels while (m_o,n) and (m_i,n) are the pair of pixels adjacent to (m,n) in the same column, outside and inside $c(T)$, respectively. In Figure 9 $F[c(T)]$ has been normalized and plotted as a function of the threshold value T: its maximum corresponds to a value of T leading to the extraction of the optimal mouth contour as shown in the picture of Figure 11.

The jaw contour is approximated by two parabolic arcs smoothly connected in correspondence of the chin, assumed to lay on the face symmetry axis under the mouth. The image luminance distribution is filtered through the following operator $V[x(m,n)]$:

$$V[x(m,n)] = \sigma^2_{(m,n)} \quad (5)$$

The $V(m,n)$ filtered signal is then thresholded with respect to the value S according to:

$$V_S(m,n) = \begin{cases} V(m,n) & if\ V(m,n) < S \\ 0 & if\ V(m,n) > S \end{cases} \quad (6)$$

and analyzed along the line passing through the mouth extremes to find out the intersection points with the face silhouette. The intersecting points have the following characteristics:

- their $V(m,n)$ value exceeds the threshold S ($V_S(m,n) \neq 0$);
- they are roughly at the same distance from the face symmetry axis;
- they lay on the mouth-through-line roughly in correspondence of the projection of the external extremes of the eyes (see Figure 2).

Let us call cx_1 and cx_2 the silhouette intersecting points and $p(t)$ the position of the chin constrained to lay on the symmetry axis $s(t)$, expressed as a function of the parameter t. For each value of t, the two parabolic arcs $a_1(t)$ and $a_2(t)$ passing through $\{(cx_1,\ p(t)\}$ and $\{cx_2,\ p(t)\}$ are computed. The following matching functional $W(t)$ is computed:

$$W(t) = \sum_{\forall(m,n)\in a_1(t),a_2(t)} V_S(m,n) \quad (7)$$

The value of t for which $W(t)$ is maximum, identifies the point $p(t)$ taken as an estimate of the chin position. In Figure 10 $W(t)$ is plotted as a function of the variable t: its maximum corresponds to a value of t leading to the optimal chin and jaw extraction shown in Figure 11.

4 Experimental results

The above described analysis-synthesis algorithms have been applied for coding standard "head-and-shoulder" monochrome videophone sequences like "Miss America" and "Claire" (256x256 pixels, 8 bpp, 10 frame/sec.) achieving an average rate of 0.5 Kbit/sec for facial parameters coding. The analysis algorithms have proven to be precise and robust both for the estimation of the face symmetry axis, as described in Figure 12, and for the extraction of the somatic features. As illustrated in Figure 13, facial mimics is synthesized from the model very effectively, providing appreciable reconstruction quality with very low decoding complexity. On-going research, oriented at the exploitation of the acoustic information to integrate the visual analysis, is presently opening new promising perspectives in lips synchronization (Morishima, Aizawa and Harashima, 1988; Yuhas, Goldstein Jr. and Sejnowski, 1989).

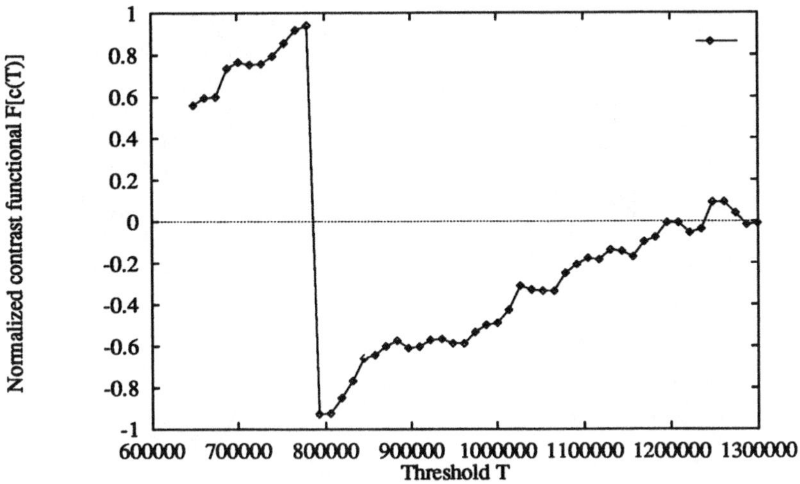

Figure 9: Normalized contrast functional $F[c(T)]$ plotted as a function of the threshold value T. Its maximum, just before the discontinuous transition from positive to negative values, corresponds a value of T leading to the extraction of the mouth contour shown in Figure 11.

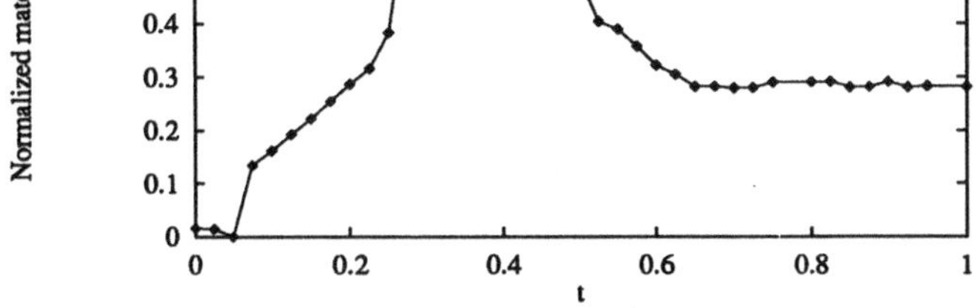

Figure 10: Normalized matching functional $W(t)$ plotted as a function of the variable t. Simulation performed on the sequence "Miss America", frame n. 20.

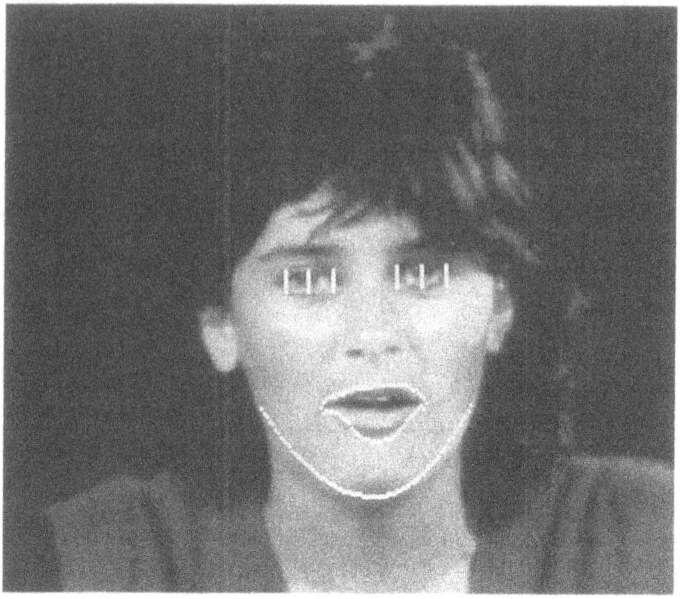

Figure 11: Chin and jaw contour have been extracted.

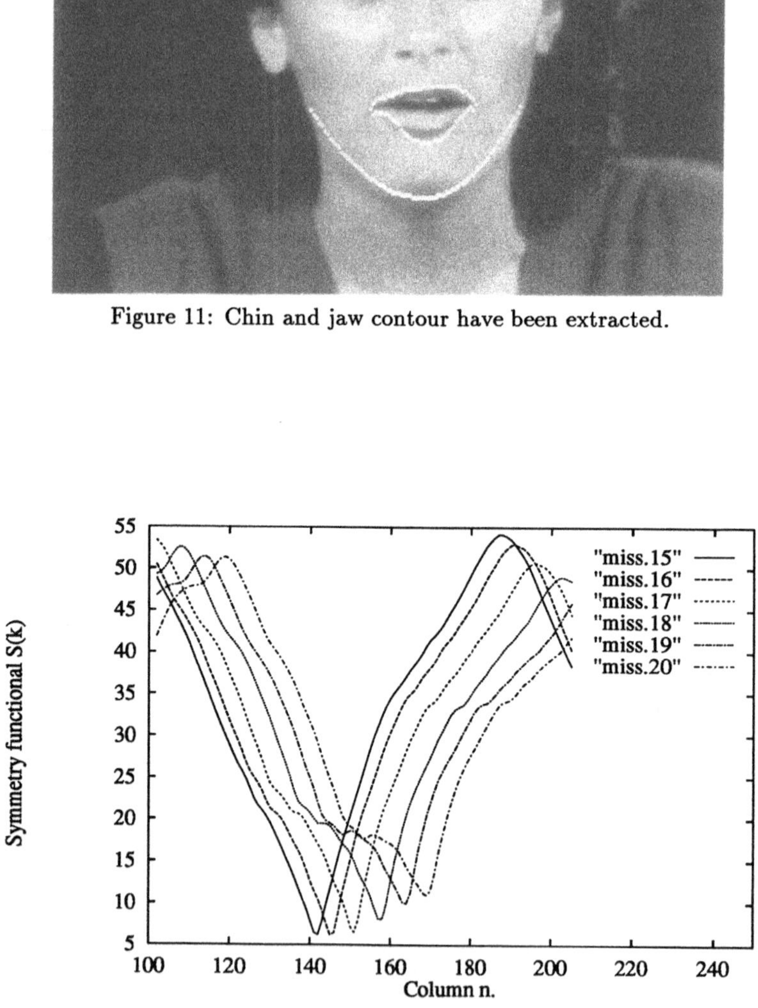

Figure 12: The face symmetry axis is tracked from frame to frame. The symmetry functional always exhibits a single sharp minimum leading to good estimations. Simulation performed on the sequence "Miss America".

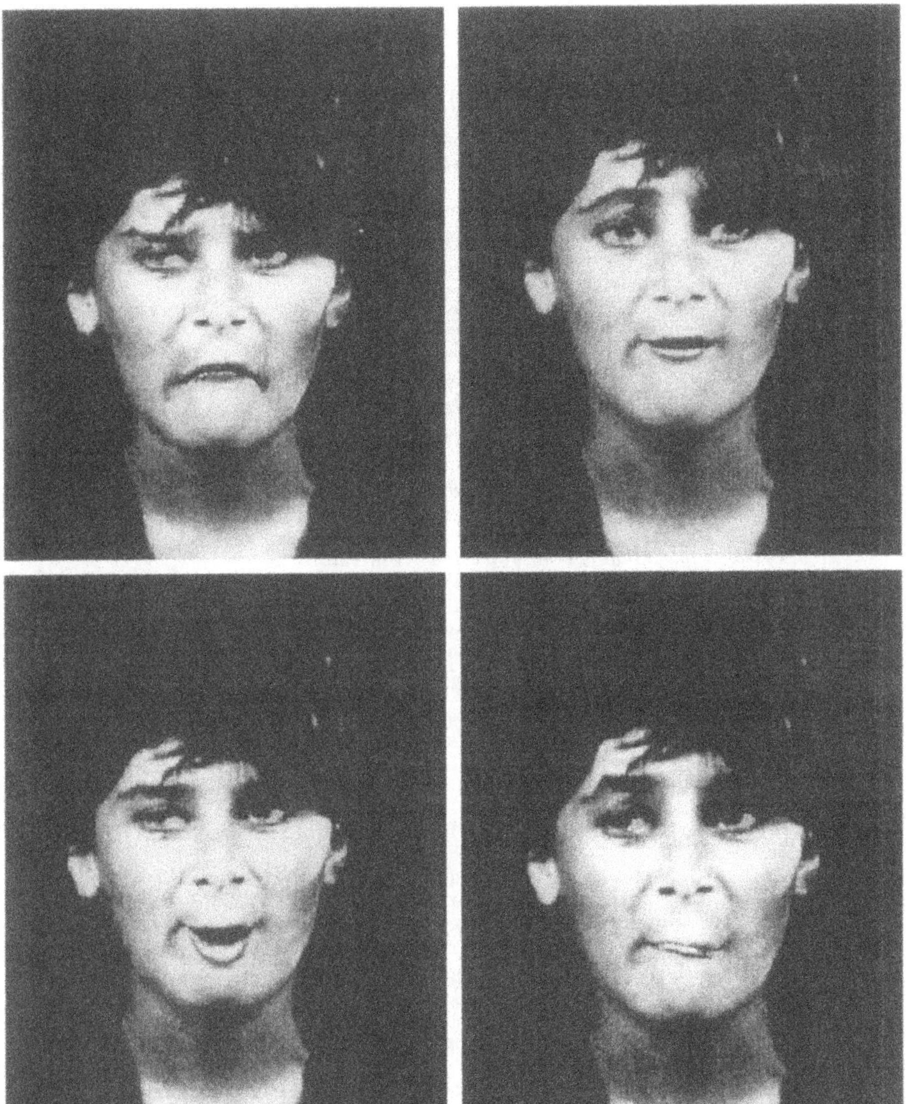

Figure 13: Examples of synthesized facial expressions showing the achievable reconstruction quality.

References

Aizawa, K., Harashima, H. and Saito, T. (1989) Model-Based Analysis - Synthesis Image Coding (MBASIC) System for Person's Face. *Image Communication* 1:139-152.

Badique', E. (1990) Knowledge-based Facial Area Recognition and Improved Coding in a CCITT-Compatible Low-Bitrate Video-Codec. *Proc. PCS-90, Cambridge Ma* 9-1.

Buck, M. and Diehl, N. (1990) Segmentation and modeling of head and shoulder scenes. *Proc. II Int.Conf. on 64Kbit/s Video Coding, Rotterdam* 4-3.

Buck, M. (1990) Segmentation of moving head-and-shoulder shape. *Proc. PCS-90, Cambridge Ma 1990* 9-2.

CCITT Recommendation H.261: Video codec for audiovisual services at p*64 kbits/s (1990) *CCITT White book.*

Choi, C.S., Harashima, H. and Takebe, T. (1991) Analysis and Synthesis of Facial Expressions in Knowledge-Based Coding of Facial Image Sequences. *Proc. ICASSP-91, S.Francisco CA* 2737-2740.

Forchheimer, R. and Kronander, T. (1989) Image Coding - from Waveforms to Animation. *IEEE Trans. on ASSP* 37:2008-2023.

Ekman, P. and Friesen, W.V. (1977) Facial Action Coding System. Consulting Psychologists Press, Stanford University, Palo Alto.

Gilge, M., Engelhardt, T. and Melhan, R. (1989) Coding of Arbitrarily Shaped Image Segments Based on a Generalized Orthogonal Transform. *Signal Processing: Image Communication* 1:103-116.

Hoetter, M. and Thoma, R. (1988) Image Segmentation Based on Object Oriented Mapping Parameter Estimation. *Signal Processing* 15:315-334.

Kunt, M., Ikonomopoulos, A. and Kocher, M. (1985) Second-Generation Image Coding Techniques. *IEEE Proceedings* 73:549-574.

Kunt, M., Benard, M. and Leonardi, R. (1987) Recent Results on High-Compression Image Coding. *IEEE Trans. on Circuits and Systems* 34:1306-1336.

Lavagetto, F., Grattarola, A.A., Curinga, S. and Braccini, C. (1992) Muscle Modeling for Facial Animation in Videophone Coding. *Proc. IEEE Int. Workshop on Robot and Human Communication, Tokyo* 369-375.

Magnenat-Thalmann, N., Primeau, E. and Thalmann, D. (1988) Abstract Muscle Action Procedures for Face Animation. *The Visual Computer* 3:290-297.

Morishima, S., Aizawa, K. and Harashima, H. (1988) Model-based facial image coding controlled by the speech parameter. *Proc. PCS-88, Turin, I* 4-4.

MPEG Video Simulation Model Three SM3 (1990) *Doc. ISO-IEC/JTC1/SC2/WG8 N/MPEG90.*

Musmann, H.G., Pirsh, P. and Grallert, H.J. (1985) Advances in Picture Coding. *IEEE Procedings* 73:523-548.

Musmann, H.G., Hoetter, M. and Ostermann, J. (1989) Object-Oriented Analysis - Synthesis Coding of Moving Images. *Signal Processing: Image Communication* 1:117-138.

Nakaya, Y., Chuah, Y.C. and Harashima, H. (1991) Model-based/waveform hybrid coding for videotelephone images. *Proc. ICASSP-91, S.Francisco, CA* 2741-2744.

Parke, F.I. (1982) Parameterized Models for Facial Animation. *IEEE Computer Graphics and Applications* 2:61-68.

Pereira, F. and Masera, L. (1990) Two-layers knowledge-based videophone coding. *Proc. PCS-90, Cambridge Ma* 6-1.

Terzopoulos, D. and Waters, K. (1990) Analysis of Facial Images Using Physical and Anatomical Models. *Proc. IEEE 3rd Int, Conf. on Computer Vision, Osaka* 727-732.

Waters, K. (1987) A Muscle Model for Animating Threedimensional Facial Expression. *Computer Graphics* 22:17-24.

Yuhas, B.P., Goldstein Jr., M.H. and Sejnowski, T.J. (1989) Integration of Acoustic and Visual Speech Signal Using Neural Networks. *IEEE Communications Magazine* 65-71.

Chapter 8

Modeling for CIM Applications

Reasoning about Physical Solids and Processes

Aristides A. G. Requicha
Programmable Automation Laboratory
Computer Science Department and
Institute for Robotics and Intelligent Systems
University of Southern California
Los Angeles, CA 90089-0781, USA

Introduction

The development of solid modeling has been motivated primarily by its potential for supporting automated applications. Analytic applications have been addressed successfully, and algorithms are available for visualization, mass property calculation, static interference analysis, kinematic simulation of mechanisms, and simulation of manufacturing processes such as machining. Work on automatic meshing for Finite Element Analysis (FEA), simulation of semiconductor fabrication operations, and electronic packaging is progressing nicely.

But automation of applications that involve synthesis or *spatial planning* remains an elusive goal. This paper discusses recent research at USC's Programmable Automation Lab on three problems that involve reasoning about solid mechanical parts and physical processes that act upon them: numerically controlled (NC) machining, dimensional inspection, and fixturing.

Numerically Controlled Machining

The problem addressed by machining-planning research may be stated as follows. Given solid models of the desired part and the raw material, plus tolerancing, material and other ancillary specifications, generate automatically a plan for manufacturing the part, and actual instructions to drive NC machine tools and other manufacturing equipment. Automatic machining planning may be decomposed into the following subproblems or tasks, illustrated in Figure 1.

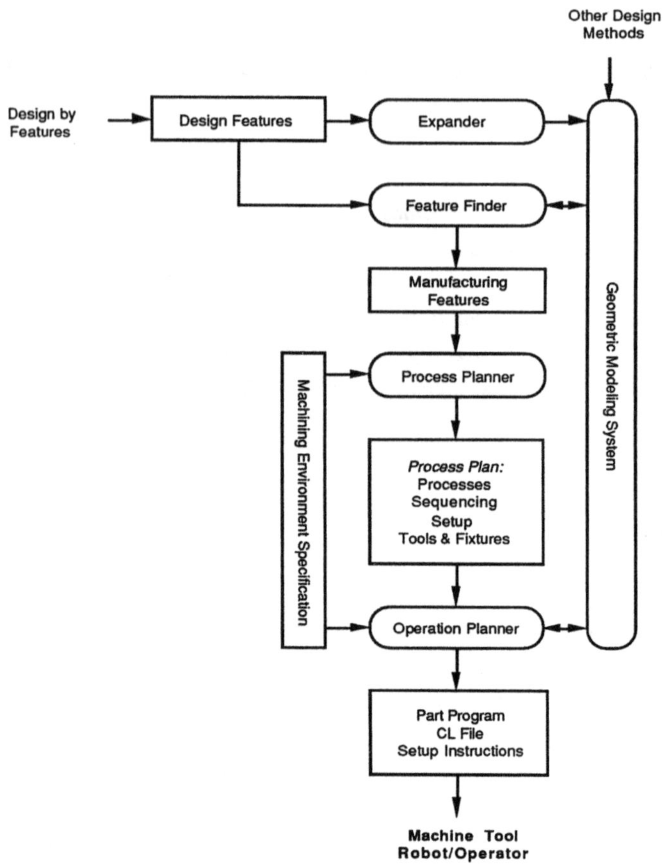

Figure 1 – Automatic Machining Planning

Recognition of machinable features such as holes, slots and pockets. For example, a planner must "know" that a certain surface or surfaces are associated with a hole feature, otherwise it will not be able to infer that a drilling and a reaming operation are needed. Although some feature information can be captured directly at the design stage, recognition is needed because manufacturing features differ from those used in design. For example, a web is a design feature that is machined indirectly, typically by removing pockets that share portions of their boundaries with the web. As shown in the figure, we favor systems in which design is accomplished through *design* features and perhaps other means, and the design data are used both to construct a geometric model of the part *and* to facilitate the operation of a feature recognizer. We defer discussion of OOFF, USC's feature finder, to the end of this section.

Process selection for each individual feature of a part. The RTCAPP planner developed at USC by Prof. Khoshnevis and his students provides an example of a state of the art system [Park 1990]. It is a rule-based expert system that manipulates "symbolic geometry", i.e., sets of geometric attributes and predicates. For example, a hole is represented by a data structure containing the feature type, plus attributes such as diameter and tolerances. A typical process selection rule stipulates that "if the size tolerance is less than a prescribed value *T* the hole must be drilled and then reamed". The process selection system does not perform geometric computations (e.g., intersections), and it does not even have a global model of the part and its environment. It assumes that all the necessary features and attributes have been pre-computed or are entered manually. Choice among competing alternative processes involves search, guided by cost considerations. On-going research by Dusan Sormaz at USC seeks to couple the process planner with OOFF, so as to use the geometric information produced by the feature recognizer to derive the attributes needed by the planner.

Process ordering. Selected processes must be partially ordered to reflect precedence relations. Process selection and ordering are closely related. Systems such as RTCAPP address both subproblems. Features contain predicates such as "intersects slot *S*", and sequencing rules stipulate, for example, that "if the depth of hole *H* is larger than a threshold *T*, and *H* intersects slot *S*, then *H* must precede *S*".

Setup planning, which involves the selection of part orientation and location with respect to machine tools, as well as the selection and placement of clamping devices and other fixtures. This is perhaps the least understood and most complex aspect of machining planning. We discuss setup planning for *inspection* (which is a related problem) in the next section, and address clamping in the section on Fixture Design and Assembly.

Cutter and machine selection. Process planning systems such as RTCAPP select tools by using rules and tables, using methods largely independent of solid modeling concepts.

The outcome of the tasks just described is usually called a *process plan*, which is a list (or perhaps a graph including precedence information) of machining and setup operations, plus associated resources such as tools and machines. Existent systems other than feature recognizers make essentially no use of solid modelers, and operate primarily on feature data and associated attributes. Whether this is desirable or not is unclear at present.

The process plan must be expanded, through *operation planning*, into executable instructions for machine tools and human operators. Operation planning consists of two main tasks.

Parameter and strategy selection. This involves the choice of parameters such as feeds, speeds, depth of cut, and so on, as well as strategies for plunging into the material and for cutting it. For example, one might decide to clear a pocket by using either a ziz-zag or a spiral cut. These parameters and strategies, together with geometric data about the features to be cut, constitute the information that must be passed to NC code generation modules. At USC we have an on-going project to automate the generation of such information, in collaboration with EDS/Unigraphics.

Cutter-path generation. This task produces the actual code for driving the NC machinery, and often involves expensive geometric computations. Traditional cutter-path generation, implemented in most of the current commercial CAD/CAM systems, is not based on solid models. It uses surface or wireframe models, is based on iterative surface-following methods or offset computations, and requires extensive user intervention. Feature-based machining systems were demonstrated in Chan's thesis at the University of Rochester, and are beginning to appear commercially. Such systems operate on solid models of features and parts, can ensure program correctness, and do not require user intervention. At USC we are attempting to couple our feature finder output, plus process information added by Sormaz' planner, and strategy and parameter data, to Unigraphics NC software.

Let us now focus on OOFF (Object-Oriented Feature Finder), which was developed by Jan Vandenbrande in his 1990 PhD thesis [Requicha & Vandenbrande 1989, Vandenbrande 1990, Vandenbrande & Requicha 1990, 1993]. The recognizer uses a rule-based approach for generating clues or hints about potential features from partial information gathered from several sources—nominal and toleranced geometry, attributes (e.g. threads), and functional features specified by a designer. (One could use most of the methods proposed in the extant feature recognition literature as additional hint generators.) Hint validity is assessed by using geometric tests based on criteria closely associated with machinability constraints such as accessibility and non-invasive machining. Complex interactions among features are accommodated because the search process does not rely on complete information, and missing portions of a feature are inferred by growing (or "completing") the feature volumetrically. This strategy is reminiscent of some computer vision systems, which also must deal with incomplete data, because of occlusion phenomena.

The "generate and test" cycle continues until the recognized features are sufficient to transform the raw material into the desired part. The final output of the feature finder is a decomposition of the volume to be removed into a set of volumetric (solid) features that correspond to manufacturing processes typically performed in 3-axis machining centers. Solid features are crucial for performing geometric tests, and should prove very useful to process planning systems for calculating intermediate workpieces, testing for potential collisions, determining feeds and speeds from the volumes to be removed, and so on. The features may overlap in common regions, which are classified as "optional", and alternative feature decompositions may be produced. Adjacent features with common properties are grouped together into composite features. Accessibility and adjacency information are provided to facilitate reasoning about precedences and process sequencing.

The feature recognizer is implemented in our AI/SM (Artificial Intelligence/Solid Modeling) test bed, which consists of the KnowledgeCraft (KC) AI environment, tightly coupled to the PADL-2 solid modeler. (Our latest version uses the Parasolid modeler instead of PADL-2.) In the current experimental implementation the boundary representations of the stock and the delta volume (which equals the difference between the stock and the desired part) are enhanced with adjacency links and other useful information, and converted into a frame-based structure in KC. This structure is processed by OPS-5 rules which fire when certain face patterns and geometric conditions are satisfied. Some of these conditions are checked by calls to the modeler. Most of the computation is associated with feature completion, growing and verification, which involve geometric tests performed by the modeler and additional processing in KC.

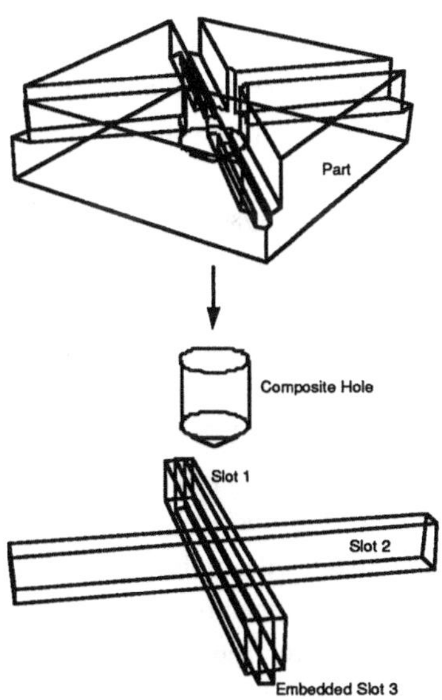

Figure 2 – Automaticaly-generated feature decomposition.

Figure 2 shows a feature decomposition for a deceptively simple object that involves complex interactions. (The figure was generated directly from the recognizer output; not shown are alternative interpretations of the slots as "open pockets", and slabs that correspond to face milling operations used to "square" the stock.) The decomposition consists of one composite hole (a cylindrical hole adjacent to a conical hole) and three slots. Slot 3 is embedded in Slot 1, both of which cross slot 2 and the composite hole. The features are extended towards the stock because of the feature completion process. For Slot 3 this is most noticeable because its volume extends upwards through Slot 1. The volume common with Slot 1 is considered "optional" because it can be removed by machining either Slot 3 or Slot 1. This extended volume implies that there is no strict ordering between Slot 3 and Slot 1 because both are accessible. It may not be as efficient to make Slot 3 before Slot 1, but both sequences produce correct results. The feature finder currently does not output precedence information, but a process planner should be able to reason about precedence from the volumes produced by the finder. For example, it should be possible to infer that the composite hole must be machined before the adjacent features by analyzing the interaction of the volumetric hole and slot features.

Dimensional Inspection

Dimensional inspection is a quality control task that consists of measuring a mechanical part so as to determine whether it meets its nominal and tolerancing specifications. Coordinate Measuring Machines (CMMs), which, in essence, are very accurate 3-D digitizers, are versatile and well suited for automated dimensional inspection.

We are developing an inspection system with the architecture shown in Figure 3. The input is a solid model of the part to be inspected, together with a set of surface features and associated tolerances. (A surface feature here is simply a set of "faces" of the part.) The high-level planner produces a partially-ordered collection of *setups*, and a partially-ordered set of *operations* for each setup. A setup is characterized by a fixed workpiece orientation with respect to a CMM, and by the associated fixtures and clamping equipment. An operation essentially consists of inspecting a surface feature, and has one or more generic probes and probe directions associated with it. The low-level, operation planner takes into consideration the available machines, probes and fixtures, determines appropriate sampling points to inspect each feature, and produces probe paths and specific part-positioning information. Probe paths are translated into actual commands for the CMM, and part positioning information is communicated to a human operator (or, eventually, to a robot). Measured points are interpreted by a soft gaging module, which determines if a part meets its tolerance spec. (Additional output information may also be useful to determine, for example, why a part is out of spec.)

We think that accessibility is a major concern in high-level planning for inspection. It strongly influences the part orientation in each setup, which features may be inspected in a setup, and the probe orientations. We developed an accessibility analysis module, whose underlying theory is based on semi-infinite line models for probes, and on the properties of *direction cones*, which represent the sets of accessible directions — see [Spyridi and Requicha 1990, 1991]. The algorithm may be summarized as follows. To compute the global accessibility cone (GAC) for a face of a solid, (i) sweep a shrunk version of the face over the boundary elements (faces, edges and vertices) of the solid, (ii) compute the "silhouette" or "shadow" of the sweep as seen from a reference point in the face, (iii) union all the cones that correspond to the silhouettes, and (iv) complement the result. To compute the sweeps, or Minkowski sums, it suffices to calculate the contributions from those solid's faces, edges and vertices whose normal vectors (Gaussian images) overlap those of the face (plus its bounding edges and vertices) being considered. Importantly, all of the required sweeps can be computed in the plane and produce polygons, rather than 3-D sets.

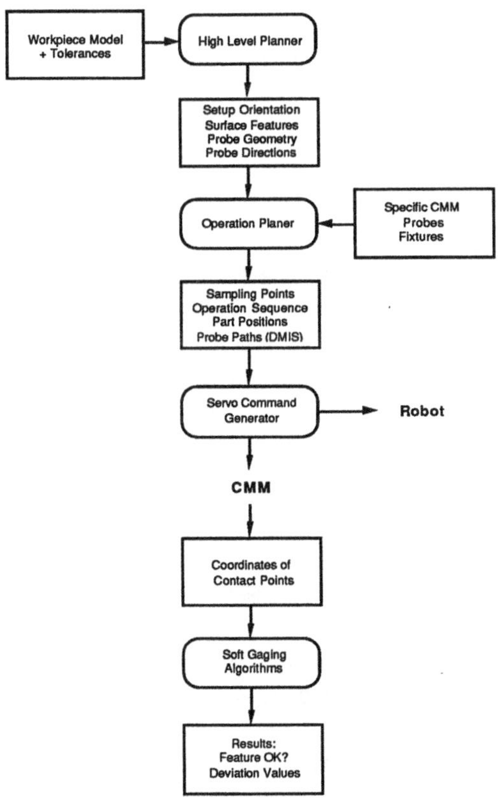

Figure 3 – CMM Inspection

When the intersection of the GACs of all the features is non-empty, any direction within the intersection cone may be used to inspect all the features. Usually, however, the intersection is empty, and one must arrange the cones into *clusters*, so that the cones in each cluster have a non-empty intersection. A minimal number of clusters is desirable, to ensure that a small number of probes and setups are used.

Our current work is centered on the design of the high-level planner. Our approach casts the planning problem as search in a space of partially-completed plans. Plans evolve towards completion through the effects of operators that map plans into plans. The state is represented by sets of 4-tuples (SF, PG, PD, SU), where SF is a (possibly compound) surface feature to be inspected, PG are the acceptable probe geometries (selected from a given set of physical probes), PD are the accessible directions represented by cones, and SU are the setup orientations. We follow a least-commitment strategy, and attempt to reason about all the possible solutions, gradually narrowing their range by applying constraints such as accessibility, same-setup (for related features), and so on. Results will be reported in a forthcoming PhD thesis by Tonia Spyridi.

Fixture Design and Assembly

Setup and fixturing are amongst the least automated of all the production activities for mechanical components and assemblies, and yet they contribute significantly to overall factors such as cost and lead time. We have just been awarded a NSF Strategic Manufacturing Initiative grant to study fixturing. This is a collaborative project whose principal investigators are Ari Requicha, George Bekey and Ken Goldberg of USC/IRIS and Lucy King of the GMI Management and Enginering Institute, and involves the Rocketdyne Division of Rockwell International as industrial partner. No results are available yet. The following is a description of what we intend to do.

Mechanical parts must be fixtured by using clamps and other devices to ensure that part poses (positions and orientations) do not change while manufacturing, assembly, and inspection operations take place. The fixtures depend on the specific operations or *tasks* to be performed. For example, a machining fixture must resist the cutting forces, and must ensure that the volumes to be removed are accessible to the cutting tools. Thus, the input to the proposed fixturing design and assembly system includes solid models for the parts to be fixtured, plus a description of the task or tasks to be performed while the parts are attached to the fixture. Part models must contain tolerances, surface finishes, and other ancillary information required for fixturing. Tasks will be expressed in a *task-description language*, which is likely to be based on *geometric features* such as solids, surfaces and curves.

We decompose the fixturing design and assembly process as shown in Figure 4. A *fixture specification generator* reasons about the input data so as to produce an abstraction or high-level, functional description of the fixture. We call such an abstraction a *fixture specification*. We envision fixture specifications that contain information on the relative orientation between part and fixture, estimates of the forces and torques to be applied to the part by the fixture, surfaces available for clamping, surfaces that must be kept clear, and so on. Fixture specification generation involves accessibility analysis, recognition of fixturing features, tolerance analysis, and perhaps other activities not yet identified.

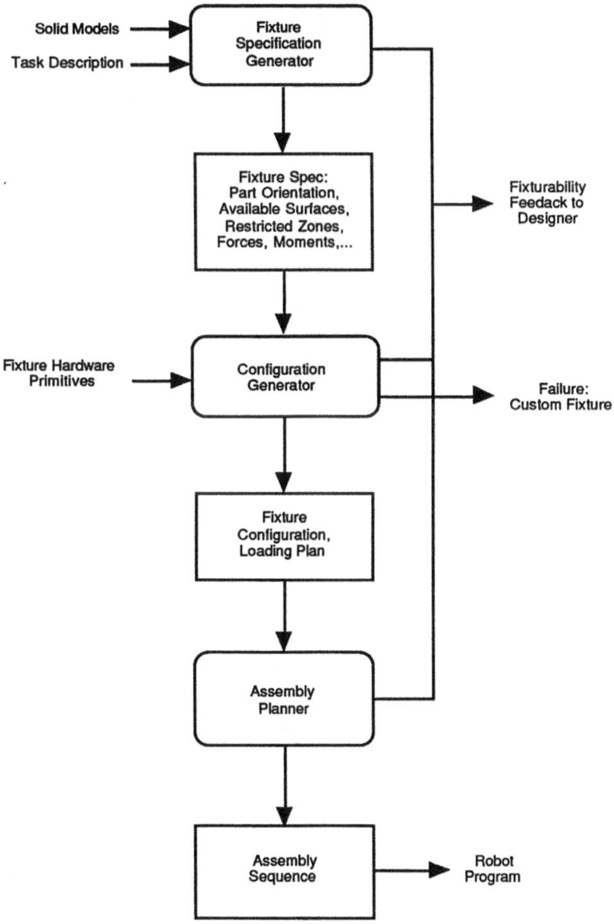

Figure 4 – Fixture design and assembly process

The *fixture configuration generator* produces (a representation for) a set of suitably positioned devices that constitutes an embodiment, or physical realization, of the abstract fixture specification. The devices are selected from a finite list of modular fixturing components, or *hardware primitives*. Here we perform a kinematic analysis of form and force closure, consider the problem of loading the part into the fixture, and use cost/performance criteria such as minimal number of modular components. We also attempt to ensure that the fixture configuration is *foolproof*, i.e., that the part can only be loaded in the fixture in a unique pose. This facilitates correct loading, whether done by humans or robots.

If the generator cannot synthesize an acceptable fixture configuration, it exits with a failure message, and a custom fixture must be designed manually. Failures may stem from the non-existence of solutions (e.g., because of a lack of suitable hardware primitives), or (infrequently, we hope) from the generator's own reasoning limitations.

Finally, the *assembly planner* finds a sequence of operations for assembling the chosen fixture configuration. The operations can either be executed by humans, or converted into programs for robots.

Each step of the process—specification generation, configuration generation, or assembly planning—may produce feedback information for the part designer. The feedback reflects the *fixturability* of the part. It can range from a simple estimate of how difficult or costly the fixture is, to elaborate advice on how to modify the part so as to improve its fixturability. This feedback is important in a concurrent engineering scenario, in which a part designer seeks advice from a fixturing expert—in our case, an automaton.

The ability to learn from previous experience and to re-use proven fixture designs should significantly enhance the efficiency of a fixture design system, and also lead to higher-quality designs. A previous design must be augmented with information on intent and rationale, so that it can be retrieved and modified in situations for which the design is relevant. Describing function, behavior, intent, or rationale of mechanical products is a wide open and difficult research area. We think that fixture design may provide a relatively simple instance of the more general problem of automatic design, and that there are good chances to make progress in such a restricted domain. Successful fixturings will be encoded and stored so as to allow case-based reasoning in the evaluation of new fixturing requirements. Reasoning about shape and function will generate information on design modifications necessary to achieve the new requirements. A system can either attempt to carry out these modifications automatically, or can provide them as re-design advice to a designer.

Summary and Conclusions

Total automation of a wide range of design and manufacturing activities has proven more difficult than expected in the pioneering times of solid modeling. Analytical applications have been tackled successfully but applications that involve synthesis or planning have progressed slowly.

This paper describes recent research on spatial planning for machining, inspection and fixturing. The key characteristic of this work is the use of a hybrid approach that brings together concepts and techniques from computational geometry and artificial intelligence. Three planners under development at USC are discussed. One extracts features from a solid model of a part and plans the removal of the associated volumes. Another produces a high-level plan for for the dimensional inspection of a part with a coordinate measuring machine. It selects part and probe orientations, and plans measurement operations for each setup. The last has just begun to be developed, and is intended to produce designs for fixtures, and assembly plans for constructing them from modular components.

One thing we have learned from our research of the past few years is that spatial reasoning is hard! Solid modeling is but one of the technologies needed to fully automate design and production activities. It is especially relevant to issues of collisions, gouging, precedence, accessibility, and in-process workpiece modeling. In addition to the usual Boolean operations, computational support is needed for Minkowski operations and other configuration-space manipulations. Geometric information also is important for other tasks such as cutter path generation for numerically controlled machining, but surface or wireframe models often suffice, once accessibility has been established through analysis based on solids. Non-geometric information, for example on material and available resources, also plays a crucial role.

Acknowledgements

The research reported in this paper was supported in part by the National Science Foundation under grants DMC-87-96192, DDM-87-15404, CDR-87-17322, DDM-92-14996 and DDM-92-15362, by the industrial members of the Institute for Manufacturing and Automation Research (IMAR), and by the Industrial Associates of the Programmable Automation Laboratory, Institute for Robotics and Intelligent Systems (IRIS) of the University of Southern California.

References

Park, J. Y. (1990). "Incremental process planning as a support tool for economic product design", Ph.D. Dissertation, Industrial and Systems Engineering Department, University of Southern California, June.

Requicha, A. A. G. and Vandenbrande, J. H. (1989). "Form features for mechanical design and manufacturing", *Proc. ASME Int'l Computers in Engineering Conf.*, Anaheim, CA, pp. 47-52, July 30-August 3.

Spyridi, A. J. and Requicha, A. A. G. (1990). "Accessibility analysis for the automatic inspection of mechanical parts by coordinate measuring machines", *Proc. IEEE Int'l Conf. on Robotics & Automation*, Cincinnati, OH, pp. 1284-1289, May 13 - 18.

Spyridi, A. J. and Requicha, A. A. G. (1991)."Accessibility analysis for polyhedral objects", in S. G. Tzafestas, Ed., *Engineering Systems with Intelligence: Concepts, Tools and Applications*. Dordrecht, Holland: Kluwer Academic Publishers, Inc., pp. 317-324.

Vandenbrande, J. H. (1990). "Automatic recognition of machinable features in solid models", Ph. D. Dissertation, Electrical Engineering Department, University of Rochester, May. (Available also from University Microfilms, and as IRIS Rept. No. 260, Institute for Robotics and Intelligent Systems, University of Southern California.)

Vandenbrande, J. H. and Requicha, A. A. G. (1990). "Spatial reasoning for automatic recognition of interacting form features", *Proc. ASME Int'l Computers in Engineering Conf.*, Boston, MA, Vol. 1, pp. 251-256, August 5-9.

Vandenbrande, J. H. and Requicha, A. A. G. (1993). "Spatial reasoning for the automatic recognition of machinable features in solid models", *IEEE Trans. Pattern Analysis & Machine Intelligence*, in press.

Integration of Design by Features and Feature Recognition approaches through a Unified Model

T. De Martino B. Falcidieno* F. Giannini**
S. Haßinger° and J. Ovtcharova°

** Istituto per la Matematica Applicata, C.N.R.*
Via De Marini 6, 16149 Genova, Italy
° Fraunhofer Institut für Graphische Datenverabeitung
Wilhelminenstraße 7, 6100 Darmstadt, Germany

Abstract

Features are real existing constituencies of product parts that associate engineering significance with shapes. A feature-based representation of product models is an essential prerequisite to the development of a new generation of Computer Aided Design systems.

In this paper, we propose a system architecture for feature-based modeling which is founded on the integration of two approaches: feature extraction from existing solid models and design-by-features. This integration is obtained through the definition of a common feature library and a Unified Model, which plays the role of communication link between the geometric model and the feature-based model. This system should enable the user to mix the two modes of definition allowing him to design an object directly with features or to start with a geometric model and to extract a feature model from it.

1 Introduction

The current state of Computer-Aided Design (CAD) can be identified as a transition state from traditional geometry-based design systems to Computer-Aided Engineering (CAE) systems in which pure geometric information is not the only basis of the entire design enterprise. For instance, the design of complex mechanisms requires information on material properties, cinematic joints, neighbour relationships and functional conditions in addition to shape properties.

Future CAD systems, therefore, must be equipped with facilities expressive enough to incorporate various kinds of information, beside geometric information. Thus, comprehensive models, called *product models* are being widely investigated as a uniform modeling basis for CAD [Wilson 1990] [ISO 1992]. Activities of the product modeling process are concerned with representing and supporting all information about the product in a way that allows to capture the whole design, analysis, manufacture, test, inspection and maintenance sequence, with no loss of information at any stage.

Recently, features have been discussed in the engineering community as the elements which provide a convenient language for modeling product parts in order to include non geometric information. Feature-based models allow each application to have its own view of the product.

Two distinct approaches have been considered by researchers to incorporate features into a part model, namely *design-by-features* and *feature extraction* from geometric models.

The purpose of this paper is to outline a system architecture for feature-based modeling which integrates these two strategies. This system should enable the user to design a part using features, or to start with a geometric model and create a feature-based model from it. Also, it should allow the user to mix the two modes of definition and to extend the feature library. To this end, we propose a unified feature-oriented model as communication link between design-by-features and feature recognition, together with some mechanisms to map a geometric model into the unified model, and from this intermediate representation to a context-dependent feature-based model and viceversa.

2 Generation of Feature Information

Features are high-level semantic data which provide a concise description of the part characteristics. Since there is no real consensus in the definition of what a feature is, an attempt to unify them leads to the following definition: *features are real existing elements constituting parts that associate engineering significance with shapes* [CAM-I 1988].

The main advantages of features include, *firstly* a vocabulary which is more natural for expressing the product part than geometric models; *secondly* the possibility of using features as a basis for modeling product information in different phases and *thirdly* an increase in the designer's productivity and cost effectiveness.

A feature based model can be created by following two different approaches: *design-by-features* and *feature extraction*.

Using the first strategy, the feature-based model is created during the design stage, when features are used as primitives constituting the object. The main advantage of this approach is the possibility of building the model immediately including the information available to the designer. On the other hand, the problem with design-by-features systems is that the user needs definitions of features prior to design which are oriented to specific applications. In this way, the set of features used in design is limited. Moreover, the resulting feature-based model is strictly context-dependent and it cannot be shared between different application viewpoints [Cunningham Dixon 1988], [Shah Rogers 1988].

In feature recognition, features are extracted from the geometric model of the part. In this way no restrictions are imposed to the designer who defines the object shape by using geometric primitives. This approach can be adapted to different application contexts, but here the key problem is that it is possible to recognize only what is already implicitly stored in the database, since features are extracted after the completion of design [Falcidieno Giannini 1989], [Requicha Vandenbrande 1989], [Sakuray Gossard 1990], [Joshi 1990].

As a consequence, both design-by-features and feature recognition approaches are inadequate when performed alone or strictly in sequence. Thus, the solution to efficient feature-based modeling seems to be a combination of both.

Some attempts in this direction have been already proposed [Sreevalson 1990], [Dixon, Libardi 1990], [Falcidieno, Giannini, Porzia, Spagnuolo 1992], [Lakko, Mäntylä 1992].

A feature modeler joining recognition and design approaches would combine the positive aspects of both methods. A system based on an integrated approach should give the possibility of generating features during design evolution, creating application specific feature taxonomies and mapping feature sets between different application contexts, so that the user can design part of the model directly with features and part of it with the underlying solid modeler.

Let us give an example. Suppose we want to define a simple part like the object in figure 1a. How this part is modeled in terms of features varies from one context to another. For example, it can be interpreted as having a slot, a step and an array pattern of four through-holes, or two ribs and the same pattern of holes (see figures 1b and 1c).

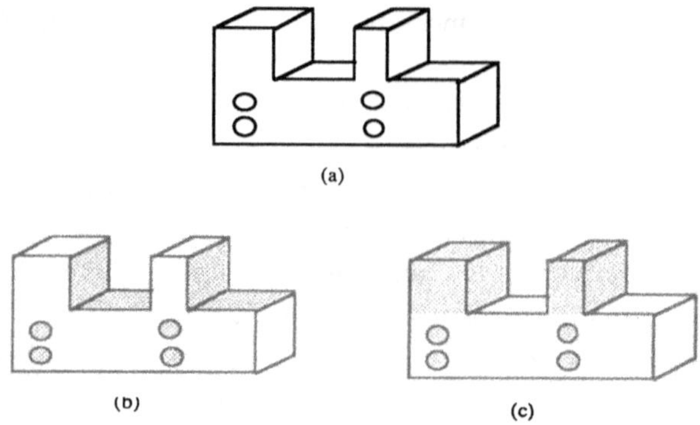

Figure 1 : A simple part (*a*) and two different interpretations (*b* and *c*)

If the part is modeled with features the application context must be *a priori* chosen, thus using the array pattern of through-holes and either the slot and the step features (see figure 2 a), or the two ribs (see figure 2 b).

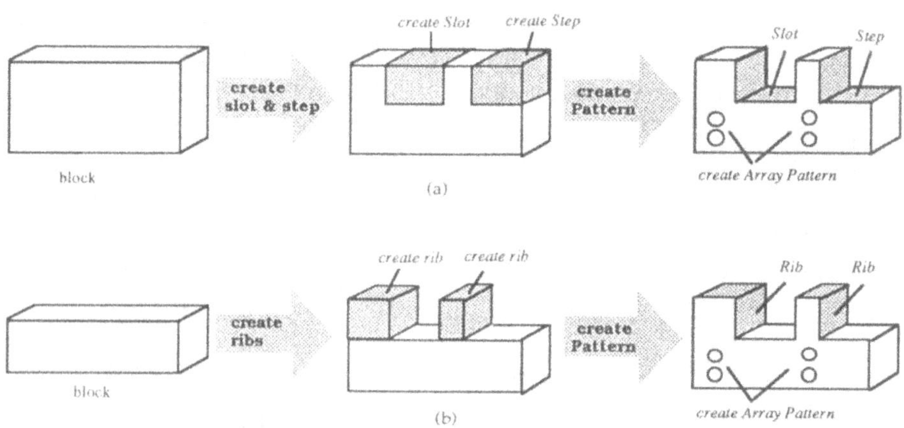

Figure 2: The part of figure 1 designed by features in two different ways

On the other hand, if a recognition approach is adopted, the decision on the application context may be postponed and it is possible to recognize both the two ribs and the step and the slot, by using different sets of rules.
More difficulties may arise in the identification of the compound feature "array pattern of four through holes" that was already known to the designer.
In this case, a more efficient solution seems to be a mixed approach which allows the designer to create the model of the object partly with the underlying solid modeler and partly with a design-by-features approach. In figure 3 the object of figure 1 is built by using both a sweeping function of the solid modeler and the "make pattern" function of the design-by-features system. Successively, and

according to the specific task, the model can be interpreted, as depicted in figures 1b or 1c.

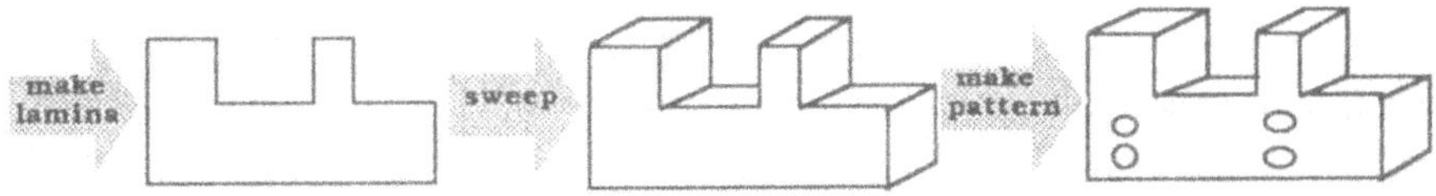

Figure 3: The part of figure 1 defined by using a mixed approach

3 Various Levels of Modeling in Integrated Systems

One of the main difficulties in integrating design-by-features and feature recognition is that in the first approach the user creates context-dependent representations specific and rich enough to meet the requirements of a given application, while in the second one the user builds the geometric model of a part which is successively extended to a feature-based model through a recognition process. The information content of the two representations is different since, in its broadest sense, a feature-based model not only encapsulates information about geometric form, but also about engineering meaning and function. As figure 4 shows, the geometric model is only the kernel of the product model and, in particular, of all the possible feature-based models created for every application context.

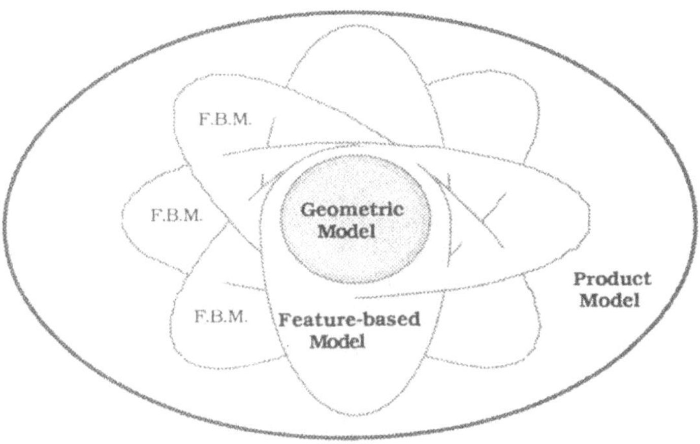

Figure 4: The increasing information content in the various representations

From a theoretical and algorithmic point of view there is no problem in deriving a geometric representation from the higher level model, since each feature is

associated with a solid model defined in terms of dimensional parameters. What is more difficult is the inverse transformation: to map a geometric model into a feature-based representation. To go towards this direction requires the modeling of the perception, understanding and synthesis performed by the expert. The problem here is not only modeling parts, but also modeling their context of use.
Thus, for integrating a design-by-features system with an automatic recognition system, both the representation model of the object and the description of the context must be consistent.
The solution seems to be the definition of an intermediate representation, which should be an explicit evaluated model containing all the geometric and topological information about features which can be derived from a feature-based model or can be extracted by interactive or automatic recognition.
In our integrated system, this intermediate model is called Unified Model and plays the role of communication link between the geometric model and the feature-based model (see figure 5). The Unified Model is considered the framework of the feature-based model, expressly built to hold additional information which describes the context of application.

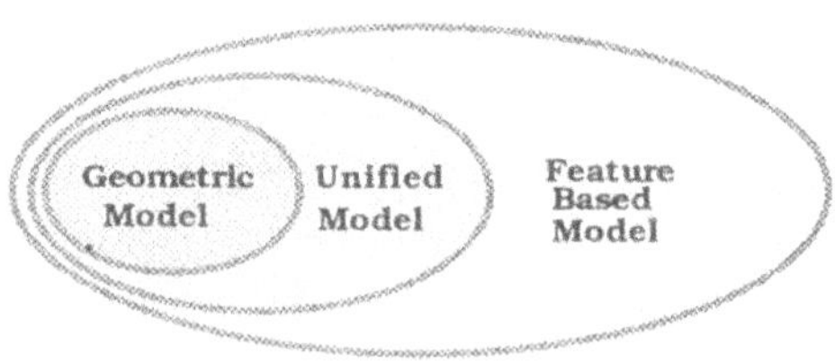

Figure 5: The Unified Model as an intermediate representation between the Geometric Model and the Feature-based Model

The Unified Model, though feature oriented, is still a geometric model, which benefits from the use of representations having a hybrid nature rather than traditional solid models (B-rep or CSG).
At present the Unified Model is expressed as a hierarchical graph where each node corresponds to a shape feature volume represented in a boundary form and the arcs represent connections between volumes expressed by their common boundary elements, i.e. overlapping faces. Every non root component represents a shape feature of the object. More details on it can be found in [Falcidieno, Giannini 1989].
A qualifying aspect of the Unified Model is its dynamic structure which can be updated through two different mechanisms: simplification and subdivision. By simplification we can merge some components, thus reducing the complexity of

the representation, while subdivision is the dual operation. Figure 6 shows how these operations can act on the feature graph. The object depicted in figure 6(a) could be represented like in figure 6(b) as the result of a design process, then the representation can be adapted either for an assembly task by a simplification operation on the graph, see figure 6(c), or for a manufacturing application by applying successively a subdivision operation, as figure 6(d) shows.

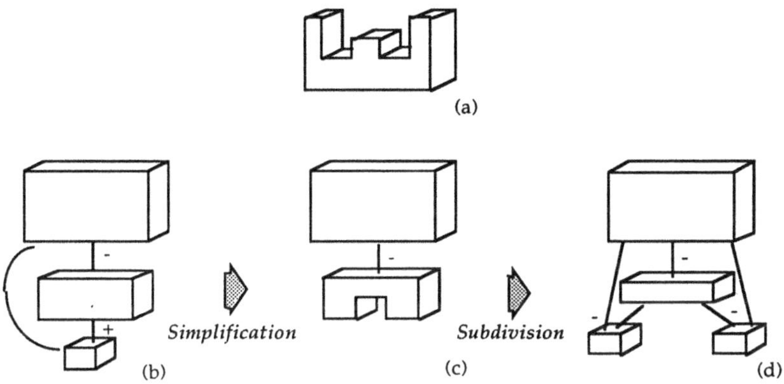

Figure 6: Updating the feature graph through simplification and subdivision operations

4 The System Architecture

To make the definition of design features compatible with the feature description in the recognition system, the user should be allowed to define a library where every feature has to be formalized and archived in a way consistent with both processes. Also the geometric model and the feature based descriptions of the parts should be strictly correlated and manipulated.

Based on these two main requirements, an ideal architecture like that in figure 7, could be devised. Here the user interacts with the system in three ways: through the Feature Editor, the Feature Modeler and the Solid Modeler.

The user can create the solid model of an object through the Geometric Modeler or he can design the object parts directly by features using the Feature Modeler. The Feature Library is created through the Feature Editor by specifying a set of parameters for pre-defined features, or by using the Geometric Modeler depending on the feature shape complexity.

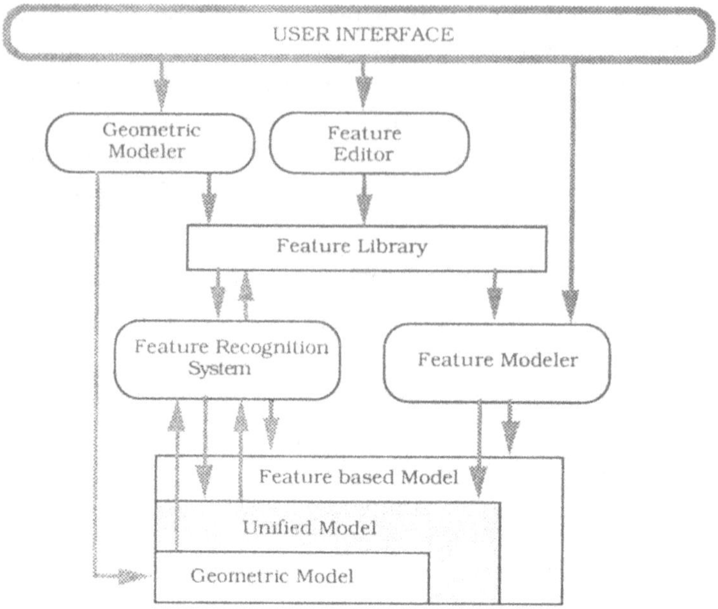

Figure 7: The proposed system architecture

In this architecture, the keys for the integration between design-by-features and automatic recognition are the Unified Model and the common feature library. If the user creates the solid model of the part, this model is automatically converted into the Unified Model through the recognition mechanism and then transformed into a feature-based model by using a data-driven mechanism which interprets the model for a specific application context. If the user directly creates the model by features, the set of data defined within the feature model is linked to the elements of the solid model via the Unified Model.

The mapping of feature-based models between different application contexts is performed by the recognition module which makes use of context-dependent feature libraries, and works on the Unified Model of the part.

At present, prototypes of some parts of this architecture exist: a parametric feature modeler [Ovtcharova, Haßinger 1991], an automatic recognition module from a geometric model (B-rep) to the Unified Model [Falcidieno Giannini 1989] and a mechanism allowing users to define their own feature library to convert the Unified Model into a feature-based model [De Martino Falcidieno Giannini 1991].

4.1 The Feature Library

The feature library is primarily used to store the description of design features. Here, two types of features are distinguished: (1) pre-defined features which are always available and define the fixed part of the library, and (2) user-defined features which complete the previous set and allow a dynamic management of the library.

The set of pre-defined features consists of standard design features, such as cylindrical holes, rectangular pockets, simple slots. Each pre-defined feature is implicitly described by a set of parameters and the user can model the part by instancing features from the library. The feature description includes a name, an identifier, the type of the corresponding form feature (depression, protrusion), the type of representation (explicit or implicit), a list of parameters and some constraints on these parameters, a set of attributes which are application dependent and a set of procedures which are necessary for creating and manipulating the feature.

In figure 8 an example of a pre-defined cylindrical hole is shown. In order to define an instance of such hole from the library the user has to call the procedure create_cylindrical_hole() specifying a value for each parameter. Then the system automatically updates the Unified Model, inserting the defined feature in the graph structure. Transformations and modifications of the feature model can be provided by the procedure manipulate_cylindrical_hole(), while the consistency checking is performed by the procedure validate_cylindrical_hole().

If the set of pre-defined features is not sufficient, the designer can specify his own set of features, which will be included in the feature library.

User-defined features can be created by means of the feature modeler or of the solid modeler, depending on their geometric complexity. The feature modeler can be used when it is possible to describe a design feature as composition of pre-defined features. The stepped hole described in figure 9 is an example of feature defined by the user through standard design features.

If the description of a feature as composition of standard features is too complex or impossible to be defined, the user can create his own features by means of the solid modeler. He has to define the feature volume which affects the main shape of the object. The shape feature is then explicitly represented by the geometric model in the library but the information describing this type of feature is not complete as for pre-defined features: implicit representations are not considered and manipulations cannot be provided. The user can only associate a name and a set of technological attributes to the part.

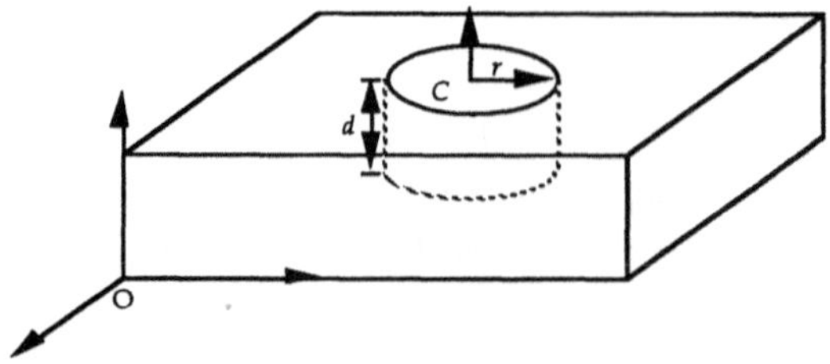

TYPE:	*cylindrical_hole*
IDENTIFIER:	0001
FORM FEATURE TYPE:	*depression*
REPRESENTATION TYPE:	*implicit*
PARAMETERS:	*r, d* /* *radius, depth* */
CONSTRAINTS:	*r, d > 0*
POSITION:	*location (point C) and orientation (normal and reference directions)*
ATTRIBUTES:	*surface finish*
PROCEDURES:	*create_cylindrical_hole()* *manipulate_cylindrical_hole()*
	delete_cylindrical_hole() *validate_cylindrical_hole ()*

Figure 8: An example of pre-defined features: a cylindrical hole

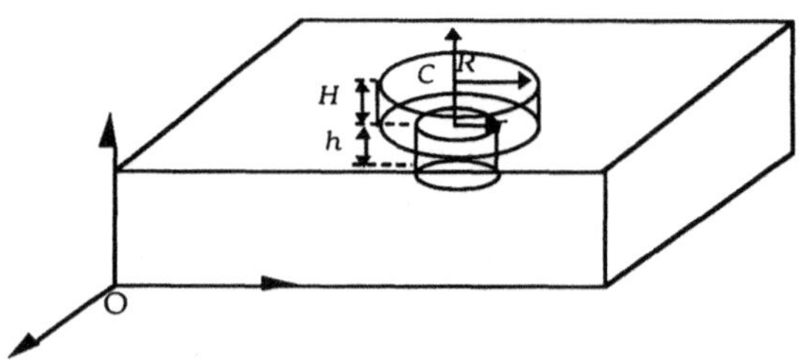

TYPE:	*stepped_hole*
IDENTIFIER:	0011
FORM FEATURE TYPE:	*depression*
REPRESENTATION TYPE:	*implicit*
PARAMETERS:	*r, h* /* *first hole radius and depth* */
	R, H /* *second hole radius and depth* */
CONSTRAINTS:	*r, R, h, H > 0; r=2R; h=H*
POSITION:	*location (point C) and orientation (normal and reference directions)*
ATTRIBUTES:	*surface finish*
PROCEDURES:	*create_stepped_hole()* *manipulate_stepped_hole()*
	delete_stepped_hole() *validate_stepped_hole ()*

Figure 9: A stepped hole defined as composition of two cylindrical pre-defined holes

Figure 10 shows an example of a feature defined by the user through the solid modeler, and the corresponding description stored in the library.

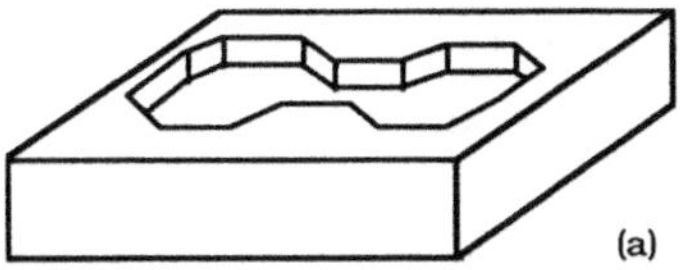

(a)

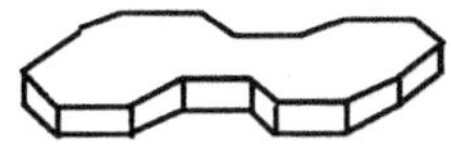

(b)

TYPE:	*pocket*
IDENTIFIER:	0111
FORM FEATURE TYPE:	*depression*
REPRESENTATION TYPE:	*explicit*
PARAMETERS:	*NULL*
CONSTRAINTS:	*NULL*
POSITION:	*location (point C) and orientation (normal and reference directions)*
ATTRIBUTES:	*surface finish, ...*
PROCEDURES:	*create_feature()* *delete_feature()*

Figure 10: The complex shaped pocket in (a) as an example of feature defined by the user through the solid modeler (b) and its representation in the library

4.2 The Design by Features System

The design-by-features system allows the user to design a product part directly with features. The two main modes in which the system operates are: creating and manipulating instances of predefined features from the library and updating the library with user-defined features which are mostly application specific [Ovtcharova Haßinger 1991].

The design-by-features system follows the top-down and bottom-up approach of design using a hierarchical data scheme, which makes it possible to trace from design features specification (application-oriented) to form features definition (generic) and their representation and geometric evaluation [Ovtcharova 1992], [Ovtcharova Pahl Rix 1992].

The central idea is that the design features defined on the top level and instanced from the feature library are used to model a product part in a concrete application context. Their description derives specific meaning from the view of the function of the product part, including shape data as well as non-shape data.

At the second level, the shapes of design features are usually expressed by form features defined in parametric way. The parametric definition is provided in terms of positive feature volumes (protrusion, connection) and negative feature volumes (depression, passage) which are specified by a cross section. The cross sections can be pre-defined such as circular, rectangular, racetrack, or used-defined cross section, stored in the feature library.
At the third level, form features are represented in two main forms: implicit and explicit. The implicit representation (for example, by sweeping) can be considered as consistent, but not detailed. For example, a racetrack depression might be represented by giving the width and length parameters of the racetrack sweep profile, as well as the sweep depth, rather than a racetrack surface. The explicit representation allows referencing of feature constituencies. If feature parameters, such as depth, are needed, however, they must be derived.
Feature representations are typically used in association with geometric models. At the fourth level, form features are geometrically evaluated using the solid modeler. The feature data at different levels are linked by mapping in top-down and bottom-up fashion, such as "have as shapes" and "are shapes of", or "are represented by" and "are representations of".
As a consequence, in the design system, features are always represented by explicit detailed descriptions which are associated with implicit and concise descriptions through a set of parameters. Two descriptions of each design feature are considered: an ideal version which is of the implicit type and is associated with a canonical feature volume, and the real version which explicitly describes the real feature volume in boundary form. The real volume is obtained taking into account any interaction of the ideal feature with the main part or with the other interacting features. An example may help to clarify the feature volume creation. Figure 11 shows the generation of a rectangular slot on a prismatic object. In figure 11(a) the canonical feature volume is depicted while in figure 11(b) its real volume is represented.

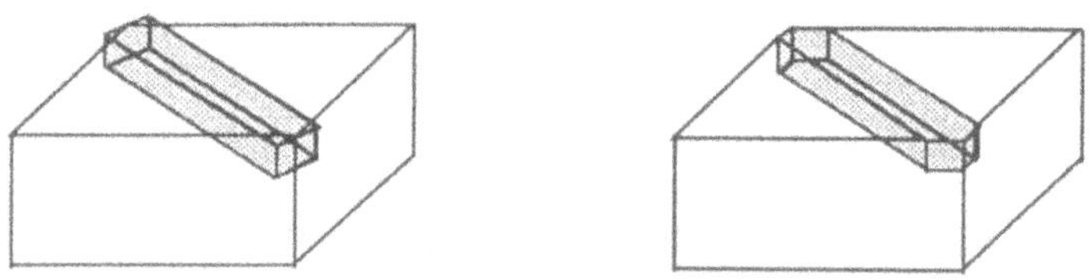

(a) (b)

Figure 11: (a) The ideal volume associated to a slot feature and (b) its real representation

4.3 The Feature Recognition System

In the design by features approach the description of the object is connected to the application context. In the recognition approach the shape model of the object and the description of the context are not related. Thus the problem to solve is their correlation in a consistent way. To do this the recognition module is structured in two parts: the Shape Feature recognizer which converts the object geometric model into the Unified Model, and the Shape Feature Interpreter, which maps the Unified Model into a specific context. How these two modules act on the data is shown in figure 12.

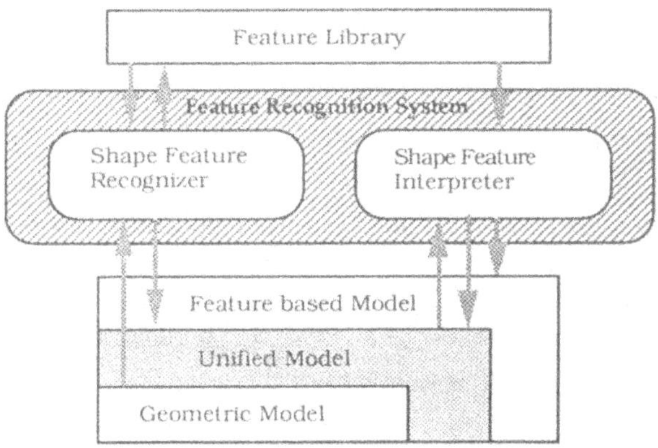

Figure 12: The Feature Recognition System

The Shape Feature Recognizer is based on context independent rules which identify shape features by analyzing adjacencies between faces in the boundary representation and classify them as *Protrusions* or *Depressions*.
The set of faces recognized as protrusions and depressions are then completed in order to obtain the corresponding positive and negative volumes by using the solid modeler. Eventually, these volumes are organized in the Unified Model. Details on this module are described in [Falcidieno, Giannini 1989].
Shape features, recognized and extracted by this set of rules, independent of the context, not always meets the specific requirements of the application. Then, the Shape Feature Interpreter performs the necessary transformations on the Unified Model, applying context dependent rules. These rules are not expressed as code inside the system, but given by the user through a "teaching by example" technique [De Martino, Falcidieno, Giannini 1991]: the user shows an example of

a specific feature to the system, thus creating the link to the application. In this way the user can specify which features have to be represented in the model, and how to represent them.

Once the user has indicated the feature example, which can be selected from the feature library or created through the available solid modeler, the system automatically extracts the feature graph of the example and analyzes the object model searching for subgraphs which could correspond to instances of the feature examples. Then, the user specifies the kind of operation to perform on each recognized subgraph.

Consequently, the geometric description satisfies the application requirements and the Unified Model is ready to be completed with application specific information in order to become a Feature Based Model.

5 Summary and Conclusions

In this paper we have discussed the need of feature-based modelers as a prerequisite to more complete product modeling systems. Such systems need to be able to support different points of view, and this can only be provided by feature-based representations.

A system architecture for integrating design-by-features and automatic recognition has been proposed. This integrated approach to feature-based modeling seems to be an ideal way to give the user the possibility of directly dealing with features, storing them in the data base and relating them to a variety of engineering applications. It can be successively used for concurrent engineering activities and computer integrated manufacturing applications where downstream activities are performed simultaneously, not sequentially.

One key to such a flexible system seems to be the development of more intertwined data structures which associate the geometric model of a part with its feature-based description.

Another key is related to the possibility for users to define their own features and to support the necessary procedures to convert these descriptions into the different contexts.

At present the proposed architecture has not yet been fully tested and the integration between design-by-features and feature recognition is performed conceptually through the definition of a common Unified Model.

References

CAM-I (1988) Shah, J., Streevalsan, P., Rogers, M., Billo, R., Mathew, A.*Current Status of Feature Technology,* Technical Report, R-88-GM-04, August

Cunningham, J.J., Dixon, J.R. (1988), *Designing with Features: The Origin of Features,* in: ASME Computers in Engineering Conference, San Francisco, July/August, pp. 237-243.

De Martino, T., Falcidieno, B., Giannini, F. (1991) *Feature-based Model transformations between different Application Contexts,* Proceedings of Computer Applications in Production and Engineering: Integration Aspects, CAPE'91, Bordeaux, France, 10-12 September, pp. 361-368

Dixon, JR., Libardi, EC. (1990) *Unresolved Research Issues in Development of Design with Features Systems,* in: Geometric Modeling for Product Engineering, North Holland, IFIP1990, pp. 183-196

Falcidieno, B., Giannini, F. (1989) *Automatic Recognition and Representation of Shape-based Features in Geometric Modeling System,* Computer Vision, Graphics and Image Processing 48: pp. 93-123

Falcidieno, B., Giannini, F., Porzia, C., Spagnuolo, M. (1992) *A Uniform approach to represent features in different application contexts,* Computers in Industry 19: pp. 175-184

ISO (1992) Industrial Automation Systems, Product Data Representation and Exchange - Part 48: Integrated Generic Resources: Form Features, Working Draft, ISO TC 184/SC4 WG3 N102 (P5), January 2

Joshi, S. (1990) *Feature recognition and geometric reasoning for some process planning activities,* Geometric Modeling for Product Engineering, M.J.Wozny, J. Turner, K. Preiss Editors 1990 (IFIP '88), pp. 363-383

Lakko, T., Mäntylä, M. (1992) *Feature-based Modelling of Families of Machined Parts,* In: Proceedings of the IFIP TC5/WG5.3 Eighth International PROLAMAT Conference, Man in CIM, Tokyo, 24-26 June, pp. 351-360

Ovtcharova, J., Haßinger, S. (1991) *Feature-Based Reasoning in Product Modeling,* in: Proceedings of the Fourth International IFIP TC5 Conference on Computer Applications in Production and Engineering, Integration Aspects, CAPE'91, Bordeaux, France, 10-12 September, pp.379-387.

Ovtcharova, J., Pahl, G., Rix, J. (1992) *Towards a Feature Classification Schema and Concept for Feature-Based Modeling,* Computers & Graphics, Vol.16, N.2: pp. 187-195.

Ovtcharova, J. (1992) *A Hierarchical Data Schema for Feature-Based Design Support* , in VDI Berichte Nr.993.3, 1992, pp. 33-47

Requicha, A.A.G., Vandenbrande, J.H. (1989) *Features for Mechanical design and Manufacturing* Computer and Engineering, Book n.G0502A: pp.376-381

Sakuray, H., Gossard, D.C. (1990) *Recognizing Shape Features in Solid Models,* IEEE Computer Graphics & Applications, sept. pp. 22-32

Shah, J., Rogers, M.T. (1988) *Functional Requirements and Conceptual Design of the Feature-Based Modeling System,* Computer-Aided Engineering Journal, February, pp. 9-15

Sreevalson, P.C. (1990) *An Investigation into the unification of form feature definition methods,* Master Thesis, Arizona State University

Wilson, P.R. (1990) *Feature Modeling Overview,* SIGGRAPH'90, Course Notes 12, Dallas, August 6-10, pp. XII.1-XII.56

Chapter 9

Modeling for Rendering Complex Objects

Modeling in Volume Graphics

Arie Kaufman[*], *Roni Yagel*[**], *and Daniel Cohen*[***]

[*]*Department of Computer Science*
State University of New York at Stony Brook, Stony Brook, NY 11794-4400, USA

[**]*Department of Computer and Information Science*
The Ohio State University, Columbus, OH 43210-1277, USA

[***]*Department of Mathematics and Computer Science*
Ben Gurion University, Beer-Sheva 84105, ISRAEL

Abstract

In traditional CAD and solid modeling, 3D objects are represented in terms of their geometric components. In contrast, in volume graphics 3D objects are represented by a discrete digital model, which is stored as a large 3D array of unit volume elements (voxels). The rapid progress in hardware, primarily in memory subsystems, has been recently transforming the field of volume graphics into a major trend which offers an alternative to traditional 3D surface graphics. This paper discusses volume graphics and several related modeling techniques.

1. Introduction

This paper introduces a discrete representation scheme that is different from the surface or solid representation schemes traditionally used in 3D computer graphics. This discrete representation employs a *volume buffer*, that is, a *3D raster* of unit volume elements (in short, *voxels*) to store the 3D digital representation of the 3D objects. A voxel is the 3D counterpart of the 2D pixel; in the same way that a pixel represents a unit of area, a voxel represents a unit of volume. Each voxel has a numeric value associated with it, which represents some measurable properties or independent variables (e.g., color, opacity, density, coverage proportion, time) of the real object intersecting that voxel. The aggregate of voxels tessellating the volume buffer forms the *volumetric dataset* which represents all the regions in the 3D volume, whether in the interior or on the boundary of the objects. *Volume graphics* is an emerging subfield of computer graphics concerned with the synthesis, manipulation, and rendering of 3D objects represented by a volume buffer (Kaufman, Cohen, and Yagel 1993).

Volume graphics employs a conventional 2D frame-buffer and a raster screen for display purposes, but employs a volume buffer as a medium for the representation and manipulation of 3D scenes. The 3D scene is pre-discretized, and the resulting 3D discrete form is used as a database of the 3D scene for manipulation and rendering purposes, which in effect decouples discretization from rendering (viewing and shading). Furthermore, all objects are converted into one uniform meta-object – the voxel, where each voxel is atomic and represents the information about no more than one object that resides in that voxel.

Volume graphics offers the same benefits as surface graphics, with several advantages. The volume data is viewpoint independent, that is, it is generated once, and can be rendered under changing viewing parameters. The rendering phase in volume graphics is insensitive to scene complexity, that is, the performance of the volumetric renderer depends only on the constant resolution of the volume buffer and is independent of the number of objects in the scene. Similarly, the performance of the renderer is insensitive to object complexity since it renders only voxels regardless of the complexity of the source object, whether simple (e.g., polygon, sphere) or complex (e.g., fractal, algebraic surface). Volume graphics supports a variety of modeling techniques, such as Boolean and block operations and constructive solid modeling, as described later. When 3D sampled and simulated data are available, such as those generated by medical scanners (e.g., CT, MRI) or scientific simulations (e.g., computational fluid dynamics), they too can be accommodated by volume graphics. We later describe the capability of volume graphics to represent amorphous phenomena and to have information on both the interior as well as exterior of 3D objects.

Several disadvantages of this approach are related to the loss of geometric information and to the discrete nature of the representation, namely, aliasing artifacts, discrete transformations, and shading performed in discrete space (Yagel, Cohen, and Kaufman 1992a). In addition, this approach requires substantial amounts of storage space and processing time. Finally, since objects are represented by a finite grid, accuracy is also restricted to the grid resolution. However, these problems echo similar problems encountered when 2D raster graphics emerged as an alternative technology to vector graphics and can be alleviated in similar ways. For example, antialiasing techniques, which have been developed to alleviate discretization artifacts in 2D rasters, can be extended to ease the same problem in 3D voxel space.

The same appeal that caused the migration of the computer graphics world from vector graphics to raster graphics, once the memory and processing power became available, is starting to drive a variety of applications from surface-based representation of 3D scenes to voxel-based representation. Naturally, this trend first appeared in applications involving sampled and computed 3D data, such as biomedical and scientific visualization in which the datasets are in volumetric form. Volume graphics when applied to empirical imagery is usually termed *volume visualization*. The diverse applications of volume visualization still provide a major driving force for advances in volume graphics. Some examples of these applications are medical imaging, biology, geoscience, industrial testing, meteorology, computational fluid dynamics, computational chemistry, and molecular systems (see (Kaufman 1990) Chapter 7).

Although 3D raster representation seems to be more natural for empirical imagery, the advantages of this representation are also attracting traditional surface-based applications that deal with the modeling and rendering of synthetic scenes such as CAD and flight simulation (see Figures 2-4). Furthermore, in many applications involving sampled data, like surgical planning and radiation therapy planning, the data need to be visualized along with synthetic objects that may not be available in digital form, such as prosthetic devices, scalpels, injection needles, isodose surfaces, and radiation beams. These objects can be voxelized and intermixed with the sampled organ in the volume buffer and then rendered to the screen (Kaufman, Yagel, and Cohen 1990).

We describe next the relationships between volume graphics, surface graphics and volume visualization. We then survey some basic definitions in 3D discrete topology which are essential to the understanding of the nature of discrete objects. Finally, we describe several modeling techniques that find a particular attractive implementation in volume graphics.

2. Taxonomy of Volume Graphics

Volume visualization is a method that facilitates the interpretation of volumetric datasets by supporting visually-based exploration using interactive graphics and imaging. Its objective is to provide mechanisms for peering inside the volumetric objects and for probing into the voluminous and complex structures and their dynamics. It encompasses an array of techniques for extracting meaningful information from a volumetric dataset and for displaying it in a visual manner ((Kaufman 1990) Chapter 1). Volume graphics employs a volume buffer for object representation, and it consists of a set of techniques for representing, synthesizing, manipulating, and rendering of 3D objects in a volume buffer. However, unlike volume graphics, which deals with volume-represented imagery generated from 3D geometric models, volume visualization focuses on sampled or simulated datasets, does not necessarily use regular voxel grids, and is not necessarily limited to the volume buffer representation or volume rendering. In many cases, effective visualization of datasets is achieved by other means, including traditional surface rendering. Furthermore, volume graphics is concerned with handling synthetic scenes as an alternative to surface graphics and has the potential to greatly advance the field of 3D graphics by offering a comprehensive alternative to surface graphics in many applications.

Figure 1 presents the dataflow for volume visualization and volume graphics. The two major sources of volumetric data are sampled/computed data (top left) and geometric models (top right). The sampled data is 3D reconstructed to fill in gaps of missing information and then stored in the volume buffer. The geometric model, represented by a geometric formula, has to be converted (voxelized) into a set of voxels that is stored in the volume buffer. We later discuss this process, called *voxelization*, in more detail. The combined volume is then rendered to the screen by employing a *volume rendering* algorithm. Volume rendering involves both the viewing and the shading of the volume image and can be accomplished by forward projection (Drebin, Carpenter, and Hanrahan 1988), by ray casting (Levoy 1988), or by discrete ray tracing (Yagel, Cohen, and Kaufman 1992b). Alternatively, the sampled data can be converted into a geometric model by fitting geometric primitives to surfaces detected in the volume. This set of primitives is then rendered to the screen by employing a traditional surface rendering algorithm.

The volume graphics dataflow is marked with solid arrows in Figure 1. The primary source of volume data for volume graphics is a 3D continuous geometric model. Such a geometric model is *3D scan-converted (voxelized)* into a set of voxels that "best" approximates the synthetic model within the discrete volume buffer (see (Kaufman 1990) Chapter 5). Once converted, the digital synthetic model may be intermixed with a sampled dataset to form a hybrid voxel model. The fundamentals of voxelization and the related 3D discrete topology issues are presented in the next section. In order to visualize the dataset in the volume buffer, the volume primitives are directly projected using volume rendering.

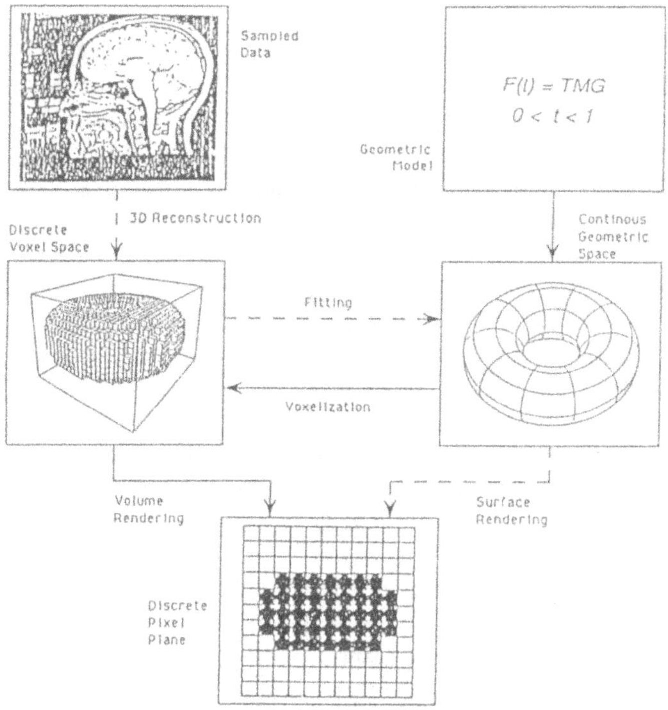

Figure 1: Dataflow for volume visualization and volume graphics.

3. 3D Discrete Topology

One way to model 3D scenes is by using traditional surface modeling techniques. The resulting geometric components can then be converted into voxel representation (voxelized). Intuitively, one would assume that a proper voxelization simply "selects" all voxels which are met, even partially, by the object body. Although this approach could be satisfactory in some cases, commonly the entities it generates are either too coarse and may include more voxels than are necessary or are too thin and do not properly "separate" the two sides of the surface.

One practical meaning of separation is apparent when a voxelized scene is rendered by casting discrete rays from the image plane to the scene. The penetration of the discrete ray traversing background voxels through the voxelized surface causes the appearance of a hole in the final image of the rendered surface. Another type of error might occur when a 3D flooding algorithm is employed either to fill in an object or to measure its volume, surface area, or other properties. In this case the non-separability of the surface causes a leakage of the flood through the discrete surface.

Unfortunately, the extension of the 2D definition of separation to the third dimension and to surfaces is not straight forward since voxelized surfaces cannot be defined as ordered sequences of voxels and a voxel on the surface does not have a specific number of adjacent voxels. Furthermore, there are important topological issues, such as the separation of both sides of a surface, which cannot be well defined by employing 2D terminology. The theory that deals with these 3D topological issues is called *3D discrete topology*. We sketch below some basic notions and informal definitions used in this field. For more information see (Cohen and Kaufman 1991).

The 3D discrete space is a set of integral grid points in 3D Euclidean space defined by their Cartesian coordinates (x, y, z). A voxel is the unit cubic volume centered at the integral grid point. The voxel value is mapped onto $\{0,1\}$: the voxels assigned "1" are called the "black" voxels representing opaque objects, and those assigned "0" are the "white" voxels representing the transparent background. Outside the scope of this paper are non-binary approaches where the voxel value is mapped onto the interval $[0,1]$, representing either partial coverage, variable densities, or graded opacities.

Two voxels are *26-adjacent* if they either share a vertex, an edge, or a face. Every voxel has 26 such adjacent voxels: eight share a vertex with the center voxel, twelve share an edge, and six share a face. Accordingly, face-sharing voxels are defined as *6-adjacent*, and edge-sharing and face-sharing voxels are defined as *18-adjacent*. The prefix N is used to define the adjacency relation, where $N \in \{6, 18, 26\}$. We say that a sequence of voxels having the same value is an *N-path* if all consecutive pairs are N-adjacent. A set of voxels A is *N-connected* if there is an N-path between every pair of voxels in A. An *N-connected component* is a maximal N-connected set.

Assume that a voxel space, denoted by Σ, includes one subset of "black" voxels S. If $\Sigma - S$ is not N-connected, that is, $\Sigma - S$ consists of at least two white N-connected components, then S is said to be *N-separating* in Σ. Loosely speaking, in 2D, an 8-connected black path that divides the white pixels into two groups is 4-separating and a 4-connected black path that divides the white pixels into two groups is 8-separating. There are no analogous results in 3D space.

Let A be an N-separating surface. A voxel $p \in A$ is said to be an *N-simple voxel* if $A - p$ is still N-separating. An N-separating surface is called *N-minimal* if it does not contain any N-simple voxel. A *cover* of a continuous surface is a set of voxels such that every point of the continuous surface lies in a voxel of the cover. A cover is said to be a *minimal cover* if none of its subsets is also a cover. The cover property is essential in applications that employ space subdivision for ray tracing (Glassner 1984), where the subspaces (voxels) which contain objects have to be identified by the rays. Note that a cover is not necessarily separating, but on the other hand, as mentioned above, it may include simple voxels. In fact, even a minimal cover is not necessarily N-minimal for any N. When voxelizing a surface, one should strive to generate an N-separating, N-minimal, and covering set of voxels.

4. Volume Based Modeling

We now turn to describe the volumetric approach to several common modeling techniques. We describe the generation of object primitives (voxelization), texture and photo-mapping, solid-texturing, modeling of amorphous phenomena, modeling by block operations, and constructive solid modeling. For each of the techniques, we identify the advantages of the volume graphics approach.

4.1. Voxelization of Geometric Objects

An indispensable stage in volume graphics is the synthesis of voxel-represented objects. This stage, which is called *voxelization*, is concerned with converting geometric objects from their continuous geometric representation into a set of voxels that "best" approximates the continuous object. As this process mimics the scan-conversion process that pixelizes (rasterizes) 2D geometric objects, it is also referred to as *3D scan-conversion*. In 2D rasterization the pixels are directly drawn onto the screen to be visualized, and filtering is usually applied to reduce aliasing artifacts. However, the voxelization process does not render the voxels but merely generates a database of the discrete binary digitization of the continuous object. Nevertheless, non-binary antialiased voxelization can be employed as an alternative to binary voxelization, which may support superior rendering.

In the past, digitization of solids was performed by spatial enumeration algorithms which employ point or cell classification methods in either an exhaustive fashion or by recursive subdivision (Lee and Requicha 1982). However, subdivision techniques for model decomposition into rectangular subspaces are computationally expensive and thus inappropriate for medium or high resolution grids. Instead, objects should be directly voxelized, preferably generating an N-separating, N-minimal, and covering set, where N is application dependent. The voxelization algorithms should follow the same paradigms as the 2D scan-conversion algorithms; they should be incremental, accurate, use simple arithmetic (preferably integer only), and have a complexity that is not more than linear with the number of voxels generated.

The literature of 3D scan conversion is relatively small. Danielsson (Danielsson 1970) and Mokrzycki (Mokrzycki 1988) developed similar 3D curve algorithms, where the curve is defined by the intersection of two implicit surfaces. Voxelization algorithms have been developed for 3D lines, 3D circles, and a variety of surfaces and solids, including polygons, polyhedra, and quadric objects (Kaufman and Shimony 1986). Efficient algorithms have been developed for voxelizing polygons using an integer-based decision mechanism embedded within a scan-line filling algorithm (Kaufman 1987b), for parametric curves, surfaces, and volumes using an integer-based forward differencing technique (Kaufman 1987a), and for quadric objects such as cylinders, spheres, and cones using "weaving" algorithms by which a discrete circle/line master sweeps along a discrete circle/line base (Cohen and Kaufman 1990).

The voxelized representation is especially attractive when dealing with very complex models, due to the insensitivity of the volumetric representation to the scene complexity. Some examples are fractals (Norton 1982), terrain models (Cohen and Shaked 1992; Wright and Hsieh 1992), and other complex models (Snyder and Barr 1987). Figures 2-3 show volume rendering of terrain models which have been voxelized from a geometric model and have been used in flight simulations.

4.2. Texture and Photo Mapping

One of the attractive attributes of volume graphics is its insensitivity to object complexity. One type of object complexity involves objects that are enhanced with texture-mapping, photo mapping, environment-mapping, or solid texturing. Texture-mapping is commonly implemented during the last stage of the rendering pipeline, and its complexity is proportional to the object's complexity. In volume graphics, texture-mapping is performed during the voxelization stage, and the texture color is stored in each voxel.

Figure 2: A voxelized landscape that has been mapped with aerial photos.

We have also implemented a photo-mapping technique where six orthogonal photographs of the real object are projected back onto the voxelized object (see Figure 4). Once this mapping is applied, it is stored with the voxels themselves during the voxelization stage, and therefore does not degrade the rendering performance. Texture and photo-mapping are also viewpoint independent attributes implying that once the texture is stored as part of the voxel value, texture-mapping need not be repeated. This important feature is exploited by voxel-based flight simulators (see Figures 2-3) and in CAD systems (see Figure 4).

4.3. Solid Texturing

A central feature of volumetric representation is that, unlike surface representation, it is capable of representing inner structures of objects, which can be revealed and explored with appropriate manipulation and rendering techniques. This capability is essential for the exploration of sampled or computed objects. However, synthetic objects are also likely to be solid rather than hollow. One method for modeling various solid types is "solid texturing", in which a function or a 3D map models the color of the objects in

Figure 3: A volumetric model of an airport enhanced with photo-mapping of satellite images. The buildings are synthetic voxel models raised on top of the terrain.

3D. During the voxelization phase each voxel belonging to the objects is assigned a value by the texturing function or the 3D map. This value is then stored as part of the voxel information. Again, since this value is view independent, it does not have to be recomputed for every change in the rendering parameters.

4.4. Amorphous Phenomena

While translucent objects can be represented by surface methods, these methods cannot efficiently support the modeling and rendering of amorphous phenomena (e.g., clouds, fire, smoke) that are volumetric in nature and do not have any notion of tangible surfaces. A common modeling and rendering approach is based on a function that, for any input point in 3D, calculates some object features such as density, reflectivity, or color. These functions can then be rendered by ray casting, which casts a ray from each pixel into the function domain. Along the passage of the ray, at constant intervals the function is evaluated to yield a sample. All samples along each ray are combined to form the pixel color. Some examples for the use of this or similar techniques are the rendering of

Figure 4: The space shuttle. A voxel-based model of the shuttle was generated by voxelizing a polygon mesh model. The voxels were photo-mapped during the voxelization stage using six orthogonal photographs of a physical model of the space shuttle.

fractals (Hart, Sandin, and Kauffman 1989), hypertextures (Perlin and Hoffert 1989), fur (Kajiya and Kay 1989), and gases (Ebert and Parent 1990).

The process of function evaluation at each sample point in 3D has to be repeated for each image generated. In contrast, the volumetric approach allows the pre-computation of these functions at each grid point of the volume buffer. The resulting volumetric dataset can then be rendered from multiple viewpoints without recomputing the modeling function. As in other volume graphics techniques, accuracy is traded for speed, due to the resolution limit. Instead of accurately computing the function at each sample point, some type of interpolation from the precomputed grid values is employed.

4.5. Block Operations

An intrinsic characteristic of rasters is that adjacent objects in the scene are also represented by neighboring memory cells. Therefore, rasters lend themselves to various meaningful grouping-based operations, such as *bitblt* in 2D, or *voxblt* in 3D (Kaufman 1992). These include transfer of volume buffer rectangular blocks while supporting voxel-by-voxel operations between source and destination blocks. Block operations add a variety of modeling capabilities which aid in the task of image synthesis and form the basis for the efficient implementation of a 3D "room manager", which is the extension of window management to the third dimension.

4.6. Constructive Solid Geometry

The volume buffer lends itself to Boolean operations that can be performed on a voxel-by-voxel basis during the voxelization stage. This property is very advantageous when Constructive Solid Geometry (CSG) is the modeling paradigm. Subtraction, union, and intersection operations between two voxelized objects are accomplished at the voxel level, thereby reducing the original problem of evaluating a CSG tree during rendering time down to a 1D Boolean operation between pairs of voxels during a preprocessing stage. Once a CSG model has been constructed in voxel representation, it is rendered in the same way any other volume buffer is. This makes discrete ray tracing of constructive solid models straightforward (Yagel, Cohen, and Kaufman 1992b).

5. Conclusions

We have explored modeling by volume graphics, which is based on the employment of a volume buffer for 3D scene representation. Modeling with volumes has advantages over modeling with surfaces because it is viewpoint independent, insensitive to scene and object complexity, and being suitable for the representation of sampled and simulated datasets and mixtures thereof with geometric objects. It supports the visualization of internal structures such as solid textures, and lends itself to the realization of block operations, surface texturing, amorphous phenomena, and CSG modeling. The problems associated with the volume buffer representation, such as discreteness, memory size, processing time, finite resolution, and loss of geometric representation, echo problems encountered in 2D raster graphics, and can be alleviated in similar ways. The progress so far in volume graphics, in computer hardware, and memory systems guarantees that volume graphics will develop into a major trend in computer graphics. It has the potential to supersede surface graphics for handling and visualizing volumes as well as for modeling and rendering synthetic scenes composed of surfaces and solids.

Acknowledgments

This work has been supported in part by the National Science Foundation under grants IRI-9008109, CCR-9205047, and CCR-9211288, and grants from Hughes Aircraft Company, Hewlett Packard company, and the Center for Biotechnology, SUNY at Stony Brook, which is sponsored by the New York State Science and Technology Foundation. Daniel Cohen acknoweledges the support of Arie Kaufman for his research visits to SUNY at Stony Brook during which he worked on this research. Figure 2 is courtesy of Tiltan System Engineering, and Figure 3 is courtesy of Hughes Aircraft Company.

6. References

Cohen, D. and Kaufman, A., "Scan Conversion Algorithms for Linear and Quadratic Objects", in *Volume Visualization*, A. Kaufman, (ed.), IEEE Computer Society Press, Los Alamitos, CA, , 280-301, 1990.

Cohen, D. and Kaufman, A., "Fundamentals of Surface Voxelization ", Technical Report 91.06.09, Computer Science, SUNY at Stony Brook, June 1991.

Cohen, D. and Shaked, A., "Pyramidal Ray Casting", *ACM Volume Visualization Workshop*, Boston, MA, October 1992.

Danielsson, P. E., "Incremental Curve Generation", *IEEE Transactions on Computers*, **C-19**, 783-793, (1970).

Drebin, R. A., Carpenter, L., and Hanrahan, P., "Volume Rendering", *Computer Graphics (Proc. SIGGRAPH)*, **22**, 4, 65-74, (August 1988).

Ebert, D. S. and Parent, R. E., "Rendering and Animation of Gaseous Phenomena by Combining Fast Volume and Scanline A-buffer Techniques", *Computer Graphics*, **24**, 4, 367-376, (August 1990).

Glassner, A. S., "Space Subdivision for Fast Ray Tracing", *IEEE Computer Graphics and Applications*, **4**, 10 , 15-22, (October 1984).

Hart, J. C., Sandin, D. J., and Kauffman, L. H., "Ray Tracing Deterministic 3-D Fractals", *Computer Graphics*, **23**, 3, 289-296, (July 1989).

Kajiya, J. T. and Kay, T. L., "Rendering Fur with Three Dimensional Textures", *Computer Graphics*, **23**, 3, 271-280, (July 1989).

Kaufman, A. and Shimony, E., "3D Scan-Conversion Algorithms for Voxel-Based Graphics", *Proc. ACM Workshop on Interactive 3D Graphics*, Chapel Hill, NC, 45-76, October 1986.

Kaufman, A., "Efficient Algorithms for 3D Scan-Conversion of Parametric Curves, Surfaces, and Volumes", *Computer Graphics*, **21**, 4, 171-179, (July 1987).

Kaufman, A., "An Algorithm for 3D Scan-Conversion of Polygons", *Proc. EUROGRAPHICS'87*, Amsterdam, Netherlands, 197-208, August 1987.

Kaufman, A., *Volume Visualization*, IEEE Computer Society Press Tutorial, Los Alamitos, CA, 1990.

Kaufman, A., Yagel, R., and Cohen, D., "Intermixing Surface and Volume Rendering", in *3D Imaging in Medicine: Algorithms, Systems, Applications*, K. H. Hoehne, H. Fuchs, and S. M. Pizer, (eds.), , 217-227, June 1990.

Kaufman, A., "The *voxblt* Engine: A Voxel Frame Buffer Processor", in *Advances in Graphics Hardware III*, A.A.M. Kuijk, (ed.), Springer-Verlag, Berlin, , 85-102, 1992.

Kaufman, A., Cohen, D., and Yagel, R., "Volume Graphics", *Computer*, July 1993.

Lee, Y. T. and Requicha, A. A. G., "Algorithms for Computing the Volume and Other Integral Properties of Solids: I-Known Methods and Open Issues; II-A Family of Algorithms Based on Representation Conversion and Cellular Approximation", *Communications of the ACM*, **25**, 9, 635-650, (September 1982).

Levoy, M., "Display of Surfaces from Volume Data", *Computer Graphics and Applications*, **8**, 5, 29-37, (May 1988).

Mokrzycki, W., "Algorithms of Discretization of Algebraic Spatial Curves on Homogeneous Cubical Grids", *Computers & Graphics*, **12**, 3/4, 477-487, (1988).

Norton, V. A., "Generation and Rendering of Geometric Fractals in 3-D", *Computer Graphics*, **16**, 3, 61-67, (1982).

Perlin, K. and Hoffert, E. M., "Hypertexture", *Computer Graphics*, **23**, 3, 253-262, (July 1989).

Snyder, J. M. and Barr, A. H., "Ray Tracing Complex Models Containing Surface Tessellations", *Computer Graphics*, **21**, 4, 119-128, (July 1987).

Wright, J. and Hsieh, J., "A Voxel-Based, Forward Projection Algorithm for Rendering Surface and Volumetric Data", *Proceedings Visualization '92*, Boston, MA, 340-348, October 1992.

Yagel, R., Cohen, D., and Kaufman, A., "Normal Estimation in 3D Discrete Space", *The Visual Computer*, 278-291, June 1992.

Yagel, R., Cohen, D., and Kaufman, A., "Discrete Ray Tracing", *IEEE Computer Graphics and Applications*, 19-28, September 1992.

Multi-resolution 3D approximations for rendering complex scenes

Jarek Rossignac and Paul Borrel

Interactive Geometric Modeling
IBM T.J. Watson Research Center
P.O. Box 704
Yorktown Heights, New York 10598

Abstract

We present a simple, effective, and efficient technique for approximating arbitrary polyhedra. It is based on triangulation and vertex-clustering, and produces a series of 3D approximations (also called "levels of detail") that resemble the original object from all viewpoints, but contain an increasingly smaller number of faces and vertices. The simplification is more efficient than competing techniques because it does not require building and maintaining a topological adjacency graph. Furthermore, it is better suited for mechanical CAD models which often exhibit patterns of small features, because it automatically groups and simplifies features that are geometrically close, but need not be topologically close or even part of a single connected component. Using a lower level of detail when displaying small, distant, or background objects improves graphic performance without a significant loss of perceptual information, and thus enables realtime inspection of complex scenes or a convenient environment for animation or walkthrough preview.

1. Introduction

The interactive 3D navigation through scenes defined by millions of polygons is vital for industrial CAD applications, such as the design reviews for large mechanical assemblies. Yet, it cannot even be supported on emerging multiprocessor high-end graphic servers (see [Garlick et al., 1990] for recent progress). Since the galloping hardware developments will only stimulate the demand for support of even larger data-sets, a distinction must be made between (1) the accurate geometric models necessary for representing mechanical parts and (2) specialized representations of these parts tailored for efficient graphics.

Previously developed graphics performance improvements that deal with scene complexity by quickly eliminating objects that do not project on the screen, or by displaying crude approximations of objects whose projection is very small, are insufficient and exhibit important short-comings. Pre-computed hierarchical spatial directories [Airey et al., 1990] [Teller and Séquin, 1991] help to quickly prune portions of the model lying outside of the viewing space, but have no effect when the entire scene fits in that space. The graphics performance increases achieved by rendering isolated dots, mini-max boxes, or other geometrically simple bounds instead of distant or small objects are often offset by a significant loss of visual information and by distracting abrupt shape changes that occur when objects slowly approach the viewer. Geometric approximations with minimal rendering cost and a close resemblance with the original solids from all directions are the key to an acceptable solution for realtime graphics of complex scenes [Clark, 1976] [Crow, 1982]. Furthermore, a sequence of approximations offering different trade-offs between visual accuracy and graphic performance will prove effective for revealing details as objects approach the viewpoint, only if the transitions between one approximation and the next are barely noticeable.

Since a major factor of the shading cost for a polyhedron is the number of vertices that must be processed by the graphics pipeline when rendering the object's faces, approximations should strive to reduce the number of vertices and faces while preserving the overall aspect of the model.

We present here a new simplification technique that operates on boundary representations of an arbitrary polyhedron and generates a series of simplified models with a decreasing number of faces and vertices. The resulting models do not necessarily form valid boundaries of 3D regions—for example, an elongated solid may be approximated by a curve segment. However, the error introduced by the simplification is bounded (in the Hausdorf distance sense) by a user-controlled accuracy factor and the resulting shapes exhibit a remarkable visual fidelity considering the data-reduction ratios.

2. Alternative solutions and related work

Most polyhedra are used to approximate more general shapes and are constructed as tesselations of curved faces. Approximations with fewer vertices and faces can thus in principle be produced by using coarser tesselation parameters. Indeed, emerging high-end graphic architectures support adaptive tesselation for trimmed NURBS surfaces [Rockwood et al., 1989]. However, in practice, polyhedral representations often result from Boolean operations (poorly supported for curved geometries) or from procedural models which are not available to the graphics system and are too expensive to regenerate in realtime. Consequently, re-tesselation of curved surfaces is not always an acceptable alternative for simplifying the vast majority of existing polyhedral models. The simplification process should be made independent of the design history and should be automatic [Crow, 1982].

Recursive difference techniques [Kim, 1990] replace a solid S by the difference, H − D, between its convex hull H and a delta solid, D = H − S, and apply recursively this process to (a subdivision of) the connected components of D. The resulting CSG tree may be truncated, replacing all delta solids at a given recursion depth d by their convex hull. The truncation removes cavity or protrusion details, depending on the parity of d. Unfortunately, this process does not simplify convex objects; tends to increase the number of faces; and, for small values of d, produces approximations whose overall shape considerably differs from the original solids.

Line simplification algorithms (also called "line generalization") used in Cartography [McMaster, 1987] apply recursive subdivision to approximate a plane polygonal curve by a small number of vertices lying on that curve. The maximum deviation between the curve and an "anchor-floater" line joining the end-points is evaluated. If the deviation exceeds a given threshold, the curve is split at the maximal deviation point for further iterations, otherwise, the curve is replaced by the line segment. We have designed a 3D extension of this approach requiring the construction and coarse triangulation of the topology of the object's boundary. After considering its algorithmic complexity and storage requirements, we have opted for the simpler and more efficient solution described in the remainder of this paper. The approach is however very effective for models with a regular (mesh) topology [Williams, 1983].

Surface fitting techniques to regularly spaced scanner data points [Schmitt et al., 1996] may also be used for producing levels of detail polyhedral approximations [DeHaemer and Zyda, 1991]. These techniques have been recently extended to unorganized data points [Hoppe et al., 1992] [Scarlatos and Pavlidis, 1992] [DeRose et al., 1992] and to new sparse points automatically distributed over an existing triangulated surface (either evenly or according to curvature) [Turk, 1992].

Several simplification techniques of dense triangular meshes approximating smooth surfaces have been proposed. Flat vertices (defined in terms of the normals to abutting triangles [Kalvin et al., 1991] or in terms of the distance to a locally approximating plane [Schroeder et al., 1992]) may be removed and the so created hole triangulated. The process may be repeated by progressively increasing the tolerance until a sufficiently low number fo vertices is reached.

The approach presented here is aimed at very complex and fairly irregular CAD models of mechanical parts. It has several advantages over the methods briefly mentioned above:

- The computation of the simplification does not require the construction of a topological adjacency graph between faces, edges, and vertices. It works of a simple array of vertices and of an array of triangles, each defined in terms of three vertex-indices.
- The algorithm for computing the simplification is very time efficient. In its simplest form, it needs to traverse the input data (vertex and triangle tables) only once.
- The tolerance (i.e. bound on the Hausdorf distance between the original and simplified model) may be arbitrarily increased reducing the triangle count by several orders of magnitude.
- To further reduce the triangle count, the simplification algorithm may produce non-regularized models. Particularly, when using the appropriate tolerance, thin plates may be simplified to "dangling" faces, long objects to isolated edges, and (groups of) small solids into isolated points.
- It is not restricted by topological adjacency constraints and may merge features that are geometrically close but are not topologically adjacent. Particularly, an arbitrary number of small neighboring isolated objects may be merged and simplified into a single point.

Figure 1 illustrates the result of one simplification pass on a small assembly of mechanical parts.

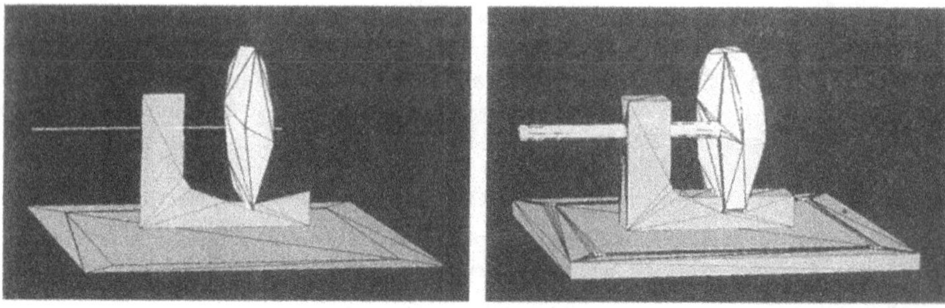

Figure 1: Example of simplification. *The solids are triangulated (left) and simplified (right). Note that the simplification of regular solid that are either flat or elongated generates lower-dimensional elements.*

Below, we describe the algorithm for producing such a single simplification. Section 4 discusses how the algorithm may be used for producing level of detail representations. Section 5 presents various rendering modes that exploit the level of detail models to significantly increase the graphics performance.

3. Single simplification process

The original model of each object is represented by a vertex table V containing vertex coordinates and a face table F containing references to V, sorted and organized according to the edge-loops bounding the face. The simplification involves the processing steps presented below and summarized in Figure 2. They manipulate the data-structure of Figure 3.

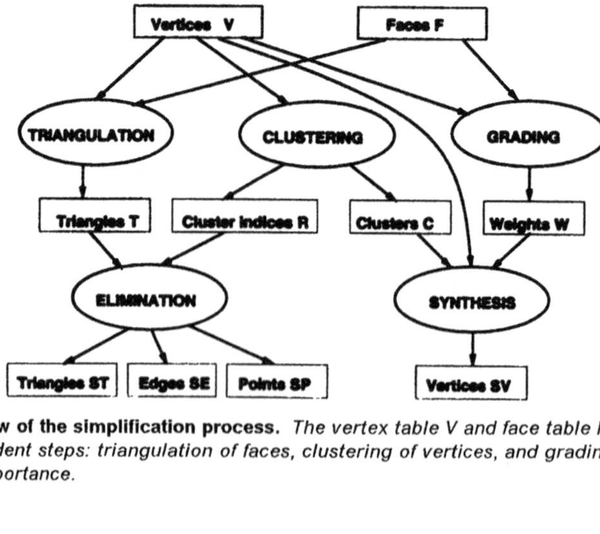

Figure 2: Overview of the simplification process. *The vertex table V and face table F are processed by three independent steps: triangulation of faces, clustering of vertices, and grading of vertices as to their visual importance.*

3.1 Grading

A weight is computed for each vertex of V and stored in the W table. The weight defines the relative perceptual importance of the vertex. The subjectivity of our approach is confined to the choice of criteria for weight evaluation. We favor (1) vertices that have a higher probability of lying on the object's silhouettes from an arbitrary viewing direction and (2) vertices that bound large faces that should not be affected by the removal of small details. The first factor may be efficiently estimated using the inverse of the maximum angle between all pairs of incident edges on the candidate vertex. The second factor may be estimated using the length of the longest among all of the edges incident upon the vertex.

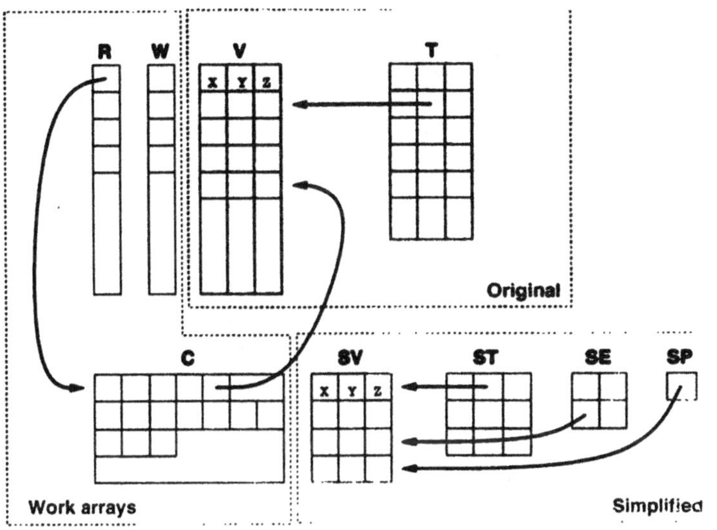

Figure 3: Data-structures and their interdependencies. *Given the input arrays of vertices V and triangles T, the algorithm computes auxiliary structures, R, W, and C and produces the resulting vertices, SV, triangles, ST, edges, SE, and points, SP. There is one entry per initial vertex in V, R, and W. There is one entry per resulting vertex in C and SV.*

3.2 Triangulation

Each face is decomposed into triangles [Edelsbrunner et al., 1990] supported by its original vertices. Because CAD models typically contain faces bounded by a large number of edges, a very efficient triangulation technique is used which does not require the a priori decomposition of the face into monotonic or convex regions [Ronfard and Rossignac, In preparation. 1993.].

The resulting T table contains 3 vertex-indices per triangle.

3.3 Clustering

Based on geometric proximity, the vertices of V are grouped into clusters. Clusters are numbered by the order in which they are created. The R table indicates, for each vertex of V, the corresponding cluster number. Conversely, the C table contains, for each cluster, a list of references to the vertices falling into that cluster. We have opted for a simple clustering process based on the truncation of vertex coordinates. A box, or other bound, containing the object is uniformly subdivided into cells. Vertices falling within one cell form a cluster and will be replaced by a unique vertex. The clustering procedure takes as parameters the box in which the clustering should occur and the maximum number of cells along each dimension. The solid's bounding box or a common box for the entire scene may be used.

The list of vertex indices stored in the cluster table C is used in the synthesis stage (below) for computing an "optimal" vertex representative for each cluster. For example the vertex closest to weighted the average. This list may be omitted if one decides to compute the representative vertex for each cluster in an incremental manner. For example, one could use the first vertex encountered for the cluster or the running weighted average. These only require storing three vertex coordinates (and possibly a vertex count) for each cluster. The restriction permits to compute the cluster representative vertices without reading the input data twice, which leads to important performance improvements when the input vertex table is too large to fit in memory.

3.4 Synthesis

For each cluster, a representative vertex is computed using the C, W, and V tables and is stored in the SV table of simplified vertices. For data smoothing, the representative vertex may be defined as the center of mass of all the vertices of the cluster weighted with the values stored in W. For removing details without perturbing retained faces, the vertex with maximal weight may be selected. The synthesis maps each vertex, V(i), into the representative vertex, SV(R(i)), of the corresponding cluster. The mapping is typically many-to-one and thus reduces the total number of vertices.

3.5 Elimination

Table R maps the vertices of the original triangles into new representative vertices. When all three representative vertices are equal, the triangle degenerates into a point. When exactly two representative vertices are equal the triangle degenerates into an edge. Such edges and points, when they do not bound any other triangle of the simplified object, are stored in SE and SP tables, and rendered as part of the solid's approximation. Significant graphics performance improvements are obtained by removing, from the simplified model, all triangle-duplicates, all edge-duplicates, all point-duplicates, all edges bounding a retained triangle, all points bounding a retained edge, and all points bounding a retained triangle. The elimination process performs these tasks and produces three tables: the simplified triangles, ST; the dangling edges, SE; and the isolated points, SP. They respectively contain three, two, and one reference to entries in the SV table.

The search for duplicates uses a temporary data-structure, which associates, with each cluster, a list of incident edges and, with each edge, a list of triangles. Triangles are stored only once in this data-structure using their lowest-index vertex for locating the cluster, using the intermediate-index vertex for locating the edge incident upon that cluster, and using the last vertex for locating the triangle. Dangling edges are implicitly defined as edges with empty triangle-lists. Isolated points are defined as clusters with empty edge-lists.

3.6 Adjustment of normals

A final step computes new normals for all the triangles in ST using its simplified vertex coordinates. The normals are only used for rendering. Normals of back-facing triangles are automatically inverted by the graphics processor.

4. Series of increasing simplification

Approximate models of the same objects with increasing degree of simplification may be obtained by executing the above process several times, with decreasing clustering resolutions.

A more efficient approach performs a first simplification with the highest resolution, then recursively merges adjacent clusters into new ones to produce the other simplified models. An octtree used to store the representative vertices for all the clusters of the first simplification provides a convenient data-structure for merging adjacent clusters.

A series of models with different degrees of simplification is shown Figure 4.

5. Rendering modes

Simplified models may be used in different ways, depending on the application and the type of user interaction.

5.1 Preview on simplified models

If the full precision model does not fit in the graphic workstation's memory and paging from disk is expensive, a simplified version may be loaded and used to specify interactively viewing angles or walkthrough trajectories for a camera. Full precision images or walkthrough animations may be computed in batch mode and viewed later.

5.2 Simplified models during motion

If the full precision model fits in memory and can be displayed at acceptable but non-interactive rates, a crude simplified model is constructed and stored. (It typically only increases the storage requirements by a few percents.) The user may then toggle between the full resolution original data and a crude approximation of all the objects, used mainly for realtime feedback during interactive navigation.

5.3 Simplified background

In the above scheme, selected details of the scene may be rendered with full precision, while the other objects, considered as background information are rendered using simplified models (see Figure 5).

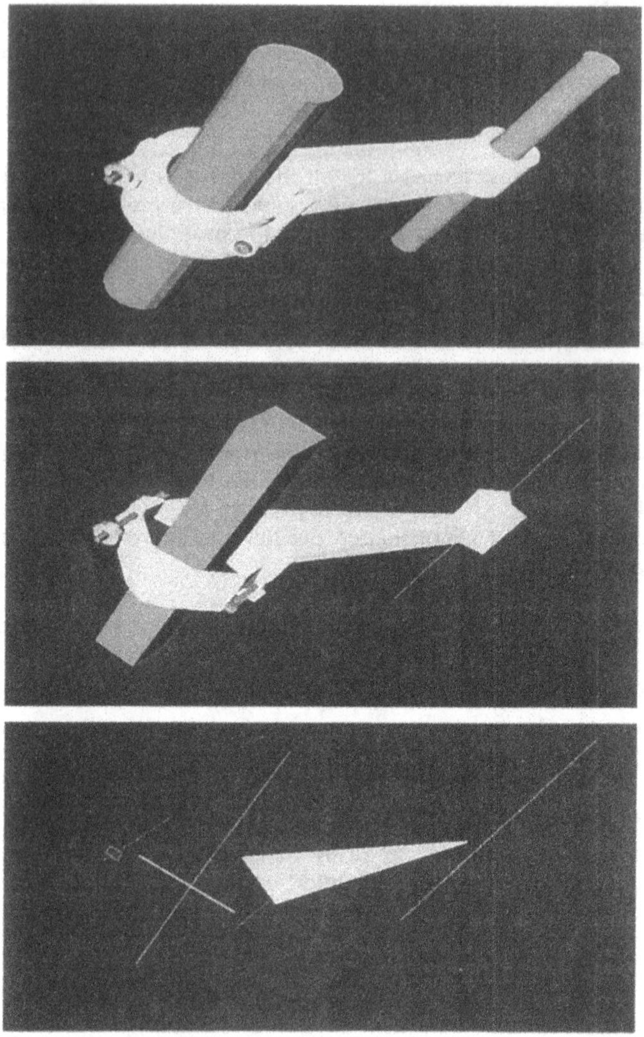

Figure 4: Increasing levels of simplification. *The original solid (top) has 4804 triangular faces. The two approximating models below have respectively 218 faces plus 1 dangling edge and 1 face plus 9 dangling edges.*

5.4 Dynamic selection

Simplification levels may be selected adaptively depending on the viewpoint. Models that are further away from the viewer are displayed with less details. The distance to the viewer may be estimated using precomputed spherical or other simple bounds for each object. Figure 6 shows the same parts as in Figure 4, but with different degrees of approximation selected automatically according to the distance from the viewer.

Figure 5: Simplified background. *Only one table and its set of chairs are rendered with full precision, the others sets are rendered using simplified models (top), which reduces the rendering time by 80%. A detailed view comparing the approximated and the original models is shown (below).*

5.5 *Continuous evolution*

When the more simplified models are derived from less simplified ones, one can produce parametric models, which simulate the metamorphosis between two consecutive simplification levels. We use the technique described in [Kaul and Rossignac, 1992], where each vertex of the polyhedron is replaced by a linear parameterized trajectory. As the object moves closer to the viewer, the common parameter for computing all the vertices is smoothly adjusted. The result simulates the migration of all the vertices towards the representative vertex of their clusters. As the model, moving towards the viewer, traverses a threshold between two consecutive simplification levels, the system automatically switches between consecutive interpolating models at their common limit shape.

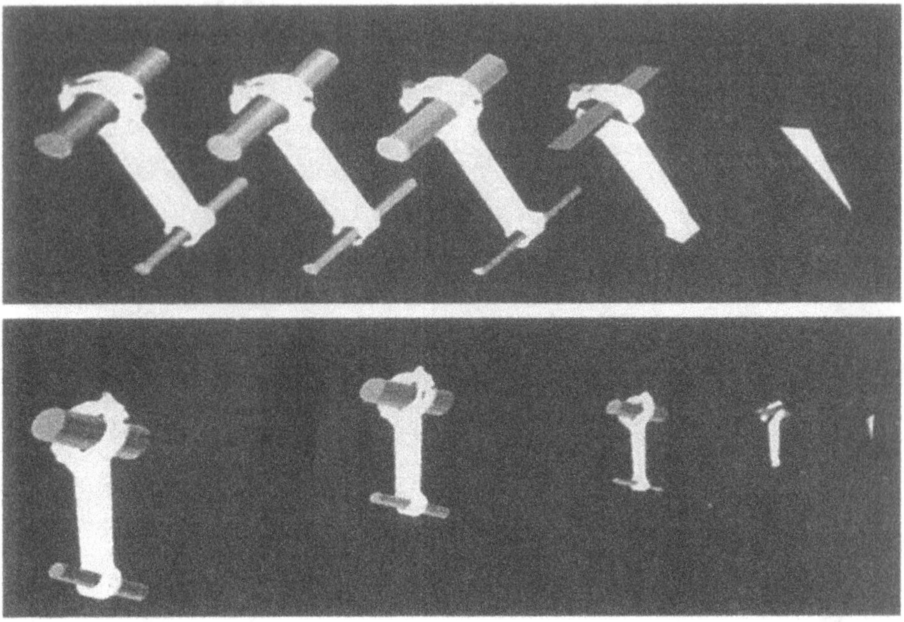

Figure 6: Levels of detail. *Five instances of the same assembly (top) are shown using different levels of approximation that depend on their distance to the viewer. For comparison, the five approximations are shown with the same scale (below).*

6. Conclusion

Although the performance of state of the art hardware graphics is growing rapidly, price constraints and the growing needs to industrial customers call for algorithmic improvements that improve the visualization speed of complex 3D scenes. We have presented a new technique, which automatically computes one or several simplified graphics representations of each object. These representations may be used selectively in lieu of the original model to accelerate the display process while preserving the overall perceptual information content of the scene. The described method clusters vertices of the model and produces an approximate model where original faces are approximated with fewer faces defined in terms of selected vertices. Several simplified representations with different simplification factors may be stored in addition to the original model. Actual viewing conditions are used to establish automatically for each object which representation should be used for graphics.

References

Airey, J., Rohlf, J., and Brooks, F. Towards image realism with interactive update rates in complex virtual building environments. *ACM Proc. Symposium on Interactive 3D Graphics*, 24(2):41-50, 1990.

Clark, J. Hierarchical geometric models for visible surface algorithms. *Communications of the ACM*, 19(10):547-554, October 1976.

Crow, F. A more flexible image generation environment. *Computer Graphics*, 16(3):9-18, 1982.

DeHaemer and Zyda, M. Simplification of objects rendered by polygonal approximations. *Computers and Graphics*, 15(2):175-184, 1991.

DeRose, T., Hoppe, H., McDonald, J., and Stuetzle, W. Fitting of surfaces to scattered data. In J. Warren, editor, *SPIE Proc. Curves and Surfaces in Computer Vision and Graphics III*, 1830:212-220, November 16-18 1992.

Edelsbrunner, H., Tan, S.T., and Waupotitsch, A. A polynomial time algorithm for the mini-max angle triangulation. *6th ACM Symp. on Computational Geometry*, 44-52, 1990.

Garlick, B.J., Baum, D.R., and Winget, J.M. Interactive viewing of large geometric databases using multiprocessor graphics workstations. *SIGGRAPH Course Notes*, 28:239-245, 1990.

Hoppe, H., DeRose, T., Duchamp, T., McDonald, J., and Stuetzle, W. Surface reconstruction from unorganized points. *Computer Graphics*, 26(2):71-78, July 1992.

Kalvin, A., Cutting, C., Haddad, B., and Noz, M. Constructing topologically connected surfaces for the comprehensive analysis of 3D medical structures. *SPIE Image Processing*, 1445:247-258, 1991.

Kaul, A. and Rossignac, J. Solid-Interpolating Deformations: Constructions and Animation of PIPs. *Computers and Graphics (Best Paper Award at Eurographics'91)*, 16(1):107-115, 1992.

Kim, Y.S. *Convex decomposition and solid geometric modeling*, PhD thesis. Dept. of Mechanical Engineering, Stanford University, 1990.

McMaster, R.B. Automated Line Generation. *Cartographica*, 24(2):74-111, 1987.

Rockwood, A., Heaton, K., and Davis, T. Real-time Rendering of Trimmed Surfaces. *Computer Graphics*, 23(3):107-116, 1989.

Ronfard, R. and Rossignac, J. Flooding: Efficient triangulation of multiply connected polygons. IBM Research. In preparation. 1993.

Scarlatos, L. and Pavlidis, T. Hierarchical triagulation using cartographic coherence. *CVGIP: Graphical Models and Image Processing*, 54(2):147-161, 1992.

Schmitt, F., Barsky, B., and Du, W. An adaptive subdivision method for surface-fitting from sampled data. *Computer Graphics*, 20(4):179-188, 1996.

Schroeder, W., Zarge, J., and Lorensen, W. Decimation of triangle meshes. *Computer Graphics*, 26(2):65-70, July 1992.

Teller, S.J. and Séquin, C.H. Visibility Preprocessing for interactive walkthroughs. *Computer Graphics*, 25(4):61-69, July 1991.

Turk, G. Re-tiling polygonal surfaces. *Computer Graphics*, 26(2):55-64, July 1992.

Williams, L. Pyramidal parametrics. *Computer Graphics*, 17(3):1-10, 1983.

Volume Tracing Soft Objects

Masa Inakage
The Media Studio Inc.
2-24-7 Shichirigahama-Higashi
Kamakura, Kanagaw 248 JAPAN

ABSTRACT

This paper presents a volume rendering technique called the volume tracing. Volume tracing is an extension to ray tracing rendering technique. In this paper, we focus on the rendering of soft objects. Soft objects include implicit surfaces which are called "the metaballs". The visualization of volume data defined by soft objects is achieved by the use of volume tracing.

Keywords: fuzzy objects, implicit surfaces, metaballs, stochastic metaballs, volume rendering, volume tracing

1. INTRODUCTION

Three dimensional computer graphics modeling and rendering technqiues have achieved photo-realistic image synthesis of objects with solid surfaces. In many cases, the techniques assume surface models in which only the surfaces of objects are defined. Hence, the surface models cannot visualize the internal data of objects. Solid models are used in CAD/CAM applications. The shape of objects defined by solid models are limited to combinations of geometric functions such as spheres and cones. There are many objects such as fuzzy objects that are inadequate to be defined by the surface models or solid models. It is necessary to use special modeling and rendering techniques for image synthesis of fuzzy objects.

Several researches in modeling and rendering the fuzzy objects have been reported. Blinn[1] and Nishimura[5] used ray tracing to render the soft objects. Since the soft objects are defined by high order functions, both papers adopted quadric functions to approximate the modeling of soft objects. Wyvill[8,9,10] used polygonal approximations so that traditional rendering techniques can be used. Karla[4] and Wyvill[11] have presented techniques to accurately render the soft objects by ray tracing. However, these techniques are mathematically complicated. Reeves[7] described a modeling technique called the particle systems to model fuzzy objects. The particle systems are effective for modeling a group of particles such as fireworks, splashes. However, the particle systems are not suitable for modeling clouds and flames. Perlin[6] describes texture synthesis techniques using soft objects of iso-surfaces. Volume tracing is used to render the synthesized textures. In Inakage[3], laminar flames are modeled by an anisotropic density function. Volume tracing is used to render the flames. However, it does not describe general features of soft objects such as the blending effects.

In this paper, we first present the volume tracing technique, in section 3.1 we apply the technique to render the soft objects of iso-surfaces. The technique is extended in section 3.2 to account for soft objects with opacity and stochastic particles. In section 4, examples of the technique are shown.

2. VOLUME TRACING

Volume tracing extends the notion of ray tracing to account for the volume model. In ray tracing, screen sampling is used to calculate the intensity of the screen pixel. This screen sampling determines the eye ray. Each screen sampled eye ray is tested for an intersection with objects. The intersecting surface is analytically calculated. Ray tracing ignores all the volume data between the surface intersection and the screen because ray tracing assumes a vacuum space. When the space is filled with gas particles or any scalar fields, the fundamental assumption of the ray tracing technique fails.

The volume sampling process is a sampling process performed along a given ray. The eye ray is extended incrementally until it is clipped by the maximum distance (clipping volume) or it intersects with an opaque object, as shown in figure 1. It is noted that the sample volume of a ray is not dependent on the voxel vertices.

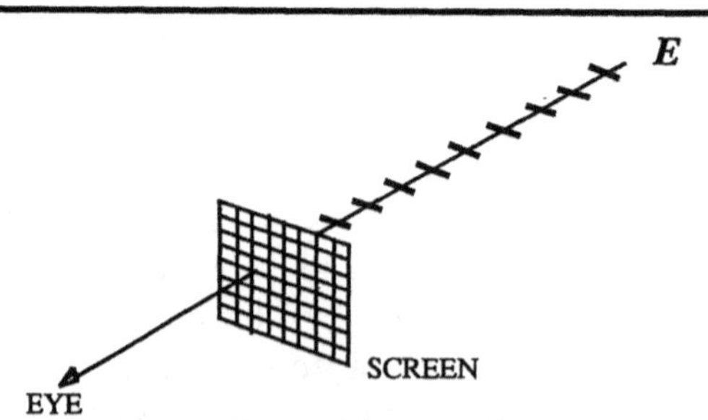

Figure 1 Illustration of the volume sampling

Once the sample volume is obtained, a scalar value that occupies the sample volume must be calculated in order to apply an appropriate shading model for the volume. The algorithm accounts for volume data of both voxel and functional models. Scalar value can be directly calculated if the volume data are functionally defined. To determine the scalar value of a voxel-based sample volume, numerical interpolation is used. First, the distances between the sample point and the neighboring voxels are calculated. The distance is used to determine the weight factor for averaging. The weighted averaging technique is applied to calculate the scalar value of the sample volume.

3. SOFT OBJECTS

In this section, we first describe iso-surfaces or metaballs. Then, the extensions of soft objects to model flames and other fuzzy objects are presented.

3.1 Metaballs

Metaballs are defined by iso-surfaces of the density function. It is a spherical function that has a center point with maximum influence. The influence factor decreases as a function of the distance from the center point. A suitable density function is proposed in Wyvill [11]. The density function $F()$ we used in this paper is

$$F(a) = -0.4444\,(a^6 / b^6) + 1.8888\,(a^4 / b^4) - 2.4444\,(a^2 / b^2) + 1.0$$

$$a \leq b$$

where a is the distance from the center point of the spherical density function to a given point P, and b is the maximum distance which the density function influences. Hence, b defines the amount of influence at the center point. To obtain the iso-surfaces, we define the surfaces by all points that satisfy $F(a) = val$. Wyvill [9] found that val = 0.5 provides a good set of points to constitute the metaballs. For multiple metaballs, the summation of F(a) for all the metaballs defines the iso-surfaces. This summation results in the blending effects of metaballs. A negative value of b implies that the amount of influences by the surrounding metaballs is decreased. This subtraction operation creates holes in the iso-surfaces.

In order to volume trace the metaballs, we render all the points in the density function that satisfy $F(a) \geq val$, as shown in figure 2. The algorithm can be summarized as follows:

1. Obtain an eye ray from screen sample.
2. Obtain a point *P* by volume sample the eye ray.
3. Calculate *F(a)* for each metaballs, and sum them.
4. **If** (*F(a)≥val*) **then**
   4-1. Calculate the surface normal.
   4-2. Calculate the intensity of light at point *P*.
   4-3. **goto** 1.

else

5. **While** (point *P* < maximum distance) **goto** 2.

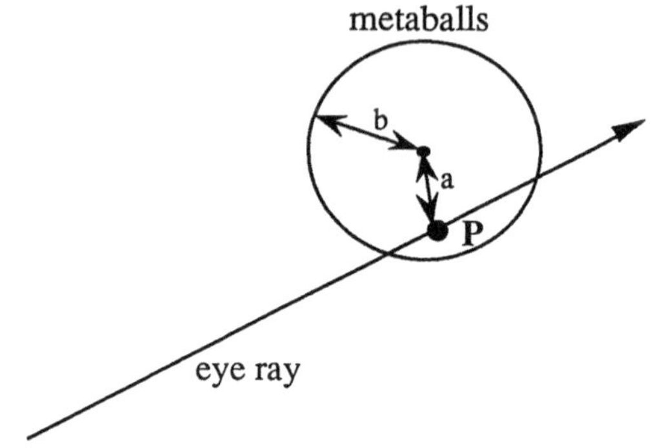

Figure 2 Volume tracing metaballs

3.2 Extensions

3.2.1 Anisotropic Density Function

The density function can be modified to an anisotropic density function. The basic primitive of the function becomes the ellipsoids. For a given point P(x,y,z), the anisotropic density functionF() is written as

$$F(a) = -0.4444\ (a^6 / c^6) + 1.8888\ (a^4 / c^4) - 2.4444\ (a^2 / c^2) + 1.0$$

$$a \leq c$$

where
$c = f(b, q, \phi)$

Function *f()* defines the anisotropy which is dependent on the angles$q$, ϕ in polar coordinates.

3.2.2 Fuzzy Volumes

The density function may be used to control the opacity and color. Instead of thresholding at $F(a) \geq val$, we use $f(F(a))$ to be the opacity factor. At $f(F(a)) = 0.0$, we assume that it is transparent. The same method may be used to manipulate the colors of soft objects.

Another modification to the density function is the use of stochastic factors. As an example, we apply the particals technique. In Inakage[2], the particals technique is presented to stochastically break the spherical surfaces into small segments. We apply the particals to create stochastic metaballs.

For a given point P(x,y,z), the stochastic density functionF() is expressed as

$$F(a) = -0.4444\ (a^6 / c^6) + 1.8888\ (a^4 / c^4) - 2.4444\ (a^2 / c^2) + 1.0$$

$a \leq c$

where
$c = noise(b)$

Note that the noise function is dependent on the volume sampled point P. It does not have frame-to-frame coherency.

4. EXAMPLES

Figure 3 shows the blending effects of soft objects by volume tracing. As two metaballs are placed close together, they start to merge. Figure 4 is an example of 5 blended metaballs. Figure 5 uses the same set of data that is used to render figure 4. In this example, metaballs are given stochastic factors to generate fuzzy particles. Figure 6 is an example of fuzzy volume in which the opacity is controled by the density function.

Examples were rendered on NEC PC9801 VX2 16-bit personal computer with 8087 floating point accelerating chip. Images are rendered in 24 bits full color. Computation time for figure 3 was approximately 1 hour at 160 x 100 x 250 sampling resolution.

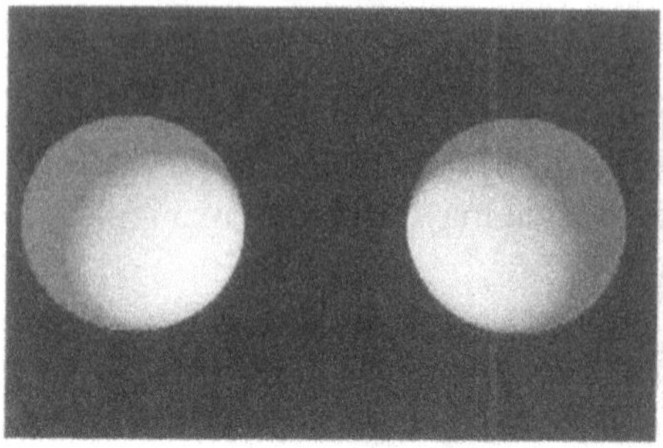

(a)

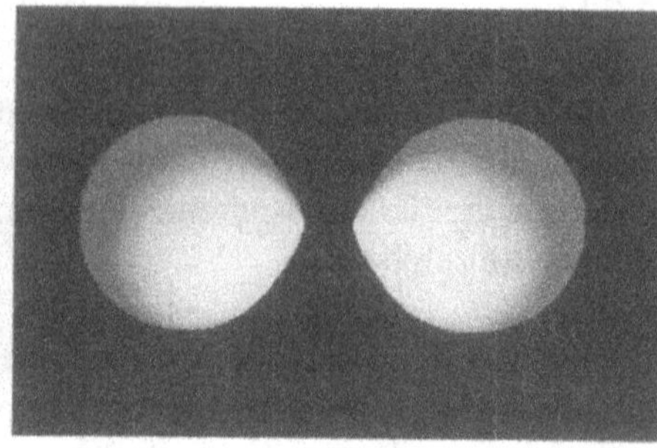

(b)

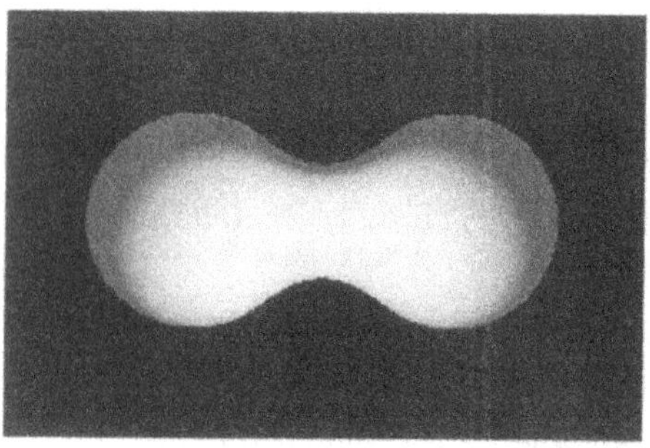

(c)

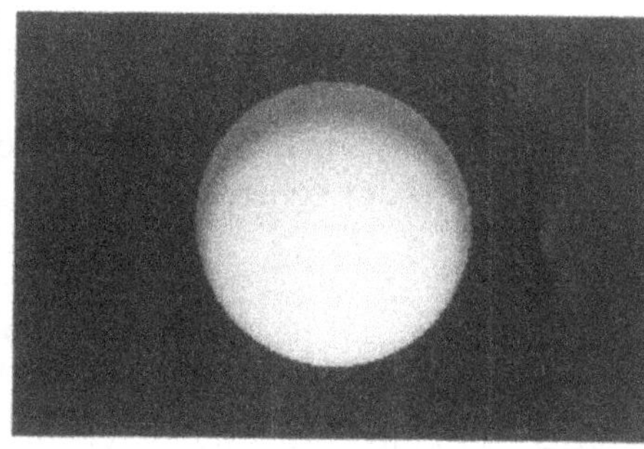

(d)

Figure 3 (a)-(d) illustrates the changes in the blending effect with 2 metaballs.

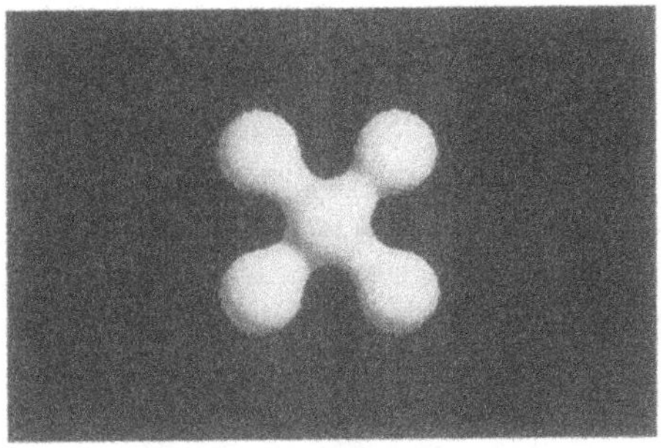

Figure 4 The blending effect with 5 metaballs

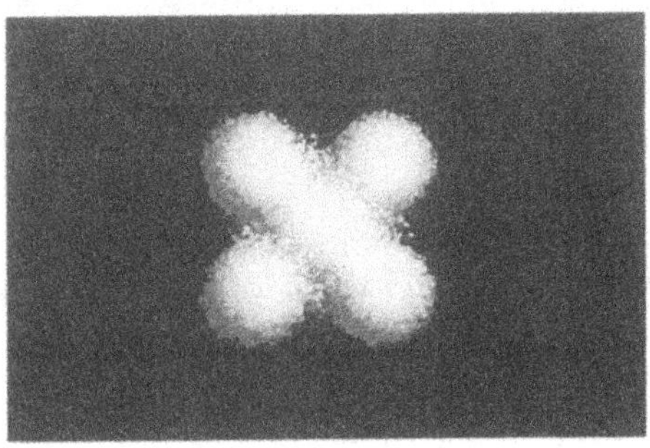

Figure 5 5 stochastic metaballs

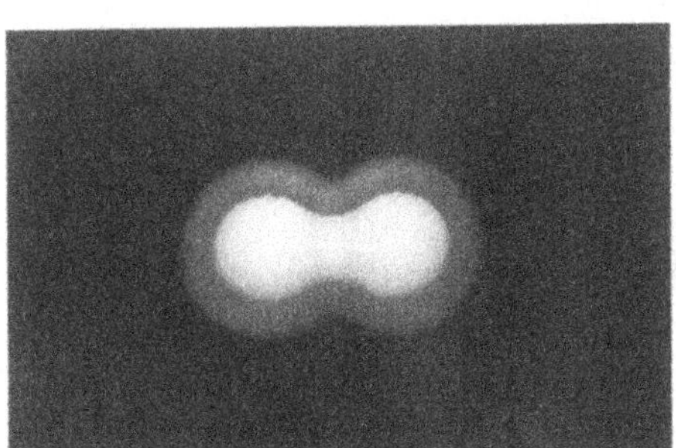

Figure 6 Opacity controled by the density function

5. FUTURE WORKS

Volume tracing is a computationally expensive technique. Techniques to improve the rendering performance is necessary for production environment. Anti-aliasing of volume sampling is appreciated for rendering curved surfaces such as surfaces of soft objects. The algorithm is currently modified to adaptively supersample the volume. We are investigating various density functions that produce visually interesting shapes.

REFERENCES

[1] Blinn, J., "A Generalization of Algebraic Surface Drawing," *ACM Transactions on Graphics,* 1, 1982, pp.235-256

[2] Inakage, M., "PARTICALS: An Artistic Approach to Fuzzy Objects," *proceedings of CG International '88,* pp.126-134

[3] Inakage, M., "A Simple Model of Flames," proceedings of CG Int*ernational '90,* pp.71-81

[4] Karla, D. and Barr, A.H., "Guaranteed Ray Intersection with Implicit Surfaces," *Computer Graphics, 23,* 3, 1989, pp.297-306

[5] Nishimura, H., Hirai, M., Kawai, T., Kawata, T., Shirakawa, I. and Omura, K., "Object Modeling by Distribution Function and a Method of Image Generation," *proceedings of the Electronics Communication Conference '85,* (in Japanese)

[6] Perlin, K. and Hoffert, E.M., "Hypertexture," *Computer Graphics, 23,* 3, 1989, pp.253-262

[7] Reeves, W.T., "Particle Systems - A Technique for Modeling a Class of Fuzzy Objects," Computer Graphics, 17, 3, 1983, pp.359-376

[8] Wyvill, B., McPheeters, C. and Wyvill, G., "Animating Soft Objects," *The Visual Computers, 2,* 4, 1986, pp.235-242

[9] Wyvill, G., McPheeters, C. and Wyvill, B., "Data Structure for Soft Objects," *The Visual Computers, 2,* 4, 1986, pp.227-234

[10] Wyvill, G., Wyvill, B. and McPheeters, C., "Solid Texturing of Soft Objects," *IEEE Computer Graphics and Applications, 7,* 12, 1987, pp.20-26

[11] Wyvill, G. and Trotman, A., "Ray Tracing Soft Objects," *proceedings of CG International '90,* pp.469-476

List of Contributors

Springer-Verlag and the Environment

We at Springer-Verlag firmly believe that an international science publisher has a special obligation to the environment, and our corporate policies consistently reflect this conviction.

We also expect our business partners – paper mills, printers, packaging manufacturers, etc. – to commit themselves to using environmentally friendly materials and production processes.

The paper in this book is made from low- or no-chlorine pulp and is acid free, in conformance with international standards for paper permanency.

www.ingramcontent.com/pod-product-compliance
Lightning Source LLC
Chambersburg PA
CBHW071408230926
51846CB00001B/34
9783642781162